A HISTORY
OF ENGLAND

COUNTIES OF
ENGLAND AND WALES

MILES

0   20   40   60   80

SCOTLAND

NORTHUMBERLAND

CUMBERLAND

DURHAM

WESTMORLAND

Isle Of
Man

ENGLAND

YORKSHIRE

ANGLESEY

FLINT

LANCASHIRE

CAERNARVON

DENBIGH

CHESHIRE

DERBY

NOTTINGHAM

LINCOLN

MERIONETH

STAFFORD

RUTLAND

MONTGOMERY

SHROPSHIRE

LEICESTER

NORFOLK

WALES

RADNOR

WARWICK

NORTHAMPTON

HUNTINGDON

PEMBROKE

CARDIGAN

WORCESTER

CAMBRIDGE

SUFFOLK

BRECKNOCK

HEREFORD

BEDFORD

CARMARTHEN

OXFORD

BUCKINGHAM

HERTFORD

ESSEX

GLAMORGAN

MONMOUTH

GLOUCESTER

MIDDLESEX
LONDON

BERKSHIRE

SURREY

KENT

WILTSHIRE

HAMPSHIRE

SUSSEX

SOMERSET

DEVON

DORSET

Isle Of
Wight

CORNWALL

Clayton Roberts

The Ohio State University

David Roberts

Dartmouth College

THIRD EDITION

A HISTORY
OF ENGLAND

Volume II
1688 to the Present

Prentice Hall, Englewood Cliffs, New Jersey 07632

Library of Congress Cataloging-in-Publication Data

Roberts, Clayton.
    A history of England / Clayton Roberts, David Roberts. — 3rd ed.
      p.   cm.
    Includes bibliographical references and index.
    Contents: — v. 2. 1688 to the present.
    ISBN 0-13-390410-5 (v. 2)
    1. Great Britain—History 2. England—Civilization.
I. Roberts, David, 1923-   . II. Title.
DA30.R58 1991b
942—dc20   90-7461
                                        CIP

Editorial/production supervision: bookworks
Cover design: Lundgren Graphics, Ltd.
Manufacturing buyer: Debbie Kesar/Marianne Gloriande
Cover photo: The Court of Kings Bench at work in the fifteenth century
(Courtesy of the Masters of the Inner Temple).

Printed in the United States of America

10 9 8 7 6 5 4 3 2 1

ISBN 0-13-390410-5

Prentice-Hall International, Inc., *London*
Prentice-Hall of Australia Pty. Limited, *Sydney*
Prentice-Hall Canada Inc., *Toronto*
Prentice-Hall Hispanoamericana, S.A., *Mexico*
Prentice-Hall of India Private Limited, *New Delhi*
Prentice-Hall of Japan, Inc., *Tokyo*
Simon & Schuster Southeast Asia Pte. Ltd., *Singapore*
Editora Prentice-Hall do Brasil, Ltda., *Rio de Janeiro*

Contents

Preface

The history of England has exercised a perennial fascination over the minds of mankind. A people who gave us Shakespeare and Newton, created the common law and Parliament, built the world's largest empire, transformed industry, and defended the liberties of Europe against Napoleon and Hitler cannot be dull or insignificant. But though the fascination remains perennial, the story to be told changes with the mounting literature on the subject. In the past twenty years scholars have written and published a flood of articles and books on the history of England. They have examined or reexamined every event, left nothing untouched, from the building of Stonehenge to the discovery of North Sea oil.

It is our purpose to incorporate this recent scholarship into a history of England that is broad in scope and interpretive in nature.

The time has long since passed when a history of England could be a history of past politics. We have endeavored, therefore, to write a history of society as well as of the state, a task which the works of J. Z. Titow, M. M. Postan, Lawrence Stone, Peter Laslett, E. P. Thompson, Eric Hobsbawm, David Landes, and many others have made possible. Demographers, intellectual historians, social historians, historians of technology, and historians of popular movements have opened up a new world, a world which general histories of England have previously ignored. We have sought to illuminate this broader, richer world, even though it means saying less about the rise and fall of ministries.

We have sought throughout to wed a narrative form to a concern for interpretation, both to trace how and to explain why events came about. Without embracing any single interpretation of English history, we have sought to stress the dominant themes that run through it: the coming of Christianity, the creation of the English monarchy, the growth of English power and empire, the triumph of Protestantism and religious diversity, the winning of political liberty and parliamentary government, the emergence of a capitalistic and industrial economy, the triumph of the scientific method; and, in the twentieth century, the emergence of the welfare state, the decline in English power, the loss of empire, the faltering of the economy, and the decay of religious belief.

The historian's task is by no means limited to tracing such developments; he or she must also study past ages for their own sake. Thus we have sought to explain in terms of the society they served such institutions as the Anglo-Saxon manor, the medieval Exchequer, the Tudor council, the Stuart Parliament, the Hanoverian Cabinet, and the nineteenth-century economy, and also to portray in their own terms medieval piety, Elizabethan humanism, Augustan manners, Victorian morality, and twentieth-century popular culture.

Although we have paid close attention to analysis and explanation, we have not sought to write an abstract and impersonal history. At bottom, men and women, with their fervor and heroism, their steadfastness and suffering, their folly and stupidity, their greatness and meanness, make history. We have endeavored to capture those dramatic confrontations, those acts of heroism, those eruptions of passion, and those moments of illumination that give history its vividness, its color, and its drama and that help to shape its course.

The help of other scholars has been invaluable to us in the writing of this history. Bryce Lyon of Brown University, Donald Sutherland of the University of Iowa, and Mavis Mate of the University of Oregon read with care and commented upon the chapters on Medieval England. Paul Seaver of Stanford University, Stephen Baxter of the University of North Carolina, Barrett Beer of Kent State University, and Roger Manning of Cleveland State University read with equal care the chapters on Tudor and Stuart England. Sidney Burrell of Boston University kindly loaned us his paper on the origins of the first Bishops' War, a paper whose insights proved most helpful. Henry Snyder of Louisiana State University read Chapters 21 through 23, while Peter Stansky of Stanford University, Sheldon Rothblatt of the University of California at Berkeley, and Anthony Wohl and Donald Olsen of Vassar College read the chapters on the eighteenth, nineteenth, and twentieth centuries. To all these scholars we owe a great debt. They qualified our bold assertions, corrected our minor inaccuracies, and questioned our doubtful interpretations. The story as finally told, however, remains ours; we bear sole responsibility for it.

CLAYTON ROBERTS
DAVID ROBERTS

War and society

16

The Glorious Revolution made war with France inevitable, for William had not led an army to England merely to win the title of King; he had led an army there principally to bring England into the balance of power against France. This fact became clear in May 1689 when William, as King of England, with the support of Parliament, declared war on France. The war upon which England then embarked continued (with one short interruption between 1697 and 1701) until 1713. The nation was at war for twenty-one of the twenty-five years William and Anne reigned in England. It was a far-flung war. English armies fought in Ireland and Flanders, on the banks of the Danube and on the plains of Spain, at Port Royal in Acadia and at Port Mahon in Minorca. The fleet fought in the Channel, in the Mediterranean, and on the high seas. England maintained 40,000 men on the Continent, built and manned 323 ships of war, sent 9,000 men to Spain, and spent over £5 million a year to support its forces and subsidize its allies.

Such an effort could not fail to affect English society. Because of the war, Parliament met every year and became an indispensable part of the government. Because of the war, the royal administration grew in numbers and efficiency. Because of the war, new financial institutions emerged, which split propertied society into landed and monied interests. At the same time, the values of commerce permeated all ranks of society and helped shape English civilization. England entered the war a second-rate European power, divided from Scotland, unstable in its politics, and unsure of its colonies. It emerged a major European power, united with Scotland, politically stable, and set on the path of imperial greatness. England became Great Britain. A nation that had endured a century of discord and revolution now entered on a century of peace and stability.

THE WAR OF THE LEAGUE OF AUGSBURG

In 1667 the armies of Louis XIV invaded the Spanish Netherlands; in 1672 they attacked the Dutch; in 1681 they seized Strasbourg; and in 1688 they laid waste the Palatinate. These acts persuaded William to devote his public life to the task of curbing the power of France in Europe. They also drove the nations of Europe (Austria, Spain, Sweden, Bavaria, Saxony, and the Palatinate) to form the League of Augsburg in 1686 and to ally with the Dutch and the English in 1689 to resist French aggression. The English shared these fears that the greatness of France would endanger the liberties of Europe, but they had a further reason for declaring war: Louis XIV in March 1689 gave James II the men, money, and ships with which to return to Ireland to recover the Crown he had lost. For the English, the War of the League of Augsburg was also the War of the English Succession

James landed in Ireland only to discover that the Irish were more intent on recovering the lands Cromwell had stolen from them than helping James recover the Crown of England. Ireland for the Irish was their program, "Now or Never" their motto. An Irish Parliament repealed the Act of Settlement of 1661 and confiscated the lands of 2400 Protestants who had fled to England. But the Presbyterians in Ulster did not flee; they sought safety behind the walls of Londonderry and Enniskillen. Their stubborn resistance, withstanding siege and assault, secured Ulster for William, thus providing him with a base from which, in the summer of 1690, he could lead 35,000 well-disciplined men south toward James's retreating and ill-equipped army of 21,000. Outnumbered, outmaneuvered, and outfought, the Irish could not prevent the English from storming across the river Boyne on the first of July. Among the first to flee the battlefield was James himself; a week later he took ship for France. His flight made the defeat of the Irish at the Battle of the Boyne the decisive engagement in the Protestant reconquest of Ireland.

In the next twenty years, the English reduced the Irish to a condition of virtual slavery. The Catholics, who composed four-fifths of the population, now owned but one-seventh of the land. A series of penal laws kept Catholics from public life. A Catholic could not hold office, sit in Parliament, vote in elections, serve on a jury, practice law, teach school, purchase land, or own a horse worth more than £5. And no Irishman whatever, not even the industrious Protestants, could export woolen cloth, sell cattle in England, or trade with the colonies. The Irish became, in Jonathan Swift's words, "hewers of wood and drawers of water" to their English conquerors.

In 1690 Ireland was the pivot of Europe; in 1692 the Channel was. Emboldened by a naval victory over the English at Beachy Head in 1690, Louis XIV in 1692 prepared to invade England. He assembled an army at Barfleur, which James II joined. But a French fleet sent to clear the Channel met defeat at La Hogue at the hands of a combined English and Dutch fleet that outnumbered the French fleet by 99 ships-of-the-line to 44. The French lost fifteen ships

A contemporary engraving of the Battle of the Boyne (*Bettmann Archive*).

and Louis never again sent out the fleet. Seapower had saved England from invasion, as it had done once before when Philip II launched the Armada and as it was to do again when Napoleon and Hitler threatened to hurl their armies across the Channel.

Victory at the Boyne and victory at La Hogue secured the Protestant succession in England, but the war to lessen the power of France raged on in Flanders. Louis XIV won the battles but could not win the war. William was not a brilliant soldier, but what he lacked in brilliance he made up for in perseverance. Not until the sixth year of the war could the Allies hold their own against the French, but in that year, 1695, they captured the great fortress-city of Namur. The fall of Namur and the financial exhaustion of France led Louis XIV in 1697 to negotiate the Peace of Ryswick. Louis agreed to recognize William as King of

England and to restore all the territories he had seized since 1678, except Strasbourg.

THE FINANCIAL REVOLUTION

The money that paid for the siege and capture of Namur came from the newly created Bank of England, the establishment of which marked a revolution in the financial affairs of England.

During the reigns of Charles II and James II the English government spent about £2 million every year; during the reigns of William and Anne it spent nearly £6 million. The ability to tap the wealth of all Englishmen allowed this vast increase in public expenditure and permitted a nation with less than 6 million inhabitants to send out a powerful fleet and support a formidable army. Two-thirds of the money needed for the war came from taxes, of which the land tax was the most important. Each year a Parliament elected by the landowners of England voted that the landowners of England should pay the government 4 shillings on the pound on the rents they collected, the equivalent of an income tax of 20 percent. When it came to raising money—the very sinews of war—the parliamentary monarchy of England proved far more effective than the royal absolutism of France.

Government borrowing provided for that part of the budget not met by taxes. In times of need both Charles I and Charles II had borrowed from wealthy individuals, often pledging crown revenues for repayment. But such loans were short-term, expensive, and destructive of future income. What England needed were long-term loans, secured by parliamentary revenues, and participated in by prosperous subjects from all walks of life. Such a loan Parliament devised in 1693, when it authorized the sale of life annuities, secured on an excise voted by Parliament for ninety-nine years. In effect, the government would not repay the principal, but would pay 14 percent interest on it until the holder died. The act of 1693 marks the beginning of a permanent national debt in England, one in which any person with a few extra pounds could participate. The Dean of Norwich, for one, rushed out to buy his daughter an annuity.

The idea of a permanent national debt gained a more solid foundation in 1694 with the establishment of the Bank of England. The idea for a bank arose from the fertile mind of William Patterson, son of a Scottish farmer, successful London merchant, and traveler to Holland (where he studied their bank) and to America (where he was, according to his friends, a missionary; according to his enemies, a buccaneer). But it was Charles Montagu, the brilliant Whig politician, who translated Patterson's idea into legislation and who steered it through Parliament. According to that legislation, a bank should be created that would lend the government £1.2 million. In return, the government would pay 8 percent interest on the money and would empower the bank to sell stock, receive deposits, make loans, and issue banknotes. The scheme was an immediate success; within twelve days subscribers bought up all the bank's stock. In the years that followed its notes retained their value, and the government found in the bank an indispensable source of further credit.

The Bank of England was the first joint-stock bank in England, but not the first bank. Private banking emerged in England during the 1650s, when the goldsmiths of London began to accept gold and silver for safekeeping and to lend out part of it at interest. Soon the receipts the goldsmiths gave for the gold and silver deposited with them began to circulate as paper money. By 1675 bankers were performing the three essential functions of banking: accepting deposits, lending money, and issuing notes. To these functions banks founded by scriveners, whose trade was the conveyance of property, added a fourth: the loaning of money on the security of a mortgage. Soon politicians saw that banks, by providing more generous credit and by increasing the supply of money, promoted new enterprises and thereby the employment of the poor. In the 1690s England needed credit and a circulating medium more than ever before, and the new Bank of England provided them.

The establishment of a stock exchange was the third step in the financial revolution of William III's reign. Stockbrokers were already gathering at Jonathan's and Garraway's coffeehouses in Exchange Alley and were dealing in company stocks and government securities. Because many brokers sold bogus stock or stock at double its price, Parliament decided in 1697 to limit their number to 100 and to require those selling government securities to register with the government. Pamphleteers continued to denounce "stock-jobbers," but without them there would have been no capital market.

THE POLITICS OF WAR AND PEACE

The authors of the revolution settlement did not intend that Parliament should meet every year, only every three years. But the insatiable demands of war forced William to summon it every year so it could vote the taxes and float the loans needed to pay for the war. William's dependence on Parliament had a profound influence on the development of the constitution, especially when coupled with the passions of party. Virtuous men decried the spirit of party, but they could not extinguish it. Division lists (that is, lists of how men voted on certain issues) survive for eight votes taken in the House of Commons during William's reign. They show that among those who voted, 85 percent cast votes solely on the Whig or solely on the Tory side. These party divisions were not fortuitous, for social differences and political principles divided people. Most squires were Tories, though not all, or else the Whigs would never have won an election. Most merchants and bankers were Whigs. The Tories favored the persecution of Dissenters, a naval war only, and the inviolability of the hereditary succession, which many of them placed in the House of Stuart. The Whigs favored religious toleration, a land war in Europe, and the revolution settlement.

William III by Candelight, portrait by Gottfried Schalcken (*National Trust*).

William III desired to be King of all the English, not merely of the Whigs. He therefore chose to govern with a mixed ministry composed of statesmen from both parties or none. But the partisan passions of the Whigs in 1690 drove him to turn to the Tories from 1690 to 1692. The Tories, however, failed to defend English shipping at sea, grew hostile to the land war, and proved unable to manage Parliament. Their failure gave the Whigs their opportunity. Gaining a predominant influence in Parliament, they gradually forced William to give them high office. By 1696 only Whigs sat in the Cabinet, that inner group of advisers who now replaced the Privy Council as the mainspring of government. It was the first party ministry in English history.

In 1697 William, who kept a tight grip on the reins of foreign policy, negotiated the Peace of Ryswick. The coming of peace spelled doom for the Whigs, for the Tories were now able to turn against them the country members' anger at the courtiers who had grown rich during the war. The split between Court and Country was as important in the politics of William's reign as the division between Whig and Tory. "If an angel came from Heaven that was a Privy Councilor," cried one member, "I would not trust my liberty with him for one moment." This spirit of distrust led Parliament in 1698 to deny William a standing army of more than 7000 men, for a standing army was seen as an instrument of tyranny. It also led the Commons in 1701 to impeach the Whig ministers who dared to negotiate treaties without first seeking the advice of Parliament. And it led Parliament that same year to add to the Act of Settlement (passed in order to settle the succession on the House of Hanover) a whole charter of liberties: no person who held an office of profit under the King should sit in the House of Commons; all resolutions taken in the Privy Council should be signed by the councilors; judges should be removable only upon the address of both Houses of Parliament; no pardon should be pleadable to an impeachment. Parliament in 1705 repealed the first two of these clauses, thus allowing the growth of cabinet government in England, but their passage in 1701 shows how deep was the countryman's distrust of the Court. The spirit of Eliot and Pym was not wholly dead.

The Tories, by exploiting the countrymen's fury against the Court, were able, between 1698 and 1700, to drive the Whigs from office. In the autumn of 1700 William was forced to bring the leading Tories into the Cabinet, but his mind was less absorbed by these domestic quarrels than by the question of the Spanish succession. Because the Treaty of Ryswick had made no provision for the succession to the Spanish crown after the death of Charles II, its sickly, childless, imbecile king, William had to negotiate two partition treaties with Louis XIV. The second of these allotted to the Austrian claimant Spain, its colonies, and the Spanish Netherlands, and to the French claimant Naples, Sicily, and Milan. But this treaty, which the merchants of London detested because it surrendered the Mediterranean to French dominance, never came into effect.

In 1700, Charles II left behind him a will that bequeathed to Philip, Duke of Anjou, Louis XIV's grandson, the entire Spanish empire. Most people, though not William, preferred the will and peace to partition and war. But Louis XIV then embarked on a series of arrogant actions that turned English public opinion in favor of war. He sent French armies into the Spanish Netherlands, seized the Dutch fortresses there, forced the Spanish to grant a French company the contract for supplying African slaves to Spanish America, and refused to demand from Philip a renunciation of his rights to the French crown. The threat posed to the balance of power no doubt alarmed the English, but many were even more alarmed at the threat posed to the markets for English cloth in Spain, the Netherlands, and the Mediterranean.

William in the summer of 1701 skillfully edged Parliament toward war and negotiated an alliance with the Dutch and the Emperor. This alliance was completed in September, several weeks before Louis XIV, standing at the death-bed of James II, recognized James's son, James III, as King of England. By this act Louis guaranteed that the English, Tories as well as Whigs, would rally behind the war. William, however, did not live to lead the armies of England once more against France. In February 1702, riding in the park of Hampton Court, his horse stumbled on a mole hole and pitched William to the ground. Two weeks later he died, leaving to others the prosecution of his life-long duel with Louis XIV.

THE WAR OF THE SPANISH SUCCESSION

Princess Anne, daughter of James II, ascended the throne in 1702. She was 37 years old, exceedingly fat, red and spotted in complexion, and wracked by gout. She had to be carried to her coronation. She was slow-witted, uninformed, obstinate, and narrow-minded; yet also pious, sensible, good-natured, and kind. She bore fifteen children and buried them all. She loved the Church and those who defended it, but had no interest in art, music, plays, or books. Her one hobby was eating; her husband's, drinking. This orindary woman, whom the laws of hereditary monarchy raised to the throne, helped shape events during these years in two ways: first, by naming the Earl of Marlborough in 1702 to command her troops, and secondly by dismissing him from that command in 1711. By the first act she brought England unparalleled military victories; by the second she brought peace to her kingdom.

During the War of the Spanish Succession, John Churchill, Earl (later Duke) of Marlborough, waged ten campaigns, fought four major battles, and besieged over thirty towns. In all this fighting he never lost a battle or a skirmish or a siege. He was one of the great generals of history. His skill in war was no accident, for he had chosen the career of arms as a young man. The son of a royalist gentleman who had lost his lands fighting for Charles I, he was poor, obscure, and ambitious. He rose at Court through his own charm and through the charm of his sister, who was mistress to James, Duke of York. He rose in the army through his great courage and skill. He learned the French way of war when fighting for Louis XIV at Maestricht. He proved his own tactical

Queen Anne, according to the Studio of J. Clostenian (*National Portrait Gallery*).

John Churchill, Duke of Marlborough
(*National Portrait Gallery*).

genius by defeating the Duke of Monmouth at Sedgmoor. At Walcourt in 1689 he fought side by side with the Dutch, while at Kinsale in 1690 he displayed a keen strategic sense. To the skills of a soldier he added the talents of a courtier and diplomat. He was handsome, urbane, charming, never without a compliment, always persuasive, impossible to anger. Yet he was also crafty and dissimulating, kept his counsels to himself, and seized every opportunity to advance his family and fortune. Under William III he fell into disfavor, but the succession of Queen Anne saw his star rise again, for Sarah Jennings, whom he married in 1678, was the close confidante of the Queen.

Marlborough assumed command of the Allied armies at a moment when the nature of European warfare was changing profoundly. It was his genius to adapt his tactics to these changes; it was the misfortune of the French that they did not. Three technical innovations lay behind these changes: the flintlock musket, the prepacked paper cartridge, and the socket bayonet. The flintlock musket was several pounds lighter than its predecessor, the matchlock, misfired only twice in ten shots, and could be discharged eight times faster (about two shots a minute). The prepacked paper cartridge, containing powder and a one-ounce ball, simplified reloading. The socket bayonet, which allowed a soldier to fire his musket or stab with it, made the pike unnecessary. Marlborough saw that these innovations made the infantry a source of firepower, not blocks of resistance. He therefore placed his men in three lines, staggered, so that an entire platoon could fire at once. The French clung to the column, four or five deep, with only the front line firing. The French were equally old-fashioned in their use of the cavalry. Marlborough adopted the tactics of Gustavus Adolphus

Sarah Jennings, Dutchess of
Marlborough (*National Portrait Gallery*).

and Cromwell: the cavalry should ride hard against the enemy, disrupt them
with the shock of the impact, and cut them down with naked steel. The French
still regarded the cavalry as a mobile source of firepower, riding to within thirty
paces of the enemy and discharging their pistols. The tactic cost them dearly
at Blenheim.

Marlborough was equally innovative in his strategy. For forty years the
armies of Europe had fought by siege. Having besieged and captured one town,
an army would lay siege to the next. At this rate it would take thirty years to
cross Flanders. Marlborough preferred a war of movement, leading to a decisive
battle.

The supreme instance of such a war of movement occurred in 1704. Bavaria's entry into the war on the side of France posed a threat to Vienna and to
Austria's continuance in the Grand Alliance. Marlborough resolved to save Austria. With his usual painstaking attention to supply and with the gold of England
behind him, he marched his army 250 miles across Europe, from the Netherlands
to Bavaria. He momentarily paralyzed the French army by making a feint toward
the Moselle; he then crossed the Rhine and marched on to Bavaria. At Heidelberg
he had a new pair of shoes ready for each soldier. After driving the local Bavarian
forces into Augsburg, he turned to face Marshall Tallard, who had pursued
him at the head of a French army.

Though Marshall Tallard's army outnumbered that of the Allies by 56,000
men to 52,000, it was Marlborough, not Tallard, who sought battle. At the
village of Blenheim, on the banks of the Danube, on August 13, Marlborough
launched his attack. By bringing relentless pressure on the village itself, he

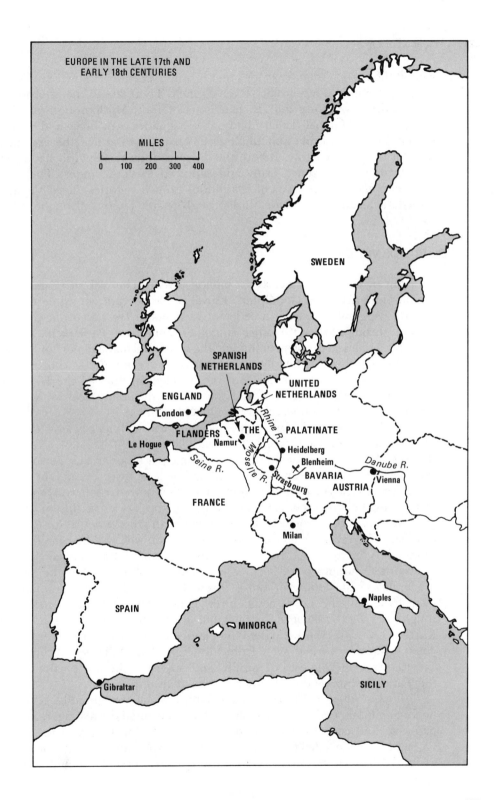

EUROPE IN THE LATE 17th AND
EARLY 18th CENTURIES

MILES

0   100   200   300   400

SWEDEN

SPANISH
NETHERLANDS

UNITED
NETHERLANDS

ENGLAND

London

FLANDERS   THE   PALATINATE

Le Hogue   Namur

Rhine R.

Heidelberg

Blenheim

Moselle R.   Danube R.

Seine R.   Strasbourg   BAVARIA   Vienna

FRANCE   AUSTRIA

Milan

SPAIN

Naples

MINORCA

Gibraltar   SICILY

caused the French to move troops there from the center. Sixteen English battalions thus pinned down twenty-seven French. Then late in the afternoon, with 81 squadrons of horse and 18 battalions of foot, Marlborough attacked the center, where Marshall Tallard had only 64 squadrons of horse and 9 battalions of foot. The center broke and the English raced to the Danube, thereby encircling most of the French army. Before the day was done the English had destroyed two thirds of the French army and captured its commander. The Battle of Blenheim ended forty years of continuous French victories, saved Vienna, preserved the alliance, and made Marlborough's name famous throughout Europe.

THE POLITICS OF VICTORY

The cost of victory was nearly £9 million a year. The task of raising this sum fell on Sidney, Earl of Godolphin, a loyal public servant, an astute financier, a compulsive gambler, and a breeder of racehorses. He raised one-third of the amount through loans; the other £6 million came from Parliament. This posed the central political problem of the age: the successful management of Parliament. The Queen solved it initially by relying on Tory ministers who enjoyed the support of a Tory Parliament. But the unrelenting fury of the High Church Tories against the Dissenters, and the Tories' dwindling zeal for waging war on the Continent, soon wrecked the Queen's scheme.

The High Church Tories directed their special anger against the practice of occasional conformity, a practice that allowed the Dissenters to circumvent the Test Act. That act denied state or municipal office to any person who did not take communion in an Anglican Church at least twice a year. The Dissenters circumvented the Act by taking communion as required, then worshipping every Sunday in their own chapels. The anger of the Tories at this practice arose less from a desire to correct religious error than from a desire for a monopoly of office. The religious fervor of the age of Cromwell had become the political passions of the age of Anne. In 1702 the extreme Tories carried through the House of Commons a bill against occasional conformity, but the Whigs and moderates in the House of Lords threw it out. In 1703 the Commons again passed the bill; the Lords again threw it out. The extreme Tories therefore sought in 1704 to tack it to a money bill, so that the Lords could not refuse it. But the Queen's servants and the Whigs joined forces to defeat it in the Commons. The Queen now turned away from the High Church Tories. By dividing her subjects, endangering bills of supply, and opposing the war on the Continent, the Tories had made their further employment impossible.

Though they had to rely on the Whigs, Marlborough and Godolphin did not intend to surrender power to them. They remained the managers, dispensing patronage, advising the Queen, governing the realm. But in order to manage Parliament they needed the help of the Whigs, who had increased their numbers in the 1705 elections: together with the Queen's servants, they now formed a majority in the Commons. It was Godolphin's plan to manage Parliament through an alliance of Whigs, courtiers, and moderate Tories; and it was the Queen's hope that such an alliance would allow her to retain the right to appoint ministers of her own choice. Both were to be disappointed. The passions of party swept away all such reconciling schemes. For the support they gave Godolphin in Parliament the Whigs demanded payment: the appointment of William Cowper as Lord Keeper in 1704, of the Earl of Sunderland as Secretary of State in 1706, of Lord Somers as President of the Council and Lord Wharton as Lord Lieutenant of Ireland in 1708, and of Lord Orford as First Lord of the Admiralty in 1709. Fiercely, stubbornly, then pathetically, Queen Anne opposed all these appointments. She was resolved not to become a prisoner of party. By 1709, however, she was. A Whig landslide in the general elections of 1708 left her no choice. The power of the purse allied to the passions of party had proved too strong for the royal prerogative.

The fact of party permeated all the politics of the reign of Queen Anne. Out of 1,064 members returned to Parliament between 1702 and 1714, only 71 cannot be clearly identified as Whig or Tory. And the rage of party flowed out from the Houses of Parliament to divide people in the counties, in the boroughs, in the city of London, in the Church, in the army, in coffeehouses, in the theater, in the journals—everywhere. The chief effect of party was to place political power in that party that prevailed at the polls and so won a majority in the House of Commons.

The House of Commons represented a narrow social elite, those who owned property, principally land. The ranks from which members of Parliament were drawn made up only 0.5 percent of Englishmen. Even then the country squires who crowded the benches of St. Stephen's—where the Commons met—protested against the chance army officer or merchant who strayed into the House. In an attempt to keep them out, they passed the Property Qualification Act of 1711, which required county members to own landed property worth £600 a year and borough members, property worth £300—though the act was easily evaded by temporarily transferring land to a new member.

Those who had the right to vote for members of Parliament were more numerous, but still an elite. Only 4.3 percent of the population had the vote, about one adult male in five. And many of these voters were freehold tenants whom the landlord marshaled to the polls or townsmen in a borough where a great peer had a predominant influence. Of 513 seats in Parliament, perhaps 120 were at the nomination of a great magnate; another 20 were at the nomination of the Crown. In many constituencies a Whig or Tory family would have so firm a grip on the seat that the election would go uncontested. During Anne's reign only about 100 seats were contested in a general election, though in those contests the battle between Whig and Tory raged furiously.

The power of the squirarchy in local government was even greater than its power in the House of Commons. The squires, as justices of the peace, sat on the county bench, where they judged, administered, and taxed their countrymen. And the Revolution of 1688 had taught the Crown not to interfere in local government. In Cromwell's England the middle classes had endeavored to seize power; draymen, leather merchants, and the sons of butchers were found among those who governed England. The Restoration and the Glorious Revolution restored the rule of the wealthy. England became an oligarchy, in which the divine right of property replaced the divine right of kings.

THE NEW WORLD OF TRADE

The society over which this oligarchy ruled was one made rich by commerce. The hub of this new world of trade was London, with its half-million inhabitants. Below London Bridge the Thames was a forest of masts. Out of the Thames sailed the great East India ships, to bring back the tea that was to make the English a nation of tea drinkers. From North America came the beaver, with which to manufacture hats for gentlemen of fashion, and tobacco, with which to fill their pipes. From the Levant came coffee and cotton; from the African coast ivory and dyewood; from the Baltic hemp, tar, and timber. A steady stream of colliers brought coal from Newcastle, a trade that tripled in the seventeenth century. The small pinks, which carried more cargo and employed fewer men than the older ships, challenged the supremacy of the Dutch flyboat in the North Sea. By 1700 shipping owned in London reached 140,000 tons, and one in every four Londoners depended on the sea for a living.

Though London was the hub of trade, it did not dominate trade as it had under the Tudors. Merchants in London owned 140,000 tons of shipping, but those in the outports owned 183,000 tons. Every year 240 ships went in and out of Bristol harbor, carrying English manufactures to the colonies and bringing back tobacco and sugar. Exeter became a thriving port on the export of woolen cloth. Liverpool grew wealthy by refining the sugar its ships brought from the West Indies. The reexport of colonial products, principally tobacco, accounted for nearly a third of England's total exports. Once dangerously dependent on its trade to northern Europe, England now became a world entrepôt, one-third of whose imports came from America, the West Indies, and the East. The volume of trade also increased. English imports rose by £1.4 million a year; exports, by £2.3 million. But what truly brought joy to the hearts of the mercantilists was the fact that during these same years a trade deficit of £300,000 a year became a trade surplus of £600,000. England now enjoyed a favorable balance of trade.

Large as England's foreign trade was, its domestic trade was three times greater. Ships and barges carried grain, coal, salt, bricks, and iron from port to port and up the navigable rivers. Cloth was still the greatest of English manufactures and was still organized according to the domestic system. But the salt panners on the Tyne, the sugar boilers on the Mersey, the tin smelters of Cornwall, the brewers of London, and the glass makers of Newcastle formed a semi-industrialized society. And each of these industries by 1700 had solved the problem of how to pan salt, boil sugar, smelt tin, brew beer, and make glass with coal rather than charcoal, thus escaping from the shortage of wood in England. Then in 1709, in Shropshire, a Quaker ironmaster, Abraham Darby, discovered how to smelt iron ore with coke (coal heated in an oven in order to drive off impurities). In time his discovery would transform the iron industry, but for the moment the greatest advances in manufacturing arose from an act of religious intolerance, not an advance in industrial technology. By revoking the Edict of Nantes in 1685, Louis XIV drove 15,000 Huguenots, mostly skilled artisans, to settle in London, at Spitalfields, Soho, and Bethnal Green. There they manufactured for peers and squires, for merchants and lawyers, the crystal, fine paper, cutlery, watches, and precision instruments the wealthy prized. Above all, the silk manufacturers of Spitalfields produced the velvets, satins, and brocades that an age of elegance required.

The spirit of commerce pervaded English society. Even the gentry engaged in economic activity. Sir John Lowther produced coal as well as grain on his Whitehaven estates. Thomas Foley, who founded a family in the West Midlands, mined iron ore on his property. Not all landlords had coal or iron on their land, but most of them produced timber or wool or wood for sale to the manufacturers of England. Angry squires might curse the monied men over tankards of October ale, but the Marquis of Tavistock had no qualms at marrying the granddaughter and heir of Sir Josiah Child, once a brewer, now an East India merchant, and one of the wealthiest men in England. Prosperous merchants, on their part, bought land and became gentlemen.

The growth of joint-stock companies permitted all men of wealth, whether great courtiers or successful landlords or wealthy lawyers or well-placed clergymen, to invest in the trade of England. In 1688 there were only fifteen joint-stock companies in all England; by 1696 there were over a hundred. One could invest not only in the great companies—the Bank of England, the East India Company, Hudson's Bay—but also in companies to manufacture gunpowder, smelt copper, produce hollow swordblades, and carry water from Hampstead to London. The luckiest of all were those who invested in William Philips's company to salvage a Spanish plate ship that had sunk off Hispaniola. The company found gold and silver equal to that which Drake had brought home, and returned to each investor £100 for every £1 invested, a return of 10,000 percent!

This structure of trade and manufacturing rested securely on the agricultural wealth of England. This wealth was astonishing. Yields of wheat per acre in the seventeenth century were close to modern yields. In 1720 dairy cows gave a gallon and a third a day, only a little less than what they give today. Between the later Middle Ages and the end of the seventeenth century grain and grass yields rose about fourfold, and the increase in sheep and cattle was even greater. On the average, agricultural output rose fivefold between 1400 and 1700. Medieval agriculture was hardly able to support 3 million people; by 1700 England could feed 5 million and still export grain.

The explanation for this great increase in productivity lies in the agricultural revolution that occurred between 1560 and 1720. The heart of this revolution lay in the replacement of permanent tillage (with the arable lying fallow every third year) and permanent pasture with a system of alternation called up-and-down husbandry. Under this system, a farmer would grow wheat or barley on a piece of land for four or five years, then put it to grass for seven or eight years, then return it to tillage. This alternation preserved the fertility of the land, and though no more grain was produced, far more grass nutrients were. This meant more dairy products and more lamb, mutton, and beef. The introduction of up-and-down husbandry was accompanied by other changes. Turnips and clover were introduced as field crops and allowed the farmer to feed livestock during the winter. Permanent meadows were watered to give more and better grass. Marshes, such as the Fenland in East Anglia, were drained and their rich soil exploited. Marl, sand, lime, and manure were spread on fields to increase their fertility. Selective breeding improved cattle and sheep; during these years the Cotswold sheep were transformed—their legs shortened and their carcasses made larger and fleshier (for it was not their wool but their flesh that made them profitable). The sum total of these changes—themselves the product of the enterprise and ingenuity of English farmers—was to end the curse of widespread famine that hung over medieval England.

THE SOCIAL PYRAMID

The wealth this labor and enterprise produced was distributed among England's 5 million inhabitants in a highly inequitable manner. There was nothing new in this. What was new was the rise of "political arithmetic," a science that allowed the distribution of wealth to be measured. The greatest of the political arithmeti-

Blenheim Palace, designed in the English baroque style by Sir John Vanbrugh and built at the public expense for the Duke of Marlborough (*The Central Press Photos Limited*).

cians was Gregory King, son of a Lichfield surveyor, a skillful mathematician, an ingenious statistician, and a minor civil servant who loved curious facts. During the reign of William III he described the structure of English society in table form.

At the apex of the pyramid were 160 noblemen, with an average income of £3200 a year, and 26 bishops with incomes ranging from the bishop of Britol's £360 a year to the bishop of Durham's £6000. The nobility used their opulent fortunes to build great country houses, to retain a phalanx of servants, to serve sumptuous meals, to purchase pictures from Italy, to buy furniture from France, to spend the season in London, and to wager vast sums at the gaming table.

Below the peers came the gentry, some 16,400 baronets, knights, esquires, and gentlemen, the richest of whom might be worth £2000 a year, the poorest only £200. Their average income was £354 a year. The rustic squire spent his business hours selling grain and buying livestock, his leisure hours hunting, shooting, and drinking. He spoke with a provincial accent, and his library had few books besides the Bible and Foxe's *Book of Martyrs*. He rarely visited London, but when he did he stood out in the crowd because of his old-fashioned coat without sleeves. The more prosperous among them built manor houses in the style of Wren, simple yet elegant. Paneling now replaced tapestries, and the sash window, often 5 feet high, replaced the mullioned windows of the Elizabethans. Their wives avidly collected chinaware brought from the East.

Below the gentlemen came the yeoman, a man who owned the land he

Eltham Lodge, a modest country house built in the late seventeenth century (*Country Life*).

farmed, but who possessed no coat of arms and presumed to no gentility. Gregory King called them the freeholders of England and numbered them at 160,000. The better sort made, on average, £91 a year; the lesser sort only £55. To their numbers may be added 150,000 farmers, or husbandmen, who rented land as copyholders or leaseholders and who earned, on average, £42 a year. The squires showed their contempt for these classes by passing a law that prevented all freeholders worth less than £100 a year from killing game—even on their own land. The partridges were to be reserved for gentlemen.

More numerous than the yeomen were those whom Gregory King called the laboring people and outservants. They worked in the fields as employees of the yeomen and farmers. They numbered some 364,000 families, and the average income of a family was about £15.

Life for these husbandmen and laborers was simple, arduous, but not intolerable. More of them ate wheaten bread than ate rye or barley bread. They saw roast meat on the table at least twice a week, perhaps more often when beef fell to 2½ pence a pound and mutton to 2 pence. They had yet to learn to drink coffee and tea, but they drank enormous quantities of beer—between 2 and 4 pints a day. Foreigners were impressed with their clean, neat cottages. Hours of labor were long. The husbandmen returning from the fields, complained the pious, were too tired to say prayers. Child labor was common, and praised. Daniel Defoe rejoiced that around Halifax hardly anyone above the age of 4 was idle. Wages in the fields ran from 8 to 12 pence a day, too little to feed a wife and children. Only where the wife could earn 9 pence carding wool and the children 4 pence each spinning yarn could the working family fare well.

Trade, then as now, was where fortunes were made. Three million people earned £25 million in agriculture (or about £8 a person), while 300,000 earned £10 million in trade (or about £33 a person). According to Gregory King's calculation, some 2,000 eminent merchants earned £400 a year; another 2,000 merchants earned £198. Shopkeepers and tradesmen, of whom there were 50,000 families, earned £45 a year, while artisans, 60,000 in number, earned £38. The professions offered a second avenue to wealth. Lawyers earned £154 a year, eminent clergymen £72, lesser clergymen £50, naval officers £80, and army officers £60. Common seamen earned only £20, common soldiers £14. Great offices of state brought an income of £240 a year, lesser offices £120. These, then, were the classes—common seaman, soldier, and husbandman apart—who enjoyed the new wealth of England.

At the very base of the pyramid were 400,000 families of cottagers and paupers, the largest class of all and the poorest. Their yearly income averaged £6 10s. The terms "cottager" and "poor" were nearly synonymous, for a cottage was a small house or hovel with little or no land. Sir Francis Bacon called cottagers "but housed beggars." Since there was little regular employment on farms in the early eighteenth century, the squatters eked out a livelihood by squatting on the commons, keeping geese, cutting wood, and poaching. Their inadequate incomes often had to be supplemented by parish poor relief and private charity. The first provided about £900,000 a year; the second, about £200,000. Together they yielded about £1 per person a year for the poor—quite unevenly distributed. This was merely enough to stave off the worst hunger and cold. Each parish sought to exclude from its boundaries the poor from other parishes. By the Act of Settlement of 1662, a parish in which a person sought to settle could send him back to the parish from which he came if they thought he might someday be a burden. The true answer to this appalling problem of poverty, as Daniel Defoe saw, was not charity, but the employment of the poor. Sir Josiah Child, a governor of the East India Company and a writer on economics, even proposed that the government buy land, build work-houses, and set the poor to work. His advice went unheeded.

THE AUGUSTAN AGE

London, which was the center of trade, was also the center of a new middle-class culture. It was here that men conversed in their favorite coffeehouses, dined at taverns, read *The Spectator*, applauded the latest play, heard the new Italian opera, and purchased their waistcoats, cravats, and wigs (which even tradesmen now wore). The center of gravity in London moved westward as the great deserted the city and built townhouses in Bloomsbury, Piccadilly, and St. James's Square. Christopher Wren, after the Great Fire, had proposed rebuilding London with wide, straight streets meeting in a star-shaped open space. This was the principle of the *rond-point*, adopted by the French under Louis XIV. But Charles II, after a few days' thought, rejected the proposal. London's contribution to town planning in the seventeenth and eighteenth centuries was to be the square, a garden or field around which were built privately owned houses of similar design. These houses were usually of brick, of uniform height (three or four stories), sparsely decorated, the façade broken only by sash windows that diminished in size as they rose from story to story. As the *rond-point* reflected the majesty of an absolute monarch, so the London square reflected the wealth, power, good taste, and independence of the English gentleman.

Though the English in Charles II's reign had condemned coffee as useless, "since it serves neither nourishment nor debauchery," by Queen Anne's reign there were over 500 coffeehouses in London. Everyone had a favorite coffee-house. Men of fashion went to White's in St. James's Street. Poets drank their coffee and chocolate at Will's, scholars at The Grecian. Merchants wrote marine insurance at Lloyd's and brokers traded in stock at Jonathan's. At coffeehouses great noblemen conversed easily with private gentlemen and persons of all ranks learned the latest news from abroad and at home.

The theaters opened their doors at 6 P.M. In the London of Queen Anne there were two theaters—at Lincoln's Inn Field and in Drury Lane. Then in 1705 John Vanbrugh, soldier, playwright, and future architect of Blenheim

Palace, built a theater in the Haymarket, called the Queen's Theater or the Italian Opera House. Though literary critics found Italian opera to be merely "nonsense well tuned," it conquered London during the reign of Queen Anne. England had its native composers, of whom Henry Purcell was the greatest. But even Purcell came under the Italian influence, bringing melodic expressiveness and dramatic declamation to his opera, *Dido and Aeneas*. Throughout Europe a new spirit entered music; the religious gave way to the secular.

Despite the power of Thomas Betterton's Hamlet, the theater did not flourish during the reigns of William and Anne. Most of the plays performed were comedies of manners by the Restoration dramatists. The plays were witty, cynical, and indecent, which led the clergy to denounce the immorality of the stage and the government to prosecute actors for lewdness. During these years there occurred a shift in taste away from the brilliant and cynical world of the Restoration wits to the amiable morality and sentimentality of eighteenth-century comedies.

The Augustan age of Queen Anne—so called because the greatness of its literary achievement resembled that of Rome under Augustus—was not an age of drama, nor of poetry, but of prose. Its characteristic literary forms were the newspaper, the pamphlet, and the review, all of which enjoyed a new freedom with the ending of the Licensing Act in 1695. An author could now, within the law of libel and sedition, write what he pleased. In the opening months of Queen Anne's reign the first daily newspaper in England, *The Daily Courant*, began; before she died the circulation of all newspapers had reached 67,000 a week. But the newspapers of that day, a single sheet printed on both sides, carried only news and advertisements; there was no editorial comment. The political pamphlet and the review provided that. The greatest of these pamphleteers and reviewers were Daniel Defoe and Jonathan Swift. Defoe's ironical attack on intolerance, in *The Shortest Way with the Dissenters*, led him to the pillory; and Swift's bitter denunciation of the Dutch in *The Conduct of the Allies* helped bring peace to England in 1713. For eight years Defoe wrote *The Review* to win people over to moderation and for two years Swift wrote *The Examiner* to make them Tories. Never before had the pen been so powerful, for never before had the politician so great a need to sway public opinion. The control of Parliament might depend upon it.

Swift and Defoe appealed to the public's interest in politics; Richard Steele and Joseph Addison, to its interest in society. Richard Steele, at various times a captain in the Life Guards, playwright, theatrical manager, and projector of commercial schemes, began *The Tatler* in 1709 and *The Spectator* in 1711. He prevailed on his friend, Joseph Addison, a shy Oxford scholar, an undersecretary of state, and a literary genius, to contribute to both. *The Tatler* and *The Spectator* were instant successes, for their satire of vice and praise of virtue taught the newly enriched gentlemen, merchants, lawyers, and government servants how to act and how to spend their money.

The Spectator sought to reform the manners and quicken the moral life of

English men and women. It prized good sense over great learning and preferred virtue to mere politeness. It satirized boorishness and ridiculed dueling. It directed men away from both political fanaticism and religious enthusiasm. "Reason," it urged, "should govern passion." It praised honesty above the affectation of good breeding: "The Tradesman who deals with me, in a commodity which I do not understand, with uprightness, has much more right to the character of a gentleman than the courtier who gives me false hopes or the scholar who laughs at my ignorance." It contrasted the "pride and beggary" of the European nobility with the willingness of English gentlemen to send their younger sons into trade. *The Spectator* was both a manual of deportment and a model of correct style. Its prose was balanced, graceful, polished, and clear—a style that suited an age that believed in reason, good sense, elegance, and sobriety.

The same spirit pervaded religion, where the fury of the High Churchmen against the Dissenters could not conceal the growth of moderation and toleration within the Church (a movement soon to be called Latitudinarianism). Under the influence of Newton and Locke, people began to emphasize the reasonableness of Christianity. They also sought a practical divinity, one that would teach people how to live. To this end, a group of clergymen founded the Society for the Reformation of Manners, which did much to reduce swearing and drunkenness, but perhaps did even more to promote the gloomy English Sunday. Even the Quakers grew more mellow, devoting their energies to the counting house rather than to the disruption of church services. As Daniel Defoe, the spokesman for the Dissenters, remarked, after riding through much of England, "the main affair of Life" is "getting money."

MARRIAGE, COURTSHIP, AND THE FAMILY

Public affairs loom large in works of history, but for most people public affairs are a very small thing compared to their private lives. And nothing is more central to a person's private life than the choice of a husband or wife. In the sixteenth century, among the landed classes, one's parents made that choice for one and based it on considerations of lineage, property, power, and honor. The family line must be continued, the estate augmented, political alliances cemented, and social degradation avoided. The system allowed little time for courtship, the bride and groom often seeing each other for the first time after the marriage had been negotiated. "People in my way," wrote the daughter of a marquess, "are sold like slaves."

This system of arranged marriages slowly decayed, weakened by the Protestant insistence on affection within a marriage, by the seventeenth-century emphasis upon personal liberty, and by the eighteenth-century celebration of sentiment. The change was slow and uneven. The great peers with great estates clung to arranged marriages the longest. Yet the forces of change were inexorable. In 1660 Parliament abolished the Court of Wards, where the Crown auctioned

Courtship in High Life, an etching by Thomas Rowlandson (*The Metropolitan Museum of Art, The Elisha Whittelsey Fund, 1959. [59.533.117]*).

off the right to select husbands and wives for fatherless heirs and heiresses. In 1680 Aphra Behn, a zealous feminist, launched an attack upon arranged marriages. In 1705 Daniel Defoe denounced "marriages for the preserving of estates" as equivalent to rape. And Joseph Addison called for long courtships. By 1700 most children of squires and merchants possessed the right to veto their parents' choice; by 1800 they possessed the right of choice, with a veto left to their parents. This change made necessary opportunities for courtship, which were soon established. In the eighteenth century there grew up that world celebrated in the novels of Jane Austen, a world of balls, card parties, teas, assembly rooms, and the London and the Bath seasons.

Not all English men and women married and those who did often married late in life. The average age at marriage for daughters of the nobility was 20 in the sixteenth century, 23 in the eighteenth. The median age at marriage for the heirs of squires rose from 21 in the sixteenth century to 28 in the eighteenth, while younger sons in the eighteenth century did not marry until their thirties. The explanation for this trend lies in the turn towards choice in marriage, in the greater number of years spent at school and university, and in the need for younger sons to accumulate the wealth necessary to support a marriage. Many of these younger sons never accumulated that wealth, with the result that they chose to be bachelors. Their choice in turn increased the number of spinsters. In the sixteenth century 5 percent of the daughters of the landed classes never married; in the eighteenth century 25 percent never married. Because of their high social background they would not work, so they either served as housekeepers to a sister's family or existed in lonely lodgings on small pensions.

In the sixteenth and seventeenth centuries the children of shopkeepers, artisans, and yeomen enjoyed somewhat greater freedom in the choice of wives and husbands than did the children of the rich, but where there was property—a shop or a copyhold—parental control was exercised. By the eighteenth century that control had lessened; children from the lower middle class often married by free choice, even without their parents' consent. Among the propertyless poor, young men and women chose each other freely, with hardly any interference from parents. Courtship within the lower middle class tended to be decorous and the motives leading to marriage prudent. Courtship among the poor, who could afford few pleasures beyond sex and drink, was far less inhibited, as the figures for prenuptial pregnancies demonstrate. A prenuptial pregnancy was a pregnancy that resulted in the birth of a child 8½ months after the wedding, or earlier. In the sixteenth and seventeenth centuries recorded prenuptial pregnancies ran well below 20 percent of all first pregnancies; in the eighteenth century it shot up to 40 percent. In part this was a result of the revival between 1620 and 1720 of the belief that a betrothal (an exchange of promises to marry) justified the consummation of the sexual act, but many pregnancies occurred long before the wedding day and can only be explained by a decline in the moral, legal, and economic inhibitions against premarital sexual intercourse. The collapse of the Puritan movement lessened the moral inhibitions; the decay of Church courts lessened the legal impediments; and the rise of a landless laboring class able to find employment in cottage industries increased the opportunities. As a result, among the poor in the eighteenth century most brides had had sexual intercourse with their future husbands before marriage.

Once married, the bride was wholly subject to her husband. The principle of patriarchy held sway throughout the sixteenth and seventeenth centuries. In law, wrote Blackstone, "the husband and wife are one, and the husband is that one." Both their property and their children belonged to the husband alone. This subjection of the wife was accompanied by deference and distance; wives called their husbands "Sir"; husbands, their wives "Madam." The Reformation and the Renaissance state both deepened the subjection of women. Protestantism laid on the husband the duty, once exercised by the priest, to supervise the religious and moral conduct of the family—family prayers took the place of the confessional. The Renaissance state regarded deference to the father as a guarantee of law and order, the equivalent of obedience to the monarch. Not without reason did James I call himself "the politic father of his people." Among the lower middle classes the fact that marriage was an economic partnership gave the wife some leverage, but she was more often treated as a servant than as a partner. Among the laboring poor, wives were subjected to a crushing burden of toil and to beatings by their husbands.

During the eighteenth century, among the wealthier classes, a more intimate, more affectionate, more equal, and less patriarchal marriage appeared, a companionate marriage, in which wives and husbands addressed each other by their first names. Since Elizabeth's reign, if not earlier, such companionate marriages were common among craftsmen and tradesmen; now they spread to the upper classes. The forces producing the companionate marriage were many. The decline in religious enthusiasm led to a decline in family prayers and to the authority the father exercised there. The growing belief in religious toleration and respect for the individual conscience furthered personal autonomy within the family. The Glorious Revolution, by discrediting patriarchy in the state, made it harder to justify it in the home. A growing revulsion against cruelty of all kinds led to the condemnation of wife-beating. In 1782 there was a public outcry when a judge sought to revive the doctrine that it was lawful for a husband to beat his wife, provided that the stick was no thicker than a thumb. But perhaps the most powerful force was the growing education of women. It was good conversation, wrote John Milton, that made for a good marriage, and it was education, asserted Dr. Johnson, that made for good conversation. In 1600 only one woman could sign her name to every eight men who could; by 1750 the ratio was one to two. And by then numerous boarding schools were turning out women well-versed in history, poetry, French, music, and dancing.

Parallel to these changes in marriage were changes in the attitude of men and women towards sexuality. Medieval theologians had condemned all sex as unclean and had made an ideal of virginity. The Protestant reformers replaced the ideal of virginity with that of holy matrimony, citing the Biblical injunction to be fruitful. But the Protestant theologians condemned all sexual activity that was not designed for procreation. There should be no sexual activity when conception is not possible, as during pregnancy. There should be no oral or manual sexual play. There should be no use of birth control practices, of which the commonest was *coitus interruptus*. There should be no expression of passionate love in marriage, which they regarded as no better than adultery. Actual practices may have differed considerably from these precepts, yet there were other obstacles to a high level of sexual activity in these years. Lack of personal hygiene, frequent illness, prudishness about appearing naked, and fear of pregnancy all inhibited sexual activity. During the eighteenth century, however, a desire to limit families and the new ideal of the pursuit of pleasure led to the liberation of sexuality among the upper classes. The new hedonism separated the pleasures of sex from the procreative function. Authors such as Aphra Behn, Mrs. Manley, Bernard de Mandeville, and John Wilkes unblushingly celebrated the pleasures of sex. From 1675 onwards the upper classes practiced birth control. And the bookstores of London freely sold pornographic books and pictures. But the new hedonism was largely for men. During these centuries, as during most of human history, there existed a double standard of sexual behavior. A bride was expected to be a virgin on her wedding night; a man was expected to have had some sexual experience. Fornication and adultery by men were regarded as minor sins; for women they brought the deepest dishonor.

This double standard was only possible because the bachelors and adulterous husbands of the upper classes found sexual partners in the actresses, milliners, maids, and whores of the lower classes. Promiscuity and prostitution among the poor supported female chastity among the rich. There is evidence to show that such promiscuity existed even in Elizabethan times. In Essex during Elizabeth's reign 15,000 persons out of a population of 40,000 adults were summoned before church courts for sexual offenses, which meant that an adult during those years had one chance in four of being summoned before a court for adultery, fornication, incest, or homosexuality. The rate of illegitimacy in Elizabethan England was 4 percent. Under the pressure of Puritan preaching a stricter standard of sexual morality was achieved in the seventeenth century; the rate of illegitimacy fell to 1½ percent. But in the eighteenth century both promiscuity and prostitution flourished, with the rate of illegitimacy rising to over 4 percent in 1760 and to 8 percent in the 1780s. London became the scene of a vast sexual underworld, made up of kept mistresses, high-class houses of assignation, general and specialized brothels, and common street whores. Men of all classes made use of prostitutes, the demand for which increased with the growing number of bachelors and late marriages. Poverty drove young girls to become prostitutes, in accordance with Francis Place's law that "chastity and poverty are incompatible." The growing culture of sexual promiscuity among the poor also helped swell the ranks of prostitutes. Many were recruited from unwed mothers. Prostitutes ranged in age from 15 to 22; the median age was 18; none was active after 22. They were an abject, wretched, hopeless class, the most pitiable class of persons in England.

The begetting of children was one of the principal purposes of marriage, though among the landed classes daughters were less welcome than sons (since the dowries needed to find them husbands could bankrupt a family). Among the poor few, if any, children were welcome (since it was a struggle to find the food to feed them). In the sixteenth and seventeenth centuries parents were negligent in the care of infants, with the result that infants were weaned from the mother's breast at a later date than they are today and were not subjected to severe toilet training. In other ways, though, they were more severely treated. In order to keep a child from breaking its leg or scratching out its eyes or tearing off its ears, it was wrapped tightly in bandages for the first four months of its life, a practice called swaddling.

Once the child had left infancy for childhood, he or she entered a world marked by formality, distance, deference, and obedience. Children of the upper classes saw little of their parents, being entrusted to a wetnurse as an infant, then to nurses and tutors, and finally, at about ten, to the master or mistress of a boarding school. Boys and girls lower in the social scale left home at about the same age to become domestic servants or apprentices. Not only deference

A swaddled child; the infant child of Sir John St. John at Lydiard Tregoze, Wiltshire (*Lawrence Stone*).

but cruelty marked the years of childhood. This was in part a product of Puritanism, which taught the doctrine of Original Sin and regarded the child in the cradle as a sinner. His will must be broken, he must be taught obedience to God's commandments, he must be made virtuous; otherwise the dream of creating a Godly society on this earth could not be realized. To this end parents and masters used not a system of rewards but of physical punishment, to which was added the psychological terrors of death and Hell. The children's books of the time threatened divine vengeance on the sinner. It was even believed that schoolmasters could by flogging teach boys Latin grammar. The commonest form of punishment of an errant boy was to lay him over a bench and flog his naked buttocks with a bundle of birches until the blood flowed. Many apprentices were exposed to similar sadism from their masters. The one redeeming feature to the Puritan approach to childhood is that, unlike the earlier indifference shown children, it arose from a concern for the child's future.

During the eighteenth century this gloomy picture changed. Signs of greater warmth, affection, intimacy, cheerfulness, and permissiveness appeared within the family. Swaddling gave way to the use of loose clothing. Maternal breast feeding, which deepened the affection of the mother for the child, replaced wetnurses. More affectionate modes of address, as "Mamma" and "Papa" replaced "Sir" and "Madam." Symbolic acts of deference, such as kneeling or standing when in the presence of parents, faded away. Children's books that offered plain entertainment and fun replaced those that threatened divine vengeance. Toy shops sprang up in the towns and dolls with changeable clothing were mass produced. Parents limited the size of their families in order to have the means to educate their sons and marry off their daughters. Increasingly parents educated their children at home in order to save them from the brutality of the schools. But that brutality diminished as flogging students simply for academic lapses declined. The causes for these changes were many. John Locke provided the intellectual premise for them by arguing that man was not born evil, as Calvin taught, but a blank slate, a *tabula rasa*, upon which a favorable environment might inscribe virtue. This view, joined to the growing individualism of the age, made abhorrent the doctrine that the purpose of childrearing was to break the will of the child. Then there were those eighteenth-century ideals of the pursuit of happiness and the cultivation of sentiment, which inevitably led to a more cheerful, affectionate home. And finally there was that movement against cruelty that led not only to the abolition of the slave trade and the suppression of cockfighting but to the decline of flogging.

These changes took place first in the families of the urban, literate middle class, but they spread to the landed gentry, and later to the nobility. These new ideas had less influence upon the lower middle class, who were often Nonconformists. Such families became increasingly child-oriented but remained authoritarian. Among cottagers and artisans parents often treated their children brutally, but prized them as economic assets. Among the very poor, parents were careless, indifferent, and cruel. Where they could exploit their children's labor they did so; where they could not, they neglected them. Death by neglect contributed significantly to the child mortality of the eighteenth century. The new, affectionate, happy family was rarely to be found among the poor.

THE ACT OF UNION WITH SCOTLAND

The most important public act of Queen Anne's reign may well have been the Act of Union, which led the English and the Scots to bury centuries of strife. The Scotland of Charles II's reign was a monument to fanaticism. At the Restoration Scotland recovered its Parliament, which Cromwell had abolished, but that Parliament was subservient to the Privy Council in Edinburgh, which Charles II controled from London. Charles used his power to restore episcopacy and to force the Presbyterians to renounce the Covenant (a solemn agreement, sworn to by the Scots, to defend their Church). Unwilling to take the tests imposed on them, a third of the clergy—the Covenanters—left their churches and conducted religious services on lonely hillsides or in thick forests. The government sent the militia to suppress these conventicles; the fierce Covenanters answered with rebellion, which the government then ruthlessly crushed. But though the English denied the Scots political and religious independence, they forced on them an unwanted economic independence. By the Navigation Acts the Scots were forbidden to trade with the English colonies or to engage in the English coastal trade.

By no means did all Scots favor the Covenanters, for their tyranny was as dreaded as the Court's, but all did oppose the popish designs of James II. Thus when James withdrew his troops from Scotland to resist William, the government in Edinburgh found itself powerless. A group of Scots hurried south to persuade William to summon a convention in Edinburgh. It met in March 1689 and drew up a Claim of Right similar to the English Declaration of Rights, only more radical: Where the English said James had "abdicated," the Scots boldly said he was "deposed." The convention also forced William to reestablish the Presbyterian Church and to abolish the Lords of the Articles, the committee through which the Crown controled Parliament. For the first time in centuries, the Scottish people enjoyed both religious and political independence.

But though a free Parliament quickened the political life of Scotland and a restored Presbyterianism calmed its religious quarrels, the Scots remained poor. A million inhabitants scratched a meager existence from the soil or engaged in a limited local trade. Scottish agricultural methods were medieval; no money was invested in the land; improvements proved impossible because of short leases and insecurity of tenure. The per capita wealth of Scotland was thought to be one-fifth that of England. What the Scots wanted most was a chance to participate in the English trading empire, but the English persisted in excluding them. The Scots therefore resolved to create their own commercial empire. In 1695 they founded a Company to Trade with Africa and the Indies, and in 1698 that company founded a colony at Darien, on the Isthmus of Panama. From here they hoped to dominate the trade of both Atlantic and Pacific. But the Darien adventure, in which so many people had invested, proved a fiasco. The company placed its colony in the center of a swamp, sent out woolens and Bibles the natives did not want, and offended Spain, then the ally of England. Disease, bankruptcy, and Spanish troops soon ended the life of the colony. The Scots now saw that their only salvation was to enter into a union with England, a union that would bring them within the Navigation Acts.

The Scots had sought such a union in the past—in 1667, in 1670, and again in 1689—but had always been repulsed. They now found a lever with which to pry open the English commercial empire. In 1703 the Scottish Parliament passed an Act of Security which provided that the Parliament should meet on Queen Anne's death and choose a successor. That successor would not be the person the English chose unless England had previously conceded Scotland freedom to trade with England and its colonies. The passage of the Act of Security forced the English to choose between the perpetual hostility of a separate Scottish kingdom or a union that guaranteed full reciprocity of trade.

The English chose union and reciprocity. In 1706 Queen Anne, with the consent of both Parliaments, named commissioners to negotiate a Treaty of

Union. The treaty was a triumph of good sense and compromise. The two kingdoms became one, under a single Crown, with a single Parliament, and with trade laws that applied to all the inhabitants of "Great Britain," as the new kingdom was to be called. Though Scotland surrendered its Parliament, it retained its own system of law, so different from the English Common law, and the Presbyterian Church, whose privileges the treaty guaranteed for all generations to come. The taxation and tariff systems of Great Britain were to be one, though Scotland, in consideration of its poverty, was to pay only one-fortieth of the land tax.

The English Parliament ratified the treaty with little debate, but a bitter struggle ensued in the Scottish Parliament. Popular opinion in Scotland opposed the treaty, or did so until the Presbyterians saw that it offered adequate safeguards for their Church. But the final decision rested with Parliament. In 1707 the Scottish Parliament ratified the treaty. Some English money no doubt lubricated the process, but bribery alone cannot explain ratification. The true explanation lies in economic interests. The Scottish merchants who hoped to trade with the colonies and the Scottish landlords who wished to export corn, cattle, and coal to England had the numbers and the power to persuade the Scottish Parliament to ratify the treaty. Their calculations were not mistaken, for the Act of Union made possible the unprecedented prosperity of Scotland in the eighteenth century.

THE TREATY OF UTRECHT

The Act of Union was one of the most constructive acts carried out by the Whig ministers during these years. Their most destructive act was the failure to negotiate peace with France in 1709. The problem was Spain. In order to secure Portugal's adherence to the Grand Alliance, England in 1703 had promised not to make a peace that left Spain in the hands of the Bourbons. "No peace without Spain" became the slogan that imprisoned the minds of the Whigs. It proved particularly inappropriate when in 1707 a French and Spanish victory at the Battle of Almanza ended all hopes that Charles III, the Austrian claimant, could ever gain the Spanish throne. True, the next year Marlborough won another great victory and in 1709 France suffered the worst frost in living memory. A bankrupt Louis XIV even agreed to surrender Spain to Charles III, but when the English and Dutch demanded that he send French troops to drive his own grandson, Philip V, from Madrid, he refused. "If I must wage war," replied Louis XIV, "I had rather wage it against my enemies than against my children." The peace negotiations at Getruydenberg collapsed and the costly war dragged on.

In 1710 the nation grew weary of the war and Queen Anne grew weary of the Whigs. Not only did the squires groan under the heavy taxes, but shipping and trade suffered, as it had during William's war. Between May 1702 and

Christmas 1709 the English lost 1146 merchantmen. The nation longed for peace, but the Whigs drove on the war. They then made a serious tactical error; they impeached Dr. Henry Sacheverell, an unimportant High Church clergyman, for preaching a sermon against the principles of the Glorious Revolution. In the ensuing trial the Whig lawyers duly exposed the fallacies of passive obedience and the Lords found Dr. Sacheverell guilty, but they only suspended him from preaching for three years. The sentence was in fact an acquittal. The long trial, the publicity that attended it, and the virtual acquittal of Sacheverell turned public opinion away from the Whigs and the Dissenters and toward the Church and the Tories.

At this very moment, Robert Harley, a country Whig in William's reign, a Speaker of the House in 1701, a Tory secretary of state under Queen Anne, and a politician famous for his skill in managing the Commons, found his way up the back stairs of Kensington palace. Winning the Queen's favor, he skillfully directed her actions and quietly undermined the power of Godolphin and the Whigs. In August the Queen dismissed Godolphin and in September removed the Whigs. Harley himself became Chancellor of the Exchequer, and moderate Tories filled the other offices. It was a splendid illustration of the power that remained in the Queen's hands, but Harley could not hope to remain in office unless he could manage Parliament successfully for her—and it was a Whig Parliament he must meet in the autumn. He therefore persuaded the Queen to dissolve Parliament and send out writs for the election of a new one. Desperate for peace and angered by the Sacheverell trial, the voters returned a Tory majority, a majority which Harley, himself a moderate Tory, skillfully managed to bring the country the peace it sought.

The greatest obstacle to peace lay with England's allies, particularly Austria, whose claims at the peace table far exceeded its contributions on the battlefield. To circumvent the allies, the new Tory ministry negotiated a separate peace. It began secret negotiations in August 1710 and reached a preliminary agreement with France in October 1711. It provided for a peace without Spain, which provoked the fury of the Whigs. Only by persuading the Queen to name twelve new peers was Harley able to win the support of the House of Lords for the preliminaries; and only by withdrawing English troops from combat in June 1712 could he force the allies to join in the negotiations at Utrecht. Britain undoubtedly deserted its allies and made a separate peace, but it is difficult to see how it could have made peace otherwise.

The resulting Treaty of Utrecht showed once again that most peace treaties reflect the disposition of military forces at the end of hostilities. The forces of Philip V had conquered Spain and the treaty acknowledged him as King of Spain, with the provision that the crowns of France and Spain should never be joined in one person. Marlborough had won that part of the Netherlands which is now Belgium; it became the Austrian Netherlands. The Dutch received the right to garrison the barrier fortresses in the Austrian Netherlands. Above all the treaty reflected the dominance of English seapower. Since 1694, the English fleet had wintered in the Mediterranean. In 1704, a week before the

Battle of Blenheim, the fleet had seized Gibraltar, and four years later it captured Minorca, with its splendid harbor at Port Mahon. By the Treaty of Utrecht Britain retained both. In September 1710, 400 British marines and 1500 New Englanders captured Port Royal in Acadia, which was renamed Nova Scotia. The Treaty of Utrecht recognized it as English. The treaty likewise gave Britain a clear title to Newfoundland and the Hudson's Bay region, and granted to it the island of St. Kitt's in the West Indies. Finally, Britain wrested from Spain the Asiento, an agreement whereby Spain gave Britain the exclusive right to carry black slaves to the Spanish Indies and permission to send one English ship of 500 tons each year to trade at the annual fairs in the Caribbean.

Britain had not yet won Canada or gained India, but it was firmly set on the path of imperial greatness. The Treaty of Utrecht made that plain, but so did the demographic facts. In 1688 there were only 200,000 British settlers in North America; by 1713 there were 350,000.

THE HANOVERIAN SUCCESSION

The succession question dominated the last years of Queen Anne's reign, but intermingled with it was the question of the unity of the Tory party. Robert Harley, who became the Earl of Oxford in 1711, sought to govern above party, as Godolphin and Marlborough had tried to do in the early years of Anne's reign. But once again the managers came up against the insatiable demands of party. The Tories wanted every Whig thrown out of office and replaced with a Tory. These Tories found a leader in the brilliant and mercurial Henry St. John, Viscount Bolingbroke. Bolingbroke believed that a government could no more be carried on with mixed hands than a coach could be driven with unequal wheels. He vowed to drive every Whig from office, even the most minor. The Earl of Oxford, who as Lord Treasurer and the Queen's favorite controled patronage, protested and delayed, but finally yielded. Gradually Tories replaced Whigs in the government, but not fast enough for Bolingbroke, who now sought to curry the Queen's favor behind Oxford's back.

Allied with Bolingbroke were the High Churchmen, who wished to suppress the Dissenters totally. In 1711 they secured an act against the practice of occasional conformity and in 1714 a Schism Act that would close down all Dissenting academies and schools. The hatred of the High Churchman for the Dissenter remained unabated to the bitter end.

But the time was running out for the Tories. The Queen's health declined and the prospect of the succession of the House of Hanover plunged the Tories into gloom, for they had offended Hanover. The Tories had on their right wing the Jacobites, so called because they supported the claims to the crown of James II and his son, James III, whose names in Latin would be Jacobus. Jacobitism was largely a sentimental movement, but the Jacobites were noisy and powerful enough in the Tory party, particularly among the Scottish members, to frighten Hanover. The Earl of Oxford, now descending into indolence and drink, probably remained loyal to Hanover, but Bolingbroke in the last few months of the Queen's reign appeared to cast his lot with the Jacobites. Winning the Queen's favor, he was able to engineer Oxford's dismissal and plan the admission of Jacobites to the Cabinet. But he had only two full days in power before the Queen died on August 1, 1714. Had she lived another six months, Bolingbroke might have sought to bring in the pretender, but he also might have shrunk from so hopeless an enterprise. It is almost certain that he could not have found a majority to repeal the Act of Settlement, and rebellion brought with it too many risks. The one certain fact is that Bolingbroke in these last months shattered the unity of the Tory party, thereby assuring that when the Whigs came to power under George I they would face a divided and discredited opposition. The Whig ascendancy of the eighteenth century was prepared in the last months of the Queen's reign.

FURTHER READING

DAVID OGG. *England in the Reigns of James II and William III*. Oxford, 1955. A narrative of political events, with chapters on law, government, religion, economics, and social thought; a lively, engaging book, offering a traditional interpretation of the Revolution.

HENRY HORWITZ. *Parliament, Policy, and Politics in the Reign of William III*. Manchester, England, 1977. Narrowly political; focuses on how the King's business was transacted in Parliament; not easy reading but incorporates in its narrative the most recent scholarly work on the reign.

GEORGE MACAULAY TREVELYAN. *England Under Queen Anne*. 3 vols. London, 1930, 1932, 1934. An epic survey of the reign, written with charm, acuity, and authority by a distinguished English historian.

GEOFFREY HOLMES. *British Politics in the Age of Anne*. London, 1967. A penetrating and vivid picture of the politics of the age, not only in Parliament but in the counties, coffeehouses, theaters, and the press.

DAVID CHANDLER. *Marlborough as Military Commander*. New York, 1973. Not as limited as the title suggests; rather, a well-written biography by a leading authority on eighteenth-century warfare.

P. G. M. DICKSON. *The Financial Revolution in England: A Study in the Development of Public Credit 1688–1756*. London, 1967. A scholarly, technical, yet important study of the origins of the national debt, the money market, and the Stock Exchange.

ERIC KERRIDGE. *The Agricultural Revolution*. London, 1967. A study of alternate husbandry, fen drainage, the use of fertilizers, water meadows, and new crops such as turnips and clover; its thesis that these amounted to an agricultural revolution is controversial.

JUDITH HOOK. *The Baroque Age in England*. London, 1976. Discusses art and architecture during the whole seventeenth century, though the baroque, narrowly defined, flourished only after 1690.

*RALPH A. HOULBROOKE. *The English Family 1450–1700*. New York, 1984. A useful survey and critical analysis of current work on the early-modern English family; rejects the negative view of parent-child relations advanced by Lawrence Stone in *The Family, Sex, and Marriage in England 1500–1800* (New York, abridged ed., paperback, 1980).

*RICHARD GOUGH. *The History of Myddle*. Penguin Books, 1981. The history of a seventeenth-century parish, written in 1701 by Richard Gough, a resident of the parish; filled with vivid insights into the lives of ordinary English countryfolk.

An age of stability: 1714–1760

17

On the evening of September 18, 1714, George I, Elector of Hanover, great-grandson of James I, and King of England by act of Parliament, landed with his mistress and his son, the future George II, at Greenwich. The next day some two hundred coaches of the gentry and nobility escorted the two Georges to the city, where they were greeted by the Lord Mayor and the cheers of thousands. The carriages and the cheers expressed relief that England had escaped a civil war and a Catholic king far more than it did any great love of the two Georges.

About to enter upon an age of stability, imperial triumph, and intellectual enlightenment, the England of 1714 appeared to contemporaries politically unstable and diplomatically isolated. What could be said of a nation that beheaded and deposed kings, fought civil wars, suppressed the Irish, endured Titus Oates's mobs, divided into political factions, and preferred the quarrels of representative government to the order of absolute monarchy? Who could have confidence in England after the Peace of Utrecht, which allowed a Bourbon to rule Spain, abandoned allies, and left France dominant in Europe and a threat in America. But forty-six years later, in 1760, the England that mourned the death of George II had proved the soundness of constitutional government, acquired a world empire, and become the champion of reason in all fields of endeavor and inquiry.

THE ACHIEVEMENT OF POLITICAL STABILITY

Representative governments have rarely lasted long. Every age is littered with its failures: neither wise Athenians, practical Romans, nor ingenious Florentines could make it last. All the more remarkable then was the development in eighteenth-century England of an art of sharing power and governing others that still endures.

How did they do it? Any answer to that question must begin with the English constitution and particularly with its separation of powers. Many contemporaries thought this tripartite separation of powers the key to English liberty, though they could not agree as to the particular triad. Some saw it in King, Parliament, and the courts of law; others in King, Parliament, and local government. The truth is that there was no tripartite division; the power to govern was widely distributed. It did reside, to be sure, in King, Parliament, and the law courts, but it also resided in the counties with their lord lieutenants and justices of the peace, in the parishes with their overseers and constables, in the dioceses with bishops and arch-deacons, and even in commercial matters with the Bank of England. This wide distribution of power brought into the governance of the country those powerful oligarchies that dominated England's economy and society and contributed to its political stability.

Too broad a distribution of power can, if there is no agreement where sovereignty lies, lead to confusion. Although in theory many viewed the King as the supreme executive, in crises it became clear that sovereignty lay with Parliament. Through the control of the purse it could bring the King's government to a halt. It could also enact or repeal any law, abolish, create, or reform law courts, and dismiss judges. The Lord Chancellor and the Attorney General sat in Parliament, and Parliament's leaders advised the King whom to appoint as the judges of the leading courts. The same leaders also advised the King whom he should employ as his chief ministers, though how far the King had to obey that advice was the great constitutional question of eighteenth-century politics. In theory the King could appoint and dismiss any minister he wished. The ministers were also answerable to the King for day-to-day government. But ultimately, on great issues and in great crises, the ministers followed the will of that Parliament which alone voted the money to carry on the government. When it came to daily government, therefore, a great deal depended on the personality of the King, which from 1714 to 1760 meant George I and George II.

George I was neither brilliant nor ambitious nor, since he was shy, private, and spoke English poorly, very sociable; but he was not cold and unfeeling, and if wooden and formal in public, in private he was witty and pleasant. Calm, shrewd, and realistic and no mere cipher, he ruled as firmly as his son, who was more sociable, though as ill-tempered, opinionated, and irascible. But because of his intelligent and vivacious wife, Queen Caroline, he did preside over a lively Court. He also loved the business of governing, which he did with a clear but narrow intelligence, a passion for detail, and in crises, a dependence on the stronger wills of his wife and his ministers. George I and George II were not figureheads. They made all military appointments, supervised civil ones, distributed favors, presided over the courts, decided foreign policy, and chose and dismissed ministers, whom they and Parliament considered their servants. Yet their energy had its limits. After 1717 George I ceased to attend meetings of the informal cabinet council, a council George II only occasionally attended. By 1760 this small inner cabinet used the patronage it controlled to build strong ministries that the King had difficulty dismissing. In 1756, on failing to dismiss a ministry, George II exclaimed: "I do not look upon myself as King while I am in the hands of these scoundrels."

A constitution that not only allowed landed wealth dominance in Cabinet and Parliament and, as Justices of the Peace, in the countryside, but also gave representation to the counties' "40-shilling" freeholders (those who owned a freehold that would rent at 40 shillings a year) and to townsmen in open constituencies and gave liberty of the press and assembly to all subjects was a constitution that by allowing wealth its role and discontent its expression, greatly furthered stability.

A second major reason for stability was the absence of those three explosive issues—war, succession, and religion—that violently divided Whig and Tory in

George II, King of England from 1727 to 1760 (*National Portrait Gallery*).

the reign of Queen Anne. The war was over, the Hanoverian succession a *fait accompli*, and religious differences, if as pervasive as ever, was forced to give opposing sects a grudging tolerance. The Lutheranism of Georges I and II made the hopes of High Church Tories for the suppression of Dissent quite as improbable as James III's Catholicism made improbable High Tory hopes for the restoration of the Stuarts. Yet many Tories sought both improbabilities, those wanting James III as King earning the name Jacobites and the label traitor. In 1715 Jacobite Tories in northern England had joined a 10,000-man Scots army in an attempt to restore James III. George I thus proscribed all Tories from office, national or local, a proscription his son, even more hostile to Tories, continued. The result was to drive all Tories, even loyal ones, to rhetorical talk of a Stuart restoration and toasts to the King across the water. Although most were actually not traitors they were caught in a dilemma: by solemn oaths and by their beliefs in a divine right monarchy and the sacred laws of inheritance, they were attached to the Stuarts, but by an equally deep belief in passive resistance and loyalty to lawful authority, as well as from practical interests, they could not take up arms against the Hanoverians. The result was a distinct Tory party, an Anglican one, one with distinct policies and supporters, one returning 178 members of Parliament (MPs) in 1722 and 149 in 1734, but a party paralyzed and proscribed, doomed to submit to the rule of the Whigs.

The one-party government of the Whigs from 1714 to 1760—and of Robert Walpole from 1719 to 1742—was a third reason for stability. Sir Robert Walpole was a country squire from Norfolk, with an appetite for fine food, grand houses, coarse wit, and political power. He had an unrivaled ability to understand and use men, an ability he displayed in dealing with the South Sea Company. The company, though formed to trade in the South Seas, was used mainly to refinance the huge war debt at a lower rate of interest. The directors sold stock worth far more than the company's earning power, and just before the public realized it, many of them sold their shares. The price of stock plummeted from £1,050 per share to £140, and then the company collapsed. Some of Walpole's chief rivals in the Whig government were deeply involved and so disgraced. Walpole, who was not implicated, wisely came to their defense. The disgrace of some rivals and the death of others suddenly created a vacuum the astute squire from Norfolk eagerly filled. Popular with Parliament, he had only to win the confidence of George I, and after 1727, George II, to become the most powerful politician in England.

By persuading Parliament to vote George I a larger income, by managing Parliament with firmness, and by tact and shrewdness, he won the King's favor. That favor gave him influence over appointments to offices at Court. Deftly combining this court patronage with the even greater patronage of the government, he built up a political machine that survived even his own fall in 1742 and that, in the less brilliant hands of Henry Pelham and his brother the Duke of Newcastle, continued the stable rule of the Whig oligarchy. The Pelhams were from the aristocracy. The Duke of Newcastle, one of the richest landowners

Robert Walpole, unrivaled leader of the Whigs, the House of Commons, and the Government from 1720 to 1742 (*National Portrait Gallery*).

in England, was Lord Lieutenant of Nottinghamshire and Middlesex, and controlled the election of sixteen members of Parliament. From 1722 to 1760 Walpole, Henry Pelham, and Newcastle, working with the two Georges, bestowed upon their friends places, pensions, honors, government contracts, and electoral assistance.

That system brought a needed cohesion to political life. In the nineteenth century political parties performed that function; in the early Georgian period after the Walpole-Whig monopoly ended, political parties rested less on coherent differences of ideologies and interests than they did on aristocratic connections whose coalescings could win the patronage of court, government, Church, army, and navy. Walpole and the Pelhams realized this fact and made the best of it. By 1742 a full 142 MPs had places, 24 at court, about 50 actively in government, and the remainder with sinecures and other emoluments. Grooms of the King's bedchamber received £500 a year, clerks of the green cloth, £1,000. Sinecures in the civil government—that is, offices with a salary but requiring no work—also paid handsomely. For men ambitious for both power and income, the desirable offices were First Lord of the Treasury, Lord Chancellor, President of the Council, Lord Privy Seal, one of the two Secretaries of State, or other offices of cabinet rank. Serving these ministers were undersecretaries and members of the Treasury, Admiralty, and Ordinance boards. Equally attractive to the thirty barristers in the Commons were appointments as Solicitor General, Master of the Rolls, or Admiralty Judge. All told, fifty "men of business" earned good incomes administering the government's business and defending its policies in debate. The patronage system also included the House of Lords. To be made a peer, spiritual or temporal, was the highest honor. Its twenty-six bishops were quite as loyal to the great Whigs who appointed them as were that fourth of the Lords who enjoyed rewarding places at Court.

The constant complaint was that there were not enough places. There were, however, other rewards. MPs loyal to the government won pensions, military promotions, contracts for supplying the army and navy, and if the MP were in electoral trouble, either a safe government seat or money and influence to help win another. Finally, there were honors, knighthoods, baronetcies, and the Order of the Garter. The system of influence extended beyond Parliament. The government controlled many rich benefices and cathedral appointments. Ecclesiastical preferments, said Walpole, are as useful to the government as civil appointments. Civil appointments were many and at all levels, particularly in the customs, excise, and stamp offices. It was more exalted, of course, to be named a lord lieutenant or justice of the peace. These ecclesiastical, civil, and local appointments were carefully dovetailed with the interests of Whig families in order to elect friendly MPs. It was a world of family ties, local friendships, aristocratic connections, mutual obligations, and influence.

As vast and labyrinthine as this system of influence was, its critics at the time exaggerated its effects. In 1742 it could not save Robert Walpole from having to resign when Parliament blamed him for listless conduct of the war against Spain. Neither could it save Newcastle in 1756, when his fumbling conduct of the war against France angered Parliament. In both cases George II supported his ministers fully, but to no avail. The majesty of prerogative and the power of patronage could not, even when combined, withstand the anger of Parliament. The fall of Walpole and Newcastle reveals both that ministers were ultimately responsible to Parliament and that the patronage system could not, in itself, always ensure a majority. There never were, in fact, more than 150 or 160 MPs at any one time who held place, nor did holding place mean they would not vote against the government. Perhaps 40 or 50 more, particularly officers in the army and navy, felt obliged to support the government—that is, unless it did badly. Some 300 independent country gentlemen, Whig and Tory, and some 50 rival Whig politicians out of office owed nothing to the government. The patronage system provided an important but not a sufficient basis for a stable government. Of equal importance was the electoral system by which 558 men won seats in Parliament.

That the British electoral system could contribute to stability seems utterly paradoxical. Its chaotic nature promised anarchy, not order. Scotland elected 45 MPs, Wales 24, and England 489. Forty English counties, representing 160,000 voters, elected but 80 MPs, while 203 English boroughs, representing only 101,000 voters, returned 409 MPs, and the two English universities, 4. In the counties all who owned a freehold that would rent at 40 shillings a year could vote. It was a franchise that in 1761 allowed 800 to vote in Rutland and 20,000 in Yorkshire. So far the system seems reasonably ordered. But little order defined the franchise and sizes of the 203 English boroughs.

Boroughs returning MPs varied greatly. Some, but not many, were large towns where thousands voted, others, like Old Sarum, were unpopulated sheep walks. Most were in the south of England. Though their franchises differed greatly, most fell into five categories: pot wallopers, scot and lot, freeman, corporation, and burgage. In the pot walloper boroughs all householders *not* on poor relief could vote, and in scot and lot all could vote who *paid* poor rates. These broad franchises prevailed in only 48 of the 203 boroughs. Far narrower were most of the 92 freeman boroughs, where only those whom the town corporation designated freemen could *vote*, but it was a variable franchise that allowed 20 to vote in Camelford and 7,000 in London. In the 27 corporation boroughs, only the mayor and aldermen or town councilors could vote, which usually meant 30 or 40 and never over 60. In the 29 burgage boroughs, only those who held property of a very special tenure called burgage could vote. Most burgage boroughs were so dependent on one patron that they became known as pocket boroughs. Such boroughs could be bought and sold, and in 1761 the going price was £2,000.

Boroughs of all types came under the influence of patrons. Since only one in five boroughs had more than 500 voters, and most far less, the more powerful local landed families were able to control elections. They did so usually by exploiting that deference, dependence, and friendship that borough elites owed them, but if necessary they used entertainment or bribery—49 hogshead of strong beer helping win one borough in Sussex, £10 a voter in another. By such influences 55 peers and 56 commoners controlled the election of 205 MPs, and the government controlled another 30. MPs who ran in larger constituencies had to work harder and spend more in managing their boroughs. The 80 MPs from the counties, mostly from old gentry families, also represented large electorates, but they were rural ones whose voters were dependent on the ruling families, families both Whig and Tory, who often agreed not to contest the constituencies. In 1761, for example, only 53 of 314 constituencies were contested.

The House of Commons elected by this system reflected the predominance of the landed classes. One-fifth of the MPs were sons either of English or Irish peers, another sixth were baronets or the sons of baronets, and most of the remaining came from the gentry class. One-third were professional men, mostly in law, the army, and the navy; they were often the younger sons of peers and gentlemen. Fifty merchants sat in the Commons, nearly all wealthy ones from

THE CITIES AND RESOURCES
OF BRITAIN IN 1800

MILES

0   20   40   60   80

SHIPYARDS

Glasgow   Edinburgh

COAL

R. Tweed

Newcastle
upon Tyne
SHIPYARDS

R. Tyne

Sunderland

COAL

Stockton on Tees

R. Tees   IRON

York

Leeds   Hull

COAL   COAL

Huddersfield

Liverpool   Manchester

COTTON

Sheffield

COAL   STEEL

R. Trent

COAL

Derby   Nottingham

Shrewsbury

Birmingham   Leicester   Norwich

R. Severn

COAL

Aberystwyth

R. Ouse

COAL   Northampton   Cambridge

R. Avon

Carmarthan   Rhondda

COAL   Oxford

IRON   London

Cardiff   Bristol

Bath   R. Thames

Dover

COAL

Southampton   Brighton

Plymouth   Portsmouth

452

London, and a handful of MPs who had won fortunes in India. Wealth was the universal solvent; it could buy burgage tenures or win elections. The electoral system was not closed. Businessmen and professionals could enter it—and potentially in vast numbers. But in 1760 they were a small minority; the landed classes dominated most elections.

In numbers the landed classes were few; in wealth, amply provided; in outlook, homogeneous. Some 400 great families owned some 20 percent of the cultivated land and enjoyed incomes from £5,000 to £40,000; 700 to 800 families owned nearly 30 percent of the land and enjoyed incomes from £3,000 to £4,000. These families formed the core of the landed elite. They had the status and commanded the deference to win county elections and the money and influence to manage borough ones. In the some 3,000 lesser gentry who owned another 30 percent of the land they found allies at the elections, as they did among the landed classes' younger sons in the Church, in the law, or home on half pay from the army. United by marriage, similar educations, common economic interests, and the power to govern locally, they were of the same class as the politicians who governed England. Powerful, assured, and themselves often active in commerce and industry, they could welcome into their world their mercantile and urban cousins. The social and economic unity of the landed and commercial elite and their control of the electoral system underlay the stability of early Georgian England quite as much as did the constitution, the wise rule of the two Georges, the dominance of Walpole and the Whigs, and the patronage system. All these factors explain why the government not only provided sound if undistinguished rule between 1716 and 1756, but could in 1756 prove its flexibility by placing in power the grandson of an Indian merchant and the fiercest critic of the King, William Pitt the elder, and then support his audacious attempt to wrest an empire from France.

THE WINNING OF AN EMPIRE

Though Britain in 1714 had a new and vulnerable dynasty and was without allies, it did not abandon its two traditional diplomatic goals, the protection of trade and the preservation of a balance of power in Europe. To these goals George I added a third, the interests of the Electorate of Hanover, a concern that aroused fierce opposition from MPs who felt it should form no part of British diplomacy, whose sole aim should be national self-interest. But diplomacy is rarely that rational, and dynastic concerns counted for much in eighteenth-century Europe, as did the pride of monarchs, the vanity of foreign ministers, and in England the passions of the people.

In the dour George I and the scholarly Lord Stanhope monarchical pride and ministerial vanity combined to define, from 1715 to 1721, Britain's foreign policy. It was a bold, elaborate, and convoluted policy, one that George I insisted should protect Hanoverian interests in the Germanies and that Stanhope insisted

EUROPE IN THE MID-EIGHTEENTH CENTURY

MILES

100 200 300 400

NORWAY

SWEDEN

RUSSIA

DENMARK

AUSTRIAN
NETHERLANDS

Bremen

Verden

PRUSSIA

POLAND

ENGLAND

HOLLAND

HANOVER

SILESIA

HOLY ROMAN EMPIRE

BAVARIA

FRANCE

SWITZERLAND

AUSTRIA

HUNGARY

MILAN

SAVOY

OTTOMAN EMPIRE

PORTUGAL

SPAIN

CORSICA

PAPAL
STATES

SARDINIA

SICILY

should protect Britain's security and peace. Stanhope hoped to attain his goals by ensuring that there be no disruptions of the settled European system. To make Britain the effective policeman of that system, Stanhope kept the army strong, taxes high, and alliances many and complex. But his greatest scheme, to use powerful Prussia as a check on Russia and Austria and as an anchor of a Protestant alliance, fell afoul of George I's Hanoverian quarrels with Prussia over Mecklenburgh. Instead, a fourteen-year alliance was formed with France, an apparently anomalous treaty since France was Britain's historic enemy but one that pleased George I since it guaranteed his throne from French-sponsored Jacobite invasions. It also allowed Europe's two great powers to recover from thirty years of war, to rebuild armed forces and replenish treasuries. Stanhope, emboldened by the French alliance and his grand schemes, opposed in 1718 Spain's territorial ambitions in Italy, ambitions that meant nothing to British subjects, and that led, in 1718, to a useless war, but one that luckily resulted in Britain's Admiral Byng sinking, off Sicily, most of Spain's fleet.

Stanhope died in 1721. His successor, Lord Townshend, in continuing Stanhope's grand system, found it costly, difficult, and in its preference of Hanoverian interests over British commerce, and French alliances over Dutch territorial integrity, quite unpopular. When in 1730, Townshend replaced the Anglo-French with a weaker Anglo-Austrian alliance one-half of Stanhope's system collapsed. In 1732 when the Austrian alliance, the other half of that system, failed, British active involvement in Europe also collapsed. In its place Robert Walpole, now Secretary of State, adopted a policy of isolation. He even insisted that George I stay neutral in the war of Polish succession.

Isolation was at first popular. The land tax, 4s in 1727, was only 1s in 1732. Not so popular was Walpole's pacific view of Spanish depradations of British trade in the Caribbean. On the question of Spanish seizure of English ships, Walpole patiently negotiated a compromise, the Convention of Pardo, of January 1739. It was a compromise that imposed checks on British trade, and any checks on trade evoked the fiery eloquence of William Pitt and the resolute anger of the merchants. Parliament, in 1739, voted to go to war with Spain.

The Spanish war proved costly and humiliating. England won no great victories or territories and did not force Spain to abandon the right of seizure. No more glorious was the War of the Austrian Succession, which England entered in 1740. Walpole had promised Austria that when Charles VI of Austria died and his daughter, Maria Theresa, succeeded to the throne, England would help her empire. At Charles's death Prussia and Bavaria, with French support, began to dismember the empire, and Parliament, against Walpole's advice, came to Maria Theresa's rescue. England could not, said those anxious to rescue Maria Theresa, allow a France of 22 million people and with an army of 130,000 men and a navy of 80 men-of-war, destroy Austria and dominate Europe. The cynical Walpole saw no threat to Europe; he only saw German princes hungry for territory. After Parliament forced him from office, he told his successors:

"This war is yours . . . I wish you joy of it." For eight years England fought desultory, losing battles that formed no part of an overall strategy and that were waged by inept commanders. During the same eight years diplomats failed to gain a winning alliance or a peace until in 1748 both sides settled for a peace based on the status quo ante bellum (that is, on the status of Europe before the war). It had been, said Thomas Carlyle, "an unintelligible huge English-Foreign-Delirium."

But it was a war not without some romance and some lessons. The romance came in July 1745 when Charles Edward landed in Scotland, declared his father, James III, King of England, raised an army, and defeated the English at Prestonpans. He then invaded England. The English neither rose to support him nor took arms to oppose him, but awaited the return from Flanders of George II's younger son, the Duke of Cumberland, and his army. Facing little resistance, Prince Charles Edward moved to Derby, where he was poised for a dash to London. But he lost his nerve, retreated to Scotland, lost disastrously at Culloden, and fled first into the hills and then to France. The Duke of Cumberland turned romance into tragedy by ordering his army to massacre the defeated Highlanders.

The lesson of the war was that naval power was crucial. English naval victories so decisively cleared the seas of the French navy that England had France's overseas trade and colonies at her mercy. France, though triumphant in Flanders, had thus to agree to the peace of Aix-la-Chapelle.

The peace did not last long. In 1754 France and Britain again fought each other in India and North America. In the summer of 1756 they also went to war in Europe, only with different allies. In the 1740s England allied with Austria against France and Austria. This famous diplomatic revolution reflected both the shrewd calculations of Austria's Count Kaunitz and the trial-and-error diplomacy of England's greatest manager of parliamentary boroughs, the Duke of Newcastle. Kaunitz knew what he wanted, an alliance with a powerful France; Newcastle only knew that he wished to use subsidies to collect allies as he collected boroughs. Newcastle thus offered to subsidize Russia, which agreed. This unsettled Frederick II of Prussia, who asked for a subsidy and obtained it, which unsettled Louis XV, who yielded to Kaunitz's designs and allied with Austria. Russia was meanwhile piqued at England for subsidizing Frederick and so joined Austria, France, Sweden, and the Imperial Circle of Germany against the common enemy, Prussia. Frederick II's 5.5 million Prussians faced countries with a combined population greater than 100 million. Prussia could not expect much help from England's 6 million inhabitants, particularly since England had committed its resources to colonial wars and faced a France whose seventy heavily armored ships-of-the-line and numerous frigates threatened the sea lanes to India, Africa, and North America. France also had forts extending from the St. Lawrence to New Orleans, enjoyed alliances with Indian nations, and possessed armed forces far stronger than those of England's apathetic and disarmed colonies. France seemed destined to dominate North America.

In the fall of 1756 England's plight looked alarming. In 1755 the French had destroyed General Braddock's army in Pennsylvania. In May 1756 the French routed Britain's Mediterranean fleet and captured Minorca and in August captured Fort Oswego on Lake Ontario. The timid, faltering, and procrastinating Duke of Newcastle could do no more than execute the admiral who lost Minorca. All was pessimism and defeatism: the young Lord Shelburne said he could find no one "who did not believe we were utterly ruined." A year later that ruin seemed as inexorable. That scathing critic of past weakness, William Pitt, replaced Newcastle as the chief minister, but the failures continued. In June the Austrians defeated Frederick in Bohemia and in July news arrived from India of the loss of Calcutta. In September the Duke of Cumberland surrendered to the French and declared Hanover and Hesse neutral. In October the daring descent on Rochefort on the French coast proved a debacle. In November Fort William Henry in New York fell to the French. Also in November a storm destroyed the British expedition sent to capture Cape Breton just north of Nova Scotia.

Disasters that would discourage most men did not lessen Pitt's confidence. He outlined bold strategies, laid out tactical plans in detail, promoted and inspired talented officers, and recruited rugged Scottish Highlanders. Under Pitt the army grew to 100,000, the navy to 70,000, shipyards expanded, and foundries for making cannons multiplied. By 1759 England had a fleet twice the size of France's. British commerce flourished as France's shriveled. A hum of ceaseless activity swept over Pitt's England, but only time could translate it into victories. Heartening though it was to hear of General Forbes's capture of Fort Dusquesne (promptly renamed Pittsburgh), of Clive's victory at Plassey in Bengal, of the fall of Goree (France's outpost in West Africa), and of the capture of Cape Breton, the summer of 1759 still found France firmly entrenched in Canada, southern India, and the West Indies, and her armies pressing forward in Germany. France was also preparing to invade England. In June of 1759 the English still worried about the future.

Then, with a rush, came the victories. The church bells, said Horace Walpole, were worn threadbare from ringing. In July the British captured Guadeloupe in the Caribbean, in August a British-German army won a great victory at Minden in Germany, and in September James Wolfe and his small army scaled the Plains of Abraham to seize Quebec. France's chief minister, Choiseul, decided that the only recourse was to invade Britain. He ordered his Mediterranean fleet to join the main fleet at Brest. Together with hundreds of transports carrying troops, they would conquer defenseless England. But the Mediterranean fleet never made it to Brest. Britain's Admiral Boscawen caught it passing Gibraltar, sank four ships-of-the-line, and drove the rest onto the beaches. A smaller French fleet nevertheless left Brest, but a British fleet sailed through the night and forced the French to retreat to Quiberon Bay. Daring tricky shoals and a gale, the British penetrated the bay and destroyed the French. England now ruled the seas.

But the war continued until 1763. Spain entered, foolishly, in 1761. Britain

It was ships-of-the-line of the British Navy, sailed by sailors of unrivaled experience, that won an Empire (*Science Museum, South Kensington*).

promptly took Cuba and Manila from them. France also suffered humiliations, not only by losing Martinique, but enduring the embarrassment of a British occupation of Belle Isle in its own Bay of Biscay. At the Treaty of Paris of 1763 Britain returned to France Belle Isle, Guadeloupe, Martinique, and Gore, and those factories in India held before 1749 (but which were not to be fortified). Britain gained all of Canada and the lands between the Allegheny and the Mississippi, Senegal in Africa, Granada, Dominica, St. Vincent and Tobago in the West Indies, a free hand in India, and the return of Minorca. The British wrested these possessions from France because they won on the seas. That supremacy came, in turn, because they had more ships manned by many more experienced officers and seamen. The French built equally good ships and trained excellent officers, but the British displayed superior seamanship. Their officers and crews had greater experience at sea. The British officer rank was far more open to the talented of all classes. The blockade of France, by forcing the French into their harbors and by demanding of the British constant sailing off the French coast, only accentuated the differences in their seamanship.

That Britain enjoyed a naval supremacy over France was also due to William Pitt, Frederick II, and the political, social, and geographic differences between the two nations. Under Pitt's loose guidance British genius of every sort flourished: not only improvising generals, ingenious admirals, and hard-working statesmen but clever gun makers, adroit seamen, intrepid soldiers, and landed and mercantile classes willing to pay the bill. Without any overall strategy and in an ad hoc manner, and with much flexibility, the war was won. Dominance of the Atlantic and the conquest of Quebec were the most dramatic of victories, but equally crucial were destructive attacks on France's Western ports and the brilliant defensive actions of the heavily subsidized and heroic Frederick II of Prussia. "America," it was said, "was won in Europe."

Pitt realized Frederick's value. For seven years Frederick involved France in a war that diverted its money, men, and energies from the building of a great navy and the defense of its colonies. France's ministers and king wanted victories in Europe, not in America and India. Britain, by contrast, was landed and mercantile, an aristocratic and middle-class society with representative government. Its naval officers could come from the middle classes, and its ablest statemen rose to power despite having angered the King, as Pitt angered him in 1743 by calling Hanover a "despicable Electorate." Because England had a free Parliament, Pitt could and did take command. Louis XV would not have tolerated this quarrelsome, ungracious, moody politician. Most English aristocrats also would not, but in the crisis of 1756 so powerful were the shouts of the public, so insistent the demands of commerce, that Parliament demanded that the great commoner lead. Pitt once told Parliament, "when your trade is at stake, you must defend it or your country will perish." This was not as true of France as it was of England, where the middle classes contributed so substantially to the kingdom's wealth and power. That middle class would eventually define English culture, but before that happened, aristocratic England was to make a grand and noble attempt to order its culture on the fixed and certain principles of reason and nature.

THE SEARCH FOR AN ORDERED CULTURE

The Elizabethan educated classes enjoyed a reasonably unified world outlook. The scientific revolution of the seventeenth century destroyed that outlook: objects no longer moved because of their essences, the universe did not include empyrean heights, and a mechanical pump called the heart and not the four humors governed human beings. But not all was destruction: science and learning had also revealed a simple and rational world, one in which natural law governed the planets; in which Chinese, Persians, and Europeans believed in the same ethics; and in which, as John Locke said, empirical observation and the laws of reflection can disclose the secrets of nature. But it was Isaac Newton's mathematical demonstration of the workings of the universe that led to an unbounded confidence in the power of reason and the order of nature. "Nature, and nature's law lay hid in night," sang out Alexander Pope in 1734, "God said let Newton be, and all was light."

For many all indeed was light, the light of reason and of nature. Upon nature's law—ethical, esthetic, political, and historical—people could build a rational society and a culture of beauty and elegance. Reason and natural law could even rescue religion, so rudely set adrift from its Elizabethan moorings by doubts of biblical revelation and the collapse of the Ptolemaic universe. Nature itself proved the existence of an intelligent creator. How splendid it all was! "O Glorious Nature," exclaimed the third Earl of Shaftesbury, in his *Characteristics of Men* of 1711, "supremely Fair and sovereignly Good! All-loving, All-lovely, All-Divine!" Shaftesbury was a deist—that is one who believes in an impersonal God, a God who, like a watchmaker, having created the universe, no longer interferes. The laws of nature, not a particular revelation, demonstrate to the deist the existence of God.

For many people, Shaftesbury's celebration of nature only belittled biblical truth. For them the great book was Joseph Butler's *Analogy of Religion*, published in 1736. Butler, an Anglican bishop, said that nature was not perfect, that it had blemishes and was, like the Bible, an imperfect revelation. But still intelligence and order did predominate in nature as divine truth did in the Bible. Nature's very blemishes might even be a necessary part of God's larger schemes. For nearly a century Butler's judicious combination of reason and revelation provided a bulwark against doubt. But it was a combination in which reason threatened to predominate, as it did in David Hartley's *Observations on Man* of 1749. Hartley only briefly acknowledges the claims of revelation. His main argument is that by the association of ideas derived from the senses, we learn about chairs, tables, beauty, motion, and God. Religion, like all knowledge, rests on reason and nature. So does morality. Both Shaftesbury and Butler argued that humans had an innate faculty for judging right and wrong, though they differed as to the nature of this faculty. Shaftesbury based it on natural sympathy and reason and Butler on reason and an innate moral sense. Hartley, in contrast, denies that there is an innate moral sense, since morality arises only from the empirical association of virtuous action with pleasurable sensations.

Reason and nature could also define beauty. Poetry and painting, like religion and morality, reflected natural law: so argued Alexander Pope as early as 1711 in his *Essay on Criticism*, Dr. Johnson in 1778 in *Lives of the Poets*, and Sir Joshua Reynolds in 1779 in *Discourses on Art*. Between those dates "classicism"—the belief that art reflects universally valid principles—dominated England's artistic circles. Pope found that ideal in balanced rhythms, rhyme, correct diction, and a rational and detached irony. Poetry's highest form was the heroic couplet, which he used brilliantly in *Essay on Man* to argue that however inscrutable, imperfect, and complex nature seems, it does accord with reason and God's laws. Though Dr. Johnson found Pope's arguments, many of which came from Shaftesbury, weak and commonplace, he did share Pope's belief in fixed esthetic

A self-portrait of Sir Joshua Reynolds, one of the age's most heralded painters (*Royal Academy of Arts*).

principles. Johnson, son of a bookseller and a scholarship student at Oxford, earned his living writing poems, tales, biographies, and essays. He won fame for his brilliant conversation and his *Dictionary of the English Language* of 1735 in which he sought the correct meaning of words, just as he sought correct principles of poetry in his *Lives of the Poets* and universal and unchanging moral standards in all that he wrote. For Johnson morality, like poetry, rested on those rational principles of order, taste, and good sense that people everywhere saw to be in accord with reason and the laws of nature. Sir Joshua Reynolds, greatest of eighteenth-century portrait painters, said in the *Discourses* that whatever pleases in art is "analogous to the mind, and is, therefore, in the highest and best sense of the word, natural." "Reason," he told aspiring painters, "ought to preside from first to last." Beauty he defined as an idea that subsists in the mind of great artists, reflects "the perfect state of nature," and leads to "universal

Chiswick House, with its symmetrical stairways, ordered columns, balanced windows, and classical statues, is a superb example of Palladian architecture (*Department of Environment*).

rectitude and a taste for virtue." His own paintings, like Pope's verse, were gracious, polished, and elegant.

Since reason and nature disclosed the secrets of the universe and demonstrated the truth of religion, morality, and beauty, why not apply them to all aspects of life, to houses, to gardens, and to manners? This is precisely what some of the wealthy did with their Palladian villas, poetic gardens, and worldly advice to their sons. Andreas Palladio's *Four Books on Architecture*, translated into English in 1713, taught the mathematical proportions, rigid symmetries, and severe order of the Roman style. Its message fitted well with Christopher Wren's claim that geometric and not irregular figures best accord with the laws of nature and Alexander Pope's praise of the ancients, "To copy Nature is to copy them." Mereworth Castle in Kent and Chiswick Villa near London, both built in the 1720s, represent fully the precise balance and imposing grandeur of the Roman style. Mereworth, with its four identical rooms in each quarter and its stately Doric columns, reflects the perfect order Englishmen then sought, while Chiswick, with its Roman rotunda, grand octagonal central hall, and rows of statues, reminded its aristocratic visitors that, like Roman senators, they enjoyed refined tastes and imperial power.

Gardens must also be classical, proportioned, and natural. William Kent, of the Palladian school, laid out the gardens at Rousham, Oxfordshire, with their ordered hedges, fountains, bridges, and imposing mausoleum. Rationalism, restraint, decorum, moderation, and correctness ruled manners as well. Lord Chesterfield gave an entertaining, if rather cynical, expression of this outlook in 1774 in his *Letters to His Son*. The advice is worldly. He recommends the

The formal gardens of Harewood House also reflected the eighteenth century's love of a strict and rational order (*Aerofilm*).

"elegant pleasures of a rational being" which include those of the table, amusing play, conversation, and women—though all in moderation. He suggests that his son dress according to his rank, flatter women's understanding, eschew prejudice, refrain from laughter (a disagreeable noise), and follow "the plain notions of right and wrong." He should also realize that perfection resides in "the noble manners of the court." Above all he should seek happiness by conforming "to the rule of right reason which is the great law of nature."

Enlightened Englishmen believed that nearly everything must yield to reason and nature. The antiquarian Sir John Hawkins believed that reason would show that music rested on harmonies as mathematical as Newton's optics. Hawkins never found those harmonies, nor did Reynolds his canons of beauty. And Chesterfield's manners based on "right reason" taught, according to Dr. Johnson, "the morals of a whore and the manners of a dancing master."

But reason in fact could be a corrosive force in the eighteenth century. David Hume, the age's greatest philosopher, argued in 1738 in his *Treatise on Human Nature* that no matter how logically it was applied, reason could not prove the existence of the external world. Hume was exceedingly skeptical of what reason alone could do. But when he left his philosopher's den a vivid and confident sense of the external world replaced skeptical reason, and he was assured that natural laws governed all, including history, which, far more than pure reason, revealed the truth of nature. It was also nature, far more than reason that Pope, Reynolds, and Johnson considered the source of esthetic principles. "Nothing could please many and please long," announced Dr. Johnson, "but just representations of general nature." If you wish to understand the French and English, wrote Hume, study the Greeks and Romans. To delineate that unchanging human nature, David Hume published his *History of England* in 1754, Edward Gibbon the first volume of his great *Decline and Fall of the Roman Empire* in 1776, and many other scholars many other learned histories of the past.

But English culture in the eighteenth century was far too lively, creative, varied, and spontaneous to be constricted by any law of nature. The aristocracy might have relished Pope's clever verse, Reynolds's suave portraits, and Chesterfield's witticisms, but the middle classes loved the earthier engravings of William Hogarth, the novels of Henry Fielding and the bawdy lines of John Gay's *The Beggars Opera*. Among the lower orders there were also Methodists who considered John Wesley's call for a rebirth through Christ more natural than listening in church to arguments from Butler's *Analogy*. Who in fact was to say what was natural? Was it sheer popularity? If so, then Hogarth's engravings and Fielding's *Tom Jones* were among the most natural. They were also among the most inventive, Hogarth using a series of paintings or engravings to tell a moral

"The wages of sin is death," according to the moralist William Hogarth, as the idle apprentice (in the carriage) is taken to the gallows (*British Museum*).

tale, Fielding developing the novel as an extended, highly unified narrative. In a series of twelve prints entitled "Industry and Idleness," Hogarth tells how the pious, obedient Francis Goodchild rises from being a weaver's apprentice to become lord mayor of London, while his fellow apprentice, the lazy, disobedient Tom Idle, descends into a life of crime that leads to the gallows. Fielding's *Tom Jones* is equally earthy, exciting, and moralistic. It relates how Tom Jones, brave, good, and openhearted, suffers vicissitudes and treacheries but finally wins love and riches, while the evil, deceitful Bilfil wins disgrace and ignominy. Neither Hogarth nor Fielding dealt much with aristocrats or grand and heroic themes, nor did they limit themselves to the decorous and correct. Ugly, ungracious harlots, rakes, and criminals populate Hogarth's scenes, just as vulgar adventurers and profane squires fill the pages of *Tom Jones*.

Earthy as were their stories and grotesque their caricature, both Hogarth and Fielding were very Georgian in their adherence to definite rules of morality and art. Hogarth in 1753 wrote an *Analysis of Beauty* in which he too sought universal principles of beauty, while Fielding prefaced many of his chapters in *Tom Jones* with essays on the true rules and principles of novel writing, one of which was that "the picture must be after Nature herself."

Hogarth also teaches that success is the reward of virtue, as he pictures the industrious apprentice (in the carriage) about to become lord mayor (*British Museum*).

Fielding's "Nature herself," however, was broad and variegated, and his sense of morality not a little ambiguous. Hogarth and Fielding, to be sure, told of virtue rewarded and vice punished, but they also parodied the pompous, satirized the rich, ridiculed authority, and showed compassion for the lower orders, all of which reflected a new class of readers, new social forces, new ideas, and new tastes. A static classicism based on reason and nature was not possible. In the last half of the eighteenth century, architects turned to the Gothic style, poets to the romantic, and gardeners to the picturesque, while the philosopher Jeremy Bentham, in his *Fragment on Government* of 1776, even called natural law metaphysical nonsense. The dream of unifying culture around those proofs of God, esthetic principles, and notions of right and wrong that accorded with reason and nature was bound to fail. Intellectual and artistic changes alone would have undermined it, but being based largely on a "circle of polished life," it could not have withstood the vitality, worldly interests, broad tastes, and constant questioning of new institutions, groups, and classes.

THE PEOPLE AND THEIR RULERS

Most subjects of George I and II were poor and illiterate and cared nothing about the philosophy of David Hume, the paintings of Sir Joshua Reynolds, the fall of ministries, or the reversal of alliances. For them, the prominent events of their lives were the elemental ones—births, marriages, and deaths, or poverty, confrontations with the law, and small improvements that economic progress or philanthropy brought.

Births, marriages, and deaths overshadowed all other events in importance, providing both the solemn and joyous occasions of life, and affecting the ebb and flow of population growth. They determined, for example, that from 1690 to 1720 the population of England grew rapidly, that from 1720 to 1750 it stagnated, and that thereafter came an unprecedented two centuries of growth. The main cause for the stagnation after 1720 was disease. For centuries epidemics had periodically checked England's population. They did so again in 1720–21, 1736, and 1740–41—in some places typhus or smallpox, in others malaria or influenza. In rural areas disease could wipe out half a village, in London cause a death rate twice that of births. London's wretched sanitation, overcrowded tenements, and cheap gin made its inhabitants vulnerable to epidemics. Gin drinking was a curse. The English consumed some 7 million gallons of gin in the 1740s compared to some 1 million gallons of heavily taxed gin in the 1780s. One in eight Londoners, said one doctor, died from too much gin. Money wasted on drink also meant less food and increased malnutrition, one of the major causes of death.

Death everywhere was a vivid fact of life. One in three English children died before 21, and the average life span was only 29. From 1721 to 1751, 34 out of every 1,000 died annually, a figure close to that of 35 births per 1,000.

From 1751 to 1758, the death rate fell to 30 deaths a year for every 1,000 inhabitants and the birth rate rose to 37 births for every 1,000. Population thus expanded rapidly, and for the first time no epidemics checked it. Except for the great success of small pox inoculations, the reasons why no serious epidemics occurred after 1741 are obscure. Medicine was still too crude and hospitals too crowded and dirty to prevent them. Cleaner hospitals, such as those at York and Manchester, did, however, lower the death rate. So did ampler diets for those so privileged. Dr. Cadogan's *On the Nursing and Management of Children*, with its plea for cleanliness, warm clothing, and ample diet, went through twenty editions in the 1750s. His pleas, and those of many others, may well have so improved the environment and diet that disease had greater difficulty in flourishing. Improved economic conditions also led women to marry earlier and so raise the birth rate. In 1717, the average age at marriage was 30, after which it steadily declined to 23 in 1825. Plentiful jobs in manufacturing areas provided incentives for early marriages; such areas in Nottinghamshire had a birth rate 25 percent higher than that in rural areas. It was both a rising fertility and a falling death rate that gave England a population explosion.

The millions of English people involved in that event were quite unconscious of it. Of far greater concern to them was the avoidance of poverty. Nearly all below the skilled laborer suffered undernourishment. In rural areas laborers earned only 6 or 7 shillings a week, in more expensive London, only 9 or 10 shillings. And in both places they worked more than 12 hours a day. From 1700 to 1730, half of the rural laborer's 6 shillings went for bread, leaving only 3 or 4 for cheese or meat, or for rent, clothes, candles, and fuel. Their small one-room cottages had dirt floors, usually no windows, and one open hearth where peat or furze was burned and all cooking done. London weavers lived in no better conditions, often having no hearth at all. Their one room was also overcrowded, producing the same sexual promiscuity and disease as rural hovels. They faced acute fluctuations of trade that, like the severe winters in rural areas, meant unemployment and the disgrace of being a pauper.

Most of the ruling classes did not like paupers: they were a nuisance and cost £1 million a year in poor relief. In the past a strong central government had attempted to force the Elizabethan and Stuart gentry to treat paupers well, but after 1688 power in these matters devolved completely onto the local justices of the peace, the vestry, and the vestry's overseers, all of whom had very strong opinions about paupers. Increasingly they agreed to relieve the destitute only if they entered a workhouse. Such a test would deter them from applying, and if not, at least their labor in the workhouse might earn a few shillings for the parish. The work would also train them in habits of industry. Most workhouses, however, had no scheme of classification, little available work, and much over-crowding. The workhouses neither earned a profit nor trained the poor; they produced instead corruption and brutality. Many parishes sought to rid themselves of paupers by farming them out to contractors who hoped to profit from pauper labor. Profitability and economy were popular idols in an age when the cash nexus was replacing paternal relations. Everything was to be "contracted" out: the parish contracted with farmers to hire paupers as laborers, contracted with nurses to care for foundlings, contracted with craftsmen to take on for seven years the young as apprentices, and, if possible, entered into agreements with large contractors to care for all their poor. It was to the contractors' interest to skimp on food and clothing and to exact the hardest labor. Of all these schemes, only that of apprenticeship became widespread, but more often as a form of servile labor than as a means of training. The other schemes all failed, as did the workhouse test. By midcentury most parishes simply gave the paupers outdoor relief, 1 shilling a week in the north and 1 shilling 6 pence in the south. Its inadequacy led many to beg or steal and so fall afoul of the law of the land.

The law of the land imposed its discipline not only on paupers but on laborers higher up the social pyramid, such as husbandmen or artisans who earned more than 10 shillings a week and lived in two-story brick cottages. There was no typical worker in early Georgian England and no homogeneous proletariat. There were instead various communities with hierarchical relations that were vertical and paternal, running from landlord or master to the various ranks below. But as these relations increasingly yielded to the needs of a market economy, paternal and vertical lines were bisected by horizontal lines dividing the rich and privileged more markedly from the lower orders. The crucial test was ownership of property, particularly land. Landlords, as never before, were building up large estates. Small freeholders became tenant farmers, husbandmen descended to agricultural laborers, and the enclosure of the commons denied cottagers their rights to collect peat and furze and to graze their pigs. The game laws also denied all but landowners with £100 income the right to hunt, thus tempting thousands to become poachers and, if caught, criminals. Exceedingly high tariffs on tea, 4 shillings a pound, encouraged some 20,000 persons to smuggle 3 million pounds a year into England.

A large number of laborers found themselves at war with property, the law, and the three thousand justices of the peace who virtually ruled England. These local justices were indeed potentates. They imposed taxes; had prisons and workhouses built; supervised bridges and roads; appointed overseers of the poor and surveyors of highways; ordered paupers not resident in the parish to leave; made the fathers of bastards support them; and sent to prison vagrants, poachers, thieves, and drunken brawlers. They could also fine a person for absence from church, profanity, harboring vagrants, taking wood from the commons, or speaking slanderously to his wife. Huge as were their tasks so too, all too often, were their incapacities.

The most serious crimes—sheep stealing, arson, murder—came before the quarterly assize. Presided over by a King's justice from London, and attended by the Lord Lieutenant, the justices of the peace, the leading gentry, and a host of onlookers, it was a solemn ceremony. The scarlet-robed judge, after lecturing on the majesty of the law, sentenced poachers and smugglers to prison

Not all was harmony in the Age of Stability: angry peasants burned ricks and judges hanged them as well as poachers (*British Museum*).

or, if the poachers had blackened their faces to hide their identity and were hunting in the King's forests, to death by hanging. That punishment was required by the Black Act of 1723. The act was originally designed to apply to poachers who blackened their faces and hunted in the King's forests, but the judges extended it to all poachers whether in the King's forests or disguised. It was an age persuaded of the efficacy of hanging. In 1688 some fifty statutes prescribed hanging as a punishment; by 1820, two-hundred did. The gallows awaited anyone who from a person's pocket took goods worth 1 shilling or shop-lifted goods worth 5 shillings. The governing classes also liked the pillory, whipping, and jail: the pillory for drunken brawlers, the whipping for vagrants—"until their backs were bloody"—and jail for thieves. Severe punishments, they felt, deterred crime just as pardons and mercy properly given won deference and obedience. Despite the increase in statutes calling for hanging, the eighteenth century saw no great increase in death on the gallows. Juries, judges, and home secretaries at the last moment preferred mercy. Such a personal and flexible use of the law was of the very essence of the paternalism that ruled England. But its arbitrary nature could also rouse anger when severe sentences were imposed on poachers and smugglers who did not consider themselves truly criminal. Far from deterring crime it only convinced them of the truth of Oliver Goldsmith's dictum, "Laws grind the poor, and rich men rule the law."

In the 1720s the people of Windsor forest fought the King's gamekeepers and judges in defense of their rights to collect wood, and to fish and hunt, rights they had long enjoyed; in the 1740s gangs of smugglers in Sussex fought the King's excise officers to preserve their share of a trade that polite society indulged in; and in 1750 the farmers and cottagers of Staffordshire killed 10,000 rabbits belonging, according to the game laws, to the Earl of Uxbridge. The rabbits had destroyed their crops. In each of these struggles the law won out, the poachers and smugglers were hung, the rabbit slayers jailed. The lower orders, awed by paternal authority, returned to deferential ways—but only to erupt later in riots, drunkenness, crime, and turbulence. Beneath the decorous society of gentry and merchants the many lived just above the subsistence level, a perilous state one could not sustain if ill, jobless, old, or, as many were, the victims of bad harvests and high food prices. Life was hard and brutish and the struggle to be warm, clothed, and fed was unending. Solace there was in drunkenness, and it was, through gin, endemic. Anger was also widespread and robberies, poaching, vendettas, quarrels, duels, and murder.

Such endemic violence and riot was contained not only by the authoritarian rule of the wealthy but by both philanthropy and economic progress. Philanthropy in the form of endowed charities to support schools for the young, almshouses for the aged, and doles for the poor was an old tradition, one that the eighteenth century continued by founding 973 such trusts. Its buoyant humanitarianism also led to a new form of benevolence, the philanthrophic society, an association of many contributors whose annual subscriptions were applied to larger schemes for the education of the poor or the mitigation of their sufferings. Zealous philanthropists founded charity schools and hospitals of all kinds. But the charity schools taught little and few lasted long, and many hospitals only spread disease. But some were great successes, none more than London's famous Foundling Hospital for orphans. It won the support of Hogarth, Reynolds, Handel, and the leading noblemen of England and was salvation for countless children. But philanthropy could do little compared with economic progress toward the improvement of the condition of the poor.

From 1714 to 1760 that progress was slow but steady. In agriculture enclosed fields continued to replace open ones, crops were more productively rotated, cattle and sheep better bred, and fields drained and manured. Manufacturing also progressed. Abraham Darby discovered how to use coke instead of charcoal to smelt iron, Thomas Newcomen employed steam to run his atmospheric engine, and John Kay developed the flying shuttle to speed up weaving. In Newcastle Ambrose Crawley built his great iron works and in New Haddington, Scotland, one textile factory employed 700 workers. In the north cottagers spun and wove more wool, linen, and cotton, while clothiers grew richer. Yet economic growth did not keep pace with technological advance. No industrial revolution occurred. The demand for goods was too small, in part because of the slow growth of population. With fewer people to buy bread, the price of grain fell; with fewer people available to work, wages rose and agriculture languished. But for those laborers fortunate enough to survive the epidemics, higher wages and cheaper bread meant an improved standard of living. After 1760 and a decisive rise in population, prices again rose, farms and workshops prospered, and England approached the eve of the Industrial Revolution. By then both George I and II had died. No revolutions disturbed their stable reigns. Their politicians had fashioned a political system based on representative government, constitutional principles, and the rule of the wealthy; their shipbuilders and seamen built and manned a navy that won an empire; and their artists and writers produced a polished and elegant culture. Revolutions and social transformations were to be reserved for a later age.

FURTHER READING

BLACK, JEREMY, ed., *Britain in the Age of Walpole.* New York: St. Martin's Press, 1984. Eight essays by different authors on the theme of the age's stability, all intelligent, particularly the editors masterful analysis of foreign policy.

HATTON, RAGNALD. *George I, Elector and King.* Cambridge, Mass.: Harvard University Press, A spirited defense of George I as a much abler statesman, warmer person, and governing monarch than previously thought.

Marshall, Dorothy. *Eighteenth Century England.* London: Longmans, 1974. A new edition of an old classic, a richly detailed and thoughtful interpretation of the history of England from 1714 to 1784, one strong on social life.

Mingay, G. E. *English Landed Society in the Eighteenth Century.* London: Routledge and Kegan Paul, 1963. A clear and incisive description of the structure and growth of the landed classes and their day to day activities as managers of their estates, magistrates, members of parliament, and leaders of society.

OWEN, JOHN B. *Eighteenth Century England.* Totowa, N.J.: Rowman and Littlefield, 1975. A shrewdly observant account of English history from 1714 to 1815 with chapters on economic, social, and cultural developments and with a good bibliography.

PLUMB, J. H. *Robert Walpole:* Vol. 1, *The Making of a Statesman;* Vol. 2, *The King's Minister.* London: Cresset Press, 1956 & 1961. A masterful biography revealing of the inner workings of politics during the ascendancy of the Whigs, an account that views the shrewd and worldly Walpole by eighteenth-century standards.

PORTER, ROY. *English Society in the Eighteenth Century.* London: Allen Lane, 1982. A social and cultural history that views the eighteenth century as capitalist, materialistic, and pragmatic while still hierarchical, hereditary, privileged, and ruled by custom and traditions.

ROGERS, PAT. *The Augustan Vision.* London:

Weidenfeld and Nicolson, 1974. An analysis of the intellectual and artistic assumptions of mid–eighteenth-century England and how they differed from modern ones.

SPECK, W. A. *Stability and Strife in England, 1714–1760.* Cambridge, Mass.: Harvard University Press, 1977. Primarily a political history, and a most discerning one, it opens with a keen analysis of the economic, social, and constitutional foundations of early eighteenth-century England.

TURBERVILLE, A. S., ed. *Johnson's England: An Account of the Life and Manners of His Age*, 2 vols. Oxford: Clarendon Press, 1933. Thirty articles ranging from the Church and the army and navy, to meals, costumes, and sports, as well as painting, drama, education, and medicine.

WILLIAMS, E. NEVILLE. *The Eighteenth Century Constitution.* Cambridge: Cambridge University Press, 1960. The fullest collection of documents available on the constitution and government of eighteenth-century England.

WILLIAMS, BASIL. *The Whig Supremacy, 1714–1760.* Oxford: Clarendon Press, 1962. One of the clearest and fullest accounts of early Hanoverian England; its more out-of-date views have been revised by its new editor, C. H. Stuart, without lessening its wise observations.

The economic and social transformation of England: 1761–1815

18

When George III began his sixty-year reign in 1760, he had no reason to believe he would not also preside over an age of stability. For many people, of course, there was stability. In 1820 Norfolk farmers rotated crops, London barristers argued cases, Bristol merchants imported sugar, Sussex gentry managed elections, and Devon sailors manned ships in much the same manner as they had in 1760. Neither in those sixty years did the landed gentry and nobility lose their predominance. No age is composed wholly of change, not even ages of transition, just as no age is characterized solely by permanence, not even ages of stability. But for many people, the changes were momentous. For laborers who lost their cottages to an enclosure, for rural children sent to a cotton factory, for handloom weavers unable to compete with power looms, for small clothiers transformed into captains of industry, and for farmers grown rich on wartime profits, the England of 1820 differed profoundly from that of 1760. Indeed, even to live in a nation that had grown from 6.5 to 12 million during these years was itself a striking difference.

A population explosion was but one of many changes that transformed the England of George III. Equally important was the Industrial Revolution, which harnessed the power of steam to machines for spinning, weaving, iron making, mining, and the driving of ships and railroads. Less dramatic than the Industrial Revolution, but equally important and far more extensive, were those advances in farming and that expansion of handicraft manufactures that truly made England the workshop of the world.

These changes in population, agriculture, and industry lie at the heart of the economic and social transformation that occurred in the England of George III. These changes interacted with each other and with other economic and social developments to create the foundations for the industrial, urban, democratic, and imperial England of the nineteenth century. In that foundation the first requisite was a populated and well-fed kingdom.

MORE PEOPLE AND MORE FOOD

Few facts in the history of England are more dramatic than the multiplication of its people between 1760 and 1820 from 6.5 to 12 million. That a falling death rate and a rising birth rate lay behind this astonishing explosion is agreed on by historians and demographers. There is, however, no agreement on which of the two factors is more important. Some demographers believe the falling death rate was decisive, and they argue that better medical care and hospitals lessened the ravages of disease. Other demographers, who are dubious that medical or hospital practices reduced the death rate, argue instead that economic prosperity and growth, particularly in manufacturing areas, encouraged earlier marriages and so a higher birth rate. A third group, while admitting that medical practices did not lead to a fall in the death rate, still consider such a fall the crucial factor. They attribute it to an improved environment, to better houses, purer water, better disposal of refuse, cleaner clothing, and above all a better diet. The population explosion that ensued created a great demand for food, a demand that the farmers met successfully.

How did they do it? The answer is by the use of more land more efficiently, with the emphasis on more land. In the eighteenth century grain production increased around 43 percent, just keeping up with a population increase of between 40 and 50 percent. There were two reasons for this increased productivity, a 10 percent increase in production per acre and a 25 percent increase in the number of acres cultivated. Increase in efficiency resulted from the spread of those enclosures and advanced farm techniques that had their roots in the Tudor period. Of the advanced techniques none was more important than a more efficient crop rotation. In Norfolk they rotated—every four years—wheat, barley, turnips, and clover, never leaving the land fallow. The turnips and clover both refreshed the soil and provided winter feed for sheep and cattle. The sheep and cattle in turn produced manure which enriched the soil. The soil was also improved by better drainage and by adding, where it was needed, lime, chalk, or marl. By adding marl to sandy soil Thomas Coke, one of the greatest of the century's agricultural improvers, quadrupled, in fifteen years, his revenue from grain. Coke was also a great breeder of sheep and cattle, as were other farmers, who found that they could double their weight. Horses also replaced oxen as draft animals. All were in fashion by 1750 and none involved improved machinery. Indeed, except for the threshing machine, widely adopted during the Napoleonic wars, there were no revolutionary changes in agricultural machinery. If there was a revolution between 1750 and 1820, it was either in the spread of old techniques to new areas or in changes in the mode of owning property and hiring laborers.

Enclosure and capitalist farming are the key events defining late eighteenth-century agricultural changes. From 1760 to 1820 the landlords of England, by four thousand acts of Parliament, enclosed 8 million acres: first, by fencing in and consolidating, from 1760 to 1780, many open fields of arable land and, second, during the French wars, by fencing in waste lands and commons. A single proprietor could now carry out the most scientific techniques in the most capitalist manner. Crops multiplied, farm jobs increased, rents doubled, villages grew in population, and food prices fell.

But these advantages involved social costs. Small holders often gave up their few acres, while cottagers frequently lost their garden plots and both their grazing and gleaning rights on common pastures and their access to wastelands and woods for fuel. In pounds and shillings these weighed little against the bountiful crops and wider employment brought by enclosures, but to many villagers they were a painful and irreparable loss. True, the enclosure commissioners appointed by Parliament often compensated the cottager with money and the lesser occupiers with a small part of the enclosed fields, but most cottagers quickly spent the money and most occupiers could not afford to fence and develop their land. They sold out to the larger landlords. Some then became tenant farmers, some went to town or the colonies, but most sank into the rural proletariat. No longer could they graze their cows, pigs, or geese on the

Threshing machine (*Illustrated London News*).

common; grow vegetables on small plots; collect peat and furze for fuel; and, as squatters, erect desperately needed hovels. Loss of fuel not only meant cold cottages but little cooking, and without a cow or pig, their diet became a monotony of bread and cheese in the south and oatmeal and oatbread in the north. Enclosures also increased winter unemployment, moved cottages farther away, and led to feelings of isolation and anger. The same enclosures that were so necessary for feeding England's 12 million also brought, as so often happens in the process of economic growth, economic and social injustices.

Some landlords, aware of the injustices, did promise small garden plots, but few appeared. "By 19 of 20 enclosures," wrote Arthur Young, the century's greatest agricultural authority, "the poor are injured and most grossly." Enclosures were in fact only part of a more profound development, the rise of a more intensely capitalist agriculture and of a rural proletariat. From the late seventeenth century on, landlords had built larger and larger estates and rented their acres to tenant farmers in larger units on shorter leases. The landlord increasingly treated his estate as a business venture. He mortgaged the property, added farms to it, consolidated, organized enclosures, insisted on shorter leases and higher rents, and sought out farmers who were as enterprising and capitalist as millowners. The tenant farmer with his 150-acre farm emerged as the linchpin of a three-tiered structure of landlord, farmer, laborer. He was a sharp, calculating, often ruthless capitalist. He grew rich on wartime profits, sported a carriage, built a fine house, and fancied himself a gentleman, a fact which led William Cobbett, the age's greatest journalist, to observe, "When farmers become gentlemen their labourers become slaves." Farmers now paid laborers by the week instead of the year so that when frosts hit they could dismiss them. They also no longer had them live in their houses. Because manufacturers competed for labor in the north, farmers there had to pay agricultural workers 11 to 13 shillings a week, but in the south, where the population explosion created a surplus of laborers with no alternative jobs, the farmer paid 7 to 9 shillings and pocketed the rest as profit.

A market economy and a commercial spirit ruled in the rural areas. The rents and profits of landlord and farmer nearly doubled between 1790 and 1820, while laborers' real wages remained unchanged and near the subsistence level. In close parishes, those controlled by one or two landlords, cottages were pulled down or not built. Why build cottages that only attract the poor whose inevitable pauperism would drive up the rates. The excluded poor crowded into the one- or two-room thatch and mud hovels of open parishes or the slums of nearby towns. Overcrowding was intense, cold and damp the rule, and sexual promiscuity impossible to prevent.

When the three worst winters of the eighteenth century climaxed in the bad harvest of 1795, some landowners mitigated the new capitalism with a dose of old paternalism. With bread at an unprecedently high price because of the French wars, the justices of the peace of Berkshire, meeting at the town of Speenhamland, voted to grant poor relief to all laborers earning insufficient wages. In aim the act was benevolent and reflected the paternal solicitude of the squire of older times; in fact it had disastrous results, since it tempted farmers to keep wages low and independent laborers to go on relief. Why pay a laborer 9 instead of 7 shillings if the parish will pay the additional two? And why work hard if the parish keeps up the wages of lazy and energetic alike? Speenhamland was not an act of Parliament but a decision of the Berkshire justices of the peace and it was never universal in England. Yet the use of parish relief in support of low wages was widely adopted in the south at the turn of the century. The result was the pauperization of many laborers. And though the practice of giving relief in aid of wages had declined by 1834, there was no increase in wages. As farmers and landowners grew wealthier, agricultural workers, paid subsistence wages, often denied a cottage, deprived of rights to the commons, became isolated and oppressed.

But it was also an age in which the farmers of England increased the production of grain from 17 million quarters in 1760 to 28 million in 1820. Enclosures, capitalist farming, and the spread of efficient methods, not technological breakthroughs, explain the great increase in food production. If there was an agricultural revolution between 1760 and 1820, it came in the organization of property and labor not in the rotation of crops. It was a more capitalist organization, one in tune with the even more dramatic changes in industry.

THE INDUSTRIAL REVOLUTION

In the 1760s English industry was prosperous and expanding, but at too slow a pace for many ambitious entrepreneurs. Three problems in particular frustrated their desire for greater productivity: the inability to spin great quantities of inexpensive cotton thread; the limits that dwindling supplies of charcoal and forge work placed on the production of a tough wrought iron; and the inadequacies of wind, water, and muscle as sources of power. These were perennial problems: for millennia the agile fingers of humans had spun thread; the pure heat of charcoal had melted iron for the forge; and horses, windmills, and waterwheels ground corn and raised coal from mines. For millennia these limits were accepted. But in the 1760s economic prosperity, entrepreneurial vitality, and technological advances led the English to believe they could be overcome.

Three specific inventions of the early eighteenth century were crucial in eliciting the technological creativeness that came in the 1760s: Thomas Newcomen's atmospheric engine of 1705, Abraham Darby's use of coke to produce pig iron in 1709, and John Kay's flying shuttle of 1733. Each of these inventions made further ones necessary. Kay's flying shuttle, for example, allowed just one person to weave broader cloth and to do so more rapidly. This increased efficiency in weaving heightened the demand for the thread and so for a faster spinning process. It was a challenge met by James Heargraves and his spinning jenny of 1765 and Richard Arkwright and his water frame of 1767. Heargraves's solution was to place at one end of a rectangular frame a row of 8 or 10 vertical spindles and at the other end a carriage on small wheels through which 8 or 10 carded slivers of cotton ran. The spinner pushed the carriage back and forward with one hand while he or she turned the wheel that turned the spindles with the other. It was a multiple spinning wheel and still worked by hand. Furthermore, its thread was too weak for the warp of a loom. Richard Arkwright's water frame produced a harder thread mechanically by running the carded cotton slivers through two pairs of rollers. Each pair had a top and bottom roller pressing against each other and between which the cotton sliver traveled. Since the second pair moved a little faster than the first, it pulled the cotton out into a thread. The spindles at the end strengthened it by giving it a twist. The result was a hard, strong thread good for warp and weft. It was a thread produced totally by a machine. Since it took a waterwheel to turn the machine, it became known as the water frame.

A steam engine could also drive it and did so sixteen years after James Watt filed a patent in 1769. Watt, a maker of scientific instruments for Glasgow University, was given a Newcomen engine to improve. Newcomen's engine posed a challenge because of its inefficiency. It used a coal fire to produce steam, which it sent into a cylinder with a piston, but it did not use the expanding

Richard Arkwright's water frame (*Science Museum, South Kensington*).

An early model of James Watt's steam engine (*Birmingham Public Library*).

force of this steam directly. Instead, by injecting cold water into the steam-filled cylinder, it caused the steam to condense, thus creating a vacuum which caused the air pressure outside to force the piston down and so move the pump. Bothered at the loss of energy involved in the cooling of the cylinder, Watt designed an engine in which the expansive pressure of the steam was applied alternately to each side of the piston, pushing it back and forth. He also designed a way to translate the back-and-forth motion of the arm extending from the piston into the circular motion of a revolving wheel. The double-acting, rotating steam engine was thus born.

Watt's steam engine demanded a hard, tough, wrought iron, an iron much tougher than Darby's pig iron. The Quaker Darby was the first to use coke—that is, preheated coal—to separate iron from its ore. To make that iron tougher it had to be reheated in a charcoal fire and much hammered at the forge, a costly and laborious process. Henry Cort in 1783 found a cheaper method with his puddling and rolling process. He placed the pig iron into a reverbatory furnace in which the heat of a coal fire in a separate chamber was channeled into the pig iron until it was molten. He then put in clinkers rich in oxides of iron and had workers stir the mixture with rods so that the oxygen would cause carbon and impurities to burn off instead of corrupting the iron. The iron was then poured off, its impurities hammered out, and the molten metal run through rollers to give it the desired shape. Fifteen tons of iron could now be produced in the time formerly taken to produce one. The stronger iron could make stouter steam engines that could pump water and lift coal from deep mines or power steamships and railways. They could also drive the mule, a spinning machine that combined the best features of the spinning jenny and the water frame, and the power loom for weaving cotton and wool cloth. Samuel Crompton, the son of a small landholder in Lancashire, invented the mule in 1779, and Edmund Cartwright, Oxford scholar and Anglican clergyman, invented the power loom in 1785. Quantities of good cotton cloth could now be produced at unbelievably low prices. In 1812 one spinner could produce what it took 200 spinners to produce before the new machines and one calico printing machine could do the work of 100 hand-block printers. Cotton cloth that sold at 11 shillings a yard in 1784 sold for 1 shilling in 1832.

Pouring iron (*Illustrated London News*).

At the heart of the Industrial Revolution lay those mechanical inventions that burst forth in the twenty years after 1765. Once started, the technical advances never ceased, the Industrial Revolution being a continuing and almost self-generating event. But it involved more than inventions. It also required the more systematic and rational use of capital, labor, and management. It meant a keener search for raw materials, cheaper transport to the workshop, efficient division of labor, concern for mass production, lower costs, and mass markets. Such an entrepreneurial spirit was personified in the king of potters, the imperious Josiah Wedgwood of Burselm, Staffordshire. Believing that "all things yield to experiment," he made over 10,000 trial pieces before achieving the high-quality blue and white jasperware for which he became famous; then by a rigorous division of labor, he lowered the costs to allow for mass consumption.

Cottage and workshop manufactures multiplied and improved their tools and skills as fast as factories grew, and they employed far more workers. The economic transformation of England was not all steam engines and textile mills. In 1800 only 490 of Watt's steam engines were in use. King Cotton employed only 100,000 hands in 1814 and less than half were adult males. Shoemakers and cobblers outnumbered factory workers just as tailors did coal miners and blacksmiths iron workers—and that by three times. Only 10 percent of workers in 1830 had experienced factory employment.

By the middle of the nineteenth century, the spinning machines were far larger, vaster, more complicated, and more efficient, but still used rollers and spindles (*Illustrated London News*).

Great too was the expansion of the world of finance and trade, long the wealthiest part of Britain's economy. From wool trading in the west country and cotton speculation in Manchester arose the Barings and Rothchilds. By shrewd wartime speculation in gold and silver and private and government bonds they established themselves as two of the greatest banking firms of the nineteenth century. The great trading companies and banks of the City were as important as the captains of industry of the north to the economic transformation of England. These traders, bankers, brokers, and insurers dominated world finance and trade, much as England's merchant marine—9,400 ships as early as 1776—dominated the seas and the commerce thereon. The vigor of the bustling world of craftsmen and shopkeepers and the wealth and power of the world of finance and trade must never be overlooked when addressing the question: Why did the Industrial Revolution occur in eighteenth-century England?

The Causes of the Industrial Revolution.   The origins of the Industrial Revolution lie in four characteristics of the economy of eighteenth-century England. The first was an abundance of capital, labor, and raw materials; the second, a vigorous demand for manufactured goods; the third, an economy free from undue regulation; and the last, an economy whose expansion was blocked by crucial bottlenecks that could be overcome by innovation.

Abundant capital and labor are of course necessary for healthy growth, with most economists according the accumulation of capital the premium position. One could not produce Watt's steam engine, puddle iron in Cort's reverberatory furnaces, or fill factories with water frames without thousands of pounds and hundreds of laborers. Happily, late eighteenth-century England possessed a plentiful supply of both. A population explosion and a marked rise in food production freed thousands to work in the new industries just as a prosperous commerce, manufacturing, and agriculture provided considerable capital. That capital was further enlarged by the expansion of credit offered by some 600 country and 70 London banks. In 1763 the interest rate on loans fell to 3.75 percent. The capital spent on wars and country homes, whether in England or in France or Germany, far exceeded that needed to develop the water frame, spinning jenny, or steam engine. The availability of capital was not the crucial factor explaining why the Industrial Revolution occurred in England and not on the Continent.

Perhaps the key was abundant raw materials. Yet again there are doubts; the first breakthrough came in cotton, of which England had none. The second and third came in the conversion of coal to steam power and its use in making wrought iron. Although both advances meant exploiting England's vast coalfields, both were responses to a lack of resources—charcoal in the case of making iron and water and horses in the case of steam. Dearth may present a greater challenge than abundance. The great forests of France gave it such a preeminence in iron production that the French did not search for techniques to smelt iron with coal. An abundance of capital, labor, and coal was to be vital to industrial growth after 1790, but their abundance does not provide the explanation for the technological advances of the 1760s and 1770s.

What drove Hargreaves, Watt, Cort, and their capitalist partners to invent and manufacture spinning machines, rolling mills, and steam engines was the overwhelming demand for cloth, iron, and power. In no other country was there a greater demand for goods that were both standardized and of good quality. It was this demand that made possible mass production at good profits. One of the most striking reasons for that great demand was England's expanding overseas trade. Sailing ships bound for Europe, the American colonies, West Africa, and India were loaded with exports. There was also Ireland, which at midcentury was a good customer when overseas exports lagged. But the largest market was the domestic. In 1770 it consumed 77 percent of all manufactures. There were more English with more money in 1770 than in 1700. There were also more canals, deepened rivers, and improved roads, all of which lowered the cost of cloth, iron wares, and pottery. Added to the 1,000 miles of navigable rivers and many miles of coastal sea routes, the new canals and roads made England the largest and most compact free trade area in the world. With the average wage 15 percent higher than a century earlier and twice that received by workers in the Rhineland and France, and with the price of food 15 percent less in 1750 than in 1720, workers had more to spend on manufactured goods. Since the largest share of the rising income went to the middle and upper classes and to the artisans engaged in manufacturing, there grew up a healthy market for Wedgwood's jasperware, sporting guns, handsome cutlery, sturdy pots, and cloths of all kinds.

The third characteristic of the economy that favored the Industrial Revolution was freedom from undue restrictions. No guild told Arkwright how much cotton thread to produce, no town corporation prohibited the use of power looms, no internal tolls hampered trade, and no village dictated agricultural practices. England was not, to be sure, without mercantilist regulations: the Navigation Acts gave England's manufacturers a monopoly of colonial trade, while other acts protected domestic clothiers. Government measures that helped industry were accepted, those that hampered trade were repealed. Free of burdensome taxes, left alone by government, and unhampered by old trade associations or new trade unions, the Industrial Revolution was born of a *laissez-faire* economy.

French entrepreneurs, though less free than the British, still enjoyed considerable freedom. France's mercantilism, large in theory, was less effective in practice. France also had a rapidly growing overseas trade, an increasing population, rising incomes, a strong demand for goods, and ample capital, labor, and materials. Yet its trade, wage levels, demand, and capital were not, in the eighteenth century, the equal per capita of those in England.

France also lacked three bottlenecks that challenged British entrepreneurs: a lack of spinners and weavers in the clothing districts of Lancashire and Yorkshire, dwindling supplies of charcoal for producing wrought iron, and the need in coal mining and iron smelting for a steadier and greater source of power than that provided by horses and waterwheels. Given the unprecedented demand for cottons, iron, and power, these bottlenecks were a distinct stimulus to invention. The lack of laborers to spin and weave was of course local, since England as a whole enjoyed a surplus of laborers. But though local it was no less aggravating. Clothiers in Lancashire and Yorkshire had increasingly to travel 7 or 8 miles to find cottagers who could spin and weave. The spinners and weavers, knowing that their labor and the articles they produced were in great demand, stole thread, adulterated cloth, and charged high prices. The clothiers could not move to areas where labor was more abundant and so cheaper, since they needed the streams of the Pennine mountains to run carding and fulling machinery. A machine that would spin cotton thread would free these ambitious men from rising costs of labor that were cutting into profits.

Those who produced iron faced the mounting cost of charcoal. It was this problem that caused Henry Cort and others to search for a means of using coal to produce wrought iron. Coal would then be of even more value, though its widespread use in the production of glass, soap, salt, and dyes and its use for the heating of homes already made it a most desired item. But the mining of coal had itself run into bottlenecks. By 1750 accessible seams of coal had worn out. But to go deeper, to drain flooded seams, and to bring needed ventilation required a powerful engine, one less cumbersome than the 500 horses one colliery used and one far more efficient than the energy-wasting Newcomen atmospheric engine. Watt's steam engine provided just the answer, an answer that the bottleneck in coal had evoked.

Technological advances and economic growth involve the interaction of many forces. From 1767 to 1790 the most important one was the great demand for goods engendered by a prosperous domestic market, a buoyant overseas trade, and a growing population. It was a pervasive force which, when challenged by bottlenecks in the production of cloth, iron, and power inspired men to invent water frames and steam engines. It was a force that reflected, in turn, other economic forces. An abundance of capital and labor, for example, does not directly explain the discovery of the spinning jenny and the water frame, but it does help explain England's ability to construct canals and turnpikes. These canals and turnpikes helped reduce transportation costs for raw cotton coming into the clothing districts and for cotton cloth going out, a reduction crucial to lowering the price of cottons and thereby increasing the demand. Abundant capital and labor also proved vital to the second phase of the Industrial Revolution that came in the early nineteenth century, in which captains of industry built huge shipyards, vast railway networks, many-storied factories, and gigantic iron and steel works.

This analysis of the causes of the Industrial Revolution has been in terms of economic forces, of capital, labor, trade, demand, transportation, and standardized production. But were there no social, political, and cultural forces that help explain the economic changes that led to the Industrial Revolution? The answer is yes, there were, though their action is so interwoven with the economic changes that they are hard to isolate. This is particularly true of social forces. English society in 1760 was, though definitely pyramidal, more open, mobile, and freer of class prejudice than continental societies. Lords and gentlemen mixed with merchants and farmers at the assizes, merchants drank with mechanics, the younger sons of peers entered trade, wealthy tradesmen became gentry. The result was the spread of an entrepreneurial spirit among all classes, and the growth of similar tastes for clothes, pottery, and hardwares and hence a stronger demand for standard goods that could be produced in numbers large enough to require machinery. Britain's political system also helped. A Parliament that included improving landlords and great merchants could guarantee both enclosure acts and the defeat or repeal of measures restrictive of commerce. That Britain's economy was the freest in Europe was not unrelated to its having a representative government.

Social and political forces thus provided a framework favorable to a revolution in industry, but these forces did not act as directly on the creators and exploiters of the new machines as did the intellectual outlook of the inventors and entrepreneurs. Of these men only Cartwright went to University, and that was to an Oxford that taught no science. James Watt, who taught himself science, was neither a student nor a lecturer at Glasgow University but a repairer of scientific instruments. He was a tinkerer, an experimenter, a repairer, an improver, as were the many millwrights and iron forge workers and gentleman farmers whose stream of innovations owed scarcely anything to theoretical advances in physics and chemistry. Belief that scientific advances brought technical progress did abound, being an article of faith in the Royal Society for Improving Natural Knowledge, founded in 1660, and the Royal Society of Arts, founded in 1754, but no pioneering invention came from their publications, nor did any advances come from France and Germany whose eighteenth-century record for scientific advances and scientific education far outdistanced Britain's. But though Newton's laws of motion and Boyle's law of gases did not lead to Watt's steam engine and Cort's puddling process, both the discovery of those laws and these inventions reflect that pervasive belief in systematic observation and experiment that, from Robert Grosseteste to Francis Bacon and from Thomas Hobbes to John Locke, constituted the core of British empiricism. The same belief in the rationality of the empirical method even inspired those myriad entrepreneurs whose economic experiments, and calculations of profit and loss, also help to explain why the first Industrial Revolution occurred in England.

A second strain in the outlook of these inventors and entrepreneurs was puritanism. Half the inventors and entrepreneurs who were active in the Industrial Revolution were Nonconformists, though only 5 percent of the English were. The German sociologist Max Weber argues in his *Protestant Ethic and the Spirit of Capitalism* that the Calvinist belief that God gave each man a calling to perform made businessmen more dynamic capitalists, particularly when this belief was combined with a Puritan morality of thrift, industry, and sobriety. The existence of flourishing capitalist systems in Catholic countries has raised doubts about his theory; yet the fact remains that half the inventors and entrepreneurs of these years were Nonconformist. Some suggest that the excellence of Nonconformist education in Lancashire and Yorkshire explains this fact, others that their exclusion from the army, law, politics, universities, and the Church led them to compensate by achieving success in business. Like the experimentalism of the inventors and the rationalism of the entrepreneurs, the Puritan ethic is quite evidently at work. But its exact nature, the extent of its influence, and its origins are elusive and obscure.

The Consequences of the Industrial Revolution.

In the long run, the Industrial Revolution made England a wealthy and urban nation. Industry created new goods and services and multiplied old ones. It built large cities and linked them together with railways, automobiles, and airplanes. It also produced a large middle class and a powerful proletariat, both of which sought and won political power and a larger share of the national wealth. The new technology—rapid presses, the cinema, radio, and television—also transformed the culture of Britain. In the long run, the Industrial Revolution brought material improvement, political power, and a transformed culture to all classes. But how beneficial was it in the short run? Did it improve the material life of most people from 1790 to 1850? Historians disagree in their answers to this question. One group, called the pessimists, has drawn up a formidable indictment against the Industrial Revolution: it forced children to work 16 hours a day, crowded workers into slums, reduced their standard of living, destroyed their craft industry, robbed them of their tools and dignity, and placed them in soulless factories and cities. Other historians, called the optimists, counter this indictment with a spirited defense.[*] The Industrial Revolution created cities full of opportunities; it provided jobs for millions, raised their standard of living and education, and gave them greater freedom and a greater role in government and culture. It is a dispute that reveals much about the economic and social changes that, from 1790 to 1850, transformed the nature of English life.

The Pessimist Indictment.

At the core of the Industrial Revolution lay the factory and mine with their steam-powered machinery. Many of these factories and mines employed children because their labor was cheaper. Children in textile mills ranged in age from 4 to 20. "Six is not uncommon," said one witness in 1832. A similar judgment, "five and one half is not uncommon," was made in 1842 of children in coal mines, and the witness added that some entered the mines at four. The hours of work in mines and mills averaged 12, though if a mill faced a rush order it worked much longer. In the mines, the

---

[*]The pessimist case is best stated in the writings of John and Barbara Hammond, E. P. Thompson, and E. J. Hobsbawm. The optimist case is given in the writings of J. H. Clapham, T. S. Ashton, and R. M. Hartwell.

smallest children spent 12 hours alone in total darkness. Children in textile mills tended spinning machines, a job demanding constant attentiveness and often considerable moving about. Factory discipline was exacting and severe, as was that in the mines. Neither mine nor mill were healthy places for children. The employment of mothers was also harmful to family life. One out of five infants born to mothers working in the slums of industrial towns died before their first year. Since 60 percent of cotton workers were women, the resulting deaths of infants was quite appalling. If they survived to adulthood, they were often dismissed. Weak and uneducated they were unsuited to other work. These factories were, as the poet William Blake wrote, "dark, satanic mills."

The pessimists also charge that the Industrial Revolution destroyed the handicraft trades in which workers spun the thread, wove the cloth, hammered the nails, knitted the stockings, and stitched the shoes needed by millions of others. Most of these artisans enjoyed great prosperity in the 1790s and 1800s, since spinning machines had greatly reduced the cost of thread and yarn and the puddling and rolling processes the cost of iron rods. These were the materials handicraft workers converted into cloth, stockings, and nails. In those golden days they earned more than 20 shillings a week, a handsome return that unfortunately greatly increased their numbers by attracting other workers. It also encouraged entrepreneurs to assemble weavers, knitters, and nailers in larger workshops. Even before the wide use of power looms, hosiery knitting machines, and mechanical nail presses, the handicraft workers found their earnings reduced. The machines run by steam did finally wipe out these craftsmen, just as the gig mill undermined the artisans who cropped cloth by hand.

These artisans had worked at home, earned a good living, and enjoyed a high status. Because the regimentation of the factory was humiliating to them, or because no such jobs were to be had, they chose in the 1830s to work 16 hour days at only 4 shillings a week in defense of their independence, and it was a losing battle. Handloom weavers were, after agricultural laborers and servants, the third largest category of workers; as late as 1834, there were 840,000 dependent on that trade. By 1850 few wove cloth by hand. Thousands of knitters in the Midlands and hundreds of cloth croppers in Yorkshire met the same fate. It is thus not surprising that in 1811 and 1816 the angrier of these artisans in Lancashire, Yorkshire, and the Midlands burned down gig mills, broke up power looms, and destroyed the knitting frames of employers who violated customary practices. Their attempt to stem the tide of technological progress proved futile. It is true that at first their distress was due not to machinery but to the enormous increase in those who wove, knitted, and cropped. But ultimately machine-produced goods destroyed a handicraft trade that had given thousands not only an adequate living, but dignity and independence.

Many of the worst evils endured by the industrial working classes were the result of living in rapidly growing, overcrowded, and filthy towns. The miserable conditions of these towns forms the third charge in the pessimists' indictment. In 1750 only a fifth of the English lived in towns over 5,000, in

The Industrial Revolution brought polluted rivers, like the Irwell in Manchester, and heavy smoke and crowded slums.

1850, over three-fifths did. During those years population doubled every twenty years. Manchester in 1760 had 17,000; in 1851 it had twenty-one times as many, or 367,000. These hurriedly built cities were not happy places in which to live. At first the new tenements seemed roomier and warmer than the damp clay hovels of rural areas, but overcrowding and constant use soon led to their deterioration. Families of six or seven crammed into 12 by 10-foot rooms. Cooking facilities were rare, running water and indoor toilets nonexistent, windows few, and outhouses and wells in the courtyards full with refuse. The overcrowding produced sexual promiscuity and the filth produced disease. Nearby breweries, tanneries, dye works, and factories polluted the rivers and added their odors to an atmosphere already heavy with the stench of animal and human excrement. Countless coal furnaces belched sulfurous black smoke. Disease was rampant. In the 1840s one in forty-five of the English died each year; in the slums of Macclesfield it was one in twenty. An average laborer in Manchester could expect to live to the age of 17 and a professional worker to 38, while in rural Rutland a laborer could expect to enjoy 38 and a professional 52 years of life—and a life breathing clean air. Polluted water, not air, was the villain, it being too often full of cholera, typhoid, and diphtheria bacteria. The close proximity of

London, a city of commerce and hand manufacturers more than large factories, also had miserable slums, as Gustav Doré depicts.

outhouses and courtyard excrement to wells, streams, and cisterns made the working-class slum a deathtrap.

The more England became urbanized, the greater the crime. In 1805 criminals numbering 4,605 were tried; by 1846 their numbers rose to 30,349, most of whom dwelled in towns. Towns also witnessed a rise in drunkenness, since gin and beer shops provided the best escape from miserable conditions. Parks and public walks, like music halls, libraries, and cricket and football grounds, were some years away. There were also few schools. A survey in 1818 showed that only one in four children in towns were being educated, and then meagerly. Life in towns was dedicated to work.

Yet at times they could not even provide that. In 1826, from 30 to 75 percent of those in the manufacturing towns of Lancashire and Yorkshire were unemployed. The depression of 1842 was even more severe. In Bolton 60 percent were jobless, and in Leeds 20 percent of its peoples existed on 1 shilling per head per week. The years 1801, 1811, and 1816 were also depression years, as was 1847: they came periodically as part of the trade cycles of industrial capitalism. But even in good years there were many underemployed. From 1800 to 1850, the cotton town of Oldham had an unemployment rate that left 40 percent of its citizens in poverty. Henry Mayhew, one of England's most knowledgeable journalists, estimated in 1850 that one-third of the working class "are fully and constantly employed," one-third "employed half their time," and one-third "wholly unemployed, obtaining a day's work occasionally by the displacement of some of the others." This constant underemployment combined with periods of mass unemployment forms the fourth charge in the pessimists' indictment.

A final charge was the alienation and isolation of the worker in impersonal factories and friendless, crowded towns. Workers no longer owned their own tools, determined the time and pace of production, or worked in their own homes. They tended machines that ran at ever-increasing speeds. For minor lapses they were heavily fined and for major ones dismissed. They also no longer lived in villages and small towns held together by loyalties of kind neighbors and the paternal rule of squire and parson. In what the novelist Charles Dickens called "coketowns," the employer was remote and unknown, a resident of a distant suburb. A great gulf divided rich and poor in these towns. All was reduced to cash relations that were often exploitive, as in company stores where employees had to buy, at inflated prices, their groceries and dry goods. The practice of requiring employees to buy in company stores was called the truck system and was a source of additional profit to employers. It formed part of the cold, calculating capitalist world that workers found so alienating.

The Optimist Defense.   The first and most important fact about the Industrial Revolution is its astonishing productivity. From 1782 to 1852, industrial production grew 3 to 4 percent a year. In 1850 Britain produced eight times as much iron, five times as much coal, and six times as much cloth as in 1800, and the production of these commodities in 1800 was far more than in 1760. In 1830 Britain produced about 70 percent of the world's coal and 50 percent of its cotton and iron. Railway lines rose from a few mining lines in 1825 to 6,308 miles in 1850. British industry was a giant cornucopia pouring forth inexpensive but quality cottons, woolens, stockings, sheets, blankets, plates, cups, teakettles, pots, stoves, and iron grates. To fill the stoves and grates, Britain produced cheap coal transported on the same railways and steamships that brought in fresh produce and cheap grain and offered workers cheap transport. Though population doubled between 1800 and 1850, per capita income, measured in goods and services, rose some 85 percent. Industry was providing the English with more goods than ever before.

Industry also provided more jobs than ever before, a fact that forms the second argument in the optimist defense. There were, to be sure, many unemployed in 1826 and 1842, but in the boom years of 1835 and 1845 jobs were

Steamships like the *Great Eastern*, the product of Watt's steam engine and Henry Cort's tough, cheaper iron, gave Britain dominance of the sea lanes, commercial prosperity, and Empire (*Illustrated London News*).

One of the greatest miracles of the Industrial Revolution was the railway, also an offspring of the marriage of iron and steam (*Illustrated London News*).

plentiful in manufacturing towns. At midcentury there were jobs for more than 5 million people, jobs that enabled them to support a population twice what it had been in 1800 and at a higher standard of living. Nor were these standards markedly more miserable than before the Industrial Revolution. Many textile mills kept families together and most of them paid them, collectively, from 25 to 30 shillings a week, an unheard-of sum to the agrarian poor and one that would buy meat, good clothing, and a glass of ale at the pub. Many workers found factories warm, dry, and usually clean and whitewashed, and preferred them to the cold and damp from which farm laborers suffered. Skilled workers in the factories were certainly better paid than were field hands. The machinists who made, repaired, and operated these complex machines formed an aristocracy of highly paid laborers. The same Industrial Revolution that destroyed the handicraft trades opened up opportunities for other skilled workers. There were more avenues for upward mobility in 1850 than in 1760 not only in the elite world of skilled workers, but in the enlarged world of commerce that flourished in the new towns. These towns, for all their congestion and smoke, still offered workers a more liberated and interesting, if briefer, existence than life in a village. The amenities of town life form the third argument in the optimist defense.

Early industrial towns were not without excitement and pleasure. Manchester, for example, was dense with pubs. Their exteriors were richly ornamented and their interiors were brightly lit with gaslight and warmed by coal fires, strong ale, and fellowship. They were home for all single and many married men. Manchester and other large towns also had theaters, shops, and eating places, and for the poor the busy street itself, with stalls, peddlers, barrows full of trinkets, and organ grinders. However oppressive the factory and the tenements, they did create a working-class culture, one that gave people freedom, an identity, and a sense of community. Agricultural laborers lived under the patriarchal rule of squire and parson and could be fined for drunkenness or not attending church. The city dweller lived a freer life, one that not only saw the extended family flourish, but saw the emergence of a working-class consciousness.

That consciousness itself offers a defense of the Industrial Revolution. There is an irony in listing the emergence of working-class consciousness as a benefit, since the trade unions and political organizations which heightened that consciousness arose as protests at the injustices of the Industrial Revolution. The trade unions in particular protested against long hours, low pay, and wretched working conditions. From 1790 to 1850 the trade unions experienced many vicissitudes. The Combination Acts of 1799 and 1800 declared them illegal. Even after the repeal of those acts in 1824, the unions faced widespread hostility and frequent legal harassment. They suffered broken strikes, empty treasuries, and ignominious failure in their attempt in 1834 to organize a "grand consolidated union" of all workers. But despite these failures they grew stronger, and by 1850 the skilled workers among them had established effective unions.

The emergence of trade unions was not the only force that awakened a class consciousness; there were also the radical press, social and educational organizations, and the agitation for parliamentary reform. It was in London and the northern towns that the presses published and the workers bought cheap editions of Thomas Paine's *Rights of Man* in the 1790s and William Cobbett's *Political Register* in the 1810s. It was also in these towns that the middle class established mechanics institutes to educate the workers in the virtue of self-help and that the workers founded cooperatives to purchase goods cheaply, and friendly societies to care for members when they were ill, jobless, or old. Above all, it was the workers in the towns who from 1818 on agitated for the vote. Although unsuccessful, they increased their proletarian solidarity.

A fifth salutary consequence of industrialization was those social and administrative reforms called forth by the fact of industrialization. The early manufacturing towns were, to be sure, without social services and poorly governed, but these very deficiencies evoked reform. In 1835 the Municipal Reform Act abolished the rule of self-appointed elites that had brought corruption to the towns of England. In its place the act established the rule of officials elected by all householders. Between 1790 and 1850 countless local improvement acts also established authorities to improve sewerage, paving, water supplies, lighting, and police. The national government also responded to the challenge of industrialization. Factory Acts in 1833 excluded children from textile mills and in 1847 limited women and young people to 10 hours of work a day, while an act of 1842 excluded women and children from the mines. Education grants in 1839 and 1847 helped local schools, and the Public Health Act of 1848 encouraged the improvement of water and sewerage systems. The Health Act required the adoption of 6-inch, tubular, glazed, earthenware pipes that, along with the flush toilet, are one of the less heralded but no less significant consequences of the Industrial Revolution.

A Balancing Up.   In making a final judgment on the merits of the pessimist indictment and the optimist defense, two questions must be asked: How much of the exploitation and misery that occurred between 1790 and 1850 should be attributed to the Industrial Revolution, and how were the benefits and burdens of that revolution distributed?

A fair answer to the first question favors the optimists' case since economic distress arose not so much from industrialization as bad harvests, the French wars, postwar dislocations, and most of all a doubling of the population. Bad harvests and high food costs made the poor poorer in the 1790s; the collapse of the continental market brought unemployment after 1810, and huge population increases, mostly rural, caused more than one in five of the poor to go on relief. Countries such as Ireland, which experienced a similar increase but had no Industrial Revolution, suffered much greater poverty. The advent of steam engine and factories explain only part of urban squalor: the worst slums were not in factory towns but in the slums of old cities like Bristol or in overcrowded cottage industry villages. London, with hardly a single steam engine, suffered every conceivable urban ill. The small workshops of London, like those in Birmingham or Norwich, exploited children quite as much as factories and had done so for centuries. In a broad sense they were, like Wedgwood's pottery firm or the enclosed farms of the improving agriculturalist, part of an industrial capitalism that deployed labor and capital rationally in order to maximize profits.

How did this industrial capitalism distribute its burdens and benefits? The answer, not very equitably, supports the pessimist indictment. In 1801, 1.1 percent of the population received 25 percent of the nation's income; in 1848, 1.2 percent received 35 percent. The very rich did very well. From the number of the fine houses built, the works of art purchased, and the splendid furnishings bought, it is evident that the middle classes also did well. Accounts of their affluence offer a contrast to reports of 35 to 75 percent unemployed in northern towns in 1826 and 1842, of one-third of the work force constantly searching for work, and of farm workers receiving but 8 shillings a week as late as 1850. Economic historians who hold that the average national real income rose 85 percent between 1800 and 1850 forget there was no average Englishman. The top 1 percent of income owners were certainly anything but average. Tax returns figures show that they increased their share of the national income by 10 percent in those years. If these very rich could increase their share, why not the next 20 or 30 percent? Very likely they did. The middle class grew in numbers and wealth, erected imposing mansions, built resort towns, took continental tours, indulged in every luxury, and invested millions abroad and at home—all of which suggests that the middle class, far more than the working class, was the beneficiary of the Industrial Revolution.

Both the prosecution and the defense present strong arguments, a fact that reveals a striking ambivalence in the capitalism of the age: its vitality as an economic force and its injustice as a social system. The free energies of laissez-faire capitalism gave rise to a new technology, but the same capitalism proved incapable of controlling urban growth or ensuring the fair treatment of workers. Whatever the precise distribution of wealth, there was certainly enough of it available to have employed adults and not children in mines, to have built sewers and water systems in towns, and to have paid the very poor a shilling or more in wages.

Among the many reasons why the upper classes did not do more about these problems, one of the most important was their belief in political economy. Adam Smith in 1776 published *The Wealth of Nations*, a work in which he argued that there were natural and harmonious laws governing the economy, laws whereby each individual's free pursuit of gain promoted the welfare of all. The government should never interfere with these laws of supply and demand, but rather should pursue a policy of laissez-faire. Equally persuaded of the wisdom of this policy were Thomas Malthus and David Ricardo, though with less optimism. Malthus, in his *Essay on Population*, published in 1798, argued that because food increased at an arithmetic rate, (1, 2, 3, 4, . . .) and population at a geometrical rate (1, 2, 4, 8, 16, . . .) there would eventually be too little food. Only war, famine, disease, or moral restraint could check this increase in population. Since all government relief to the poor only encouraged their reproduction, he urged an end to all poor relief. David Ricardo was so impressed with the remorseless pressure of population that, in his *Principles of Economics* of 1817, he argued that the poor's propensity to multiply would drive their wages down to the subsistence level. Both Malthus and Ricardo agreed with Adam Smith that government interference did harm, not good. With the great triumphs of the Industrial Revolution demonstrating the wisdom of laissez-faire, these persuasively logical theories won the allegiance of the governing classes. They also fit well with the view that poverty is inevitable and labor the curse of man, a view that was part of the profound revival of serious religion that formed a parallel development to the social and economic transformation of England.

FURTHER READING

CHAMBERS, JONATHAN D., and GORDON E. MIN-GAY. *The Agricultural Revolution.* London: Batsford, 1966. Explains the agricultural revolution in terms of technical advances, increase in population, and growth of urban markets.

DEAN, PHYLLIS. *The First Industrial Revolution.* Cambridge: Cambridge University Press, 1965. Analyzes the causes of the Industrial Revolution in terms of agricultural, commercial, financial, and population changes and describes technological breakthroughs in cotton, iron, and power.

FLINN, MICHAEL W. *British Population Growth, 1700–1850.* London: Macmillan, 1972. A clear, accurate, and brief account of that great explosion of population that came after 1700, one in which a declining death rate is seen as more important than a rising birth rate.

HARTWELL, R. M. *The Industrial Revolution and Economic Growth.* London: Methuen, 1971. A perceptive and cogently argued explanation of the Industrial Revolution, and a favorable assessment of its consequences.

HORN, PAMELA. *The Rural World, 1780–1850: Social Change in the English Countryside.* New York: St. Martin's Press, 1981. A probing account of the changing agricultural society, one that saw capitalist enclosures replace open field villages, the French Wars drive up profits, and population increases drive down wages to subsistence level. Pamela Horn strikes a fine balance between the paternalism and harmony that covered over a world of exploitation and hostility.

LANDES, DAVID. *The Unbound Prometheus.* Cambridge: Cambridge University Press, 1969. The best analysis of the Industrial Revolution, one that puts its emphasis on the strong demand for standardized goods and a prosperous commercial and socially mobile England.

MANTOUX, PAUL. *The Industrial Revolution in the Eighteenth Century.* London: Cape, 1961. One of the best accounts of the inventions that lay at the heart of the Industrial Revolution; good also on the old domestic system and the new factories.

MARSHALL, DOROTHY. *Industrial England, 1776–1851.* London: Routledge and Kegan Paul, 1978. A discussion of the crucial transition from the traditional to the modern that underlines the dislocations, collapsing structures, and suffering as well as the opportunities and advances.

PERKIN, HAROLD. *The Origins of Modern English Society, 1780–1880.* London: Routledge and Kegan Paul, 1976. A brilliant depiction of eighteenth-century society—rural, hierarchical, paternalist—and the emergence of new social and economic forces that transformed it into an individualist, capitalist, and class society.

PIKE, A. ROYSTON. *Hard Times: Human Documents of the Industrial Revolution*. New York: Praeger, 1966. An excellent collection of documents on social conditions during the Industrial Revolution, skillfully using the reports of royal commissions, parliamentary committees, and civil servants.

THOMPSON, E. P. *The Making of the English Working Class*. New York: Vintage, 1966. A classic account of the emergence of the working class, one done with a vivid Marxist sense of class struggle and exploitation but with a non-Marxist sophistication about its complexities.

WALVIN, JAMES. *English Urban Life, 1776–1851*. London: Hutchinson, 1984. A thorough examination of how in seventy-five years England went from a largely rural to a largely urban society and of how in that transformation the working classes, though they enjoyed more limited and transient gains than did other class, still preserved those ceremonies and recreations rooted in lasting family structures.

The intellectual transformation

19

In the summer of 1739 Joseph Butler, Bishop of Bristol and author of *Analogy of Religion*, was alarmed. He had heard that a fellow of Lincoln College, Oxford, one John Wesley, was preaching to thousands in the open fields of Kingswood, a mining village near Bristol. In August he had an interview with the young revivalist and told him: "Sir, the pretending to extra-ordinary revelations and gifts of Holy Spirit is a horrid thing—a very horrid thing!" Wesley was not intimidated. "I pretend," he replied, "to no extra-ordinary revelations, or gifts of the Holy Ghost, none but what every Christian may receive and ought to expect and pray for." Wesley then expounded on the importance of the doctrine of justification by faith, which he defined as "the conviction, wrought in a man by the Holy Ghost, that Christ hath loved him and given Himself for him, and that . . . through the merits of Christ, his sins are forgiven and he is reconciled to the favor of God." To the philosophical Butler, "gifts of the Holy Ghost" opened the door to enthusiasm.

That enthusiasm, which became a vital part of evangelical religion in the nineteenth century, was for mid–eighteenth-century people a fearful thing. Dr. Johnson defined it as "A vain belief in private revelation; a vain confidence in divine favour or communication." Bishop Butler ended the interview by ordering Wesley to leave the diocese. Wesley stayed, leaving only when he felt the call to preach elsewhere, which in the next fifty-two years came often. When he died in 1791 he had traveled 25,000 miles—mostly on horseback and while reading—and preached some 40,000 sermons. With his brother Charles and a fellow Oxford student, George Whitefield, John Wesley had established Methodist churches throughout the world and had brought to England an evangelical revival that awakened nonconformity to a vigorous life, won over a large part of the Church of England to serious religion, and profoundly affected the outlook of the governing classes.

Bishop Butler had reason to be alarmed. Wesley's appeal to ordinary people to pray for the "revelations and gifts of the Holy Ghost" constituted as revolutionary a force as the steam engine, and the evangelical revival it caused transformed the lives of the English as much as did the Industrial Revolution. Since that revival arose both from the Church of England's failures to meet the religious needs of the lower classes and from a deep dissatisfaction with its dry rationalism, a closer look should first be taken at that wealthy and august establishment.

THE CHURCH OF ENGLAND

For many of those who heard Wesley at Kingswood, it was their first religious experience. Wesley and his fellow preachers addressed the many men and women the Church of England had ignored, not those who attended its services. The early Wesleyan preachers were Anglicans themselves and felt they were only filling a vacuum the parish priest could not fill. There were, to be sure, plenty of parish priests—some 13,500. To help support them, there were 11,700 livings worth some £3 million a year. A *living* was a fixed income from Church lands and tithes attached to a particular parish church. Livings differed greatly in amount, ranging from a few pounds to a few thousand pounds—the average in the diocese of Carlisle in 1747 was £59. Because many livings paid so poorly, some priests held more than one—a justifiable case of pluralism. But some held solid livings, hired curates for as little as £10 a year, and absented themselves to Oxford or London. Pluralism and nonresidency in fact were the rule, not the exception: in Devon, in 1780, 70 percent of the rectors were nonresident. But many also held more than one of the wealthier livings, and not because of need but because of political and social influence. Many wealthy pluralists appointed a curate or two at meager stipends to manage their many parishes.

As a result of pluralism there were many parishes with no resident priest—in fact, some 6,000 of them. Many of the vicars of the very poor livings and many of the meagerly paid curates had to run a school or farm in order to make ends meet, while the wealthy pluralists spent their time hunting and dining with the gentry. Sports and society, more than books and prayer, were their passions, and the rich in their rented pews up front, not the poor on the benches in the rear, received their attention. A poorly paid, ill-educated, and worldly clergy in a Church beset by pluralism and absenteeism meant that even in those rural areas where the Church was strong, it failed to meet the needs of an expanding population. The Church failed even more completely in England's mushrooming towns. In 1751 the Church of England in Manchester had but one parish church for a population of 20,000 and in 1800 had for Marylebone's 40,000 in London a church seating 200. By 1812 Dissenting chapels in London outnumbered Anglican churches 256 to 186.

The Church of England not only failed to offer the most rudimentary services to thousands of the poor, but its doctrines and services increasingly failed to inspire the educated and the wealthy. Upper-class Anglicans in the first half of the eighteenth century wanted a religion that was rational, moderate, comprehensive, and practical. They wanted morality taught, not theology. Tired of the furious doctrinal disputes of the seventeenth century, they wished their parsons to avoid the dogmatic, mystical, and emotional. To worship the supreme being, to be christened, baptized and buried by the Church, and to be edified by moral homilies was sufficient. Good Christians ought, therefore, to treat differences over doctrine with great latitude. This outlook, called Latitudinarianism, became dominant among eighteenth-century bishops, the lower clergy, and the governing classes. It had a strong utilitarian tone, seeing in edifying sermons a way to inculcate morality into the lower orders and philanthropy into the upper classes.

The Latitudinarians in the Church of England did little to promote serious religion. "In England," noted the French philosopher Montesquieu, "there is no religion." "Christianity," said Bishop Butler, "is now at length discovered to

In the late eighteenth century, many grew angry about pluralism, that is, the fact that one clergyman held two, three, four, or more livings (*British Museum*).

be fictitious." For the spiritually sensitive—for the Wesleys and Whitefields—and for the despairing lower classes—for the people of Kingswood—the Church's tepid formula and parochial neglect offered no assurance of salvation and no comfort to their forlorn existence—hence the revival of a fervent and vital Christianity.

That revival, however, did not topple the Church of England. The Anglican Church had its strengths as well as its weaknesses. The very comprehensiveness and reasonableness of its Latitudinarianism pleased many practical Christians and offered room for deists, evangelicals, and High Churchmen alike. There were also parish clergy who were conscientious shepherds of their flocks. By visiting the sick, managing schools, establishing clothing clubs, rebuking the erring, delivering sermons, and performing marriages, baptisms, and burials, they created villages where people lived in a closer communion with one another. Such clergymen, however, were in the minority. And even rarer were clergymen dedicated to reforming the Church or to using its wealth for the preaching of the Gospel to the poor. Although parliamentary grants between 1818 and 1833 led to considerable church building, not until 1836, when Parliament created the ecclesiastical commissioners, was there significant reform.

The Church of England was too intertwined with powerful interests to achieve reform. Landowners, for example, had the right to appoint priests of their own choice to half of all livings, and ministers of the crown the right to appoint all bishops, some 50 prebends, and some 600 livings. The bishops in turn had many wealthy cathedral sinecures at their disposal. The Church of England, itself a vested interest, was an inseparable part of the social and political constitution of England, which was, until 1832, largely the preserve of the aristocracy. It was thus the younger sons of noblemen and gentry who won bishoprics, cathedral appointments, and the wealthier livings; the poorer graduates of Oxford and Cambridge became impoverished vicars and ill-paid curates. All of them, though, if not quite gentlemen, had university degrees, and few cared to enter factory towns to preach to the working class. That vacuum could only be filled by men who believed that God had called them to preach the Gospel.

When John Wesley left Bristol it was not to please Bishop Butler but to preach Christ's redeeming mercy to the neglected keelmen of Newcastle, the weavers of Norwich, and the hosiers of Leicester. It was a mission that required bravery. Angry mobs jeered at him, dragged him about, shouted him down, and hit him with stones, while justices of the peace turned a blind eye and the clergy fanned the mob's fears. Undaunted, John Wesley continued to preach the Gospel four or five times a day. His brother Charles, his friend George Whitefield, and many of his disciples were equally indefatigable. Increasingly the lower orders accepted the promise of Christ's mercy and joined the burgeoning Methodist societies. By the 1750s the widespread hostility against Wesley had abated, and by the 1780s he was a respected national figure. At his death, 80,000 persons paid a penny each week to attend a Methodist society.

Wesley's success came in large part from his combining an open theology based on Christ's mercy with a warm, friendly service and a tightly knit organization. He took his theology—that sinful man gains salvation by Christ's merits and not by good works—from Luther and Calvin, but he wisely dropped the gloomy doctrine of predestination. For Wesley God had not, at the very creation, selected the few who were to be saved, but had instead, by Christ's sacrifice, offered salvation to all who had faith and were holy. To such people, conscious of their own depravity and sin, would come a conversion, a new birth, a sense of assurance, and even Christian perfection.

Methodism offered to seekers of holiness active participation in religious services. Hymns rang out in their halls as they had never rung out in parish churches. Charles Wesley himself composed 6,500 hymns, all of them promising God's love. Week after week, Methodists took part in meetings in which they could freely express themselves and gain a sense of belonging. To a theology that promised salvation and to services that brought fellowship, Wesley added

John Wesley, founder of the Methodist Church (*National Portrait Gallery*).

the security of belonging to a disciplined and authoritarian organization. Methodists in every local society also belonged to small groups called classes. They met weekly for prayer, Bible study, and self-examination. To attend a class, one purchased every three months a shilling ticket—a ticket which, if refused, meant expulsion. Wesley believed in tolerance and demanded no doctrinal tests for membership. But he also believed in righteousness and would refuse tickets to repeated sinners. Each class had class leaders, just as each society had stewards and trustees to manage finances and buildings. An annual conference chose the preachers for each society and replaced them every three years. The societies were grouped into seven circuits, and all were under the rule of an annual conference of ministers chosen and ruled by John Wesley. From 1739 to 1791 the Methodist societies were run by the man whose genius and perseverance had created them.

John Wesley was an extraordinary man. Small, neatly dressed, and self-controlled, he was calm in crisis, courageous before mobs, shrewd in his theology, flawless as an organizer, magnetic but not oratorical in preaching, autocratic in temperament, and, above all, deeply caring of the precious souls and the fragile lives of the wretched and forsaken.

His father was a High Church clergyman and his mother a pious woman who raised him with Puritan severity. Educated at Oxford, he might have risen high in the Church but chose instead to preach to the poor. He was not, however, hostile to the Church; he always wanted the Methodist societies to remain part of the Church of England. But so estranged—socially and spiritually—did most Methodists feel from the wealthy and Latitudinarian Church of England that they insisted their own preachers administer communion to them in their modest halls. Wesley agreed to allow such communions in a few select cases. In 1784 he also ordained two ministers to preach in America and empowered them to ordain other ministers in that country. This act violated the Anglican rule that only bishops can ordain ministers. Joined to the new practice of giving communion in Methodist chapels, it made the breach with the Church of England irreparable. The Methodists had become one of the free churches.

The Methodists also became divided, a result of Wesley's attempt to combine an authoritarian organization with an individualistic theology. The annual conference, composed of ministers selected by previous conferences, continued Wesley's dictatorial rule after his death. In 1797 the New Connexion Ministers split off because they wished a more democratic church; in 1812 the Primitive Methodists separated because the annual conference forbade their holding camp meetings; and in 1815 the Bible Christians separated because its preachers wanted to preach in areas forbidden by the conference. But still Methodism prospered. Although only 77,000 in 1796, in 1821, they numbered 235,000 and, in 1851, 725,000. And many more, not actually members, attended their chapels.

Why this rapid expansion? The attractiveness of Methodist doctrine, services, and fellowship, of course, explains much of it, but so also do the French Revolution and England's exploding population and economy. The French Revolution created a climate both of excitement and anxiety while England's multiplying population and growing economy created those expanding classes and towns in which the uprooted and mobile felt loneliness and unease. This vast array of clerks, skilled weavers, shoemakers, mechanics, apothecaries, plant overseers, small manufacturers, and petty shopkeepers felt socially inferior to Anglicans and uncomfortable with the exclusiveness of Dissent, yet were anxious to rise above the lowest level of the working classes. These were the people whose lives were transformed by faith in Christ.

But what effect did Methodism have on them? Did it liberate or enslave? Make them radical or submissive? It did all these things, depending on the person and the generation. For a miner steeped in ignorance, a weaver mired in drunkenness, a shoemaker alone in a desolate slum, each with a short life expectancy, a new birth into Christian holiness and the assurance of life after death was a liberating experience. Liberating also in a worldly sense was the moral discipline of the Methodists and the confidence that came from being a class leader or Sunday School teacher.

For a third-generation Methodist, one better educated and more prosperous, his religion could be less liberating. The Methodist Church's repeated call for submission to authority, its strict puritanism, its talk of hell, its Toryism, its denunciation of all politics could and did discourage political and intellectual activity. Methodism could be and often was a counterrevolutionary force. But since most workers were, after all, not Methodists and since Britain was not in the nineteenth century on the eve of a revolution, it is erroneous to attribute its stability to Methodism. Methodism was also not a foolproof antidote to radicalism. From 1838 onward some Methodists did join the Chartists in their demand for democracy. Many rank-and-file Methodists found that the church's zeal for a better world and its skills of organization could be transferred to trade unions and political clubs. Primitive Methodists were particularly active in trade unions. By these indirect means, Methodism helped create within the working classes an educated and disciplined outlook that helped form a liberal England. Within that new England, they found allies in the Nonconformist churches.

THE AWAKENING OF DISSENT

The second part of the evangelical revival that swept England from 1740 to 1840 involved the awakening of the Congregational and Baptist churches. Both had declined, as had the Presbyterians and Quakers, into religious formalism. Attendance fell and membership dwindled. Congregational and Baptist ministers worried more about the nature of predestination than the souls of the poor, and the Quakers argued over the relation of church discipline and the inner light. Presbyterians suffered the most. The rationalism that led Anglicans to Latitudinarianism led Presbyterians to Unitarianism and decline. In 1729 Hampshire had forty Presbyterian chapels, in 1812 only two. Though a stern orthodoxy allowed the Congregationalists and Baptists to withstand eighteenth-century Latitudinarianism, they wisely, in the early nineteenth century, relaxed their Calvinistic notions of predestination and embraced a freer more experiential, evangelical faith.

The zealous preaching of vital Christianity not only aroused the Congregationalists and Baptists, after 1800 it even imparted some energy to the Quakers and to the Unitarian churches that had evolved out of Presbyterianism. From 1790 to 1850 all these churches grew larger. By 1851 Nonconformists (the term now includes Methodists) had 20,399 buildings for worship accommodating 4.8 million persons, compared to the Anglicans 19,077 buildings seating 5.3 million. The religious in England were now evenly divided between Anglican and non-Anglican. On census Sunday, 1851, the attendance at the three services held in Anglican churches was 3.7 million, the attendance at non-Anglican services 3.4 million (some were Roman Catholics).

The remarkable expansion of the Congregationalists and Baptists was a result of the same forces that explain the rise of Methodism: the superior appeal of a personal evangelical faith over Anglican Latitudinarianism, the failure of the Church of England to meet people's religious needs, the increase in population and towns, and the pervasively conservative reaction to the godliness of the French revolution. In numbers the Methodists kept pace with Congregationalists and Baptists, but not in wealth and influence: the congregationalists and Baptists became, after 1815, the leaders of the free churches. They dominated many industrial towns: in Rochdale they held sixty-six services a week, compared to the Anglicans' six.

With their seventeenth-century Puritan classics and their eighteenth-century academies, they provided an educated ministry and a learned theology that the Methodists could not match—nor could most of the Anglican clergy. Congregationalists and Baptists also attracted the less well-to-do. The industrial towns of the north contained shopkeepers, skilled journeymen, commercial men, and professional men many of whom were engaged in a struggle in which the self-help morality and social friendship of the Nonconformist churches could play a crucial role. These classes also found that Congregationalists and Baptists were bolder spokesmen for their interests than the Methodists. The leaders of the Methodist Church were Tory in politics; they had a deference for Anglicans and a fear of being called subversives. The leaders of the Congregationalists and Baptists, on the other hand, were Whigs and had a long tradition of defying the Establishment. Growing in wealth, civic pride, and confidence, they led the struggle for political and religious liberty.

In 1815 those who refused to take Anglican communion could neither hold high office nor sit in Parliament; neither could they attend Oxford or earn degrees at Cambridge. Nonconformists also had to pay church rates, a tax for the repair of the parish church, and one-tenth of their income from land, the tithe, to an Anglican parson. Furthermore they had to go to an Anglican priest to get married, have their loved ones buried, or their newly born christened.

Not altars, not stained glass, not rituals and vestments formed the center of the Congregationalists' Surrey Chapel, but elevated in his pulpit, the preacher (*Guildhall Library*).

Led by the Baptists and Congregationalists in the 1820s and 1830s, the Nonconformist churches demanded an end to these disabilities. Since their increase in numbers and wealth now made their votes in borough elections crucial, they were able, in alliance with the Whigs and Radicals, to force the repeal of the Test and Corporation Acts in 1828 and so won the right to sit in Parliament and hold public offices. In 1838 they also gained the right to christen children and to perform marriages in their own churches. Although they lost their fight to abolish church rates, they did, in towns where they had a majority on the vestry, refuse to collect them. By 1856 religious liberty and equality had become the birthright of all the English: Oxford had even abolished its religious tests for admission and Cambridge its test for earning degrees.

The Nonconformists not only became an important political force, they also created a social and intellectual culture based on a sturdy individualism. Thrift, temperance, integrity, foresight, self-improvement, and hard work were the virtues that, in an unfettered economy, would promote the greatest good. All that was needed were institutions to train the lower orders in this morality of self-help. Such institutions should be voluntary; they should arise from the energies of free men, not the dictates of an aristocratic government.

The Nonconformists thus built innumerable churches, chapels, and Sunday and day schools. They also helped establish mechanics institutes to educate workers and philosophical societies to inform the middle classes. They founded periodicals and publishing houses and helped form cooperative stores, savings banks, and provident societies. They also helped support charities, hospitals, orphanages, dispensaries, and washhouses, while a few Nonconformist factory owners supplied workers with libraries, tea rooms, and social halls and helped form Bible groups and music societies. The Nonconformists often united with each other in promoting these institutions. In 1814, for example, they formed a society that by 1840 had established hundreds of schools for the working classes, schools which, like other voluntary institutions, promoted a sturdy individualism for a capitalist society. Out of these many institutions grew one of the most powerful forces in Victorian England: that serious, Puritan, resolute, ambitious, and often narrowly philistine outlook called the Nonconformist conscience.

EVANGELICALISM IN THE CHURCH OF ENGLAND

Charles Simeon, the son of a wealthy barrister, was educated at Eton, at Cambridge, and in the pleasures of society. But by 1782 he had become, as the vicar of Holy Trinity Church in Cambridge, a preacher of serious religion. Hannah More, in the same year, published her last play before her conversion from fashionable playwright and friend of Horace Walpole to evangelical reformer and friend of William Wilberforce. Wilberforce, a close friend of the prime minister, William Pitt the younger, had by 1782 abandoned the vanities of his youth in order to dedicate his £30,000-a-year income, position in Parliament, and organizing genius to evangelical religion. Simeon, More, and Wilberforce were all Anglicans, all talented, all converts from youthful worldliness, all persons of influence, and all successful in carrying serious religion to the upper classes. Charles Simeon, for example, impressed his zeal on hundreds of young Cambridge men destined for the Church, many of whom gained the livings that Simeon and wealthy evangelicals had purchased for the promotion of serious religion. Hannah More meanwhile, at Cowslip Green, Somersetshire, established Sunday and day schools and Bible groups that brought the true Gospel to the neglected poor. She wrote tracts based on her experiences, tracts that sold in the millions and that preached faith in Christ, strict self-denying morals, and social obedience. And at Clapham Common, near London, William Wilberforce and his wealthy evangelical neighbors, planned societies for the reformation of English life, drew up legislation to abolish the slave trade, and lived prayerful and righteous lives. The doctrines Bishop Butler had called horrid had finally penetrated to the center of ecclesiastical, social, and political power. At the turn of the century no less than 17 bishops supported Wilberforce's attack on drunkenness, gambling, the theater, and by 1848 an evangelical had become Archbishop of Canterbury. Although evangelical clergy numbered only one in eight by 1830 (up considerably from one in twenty in 1810), they were the leaven of the Church of England.

The conversion of these upper-class Anglicans reflected, as did the conversion of Methodists and Nonconformists, an unease with the apathy of the Church and a disgust at the cynicism and worldliness of the upper classes. In the past the governing classes lived at ease with the Church's lax doctrines and its tolerance of drunkenness, gambling, and cockfighting. But by 1790 the challenge of an evangelical morality made such indifference and worldliness seem the grossest of immoralities. Methodists, Dissenters, and many evangelical Anglicans lived lives, preached sermons, and published works that increasingly shamed the more sensitive of the upper classes. Religious movements, too, like changes in fashion, can be contagious; they can spread by their own dynamics.

Before the French Revolution evangelicalism spread slowly. After the French Revolution and the rise of a domestic radicalism, it spread more swiftly. The English saw that the French aristocracy, who had pursued pleasure, lapsed into skepticism, and neglected the poor, now faced a reign of terror and the guillotine. Just as alarming were the radical agitators in England itself, men who were steeped in the ideas of Tom Paine rather than those of St. Paul. Evangelicalism appealed to those who wished order not revolution, an order ensured by the

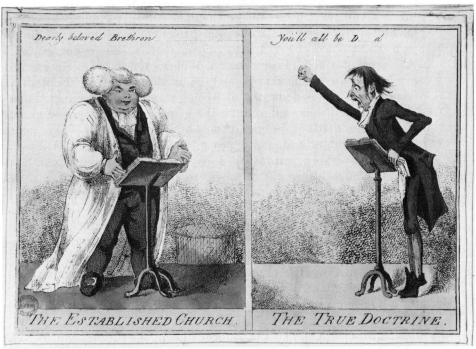

A pro-Anglican caricature of a comfortable Church of England clergyman and a ranting, emotional Nonconformist minister (*British Museum*).

righteousness of the upper and the obedience of the lower classes. Evangelicalism was also attractive because it was functional, psychologically and socially. Not abstruse theology but moral seriousness made Wilberforce's *Practical Christianity* so enormously popular. The certainties of its piety and morals erased doubts caused by the age's theological uncertainties, while the earnestness and purity of conduct it demanded brought both social advance and the moral approval of those already advanced.

It was a strenuous morality that also led to an outpouring of philanthropy at the parish, national, and world level.

The parish was crucial. It was in the parish that clergy became the shepherds of their flocks. When an evangelical took charge, all was activity. Card playing, dancing, and novel reading were condemned as vigorously as bull baiting, drinking, and horseracing. The Sabbath was to be respected: no letter writing and no long walks. But stern as were these rules, it was not all negative. The parson visited the poor and ill and managed schools, burial societies, and coal and clothing clubs. Often the parson became a magistrate and helped administer the poor laws, manage turnpikes, and judge wrongdoers. An evangelical parson could transform the life of a parish. But such parsons were never in the majority. Millions thus remained untouched, unless Christian laymen could reach them through philanthropic societies.

"Ours is the age of societies," wrote Sir James Stephen, a neighbor of Wilberforce in Clapham and one of the Clapham saints. He might have added "and philanthropy," a word as characteristic to the nineteenth century as humanitarian was to the eighteenth. A zeal to reform morals, relieve distress, and preach the Gospel informed all the works of William Wilberforce. He was the driving force behind the establishment, in 1798, of the Society for the Reformation of Manners, which was dedicated to freeing the Sabbath from such desecrations as sporting events and balls and to the general improvement of morals. It was but one of hundreds of societies formed by the evangelicals. There were societies to distribute Bibles and tracts, rescue prostitutes, relieve distressed weavers, promote temperance, improve prisons, visit the poor, and establish schools of all kinds. Philanthropy was the rage. In 1812, 3,000 persons, including lords and baronets, attended a meeting of the Sunday School Society to collect money to help 3,370 schools that taught 300,000 scholars. After 1814 Dissenting and Anglican evangelicals worked in the British and Foreign School Society to promote day schools. But these schools proved inadequate to meet the needs of a growing population. The other philanthropic societies were no more successful; what was needed was the intervention of the state. But on that point the evangelicals were ambiguous. If a more active state furthered their goals they were for it; if it interfered with their societies they opposed it.

They welcomed George III's Proclamation of 1787 condemning Sabbath breaking, they applauded the Attorney General's suppression of cockfighting and bull baiting, and they supported Parliament's outlawing of slave trading in 1807 and slaveowning in the colonies in 1833. They had, indeed, been the prime movers in the movement to abolish slavery and slave trading. On the issue of slavery they had no fear of state intervention, nor did they fear the state's role in excluding children from factories and mines. But in most fields, as in education, they opposed state action. Their real weapon was the voluntary society and their true metier the preaching of the Gospel, both at home and abroad. To preach and reform abroad was a passion that led evangelicals, whether Methodist, Congregational, or Anglican, to form the Church Missionary Society and to preach the Gospel throughout the world.

Evangelicalism was a force of incalculable power. It transformed parishes, reformed morals, abolished the slave trade, and consoled the poor, converted the lost, promoted the Sabbath, made thousands more serious, and for some brought a joyless Puritanism to English life. It was a force that could produce strong reactions, one of which was the Oxford movement.

THE OXFORD MOVEMENT

In 1833, one century after John and Charles Wesley formed the Methodist club at Oxford University, another group of devout Oxford dons came together. They met at the university's St. Mary's Church to hear the Reverend John Keble, fellow of Oriel College, preach on "The National Apostasy." The English Church, exclaimed Keble, is in danger. A reformed Parliament, open to Catholics and Dissenters, and a Whig government, secular and indifferent, could now appoint bishops, reorganize Church finance, even influence doctrine—and in the most fateful manner. Was not Parliament about to abolish half the Irish bishoprics and appropriate their incomes? The sermon aroused an immediate response among those who shared Keble's fears and longings. It marked the beginning of an Anglican revival that led to the pervasive religious seriousness that made Victorian England so profoundly different from the England of the eighteenth century.

Among those who rallied to Keble's cry were two other fellows of Oriel College, Edward Pusey and John Henry Newman. Both contributed to *Tracts for Our Times*, a series of pamphlets that had an explosive effect on religious opinion in the 1830s. Pusey was professor of Hebrew at Oxford and learned in German theology and Oriental languages. In a tract on "Baptism" and in another on "The Holy Eucharist" he argued that through such sacraments Christians could achieve grace and holiness. Sacraments, he insisted, were an integral part of the English Church. A belief that the Anglican Church was divinely inspired and catholic, that its bishops and priests were in the apostolic succession from St. Peter, and that they were therefore empowered to administer the sacraments and their saving grace was fundamental to the Oxford group and anathema to the evangelicals.

Newman in particular expressed awe and reverence for such a catholic church. Son of a London banker and conventional Anglican, he was converted at 15 to evangelicalism. But at Oxford, after much reading and friendship with John Keble, he decided that the evangelicals' emphasis on individual experience and private judgment was so excessive, subjective, and prone to error that it would never stay that advancing tide of liberalism and rationalism which threatened religion in England. Neither could a belief that the Bible alone revealed God's truth withstand rationalism, since scriptural interpretations varied widely and the new criticism had shown the Bible to be often inconsistent and historically untrue. In building a bulwark against the seductive insinuations of liberalism, the Bible was not enough; the Christian also needed creeds and dogmas firmly anchored in the wisdom of the Church Fathers and Church traditions. John Wesley, facing a Church often unashamedly worldly and deistic, sought to base Christian truth on the Bible and salvation on the workings of the Holy Spirit within each individual. Newman, facing an evangelicalism fragmented into sects and undermined by rationalism, sought to base Christian truth on the traditions of the Church and salvation on the grace which derives from the good and holy works of a truly catholic and apostolic church. Since the holy works of such a church include baptism, communion, confirmation, ordination, and confession, there was a renewed emphasis on ritual and on the altar, surplices, and candles. To many Anglicans and to all Dissenters, it sounded like popery.

In the 1830s Newman had exposed the weakness of evangelicalism and underlined the need of the creed and sacraments. In the dim light of Oxford's St. Mary's Church, in language of subtle beauty and in a voice peculiarly entrancing, he wove a spell few listeners could escape. These sermons, along with the poetry of Keble, the writings and preaching of Pusey, and the work of Newman's disciples, spread the idea of a revived Anglo-Catholic Church throughout England.

These ideas also aroused hostility. First Oxford University, then England, was torn with religious strife, a strife that reached its climax in 1841 with *Tract 90*, in which Newman argued that nothing in the Thirty-nine Articles was directly inimical to Catholic ideas. Newman withdrew from Oxford, pondered Augustine's proscription of all schisms, and converted to Roman Catholicism in 1845. John Keble, less remorseless in his logic and wiser in his appreciation of the value of existing institutions, remained Anglican because that was the faith of the people of Hursley, Devonshire, a parish in which he spent thirty years as a model vicar. Pusey also remained an Anglican, anonymously donating £6,000 to build St. Saviours Church, Leeds, just one act in a wider Anglo-Catholic effort to bring the visible Church and its saving graces to industrial England. Although Newman and a few others turned to Rome, most of the Oxford men who championed the Anglican revival remained in the Church of England. The result was the revival of a strong High Church party, one still active today, and one that did much to reinvigorate the spiritual life of nineteenth-century England.

Happy as were the results of the Anglican revival in making Church services more beautiful, priests more learned, ideals more spiritual, and the faith of thousands stronger, it also heightened dissension and made impossible the dreams of such broad Churchmen as Thomas Arnold to win back the Dissenters. Arnold, the great reforming headmaster of Rugby School, wanted to incorporate Nonconformists and Anglicans into one comprehensive Church, a Church that would be based on a Christian morality common to all. The broad Church party in the Church of England were numerous and powerful and added to the religious seriousness that pervaded Victorian England. For Newman the rationalism of broad Church beliefs promoted irreligion, while for Arnold Newman's worship and rituals and creeds were sheer romanticism. Romanticism and rationalism were in fact both powerful forces in the intellectual changes of late Georgian England.

ROMANTICISM

William Wordsworth, Samuel Taylor Coleridge, and Robert Southey, the sons, respectively, of an attorney, a vicar, and a squire, were only in their twenties when, in 1798, they published a volume of poems entitled *Lyrical Ballads*. The intense emotions, rushing rhythms, and strange imagery of the poems enraged many, delighted a few, and astonished all. The delighted were often the young, like Thomas De Quincey, later a famous essayist. De Quincey found the poems "an absolute revelation of untrodden worlds teeming with power and beauty yet unsuspected amongst men." In these poems a growing Romanticism, which in the late eighteenth-century had been contained by Neoclassical rationalism, burst forth with all the energy of a storm in a seascape by Joseph Mallard William Turner and all the boldness of a Gothic tower designed by James Wyatt.

Turner and Wyatt were also turn-of-the-century Romantics. Wyatt's Fonthill Abbey was in fact built between 1796 and 1807, when Turner's picturesque paintings of wild seas and violent avalanches were leading him toward the canvases of the 1820s, in which his swirling yellows, oranges, reds, greens, and dark hues transformed ordinary scenes into epic struggles of cosmic forces. These were years alive with the romantic impulse. In 1794 William Blake, a London printer, poet, and painter, published his passionate *Songs of Innocence and Experience*, a book illustrated by his own strange, attenuated, yet soaring drawings of demi-urges, prophets, and angels; and in 1802 Sir Walter Scott published his *Border, Minstrelsy*, the first of his immensely popular poetic tales of gallant knights, fierce battles, and passionate loves, poems later followed by historical novels also full of courageous deeds and noble loves. The Romantics produced a literary renaissance scarcely equaled since Tudor times, a renaissance to which three poets—John Keats, Percy Bysshe Shelley, and Lord Byron—made a decisive contribution.

The lives of the three were all brief and ended tragically. Keats, the son of a London stablekeeper, and Shelley, heir to a landed estate in Sussex, both died in 1821, Keats of consumption at the age of 26, Shelley by drowning in

William Blake's drawing on the biblical text "Then went Satan forth from the presence of the Lord" (*Fogg Art Museum, Harvard University, Greville L. Winthrop Bequest*).

the Mediterranean at 29. Lord Byron died of fever at age 36. Handsome, a lord, and acclaimed the greatest poet of the day, Byron was lionized by London society. But that society, when it heard of his love affair with his half-sister, turned against him and drove him to exile and the composition of his best and most satirical poem, *Don Juan*. In 1824 he died a heroic death befitting a romantic poet, fighting for the liberty of Greece.

But what was this Romanticism? What is it that ties together the *Lyrical Ballads*, the seascapes of Turner, Scott's novels, and Blake's illustrated *Songs of Innocence and Experience*? And what is it about Wyatt's Fonthill Abbey that led the art historian Kenneth Clark to say that it "concentrated in itself all the Romanticism of the 1790's"? For many critics at least three characteristics are distinctive: intense imagination, heightened emotion, and individuality. The poetry and art of the Augustans had these qualities, but they were always to be controlled, always subordinated to correct taste, the dictates of reason, and

James Wyatt's Fonthill Abbey reflects the Romantics' rebellion against Classicism (*Harvard University Art Library*).

the rules of nature. Romanticism knew no such restraints. James Wyatt's tower violated the perfect proportions of the Palladian style, just as Turner's impressionistic rendering of sea and sky violate the rules of reason and nature that, in Sir Joshua Reynolds's judgment, defined beauty. And what would Alexander Pope have said of Coleridge's lines from the *Ancient Mariner*?

> The very deep did rot: O Christ!
> That ever this should be!
> Yea, slimy things did crawl with legs
> Upon the slimy sea.

An intense imagination was a particularly important part of the romantic vision. To Romantics, the empiricism of John Locke and the mechanistic views of Isaac Newton were narrow, superficial, stultifying. They looked deep into the mind and found creative, active powers, intuitions, and insights that revealed a world beyond the senses. For Blake, imagination was "the living Power and

J. M. W. Turner's "Ulysses defying Polyphemus" shows how the Romantic painter threw over the world "a halo of prismatic light" (*National Gallery*).

prime Agent of all human Perception." Shelley and Coleridge also believed in a transcendental world of mind and ideas, a world to be understood by the shaping power of imagination. Keats and Wordsworth conceived of nature in more solid terms, but their nature was not an inanimate, cold Newtonian world; it was alive with a meaning that could only be understood by empathy, intuition, and poetic sensibility. For the Romantics the mind was not passive but active, full of an imagination that, as William Blake wrote could "see a world in a grain of sand/And Heaven in a Wild Flower"; a mind that enabled William Wordsworth to discern in a setting sun "a sense sublime, of something far more deeply interfused."

The Romantics were not shy of feeling; nature itself felt. To understand that nature, Keats invoked the "holiness of the heart's affections," and Wordsworth boasted

> To every natural form, rock, fruit or flower
> I gave a moral life: I saw them feel
> Or linked them to some feeling.

The heightened emotion of the Romantic spirit varied widely. It could be intensely private and personal, it could express a radiant optimism about human beings, as in Shelley and Blake, or explore the darker irrationalities, as in Coleridge and Byron; it could rise to the heights of joy and fall to the depths of dejection; it could move Shelley to write of "melting rapture" and "beatings [that] haunt the desolate heart" and could inspire Keats to evoke the tranquil pleasures wrought by timeless beauty. At its highest point it sought to capture the sublime in towering Gothic naves, wild elemental landscapes, or poems symbolic of the cosmic struggle of good and evil, all charged with feelings of awe, pity, fear, dread, and a final peace.

The Romantics' belief that imagination and emotion brought the discovery of the true and the beautiful led to a pronounced individuality. They loved the unique and particular in the objective world, just as they prized the singular and individual responses of the artist. Samuel Johnson would have been shocked at their departure from esthetic rules and their failure to pursue what he called "the grandeur of the general." But Romantics like William Blake no longer worshipped Johnson's dicta. "To generalize," Blake wrote, "is to be an idiot. To particularize is the alone distinction of merit."

The pronounced individuality of the Romantics led to the creation of many rich and varied visions of the world. For the young and radical there was Shelley's *Prometheus Unbound* with its gigantic struggle of liberty and reason against tyranny and superstition. For those less radical there was Coleridge's *Ancient Mariner*, a weird, moonlit world alive with the supernatural and the mysterious, and also with larger moral truths Coleridge later argued can be known only by a transcendent reason. One of the most popular visions was Wordsworth's. To an England increasingly urban and disturbed by religious doubt, Wordsworth's evocative description of nature as living, soul-filled, and divine proved as exhilarating as a spring morning alive with budding flowers and sunny meadows. For the more realistic and earthy there were the worlds of Sir Walter Scott's novels and Lord Byron's poems.

No Romantic writer was as widely read as Scott. His matchless tales of Highland chiefs, Christian crusaders, and dashing cavaliers mark the birth of the historical novel and reflect the absorbing interest in the past that was part of Romanticism. Scott himself built a huge neo-Gothic castle for a country home. For many, this turn to the past was an escape. Reading Byron's satires on the hypocrisy and corruption of the English upper classes was not. These satires with their classical mode of rhyme, measured rhythms, and grave irony were not Romantic in style. But beneath that style lay the wide-ranging passion of a Romantic: compassionate toward the exploited poor, bitter against cruel despots, melancholy over man's fate, ironical about his follies, indignant at religious falseness, mocking of society's hypocrisies and yet, withal, gaily hedonistic in

> "Let us have Wine, Women, Mirth and Laughter
> Sermons and soda water the day after"

Political Romanticism took many paths: for Blake, Shelley, and Byron, toward radicalism; for Coleridge, Wordsworth, and Scott, toward conservatism. But whatever path it took, its imaginative visions stirred and excited the intellectual life of England.

Romanticism had a dramatic impact on the outlook of early nineteenth-century England second only perhaps to the revival of serious religion. Both movements were reactions to the stagnant orthodoxies of the eighteenth century. De Quincey's delighted outcry about "revelations of untrodden worlds" sounds not unlike the cries of the converted Wilberforce. Both felt liberated from an outlook that, however fresh and appealing to Alexander Pope and Bishop Butler, had become by the turn of the century formal, rigid, and stultifying.

Romanticism was also a reflection of new and liberating forces—increasing wealth, an expanding empire, a rising middle class, a more literate working class, more and larger cities, advances in learning, better transportation, increased travel, and a multiplication of theaters, opera houses, coffee shops, newspapers, philosophical societies, and publishing houses. A great increase in wealth and building encouraged experiments in the neo-Gothic style. Bustling London produced the opportunities, schools, and professions for Blake, the son of a hosier, and for Turner, the son of a barber. The English began to travel: Turner and Wordsworth went to the Alps; Shelley, Keats, and Byron to Italy. The advance of knowledge also exhilarated people: new horizons were opened up. Even the French Revolution, in its earliest years, excited the idealism of the young Coleridge and Wordsworth. An older Wordsworth, like an older Coleridge, saw both its evils and the superficiality of the mechanistic, empirical philosophy they had learned from David Hartley. Romanticism was a complicated and protean attitude: at one moment it could celebrate the fall of kings and Hartley's laws of association; at the next it could condemn the folly of revolutions and the limits of empiricism. Built on imagination, emotion, and individuality, it always faced the dangers of subjectivity. Romanticism had departed from the fixed rules and ordered world of the eighteenth century and sought to establish its own rules and order. The result was a rich, exciting, and variegated world, but one with far less unity. An agreed-upon view of the world was also endangered by another powerful intellectual force, the spirit of rationalism.

THE SPIRIT OF RATIONALISM

Rationalism, narrowly defined, means a preference for a priori reason over empirical observation in the search for truth. More broadly defined, it refers to the belief that truth derives from both reason and observation but decidedly not from revelation, mysticism, or authority. In the late eighteenth century, rationalism also implied a belief that humans are reasonable and society rational, particularly if humans are correctly educated and society wisely planned. This rationalism, rooted in the philosophy of John Locke, flourished particularly among those of the upper classes who read David Hartley's *Observations on Man*.

Then, in 1791 and 1793, this belief in social progress through reason erupted as a political force in Thomas Paine's *Rights of Man* and William Godwin's *Political Justice*, treatises whose optimism about human perfectability was equaled in 1813 by Robert Owen's *A New View of Society*.

Thomas Paine, the son of a Quaker corsetmaker in Norfolk, was for fifteen years a journalist in America. He then returned to England, where in 1791 he wrote *The Rights of Man* in answer to Edmund Burke's *Reflections on the Revolution in France*. Burke's *Reflections*, which appeared in 1790, also angered William Godwin, the son of a Dissenting minister; it led him to write *Political Justice*. Burke argued that existing institutions were good because they reflected the wise and practical adaptations of imperfect humans living in a complex society. Such pragmatic and tested arrangements were far wiser than the untested ones that arise from the a priori and doctrinaire reasoning of ambitious revolutionaries. Burke's condemnation of the revolutionaries as doctrinaire and his defense of French monarchical and aristocratic institutions as wise infuriated Paine and Godwin, who believed these very institutions had caused the revolution in France and might cause a similar one in England.

They saw in England's parasitical monarchy, privileged aristocracy, corrupt Parliament, superstitious Church, sanguinary legal code, rotten boroughs, and tyrannical magistrates the very institutions that made people immoral and society exploitative. Abolish all monarchical and aristocratic oppressions and privileges, said Paine, and create a democratic republic that would restore to all their natural rights. Educate all in a clear and rational morality, and there will be no need for superstitious priests (a position he developed in 1795 in his *Age of Reason*). Give pensions to old people and allowances to large families, and provide lodging houses and workshops for the unemployed. But having done that, keep government small and inexpensive, with few taxes and few laws, a society of free and virtuous property owners. This was Paine's utopia. Godwin would abolish government and private property altogether. If all were well educated and free of society's corruptions, human rationality would inevitably lead people toward the good and their sympathies and intelligence would persuade them that their interests were identical with those of the community.

The government declared the *Rights of Man* seditious, and Paine fled to France. His book nevertheless sold 200,000 copies in the first three years. The government said nothing about Godwin's book: it was too expensive for the working classes. But Godwin had his disciples among the educated, including his son-in-law, the poet Shelley, and a Thomas Holcroft, who passed on some of his ideas to Robert Owen.

Robert Owen was a self-educated man who became co-owner of New Lanark, the largest cotton mill in Britain. He ran it in an enlightened manner, providing good houses, schools, and working conditions. In endless writings, lectures, and community experiments, Owen preached two grand ideas, first, that environment determines character, and second that capitalism and private property are evil. From the first idea came a deterministic philosophy that denied free will but held out the most optimistic hopes of educating all to be virtuous;

from the second came an ardor for small cooperative communities in which all property is held in common.

Owen's rich idealism and compassionate message of brotherhood moved thousands to form halls of science, cooperative stores, and model communities. But his ideas were also confused, shallow, and hopelessly optimistic. Jeremy Bentham, the very embodiment of rationalism, claimed that Robert Owen "begins in vapour and ends in smoke."

Bentham's own thought did not end in smoke but in a few seminal books, vast quantities of unpublished manuscripts, some devoted disciples, and a school of thought called utilitarianism. Bentham was a retiring bachelor with a private income and a great love of cats and music. He achieved his eminence by religiously devoting five to six hours a day for nearly half a century to thinking about the great ethical, political, and social problems of the time and to constructing a grand system that would form the basis of a rational, efficient, and happy society. That system would be based on the principle of utility—the "good" is that which brings the greatest happiness to the greatest number. He applied this principle to the institutions that in Burke's opinion embodied the wisdom of the past and found that instead they largely reflected ignorance, selfishness, and irrationality. To remove these abuses, Bentham proposed schemes for reform of the law, improvement of prisons, remodeling of education, reconstruction of local and central administration, and the establishment of a laissez-faire economy. There must also be a Parliament elected by the greatest number for only their representatives can legislate for the greatest happiness.

Bentham's application of reason to political problems was so penetrating in its exposure of abuses and so fertile in useful ideas for reform that it won him the support of many who wished to build a more rational society; he thus had considerable influence on the reform of prisons, schools, poor laws, law courts, and Parliament itself. He also inspired a few close personal disciples, the most famous of whom were James Mill, economist, historian, and publicist, and his more famous son, the philosopher John Stuart Mill. James Mill, a Scot and a stern and dour rationalist, applied reason to every problem, including the education of his son. He began teaching John Greek and Latin at age 3; by 8, on their long walks, he tested him on Herodotus and Plato. But he taught him nothing of music and poetry. Around Bentham and the Mills a group of young intellectuals formed called the Philosophical Radicals, a group which carried the utilitarian message into journalism, the civil service, the law, and Parliament, and sought to apply the spirit of rationalism and the principles of utilitarianism to the reform of society.

Those who were seriously religious or of a romantic persuasion found Bentham mechanical, narrow, and materialistic. His prisons and poor law schemes treated people as machines and his laws of economics treated them as commodities, while his claim that happiness was the sole criterion of the good was as shallow as his disdain of poetry. Bentham's utilitarianism, like Paine's republicanism, Godwin's anarchism, and Owen's utopianism, showed that the spirit of rationalism had its limits. Indeed, in the 1830s the periodicals most widely read by the educated classes condemned these rationalists. More to their taste were the poems of Wordsworth, the novels of Scott, the transcendental philosophy of Coleridge, the paintings of Turner, and the buildings of neo-Gothic architects. The religious also saw in rationalism the great enemy of Christian faith. But it was rationalism which continued, as it had in Newton's time, to produce solid triumphs in the realm of the physical sciences.

Lectures on chemistry in the 1810s and 1820s were quite popular. Londoners crowded into the Royal Institution to hear Sir Humphrey Davy or into the City Philosophical Society to listen to Davy's young assistant, Michael Faraday. Davy was the son of a wood carver, Faraday's father was a blacksmith, and both were largely self-educated. Yet both astonished the European world of science with their discoveries in chemistry and physics. In 1807 Davy isolated potassium and sodium and in 1808 calcium, barium, boron, magnesium, and strontium. He later developed the Davy lamp, which made mine work safer; discovered the elementary nature of chlorine; and with Faraday, for the first time, converted gases, such as chlorine, into their liquid form. Faraday then

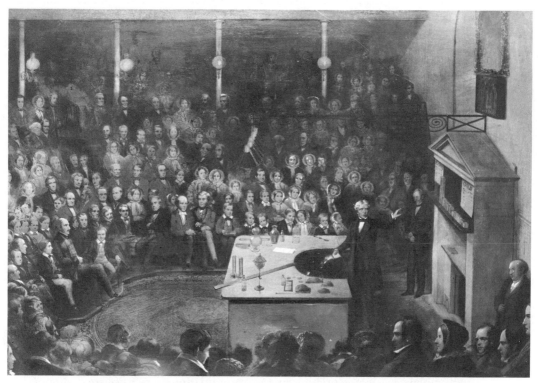

Michael Faraday, physicist, dazzles a Victorian audience fascinated with the progress of science (*The Royal Institution*).

isolated the hydrocarbon benzine, defined the laws of electroanalysis, and made, in 1831, his greatest discovery, that of electromagnetic induction, a discovery that led to the electric dynamo and the electric motor.

These discoveries were more than mere marvels; they also revolutionized old concepts that treated heat as matter, light as an imponderable fluid, and chemical qualities as peculiar bodies. Davy broke first from such materialistic concepts. He described heat as molecular motion, defined chemical qualities as the result of different molecular forms, and conceived of matter as "point atoms" surrounded by attractive and repulsive forces. Faraday continued that revolution in the field of electricity. He described electricity in terms of lines of force that worked immediately on nearby particles and in patterns similar to magnetic lines of force. Thirty years later, the great physicist Clerk Maxwell expressed Faraday's field theory in mathematical equations that helped form the basis of modern physics.

The discoveries of Davy, Faraday, and other scientists increased the already impressive reputation of science. In Birmingham's Lunar, Manchester's Literary and Philosophical, and London's Linnean societies, just as in the Royal Society and London's Institution, amateurs and professionals not only celebrated the miracles of science, but of all forms of advancing knowledge that reiterated what the eighteenth century had proclaimed, the triumph of rationalism. And although great religious movements—evangelical, Methodist, the Oxford Movement—arose in reaction to young science's brashness, materialism, and spiritual aridness, the advance of rationalism nevertheless proved remorseless and beneficent. Rationalism had witchcraft declared illegal; it treated the insane as ill and curable, not beasts and incurable; it produced the small pox inoculation; it invented the steam engine and water frame; it made more intelligible and credible the history of the past; it made the law fairer and more humane; and at torpid Oxford and Cambridge, it even began instruction in economics, geography, history, and the sciences. Diffuse and infinitely varied, rationalism became an ever more pervasive and powerful force. In inexpensive encyclopedias, in the publications of the Society for the Diffusion of Useful Knowledge, and in the multiplying periodicals it made the English a far better educated people in 1840 than in 1740. Few intellectual events in the opening decades of the nineteenth century were more significant than the rise of popular education. Though based largely on self-education and cheap mass publications, the slow expansion of schools and new methods of education also contributed much.

In few fields of learning was there a more dramatic advance than in historical scholarship. The first half of the nineteenth century saw a prodigious effort at discovering and reconstructing England's past according to a critical reading of original documents. A Public Record Office was established, government commissions edited innumerable manuscripts, local antiquary societies collected documents and published journals. The universities finally appointed outstanding scholars to professorships in history, and the press published pioneering studies on Anglo-Saxon and Norman England, on the growth of the constitution, and on Tudor and Stuart England—studies that for the first time based their conclusions on the scientific examination of primary materials.

As a result, the educated Victorian lived in an intellectual world profoundly different from that of the Georgians. The Georgians believed in a uniform natural law and a changeless human nature; they held that wars and revolutions, whether in ancient Greece or modern England, arose from similar causes. The Victorians saw the past differently. They saw the growth, development, and emergence of new institutions, new ideas, and new races, with profoundly different epochs succeeding one another. The Whig historians saw in these developments the grand progress of constitutional government and religious liberty; the Tory historians found in them, as had Burke, the tested wisdom of the past. In the 1840s no thinker was cited as often and praised as highly as Edmund Burke. The early Victorians had an extraordinary respect for history. Thus, the intellectual transformations that occurred between 1770 and 1850 produced an English people who were serious about religion, romantic in art and literature, rationalist in science, and historical in their view of the past.

FURTHER READING

ARMSTRONG, ANTHONY. *The Church of England, the Methodists, and Society, 1700–1850.* London: University of London Press, 1973. The clearest and briefest introduction, as well as one of the most discriminating, on the evangelical revival in Methodism, in the Church of England, and in Dissent.

BATE, WALTER JACKSON. *From Classic to Romantic.* New York: Harper and Brothers, 1946. An old but still profound interpretation of the crucial transition from the classical assumptions inherited from antiquity and the Renaissance to the individualism of the modern outlook.

BROWN, FORD K. *Fathers of the Victorians: The Age of Wilberforce.* Cambridge: Cambridge University Press, 1961. The fullest and liveliest account of the leading evangelicals of the Church of England, done with an irreverence and caricature that, though somewhat distorting, is also revealing.

CHADWICK, OWEN. *The Mind of the Oxford Movement.* London: Adam and Charles Black, 1970. The most scholarly and perceptive of historians of Victorian religion gives a brilliant introduction to that High Church revival that arose at Oxford with such giants as Newman and Pusey.

CLARK, KENNETH. *The Gothic Revival.* London: Constable and Co., 1928. A sharply critical study of England's "most influential artistic movement" by its most eminent art historian, one that examines the social and aesthetic demands of the epoch that brought it forth.

DAVIES, RUPERT, and GORDON RUPP. *A History of the Methodist Church in Great Britain.* London: Epworth Press, 1965. A definitive history of Methodism in Britain by a group of scholars, focusing not only on its experience of saving faith and doctrines of free grace but on its response to social change.

FORD, BORIS, ed. *From Blake to Byron.* London: Cassel & Co., 1962. A dozen critics ask of such poets as Blake, Wordsworth, Coleridge, Shelley, Keats, and Byron, what was the nature of their genius, what did they write about and why, and how did they reflect their milieu.

GILBERT, ALAN. *Religion and Society in Industrial England.* London: Longmans, 1976. An examination of the relation of religion to its social and industrial context, specifically how that context molded the conflict between Dissent and the Church of England.

HALEVY, ELIE. *The Growth of Philosophical Radicalism.* London: Faber, 1949. A logical and incisive analysis of the ideas of the political economists and Jeremy Bentham and of the contradictions between their laissez-faire economics and belief in a strong government.

RUSSELL, COLIN. *Science and Social Change in Britain, 1700–1900.* New York: St. Martin's Press, 1983. An excellent social history of science in eighteenth and nineteenth century England, one which not only describes the rise of specialization and professionalization but places great emphasis on the ideological and social uses of science.

WILEY, BASIL. *Nineteenth Century Studies: Coleridge to Matthew Arnold.* New York: Columbia University Press, 1949. A series of thoughtful essays on Coleridge, Thomas Arnold, Carlyle, Newman, John Stuart Mill, and others who struggled to preserve Christian faith in a skeptical century.

Politics in the reign of George III

20

George III was King from 1760 to 1820, the longest reign in British history until that of his granddaughter, Queen Victoria. He actively ruled but fifty-one years since illness led to his retirement in 1811 and the rule of his son as Prince Regent. In the fifty-one years of his rule three great revolutions broke out—the Industrial, the American, and the French. During the same period came two political developments of the greatest consequence, a substantial increase in Parliament's control of the executive and the growth of the democratic forces demanding Parliament's reform. When George III died, neither of these had triumphed, but both seemed inevitable.

The retiring George III would, in 1811, have denied their inevitability. Had he not, since 1760, won battle after battle with the politicians over the appointment of ministers and had he not suppressed every effort to reform Parliament? In his long reign he had resisted the encroachments of the politicians and the people with a stubborn doggedness. But though he won many battles, he lost the war. The forces released by the Industrial, American, and French revolutions made his triumphs only Pyrrhic victories. But in 1760, when George began his apprenticeship in politics, few in England could have foreseen that this would happen.

GEORGE III'S POLITICAL APPRENTICESHIP: 1760–1770

George III was 22 years old when he became King, the youngest monarch to ascend the throne since Edward VI in 1547. George had both a deeply rooted inferiority complex and a Puritan resolve to overcome it and be a strong King, two characteristics bound to create tensions. His moods were variable. Sometimes he was indolent and indifferent, sometimes withdrawn and melancholy, and

George III, who reigned from 1760 to 1820 (*National Portrait Gallery*).

sometimes exalted and vigorous, but most of all and most often, stubborn, un-yielding, sure at all times that God was with him. With an even stronger regard for kingly prerogatives than had Georges I and II, and a passionate hatred of party, especially the Whig party, he was determined not to be ruled by party men. He was scornful of politicians whom he called his "tools" and whom he treated in a cavalier manner.

He was deeply religious and moral, a chaste and loyal husband, and a model of rectitude for the nation, though for worldly politicians a bit censorious and priggish. He was no *bon vivant*, no man of fashion, but a sturdy, sober, God-fearing Englishman, popular with the middle classes as "farmer George."

His first ten years as King were very trying. They taught him many lessons, one of which was that although he could make his dearest friend chief minister, he could not sustain him in that office. He appointed his former tutor, Lord

Bute, Secretary of State in 1761 and First Lord of the Treasury in 1762. Bute had no political experience and not much political judgment: parties, he told George III, were detrimental to the constitution. His advance to power led the Duke of Newcastle, the embodiment of Whiggery, and William Pitt, the architect of victory, to resign, acts that led the petulant George III to dismiss all of Newcastle's friends. This "slaughter of the Pelhamite innocents" cleared the board for the rule of Bute. But suddenly Bute lost his nerve. Fearful of politicians who were angered by his sudden elevation and of the London mobs who hated all haughty Scotsmen, he resigned. With Pitt sulking in his tent, Newcastle dismissed and hurt, and Bute gone, George III had to turn, cap in hand, to George Grenville, a younger brother of that imperious Whig aristocrat, Lord Temple. Although Grenville was hard and domineering, and a dreadful bore, he managed the government efficiently and won majorities in the Commons. Unhappily his long, sententious, and hectoring lectures were unbearable to George III, who dismissed him in 1765.

George III's uncle, the Duke of Cumberland, next formed a ministry. Four months later he died, and the King had to turn to the Marquis of Rockingham, who lasted one year. Rockingham built his ministry on a base of over one hundred Whigs, to which he added the supporters of Grenville, Pitt, and George III, the latter loyal courtiers being known as the "King's Friends." But Rockingham's pursuit of Whig policies—a defensive alliance with Prussia to end England's isolation, the repeal of the cider tax to please the country gentlemen, and repeal of the stamp tax to conciliate America—so irritated George III that he urged the King's Friends to abandon this "hydra of faction." To escape that hydra he asked William Pitt and the Duke of Grafton to construct, in 1766, a broad-bottom ministry, one made up of the ablest from all parties. They complied, but the ministry was a weak and disorganized one. Pitt became the Earl of Chatham in 1766 and retreated to the House of Lords and his illnesses, leaving the government to Grafton, an amiable duke whose first loves were his mistress and horseracing. Four years of rudderless government followed—years that saw Americans grow angry at new taxes and Londoners indignant over Parliament's expulsion of Middlesex's duly elected MP, John Wilkes. Finally, in 1770, George III asked Lord North to lead a ministry. It astonished everyone by lasting twelve years.

Although the first ten years of George's rule seemed confusing and trivial, they were not without significance. They saw a George III who was willing to strain the constitution by appointing and dismissing ministers with little regard to majorities in his resolve not to be ruled by party, a resolve that not only foundered on an incompetent Bute, an arrogant Grenville, an absentee Pitt, and a profligate Grafton, but evoked from the Whigs an even stronger belief in party and in the principle that all ministers should enjoy the support of a majority in Parliament. But though George III strained the constitution in appointing and dismissing ministers, he did not wish to subvert the constitution by using offices, pensions, honors, and money to buy the loyalty of MPs and control elections, thus undermining the independence of Parliament. The charge was baseless, both because the offices, pensions, honors, and money were not sufficient to undermine Parliament and because such practices, on a most modest scale, were long used by Whig governments under George II and were constitutional.

The arrest in 1763 of John Wilkes and forty-eight others on a general warrant, the closing down of Wilkes's newspaper, and his imprisonment and expulsion from Parliament led to the charge that George III also desired to subvert the liberties of the English. That Parliament fully supported the prosecution of Wilkes made no more difference to radical pamphleteers, who called George III a tyrant, than did the scanty evidence of his subverting Parliament keep Edmund Burke from declaring that George III was unconstitutional. Burke, the brilliant publicist of the Rockinghamites, made that charge in his *Thoughts on the Causes of the Present Discontent* of 1770, a pamphlet which was far more persuasive when it argued that political parties were necessary and healthy.

Although many politicians in the 1760s joined George III in condemning party many in fact counted themselves Whig or Tory, the Whigs openly and aggressively as opponents of George III's threat to the constitution, the "old Tories" and the "King's Friends" more discreetly as the term Tory had Jacobite echoes. The Whigs stood for liberty, a strong Parliament, a constitutional King, religious tolerance, and an aggressive foreign policy in Europe and on the seas; the Tories stood for loyalty, a strong monarchy, the Church of England, no standing armies, an end to Whig corruption of elections and Parliament, and a more pacific foreign policy. Particular factions also formed around powerful peers and statesmen. Some, like the Pittites, Grenvillites, and Bedfords acted quite independently, but others, like the Rockinghams and Foxites were essentially Whigs.

Also active in Parliament were some 180 members of the Court and the government whose highly remunerative offices made them the King's men. And at the other extreme some 80 country gentlemen of a stalwart independence that other county MPs who listed toward Tory or Whig did not share. In the 1760s Whigs, Tories, factions, Court and treasury men, and independents constituted such a flux that the two-party system seemed nonexistent. But beneath the flux it did exist, and in the 1770s under Lord North the old Tories and King's Friends and the Bedfordites and Grenvillites came together to form that Tory party which under Pitt the younger and George III's favor dominated British politics until 1801. The Whigs under Rockingham, having absorbed the supporters of the elder Pitt and Foxites, proudly proclaimed in eloquent pamphlets by Edmund Burke that political parties were a reality, beneficial and to be desired. Public opinion agreed. In coffee houses, at public meetings, in electioneering, through pamphlets, and in London's four dailies and six weeklies, men proclaimed themselves Whig or Tory. The growth of party was remorseless and with it the insistence that ministers be wholly responsible to Parliament and not the King. Much of the London press also defended John Wilkes's right to sit in Parliament.

In 1768, the cry "Wilkes and liberty" came loud and clear from the county of Middlesex, the home of some 700,000 Londoners. John Wilkes was himself a Londoner, the son of a wealthy distiller who married the daughter of a Buckinghamshire squire and spent £7,000 to become MP from the borough of Aylesbury. Although undistinguished as an MP, he won notoriety for his love of the bottle, the gaming table, and women, his brilliant wit and charm, and his audacious and scurrilous journalism. Wilkes owned and edited the *North Briton*, and in issue No. 45 charged that George III's description of the late peace as honorable was false. He had elsewhere said that George III's mother was Bute's mistress. These libels were too much for the government. They arrested Wilkes on a

William Hogath's portrait of "that devil Wilkes" (*British Museum*).

general warrant and ransacked the offices of the *North Briton*. The use of a general warrant, one with no mention of a particular name or place, was of dubious legality, as was the arrest of Wilkes who, as an MP, enjoyed the parliamentary privilege of freedom from arrest. Wilkes was in fact released. A man of unparalleled effrontery, he reprinted No. 45 and in 1764 fled to France. Four years later he returned, stood trial, and entered prison, but not before winning election to Parliament from Middlesex. George III and the Cabinet were furious. That blackguard Wilkes! that libeler! that squint-eyed libertine! The thought of him in Parliament was unbearable. Parliament thus, on February 2, 1769, expelled Wilkes and ordered a new election. Wilkes, running unopposed, won reelection. Again he was expelled, again he ran unopposed, was reelected and again expelled. In the fourth election during 1769 he was finally opposed by a Colonel Luttrell, a man whom Parliament later declared MP for Middlesex, though he had won only 296 votes to Wilkes's 1,143. George III and the politicians had defied the will of the freeholders of Middlesex and asserted that Parliament could determine its own membership. Such arbitrary power was as intolerable to Londoners as the use of general warrants to ransack newspaper offices, a use which the Courts in 1766 declared illegal. The London radicals formed the Society of Supporters of the Bill of Rights, held mass meetings, raised subscriptions, petitioned Parliament, paid Wilkes's debts, and made him Lord Mayor. It was the eruption of the democratic forces of an urban world against an aristocratic Parliament. The freeholders who reelected Wilkes were merchants, tradesmen, and manufacturers of the middling sort. Those who owned property that rented at more than £40 tended to vote against Wilkes, while those whose property rented for less tended to vote for him. But there were also wealthy businessmen who fought for Wilkes, just as there were impoverished weavers—some 6,000—who, though without votes, championed him by keeping his opponents from the polls.

London was not alone in protesting against Parliament's arbitrary suppression of the rights of English electors. In 1770 the countryside was alive with meetings held to petition against the expulsion of Wilkes. Some 60,000 electors from fourteen counties and twelve boroughs petitioned on behalf of Wilkes. The protests, however, were not deeply rooted. By 1774 the Wilkes movement was dead. It had no definite program of reform, and despite the petitions, its main social base was London. Yet this eruption of democratic forces struck an ominous note: What would happen when the burgeoning industrial towns and their middle and working classes became minor Londons? And what would happen if a discontented part of the gentry joined these urban forces to demand parliamentary reform? The desire for reform, weak in the 1770s, became much stronger in the 1780s, after the loss of the American colonies.

THE AMERICAN REVOLUTION: 1770–1783

Britain's loss of the American colonies arose from its insistence on integrating them into the British Empire at a time when geographical isolation, local economic interests, growing nationalism, and decades of neglect had encouraged a passion for independence. The integration of the colonies demanded the creation of a standing army and a permanent civil service in America, and to pay for both required taxing the colonists. To the colonists, who had long enjoyed considerable independence from British rule, who lived on the far side of an ocean 3,000 miles wide, and who had a Whiggish fear of tyranny, a tax for the support of an army and a civil service that would be over them was intolerable.

For the governors of England it was equally intolerable that colonists who had contributed so little and benefited so greatly from the Seven Years' War should pay nothing for their own protection and governance. Parliament thus voted in 1764 to enforce a duty on molasses and sugar entering the colonies, in 1765 to levy a stamp duty on all legal business transactions, and in 1767 to impose duties on paper, paint, glass, lead and tea, and to expand the customs service in order to prevent smuggling. George III and the politicians all agreed that Parliament was sovereign over the colonies and had the right to tax them. Not all politicians, however, agreed on the mode of taxation or on its vigorous enforcement. The colonists resisted all duties and taxes and so fiercely that the Rockingham ministry in 1765 repealed the Stamp Act and the Grafton ministry in 1769 repealed the duties on paper, paint, glass, and lead. The Grafton government kept the duty on tea as a symbol of Parliament's sovereignty over the colonies as expressed in the Declaratory Act of 1766. Neither Rockingham nor Grafton nor any other minister had the ruthlessness really to tax the colonists.

Much of what they did was, in fact, improvisation. In 1772, for example, in order to help the finances of the East India Company, Parliament allowed the company to ship tea directly to the colonies, bypassing London and colonial merchants and offering the tea at a much lower price. The Boston merchants, angered at being bypassed, threw the tea into the harbor. The rebellious defiance at Boston, along with violent acts of resistance in other colonies, led Parliament in 1774 to pass four coercive acts that closed the port of Boston, deprived Massachusetts of the right to elect the governor's council, provided that in certain cases defendants should be sent to England for trial, and authorized the compulsory quartering of troops in private homes. That same year Parliament passed the Quebec Act, an enlightened measure for Catholic Canada, with its acceptance of the Catholic religion. But for the colonists to the south it was an act of tyranny since it involved compulsory church tithes, trials without juries, and the rule of a governor unchecked by an elected legislature. It was also an act that would apply to parts of the Ohio valley. By the spring of 1775 the colonists had met in the first Continental Congress and citizens of Massachusetts had fought the British at Lexington. The American Revolution had begun.

The separation of the American colonies from their mother country, although in the long run inevitable, might not have occurred in the eighteenth century if England in the 1760s and 1770s had been either consistently more forceful or consistently more conciliatory. Had England first created a standing army and an efficient civil service and then forcefully collected taxes, the colonists probably would have yielded. On the other hand, a policy of conciliation steadily pursued might have allowed the colonies to evolve an independent dominion status within the empire. In any event, the taxes, duties, and customs regulations of the 1760s angered the colonists, while the repeal of many of them only encouraged them in their defiance.

Having revolted, the colonists had now to defeat a major world power, a formidable task since the colonies were quite unprepared. The ragged and ill-equipped colonial army George Washington led in the first year of the war consisted of men who had enlisted for only one year. Had Britain moved with dispatch and sent over a large army by early 1776, it might have won the war. But it did not. George III, as head of the army, was in charge of recruiting and promoting officers, and he delayed and delayed. Lord North, as head of the government, was in charge of raising money, building up the navy, equipping the army, and directing the war, and he moved slowly and confusedly. Not until late 1777 did the British assemble their armies in North America. Even at that date their superior forces might have won the war had they carried out their master plan of isolating New England. General Burgoyne's army was supposed to invade upper New York from Canada while General Howe's army was to advance north from New York City to connect with Burgoyne. The slow and cautious Howe, receiving no clear orders from London, chose instead to occupy Philadelphia. His army was thus far away when the bolder Burgoyne overextended himself and was defeated in October 1777 at Saratoga.

News of the defeat brought France into the war. England, having allowed a quick victory to elude it in 1776–77, now faced two possibilities: grant America independence or attack France with the heroic resolve and energy of a Pitt. England did neither. George III refused to grant independence and Lord North did little to expand the navy or inspire a superior British army to defeat an inferior colonial force. George Washington's army thus grew in confidence and numbers while Lord North's government fell into disarray, confusion, and inefficiency. The most Britain could expect was a stalemate, but only if it controlled the sea. When a French fleet that had just defeated a British relieving squadron took control of Chesapeake Bay, it meant that Washington's forces could seal the trap formed when an ill-advised General Cornwallis entered Yorktown. Cornwallis surrendered on October 19, 1781. In 1783 in the treaty of peace Britain acknowledged the independence of the colonies. For Britain, seven years of war had ended in defeat.

In the coming of the American Revolution and in the loss of the war George III played an important but not dominant role. The King, for example, had little to do with drawing up the revenue and customs measures of the 1760s—his private correspondence does not even mention the Stamp Act. He was at that time more lenient toward the colonists than his ministers. But the rebelliousness of the colonists in the 1770s aroused his ire, and he urged Lord North and his other ministers forcefully to suppress those contumacious radicals, whom he mistakenly thought had little support. On August 24, 1775, he issued a Proclamation of Rebellion condemning the revolutionaries. Parliament voted overwhelmingly for the coercive acts, and merchants from Manchester, Liverpool, and Bristol sent in loyal addresses in support of the Proclamation of Rebellion. There are few greater myths in history than the myth that the tyranny of George III caused the American Revolution.

In the conduct of the war he played a more decisive role. His greatest error was to support the ministry of Lord North for seven long years, during which the war was lost. Lord North not only had no clear strategy and failed to inspire confidence, but he could not even rebuild the navy or find able, energetic generals. But George III stuck with him to the end, just as he stubbornly insisted on continuing a losing war. On June 21, 1779, George III called the Cabinet before him and delivered a half-hour exhortation on the need to continue the war. Only when Parliament in 1782 forced Lord North out of office did the King realize that peace was inevitable.

Angered by the loss of the war and by George III's support of the incompetent Lord North, the independent country gentlemen of England revived the charge that the King had used his patronage to corrupt Parliament. It was just as much a myth in 1782 as it was in 1770, but more attractive now because George III and Lord North had lost the richest part of the empire, had suffered humiliating defeats, had increased the debt, and had taxed the land heavily. Christopher Wyvill, a wealthy Yorkshire gentleman of good family and education, again raised the cry for parliamentary reform. From 1780 to 1784 Wyvill and his friends among the gentry, the wealthy merchants, and the professionals, formed county associations to petition for the reduction of expensive and corrupting placemen and sinecures and for shorter Parliaments and an additional hundred MPs to be elected from the counties. In 1780 they gained 60,000 signatures, but thereafter the Yorkshire Association, which Wyvill had organized, faded away like the Wilkite agitations had, since it was based chiefly on angry reactions to unhappy events: in 1769 the Middlesex elections, in 1780 the bungling of the American war. Urbanization and democratic ideas were still too weak to form the basis of a substantial drive for parliamentary reform. What was truly at issue in the early 1780s was that perennial issue, who would choose the ministers who ruled England, King or Parliament? Over that issue arose the constitutional crisis of 1782–1784.

THE POLITICAL CRISIS OF 1782–1784

The constitution of eighteenth-century England gave the King the right to select and dismiss any minister he wished. It also gave Parliament the right in practice to veto any ministry by refusing to vote supplies. These two principles made government impossible if the King insisted on a minister Parliament detested. This happily never occurred during the reign of George II. George III and Parliament were equally happy for twelve years with Lord North. It was thus a bitter blow for the King when the loss of America discredited North and again raised the problem of ministerial responsibility.

Lord North, first minister of George III from 1770 to 1782 (*National Portrait Gallery*).

Lord North resigned in March 1782. He told George III he did so because he could not command a majority in the House of Commons. He then added the constitutionally wise advice that Parliament's will "must ultimately prevail." The King bowed to necessity and asked the leader of the opposition, Lord Rockingham, to form a ministry. Rockingham consented, but only if the King agreed to legislation for disenfranchising revenue officers, excluding government contractors from the Commons, and eliminating certain sinecures and places from the King's Civil List, a fund which Parliament voted the King for his sole use in employing his Court and government servants. Because these reforms reduced the cost of government they were called "economical reform," but their main intent was to reduce the Crown's influence in politics. Rockingham thought that influence was growing dangerously large, though in reality it was not. A far weightier issue was the peace treaty with America, an issue which, because of Rockingham's premature death in July 1782, fell to a ministry dominated by Lord Shelburne.

Lord Shelburne, a landowner of great wealth, had a keen and imaginative mind. He had advanced ideas on free trade and parliamentary reform, yet he was also a disciple of the Earl of Chatham, hated party, and was deferential to the King. He behaved arrogantly and cavalierly toward his colleagues and often did not bother to consult them. Four of them resigned within one month, one of them being the Commons' most brilliant orator, Charles James Fox, second son of Henry Fox, a one-time foe of William Pitt the elder. This rivalry of the Pitts and the Foxes was to grow more intense and bitter with the rise of the sons to parliamentary greatness. In 1784 William Pitt, Jr., only 23, was part of Shelburne's party of 140 MPs. Fox, age 33, had a party of 90 MPs, while Lord North had 120. There were also more than 100 independent country gentlemen. Fox, having resigned in indignation at Shelburne's incapacity to work with others, joined the followers of Lord North and some of the independents and forced Lord Shelburne to resign.

There was, for a moment, no ministry. Fox would not work with Shelburne. The young Pitt, on the other hand, would not continue in the Shelburne ministry if Lord North and his followers joined it. The stalemate then led North to negotiate with Fox. It was a chaos created by ambitious politicians. Out of it, to the astonishment of contemporaries, came the "infamous" Fox-North coalition. How, they asked, could the conservative North join with the sometimes radical Fox? How could North work with a man whose scathing oratory had exposed the folly and stupidities of his American policies? The answer is twofold: first that the amiable North personally liked the immensely charming Fox, while Fox had a similar liking for the witty North, and, second, that the American issue was now dead.

It would have been a workable coalition except for one fact: George III detested it. He particularly disliked the impetuous, vain, passionate, and at times vindictive Charles Fox, and he knew that Fox would dominate the ministry. Fox lacked prudence and tact. He insisted that the King have no say in forming the ministry, he excluded the King's friend Lord Thurlow from office, he openly expressed his disdain for the King, and he befriended the young and profligate Prince of Wales (urging that the Prince should have the extravagant income of £100,000 a year). George III would do nothing to help such a ministry.

In the autumn of 1783 the Fox-North coalition introduced an East India Bill that would deprive the East India Company of control of the government of India and turn that control over to a board of seven commissioners and nine assistants, all sixteen of whom would serve for four years, would be irremovable and would be free to dispense much patronage. All sixteen were followers of Fox and North. Although the public raised a hue and cry about this gigantic piece of patronage, the bill passed the Commons 208 to 102. But its unpopularity gave George III his chance. After gaining William Pitt's promise to attempt to form a government, he denounced the bill loudly and had Lord Temple tell

Charles James Fox, orator, gambler, Whig, and defender of liberty (*National Portrait Gallery*).

the peers that those who voted for it were his enemies. The House of Lords was more of an adjunct of, than a check on, the monarchy since it included loyal placemen, obedient bishops, deferential Scots, and lords eager for more honors and favors. On December 17, 1783, it therefore rejected the India Bill. The next day George III dismissed Fox and North and gave the seals of office to Pitt.

When Parliament met on January 12, 1784, the cool and steely Pitt, at 24 the youngest Prime Minister in British history, solemnly denied knowing of or helping the King's machinations, though he had in fact promised the King to form a government. The coalition supporters were furious. The King had acted unconstitutionally; he had worked in secret to kill a bill that he had not opposed when it was in the Commons. He and the Lords had invaded the rights of the Commons. A resolution condemning those acts passed by thirty-nine votes. Pitt's own Indian bill was defeated, and for nearly three months he suffered defeat, but increasingly by smaller margins. He ignored them and cries that he resign, because he knew that public opinion, shocked that Foxite Whigs had not only joined the same Northite Tories that they had denounced as betraying English liberty but were brazenly seizing the East India Company's patronage. In Parliament itself Pitt was also helped by George III's generous use of patronage, appointments, honors, and peerages to win over needed support.

In March the King dissolved Parliament and ordered a general election. With the assiduous use of government patronage, the conscientious encouragement of public opinion, and the services of John Robinson, the century's most astute election manager, the King and Pitt won. Ninety-six of the Fox-North

BRITTANNIA ROUSED,
OR THE COALITION MONSTERS DESTROYED

Virtuous Britannia casts aside Fox and North to destroy their infamous coalition (*British Museum*).

coalition lost their seats and lost them in large boroughs and counties where the franchise was the most popular. Government patronage no doubt helped Pitt. Never in the eighteenth century had a ministry in power lost a general election and Pitt like Walpole and Newcastle knew how to win Treasury and Admiralty boroughs. It was not, however, in such boroughs that the greatest gains were made, but in the open constituencies—in counties and large boroughs—where public opinion was expressing its sovereign will.

Although Pitt's victory destroyed the Fox-North coalition, it did not immediately give the young statesman a working majority; the Commons defeated his government four times in 1785. Yet he did not resign. After 1785 his majorities grew strong and he gave George III eighteen years of stable government. George III's and William Pitt's rout of Charles Fox and Lord North was not an attempt to subvert the constitution, although many Foxites made that charge. But that rout did strain constitutional usage. George III's intimidation of peers and Pitt's refusal to resign when repeatedly defeated, violated, in the minds of many, correct constitutional usage. The King's and Pitt's defense was that Fox and North had themselves skirted close to the unconstitutional by their "storming of the cabinet." Fox's demand that the King could have no say in the appointment of lesser ministers was a denial of the King's prerogative to form a government.

The truth is that the governing classes had come to no agreement on the precise workings of the constitutional rules. In addition to the appointment of ministers, the governing classes had not defined precisely the role of the King and the House of Lords in passing legislation. Furthermore, most believed that Parliament should allow a new ministry a fair trial and that the most effective way of finally forcing ministers to resign was to refuse to vote supplies. Fox and North never attempted that because they feared it would alienate the country gentlemen.

In any case, many in the Fox-North group shifted their allegiance to Pitt, just as did public opinion. Fox's Machiavellian alliance with North, his excessive demands on the King, his grasping for patronage in the India Bill, his failure to stand consistently for any cause besides his own advance, and the Whigs' consistent opposition to any reform of Parliament lost him the support of the public. When Fox's name was raised, Londoners cried out, "No Grand Mogul! No India! No Usurper!" Pitt and Robinson exploited Fox's unpopularity through the use of newspapers, pamphlets, caricatures, and demonstrations. They also organized a party to fight the election and to win control of Parliament. In the ensuing years Pitt became a strong Prime Minister who demanded Cabinet responsibility. George III, allowing Pitt to appeal to the public, to organize a party, and to develop Cabinet government, was laying the basis for a popular, parliamentary, and constitutional monarchy. George III defeated Fox in 1784 and would force Pitt to resign in 1801. He lost few battles over ministerial responsibility, but he left a fateful legacy to his successor, who had to face the pressures of an industrial age. But before that age arrived, Pitt and George III had to face the radical forces unleashed by the French Revolution.

THE ASCENDANCY OF PITT THE YOUNGER: 1784–1806

From December 1783 to February 1801 and from May 1804 to January 1806 the son of the great Earl of Chatham directed the English government. For nearly nineteen years he grappled with the problems confronting England. He was, as a statesman, a pragmatist. He achieved power by a conservative interpretation of the royal prerogative, and he used that power to propose liberal reforms. He approached every problem on its own merits, mastered every detail, and solved it without reference to preconceived opinions. He was always the realist, always aware that politics was the art of the possible. Such pragmatism, when combined with a genius for mastering facts and analyzing issues, serves well in normal times, but not always during great crises. Pitt thus distinguished himself during the years from 1784 to 1793, but proved unable after 1793 to transcend the limits of his pragmatism and to equal his father's commanding brilliance as a great war minister.

Firmly in power in 1785, the young Pitt faced three problems: the reform of the English administration, the broadening of trade, and the government of India. The first was the most pressing. The English government in 1786 had a debt of £238 million. Its system of taxation, never the most efficient or rational, made it difficult to raise the revenues needed for useless sinecures, redundant offices, a costly army and navy, and an annual debt payment of £9 million. In 1783 a demoralized, defeated England was drifting toward bankruptcy; by 1792 Pitt had turned England around. He increased revenues by nearly 50 percent in his first eight years and cut expenditures by £10 million; in 1792 he submitted a budget of £19.5 million, £1 million of which went into a sinking fund set aside to pay off the debt.

Pitt accomplished this increase in revenues by raising the rate of existing taxes, by creating many new taxes, and by lowering the custom duties. The lowering of custom duties raised the most money, some £3 million. Lower duties made smuggling less profitable and goods cheaper, thereby increasing their flow through customs. The buoyant prosperity brought by agricultural and industrial advances also increased customs revenues. The new direct taxes, such as those on horses, hats, ribbons, clocks, shops, coal, and windows, also increased revenues. The tax on shops and coal aroused so much protest that pragmatic Pitt withdrew them, but since no fury of protest greeted the window tax, he kept it and thereby encouraged builders to construct darker, gloomier, less well-ventilated tenements.

Pitt also cut expenditures by making the administration more economical and efficient. He weeded out the deadwood, especially useless and inefficient offices that charged high fees. Some of these he abolished, others he consolidated into departments managed by salaried and professional civil servants whose work loads, but not salaries, he increased. He consolidated revenue offices, created inspectors of tax receivers, established an audit office to ensure honest accounting, developed the idea of a modern budget, and quietly retired many sinecures.

Aware that an expanding international trade both enriched revenues and made England prosperous, Pitt attempted to free trade from burdensome tariffs. His first attempt failed abysmally. A free trade treaty with Ireland led English manufacturers to cry out that the products of cheap Irish labor would ruin them. Pitt yielded, and Ireland continued an agricultural land in thralldom to a merchantilist England. Free trade with France met a better fate. French tariffs on most English manufactured goods were lowered to 10 or 12 percent, and in return England lowered her tariffs on French wines and brandy. Pitt also reestablished the Board of Trade and encouraged commerce with the Americas by setting up free entrepôts in the West Indies. All these measures showed Pitt to be what he avowed he was, a disciple of Adam Smith and political economy.

The problems of India were more complex. There had long been misrule and corruption in India, the result both of local circumstances and the greed of the East India Company. To remedy this misrule, Pitt persuaded Parliament in 1784 to create a Board of Control of six ministers, to be appointed and removed in the same way as other leading ministers of the government. The board would supervise the East India Company's rule in India. In 1786, Burke and the Foxites voted (with Pitt's help on one article) to impeach Warren Hastings, the Governor General of the East India Company, for his corrupt rule of India. Pitt then sent the Earl of Cornwallis out as Governor General. While the world of fashion crowded Westminster Hall to hear Edmund Burke's denunciation of Hastings's corruption, arbitrary government, and lust for power, Cornwallis and the East India Company were continuing Hastings's policy of increasing the company's power throughout India. Cornwallis, of course, had to work under the surveillance of Pitt and Pitt's Board of Control and thereby avoided some of the earlier excesses. But there was no fundamental change in policy. England, without any deliberate decision, and reacting to a vacuum of power in India, found itself imperceptibly drawn toward the creation of an empire. The course of history is strange and ironical. England's conscious decisions in America lost an empire, while unconscious reflexes in India won one.

With the outbreak of the French Revolution, Pitt faced a far graver crisis than India. He suddenly faced radicalism at home, rebellion in Ireland, and war abroad. The radicalism was not new. In the 1760s Londoners had shouted "Wilkes and Liberty" and in the 1780s Yorkshiremen petitioned for "Wyvill and Reform," but both movements had proved transitory. Their radicalism looked backward to ancient English liberties. The French revolutionaries and Thomas Paine broke away from these backward glances and awakened in all classes a vision of a brave new world based on the natural rights of all individuals to liberty and equality.

From 1789 to 1792 politicians and poets alike heralded the dawn of a new era. Fox called the fall of the Bastille "the greatest event . . . that ever happened in the world!" and the poet Cowper saw approaching "the most wonderful period in history." Societies of every kind were formed to work for this glorious prospect. The aristocrats formed the Society of the Friends of the

People, membership in which cost an expensive one and one-half guineas; the middle classes established the Society for Constitutional Information; and the workers', the London Corresponding Society, membership a modest 8 pence. The favorite reading of the last two societies, though not of the first, was Thomas Paine's *Rights of Man*. It was read everywhere, in weaver's shops, newspaper rooms, factories—it was even dropped into coal pits. Everywhere there was a demand for reform, reform of the sanguinary penal laws, of corrupt corporations, of unfair taxes, of a pluralistic and absentee clergy, of the cruel game laws, of a chaotic poor law, of torpid universities closed to Dissenters, and above all of an aristocratically dominated and unrepresentative Parliament.

The ideas of Thomas Paine, the radicalism of the French Revolution, and

Tom Paine, whose *Rights of Man* led many to demand radical reform (*National Portrait Gallery*).

The artist Rowlandson and the English governing class had little doubt of the evil of French liberty and the beneficence of English liberty (*British Museum*).

the demands for reform frightened as many people as they inspired. The ferment of radical ideas evoked in response counterrevolutionary fears and hates. In Birmingham in 1791 a mob egged on by Tory clergymen and justices of the peace, destroyed the homes of many reformers, including that of the scientist and philosopher Joseph Priestley. Powerful in 1791, these counterrevolutionary forces grew awesome in 1792 and 1793, as the French Revolution moved through terror, regicide, and tyranny to war with England and Europe. The war especially intensified the hostility of the governing classes to Tom Paine, French Jacobins, and the mere mention of reform.

Pitt's response to this conflict of ideas was to join in the suppression of the reformers. In 1793 he banned all seditious publications (especially *The Rights of Man*) and arrested the leaders of the Constitutional Society and the Corresponding Society and in 1794 he suspended *habeas corpus* with its guarantee of no imprisonment without trial. The members of the Corresponding Society attending a convention in Edinburgh were tried by a Scottish court that knew no juries, were found guilty, and were transported to Australia. Those in London were tried by a court that did know juries, were found not guilty, and were welcomed as heroes in London and the provinces.

Pitt, undeterred by the verdict of not guilty, had Parliament pass a law in 1795 banning all meetings of over forty people and a law making it treason to coerce Parliament, to devise evil against the King, or to incite contempt of the constitution. The two acts were, said its critics, the most serious invasion of liberties since the Stuarts. Pitt also had an army of spies and *agents provocateurs* infiltrate the reforming societies. A hysteria unknown since the days of Titus Oates swept over England. In the 1790s as in 1678 and 1679, a fear of a hostile, powerful France multiplied English fears of France's alien ideology, once Catholic, now Jacobin. Bookstores were purged, houses searched, schoolteachers fired, Dissenters harassed, and the press censured. In Somerset a basketweaver was imprisoned for saying, "I wish success to the French." In 1799 and 1800 Pitt had Parliament pass the Combination Acts, which outlawed trade unions and all other working-class associations except friendly and provident societies.

In one sense, Pitt's policy worked. By 1795 it had broken the back of the aristocratic Society of Friends and the middle-class Constitutional Society. But

An attack on Tory repression of British liberties (*British Museum*).

the Corresponding Societies withstood the repressive measures with greater toughness. Led by artisans, shopkeepers, mechanics, and schoolteachers, and supported by thousands of laborers who suffered from the high price of food in 1795 and from the decline of handicraft industries, they defied Pitt's measures until their leaders were imprisoned or in exile. They then gave up. Pitt had won, but it was a gratuitous and unnecessary victory. Historians have found no evidence that the reforming societies planned any violence against the government. Their methods were distinctly those of peaceful persuasion, petition, and demonstration. In this instance, Pitt's pragmatism did not manifest itself in an accurate understanding of the situation; instead he bowed, in the name of the politics of the possible, to the opinions of the heresy hunters.

He was also blind to the long-run results of his policy. The bitter experience of political repression, coinciding as it did in the 1790s with the bitter experiences of the Industrial Revolution, welded the working classes together as never before, and developed in them a class consciousness that would become a major political force in nineteenth-century Britain.

William Pitt, in an indirect way, also promoted the national consciousness of the Irish and so bequeathed to nineteenth-century Britain a second major political force. In 1782 Britain for the first time made the Irish Parliament fully responsible for all legislation concerning Ireland's internal affairs, a privilege that only multiplied Irish desire for independence. The government also encouraged the Presbyterians in Ulster and the mass of Catholics to demand religious equality with Anglicans. With the outbreak of the French Revolution, the Irish grew even more impatient for liberty and religious equality. The Irish Parliament in 1793 voted to give the vote to Catholics and to allow them to hold office.

The more impatient and radical formed the United Irishmen and invited the French to send an army to Ireland. Pitt acted quickly. By suppressing the United Irishmen in Ulster, he forced a rebellion in Leinster to break out before the French invaded. The Leinster rebellion was ruthlessly crushed and the French invasion proved a fiasco. Pitt, observing that the Irish were using their Parliament as a means of achieving independence, decided to abolish it. By the offer of peerages, office, and money, and by the promise of freer trade and Catholic emancipation, his government persuaded the Irish Parliament to vote its own end and to unite with the British Parliament. Henceforth Ireland would send 100 MPs and 32 peers to the British Parliament and henceforth that Parliament would legislate for Ireland. In the short run, the Act of Union of 1800 was a shrewd and pragmatic way of handling Irish discontent; in the long run, it paved the way for oppression, exploitation, violence, and rebellion.

Part of Pitt's Irish bargain was the promise of Catholic emancipation—that is, granting to Catholics the right to sit in Parliament and to hold all political, civil, and military offices. It was a promise Pitt could not deliver. George III was adamant against emancipation. Once again he announced that those proposing emancipation were not his friends. Pitt promptly resigned, whereupon George III appointed Henry Addington Prime Minister. Addington, with Pitt's loyal support, won the backing of a majority in the Commons.

Many in that majority not only disliked Catholic emancipation but realized that Pitt had failed as a war minister. Pitt had from the start overestimated Britain's military power, underestimated France's and mistakenly expected a short war. He was slow and inefficient in building up the army and planned for no invasion of France. He was too unimaginative to form a grand strategy and too compromising to exert a dictatorial direction over the war effort. Secure behind a navy far larger than France's, Pitt looked to English subsidies, elaborate alliances, and continental armies to topple Napoleon. These diplomatic efforts, which lay at the heart of England's efforts to defeat France, will be fully discussed in the next chapter. They will show that diplomacy, not war, fitted the temperament of this prudent statesman. Pitt had a clear, cogent, and analytical mind and an austere, detached, and cold temperament; he was an ideal manager of politicians and bureaucrats but no molder of a better world. Although an advocate of parliamentary reform, free trade, Catholic emancipation, and the abolition of the slave trade, he died having furthered these causes far less than those of repression, Toryism, and the exploitation of Ireland.

ROYAL MALADIES AND ROYAL DECLINE

George III in 1788, 1801, and 1804 suffered periods of acute illness. He recovered fully from the 1788 attack, but the next two left him emaciated, senile, and blind. In 1811 his illness returned for good and Parliament declared his son, the spoiled, extravagant, profligate Prince of Wales, the Prince Regent. George III died in 1820, and the regent, now George IV, both reigned and ruled until his death in 1830. Between 1801 and 1830 the physical malady of the father and moral failings of the son severely weakened the royal prerogative.

Contemporaries of George III considered his illness a form of insanity. Doctors in the 1960s argued that it was not insanity but porphyria. When the body produces an excess of pigments called porphyrians, the urine is occasionally bluish, the limbs feel weak, the skin becomes sensitive to strong light, and one suffers from hoarseness, vomiting, and colic. When acute it leads to delirium and delusions. George III's doctors recorded many such symptoms as part of his illness, including the emission of a bluish urine. Historians have also found evidence of porphyria, a hereditary disease, in George III's ancestors.

The King's illness, particularly after Pitt's death in 1806, prevented him from supervising closely the construction and conduct of the ministries that governed England between 1806 and 1815. His son, the Prince Regent, was even less attentive. He boasted, to be sure, that ministers were but his servants, and in 1812 he played a role in the construction of the Lord Liverpool government, but except on the more dramatic issues, such as Catholic emancipation, he exerted little influence. In his negotiations with the Whigs in 1812 he proved so inept and tactless that he ended up leaning on the shrewd Lord Liverpool— who then gave him sixteen years of Tory government. George IV's appetite was for pleasure, not power. He preferred a sybaritic life at his lavish Brighton

Pavilion on the south coast to an industrious one at Westminster. His life was an open scandal. His first marriage, a secret one, was to a commoner, widow, and Roman Catholic. His second marriage, after the annulment of the first, was to Queen Caroline of Brunswick. It ended in estrangement and public quarrels. These broken marriages, along with his mistresses, gambling, dissolute parties, huge debts, and extreme Toryism, made monarchy more unpopular than ever.

Other, more impersonal forces, also led to the decline of the monarchy: the evolution of Cabinet government directed by a strong Prime Minister, the development of political parties, and the growth of public opinion as a political force. Of these three forces, the emergence of the Cabinet and the office of Prime Minister is perhaps the most elusive to date. Cabinets existed in the age of Walpole, but these vaguely defined groups had little sense of collective responsibility, and Walpole himself told the Commons that he was no Prime Minister. By 1815 the Cabinet had grown more definite in membership, procedures, and sense of collective responsibility. After Lord North's twelve and Pitt's nineteen years as Prime Minister, that office had become more powerful. Ministries now had firmer control of the bureaucracy, and were clearer in policy, more decisive in managing Parliament, and bolder toward the King. From Lord Nelson's great naval victory at Trafalgar in 1805 to Wellington's successes in Spain in 1813 and defeat of Napoleon at Waterloo in 1815, the Cabinet grew in confidence as it found itself the architect of a successful war. Cabinet ministers, not the aged George III nor the dissolute George IV, planned strategy, made alliances, issued Orders in Council, commissioned ships, raised supplies, and drew up budgets. By 1815 the ministers managed most day-to-day affairs quite independently of the King.

These ministers also constructed the governments and did so increasingly according to party loyalties and political issues. In 1812 George IV turned to the Whigs for help in throwing out his father's Tory ministers, but to his surprise found that they demanded not only place but a guarantee that they would be free to pursue their own policies. He then turned to Lord Liverpool and the Tories, with whose policies he was in greater accord. Broad-bottomed ministries were now more difficult, since men increasingly formed parties not merely from bonds of kinship, friendship, and the pursuit of office, but from a concern for larger issues. The Whigs, led by Lords Grenville and Grey, increasingly allied in the Commons with men like Samuel Romilly, the barrister, Samuel Whitbread, the brewer, and Henry Brougham, the reformer, all of them commoners with slight aristocratic connections. They came to Parliament to make laws more rational, to promote education, to win religious equality, to reform corrupt corporations, and to end waste. Romilly, Whitbread, and Brougham represented the new men of wealth in England's expanding cities and towns, men who were learning how to use the electoral system to promote their causes.

William Wilberforce, the Tory evangelical, had shown the way, as had John Wilkes and Christopher Wyvill. Wilberforce was the chief organizer and agitator for the abolition of the slave trade. For years he labored to arouse public opinion against the inhuman cruelty of packing African men and women into damp, overcrowded, fetid holds, from which many never emerged alive, and from which the living were delivered into slavery. In 1807 Parliament finally yielded to public opinion and abolished the slave trade. Wilberforce would have been aghast to have an aroused public opinion made the basis of party or government. He and his contemporaries expected issues of conscience, like the slave trade, to cut across party lines. Lord Liverpool treated Catholic emancipation in this manner, allowing his supporters and ministers a free vote on the issue. But Wilberforce, quite unintentionally, was part of a development whereby larger social, economic, and religious issues would afford a basis for party alignment.

In 1780 there were 180 placemen in the Commons, in 1820 only 70. This decline in government patronage was paralleled by a decline in the great proprietory groups and increasingly great issues determined an elector's or an MP's party. Those who championed religious freedom, a more humane legal code, a freer press, the reform of corrupt corporations, and further checks on the royal prerogative aligned with Whigs; those who championed the Anglican Church's exclusive rights, the monarchy, old and tried law codes, ancient corporations, and the suppression of radicalism aligned with the Tories. The Whigs, many of whom were now reading Bentham as well as Locke and Blackstone, eventually became the Liberals of Victorian England, while the Tories, weaned on the pronouncements of Edmund Burke, became the Conservatives of that age.

In 1815 these ideological divisions had not yet matured. The Whigs were still a small, embattled minority, some 150 MPs, and were remembered by many as the friends of the Jacobins. Earl Grey, their leader, had long given up introducing motions for the reform of Parliament. Memories of the French Revolution and the Napoleonic wars were still fresh and vivid. They were reminders of Burke's warning about the dangers of tampering with institutions that had worked tolerably well in the past. The governing classes also feared the growth of manufacturing towns, with their discontented masses, their proud captains of industry, their Dissenting chapels, and their radical presses. A profound conservatism engulfed the governing classes during these years. Toasts to throne and altar were drunk throughout the land at assize meetings, at city banquets, in cathedral closes, and in London clubs. There were even cheers for the dissolute Prince Regent.

In such a deeply conservative age no one dared say that the Crown did not enjoy the prerogative of appointing and dismissing ministries. But the deeper realities were otherwise. As memories of French terror faded and demands for reform increased, the parties in Parliament divided more sharply, a reflection of the divisions of an expanded and more varied electorate. George III had passionately defended his right to choose his ministers: it was all that kept the King from being a mere figurehead. But at his death in 1820 that prerogative was fast slipping away. His own illness, his son's laziness and unpopularity, the emergence of a strong Cabinet, the rise of distinctive parties, and the growth of an articulate public opinion all conspired to make it inevitable that ministries would soon be entirely answerable to Parliament. George III was a spirited and active King, but even his stout defense of monarchy could not hold back the forces unleashed during his long, turbulent reign.

FURTHER READING

BROOKE, JOHN. *George III*. London: Constable, 1972. A full and perspicacious biography that examines those strengths and weaknesses that made him no tyrant but a largely able King, though not without serious faults.

BREWER, JOHN. *Party Ideology and Popular Politics*. Cambridge: Cambridge University Press, 1976. A more probing study of the politics of the 1760s than Namier's because it uses newspapers, pamphlets, and meetings to show there were Whig and Tory parties.

CHRISTIE, IAN. *Wilkes Wyvell and Reform*. London: Macmillan, 1962. A lively examination of the agitation for the reform of Parliament in the 1760s and 1780s, its leaders and supporters, its inspiring ideas, and why it failed.

FOORD, ARCHIBALD. *His Majesty's Opposition: 1714–1830*. Oxford: Oxford University Press, 1964. The most complete study of the many attempts and failures from 1714 to 1830 to make the ministers responsible to the Commons and not the king.

GOODWIN, ALBERT. *The Friends of Liberty*. Cambridge, Mass.: Harvard University Press, 1979. A sympathetic study of the impact of the French Revolution and British working-class radicalism on England from 1789 to 1797.

HILL, B. W. *British Parliamentary Parties, 1742–1832*. London: Allen & Unwin, 1985. A brilliant interpretation of political parties that challenges Sir Lewis Namier's claim that Whig and Tory parties hardly existed by demonstrating not only that they persisted in the 1760s and 1770s but emerged to provide the basis of Parliamentary politics.

NAMIER, SIR LEWIS. *The Structure of Politics at the Accession of George III*. London: Macmillan, 1951._____. *England in the Age of the American Revolution*. London: Macmillan, 1961. Two classics, published in 1929 and 1930, that destroyed Whig myths about the tyranny of George III, the existence of parties, the role of ideas, the wisdom of Whigs, the stupidity of Tories, and the corruptness of the age.

PARES, RICHARD. *King George III and the Politicians*. Oxford: Oxford University Press, 1953. A penetrating examination of the dramatic conflicts between King and Commons over the issue of ministerial responsibility.

WATSON, J. STEVEN. *The Reign of George III*. Oxford: Clarendon Press, 1960. Part of the *Oxford History of England* but weaker than most on economic and intellectual history, though very probing on politics, particularly during the French Revolutionary wars.

WIENER, JOEL, ED. *Great Britain: The Lion at Home, a Documentary History of Domestic Policy*. New York: Chelsea House, 1974. "A Nation Transformed," in Vol. 1, has valuable documents that range from the constitution and George III to working-class schools and speeches of radicals; full and copious selections.

Diplomacy and war in the age of revolution

21

From 1789 to 1848 revolutions threatened the monarchical and aristocratic fabric of Europe and strained its traditional modes of diplomacy and warfare. A powerful bourgeoisie, a numerous proletariate, new technologies, democratic ideas, and nationalistic aspirations disturbed that balance of power diplomacy which ambitious monarchs and wily ministers had long practiced with varying degrees of rationality and craft. Mass armies, fighting with improved cannons, rifles, and tactics, and whole peoples inspired by liberty, equality, and patriotism, now convulsed Europe. Yet the old diplomacy, like the old monarchies of central Europe, hung on tenaciously. Even revolutionary France, for all of its egalitarian ideals, proposed no new system of diplomacy. The formation of alliances and the deployment of military power still lay at the heart of international relations. The task confronting British statesmen from 1789 to 1856 was thus not to create a new system of international relations, but rather to employ old diplomatic traditions to contain and control new revolutionary forces. The first and most dramatic chapter in that effort began with the fall of the French monarchy.

THE FRENCH REVOLUTIONARY WARS

Britain and France, with but two brief interludes, fought each other continuously from April 1793 to October 1815. The first interlude began in March 1802, with the Peace of Amiens, and lasted only fourteen months; the second began in the summer of 1814 and ended when Napoleon escaped from Elba in February 1815. The first fourteen years of this protracted, costly, and frustrating war brought continuous French victories in Europe; the second period, extending from 1807 to 1812, were years of stalemate; and the last period, from 1812 to 1815, saw the final defeat of France.

The long opening phase from 1793 to 1807 was one of the most dispiriting in the annals of British diplomacy and warfare. William Pitt formed three coalitions to prevent revolutionary France from expanding, and all three failed ignominiously. The first lasted from 1793 to 1797, the second from 1799 to 1801, and the third from August to December 1805. To form an alliance whenever a great power threatens to dominate Europe and to occupy the Low Countries was long a cardinal rule of British diplomacy. Elizabeth I and William III formed such alliances to check the power of Philip II and Louis XIV. Pitt was thus following a basic maxim of British foreign policy when, in 1793, he helped organize an alliance that included four great powers, Russia, Austria, Prussia, and Britain, as well as smaller powers such as Holland, Sardinia, the two Hesses, Hanover, Baden, and Spain—countries with a total population of nearly 100 million, compared with France's 28 million.

In this alliance Britain, drawing on her expanding manufacturers, improved agriculture and world commerce, became the paymaster of armies raised by herself and her allies. By 1795 Pitt hoped to create an allied army of 283,000 and to throw the French out of the Low Countries. He did neither. Both Britain and her allies were responsible for the failure: the allies by abandoning the coalition and the British by mismanagement.

In April 1795 Prussia signed a separate peace with France, in May Holland withdrew and allied with France, in June defeated Austrian troops abandoned the Low Countries, and in July Spain quit; only Russia remained, but she, along with Prussia, had concentrated on the partition of Poland not on war with France. The allies left in large part because Pitt's government had bungled the war. Although possessing an army defective both in numbers and training, they sent troops to blockade Toulon in southern France, to help royalists' uprisings in the Vendee, and to seize France's West Indies islands, leaving the Duke of York, commander of allied forces, only 7,000 British and 22,000 Hessian and Hanoverian troops with which to recover the Low Countries. Prussia's 60,000 failed to operate as Britain delayed her subsidy. Meanwhile the French army, full of revolutionary zeal, drove the Duke of York's forces out of the Lowlands.

News in London in 1796 and 1797 was no better as reports came in of Napoleon's triumphs in north Italy over Austria, victories that gave the *coup de grace* to the first coalition. Many in London did celebrate the conquest of France's West Indian islands, Martinique, St. Lucia, and Guadeloupe and Holland's Cape of Good Hope, Ceylon, and Colombo, conquests that reflected Britain's supremacy at sea as did Napoleon's victories reflect France's supremacy in Europe. News from Ireland was also grim in 1796 as Britain stood alone against France and her new allies Spain and Holland, and the navies of all three. The revolutionary Society of United Irishmen invited France and Spain to invade Ireland in support of an uprising. The French made two such attempts, the first in December 1796 was foiled by huge gales and the second in February 1797 by the brilliant admiral, Sir John Jervis, whose fifteen ships routed the enemies' twenty-seven. A year later in May 1798 the United Irishmen did rebel, seize many towns, and conspire with France, only to be ruthlessly suppressed.

France, frustrated on the Atlantic, turned to Italy, the Mediterranean, and Egypt where Napoleon's conquests so aroused the jealousy of Austria's Francis II and Russia's Tzar Paul that Pitt's subsidies brought them into the second coalition. The British fleet went into action. Under Admiral Horatio Nelson it destroyed, at the battle of the Nile, France's Mediterranean fleet. In 1799 Austria, Russia, and Britain, with Prussia observing a selfish and myopic neutrality, formed the second coalition against revolutionary France. With the help of "Pitt's gold" it was successful at first. Great was the elation when Austria and Russia cleared the French out of most of Italy. But then Austria and Russia quarreled, divided forces, and met defeat. Tsar Paul withdrew in anger, Pitt deployed his forces on too many fronts, and Austria lost again to the returning Bonaparte. Another coalition collapsed.

The first two coalitions fell apart for many reasons. The most important

A STOPPAGE to a STRIDE over the GLOBE

Napoleon the Goliath faces the upstart John Bull (*British Museum*).

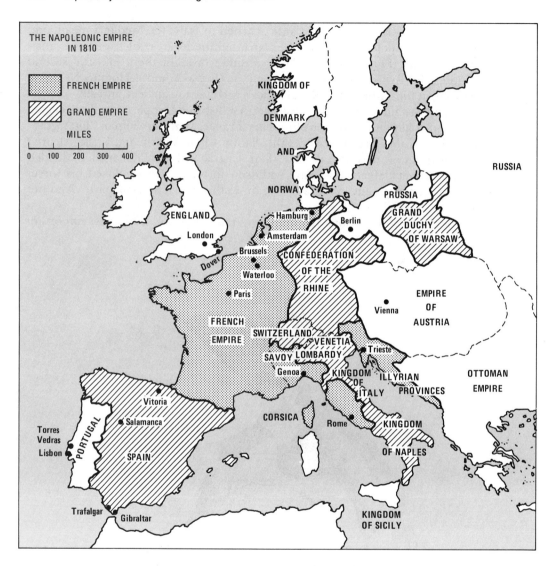

THE NAPOLEONIC EMPIRE
IN 1810

FRENCH EMPIRE

GRAND EMPIRE

MILES

0   100   200   300   400

were the selfishness, shortsightedness, and weakness of Russia's Catherine II and Paul I, of Prussia's Frederick William II, and of Austria's Francis II. All four were more anxious to make gains in their own spheres of influence than to check France. They were, Catherine excepted, inept as rulers, inefficient in directing armies, reactionary in outlook, and devoid of inspiring ideals or personal charisma. A second reason for the failure of the coalitions were the large numbers, patriotic ardor, and brilliant leadership of France's massive armies. Pitt confronted a revolutionary force never faced by his father or Marlborough. Nor did Pitt have a Frederick II or Prince Eugene to help lead the European alliance.

A final reason for the failure of the first two coalitions was Pitt's mistaken strategy and weak leadership. He squandered the energies and lives of too many men in the conquest of French and Dutch colonies that no longer weighed heavily in Europe's balance of power. He also did not build up a large army and what he did have he used in too many areas.

His successor as First Minister, Henry Addington, thus had little alternative in 1802 but to agree to the Peace of Amiens. It was a peace that returned to France, Spain, and Holland all the colonies the British had seized, except Ceylon and Trinidad, but allowed France to keep Savoy, north Italy, and a French military presence in Holland. Britain thus recognized France's predominance in Europe without any counterbalancing overseas gains. The peace also required Britain to give the strategically valuable Malta back to the Knights of St. John.

Addington in fact never did give up Malta. His procrastination over the matter grew lengthier as the restless Napoleon not only consolidated his European holdings and moved to expand his colonial possessions, but built up a large army and fleet for the invasion of England. In March 1803 the English, convinced that Napoleon would not keep the peace, declared war on France. In 1805 they persuaded Russia and Austria to form the third coalition. It quickly evaporated. Napoleon, learning that Austria and Russia were preparing for war, marched his army with astonishing speed from the Channel ports to the Danube. On December 2, at Austerlitz, he defeated their combined armies. Two months earlier, on October 20, Lord Nelson, Britain's greatest admiral, had destroyed the heart of the French fleet at Trafalgar near Gibraltar, a splendid victory that cost him his life.

Napoleon at Austerlitz and Nelson at Trafalgar won two of the most decisive victories of the French revolutionary wars and did so with similar tactics. Traditional tactics on land and sea called for the infantry or ships to form a long line parallel to the front and to advance. Napoleon and Nelson changed these tactics by throwing with great rapidity more concentrated columns of men or ships at the weaker parts of the enemy's lines. The superior numbers and revolutionary *élan* of Napoleon's conscript armies and the superior seamanship and gunnery of Nelson's fleet helped assure that these new tactics worked brilliantly.

After Austerlitz, Napoleon turned on a Prussia that had foolishly remained neutral, and at Jena on October 14, 1806, routed its armies. In June 1807 he once again put the Russian armies to flight. The new Tzar, Alexander I, was thus constrained, when he met Napoleon at Tilsit, to make an alliance in which France was very much the senior partner. France now dominated the continent as Britain did the sea. The war had reached a stalemate.

The restless, ambitious Napoleon tried to break that stalemate by establishing a continental system that would ruin the British economy. By closing all continental ports to British trade he hoped to deny Britain her greatest market and greatest source of food. Shrinking markets and supplies would bankrupt manufacturers and traders, cause unparalleled distress, and perhaps precipitate a revolution. Britain responded to this boycott by issuing the Orders of Council

Britain's greatest Admiral, Lord Nelson, leading his fleet to victory over the French at Trafalgar in 1805 (*The Tate Gallery, London*).

of November 1807. These orders required all ships going and coming from Europe to purchase licenses from and pay customs to the British and to agree to be searched in a British port. Britain wanted no contraband goods to go to France.

Between mid-1807 and mid-1808 and between mid-1810 and mid-1812, years when Napoleon vigorously enforced his boycott, the British economy did suffer, but not egregiously. Although Napoleon's decrees were severe in the first half of 1808 British exports fell only one-fourth. With three-fifths of all exports going to the Americas and the Near and Far East, the continental system could harm but not fatally. Resumed in 1811 it did, along with bad harvests, cause severe suffering, but not Britain's collapse. Napoleon could not sustain the boycott, since it also hurt France. So weakened and aggrieved were French merchants, manufacturers, and farmers, and so deprived and angry were French consumers of sugar, coffee, and cotton, that Napoleon had to relax the system, sending wine and corn to Britain in return for certain licensed imports. He was also confronted by the fact that Europe's coastline was a sieve. To stop up

The *GIANT COMMERCE* overwhelming the *Pigmy Blockade!!*

Napoleon's continental system had no chance against Britain's giant commerce (*British Museum*).

that sieve he had to conquer Spain and Portugal and coerce the Germanies and Russia. And in attempting to do this he caused his own downfall.

In order to force Spain to enforce the continental system, Napoleon replaced King Ferdinand with his brother Joseph. To compel Portugal to do the same he sent General Junot's army to Lisbon—only to see the British fleet, with Portugal's navy and King, moving slowly down the Tagus River on their way to Brazil. Napoleon now controlled every port in Europe.

At the very zenith of Napoleon's power, the Spanish and Portuguese revolted. The revolutionaries asked Britain for help and Britain answered by sending a large fleet, 30,000 soldiers, and a young general, Arthur Wellesley, to Lisbon. At Vimerio on August 21, 1808, Wellesley—a year later made Duke of Wellington—defeated General Junot. An angered Napoleon once again took command of his grand army of some 160,000 and invaded Spain. But severely distracted by the bold attack of Sir John Moore's army of 30,000 on his communications center below the Pyrenees, he saw the bitter cold of winter sweep over Spain before he could push the rebels out of that kingdom. In 1809 he again failed to clear Spain of rebels, this time because he again was distracted by the need to fight and defeat the Austrians.

In 1810, still frustrated and angered, he sent three armies to Spain with orders to throw the "English leopard" out. He nearly did. Retreating, though slowly and with great damage to the French forces, the Duke of Wellington was finally cornered in Lisbon. But he was cornered behind a line of impenetrable fortifications called the Torres Vedras. The British navy also protected his supply route up the Tagus. The French, having lost 25,000 men in the winter siege of 1810–11, had to retreat. In the summers of 1811 and 1812 Wellington patiently probed into Spain, quickly retreating to Portugal in the winters. The French grew increasingly frustrated at the elusiveness of Wellington's army and the omnipresence of the Spanish guerrillas. In 1812 Wellington defeated the French at Salamanca and in 1813 at Vitoria. The "English leopard" had driven the French eagle from the peninsula.

Britain's successes in the peninsula owed much to three forces—the British navy, the Spanish and Portuguese people, and Wellington and his army. From the initial invasion to the grim winter behind Torres Vedras the navy formed an indispensable lifeline for the British forces. It also aided those guerrilla forces whose harassments weakened the French. The revolution that had released the powerful force of French patriotism now, by its conquests, awakened a similar patriotism among the various peoples of Europe. For two decades French nationalism had disrupted Europe's balance of power. But in arousing nationalistic feelings in Spain, Portugal, and Russia it evoked a force that would create a new balance. Lord Liverpool's conservative government had the intelligence to order Wellington and his army to ally with this revolutionary force, an alliance the Duke of Wellington led with shrewdness and tact.

The Portuguese and Spanish peoples were also invaluable in the struggle against France. They supplied food, shelter, and spies, and fought courageously both as guerrillas and as trained soldiers. Wellington treated them with respect. He also treated his own army with respect, caring for their needs, disciplining them justly, and leading them brilliantly. A diligent student of strategy, he perceived the weakness that arose from Napoleon's two greatest virtues, the rapid mobility of the armies and their massive concentration on weak points. Napoleon's mobility came from traveling light and living off the countryside, while his concentration of forces came from maneuvering large armies against battle lines drawn up hurriedly and according to traditional military handbooks. In Spain and Portugal the French troops, with little food available, had to carry most of their supplies. Wellington also avoided all battles in which massive concentrations would disrupt his lines. He remained elusive until he saw a weakness in the French formation; then he would suddenly strike. His disciplined musketeers also learned to hold their fire until it could have maximum effect. At Waterloo in Belgium, in October 1815, the deadly fire of these firm lines of British musketeers decimated Napoleon's charging columns. The Duke of

Wellington's sound sense of strategy and tactics, his firm leadership of men, and his careful organization and planning helped Britain win first the peninsula and then, after Napoleon escaped from Elba, the battle of Waterloo.

The peninsular war, though dramatic, was not decisive. Both Britain and France continued their fierce economic struggle, which involved them both in other wars. Britain waged war far to the west against the United States; France, far to the east, engaged Russia in a war that led to France's downfall.

Britain's blockade of France demanded a strong assertion of British rights on the high seas. Britain thus forced American ships trading with Europe to use British ports, to pay duties there, and when on the high seas to be searched for contraband. The British also seized any sailor they suspected had earlier deserted from the British navy. These arbitrary measures finally proved too much for the republican pride of the young American nation, and it declared war in mid-June of 1812, having not heard that in the same month Britain had removed one of the main reasons for fighting. After indecisive battles on the Great Lakes and the high seas and after much argument at the negotiating table, the two powers signed a peace treaty on December 24, 1814.

For Britain, the War of 1812 was minor; for France, war with Russia was catastrophic. Unhappy with Russia's evasion of the continental system and frustrated with his inability to force Britain to surrender, Napoleon decided to conquer the continent's last independent power. In 1812 Russia's broad steppes, bitter winter, and tenacious defenses destroyed Napoleon's grand army. In 1813 and 1814 German and Russian armies, inspired by a new patriotism, completed Napoleon's defeat. The task facing the allies was now the reconstruction of Europe.

CASTLEREAGH AND THE RECONSTRUCTION OF EUROPE

In 1812 Lord Castlereagh, a cold and aloof aristocrat, and a clear-sighted and consummate diplomat, became Foreign Secretary. After Napoleon's disastrous Russian campaign, Castlereagh saw that a coalition of Prussia, Austria, Russia, and Britain could defeat revolutionary France and rebuild Europe. It could do so, however, only if the coalition were clear in its aims and resolute in its unity. The first three coalitions had failed, in part, because they lacked leadership. In 1813 and 1814 Castlereagh supplied that leadership. He was aware that the fourth coalition differed from the first three because, as he put it, "of the national character of the war." He therefore employed Britain's generous subsidies and the military presence of Wellington's army to weld together a grand alliance, one in which Britain would be dominant. To ensure its success, he went to Europe in January 1814. By early March he persuaded Russia, Prussia, and Austria to sign the Treaty of Chaumont, by which Britain promised £5 million in subsidies and one in which each ally, including Britain, promised to supply at least 150,000 soldiers. "What an extra-ordinary display of power!" exclaimed

Castlereagh. The treaty was a firm base: for twenty years the signatories were to meet regularly, principally to see that France made no more wars. By the end of March Paris fell and Napoleon surrendered.

Castlereagh's next task was to work with Tzar Alexander, Prince Hardenberg of Prussia, and Austria's Count Metternich in the construction of a European peace. For Castlereagh a basic requirement of such a peace was the fair and wise treatment of France. France should be a strong, independent member of the European system, but a nation contained by a ring of strong states. He succeeded, in the First Treaty of Paris of May 1814, in achieving these goals. That treaty gave France the boundaries of 1792 and returned to it all the colonies except Tobago, St. Lucia, and Mauritius. The Bourbon King, Louis XVIII, returned to the French throne, but not without a constitution, a decision that stemmed from Alexander's mystical liberalism, not Castlereagh's stern Toryism. Castlereagh's principal contribution was his insistence on an enlarged Netherlands under the House of Orange, a Netherlands that included Holland, Belgium, and Luxembourg and that could constitute a strong barrier to French expansion. An enlarged Prussia, much stronger on the Rhine, joined a new German Confederation, a neutral Switzerland, a strong Sardinia, and an Austria dominant in northern Italy to form a strong ring containing France.

The containment of France was the first great principle of the postwar settlement. The second principle was compensation for the victors. In theory containment and compensation, both reflected the old adage that the fruits go to the victors. Russia gained Finland, Bessarabia, and Poland. Britain won Cape Colony, Malta, and Mauritius. Prussia annexed Swedish Pomerania, much of Saxony, and territories on the Rhine. Austria picked up territories in northern Italy, on the Dalmatian coast, and in southern Germany. Most of these arrangements were made before the powers met at that greatest and most resplendent of diplomatic gatherings, the Congress of Vienna. There, amid balls, dinners, intrigues, and Mozart operas, the diplomats of the great powers ratified early arrangements, made new ones, and completed the reconstruction of Europe on the old principle of a balance of power and the new spirit of collective action, a spirit which found expression in the Concert of Europe.

Napoleon's escape from Elba, his rallying of France, and his defeat at Waterloo made it necessary to draw up a second Treaty of Paris. France's warm welcome of Napoleon and renewal of war aroused powerful passions for revenge both among the British public and the crowned heads of Europe. The aloof and cool Castlereagh, with the help of Tzar Alexander, withstood those passions. The second Treaty of Paris made only minor changes in the boundaries of France. For Castlereagh, a strong France was still indispensable to what diplomats of the time called "the just equilibrium."

In constructing this equilibrium Castlereagh was indifferent to the new forces of nationalism and liberalism. Thinking in terms of power and not of nationalism, he desired Austria to be strong in Italy, the Netherlands to include Belgium, and Prussia to have more territories in the Rhineland. Deeply fearful of liberalism, he helped place reactionary Bourbons on the thrones of Naples and Madrid. The results of these measures were not always conducive to stability. In 1820 and 1822 there were revolutions in Naples and Madrid; in 1830 the Belgians declared war on Holland, and by 1848 North Italians rose up against Austria. To suppress the Neapolitans, Metternich called for a congress of the great powers. It was an idea that reflected Castlereagh's desire to use such conferences to contain any state that disturbed Europe's balance of power. Incorporated into the second Peace of Paris as Article VI, it was in many ways the most creative of his ideas. But in the hands of Metternich and Alexander, the conference system became a method of suppressing liberalism within particular states, a proceeding Castlereagh considered a perversion of diplomacy by concert.

Lord Castlereagh's idea of using periodic conferences of the great powers to prevent wars was in fact stillborn. The conference of the four victors at Aix-La-Chapelle in 1818 was largely ceremonial, a welcoming back of France as a fully independent power. The next conference, held at Troppau in late 1820 and adjourned to Laibach in early 1821, met in order to suppress liberal revolutions in Naples, Piedmont, Spain, and Portugal. Lord Castlereagh, who did not attend, rejected its policy of suppressing liberalism. Although no friend of revolution, Castlereagh still realized the great danger involved in the great powers interfering in the domestic affairs of the smaller states. The three eastern autocrats nevertheless persisted in that tactic: in September 1822, they assembled at Verona in order to arrange for the suppression of the Spanish revolution. A month before they met Castlereagh committed suicide, though not without leaving his successor instructions to oppose the use of the congress as a means of undermining the Spanish constitutionalists.

It was Castlereagh, architect of the fourth coalition, the two Treaties of Paris, the Quadruple Alliance, the Congress of Vienna, and the idea of a Concert of Europe who first broke with that concert. He did so not because he no longer believed in diplomacy by conferences but because he believed Metternich and Alexander perverted its aims from that of creating a new public law for Europe's international relations to that of suppressing liberalism and nationalism, a use that, far from uniting Europe, only divided it between the forces of reaction and revolution. To mediate between these forces was, after October 1822, a task that fell to George Canning, a bright, eloquent, much hated and much liked liberal Tory.

THE FOREIGN POLICY OF GEORGE CANNING

Canning faced four difficult problems in his five years as Foreign Secretary: Spain, Spanish America, Portugal, and Greece. All four involved the forces of liberalism and nationalism and the outbreak of revolutions and all four loosened Britain's ties in Europe. The first of these problems arose in 1820 when the Spanish army revolted against their king, Ferdinand VII, the most reactionary, despotic, and stupid of Bourbon Kings. They forced Ferdinand to adopt a democratic constitution far beyond the capacity of the Spanish people to work. At Verona Alexander asked the great powers to intervene. Canning told Wellington, Britain's representative at Verona, "to any such interference, come what may, His Majesty will not be a party." The conference did not intervene, but Louis XVIII of France, anxious to aid a fellow Bourbon and to win a victory, threatened to invade Spain.

Canning meanwhile made bellicose speeches in and out of Parliament against those who would suppress constitutional regimes. He hoped to use an aroused public opinion to intimidate France. This was an approach to foreign affairs that Castlereagh would not have countenanced and that the Holy Alliance found dangerously democratic. The French, not intimidated by mere speeches, invaded and suppressed the revolutionaries. For Canning, it was a crushing diplomatic defeat.

French armies might occupy Madrid, but the French government would not, as many French royalists urged, impose Bourbon monarchs on Spanish colonies in the Americas that had thrown off Spanish rule. Canning believed that a French-controlled Spain, supported by a Holy Alliance that hated all revolutions, threatened these new republics. To meet this threat he asked the United States to join Britain in issuing a joint declaration against any European advance in the New World. The President of the United States, James Monroe, was not persuaded. He accepted instead the arguments of his Secretary of State, John Quincy Adams, and announced the Monroe Doctrine. In that doctrine the United States declared that the New World was out of bounds to any further encroachments by European powers. The doctrine became in time a fundamental plank of American foreign policy, made effective by the growth of the American navy.

In 1823, however, the Monroe Doctrine carried more moral authority than military clout. The American navy could not have prevented a European invasion of the Americas; only the British navy had the power to keep the Old World from interfering in the New. Canning used this fact in some long and hard conversations with the French ambassador, Prince Polignac. Polignac acknowledged it and promised that France would not use her occupation of Spain to establish monarchies in South America. Canning secretly distributed a memorandum of the conversation in order to show the new American republics that Britain was their protector and friend. Canning also persuaded the cabinet to recognize, in 1824, the republics of Buenos Aires, Mexico, and Colombia.

Canning soon found himself defending liberalism in Portugal. In April 1826 King John VI, who had given Portugal a liberal constitution after the revolution of 1820, died, leaving the throne to his son Dom Pedro. His son, content to be King of Brazil, made his 8-year-old daughter Maria Queen and his sister Isabella Regent. He also gave Portugal a more liberal constitution and betrothed Maria to her uncle, the absolutist Dom Miguel. This last unwitting piece of black humor plunged Portugal into a civil war in which Spain's Ferdinand

VII was only too happy to take part. Ferdinand gave aid to Miguel and his forces; Canning asked Ferdinand to stop. Although Ferdinand promised not to help them, he did. Canning then sent the British navy and 4,000 troops to Lisbon, a decision that won him a standing ovation in the Commons and that preserved constitutional government in Portugal.

Of all the thorny problems facing Canning, that of the Greek revolution proved the most intractable. It was, for one thing, enmeshed in the larger Near Eastern question. Britain had long considered the Ottoman Empire, however corrupt and despotic, an invaluable barrier to Russia's ambition to control Constantinople and the straits that ran between the Mediterranean and the Black Sea. Many of the English thought such control would threaten British trade and the overland routes to India. When the Greeks revolted against Turkish rule in 1821, Tzar Alexander called for a conference on the question. Although Canning refused to call a conference, he did offer to join Russia against a Turkey whose army of 10,000, victories, and ruthless atrocities had aroused Panhellenic sentiment throughout Europe on behalf of the Greek rebels. Canning knew that Tzar Nicholas desired territorial gains at Turkey's expense and that such gains endangered British influence and trade in the eastern Mediterranean, but he also knew acting in concert was a way of controlling Russia.

Canning and Nicholas I, the new Tzar, made an agreement in March 1826 that both assured Greece self-government and gave the Turkish Sultan the merely formal title of Lord Paramount. Turkey was to receive an annual tribute and to have a share in nominating officials. Canning persuaded France to accept the plan as part of the Treaty of London on July 6, 1827. Canning had broken the conservative alliance, separated Russia from Austria, championed the liberty of the Greeks, and isolated Metternich, who had long considered Canning "a malevolent meteor" and "scourge." Canning, only 57 years of age, died on August 8, confident he had won self-government for the Greeks and prevented Russian gains in the Near East. Admiral Codrington, on October 20, 1827, entered Navarino Bay, exceeded his orders, and sank the Muslim fleet, thus definitely ensuring the independence of Greece and winning at home the applause of the very vocal Panhellenic movement. But the death of Canning and the weakness of Wellington encouraged Russia to declare war on Turkey. Russia won some modest territorial gains and increased its influence in Constantinople, and these were incorporated into the Treaty of Adrianople of 1829.

The foreign policy of George Canning rested on the two traditional goals of British foreign policy: the security of British territory through a correct balance of power in Europe and the protection of its commerce by a powerful navy and empire. He never faltered in defending the territorial settlements of Vienna and in asserting the right of the Quadruple Alliance to check, if necessary, the resurgence of a bellicose France. Both policies were guarantees of that balance of power in Europe that meant a secure Britain. In all this he was the dutiful pupil of Castlereagh.

Between 1812 and 1827 the territorial settlement made at Vienna was not endangered, so Canning saw no need for the Quadruple Alliance to meet. But Britain's commerce did need protection and promotion in the Near East, in Portugal, and in the Americas. With 5 percent of British exports going to South America, with the powerful Levant Company growing rich in the Near East, and with the East India Company exploiting the wealth of India, little wonder that it was not Canning alone who recommended the de facto recognition of the new South American republics or the Greek belligerents, but the conservative Castlereagh as well. Castlereagh and Canning also agreed in supporting Turkey, quite independently of the Holy Alliance. Trade, Mediterranean or American, and the security of the British Isles and Empire gave continuity to the foreign policies of Castlereagh and Canning.

But in his pursuit of these two aims, Canning departed from Castlereagh's policies in three ways: he was more isolationist, he was friendlier to liberalism and nationalism, and he was more willing to enlist public opinion. Castlereagh, it is true, broke with the Quadruple Alliance in 1821 over the question of Naples and Spain and thereby placed Britain in a more isolated position. But he would never have said, as did Canning, "For Alliance, read England and you have the clue to my policy." Neither would he have said, "May God prosper . . . the establishment of constitutional liberty in Portugal," nor "I am still an enthusiast for national independence." Canning said these things publicly, either to cheering throngs at political meetings or to Parliament, whose debates appeared in every newspaper in the realm. As an aristocratic landlord of the eighteenth century, Lord Castlereagh kept diplomacy discreet and private, a matter for Kings and ministers, not the masses. Canning, the son of a London actress and an impoverished gentleman, loved to arouse public opinion in order to further his policy. A liberal Tory and an ambitious politician, he was born into a generation that saw an elected Parliament not a hereditary King as sovereign. He therefore sought both to guide and reflect public opinion. The passions of an aroused public, for instance, were more crucial in leading Canning to support liberalism in Portugal and Spain and revolution in Greece than were concerns for British commerce or territorial security, two interests that could have been protected quite as well by siding with the Miguelists in Portugal and the Turks in the Near East. In the early 1820s British merchants in the eastern Mediterranean were hostile to the Greeks and friendly to the Turks. Calculations of security and trade do not alone explain Canning's support of liberalism and nationalism abroad. That support also reflected English liberalism and English pride in its constitution.

It was a liberalism and a pride that expressed itself in many a toast to the triumph of constitutional liberty and the downfall of despotic Kings. In London, in Parliament, in the provinces, and in the press these toasts became increasingly common, and with them came repeated toasts to George Canning. Foreign policy reflects climates of opinion as well as national interests, cultural as well as political forces. The Romanticism that sent Byron to defend Greek liberty was alive in more than one breast in England. Panhellenic societies sprang up throughout the country. The versatile Canning, who had written youthful verses protesting Turkey's enslavement of the Greeks, could hardly fail to respond, particularly when it won him standing ovations. The age of democracy was at hand, and Canning was the first to perceive that foreign policy could not be immune from the change. In his Whig successor, Lord Palmerston, this became even more obvious.

LORD PALMERSTON AT THE FOREIGN OFFICE

Lord Castlereagh saw diplomacy as a game of chess, one in which queens and rooks are moved to achieve a rational use of power. His shrewdest move, he thought, was the castling of Belgium and Holland under the House of Orange; it would provide a buffer between France and England. But the days of dynastic states were numbered. The force of nationalism increasingly precluded the use of states as pieces in the diplomatic chess game. The people of Catholic Belgium, for example, had a dynamism and patriotism of their own, a baffling mixture of nationalism, Catholicism, revolutionary fervor, and hatred of the Dutch. In 1830 Belgium revolted against the House of Orange. The revolt destroyed Castlereagh's castling of Belgium and Holland and created a vacuum that France yearned to fill. In 1793 that yearning had led to war. It now threatened war again and posed a critical problem to the new foreign secretary, Lord Palmerston.

Palmerston, a 47-year-old Irish Viscount of great landed wealth, ebullient temperament, and long service as Secretary at War, solved the problem by relying on the force of Belgian nationalism and by insisting that Belgium be independent. It was a solution that would satisfy the Belgians and create a check on France. But creating an independent Belgium was not simple. King William I of Holland was determined to rule Belgium, and he had the sympathy of Russia, Austria, and Prussia, autocracies that opposed all tampering with the Vienna settlement of 1815. France also hungered for parts of the Lowlands.

To settle these conflicts, Lord Palmerston took a leaf from Castlereagh's book and called on the ambassadors of the great powers in London to act in the spirit of the Concert of Europe. They did so, but not easily or quickly. A revolt in Poland tied down the armies of Russia, which led the usually indecisive Frederick William III of Prussia to be even more indecisive. With neither Holland nor France able to appeal to the armies of Russia and Prussia, Lord Palmerston was in a stronger position. He used that position wisely in the ensuing negotiations over the boundaries of the new Belgium and the naming of its new king. France three times tried to make gains for itself, first in 1830, by resisting the idea of an independent Belgium; second in 1831, by insisting that the son of France's new king, Louis Philippe, be made king of Belgium; and third, in 1832, by keeping its troops in Belgium. These troops had, along with the English navy, entered the conflict in order to drive out the Dutch forces that had invaded Belgium in August 1831. In each crisis Lord Palmerston told France to accept

Viscount Palmerston, Foreign Secretary from 1830 to 1840 and 1846 to 1851, Prime Minister from 1852 to 1858 and 1859 to 1864 (*Illustrated London News*).

the conference decisions or Britain would immediately declare war on France. A similar threat by a united England and France persuaded the Dutch finally to agree to the creation of an independent Belgium under King Leopold of Saxe-Coburg. In solving the Belgian question, Lord Palmerston surprised many with his command of detail, his clarity of insight, and his patience and flexibility in negotiation, all of which he combined with a firmness that did not flinch from war itself. He used the conference system to further that balance of power which would ensure peace in Europe.

Lord Palmerston's concern for the Concert of Europe was less evident in his policy toward Portugal and Spain. In Portugal, in 1833, the constitutional government of young Queen Maria still faced the absolutist armies of Miguel, her uncle. The situation was duplicated in Spain, where Queen Christina's uncle, Don Carlos, led the forces of absolutism. Palmerston at first vowed to be neutral. But it was only a ruse. He soon allowed British naval personnel to help Queen Maria's father, Dom Pedro, in his war with Miguel, just as he allowed Colonel

De Lacy Evans to lead a legion of British volunteers in defense of Queen Christina and liberty. When Spain's Don Carlos invaded Portugal in order to help Miguel, Palmerston intervened openly and decisively. He drew up an alliance in which the two Queens, Maria and Christina, joined Britain and France in an effort to rid the peninsula of Miguel and Carlos—which they finally did, thereby strengthening constitutional government south of the Pyrenees.

The Quadruple Alliance of Britain, France, Spain, and Portugal displeased the autocrats of the Holy Alliance. Europe became more than ever divided between the adherents of constitutionalism and the defenders of absolutism. But in fact the new Quadruple Alliance was not aimed at the autocratic powers; rather, it was an attempt to contain French and British rivalry in Spain and Portugal. The return of Don Carlos to Spain and the rise in Portugal of the conservative Chartists revived that rivalry, since France now sought to gain influence in the peninsula by favoring absolutism. It was a futile attempt. Absolutism lost out in Spain because of Don Carlos's utter incompetence and in Portugal because of British power. The victory of constitutionalism in both made the jaunty Viscount popular with liberals and radicals alike.

His policy toward Mehemet Ali earned him no such popularity. Ali was Viceroy of Egypt and the father of Ibrahim, the scourge of the Greeks in the 1820s and the conqueror of Syria in 1834. This last conquest angered Sultan Mahmud II, in theory the Turkish overlord of the Viceroy of Egypt. The Turkish Empire seemed ready to dissolve. In the 1820s Turkey lost Moldavia and Wallachia (part of present-day Rumania) and also Serbia and Greece. In 1833 Russia had also won greater influence over Turkish policy and the use of the Straits.

To Palmerston, the dissolution of the Turkish Empire would make Russia dominant in the Near East. In 1839 Egypt, through the treachery of a Turkish admiral and the armies of Ibrahim, won control of Turkey's entire fleet and the rich province of Syria. With France promising Ibrahim and his father full support, the Turkish Empire was about to split in two with the Egyptian half falling under French influence and the Turkish half a prey to Russian influence. Palmerston viewed such a split as a blow to English trade and an intolerable humiliation. To prevent it he allied England with Turkey, Russia, and Austria and sent in the British fleet, a fleet which in 1840 took Beirut, Sidon, and Acre. The Syrians also revolted against Ibrahim's despotism, and Mehemet Ali sued for peace. All Syrian territory and the fleet were returned to Turkey, and Mehemet Ali promised to continue in Egypt as the Sultan's Viceroy. Palmerston had won a great diplomatic victory. But he had also tied Britain ever more tightly to the defense of a corrupt and oppressive Turkish Empire. Palmerston justified that decision by the ancient argument that Turkey was the best check to Russian ambitions in the Near East.

From 1841 to 1846 the Tory Lord Aberdeen was Foreign Secretary, and though it meant a less vigorous foreign policy, it was not ineffective. Aberdeen's judiciousness not only led to a Webster-Ashburton Treaty with America defining the Canadian boundary in Maine, but he assuaged the hurt feelings of a diplomatically defeated France. But no alliances were made. Britain had become isolated, a fact no more perturbing to Palmerston, who returned to the Foreign Office in 1846, than to Canning. Was not Britain without rival as an industrial, commercial, naval, and imperial power? Lord Palmerston was also proud of British constitutionalism, a pride that led him to favor liberal revolts against despotic kings in Paris, Madrid, and Naples—in the last two cases to the extent of sending arms to the rebels. But he did not support revolutions in general: in 1848 he opposed them in Hungary, northern Italy, and Germany. He viewed the Frankfort Parliament's talk of a united Germany as premature and visionary. He was no friend of liberalism and nationalism if such movements threatened the peace of Europe. As Secretary at War during the days of Napoleon he had learned of the horrors of war. His highest priority was peace, his greatest fear a general conflagration. He thus wanted a strong Austrian presence in the Italies, the Germanies, and the Balkans. However autocratic the Austrian Empire, it nevertheless acted as a stabilizing force. So did Prussia in northern Germany. A powerful Austria and Prussia would also check any aggressive moves by an autocratic and imperial Russia or a volatile and revolutionary France.

A second reason he did not support revolutions in northern Italy and central Europe was because he could not. The British navy could not sail to Prague, Budapest, Milan, and Frankfort, as it could to Lisbon, Cadiz, Beirut, and Alexandria; nor were the states of northern Italy and central Europe as removed from the influence of the great powers as were Portugal, Spain, Syria, and Egypt.

He was also an elected member of Parliament, a minister answerable to that body, a patriotic Englishman, and the Foreign Secretary of a country whose commerce, industry, and navy were without rival. Although ever mindful of Britain's traditional interests, Palmerston's foreign policy was also sensitive to its power and prejudices. He was always ready to send in the fleet and always ready to defend England's prestige. And just as exciting were the diplomatic victories that won him the applause of a chauvinist Parliament and press. In the Belgian crisis the preservation of a correct equilibrium was uppermost in his mind. In Portugal and the Near East he thought most about the protection of trade. Trade was also paramount in the Opium War of 1840. In that embroglio two British frigates, which Palmerston sent out, sank twenty-nine armed Chinese junks. The British then forced the Chinese to enter into formal trade relations, even though it meant buying considerable opium, which the British had previously imported from India.

At other times, as in the case of Don Pacifico, Palmerston, aware that Britain possessed the world's greatest navy, indulged in an extreme chauvinism. National security and the protection of trade routes hardly explains Palmerston's jingoistic demand—even to the extent of threatening war—that Greece pay £31,000 to Don Pacifico, a Spanish Jew of British citizenship whose house in Athens was burned by angry Greeks. Protecting Don Pacifico was not necessary to British security. The island's defense and British trade also did not require the support of Spanish constitutionalists and the insistence that other countries end the slave trade. These policies reflected public opinion far more than national self-interest. Patriots of all kinds cheered and cheered when Palmerston ended his speech on Don Pacifico with the boast that just as a Roman could find protection by declaring *Civis Romanus sum* (I am a citizen of Rome), so could a British subject in all lands find protection in the fact that "the strong arm of England will protect him against injustice and wrong."

Britain at midcentury was the wealthiest and most powerful nation in the world. Its people were urbanized, literate, and prosperous; the press free, informed, and popular; and its constitutional government the oldest in Europe. The British could and did boast of distinguished accomplishments in technology, science, and literature. These facts contributed to the creation in the English of a smug paternalism and an arrogant patriotism, a paternalism and patriotism that found expressions in the foreign policy of that equally arrogant and paternalistic landlord, Lord Palmerston.

By inheritance an Irish peer with thousands of acres, he ruled over hundreds of tenants. As fortunate in the inheritance of intelligence and buoyancy as in his broad acres and titles, he grew naturally into the part of the lordly paternalist. He found it natural to run everything in his sphere, to bully clerks in the foreign office, to keep ambassadors waiting, to lecture autocrats on constitutionalism, and to be often enough abrasive to win the nickname Lord Pumistone. But though arrogant in the Don Pacifico affair or toward his clerks, he could also be, when there was a European crisis, restrained, judicious, and responsible. He not only had a keen appreciation of the need for a correct balance of power, but he also saw the value of the conference system at the ambassadorial level in ensuring its operation. No isolationist, he both realized the usefulness of temporary alliances and European conferences. "Eternal allies or perpetual enemies," he said, are damaging to "those interests it is our duty to follow." His dismissal in 1851 by weakening British foreign policy helped lead to the Crimean War, the first major European war in forty years.

THE CRIMEAN WAR

In 1852 Napoleon III demanded and won from Turkey greater rights for Roman Catholic priests to care for holy sanctuaries in the Holy Land. Turkey's concessions angered Tzar Nicholas I who claimed that Greek and Russian Orthodox priests were the protectors of these sanctuaries. Nicholas also claimed he was the protector of the 12 million Christians dwelling in the Ottoman Empire. To fulfill these claims he sent to Constantinople in May 1852 the insolent and overbearing Prince Menschikoff. With the help of Lord Stratford, long British ambassador at Constantinople, the Sultan and Menschikoff settled the issue of the sanctuaries—but not the issue of the Tzar's claim to be the protector of the 12 million Christians.

To the Sultan and his advisors, the Tzar's claim was an intolerable invasion of Turkish sovereignty. A fateful air of doom thus hung over Constantinople as Tzar and Sultan proclaimed their irreconcilable demands. Lord Palmerston wished the British government simultaneously to call a conference of ambassadors in London and to tell the Tzar that any aggression would mean war. The Cabinet, however, overruled him. Lord Aberdeen, who as Prime Minister controlled foreign policy, chose instead to let matters drift while awaiting the decision of a meeting between the Austrian foreign minister and the Prussian, French, and British ambassadors in Vienna. On July 28 they issued the Vienna Note, reaffirming those vague sections in the treaties of 1774 and 1829 on which the Tzar based his claim. Ten days earlier Russia had occupied the independent states of Wallachia and Moldavia. Turkish and Russian troops now faced each other across the Danube, and war seemed imminent. For two months, from May 21 to July 21, the gentle and pacific Aberdeen did nothing to make it clear to Nicholas I at what point Britain would fight.

After July 21 the crucial decision lay with Lord Stratford and the Sultan. After consulting with Stratford, who, publicly urged conciliation but privately advised the Sultan to be firm, the Sultan accepted the Vienna Note, but only if it specifically said that the protection of the Christians was to be guaranteed "by the Sublime Porte"—that is, by the Sultan. That proviso was unsatisfactory to the Tzar. Negotiations continued. In September, Buol, Austria's foreign minister, persuaded the Tzar to give up the protection of the Christians for a promise

TURKEY IN DANGER.

Nicholas I said the Russian bear only wished to be a protector to Turkey; the British, including *Punch*, had doubts (*Punch*).

that they would enjoy certain immunities. Napoleon III wished to accept, but Lord Clarendon, Britain's foreign secretary, persuaded him that it was a trick; Britain and France therefore rejected the compromise. In Constantinople, meanwhile, both the Vienna Note, with its condescending tone and its infringement on Turkish sovereignty, and the Russian occupation of Moldavia and Wallachia raised war fever to a frenzied pitch. On October 23 Turkey declared war on Russia. On November 30 the Russian Black Sea fleet sank the Turkish fleet in what the London press called the "Massacre of Sinope," though it was only a normal battle in a war already declared. By March 1854 public opinion in Britain became angered at the Russian aggression. In that same month the British joined France, Austria, and Turkey in a war against Russia.

It was a useless and unnecessary war that marked the breakdown of both the Concert of Europe and the leadership of Britain. The Aberdeen government

Earl Cardigan's Light Brigade's foolish charge still overcomes the Russian artillery (*Illustrated London News*).

had been too passive in the spring of 1853 and too precipitous in the autumn. Tzar Nicholas wanted no war. Had his bluff been called in the spring he would probably have yielded, as he did in the autumn, but just at a time when British opinion, in response to menacing talk about Russian ambitions, had become uncontrollably bellicose. Britons of all kinds and classes shouted for war: the poet Tennyson, the novelist Charles Kingsley, the cotton lords of Manchester, the dockers of London, the gentry of the counties, and above all the men of the press, anxious to bring excitement to their genteel readers, grown bored with the respectability of mid-Victorian England.

In September 1854, after six months of preparation, 50,000 British and French troops landed on the Crimean peninsula in the Black Sea. They were ill-equipped, poorly supplied, and badly led, yet that autumn they won the three battles of Alma, Balaklava, and Inkerman. Alma was won by the intrepid advance of the British infantry, unsupported by cavalry or wise generalship. Victory at Balaklava resulted from the heroic resistance of a small infantry division (the 93rd Highlanders), the brilliant tactics of General Scarlett's heavy brigade, and the most foolhardy cavalry charge in history, that of the Earl of Cardigan's light brigade. At Inkerman it was the steady hand-to-hand fighting of the infantry and the superiority of the Minie rifle that won the day.

But there was a tragic irony to this campaign. It was the courage of the infantry, the famed "thin red line," and not brilliant leadership that produced these victories, yet it was an infantry treated by many officers as the scum of the earth. The officers themselves, after forty years of peace, had little experience of war. Most of them, like the arrogant and hated Earl of Cardigan, had purchased both their commissions and their promotions with cash. Under them, a soldier's life was wretched. The army paid him 7 shillings a week, half of which it took back to pay for a monotonous diet of 1 pound of bread and ¾ pound of meat every day. Soldiers were crowded into dismal barracks devoid of amenities and if subordinate flogged from 100 to 300 lashes. They had to spend two-thirds of their army career abroad, sometimes in places like Sierra Leone, where the mortality rate was 75 percent.

Yet harsh as was their regular lot, it was bliss compared to the Crimean winter that followed Inkerman. Blizzards tore down their tents; cholera, dysentery, and malaria ravaged their ranks; the sick were crammed into dirty, crowded hospital ships; medicine was lacking; food, clothing, and fuel were in short supply; and death was an hourly visitor. Florence Nightingale and her nurses, who arrived in November 1854, mitigated some of the suffering but could not make up for the gross mismanagement, penuriousness, callousness, and inefficiency that ran from the officers in the Crimea up to the cabinet and Parliament. The British soldier, grossly mistreated by the governing classes, for whom he fought and won ill-conceived and ill-directed battles, emerged from this frightful winter strong enough to capture Sebastopol and to force on the new Tzar, Alexander II, a peace in which he gave up any pretense of becoming the protector of the Christians of the Turkish Empire.

A clean hospital, unknown until Florence Nightingale and her nurses arrived (*University Library, Cambridge*).

In the sixty-seven years from the French Revolution to the end of the Crimean War, British foreign policy varied greatly: now it was interventionist, now isolationist; at one moment Britain allied with absolute monarchs, at the next with revolutionaries. Yet statesmen then and historians since have argued that underlying these changes runs a central thread, the furtherance of Britain's national self-interest. It was the unifying theme, the sovereign principle, the ultimate goal. In its purest form, the defense of English shores, it led Pitt to war on a revolutionary, expanding France and persuaded Castlereagh to make the Vienna Settlement, that exquisitely contrived balance of power which checked France, strengthened the Lowlands, redefined Germany, and secured Britain.

The furtherance of Britain's national self-interest also meant the protection of its world commerce. "British policy," said the younger Pitt, "is British trade." And so it was to Castlereagh, Canning, and Palmerston. To protect it in South America, the Tory Castlereagh countenanced revolutionary governments and Canning promised them the protection of the British navy. To extend trade to China, Palmerston fought the Opium War. The protection of Britain's self-interest, whether shores or trade, was a principle embedded in reality. That reality could be a chilling one, as when revolutionary France occupied the Lowlands, or a profitable one, as in the opening of South America and China to British commerce.

The charge of the Light Brigade was the last flourish of eighteenth-century cavalry warfare; the siege of Sebastopol saw the beginning of twentieth-century trench warfare (*Victoria and Albert Museum*).

Principles embedded in reality are convincing ones. The temptation, then, is very great to use them on less pertinent occasions as shibboleths, a temptation to which British diplomats increasingly succumbed after 1822. After that date British policy reflected two less rational forces, British public opinion and British power. Canning was the first to respond to these forces; Palmerston did so later. Loud were the cheers at Guildhall when Canning declared his support for the Portuguese liberals, even though a victory of the Portuguese absolutists would mean no danger to British shores or trade. Even louder were the cheers for Lord Palmerston when, after defending Don Pacifico, he compared Britons to Romans.

All the world suddenly became vital to British national self-interest. Russia was to be checkmated in the Near East in order to defend an overland route to India that was 7,400 miles long and, given British seapower, quite irrelevant. British public opinion became intoxicated with British power—particularly the unrivaled navy. What truly lay behind Britain's defense of the South American republics, Portuguese liberals, and Greek revolutionaries was not national security but overwhelming naval power in the Atlantic, on the Tagus, and at Navarino.

And the true explanation for Britain's ability to humiliate Mehemet Ali, win the Opium War, and support Italian revolutionaries was its invincible fleets at Beirut, Canton, and Naples. Take away the navy, and none of these areas would appear crucial to Britain's self-interest. Between 1822 and 1856 the principles guiding British foreign policy expanded. Security and trade remained, but to them were added a global policy that reflected the industrial and naval might of Britain. The foundations were thus laid for late nineteenth-century British imperialism.

FURTHER READING

BOURNE, KENNETH. *The Foreign Policy of Victorian England.* Oxford: Clarendon Press, 1970. The most up-to-date interpretation of British diplomacy after 1815—realistic, shrewd, and persuaded that diplomacy is largely the rational calculation of national self-interest.

CHRISTIE, IAN R. *Wars and Revolutions, Britain, 1760–1815.* Cambridge, Mass.: Harvard University Press, 1982. Its chapters on British diplomacy from 1760 to 1815 offer the clearest and most comprehensive discussion of foreign affairs available, and the most recent in its schoalrship.

KISSINGER, HENRY. *A World Restored.* Boston: Houghton Mifflin, 1957. A conservative interpretation of that Congress of Vienna which restored a balance of power to Europe, and the role of Castlereagh and Metternich, Kissinger's two heroes of *realpolitik.*

MARRIOT, J. A. R. *The Eastern Question.* Oxford: Clarendon Press, 1924. A systematic study of Britain's persistent role defending Turkey from Russian pressure, with Stratford Canning and Disraeli as his heroes.

POOLE, LANE. *Life of Stratford Canning, Lord Stratford de Redcliffe.* London: Longmans, Green, 1888. Although many have written of Victorian England's most important ambassador, none have analyzed his diplomacy with a defter touch.

SETON-WATSON, R. W. *Britain in Europe, 1789–1914.* New York: Macmillan, 1937. Although outdated in parts, it is still the clearest and fullest exposition of British diplomacy in Europe from 1815 to 1914.

TEMPERLEY, HAROLD. *The Foreign Policy of Canning, 1822–1827.* London: G. Bell, 1925. A magisterial portrait of George Canning, his character, ideas, and diplomacy, and how he established an English policy separate from Europe's.

———. *England and the Near East: The Crimea.* London: Longmans, Green, 1936. A close narrative of England in the Near East from 1829 to 1878 with brilliant sketches of Turkish institutions, military campaigns, and Balkan nationalities.

WEBSTER, SIR CHARLES. *The Foreign Policy of Castlereagh, 1812–1815.* London: G. Bell, 1931. A shrewd analysis of those policies that, from 1812 to 1815, transformed the map of Europe, and a brilliant portrait of their author, Lord Castlereagh.

———. *The Foreign Policy of Palmerston, 1830–1841.* London: G. Bell, 1951. A masterful account by an historian who is as tough a realist in analysis as Palmerston was as foreign secretary.

WIENER, JOEL, ED. *Great Britain: Foreign Policy and The Span of Empire, 1689–1971, a Documentary History.* New York: Chelsea, 1972. The most comprehensive collection of documents on British diplomacy: well chosen selections of parliamentary speeches and debates, treaties, dispatches, and correspondences.

Conservatism, liberalism, and reform

22

The French Revolution left England profoundly conservative. For twenty-six years England's governing classes were obsessed by its terrors and its wars. It made them fearful of change. In 1815 they were satisfied with Lord Liverpool's Tory government. It was a government that had defeated Napoleon, a government that would please the most reactionary squire and lordly earl. The austere Castlereagh, staunch friend of Metternich and staunch opponent of parliamentary reform, was both foreign secretary and leader of the Commons; the narrow-minded Lord Sidmouth, long a favorite of country squires, ruled at the Home Office with unswerving severity; the mediocre Lord Vansittart muddled through at the Exchequer; the Duke of Wellington, manly and imperturbable, sat in the Cabinet; and, most reassuring of all, the Lord Chancellor was the 64-year-old Lord Eldon, as unyielding against reform as he was stout in defense of that establishment, which, even more than the French Revolution, gave strength to conservatism. It was a most privileged establishment, one based on the fact that 1 percent of England's families owned 80 percent of the land, that their sons attended and clerical brothers dominated the public schools and universities, and that these families enjoyed universal deference. These families also counted the Church of England, Parliament, the law courts, local government, high civil and military office, and the very government of the realm quite as much their exclusive preserve as the hares and partridges and bucks that the Game Laws said they and they alone could hunt.

Beyond the pale of this most privileged, all-powerful establishment lay other forces: the burgeoning Baptist, Congregational, and Methodist chapels and Quaker and Unitarian meetinghouses; the wealthy industrial Manchesters and Birminghams; the bankers, shopkeepers, solicitors, and surgeons of the multiplying, independent-minded middling classes; gigantic London, with scores of newspapers, publishing houses, learned and philanthropic societies, and suburbs untouched by aristocrats; and finally that huge, sprawling, working class that ranged from skilled artisans providently saving for illness or death in friendly societies to the more harassed and embittered and ill-paid factory operative and declining weavers who secretly formed trade unions and to the jobless, vagrants, and ever-numerous paupers. It was the conflict of these many other forces against the establishment far more than the conflict of labor with capital that defined the course of nineteenth-century Britain. It was a conflict that began with Toryism at its most conservative and powerful.

CONSERVATIVE TORYISM

In 1816 the most pressing problem facing Lord Liverpool was financial. To pay for the costliest war in history, the government had raised taxes fivefold, had run up a debt of £861 million, and had inflated the currency by issuing cheap pound notes, notes not convertible to gold. Although the government tried to reduce spending and so taxes, it still believed it necessary to keep a 5 percent income tax. The wartime income tax had been 10 percent. To Whigs, Radicals, and Tory country gentlemen, the reduction was not enough; they therefore defeated the tax. To balance the budget, the government used loans for three years and then increased taxes on such commodities as tea, coffee, pepper, malt, cocoa, wool, and spirits—all regressive taxes that, along with many older taxes, such as those on coal, bread, and houses, fell heavily on the poor. To Whigs and Radicals taxes were an evil; they shackled the economy and oppressed the poor. Retrenchment, the cutting of swollen expenditures, was their cry.

Far more severe than unbalanced budgets was the problem of economic distress. The end of annual wartime expenditures of some £40 million combined with bad harvests and the massive discharge of soldiers and sailors caused a tragic collapse of the economy. Prices, rents, profits, and wages and employment collapsed, causing widespread suffering. Heavy rains in 1816 rotted potatoes and damaged grain crops, and for many workers the distress became unbearable. Lord Liverpool's government met the demands of the landowners by the Corn Law of 1815, which excluded all foreign grain unless the price of grain in England reached 80 shillings for a quarter of a hundredweight. It did nothing for the workers; Lord Sidmouth said it was harmful to interfere with economic laws. Faced with an indifferent government and unbearable conditions, the workers protested. In East Anglia peasants smashed machines and burned barns, in the Midlands workers destroyed stocking frames, and in London Radicals demanded universal suffrage. Hampden Clubs mushroomed, clubs named in honor of John Hampden, who refused to pay shipmoney to Charles I, and clubs where workers read William Cobbett's *Political Register*, each issue of which exposed more and more of the corruption of an oligarchic government. In Lancashire hundreds of the jobless, each with a blanket, started out for London to complain to their King of a Parliament that represented only their oppressors. A day's journey away troops dispersed these "blanketeers." The atmosphere was tense with class hatred; some believed that revolution was at hand.

The government responded with repressive legislation. It again suspended *habeas corpus* and prohibited all large public meetings. The coercion of 1817 and the prosperity of 1818 made for peaceful times, but the distress of 1819 revived the workers' discontent. Huge demonstrations were again held, one of the largest at Manchester. Henry Hunt, a tub-thumping and wildly popular orator, told 60,000 at Peterloo field that a democratic constitution would end economic and social evils. He declaimed against taxes, against corrupt government, and against a Corn Law that drove up the price of bread in order to fatten the rents of landlords. The magistrates at Manchester panicked. They ordered the yeomanry, local and amateur cavalrymen, to arrest Hunt, which they did, but not without trampling on hundreds and killing eleven. Until the yeomanry charged it was a peaceful meeting; afterward it was a riot. It left the workers bitter and the governing classes fearful. Parliament passed the famous— or infamous—Six Acts. Magistrates could now prohibit all outdoor meetings of more than fifty persons except those on county business. They could also search houses for arms, seize seditious and blasphemous publications, imprison their authors, and outlaw the cheap press by prohibitive taxes. The government was resolved to suppress public meetings and a free press, the two principal means by which the working class expressed itself.

But repression was not easy, a fact the Tories learned in the Queen Caroline affair. In 1820, George III died. His death made George IV and his wife, Caroline, King and Queen of England. That Caroline, long estranged from her husband and notorious for her love affairs in Europe, should be Queen was hateful to George IV. The new King, whose profligacy was also notorious, insisted that the government win him a divorce and exclude Caroline's name from the Prayer Book and her from the coronation. On June 4, 1820, she arrived at Dover and demanded her rights as Queen of England. Whigs and Radicals supported her in Parliament, in the press, and at public meetings. The Tory government, which tried and failed to win a divorce, was too fearful even to attempt the prohibition of public meetings on her behalf. They finally bought her off for £50,000. She left England and a year later died.

The Whigs' defense of Caroline casts little light on the differences between Whig and Tory; the Whigs in power might well have pushed for divorce. What was truly revealing about the affair was that in defending Caroline the Whigs for a second time allied themselves with public opinion. George IV, angry at the government's coolness to the divorce, had suggested the formation of a Whig government. A few decades earlier the Whigs would have accepted; in 1820 they could not because of their ties with the people. The people would not tolerate support of a George IV known largely for his profligacy, selfishness, meanness, and extreme Toryism. Whig leaders had taken the lead against the Six Acts and Tory repression. Traditionally the defenders of English liberty,

Massacre at S.t Peter's or "BRITONS STRIKE HOME"!!!

The governing classes' yeomanry at Manchester's St. Peter's field trample over the people who met to demand reform (*British Museum*).

mercantile interests, and dissent, the Whigs found themselves allied to the forces of liberalism. Indeed, it seemed in 1820 that the Whigs would be the leaders of a liberal party. Such a development did not occur until the 1830s (or perhaps the 1850s), but before then, Liverpool, without intending it, constructed a more liberal government. The event that began that development was the suicide of the most powerful of conservatives, Lord Castlereagh.

LIBERAL TORYISM

Liverpool, Prime Minister for fifteen years, was an extraordinarily adroit politician. From 1809 to 1822, when England was deeply conservative, he ruled through Castlereagh, Sidmouth, Vansittart, Eldon, and Wellington; then from 1822 to 1827, with advancing prosperity, receding fears of revolution, the triumph of political economy, and the advent of liberal ideas, he ruled through George Canning, William Huskisson, John Robinson, and Sir Robert Peel—all Tories, but all moderately so. The brilliant and ambitious Canning replaced

Castlereagh as foreign secretary and leader of the Tories in the Commons. His defense of South American republics, European constitutionalists, and Catholic emancipation had won him a reputation as a liberal. Huskisson, long the Commons' schoolmaster in economics, expounded its truths when he presented bills to reduce the tariffs on cottons, woolens, iron, coal, raw silk, and wool. Since cheaper raw materials from abroad helped the English manufacturer and since English products outsold foreign goods, the English rejoiced to see tariffs fall and trade expand. The staunch Tory country gentry did not mind as long as it did not touch their rents. But when Liverpool, Canning, and Huskisson urged a sliding scale on grain imports, one that centered on 60 shillings, not 80 shillings, as the protected price, they denounced the new free trade doctrine as part of an insidious liberal plot.

They even worried about Peel's many reforms at the Home Office. Not only was he passing bills to improve prisons, create a metropolitan police force, and reform criminal justice, but he urged a rather extensive reduction of the death penalty. Some 200 statutes prescribed hanging as the punishment for some 600 offenses. The Whigs, led by Sir Samuel Romilly and Sir James MacKintosh, had for sixteen years urged the reduction of the death penalty, only to see their bills defeated by Sidmouth and Castlereagh. But now, with Peel at the Home Office and Castlereagh and Sidmouth gone, former Whig initiatives became Tory statutes.

When Liverpool fell ill in 1827, Canning became Prime Minister. He constructed, out of the exceptional talents of Peel, Huskisson, Palmerston, and Robinson, a liberal Tory government. He even tempted three leading Whigs to join. The two-party system was in disarray. Whig leaders lamented the "dissolution" and "annihilation" of their party; liberal Tories wanted an end to the "odious distinction of Whig and Tory." The London Radical Francis Place exclaimed in 1827, "No Whigs, no Tories, mere moonshine nowadays." During the reign of Queen Anne, differences over religious and foreign policies created clear-cut Whig and Tory parties; during the reign of George III deep differences over royal prerogatives and the French Revolution sustained a two-party cleavage. Could Canning's liberal foreign policy, Huskisson's advanced political economy, and Peel's legal reforms end that cleavage?

In 1827 some said yes. Had not the party of Pitt, Liverpool, and Canning accommodated both liberalism and conservatism, those two historical ideologies that were to dominate and divide nineteenth-century Europe? Had not the public schools, universities, and the establishment won over the talented of the rising middle classes, the Wilberforces, the Peels, and the Huskissons, to Toryism? In 1827 it seemed so, but 1827 was a unique year: liberal Toryism was a passing phenomenon. Canning died in August. Brilliant as he was and esteemed as he was by the merchants of England, his views were too liberal for the extreme Tories and too Tory for the majority of liberals. The extremists could accept Peel's moderate prison and law reforms and Huskisson's lower tariffs on manufactures, but they grew restive over talks of a lower tariff on corn, the abolition of laws requiring the gallows, and the emancipation of Catholics. Some of them were also unhappy with Peel, Huskisson, and Liverpool because of their role in returning the currency to the gold standard and their opposition to provincial banks' issuing notes, policies that reduced the amount of money and so (thought many country squires) lowered prices and caused depressions. By 1828, when Wellington became Prime Minister, the extremists were tired of the liberal Tories and ready to rebel.

Whigs, Radicals, and the middle classes also became disenchanted with liberal Toryism. Its reforms were too modest. Huskisson preached free trade but dared not repeal the most prominent tariff of all, the Corn Laws. Peel consolidated hundreds of criminal statutes, but those guilty of stealing £5 or forging bank notes still went to the gallows. In 1824 Canning supported the Radicals' bill to repeal the Combination Acts of 1799 and 1800, which made trade unions illegal, but a year later he passed an act that denied these unions the rights needed to sustain a strike. The liberal Tories were practical and efficient, but too narrow, limited, and party-bound.

The word "liberal" was first used in the England of the 1820s. It came from Spain, where it referred to those who fought for liberty against abolutism. In 1820 Peel, who called liberalism an "odious principle," predicted its inevitable growth. Canning's government tried to adapt to that growth by its free trade principles and its legal and administrative reforms. But liberalism also meant Catholic emancipation and parliamentary reform.

The issue of Catholic emancipation had always been an open question in Lord Liverpool's government. Canning was for it, but Peel, who believed that Ireland needed "an honest, despotic government," was against it. Most Tories and most Englishmen shared Peel's view, but by 1828 Catholic Ireland was utterly determined on emancipation—that is, the right of Catholics to sit in Parliament and to hold high military and civil office. In a by-election at Clare county, Daniel O'Connell, a Catholic, a superb orator, and the leader of the movement for emancipation, was elected its MP. By law he could not take his seat. But if he were refused, the Irish would rebel. Peel and Wellington realized this and forced through the Catholic Emancipation Act of 1829, an act that gave Catholics in England the vote (Irish Catholics had long had the vote) and that granted all Catholics the right to hold military commissions and high office. The Tory country gentry were furious. They began to talk of the need of a larger representation in Parliament from the counties, of the need for good, solid, independent MPs far more in tune with the majority of English Protestants than were the toadies sent from the rotten boroughs. They began to talk of parliamentary reform.

So did the moderates. They urged that the parliamentary seats of East Retford and Penryn, two corrupt boroughs, be given to Manchester and the Hundred of Retford. Wellington and Peel refused, and Huskisson and his followers left the government. Wellington had fallen between two stools. He incurred the wrath of the ultra-Tories on emancipation and the anger of the moderates on East Retford and Penryn. The split weakened Wellington's government and the fissure grew greater when, on George IV's death in 1830, the English electorate, voting under an unreformed franchise, returned a Parliament of whom half favored some reform. The electorate was now more friendly to those Whigs and Radicals who, during the years of the French Revolution, during the days of Peterloo, and during the excitement of the Queen Caroline affair, had defended English liberty, the rights of Dissenters, and the interests of the middle and working classes. The spread of new ideas, the rise of new classes, and the growing power of the liberal press made it necessary for England to wrestle seriously with the problem of parliamentary reform.

THE REFORM ACT OF 1832

On June 7, 1832, King William IV, in the second year of his reign, signed the famous Reform Act of 1832. It made greater changes in the constitution of England than any event since the Revolution of 1688. It abolished the right of fifty-six boroughs to send 2 members to Parliament. These boroughs were mostly in the south and all contained less than two thousand inhabitants. Thirty other boroughs that returned 2 MPs lost one, and Weymouth's representation fell from 4 to 2. In all, eighty-seven boroughs lost the right to return 144 MPs.

The Tory William IV and the Tory House of Lords disliked the bill intensely, but both had to accept it because of the pressure of public opinion. The Lords thought the bill dangerously radical. Not only did it deny ancient corporations their time-honored rights to return MPs, but it gave to twenty-two new boroughs the right to elect 2 MPs and to twenty-one other boroughs the right to elect 1 MP. Of the 65 MPs who represented these forty-three boroughs, 8 came from London boroughs and 28 from industrial towns. Manchester, Birmingham, and Leeds, the centers of cotton, iron, and wool, now had spokesmen in the most sovereign branch of government. The boundaries of sixty-five of the remaining boroughs were redrawn so more could vote. And most alarming for the future, the act laid down a standard franchise for all boroughs. Any adult male who leased or owned a habitation worth £10 a year could now vote. The county franchise was also changed. Henceforth all 40 shillings freeholders, urban or rural, could vote, and not, as before, only those who paid a land tax. The only exception to this rule were freeholders who voted in boroughs returning MPs; they could not vote in county elections. In 1864 freeholders in towns not returning MPs made up nearly one-fifth of county voters, the rest being rural freeholders, £10 a year copyholders, and those who held land worth £10 on long-term leases or £50 on short-term leases. Before the Reform Act one in ten adult males (or about 400,000) could vote, with Cornwall's many Parliamentary boroughs and population of 192,000 returning 44 MPs while the 541,000 people in Manchester, Birmingham, Leeds, and Sheffield returned none; afterward one in five (over 700,000) voted with the four industrial cities just cited returning 8 MPs. The

Reform Acts for England, Scotland, and Ireland did have radical provisions, a fact their more conservative provisions could not disguise.

The Conservative provisions were significant ones. The House of Commons and the Whig majority of Earl Grey hoped they could persuade the landed classes that the acts did not subvert their interests. County MPs, for example, now numbered 253 not 188, a sizable number from areas almost always Tory. Likewise conservative was the provision denying freeholders with a vote in parliamentary boroughs their accustomed second vote in county elections, which freed rural counties of some urban voters. A third conservative feature was the preservation of some fifty small boroughs that were either outright pocket boroughs— that is, under the control of one person—or amenable to the influence of local families. A large number of these were in the south of England. The population of urban Middlesex, Lancashire, and the West Riding of Yorkshire equaled that of rural Buckinghamshire. Oxfordshire, and ten southern counties, yet the three urban districts had only 58 MPs to the 174 from the twelve rural counties. Landlords, not manufacturers, still controlled the Commons. Thetford with 146 voters and Reigate with 184 still returned MPs, while Doncaster and Croydon, with over 10,000, were left unrepresented. Some of the changes in the franchise were also conservative. Abolished were the democratic scot and lot and potwalloper franchise and the quite democratic 40 shillings freehold vote in Ireland—all that was kept were the sometimes democratic votes of resident freemen, but that only for the freeman's lifetime. A final conservative clause was forced into the bill by the Tory Lord Chandos. His amendment gave the vote to tenants-at-will with land worth £50. Because tenants-at-will rented land on a yearly basis, they were dependent on the landlord and would likely vote his way. The bill, in short, did much to preserve the dominance of land.

Although conservative in part, the Reform Act did end the aristocracy's near monopoly of power. The middle classes were now junior partners, rotten boroughs had been largely abolished, and, most dangerously, the precedent was set for amending the franchise. The walls of the aristocrats' citadel of power had not been razed to the ground, but they had been breached. The Tories knew this and so hated the bill. Arbitrary and wanton, said Sir Robert Peel. Most dangerous, added Wellington, a granting of "the preponderance of influence to the lowest class of inhabitants in towns." Even Whigs were dismayed. On the bill's first reading, one of them shouted of Grey's Ministry, "They are mad! They are mad!"

It was an act that many in power believed to be dangerously radical, a fact which raises an intriguing question: Why did the Commons, nine-tenths of whom represented land, a House of Lords purely aristocratic, and a Tory King pass an act that gave the middle class greater power and that eventually led to democracy? The answer to this question lies in two years of political drama. Its opening concerned the House of Commons and involved angry extreme Tories, the *noblesse oblige* of the Whigs, and two general elections. The first of these elections occurred in June and July 1830. It was an election with mixed results. Some Whigs won reelection because they espoused reform; some Tories lost because they had voted for Catholic emancipation. Electors revolted against local magnates. Counties that seldom contested elections did so because of the issue of reform. The smaller gentry, the farmer, and freeholders of all kinds asserted their independence. Never were denunciations of the old system so widespread. Deeply ominous were Thomas Attwood's Birmingham Political Union and Henry Brougham's victory in Yorkshire.

Attwood, banker, ironmonger, and crusader for cheap money as an answer to economic distress, organized workers and employers into an effective political machine that agitated for reform, a task made easier in Birmingham because its manufacturing firms were small and paternalistic. In Manchester the cotton firms were huge, the gulf between employer and employee wide, and a political union impossible. In Leeds a political union emerged, though not until November 1831. But the men of Leeds, led by Edward Baines, editor of the powerful *Leeds Mercury*, did join in 1830 with the freeholders of Yorkshire to elect as MP the redoubtable Henry Brougham, Scotsman, barrister, Whig intellectual, and a whirlwind of good causes. Attwood and Brougham, the liberal press and the political unions, and restless freeholders and those indignant at old abuses, all mounted a massive criticism of the electoral system.

The Commons that met in July 1830 was, despite the additional reformers, Tory, though barely so. Wellington could have continued in office except for some angry ultra-Tories. Persuaded that a more representative Commons would not have passed the Catholic Emancipation Act, enough ultras abandoned Wellington on a crucial vote on November 15 to bring down his government. It was now the Whigs' turn. Earl Grey, 66 years of age, long the venerated leader of the Whigs, formed a government. A friend of reform even at a time when it was viewed as treasonous, a politician uncorrupted by intrigues and office-seeking, he had the patience, tact, reputation, and courage to persuade a divided Commons, a hostile Lords, and a Tory King to adopt reform. His first act was to form one of the most aristocratic cabinets ever to govern England. Only four of its thirteen members sat in the Commons, and only one of them was from the middle class. The thirteen, said Grey, owned more land than the members of any previous cabinet; and yet, on March 1, 1831, they proposed a bill that denied to land a near monopoly of political power. The Reform Act of 1832 owed not a little to the *noblesse oblige* of the Whigs. The Whigs were, historically, the ally of dissent, commerce, the towns, and popular causes, whether seventeenth-century Exclusionists or eighteenth-century Wilkites. Their banners had, since Peterloo, included the demand for parliamentary reform.

But Whig advocacy of reform was not entirely disinterested. In a two-party system the party that is out of power is always tempted to win elections by advocating popular causes. Not a few of the Whigs became converts to reform in order to win in the election of 1830; even more were converted during the election of May 1831. Reform had suddenly caught on—it became the great popular cause. The election of May 1831 was held because on April 20 a crucial provision of the first Reform Bill was defeated in the Commons. The defeat led Grey to insist that the King dissolve Parliament in order that an election could be held solely on the issue of reform.

The general election held in May 1831 constitutes the most decisive event in the winning of reform. It gave Grey's ministry a 140-seat majority in the Commons. The counties voted overwhelmingly for reform. Only six of the county MPs who had opposed the bill won reelection. The open boroughs were also for reform. Tories gained in English and Welsh close boroughs, but lost in Scottish and Irish boroughs. The Whigs were not above using government influence, the King's name, and intimidation and bribery. But whatever the means, the result was clear: an overwhelming mandate for reform. On September 22 the Commons passed the second Reform Bill by a vote of 345 to 236. On October 8 the House of Lords rejected it by 41 votes, thereby plunging England into a political crisis.

Riots occurred in Derby, Worcester, Blandford, and Tiverton; in Birmingham 100,000 loudly protested; in London 70,000 marched; Leicester, Bolton, and Leeds formed political unions; in Nottingham rioters set fire to the Duke of Newcastle's mansion; in Bristol they burned and plundered the customs house, excise office, bishop's palace, and jails and tollhouses; the Blackburn political union talked of an armed meeting. The disorders persuaded some, but not enough, of the Lords to change their minds. On March 24, 1832, after five months of social tension and political negotiations, the Commons produced a third bill. The Lords, despite public agitation, rejected it on May 7. The Lords were as obdurate as ever. Grey had long before told William IV that the only way to overcome that obduracy was by threatening to create some forty peers. The King had agreed, but only as a last resort, and even May 7 was not the last resort. Grey therefore resigned on May 9.

Wellington, ever loyal to his King, attempted to form a ministry. Attwood held a protest meeting in Birmingham, which 200,000 attended. Francis Place and his followers in London posted placards saying "To Stop the Duke, Go for Gold!" Instructions followed on how to turn in banknotes for gold. Place wanted to empty the Bank of England of its gold and so force reform or financial panic. In ten days £1.6 million went out of its vaults. The King yielded; he would create forty or fifty new peers. The Lord's dislike of an inflated, debased peerage being greater than its dislike of reform, passed the bill. The King's threat explains why the Lords agreed. But why did the King agree? The answer may lie in part in his fear of revolution, but far more crucial was the utter impossibility of forming an alternative government. Even the great Duke, hero of Waterloo, could not form a government opposed to reform. England needed a government, and the constitution had long insisted that such a government enjoy a majority in the Commons. The elections of May 1831, the exigencies of the English constitution, and the pressure of new social forces all joined together to make reform inevitable.

Reform begets reform. The Municipal Corporation Act of 1835 followed

It was at tumultuous elections in the boroughs that the reform movement gained its inexorable strength (*Punch*).

logically the Reform Act of 1832. The members of a reformed Parliament were hardly ready to tolerate the continuance of municipal corporations more oligarchic and cliquish than the national oligarchy had ever been. Most municipal governing bodies were self-perpetuating corporations that chose their successors—often from old guilds. They had lost touch with the people of their own towns, were inefficient and extravagant, and spent the taxpayers' money on splendid banquets, not adequate sewers. The Act of 1835 abolished these ancient corporations and established instead, in 179 boroughs, town councils elected by adult males who paid rates for three years. It was a more democratic franchise than the £10 household requirement of the Reform Act. The council, in turn, elected a mayor and some aldermen. Since no one without substantial property could be a councilor or alderman, municipal government remained in the hands of the middle class.

To be a poor law guardian, one did not even need to hold property. The passage of the New Poor Law of 1834 lessened the influence of the oligarchy in the countryside just as the Municipal Reform Act had in towns. The New Poor Law declared that all ratepayers could vote for the guardians of the new poor law unions and that these guardians had the power to manage the relief of the poor. Democracy had reached the countryside, but not full democracy. The New Poor Law, like the Reform Act and the Municipal Corporation Act, had clauses favoring property and oligarchy. Those who paid large amounts of poor rates received more votes at election time than those who paid small amounts. Justices of the peace could sit *ex officio* on the boards of guardians. This arrangement led to a partnership in administering the Poor Law between peers and gentry and farmers and tradesmen, though after the 1840s the peers and gentry, tired at being outvoted by their inferiors, bowed out.

Democracy certainly did not arrive in England between 1832 and 1835, but in national, urban, and rural elections thousands of Englishmen who had never before exercised political power were now deciding who should govern them—and sometimes even becoming one of the governors themselves. It was a significant development, one that led those who had the vote to urge further reforms and those who were denied the vote to grow angry. The energy of the newly enfranchised and the anger of the disenfranchised soon led to Chartism and the Anti–Corn Law League.

CHARTISM AND THE ANTI–CORN LAW LEAGUE

On February 4, 1839, delegates representing the working class throughout the realm met at the British Coffee House at Charing Cross, London. They met to promote the National Charter, which consisted of six points: universal suffrage, the secret ballot, equal representation from equal districts, annual Parliaments, no property qualification for becoming an MP, and if a person became one, a salary. The delegates were respectable, well dressed, and sedate, yet on arrival they were forced to leave their assigned room for another. The assigned room was reserved for another set of delegates who represented the middle classes and who met to establish a national Anti–Corn Law League. The league had no interest in the six points; its desire was to repeal all tariffs limiting the importation of grain.

History is not without coincidences. A scheduling error at a London coffeehouse led to the confrontation of two national movements that in the next decade would convulse English life. The coincidence was also symbolic. The middle-class delegates won the finest rooms, and later victory in Parliament; the working-class delegates were consigned to a lesser room and met ultimate defeat. But in 1839 the delegates to the Chartist Convention knew nothing of the future—they were full of the excitement of carrying the charter through Parliament and of liberating the working class.

In 1838 and 1839 masses of working people gathered throughout the country to demand the six points. There were torchlight parades, giant processions, mammoth meetings. One procession in Glasgow was two miles long. At Peep Green in the industrial West Riding of Yorkshire, 250,000 clamored for the charter, and at Birmingham 200,000. The numbers are probably exaggerated: Manchester's meeting, called 300,000 by the *Morning Advertiser*, was calculated by another editor at 50,000. Chartist meetings were not confined to industrial cities; 6,000 attended a rally at Bath in Somerset, and 4,000 at Devizes in Wiltshire, both counties with a declining textile industry. Besides mammoth rallies there were membership drives, lectures, proliferating newspapers, and small groups modeled after the Methodists' classes. The government was alarmed but not deeply so. It not only knew that not one in twenty of the upper classes favored universal suffrage but that, as the commander of the armed forces in the north reported, "their threats . . . are miserable. With half a cartridge, and half a pike, with no money, no discipline . . . they would attack men with leaders, money, and discipline . . . and sixty rounds a man."

Why this ferment? Why these demands? The answer must be found in two fundamental facts: the political frustration of a numerous and articulate working class, and economic distress. The political frustrations were many and intense. The first was the Reform Act of 1832, an act for which many workers agitated but which denied them the vote. They felt cheated.

In the north another struggle arose, the struggle for the ten-hour day. In 1831, Richard Oastler, an agent for a landowner in Yorkshire, discovered the horrors of child labor in England's textile mills. A Tory, an evangelical, and a

A procession of Chartists delivering their giant petition demanding votes for all men (*The Museum of London*).

man of fiery and indignant passions, he promised not to rest until these evils were ended. Others joined him, and soon there were Short Time Committees throughout the factory districts, all demanding the ten-hour day. The Whigs in 1833 passed a Factory Act, but only for the children. Although it prohibited the employment of those below age 9 and limited to eight hours those between 9 and 13, it did nothing for adults. The workers again felt cheated.

A year later the Whig government again angered the working class. It passed the New Poor Law of 1834, which gave three commissioners in London the power to create poor law unions, to have workhouses built, and to order the guardians of these unions to give no relief to the able-bodied except in these grim bastilles. Throughout England there were handloom weavers, framework knitters, nailmakers, laceworkers, and other craft laborers whose incomes were declining and for whom a few shillings of parish relief was a godsend. Factory towns also had during depressions, far too many jobless for the workhouses to hold. These same towns had a local pride, local officials, and their own way of treating the poor; they resented lectures from London. The prospect of a harsh and centralized poor law caused widespread and belligerent resistance. At Bradford and Keighley the assistant poor law commissioners were assaulted; at Todmorden a mob smashed the furniture of guardians friendly to the law; and at Elland women rolled such guardians in the snow. Many of the newly elected guardians refused to carry out the commissioners' orders. For ill-paid weavers and knitters and jobless factory workers, the workhouse was a frightful prospect. Yet by 1838 and 1839 the Whig government had imposed the new unions on the manufacturing areas. The working class had lost again.

It did little better in forming trade unions. In 1834 six agricultural laborers in Dorchester were sentenced to six years' transportation for administering oaths as part of a strike for better wages. In 1837 the leaders of the Glasgow cotton spinners strike received the same sentence—transportation to prison camps in Australia. The Whig government supported these prosecutions, for neither Whig, Tory, nor middle-class Radicals liked trade unions. Employers not only destroyed Robert Owens's Grand National Consolidated Union of 1834, a grandiose effort at a nationwide union, a union claiming a million members, but defeated the more solidly based unions—the cotton spinners, the building trades, and the coal miners. The prosperous years of 1831 and 1832 had witnessed the expansion of trade unions, but worsening trade in 1837 and 1838 led to lost strikes and broken unions.

One outlet for frustration was the radical press, a medium of the first importance in heightening working-class consciousness. On this issue the workers did gain a victory. The Whigs lowered the newspaper tax from 4 pence to 1. The tax on each copy had long made newspapers too expensive for workers, and the result was the growth of an illegal press. More than one Chartist leader had spent time in prison for selling unstamped newspapers. The Whigs, both by not ending the 4-pence stamp until 1836 and by keeping a stamp on newspapers, had no chance of erasing from workers' minds the consciousness of repressive taxes. Neither did other Whig palliatives erase memories of the New Poor Law, the defeat of the ten-hour day, the breaking of unions, or the failure to do anything about England's filthy towns and lack of education for the poor. The workers had been frustrated at every turn. Compounding these frustrations was the acute economic distress of 1838 and 1839. Hungry, jobless men and women protested at advancing capitalism's threat to traditional ways of work, to cherished custom, to family, and to community. Their protests expressed their defense of a deeply rooted culture as well as a newly awakened sense of independence.

But gaining the charter was not easy. It had, first of all, only the barest of support from the governing classes. Tories abhorred it, Whigs feared it, and middle-class Radicals found it too extreme. At first, it had some middle-class, Radical support—in Birmingham, the banker Thomas Attwood; in London, the utilitarian MPs John Roebuck, John Leader, and Joseph Hume; and in Leeds, the editor of the *Leeds Times*, Samuel Smiles. But most middle-class Radicals believed in the doctrine of *laissez-faire*, were for the New Poor Law, opposed the ten-hour day, and feared universal suffrage. The Chartists were also, at first, divided over methods. The leader of the London Convention of 1839, William Lovett, preached self-improvement and moral force, while Julian Harney and Bronterre O'Brien spoke of the pike and the musket. The 235-to-46 vote of the Commons in July 1839 to not even consider their petition was a blow to the moral force Chartists. In November it was time for the pike and the musket. At Newport in Monmouthshire one hundred armed Welshmen rose in rebellion. It was quickly surpressed. By 1842 when distress again revived Chartism, it had achieved greater unity and found a national voice in the *Northern Star* and its editor Feargus O'Connor. Its circulation was the largest of provincial newspapers. Its powerful pleas along with the eloquent oratory of its editor and other Chartist missionaries rejuvenated the cause. Once again mammoth meetings, conventions, petitions—and defeat. Chartism again subsided but again would not disappear. The economic crises of 1847 revived it a third time, leading to the mammoth meeting of May 10 at Kennington Common in South London, a meeting dispelled by a thunderstorm and a formidable array of soldiers and put to rest by economic prosperity and political reform. "I defy you," said William Cobbett, "to agitate a man with a full stomach."

Although Chartism failed, it had two profound results: it gave the working class a greater sense of identity and pride, and it created an atmosphere favorable to reform. Both defy exact measurement, yet both were important. The working classes that won the vote and ballot in 1867, 1872, and 1884 owed much to that premature declaration of independence and autonomy which was Chartism. The ten-hour day, grants to education, the Public Health Act, the refusal of local unions to enforce the workhouse test, all these and more reflected the pressures of Chartism. The protests of those with empty stomachs were not wholly without effect.

The agitations of the Anti–Corn Law League, like those of the Chartists, also throve on empty stomachs. When poor harvests made bread costly—as they did from 1838 to 1842—the hungry and distressed were hardly contented with laws excluding foreign corn. Parliament in 1828 had passed such a law, one that imposed a duty of 36 shillings 8 pence on grain from abroad when the price of grain at home was 50 shillings a quarter. It was a stiff duty, and in times of poor harvests it made bread more expensive. It was also a tailor-made issue for allying middle-class Leaguers and working-class Chartists.

But the Chartists would have nothing to do with the League. To many Chartists, cheaper bread only allowed millowners to pay lower wages. Many Chartists hated the League, and were skilled at breaking up League meetings. In 1839 the League could not hold meetings in its own Manchester; a veritable class war descended on the meeting halls of the north. The landed classes, still dominant in Parliament, also opposed the League. In 1838 the Commons voted 300 to 95 against repealing the law. The obstacles appeared insurmountable, with the Chartists dominating the meeting halls and the aristocracy Parliament. Yet in 1846 the Corn Laws were repealed. How did it happen?

The answer lies largely in the League's well organized and relentless use of its moral, economic, and electoral power and, to a lesser extent, in the triumph, especially in the mind of Sir Robert Peel, of the free trade theories of the political economists. That the League was a pressure group of unrivaled, and even unscrupulous, efficiency, Chartists learned when the League's Irish bouncers used gas pipes to rout them from free trade meetings. Publications secretly financed by the League also pilloried intellectual opponents. Elections were fought and won. Two cotton manufacturers, Richard Cobden and John Bright, entered Parliament, there to blame the long depression of 1839–42, the worst of the century, on the Corn Laws. If high tariffs were abolished, European grain would pour in and the price of bread would drop. Cheaper bread would leave the workers more to spend on manufactured goods. The selling of grain to England would also give Europeans more pounds with which to buy English textiles and iron goods. Manufacturing would revive, the jobless would return to work, and distress would end. In 1842, at a time when no one knew the real causes of depression, least of all Manchester millowners, it was a plausible argument. And more than plausible was the fact that England's wheat production was increasing more slowly than its population, which meant that only cheap grain from abroad would keep down the cost of bread.

In 1843 prosperity, good harvests, cheap bread, and full stomachs took the force out of those arguments. Chartism had bowed to prosperity; would the League? Never! said its wealthy adherents. In Manchester in 1843 they completed the imposing Free Trade Hall and at it first meetings raised £50,000. The League printed, in 1843, 9 million tracts, sponsored 650 lectures, sent 156 deputations to Parliament, published a journal, *The League*, and paid for 426,000 inserts in other newspapers and magazines. For the ladies there were tea parties, bazaars, and handsomely engraved subscription cards. Most ominous of all, the League registered thousands of friendly voters and helped those needing a property qualification to purchase 40 shilling freeholds.

Resolute and efficient as this superbly organized political machine was, it had not by 1844 breached the walls of Parliament. Repeal came only when the poor wheat crop in England and a disastrous potato blight in Scotland and Ireland, both occurring in 1845, drove Sir Robert Peel and others to favor repeal. In the summer of 1846 Peel introduced and Parliament passed a bill repealing the Corn Law. He had the support of all the Radicals, all but 9 of the Whigs, and 100 Conservatives. Opposing him were 240 Conservatives led by Lord Stanley and Benjamin Disraeli. The vote split the Conservative party, the hundred who voted for repeal forming a separate group called the Peelites. The potato blight did not convert Peel, but only forced his hand. His conversion was slow and owed much to his belief in political economy. The law of comparative advantage stated that if each country is free to use its capital and labor in the most efficient manner, it will result in the largest possible production of goods at the least cost. Tariffs would mean smaller production at a higher cost. Peel

PEEL'S CHEAP BREAD SHOP,
OPENED JANUARY 22, 1846.

Punch celebrates Sir Robert Peel's conversion to free trade in corn by picturing him as the baker of cheap bread (*Punch*).

had long said that free trade was the correct policy—but only, he said, in the abstract.

But politics is not abstract, and Peel thus stoutly defended, from 1815 to 1845, the Corn Laws. But then in November 1845 Lord John Russell, leader of the Whigs, declared for free trade. Many Whigs, in fact, had long adopted this position. In the forthcoming elections the Whigs' considerable power would be united with that awesome political machine, the League. Both would be campaigning for cheaper bread at a time when bread would be costly, potatoes scarce, and people starving in Ireland and Scotland. Had Peel never converted, the Whigs and Radicals would have repealed the Corn Laws. It is a fact that may have played a role in his conversion.

In the decade after repeal, the yearly import of foreign grain doubled, thus significantly checking the rising cost of bread and so allowing both English workers and foreign farmers and landlords to buy more manufactures from Britain, thus possibly helping to explain the happy fact that sharp economic depressions ceased after 1847. And since foreign corn also rose in price while British farmers made great technical improvements, disaster did not strike English agriculture—did not, that is, until the 1870s when railroads and steamships brought in cheaper North American grain.

Throughout its campaign the League had exaggerated the law's effect. It neither caused the depression, paralyzed industry, nor created poverty. But it did symbolize, as no other law did, the privileged monopolies of the landed classes, whether in Church, army, or quarter sessions. The speeches of the repealers overflowed with abusive language. The Corn Laws were the symbol of a proud, ancient, arrogant aristocracy, an aristocracy whose monopoly in grain irritated a new middle class which believed that all monopolies were unjust. The repeal of the Corn Laws meant that the middle classes, ushered into the back of the hall by the Reform Act, had decided to come to the front and share in the leadership of England. In so doing they assumed, along with the landed classes, the responsibility of dealing with poverty, crime, and unsanitary towns. In their endeavors to solve these problems, the new ruling partners unintentionally laid the foundations of a welfare state.

THE BEGINNINGS OF A WELFARE STATE

Many people in early nineteenth-century England suffered from the cruelty and neglect of others. To suffer was common; it occurred at every level and it could be intense. It led the novelist Charles Dickens to create the cruel workhouse master in *Oliver Twist*, the hateful schoolmaster in *Nicholas Nickelby*, the cold, calculating justice in *Chimes*, the harsh millowners in *Hard Times*. Widespread suffering also led the government to issue astonishingly detailed reports on the cruelty and negligence of English society. They not only described the dramatic evils of child labor and filthy towns, but probed into abuses in every nook and cranny of life. They described the horrors of lunatic asylums, prisons, and passenger ships. They told of the room in one asylum that was crowded with wooden cribs. Most of the patients in the cribs slept naked and all lay on straw and had one blanket as a covering. On Saturday some were tied in the crib, not to be untied until Monday, when the accumulated excrement was washed away by a mop and cold water. Most managers, believing insanity incurable, simply restrained the mentally ill, often with chains and straps. A few believed that bile in the blood caused insanity and so bled them.

Life in England's 336 prisons was also ghastly. The evils of prison life arose from the indiscriminate herding of every kind of criminal into cold, cheerless, unbelievably dirty wards. In them, seasoned criminals taught the young the art of crime. There was no classification, no education, no privacy, and very little discipline, but considerable drinking, gambling, fighting, and sexual indignities. It was as hellish as the hold of a passenger ship carrying emigrants to America. In 1820, 20,000 left Liverpool on ships averaging only 250 tons.

The grimness of Newgate as drawn by Gustave Doré.

In one of these there were 36 berths for 260 passengers. The mortality rate was sometimes 50 percent. Provisions were meager, water scarce and putrid, overcrowding unbearable.

It was a wretched, risky voyage but one on which many gambled rather than go to the poorhouse. There were many poorhouses, even before the New Poor Law of 1834, and they were dismal places. Most paupers, to be sure, received relief outside these houses. There was no uniformity before 1834 among the 15,500 parishes in England and Wales; some gave relief in aid of wages, thus tempting wage earners to become paupers; others enforced a workhouse test. Even within parishes, arbitrariness ruled; one justice would grant a vagrant a meal, another order him whipped. The haphazard mixing of generosity and harshness furthered the law's demoralizing effect on the working classes, and contributed to its ever-mounting expense.

Local government was a chaos of authorities, neither uniform nor efficient. In the countryside the justices of the peace and the parish vestry (with its overseers of the poor, church wardens and constables) were the most important authorities; in the towns, municipal corporations and borough justices were, though increasingly they were joined by myriad paving, lighting, sewer, and improvement

A Victorian workhouse where husband, wife, and children lived in separate wards and ate an ample but boring diet of cheese, gruel, and stew (*Punch*).

commissions created by special acts of Parliament. Largely unpaid and usually self-appointed, these authorities, rural and urban, were free from the supervision of the central government. The service they rendered was uneven. Except for a few constables in the countryside and some hired watchmen in the towns, there was no police force. It took the military to handle riots. But the military could not handle crime, which increased with urbanization and the growth of population. In many towns, streets were abominable, as were the provisions for removing sewage and supplying water; in other towns they were adequate— again, no uniformity.

Three factors help explain the cruelty and neglect that pervaded British life. A chaotic and amateurish system of local government helps explain the state of prisons and poorhouses and the rise of crime and disease. Unregulated capitalism tolerated the evils of passenger ships, factories, and mines. And voluntarism gave rise to neglect in education and philanthropy. Voluntarism was the belief that private institutions, whether churches, hospitals, charities, friendly societies, coal clubs, or soup kitchens, provided one of the best means for a free people to meet social needs. It was, for example, through the voluntary effort of the churches that England should educate its young. But the great

The Church of England's zeal to form National Schools exceeded its ability to provide England a sound and widespread system of public education (*Illustrated London News*).

difficulty was that they were unable to do so. In 1807 the Nonconformists and liberal Churchmen formed the British and Foreign School Society. In 1811 the Church of England founded the National Society. Both resolved to educate the children of the poor, and neither succeeded. In 1840, the *Educational Magazine* said that four-fifths of London's working-class children had no schooling. In the northern towns, one-third of the children attended no schools, the others attended Sunday Schools only or crowded into a common day school run by ignorant schoolmasters (one of whom ordered two globes for his geography class, one for each hemisphere).

Neglect and cruelty were, of course, not new; they had been around for centuries. What was new was the insistence that they be diminished, even if this meant a larger central government. In 1833, for example, Parliament voted to create inspectors who were to enforce the law excluding young children from factories. In 1847 Parliament voted that all young people and women work only 10.5 hours a day. In 1842 Parliament created a mining inspectorate to see that women and children did not work in these dark, dangerous underground galleries. In 1849 Parliament increased the numbers and powers of the mining inspectors in order to reduce accidents that killed nearly one thousand miners a year. Railway and ship accidents also killed; to regulate these, Parliament created railway and merchant marine inspectors. Emigration officers had since 1803 inspected passenger ships. By 1847 they had full powers to require adequate space, provision, water, and safety. At the zenith of its enthusiasm for *laissez-faire* economics, Parliament nevertheless decreed that fatal accidents, the exploitation of children, and the wretched condition of travelers required the interference of the state.

Parliament also empowered the central government to supervise public institutions responsible for the care of paupers, criminals, and the insane. It passed the New Poor Law of 1834 which empowered three commissioners and more than a dozen assistants to supervise the elected guardians of over 500 newly formed Poor Law Unions. The commissioners' insistence that no relief be given the able bodied except in the workhouse, that married couples live in separate wards, and that beef and plum pudding no longer grace Christmas dinners evoked angry denunciations of this abominable and cruel law. The workhouses were grim, but their use was distinctly not universal; in fact throughout the 1840s and 1850s four-fifths of all relief went to those outside these houses. The commissioners also made many improvements, reducing cases of gross negligence and cruelty, improving health care and schooling, and adopting fairer, if stricter, standards of relief.

The same can be said of the prison inspectors and lunacy commissioners Parliament established in 1835 and 1845. Lunacy commissioners no longer tolerated crib rooms and prison inspectors forbid cuts in diets if a prisoner failed to turn a meaningless crank 14,000 times a day.

There was much in the old local government that was generous and much in the new central administration that was harsh, but neither was the rule.

Balancing gain against loss, it is clear that the central government made public institutions more rational, efficient, and civilized. The government not only checked industrial exploitation and reformed public institutions, but also aspired to build a better society by ensuring every citizen a good education and a healthy and secure neighborhood. To do so was to step on the toes of the powerful; in education, the Church of England; in public health, water companies and improvement commissioners; and in police, the jealousies of local authorities. Parliament therefore moved forward slowly. It promoted education by aiding, not replacing, church schools, and it improved health and security by granting new powers to local government—though in each instance there would be central inspection. In 1839 the government appointed two education inspectors and gave £30,000 in grants. By 1852 there were twenty inspectors and £200,000 in grants. In 1848 Parliament established the General Board of Health, with medical and engineering inspectors, and in 1856 it empowered the Home Office to create constabulary inspectors. Between 1833 and 1856 some twenty central commissions, boards, or inspectorates were established, all concerned with the well-being of her majesty's subjects. The early Victorians had laid the foundation of a welfare state.

It was a welfare state modest in goals, limited in powers, and built on a partnership with industry, local government, and voluntary authorities. The inspectors were few and their duties limited. In 1842 the government appointed only one inspector for England's many mines. The lunacy commissioners could not order counties to build public asylums, nor could the board of health order towns to improve sewage and water unless the town's annual mortality rose above 23 deaths per 1,000. The nearly powerless education inspectors were also frustrated as voluntary efforts failed to build enough schools to keep pace with the growing population. The English wished neither to strengthen nor weaken local government and private authorities. The result was a partnership, with local and private institutions supplying the initiative and doing the day-to-day work, while the central government advised, inspected, reported, and gave grants.

On occasion the central government interfered directly in local government in order to reform local authorities, whether they were public or private. Thousands of institutions required such reformation, institutions that ranged from small charities to the Church of England and the universities of Oxford and Cambridge. In 1820 Parliament created a Charity Commission; in 1840 that commission completed its thirty-second and final report on the mismanagement, inefficiency, and corruption of the charities. It told of endowed schools that taught no one, of almshouses whose funds went to banquets for the trustees, and of endowments for widows and orphans that helped neither. In 1853 Parliament established a permanent commission to help Oxford University reform itself. It seemed a shocking invasion of property, but there was a precedent. The Ecclesiastical Commission, established in 1836, was a permanent body empowered to help the Church abolish pluralism, end the wastefulness of cathedral

PUNCH, OR THE LONDON CHARIVARI.—July 10, 1858.

THE "SILENT HIGHWAY"-MAN.

"Your MONEY or your LIFE!"

The polluted Thames remained, as *Punch* makes vivid, a sewer of death (*Punch*).

chapters, and remove some of the more glaring inequalities in episcopal incomes. Whether universities or lighthouses or cathedrals, the government increasingly intervened in order to force them to reform themselves. Commissions to help society reform itself thus joined departments that protected the individual from exploitation and negligence as part of an administrative revolution.

A third aspect of this revolution was the improved efficiency of the civil service itself. Paid and trained professionals chosen by merit increasingly replaced the unpaid and untrained as England's civil servants. In towns, responsible and elected boards of health performed services long done badly by self-appointed commissions. In 1855 Parliament established a Civil Service Commission and introduced examinations as part of a merit system of appointment. Departments were reorganized and managed by fixed and uniform standards of fairness and efficiency.

The causes of this administrative revolution were the deep historical forces at work in early nineteenth-century England. Four of them were particularly important: the growth of an industrial and urban society, the political power of the middle and working classes, an intellectual climate combining humanitarianism and rationalism, and the government itself in the form of bureaucrats who argued for more reform.

The Industrial Revolution, of course, multiplied many evils. Child labor and dirty towns had never been so concentrated, so visible, so threatening, as in these mushrooming industrial cities. These cities also produced a wealthy middle class and an articulate working class that did not wish to tolerate such evils. The workers agitated for the ten-hour day and members of the middle class financed and organized school societies and health associations. Industrial and scientific advances also produced the wealth and technology—the glazed tubular sewer pipes and the steam engine for ventilating mines—that made the tolerance of old abuses inexcusable.

An urban England also produced a humanitarianism that considered lunatics tied naked to cribs and prisons full of putrefying matters unacceptable and a rationalism that claimed education could reduce crime, that an intelligent poor relief would lessen pauperism, and that civilized prisons and asylums might reform criminals and cure the insane. That humanitarian impulse arose from all quarters—Evangelicals, High Churchmen, cosmopolitan Londoners, and enlightened Radicals. It found perhaps its most complete expression in Lord Ashley.

To the Victorians poverty was a sin to be absolved by the hard work of breaking stones (*Illustrated London News*).

The son of an earl who cared little for him, he found in a pious nurse and a devout wife the truth and strength of evangelical religion. It led to a lifetime of devoted service to those who suffered, whether they be children in factories, mines, and slums or the mentally ill in wretched asylums and the dying in diseased towns. In 1848 he became a commissioner on the General Board of Health, working with Edwin Chadwick, a rationalist and a follower of Bentham. Chadwick wrote large parts of the Factory Report of 1832, the Poor Law Report of 1834, and the Sanitary Report of 1842. He was also secretary to the Poor Law Commission and a commissioner on the Board of Health.

Chadwick and other utilitarians had a scientific attitude toward social planning. They were the age's technocrats, its social engineers, and their elaborate schemes for prisons, schooling, poor law management, reformatories, law reform, and industrial training had a great influence on the beginnings of the welfare state. Once begun, the process never stopped. Constant investigations exposed more abuses, and endless reports and energetic administrators recommended more government action. In an industrial society whose new classes wanted a better life, in an age of bureaucracy with administrators exposing social evils, and in a climate of opinion seriously religious, humane, and enlightened, the pressures for reform were great.

The growth of a welfare state was only partly a party question. On such issues as the ten-hour day, the exclusion of children from mines, the New Poor Law, and prison and lunacy reform, Whigs and Tories voted for and against in about the same ratios. But this was not true of the establishment of the Education Inspectorate and support for the General Board of Health. From 1839 to 1854, Conservatives opposed both. The Whigs also initiated far more of these new agencies than did the Tories, whose sole agency was the Ecclesiastical Commission. It is a paradoxical fact in terms of liberalism, conservatism, and reform that the liberals who espoused *laissez-faire* doctrines were the authors of most collectivist reforms while the conservatives, who espoused paternalism, were the authors of the fewest. The reason for this paradox is that the paternalism of the Tories was local and private, one built on property, church, and locality, the very institutions most jealous of centralization, while the liberals' political economy included the seductive idea that a government could so reform a society that an educated, healthy, well-cared-for citizenry would not be dependent on government. It was not too unrealistic a dream when prosperity was strong in England, as it was from 1848 to 1879. During that period there was a momentary synthesis of capitalism, voluntarism, and government that brought well-being and progress for the many. An age of crises and change was followed by an age of equipoise.

FURTHER READING

BEALES, DEREK. *From Castlereagh to Gladstone, 1815–1885.* New York: W. W. Norton, 1969. A brilliant interpretation full of original and imaginative insights.

BRIGGS, ASA. *The Age of Improvement.* London: Longmans, Green, 1959. A wise review of events in England between 1780 and 1867 by the dean of historians of nineteenth-century Britain; a liberal interpretation, sympathetic with the rising classes and advancing ideas.

BROCK, MICHAEL. *The Great Reform Act.* London: Hutchinson, 1973. The best account of the most important reform in modern England, aware of the complexities of the forces behind the change.

CHECKLAND, S. G. *The Rise of Industrial Society.* London: Longmans, 1966. An intelligent synthesis of the many specialized works by economic and social historians, demographers, and geographers, one placed in the political context of Victorian England.

DERRY, JOHN. *The Radical Tradition.* London: Macmillan, 1967. A study of radicalism from Tom Paine and William Cobbett to Joe Chamberlain and Lloyd George, deals with political theory and mass agitation, leaders and the self-educated.

FRASER, DEREK. *The Evolution of the British Welfare State.* New York: Harper & Row, 1973. A comprehensive, reliable, and clear account of those many ad hoc reforms that, reflecting a myriad of historical forces, led to the welfare state.

HALEVY, ELIE. *The History of the English People in the Nineteenth Century*, Vols. 1–4. New York: Harcourt Brace, 1952. These four volumes provide the fullest account of the history of England from 1815 to 1850 and offer profound interpretations, most of which have stood the test of time.

KITSON CLARK, GEORGE. *The Making of Victorian England.* Cambridge, Mass.: Harvard University Press, 1962. An analysis of the factors that, from 1837 to 1850, created Victorian England; a strong emphasis on religion, but also good on population and industry.

McCORD, NORMAN. *The Anti-Corn Law League.* London: Allen & Unwin, 1958. A close and candid look at the Anti-Corn Law League, at its aims, its leaders, its organization, its middle-class nature, and its tactics, which could be as ruthless as its aims were noble.

THOMPSON, DOROTHY. *The Chartists.* New York: Pantheon Books, 1984. A comprehensive, perceptive, and sympathetic interpretation that brings in a social and cultural dimension.

WIENER, JOEL, ED. *Great Britain: The Lion at Home.* New York: Chelsea House, 1974. Volumes 1 and 2 cover the years 1760 to 1870 and include documents that are illuminating about the reform of Parliament, chartism, trade unions, and the repeal of the Corn Laws.

WOODWARD, E. L. *The Age of Reform, 1815–1870.* Oxford: Clarendon Press, 1938. A comprehensive study that is weak on economic development, strong on foreign affairs, full on education and religion—overall, sensible and sound, but not brilliant.

An age of prosperity

23

Economic prosperity was the most important fact defining mid-Victorian Britain. The repeal of the Corn Law, the Crimean War, and the Reform Act of 1867 were dramatic events, but they did not transform, as did prosperity, the lives of millions of ordinary English men and women. From 1843 to 1873 Britain enjoyed exuberant economic growth, one marred only by brief crises in 1847, 1858, and 1867. It was a case of being rich and growing richer. In 1850 Britain produced 40 percent of the world's hardwares, half of its cotton and iron, and two-thirds of its coal. It was an astonishing record, but one equaled in the next thirty years in steel, shipping, and railways. By 1870 Britain produced half the world's steel; by the 1880s it owned one-third of the world's merchant marine; by the same year it had built an even larger percentage of the world's ships and railways. All the world, said an American agent, "must get their railway iron in England where it is manufactured so rapidly and so perfectly." Britain also made remarkable advances in chemicals, in electricity, in machine tools, and in the construction of bridges, viaducts, tunnels, and huge halls. It also became in the late nineteenth century one of the world leaders in the manufacture of bicycles, sewing machines, and cameras, a part of a constant growth. In 1851 Britain's gross national product was £523 million; in 1870, £916 million. This economic miracle meant that at midcentury the per capita income of the British reached £32.6, at a time when France's was £21.1 and Germany's £13.3. The Victorians had created a giant cornucopia.

THE CRYSTAL PALACE: MID-VICTORIAN CORNUCOPIA

In 1851 examples of the endless products that flowed from Britain's cornucopia were to be found at the Crystal Palace in London, the site of the Great Exhibition

The Crystal Palace, home of the Great Exhibition of 1851 and the world's first large metal and glass building (*Illustrated London News*).

of 1851, the first world's fair in history. The Crystal Palace was also the world's first large edifice built out of metal and glass. It was an airy, light, graceful fairyland. Joseph Paxton, a gardener turned greenhouse designer, was its architect. It covered 18 acres and was built of 34 miles of pipe and 900,000 square feet of the largest panes of glass yet produced. By using prefabricated parts that were mass produced, 2,000 men built it in twenty-two weeks. When Queen Victoria opened the exhibition on May 1, it bulged with the world's industrial and artistic products. It exceeded, the historian Lord Macaulay said, the dreams of Arabian romances.

Prominent among the British contributions were dazzling feats of engineering. There were self-acting mules that spun cotton with unprecedented speed; marine engines of 700 horsepower; a gleaming locomotive of 31 tons; hydraulic presses that could lift 1,144 tons; pumps, cranes, and presses of all kinds; models of tunnels, bridges, and steamships; and innumerable steam engines—the central deity in this pantheon of machines. Here, palpable and concrete, lay the secret of Britain's economic prosperity. No foreign country could rival these astonishing creations. The new, improved self-acting mules still gave Britain the power of cotton. From 1840 to 1880 technical advances allowed the output of each cotton spinner to increase 2.5 times and enabled Britain to possess two-thirds of the world's capacity for cotton factory production. Improved steam engines, cables, elevators, pumps, and ventilation led to a great expansion in coal production, coal becoming cotton's great rival. In 1810, 50,000 British miners produced 10 million tons, and a century later 1 million miners produced 287 million tons.

One of the pumps at the exhibition was designed by Henry Bessemer, an inventor unconnected with the iron industry but destined to revolutionize it. In 1856 he developed a process for blowing air, not on the periphery, but directly into the molten metal, thus raising its heat, making it more liquid, and thereby making it easier to control its carbon content and so turn it into steel and to do so cheaply. In 1864 Charles William Siemans, and in 1871 Pierre Martin, both working in Birmingham, further improved the making of steel. By 1870 Britain produced one-half of the world's iron and steel as she did one-half of its coal.

The Bessemer and Martin-Siemens process would not work with ore rich in phosphorous. In 1878 two Welshmen, Sidney Gilchrist Thomas and his cousin Sidney Gilchrist, developed a process that allowed phosphorous-rich iron ore to be used. They thus allowed Germany and France, whose ores had much phosphorous, to rival British production.

Britain's great industrial lead at midcentury was the result of striking innovations in textiles, iron, railways, shipbuilding, and machines of every kind. These inventions so decisively reduced the cost of British goods that Britain enjoyed a near monopoly in both shipping and shipbuilding. From 1837 to 1865 British production of steamships increased twelve times. By 1870 Britain was building half of the world's sailing and nearly all of its steamships. With an unrivaled merchant marine and Empire and a head start in the industrial race, Britain gained a near monopoly in the world's markets. And her dominance as the world's banker and insurer grew greater than ever. The City of London, the center of world trade and finance, yielded a greater and more lasting wealth than did the coal, cotton, iron, and ships of the "workshop of the world."

The Great Exhibition also contained a display devoted to agriculture. It featured threshers and reapers, now widely used, and mowers, winnowers, root cutters, and seed drills, now pulled by ponderous but powerful steam tractors. Less dramatic, but equally beneficial, were the mass-produced perforated drainage pipes, which by draining Britain's heavy clay soil dramatically increased the arable land available and thereby agricultural productivity. The new machines, drainage, chemical fertilizers, and improved stock breeding created an agriculture whose luxuriant crops led to solid profits for the farmer, adequate rents for the landlord, and cheaper food for the people. It was the golden age of high farming.

To a perceptive economist, the display at the end of the eastern nave of the Crystal Palace offered a third clue for Britain's prosperity. The display featured the products of Britain's Empire. Those of the East India Company enthralled tourists, particularly the 186-carat Koh-i-Nor diamond. There were also objects of brass and bamboo that took decades to fashion and spinning wheels that revealed both Indian backwardness and need for cottons. In India, as in China, the spinning wheel was no match for Lancashire's latest self-acting mule, no more than wagons and junks were a match for the railway and steamship, miracles of transport that brought English manufactures to the farthest reaches of these vast and populated countries. The Opium War of 1840 opened China to British trade. India was long a British preserve. In 1875 Britain purchased the Suez Canal and soon took over Egypt. British-built railways, waterworks, and harbors and British textiles, hardwares, and finance soon gave Britain economic dominance in much of South America. British exports to and investment in South America doubled and redoubled. In 1871 the empire proper took 23 percent of British exports, in 1877, 5 percent. Nothing succeeds like success.

The wealthy thronged to see the marvels of an unprecedented prosperity (*The British Library*).

Between the displays of the empire and the center of Crystal Palace lay the products of Europe. The British in 1851 had no fear of them. By repealing the Corn Law in 1846 and the Navigation Acts in 1849, Britain proclaimed its faith in free trade. The more European goods the better; it only gave their producers pounds with which to buy the goods pouring out of Britain. A fourth cause of prosperity was the advance of free trade. From the tariff reductions of the 1820s and Peel's further reductions in the 1840s free trade continued its inexorable advance, culminating in the 1860s in the Cobden Treaty with France, a treaty that by 1870 had doubled British exports to that country. The Great Exhibition's display of the goods of the world was a monument to free trade.

Gold was a frequent item in the displays of the Great Exhibition, whether in jewelry, plate, or imposing nuggets. From time immemorial humans have worshipped gold. In the Bank Act of 1844, Parliament required the Bank of England to expand and contract its banknotes according to the amount of gold in its coffers. Other countries also based their currencies on gold. Thus, when gold was discovered in California and Australia, money multiplied. With more money in their pockets, more people can and will seek to buy more goods. Prices thus rose from 1848 to 1873 throughout the world. In Britain, of course,

Imposing railway stations became the age's new temples (*Illustrated London News*).

there were other forms of currency not based on gold, such as checks and bills of exchange, and their increased issue in a decade of expansion also caused an increase in purchasing power. This mounting purchasing power, in turn, led to greater sales, higher prices, rising profits, greater confidence, more investment, and a greater economic boom.

Six million people paid a pound, a half-crown, or a shilling (depending on the day of the week) to visit the Great Exhibition during its 140 days. Their numbers and their affluence point to another reason for mid-Victorian prosperity, an irrepressible population boom. The 10 million English of 1811 numbered 26 million by 1881. The more people, the greater the demand for goods and the greater supply of labor for their production.

The Great Exhibition not only contained clues pointing to the causes of prosperity—industrial superiority, high farming, imperial markets, free trade, the discovery of gold, and a population boom—but in its fantastic array of products revealed the overwhelming impact of mid-Victorian wealth on the daily life of the British. This impact can be seen in three profound social developments in Victorian England: the revolution in transportation, urbanization, and the proliferation of consumer goods.

The revolution in transport knitted together a society once parceled out in separate regions and counties—or even isolated parishes. The railway, one of the centerpieces of the Great Exhibition and the wonder of the age, trans-

Kensington Park Estate, one of London's new West End estates where the wealthy lived (*Kensington and Chelsea Public Libraries*).

formed life. In 1850 railway trains logged 67.4 million passenger miles, by 1879 the figure was 490 million passenger miles a year, a rate which meant that almost all classes were moving about freely, changing jobs, visiting relatives, going to the countryside. Railways also carried London newspapers and magazines to the provinces and brought them theatrical groups, lecturers, concert pianists, bureaucrats, and barristers. They brought back to London provincial trade union delegates, politicians, commercial agents, food, and manufacturers. Steamships on coastal routes and large rivers also helped, bringing cheap coal to flats and homes that once were cold. In 1838 the *Great Western* was the first steamship built entirely of iron and the first driven by a screw propeller; by 1870 such ships took English goods and passengers throughout the globe, and some of the passengers for good: from 1853 to 1880 they carried 2.5 million emigrants to new homes. Steamships also brought back from abroad the raw materials and foods so necessary to the workshop of the world. By 1870 Britain was importing half its meat, wool, and dairy produce, more than half its grains, and all its raw cotton. Transportation was everywhere at work, everywhere a crucial part of the mid-Victorian prosperity.

THE PURSUIT OF COMFORT: VICTORIAN SOCIETY

The transportation revolution was an integral part of urbanization. England became a nation of city dwellers. In 1851, 54 percent of the people lived in urban areas; by 1870 it was 70 percent. The suburbs of London grew the most rapidly, doubling in population in the twenty years after 1861. By 1900 one in five people lived in greater London. Other cities also mushroomed. The middle classes, in moving to the suburbs, only partially escaped the city, since most still worked in the city and all enjoyed its culture, though in differing ways. The serious attended the theater, operas, concerts, and public lectures, and visited the libraries and museums; the less serious entertained themselves at restaurants, pleasure gardens, and the new attraction of the age, the music hall. The music hall, with its glittering gas lights, its humorous skits, its drinks and delicacies, and its glorious melodies proved instantly popular. The sporting watched cricket and football, the sinful went to brothels, lovers of violence to prize fights, and lovers of drink to pubs and beer houses. There were also parks, zoos, and the grand architecture of imposing buildings and public monuments. But the cities' main attraction, as always, was jobs, some with fairly high wages and salaries.

Those fortunate enough to gain such jobs could buy a semidetached villa in the Italianate style or, closer to town, splendid terraced houses of four or five stories. These terraced houses, whose side walls adjoined the side walls of their neighbors, had on the basement level kitchens, pantries, and wine cellars; on the ground floor, a hall, a dining room, a drawing room, and a library; and on the floors above bedrooms for a large family and attic rooms for the servants. In 1850 there were 348,000 servants in England, in 1870, 1.3 million. In London one of fifteen workers was a servant. Two or three servants were as necessary to the middle-class family then as the washer-dryer and dishwasher are to today's suburban dweller. In the rear of the house was a pleasant garden. Such houses were not new to England. What was new was their numbers, the result of an exploding middle class and the vigor and inventiveness of speculative builders.

Also expansive was the growth of housing for the artisan classes. They were not at all ostentatious, like the villas of the *nouveau riche*, but plain, two-story row houses. They usually had four rooms, two up and two down. They were not commodious, not ornate, but if tidily kept provided a dwelling far more decent than the tenements from which so many of the artisans had come. They had a kitchen with an iron stove, a front room with a fireplace, probably a sofa, some reed chairs, a solid table, and upstairs, beds in separate rooms—all simple but a universe away from the hovels of the agricultural worker or the single, crowded room of a tenement. The artisan's cottage had neither flush

Victorian drawing rooms were ornate, luxurious, cluttered, and sumptuous (*National Monuments Record*).

toilets nor baths connected with water heaters—but neither did the houses of the rich outside London. Rich Londoners did have flush toilets by the 1890s, but seldom fitted baths. For artisans, the toilet was outside the house, the baths were in a tub or at one of the town's bath and wash houses. Public baths and washhouses sprang up all over urban England, and like parks, museums, and libraries were part of the new felicity of urban life.

From 1850 to 1870 most towns failed to use powers granted by Parliament to clean up their filthy and disease-ridden towns, with the result that the death rate barely declined: in London it even went up from 21 to 24 per 1,000. But by the 1880s public health service had become a more efficient part of municipal government and sanitary improvements were insured: streets were paved and cleaned and lit by gas, sewers became general, and pure water flowed to more homes. Into these homes also flowed consumer goods.

The mid-Victorian cornucopia could do nothing if it could not produce furniture, clothing, hardware, crockery, bric-a-brac, and food, drink, and tobacco. The drawing rooms of the middle classes after the 1870s had their "sociable sofas" or "tête-à-tête" sofas, heavily upholstered; tea tables in the polygonal Japanese style; and elegant marble mantels with ornate clocks. The dining room had the newest of tables, ones that could be lengthened with leaves, and richly

Corsets, tightly laced, gave them the slim waist, crinolines caged the full skirt (*Illustrated London News*).

carved mahogany sideboards full of wares from the Staffordshire potteries. In the libraries were magnificent carpets and heavy draperies, elaborate desks with numerous compartments, and padded leather chairs with coil springs, a Victorian invention and one of the prime symbols of their cult of comfort. Coziness, too, was worshipped. Some libraries had their cosy-corner, or inglenook, with shelves for books, ornaments, and bric-a-brac. It all appeared expensive, but it was not always so in reality. The decorative features of ornate looking furniture were often made of *papier mâché*. Mass production was used. And some of the elaborate carvings on the ceiling were really of molded *gutta percha*, a substance from the Niato tree of Malaya that softened when in boiling water and hardened at room temperature to look like wood. It was also used in furniture to simulate the rich carvings of wood. Taste was, of course, not impeccable and it varied from place to place and class to class—even from decade to decade. The prosperous Victorian delighted, both in architecture and design, in all sorts of styles, often considering that which was more eclectic as the more imposing.

The bedroom was also dedicated to comfort. Bedsteads were ornate affairs of brass and iron, the chamber pot was richly decorated, and the shallow and flat hip baths were filled from water cans. Flush toilets and baths with piped hot water came after the 1890s. The bedrooms' heavy mahogany wardrobes, ornately carved and decorated, were crammed with clothing, for affluent Victorians dressed elaborately. Women possessed many clothes. There were day dresses and evening dresses, ornate in design, with bodices boned and padded, and with much lace embroidery. For outdoors there were jackets, cloaks, and mantels in light woolens, velvets, and muslins; bonnets of cope, horsehair, plait, and shot silk, and gloves of kid and fawn and cashmere. Pursuit of an artificial elegance, not the cult of comfort, ruled women's fashions. Tightly laced corsets and a plenitude of petticoats produced the hour-glass figure—large bosom, slender waist, ample skirts—an elegance created at the cost of health, comfort, and mobility. In the 1850s petticoats gave way to the crinoline, a cage of light steel wire that billowed out the skirt. The Victorian woman was literally in a cage—but not so the man. His clothing aimed at comfort. Whether attired in frock coat for the day or tails for the evening, he was usually dressed in black. Color and pattern came only in the waistcoat or vest, though even these gave way to the practice of having the coat, vest, and trousers cut of the same material. The linen shirts also lost their frills, collars were lowered, the cravat approached the narrow tie. It was a warm and comfortable attire, but somber and serious as befitted an attorney or trader busy earning an income with which to buy a villa in the suburbs.

The furniture, dress, china, and kitchenware of the artisans could not compare with those of the villa, but they reached out for the same comforts and they gained from the overspill of the Victorian cornucopia a standard of living their parents and grandparents never knew. Many, but by no means all, benefited from England's remarkable economic growth. Inequality grew greater from 1850 to 1870 as it had from 1800 to 1850. A mere 0.48 percent in 1870 received

The life of the poor was simple, crowded, and miserable (*Illustrated London News*).

26.3 percent of the nation's income while 10 percent received 50.6 percent. That 10 percent included the solid middle class, the manufacturers, merchants, and professionals whose income ranged from £150 to £3,000. Beneath them was the lower middle class of clerks, drapers, managers, salesmen, and accountants, men earning from £60 to £150, and the world of skilled and semiskilled laborers, the jeweler and instrument makers at £90, cutlery and glass workers at £70, and railway engine drivers and cotton spinners at £50. The skilled and semiskilled lagged behind the middle classes until the boom of 1868–73, when their real wages increased nearly 25 percent. The sharp fall in world prices for food and raw materials after 1873 further increased their standard of living.

The 1870s were also the age of the artisans. Their housing was still usually drab and dismal, though increasingly warmer and less crowded with people and more crowded with furniture. By the 1880s and 1890s cheap trams and railways allowed the more ambitious artisans to make the exodus to the suburbs—to row houses of five and six rooms, many with the same flush toilets and bathtubs the villas possessed. But they were amenities not available to the lower fourth of society, to those sometimes called the *residuum*.

The residuum was vast and variegated, particularly in London. It included at midcentury the part-time laborer, the underemployed, the unemployable, and the sweated worker, the street people—hawkers, peddlers, ragpickers—the old, the ill and the orphaned, and the thieves and prostitutes—in a literal sense the residue. They lived in slums—some on low wages, some on poor relief, some on charities and begging, and many by scavenging or petty thievery. Their rooms were abysmal. Nearly a third of Glasgow's families lived in one room, sometimes ten or fifteen people, and some in rooms with no windows and only straw to sleep on, rooms the police judged not fit for pigs. In Liverpool a third of the families lived in cellar dwellings; every day in London 80,000 bought nightly or weekly tickets for a bed in an unventilated, filthy dormitory; the least fortunate spent the night under bridges and railway arches. Most laborers in London crowded into flats carved out of once handsome villas, now dilapidated and subdivided, or else lived in dismal and dreary tenements. The inhabitants of these crowded rooms, sparsely furnished and without piped water and sewers, enjoyed very little of the mid-Victorian wealth, and they made up over a fourth of the nation.

Many of the Victorians who were busy furnishing their villas were as indifferent to these slums as they were to open cesspools, unpaved streets, the overworking of children, and the plight of the jobless. Having excluded children from

The most wretched of all were the homeless (*Gustave Doré*).

mines and factories, they forgot the many who worked 12 and 14 and 16 hours in tailor and millinery shops producing the skirts and finery for villadom.

They also did little for the poor. In 1858 and again in 1868 severe economic crises showed how fragile and precarious was the capitalist system. In those bad years unemployed clerks and artisans found themselves slipping into the world of the disinherited and the derelict. Not a few tradesmen and small manufacturers faced bankruptcy and the appalling disgrace of pauperism. Victorian life was not as secure as its stately villas and ponderous furniture suggested. Countless suburbanites lived in genteel poverty, stretching their £80 or £90 a year to the fullest, yet aware of the abyss—the city's slum—that lay below.

The prosperity of Victorian England produced suburbs that divided rather than united classes. They not only separated the banker in his villa from the printer or mechanic in his artisan's cottage, but also the artisan in his suburb from the common laborer and the residuum. In one sense railways and trams, cheap goods and commerce, brought England together, linking Cornwall and Northumberland with London and linking consumer with consumer. But in another sense the new transport and the new manufacturing fragmented society, separating the classes in their various and exclusive neighborhoods. The ground seemed fertile for that classic struggle between bourgeoisie and proletariate that Karl Marx had predicted, a class war that tore Paris apart in 1849 and 1871 and that led German workers to embrace Marxist socialism. Yet this did not occur in Victorian Britain. Instead there arose, despite great inequalities and great neglect, a social consensus.

THE VICTORIAN SOCIAL CONSENSUS

Revolutionary Marxism failed to win over British workers. Between the revolutionary violence of the Chartists in 1842 and the Syndicalist strikes in 1910, a quiescent working class issued few threats to their masters. The middle classes even ceased pillorying the aristocracy. It would have dismayed Marx to hear many of the middle classes praise the aristocracy as England's natural rulers and to observe the workers emulating the individualism and self-reliance of the middle classes. A consensus did evolve, a harmony of classes, and though by no means without strains and hostilities, it did produce considerable agreement concerning the basic values that should underly society. It was as much a social miracle as the Victorian cornucopia was an economic one. The consensus, of course, owed a great debt to the economic miracle, since prosperity formed the most important of the four bulwarks on which the social edifice of Victorian England rested. The other three were the emerging welfare state, the Victorians' numerous philanthropies, and the culture of self-reliance and deference.

Of prosperity and the welfare state much has already been said. A country whose gross national product nearly doubled between 1851 and 1881 could please many, particularly if, while the rich were getting richer, the workers were getting richer too, with real wages rising 35 percent. That the residuum suffered is true, but that suffering was assuaged by the actions of a more active state and philanthropy.

The central government, which in the 1830s and 1840s began to take a more active role in lessening social evils, was of course modest in powers and imperfect in action. Its assiduous bureaucrats and zealous reformers, however, still pressed for further growth. The result was some local acts for town improvement, amending acts for factory, prison, and lunacy reforms, and larger grants to elementary schools—£840,000 in 1862 compared to £100,000 in 1847—but they fell far short of ending the widespread exploitation of child labor, the stench of filthy towns, or, given the growth of population, the inadequacy of English education. It was a time of inertness and apathy, one that Gladstone in 1860 pronounced "antireforming." Not a few town governments slowly improved sewers, streets, drains, and the supply of water, but mortality still remained high: by the age of 5 one-fourth of English children, mostly urban, had died. In 1866 Parliament finally passed a sanitation act compelling local authorities to use their powers to clean the towns, and in 1871 it created a Local Government Board empowered to superintend both local boards of health and poor law unions. The *Times* proclaimed the arrival of a new era in sanitation.

The year 1867, the year of the second Reform Act, ushered in a decade of social reform. The Workshop Act of 1866 banished children from all workshops of fifty or more workers, while the Factory Acts of 1874 and 1878 gave all factory workers a 56.5-hour week, Saturday afternoons off, more official holidays, and safer and cleaner factories. Parliament also repealed the Master and Servant Act, which had allowed masters to haul recalcitrant workers before justices of the peace, there to be fined, if not imprisoned. Parliament also passed the Trade Union Acts of 1871 and 1875. These acts recognized the legal status of unions, guaranteed their funds from civil suit, and assured them the right of peaceful picketing. The Local Government Board also allowed poor law unions to give outdoor relief to the able and urged them to improve the medical service on which so many workers depended. In 1861, 81 percent of hospital beds in England were in workhouses. The new welfare state—however limited—now wished to cure disease and help the poor, not just discipline them.

Parliament also decided that the state should supplement and increase voluntary efforts to educate children between the ages of 5 and 10. The Education Act of 1870 required that wherever there was no adequate school, local school boards should use taxes to provide an elementary school. The voluntary schools of the Church of England and Roman Catholics were not abolished. Parliament still voted them large grants, and so there were two systems, board schools based entirely on local taxes and fees and denominational schools based on fees, contributions, and grants from the central government. The religious instruction in the board schools could contain "no religious catechism or religious formulary," while the denominational schools that received grants had to excuse from religious instruction those pupils not of that faith and whose parents entered an objection. It was a compromise that still allowed the Church of England—heavily aided by state grants—to educate most children. It was a tepid compromise. Not until 1880 was schooling compulsory, not until 1891 free, and not until 1902 was there a system of public secondary education. In its dominant role over elementary education, as in its control of middle-class grammar schools and upper-class Etons and Oxfords, the Church not only strengthened the Anglican establishment's role but coopted into it not a few former Nonconformists, all of which increased an already powerful Anglican consensus. But it doomed many of the working class to a few years of wretched schooling and a life of isolation and separateness, ever more dependent in moments of distress on that philanthropy which formed the third bulwark of the Victorian social edifice.

Philanthropy in mid-Victorian England was massive in extent and bewildering in variety. Its dispensations exceeded those of public relief. Charities, whether endowed and managed by trustees or the work of voluntary societies, dabbled in everything. They erected water fountains in town squares, distributed Bibles to servant girls, ran the nation's lifeboat service, and founded homes for retired governesses. The 3,000 endowed schools, which ran from the poorest denominational school to the wealthiest college at Oxford, educated most English boys and girls. Some 600 charities in London sought to save people from infidelity, dirt, disease, squalor, and sin by means of churches, washhouses, hospitals, and Magdalene homes (of which there were thirty in London, designed for the rescue of prostitutes). Other societies sought to reform the law, improve prisons, build model homes, protect animals, and ensure the more pious observance of the Sabbath. Finally, philanthropy sought to relieve sheer destitution, whether by tuppence given to a beggar, almshouses provided for the aged, or the weekly grants of district visiting societies.

This generous outpouring of benevolence reached a frenetic pitch in the 1860s. Three facts explain that benevolence: urbanization, prosperity, and a profound distrust of government. Cities concentrate social evils, making them vivid and threatening. Starving urchins, pitiable old men, drunken prostitutes, courtyards stinking with excrement, and the threat of cholera cannot be lightly put aside. A wealthy city banker, who is also a sewer commissioner and opposes big government, would seek to solve the problem not by legislation but by contributing to orphanages, almshouses for the old, Magdalene homes, model housing schemes, and washhouses. An ample contribution would also assuage guilt over enormous wealth. "What luxury it is to do good," said one rich mid-Victorian manufacturer, as he dropped a £5 note into a collection for the poor.

The manufacturer added that it made him "feel good." No doubt it did. But did it *do* good? Sir Charles Trevelyan, a Secretary of the Treasury, declared that such charity encouraged deception and fraud and lured people from work. The charities of England were indeed haphazard, and much of their giving indiscriminate. To remedy these defects, mid-Victorian philanthropists founded, in 1869, the Charity Organization Society. Its aim was to impose reason and order on giving. It had three premises: that the individual was responsible for poverty, that indiscriminate relief corrupted the poor, and that state relief was indiscriminate. The depression of the mid-1880s showed these premises to be false. Philanthropy could not, in fact, handle economic depressions or urban squalor. For thirty years, for example, philanthropy built model houses, yet the resulting 25,000 units met the needs created by only six months of London's growth. Philanthropy could not solve fundamental problems, but its lavish relief did help ease the lot of the residuum. To gain a permanent share of the Victorian bounty, the answer was not begging or scavenging or workhouses but self-reliance.

Urban, capitalist, and voluntarist England provided many opportunities for advancement. It produced an array of institutions for the ambitious: mechanics institutes, athenaeums, temperance societies, improvement societies, and debating clubs. It also produced libraries, reading rooms, and book stalls, into which, like a springtime flood, poured inexpensive newspapers, magazines, and books. An increasingly literate people developed a voracious appetite for entertainment and instruction through the printed word. Self-improvement was the cry of the day. In an expanding economy, advancement went to the laborer who developed skills, the clerk who learned accounting, the self-educated attorney, the bricklayer turned builder, the spinner promoted to foreman. Self-reliance also led workers to form friendly societies and trade unions.

Four million workers belonged to friendly societies or burial societies. The burial societies guaranteed respectable funerals, the friendly societies both funerals and aid when one fell sick. The friendly societies also had banquets, ceremonies, and parades, all of which provided conviviality, fellowship, and pride. Some 700,000 found a similar fellowship in 1884 by joining cooperative stores owned and run by consumers themselves. Cooperative stores cultivated thrift, as did savings banks. By 1887 such banks had 1.6 million depositors, most from the upper levels of the working classes.

The workers also joined trade unions in order to increase their share of the national income. No social movement in Victorian England did more for the worker than the growth of trade unions. Their history runs back to the 1700s, but until the 1850s it was marked more by failure than success. After 1850 unions established themselves as a permanent part of the new industrial society. It was the skilled workers who led the way, particularly the carpenters and those mechanics, machinists, and millwrights the British call engineers. The worker in glass, tin, and iron also organized and, like the carpenters and engineers, concentrated on high wages, lower hours, avoiding strikes, building up a full treasury, and hiring skilled administrators. These administrators so favorably impressed the Royal Commission on Trade Unions of 1867 that it produced a fair report moderately favorable to unionism. The prosperous early 1870s led to more unions, but in the slump of the 1880s many collapsed. Not until the 1890s and after would the unskilled workers organize.

The leaders of the trade unions were men of self-reliance and independence. They were also polite and deferential. Deference allied with self-reliance created the Victorian formula for a social consensus. It was a formula that brought together businessmen and workers to form the basis of the Liberal party.

THE FORMATION OF THE LIBERAL PARTY

On June 6, 1859, 290 Whig, Peelite, Liberal, and Radical MPs met at Willis's Room, St. James Street, London. They cheered when Lord Palmerston, Prime Minister from 1855 to 1858, helped his rival Lord John Russell, Prime Minister from 1846 to 1851, onto the platform, for it signified the closing of the Whig ranks. They cheered again when William Ewart Gladstone's lieutenant, Sydney Herbert, and John Bright mounted the platform, a sign that the greatest of Peelites and the sturdiest of Radicals would serve under Palmerston, whose chauvinism and levity both detested. And they cheered when all four vowed to act together in a united Liberal party. Their cheers carried the hope that such a united party would end thirteen years of political confusion. That confusion which dominated English politics from 1846 to 1859 had its source in two political facts: first, that the governments of Lord Grey (1830–34), Lord Melbourne (1834–41), and Lord Russell (1846–51) did not represent the Whig party alone, but a heterogeneous coalition of Whigs, Radicals, and Liberals; and second that the Conservative party had split over the Corn Law. "Parties are at an end," said Charles Greville, secretary of the Privy Council, a remark reminiscent of Francis Place's judgment on parties during the years of George Canning.

But in history the clock can never be turned back. From 1832 to 1846 both the Conservatives and Liberals had begun, tentatively and gradually, to develop party organizations. In Parliament Grey and Melbourne had united Whigs, Reformers, and Radicals into a Parliamentary Liberal party based on the promise of reform, while Peel united the disparate Tories into a Parliamentary Conservative party based on the principles of modern conservatism, principles that would attract the middle classes. Statesmen had long known that governments fell without winning majorities and that majorities could not be won without parliamentary parties.

They also learned that party organization outside Parliament helped win general elections. In the 1830s and 1840s paid party agents coordinated the efforts of families, constituency associations, and paid local agents in the registration of voters and the management of elections. The Conservatives also established the Carlton Club in London and the Whig-Liberals, the Reform Club. Both also controlled newspapers in hopes of influencing opinion. The embryos of two national parties had come into being. These parties also reflected, however roughly, differing attitudes, traditions, and interests. For decades the electorate had seen Whig and Tory banners and heard Whig and Tory rhetoric. Whig and Tory families also had a long tradition of rivalry. Furthermore, England seemed increasingly divided between an old society based on a rural squirearchy, an old nobility, the Church of England, and the army and a new society based on the mercantile classes, an urban culture, Dissent, and the professions. Political confusion did mark the 1850s, but it was a confusion that occurred within an emerging party system.

Between 1846 and 1859 six ministries governed England. The two Conservative ones of 1852 and 1858, led by Lord Derby, were minority ministries, allowed to continue because of the internal quarrels of Whigs, Liberals, and Radicals. In 1852 the Conservatives won 290 seats, the Whig-Liberals 319, and the Peelites 45. Had the Peelites, who were good Conservatives before 1846, joined Lord Derby, who had abandoned all hope of bringing back a Corn Law, the two-party system would have resumed on traditional lines. The Peelites, who included the ablest of Peel's Conservative party, refused. They could not forgive those, led by Disraeli, who overthrew their cherished leader because he had carried the repeal of the Corn Law. They were also more interested in reform, if not of the condition of the poor, then certainly of those institutions that the Crimean War debacles revealed were urgently in need of improvement. The departure of the Peelites left a vacuum of talent in the party, a vacuum that allowed Disraeli to become the leader of the Conservatives in the Commons and, in 1852, the Chancellor of the Exchequer. Peelites such as Gladstone could not abide serving with a man they considered an unscrupulous adventurer. Political wounds, like those of jealous lovers, go deep and heal slowly.

Lord Derby became Prime Minister in 1852, in large part because the proud Peelites could no longer endure the mediocre administration of Lord John Russell. Their votes defeated Russell's government, as they did a year later Derby's. In December 1852 the only answer seemed to be a coalition of the ablest Whigs and the Peelites. The Peelite Lord Aberdeen presided over this ministry of all talents from December 1852 to February 1855. It governed efficiently at home, but abroad it not only blundered into the Crimean War but mismanaged it. The critics of those blunders brought down the Aberdeen coalition of Peelites, Whigs, and Liberals. Disraeli's remark, "the English do not love coalitions," had proved true.

But who was to rule? The answer—Lord Palmerston—astonished many. "An imposter, utterly exhausted, an old painted Pantaloon," exclaimed Disraeli. "A hoax," echoed Bright, who disliked his levity. Levity Palmerston did possess, but he was no imposter. As Lord Aberdeen's Home Secretary he displayed vigor and efficiency while his colleagues blundered. His triumph also delighted a public that saw him as the incarnation of John Bull. Palmerston ruled until February 1858, when Parliament turned him out by defeating a bill to punish English citizens involved in foreign conspiracies. In January an Italian, Orsini, had thrown a bomb at Napoleon III. The bomb did not kill Napoleon but led him to ask Palmerston to pass a law punishing any English citizen taking part in such plots. Palmerston obliged and his critics, more chauvinistic for once than he, defeated the bill and so the government. Derby, Disraeli, and the Conservatives returned for one year as a minority caretaker government. All was flux. Party lines seemed no longer to rest on ideology. Derby, for example, quite eagerly invited Palmerston to join the Conservatives, while Disraeli volunteered to allow Sir James Graham to lead the Commons if Gladstone would join the Conservatives. Gladstone, who detested Palmerston's jingoism, detested Disraeli's opportunism more. Hamletlike he wavered between liberalism and conservatism. John Bright, also hostile to Palmerston, wavered between radicalism and liberalism. With such strong-willed and independent-minded leaders, there could be no two-party system. It is for that reason that at Willis's Room on June 6, 1859, the 290 MPs cheered loudly when the leaders of the Whigs, Peelites, Liberals, and Radicals stepped onto the platform.

Gladstone joined the Liberals because of the Italian war and Palmerston's unequivocal support for Italian freedom against reactionary Austria. A passion for the freedom of European peoples and their emergence as independent nations had long inspired liberals. In 1859 that passion, along with the need to build a government to the left of Derby's and Disraeli's, led Whigs, Liberals, and Radicals to unite behind Palmerston. Gladstone's decision to join as Chancellor of the Exchequer, so crucial to Liberal unity, also reflected a shrewd note from Bright to Gladstone reminding him that Palmerston was 75 years old and that Gladstone would be his inevitable successor.

Palmerston led the reunited Liberal party from 1859 to 1865. Its record was undistinguished. Yet during these years, and during those just before and after, there grew up in the boroughs and counties of England Liberal attitudes and Liberal associations that were to be the vital cells of a national party. The growth of liberalism in English boroughs did not follow strict class lines. A study of 924 Rochdale voters in the elections of 1857 showed the following division:*

	Voting Liberal	*Voting Conservative*
Professional and commercial	88	106
Craftsmen	133	95
The drink trade	28	118
Capitalists	34	54
Retailers	167	102

After 1867, when most workers received the vote, they too divided their support in Rochdale between Liberals and Conservatives. But though capitalists and workers divided their votes, some differences are evident: craftsmen and retailers did vote Liberal more often than Conservative. A crucial fact, of course, was that the workers supported no Chartist or socialist third party. The proletariat disproved Marx's prediction of a class war. It either voted for a Liberal party that opposed state intervention in the economy and most measures to end inequality, or a Conservative party whose hierarchical and deferential principles led it to support property, authority, and the status quo whatever its inequalities. The main reason why artisans and shopkeepers voted Liberal and Conservative was mid-Victorian prosperity. "Prolonged prosperity," lamented Marx, "has demoralized the workers" and created a "bourgeois proletariat."

The more prosperous workers and small shopkeepers were, in fact, bourgeois in outlook: they were so because they did not view a master who paid good

* John R. Vincent, *The Formation of the Liberal Party.* (London: Constable, 1966).

wages and the rich who bought their goods as exploiters. Neither was inequality seen as unjust, as long as society rewarded the industrious, thrifty, and sober with promotions and their children with opportunities to advance. Sunday schools, chapels, mechanics institutes, day schools, the press, and workingclass societies all inculcated an individualistic ethic. The middle classes also enlisted artisans and petty shopkeepers—especially if they were Nonconformist—into societies for the abolition of slavery, for administrative reform, to abolish church rates, and for world peace.

Not all workers joined; many preferred the public house, the Church of England, and the Conservatives. Religion more than class determined political preference. The great expansion of the Nonconformist churches after 1850 strengthened the ranks of the Liberal party. Fewer in number but also strengthening the Liberals were those secularists whose moral earnestness and hatred of the Establishment was so akin to the Nonconformist outlook. In the 1860s these men of moral conviction and radical stance delighted in reading John Stuart Mill's *On Liberty*, published in 1859, John Bright's fiery attacks on the aristocracy, and William Gladstone's righteous indignation at the cruelties in Italian prisons and the errors of the Roman Church. Hardworking artisans and shopkeepers, self-made industrialists and professionals, crusading editors and earnest intellectuals, and the deeply religious of many faiths all found in liberalism an outlook that both denounced the exclusive privileges of the Tory establishment and promised to emerging groups equal rights and larger opportunities. These various and expanding groups also found in the forthright Gladstone a brilliant, powerful, eloquent, and manly spokesman. That he sometimes preferred hierarchy to equality and was far more passionate about a cheap, small government than about social reforms did not bother them; they only heard the thundering phrases that resounded through the press and the public halls of England. His devotion to truth, justice, liberty, and humanity made him the apotheosis of liberalism. Like a cult hero, he met the psychological needs of his supporters, one of which was the fulfillment of his promise to give the vote to all who were morally sound and politically safe. It was a promise that turned people to the question of parliamentary reform.

THE REFORM ACT OF 1867

Under Lord Palmerston's guidance, the Liberal party won the general election of 1865. Few of the 358 Liberal MPs returned in that election or of the 300 victorious Conservative MPs had campaigned for the reform of Parliament. Reform was not popular in 1865, and a year later it was still not the cry of the hour. Disraeli said reform would bring in "a horde of selfish and obscure mediocrities." In 1866 Conservatives and disaffected Liberals defeated Gladstone's moderate bill, one that would have reduced the borough franchise from £10 to £7 and that would have given the vote to those in the counties who rented households worth £14. It would have added only 156,000 voters to an electorate of a million.

One year later, the same Parliament passed a bill that gave the vote to 938,000 new voters. All urban householders would henceforth have the vote; democracy had arrived in urban England. It was not the gift of the Liberals but of the Conservatives, not of Gladstone but of Disraeli. It was a change as paradoxical as it was bizarre. It reflected the coming together of three forces: first, the growing demand for democracy; second, the frustrations of a Conservative party which had spent thirty years in the wilderness; and third, the brilliant parliamentary moves of the agile and astute Benjamin Disraeli.

Many people feared democracy, but others gradually came to demand it. During the age of Palmerston the skilled workers were busy forming trade unions and gaining better wages, and the unskilled workers remained deferential. The ruling classes, meanwhile, remained content with an electoral system in which one-fifth of the electorate, around 3 percent of the population, elected half of all MPs. They also had no objections to a system in which 246 of the 396 boroughs were associated with land, 51 of them still being family boroughs. From the Chartists' last demonstration in 1848 to the Hyde Park riots of 1867 there were no giant meetings demanding a wider franchise. But there were silent forces at work that would soon make such demands formidable; in a society of rising classes it was a question that would not go away.

From 1849 to 1866, five different cabinets discussed the question and on six occasions called for parliamentary reform. One of these came in 1858 from the Conservative government of Lord Derby and Disraeli. The bill was a conservative one and was easily defeated. But slowly the climate of opinion turned in favor of extending the franchise. Gladstone, for example, became a convert to reform when a deputation from the Amalgamated Society of Engineers came to the Treasury to ask about investing their funds in the Postal Savings Bank. Gladstone was amazed at their efficiency, thrift, and intelligence. The artisan class had indeed become impressive. They were not violent, unruly Chartists, but responsible, moderate, and educated working people. Some were poor law guardians and some improvement commissioners, others became town councilors or directors of friendly societies, cooperatives, and temperance associations. In 1866 Gladstone proposed to take the first step toward the fulfillment of his promise that all morally sound and politically safe Englishmen were morally entitled to vote.

But the proposal frightened many, even among the Liberals. One of them was Robert Lowe, a free trader and, on administrative and law issues, a Benthamite. To Lowe, the bill would open Parliament to the working class, the class most likely to contain "venality, ignorance, drunkenness . . . [and] impulsive, unreflecting and violent people." Twenty-four of Palmerston's followers agreed and joined the Conservatives to defeat Gladstone's bill. One of the Conservatives, Lord Cranborne, the future Lord Salisbury and prime minister, feared that if the working classes won power they would demand economic equality. Property itself, he believed, would be in danger. In July 1866 fear of democracy collided with demands for its first installment—and won.

That victory forced the resignation of the Liberal government on June 25 and brought in the Conservatives. The unresolved conflict between those who feared and those who demanded a wider franchise now became entangled with the frustrations and ambition of a party that had been in the minority for thirty years and out of office for twenty-eight. Could they really govern England? Were they not the party of stupidity? a party with no experienced administrators? After years in the wilderness, Lord Derby realized that if the Conservatives were to prove their mettle they must act decisively. He also knew that in 1866 agitation for reform had become great and probably irreversible. In July of 1866 a crowd of 20,000, defying a government prohibition, broke down the railings at Hyde Park and held a great meeting. In the provinces nearly a million people attended a half dozen gatherings and heard John Bright demand a wider franchise. Gladstone warned Disraeli and Lowe that "the great social forces which move onward in their might and majesty . . . are against you." In the north those social forces included the middle classes, who allied with the workers in Reform Unions to demand reform. The Reform League and the trade councils expressed more purely the voice of the proletariat. The trade councils were particularly aroused, because in the case of *Hornby* v. *Close* the court said unions were illegal combinations and their funds liable to suit.

In the spring and summer came the failure of the Overend and Gurney Bank, financial panic, and a cattle plague. By autumn Derby saw the tide of reform swell to a flood. A minority party that wished to gain a reputation for governing well could not run away. But how to meet the challenge? What of Lord Cranborne and those who feared democracy? Had not the Conservatives defeated Gladstone's bill for a £7 urban franchise? It was an embarrassing quandary. To meet it, Derby turned to Disraeli, who solved it, though not without an audacious combination of cleverness, deception, boldness, effrontery, opportunism, and courage. He also benefited from sheer muddle, confusion, and luck.

Between February 11 and March 18 Disraeli presented three plans to Parliament. The first consisted of resolutions so vague that it angered the House. The second bill was explicit. It reduced the urban franchise to £6, £1 below Gladstone's franchise. But it counterbalanced this gift to the workers by granting the upper classes some "fancy franchises" that gave the vote to all those who paid a direct tax of 20 shillings, or had £50 in savings, or who met a given educational qualification. It was much too conservative a bill to win a majority. Disraeli then produced another bill. It gave the vote to all borough householders who personally paid rates. Household suffrage was a favorite with Liberals and would gain their votes, votes Disraeli's minority government needed. But what of the Conservatives? To win them, Disraeli noted that two-thirds of all borough occupiers did not personally pay their rates, but had their landlords do so and would thus not gain the vote. (In reality compounders came to only 35 percent.) Disraeli also kept the fancy franchises. The bill was, in fact, a decidedly conservative and restrictive one and led many an MP to commit himself to it.

Then came the legerdemain. Few conjurors could rival Disraeli's tricks as he accepted amendment after amendment dismantling his fancy franchises and the requirement that householders pay their rates in person. One by one the conservative safeguards fell, leaving a democratic bill. The Liberals also carried an amendment abolishing forty-five small boroughs and transferring their seats to large towns and counties. Suddenly a bill emerged that increased the electorate from 717,000 to 2,200,000. Disraeli carried the Conservatives in part because in the drama of the moment: he made them winners. How exciting to outmaneuver Gladstone! How pleasant to outfox Bright! And how delightful to win the applause of the public! Most realized that reform was inevitable. If inevitable, why should not the Conservatives gain the credit? Social forces, as Gladstone warned, made reform only a matter of time. In 1867 riots, mass meetings, and an aroused middle class made the time very short. The fact that accidents had brought to power a Conservative party desperately needing a success and a Disraeli brilliantly adroit at Parliamentary maneuver helps to explain the paradox of a landed class giving the vote to urban workers. It was not the result of any belief in Tory democracy or any farsighted calculation that workers would vote Conservative. It was instead a result of those forces that promoted and those attitudes that defined Victorian liberalism: namely, a middle and working class that was increasingly more articulate, numerous, self-conscious, and powerful and the growing belief that others than those of the establishment should have larger opportunities and rights, including the right to share in government. These were the liberal forces behind the Reform Act of 1867, liberal forces that the clever Disraeli used to win a Conservative victory. It was his first victory in his long rivalry with Gladstone.

DISRAELI VERSUS GLADSTONE

In February 1868 ill health forced Lord Derby to resign from office and Disraeli, 64 years of age, became Prime Minister of England. Ten months later the Liberal party won the November elections and Lord John Russell resigned its leadership, whereupon Gladstone, 59 years of age, became Prime Minister. On reaching the highest political office in the land, a jubilant Disraeli exclaimed: "I have reached the top of the greasy pole." The solemn Gladstone, when selected, said he was "deeply unworthy," but confessed that "The Almighty seems to sustain and spare me for some purpose of his own."

The two statesmen were profoundly different. Disraeli, of Jewish ancestry but by upbringing an Anglican, was raised in cosmopolitan London, his father being a minor literary figure with inherited wealth and Voltairean ideas. The father sent little Ben to a Unitarian school, and after age 15 it was not a university but self-education. Gladstone's father was a Scottish Presbyterian Whig who made a fortune in shipping out of Liverpool. With his wealth he bought a rural estate, became an Anglican and Tory, and sent his son to Eton and Oxford, there to be groomed in High Church pieties, staunch Toryism, and Victorian

Benjamin Disraeli, Prime Minister, 1868, 1874–1880 (*Illustrated London News*).

seriousness. In 1832 the earnest Gladstone, 22 years of age, entered Parliament for a pocket borough. Two years later, at 24, Peel gave him office. Disraeli faced greater difficulties. He lost four elections, two of them as a Radical, before winning entry to Parliament in 1837. At 33 he could look back on many romantic escapades, the loss of a fortune gambling in stock, bankruptcy in the newspaper business, affairs with two married women, marriage to a rich widow many years older, and the publication of three novels. At literary salons his wit and charm won him more acclaim than he won from Peel or Parliament. Peel curtly refused him office, and Parliament hooted down his maiden speech. The rebuffs only made him more determined to fulfill a statement he made to Lord Melbourne in 1834, "I want to be Prime Minister."

Between 1846 and 1867 Disraeli succeeded in becoming the leading Conservative in the Commons, but not Prime Minister. As its leader, he defended, usually quite alone, the Conservative case against a battery of orators. Gladstone, whose eloquence and command of finance astonished his contemporaries, spent many of the same years resigning office because of moral positions whose subtlety

William Gladstone, Prime Minister, 1868–1874, 1880–1885, 1886, 1892–1894 (*National Portrait Gallery*).

bewildered his contemporaries. Finally, in 1859, on the issue of Italian freedom and out of aversion to Disraeli, Gladstone chose the Liberals.

Gladstone's first ministry ran from 1868 to 1874, Disraeli's second ministry from 1874 to 1880. Both were ministries of great achievement. Gladstone's measures were of three kinds—those that made institutions more efficient and fair, those that extended liberty and toleration, and those that expanded the role of government in society. An efficient not a larger government had been the highest ideal of the Peelites, of whom Gladstone had been the ablest. That government should be fair and open to all was an ideal of the Liberals, whom Gladstone now led. In his extension of civil service examinations, in his reorganization of the army and judiciary, and in his reform of the central government's control of local government, Gladstone carried forward these ideals.

The army badly needed reorganization. It was vast, confused, unfair, and on occasion, as in its floggings, cruel. The army sold commissions to wealthy aristocrats, often with scant regard to merit. Lord lieutenants nominated the officers of the county militia with the same preference for social class over military capacity. Men enlisted in the regular army for twenty-one years, and some six agencies quarreled over the management of that army. By Orders in Council and Acts of Parliament Edward Cardwell, Gladstone's Secretary for War and fellow Peelite, ended the purchase of commissions, abolished flogging in peacetime, placed the county militia under the war office, and made the Commander-in-Chief supreme over all land forces and directly answerable to the Secretary for War. He also reduced the term of enlistment to six years in the service and six years in reserve, organized regiments by territorial districts, and armed them with advanced Martin-Henry breech-loading rifles. These reforms laid the basis of the modern British army.

England's confused and overlapping central courts also needed reform. The English Judicature Act of 1873 did so by placing the functions of the medieval Queen's Bench, Exchequer, Common Pleas, and equity courts under one central court acting under a Supreme Court of Judicature. Centralization, modernization, and efficiency were the new watchwords, watchwords that also described the Local Government Act of 1871, which consolidated and expanded the principal central agencies that supervised local government into a powerful Local Government Board. Gladstone's government also insisted that all government appointments henceforth be by civil service examination. The Liberals were determined that the government be efficient, even if less aristocratic, and that society be one in which careers were open to the able, whatever their class.

The Liberals also passed measures to increase freedom. An Act of 1872, by giving the voters the secret ballot, freed them from the intimidation of landlords and employers at elections. The Trade Union Act of 1871 also freed workers from the intimidation of employers. It reversed the hated *Hornby* v. *Close* decision by declaring unions legal and giving their funds the same protection as that enjoyed by friendly societies. The government also disestablished the Protestant Church of Ireland and reduced the revenues from its wealth in land. Irish Catholics, nearly four-fifths of the population, were thus free from paying tithes to a wealthy church that claimed to be "national" but served only one-eighth of the population.

The Ballot, Trade Union, and Disestablishment acts increased the liberties of voters, workers, and Irish Catholics without expanding the role of government or encroaching on the Liberals' belief in *laissez-faire*. But in working for a more just and fair society, the Liberals also passed acts that brought greater government interference. In 1870 they passed an Education Act for the establishment of local board schools, and a Merchant Marine Act that insisted ships be safe. In 1870 they passed an act guaranteeing Irish tenant farmers fair compensation for improvements and empowering courts to revise exorbitant rents.

Better schools, safer ships, fairer rents, though it brought greater freedom for children, passengers, and tenants, also meant a larger government. To revise rents is undeniably an invasion of the rights of property. Gladstone confessed that at first he found the idea staggering. A man who tormented himself over principle, he could never square the circle of his strong belief in *laissez-faire* and the reality that the selfishness of landlords and shipowners needed to be checked by the state. At the promptings of a group of the Liberal party's strongest supporters, the Nonconformists, Gladstone also came to believe that drunkards needed to be checked. The Licensing Act of 1872 restricted the number of public houses and the hours they could be open. Philosophical consistency is seldom the attribute of a political party. In the Licensing Act the Liberal impulse to reform won out over their ideal of a society of free people, of people free to drink after 11 P.M. How to create a free society by government coercion remains to the present the great dilemma of Liberals.

Disraeli and the Conservatives after 1874 faced the same dilemma, but they did not anguish over it. In 1874 Disraeli was elated by his election triumph over Gladstone. The Commons now had 352 Conservatives, 243 Liberals, and 57 Irish. Disraeli assembled a Cabinet quite as able as Gladstone's in 1868 or as Peel's in 1841. Nearly forty years of Liberal dominance had passed. The Conservative party was again robust and it ruled for six years. It was a ministry that produced more social legislation than any other in the nineteenth century. It passed two Trade Union Acts very pleasing to the unions, one guaranteeing the right of peaceful picketing and the other ending the Master and Servant Act, which allowed the courts to treat workers as inferior servants. The government also drew up acts for promoting housing, securing pure food and drugs, strengthening the public health service, and better regulating friendly societies. In 1876 came acts for the cleansing of polluted rivers, the increased safety of merchant ships, and compulsory education. In 1878 Parliament passed a Factory Act consolidating earlier legislation. It was an impressive record, one reflective of a willingness to use government to achieve a fair and just society.

It was not, however, a reflection of a clearly defined Tory paternalism. Disraeli, to be sure, had expressed paternalistic ideas in his novels, and in his speeches of 1872 and 1873 had voiced concern over the social question. But when he met his cabinet in 1874 he had no plans for social reform. Most of the acts Parliament passed after 1874 reflected a nonpartisan, nonideological process. Royal commissions investigated social abuses, public opinion became aroused, civil servants then planned measures of reform, MPs clamored for action, and departmental ministers told the cabinet and prime minister that they must act. One such departmental minister was the Home Secretary, Robert Cross. A Lancashire businessman, a devotee of *laissez-faire*, and a pragmatic administrator of the first order, Cross, not Disraeli, was the true architect of most social reforms.

These reforms were also not very effective. *Laissez-faire* more than collectivist ideas defined them. The Artisan's Dwelling Act and the Pure Foods Acts, for example, were largely permissive. They simply allowed towns to build houses or to appoint an inspector of foods, they did not require it. Only ten of eighty-seven towns did anything about housing, and that was minimal. The Food and Drug Act was ineffective in many localities. Some of the reforms were also initiated to please vested interests. The government made education compulsory because the schools of the Anglican church needed pupils in order to get more fees.

The passage of social reform did not distinguish Liberals from Conservatives. Neither Gladstone nor Disraeli, neither Liberals nor Conservatives, favored fundamental social reforms or sought to use the powers of government to improve significantly the condition of the bottom fourth, the residuum. The parties did not divide on those issues. They divided instead on the Bulgarian massacres, on Ireland, and on Disraeli's style and Gladstone's morality.

In 1876 Turkey, which ruled over most of what is today Yugoslavia and Bulgaria, faced a series of rebellions by oppressed Christian subjects. In quelling one of these rebellions, they massacred 12,000 Bulgarians. Gladstone wrote an impassioned pamphlet denouncing this cruel atrocity; it sold 200,000 copies in three weeks. The situation festered, then reached a crisis stage when, in May 1877, Russia declared war on Turkey. Disraeli, who believed that Russia intervened in order to gain control of the Straits, supported Turkey. To Disraeli, as to Palmerston before him, a strong Turkey was vital to the balance of power in the Near East and to the defense of the British routes to India. His *realpolitik* and Gladstone's morality divided the English public as no other issue had since the Corn Law. In the spring of 1878 Disraeli attended the Congress of Berlin where, with Bismarck as the honest broker, Russia, Austria, Turkey, and Britain agreed to a treaty which made part of Bulgaria dependent on Russia, asked Austria to administer Bosnia and Herzegovina, and left the rest of Bulgaria to Turkey, though the central part was to have a Christian governor. Once more Britain propped up Turkey to check the Russian advance in the eastern Mediterranean.

To Gladstone, an independent Rumania, Bulgaria, and Serbia would provide a better check to Russia than would an unreformed and unreformable Turkey. Turkish oppression, moreover, was immoral, and Gladstone cared deeply about morality. It was a concern he expressed again and again in 1879 and 1880 in a series of public addresses as the candidate for Parliament from the Scottish constituency of Mid-Lothian. Thousands attended. All Scotland, said his daughter, wished to hear him. His speeches were read avidly in the press. His denunciations of evil were thundering, his idealism exalted, his morality pure, his praise of the working classes effusive, his righteous indignation at the cruel Turks awesome, and his strictures on the pleasure-loving upper ten thousand severe. Noble and eloquent were his appeals to truth and justice, but scant were his remarks about slums, unemployment, poverty, and sweated labor. Gladstone welded together Whig aristocrats, Anglican gentry, Nonconformist manufacturers, Radical shopkeepers, and the emerging working classes not by appeals for social reform, but by appeals to that which so many of them had in common: a record of improvement, an ethic of self-reliance, a serious religion, and beneath their deference, a hostility to a proud, exclusive, and privileged aristocracy.

Disraeli could also make stirring appeals, and they too helped weld together the Conservative party. In 1872 in the Crystal Palace he asked his audience whether they wished Britain to be "a great country, an imperial country." He called India the jewel of the Empire and in 1876 made Victoria its Empress. Disraeli realized that English nationalism was an intense emotion and that it increasingly expressed itself in a glorification of the Empire. In the Crystal Palace speech Disraeli also spoke warmly of the working classes, those classes enfranchised in part by the Conservatives in 1867. He spoke of his desire to improve their condition of life. Both Gladstone and Disraeli united their parties around the sentiments and aspirations of their supporters.

In the election of 1880 it appeared that Gladstone's lofty morality had greater appeal than Disraeli's glorification of Empire; the Liberals won 352 seats, the Conservatives 238, and the Irish Nationalists 62. It was a decisive defeat, though the result far more of economic depression than of oratory. In 1879 cheap North American and East European grain caused the collapse of the price for English grains, and English farmers suffered great losses. Unemployment also reached a record high. These harsh realities and the Conservatives' neglect of their party organization led to the Liberal victory.

A messianic Gladstone and a buoyant Liberal party governed England for the next six years. It was not a glorious period: at home economic depression kept the country discontented, abroad there were blunders. In 1881 at the battle of Majuba Hill the Boers of South Africa defeated the British and won independence for the Transvaal. Gladstone and the Cabinet disliked the burdens of Empire, yet in 1882 they stumbled into the occupation of Egypt. The government sent "Chinese" Gordon into the Sudan with inadequate forces. In 1885, after much procrastination about sending relief, the Mahdists massacred Gordon and his troops. Nothing went well, least of all with Ireland and the Irish MPs. Under the iron rule of Charles Stewart Parnell, Irish nationalist MPs repeatedly disrupted parliamentary business. In Ireland tenant farmers, ruined by cheap American grain, grew violent when evicted for inability to pay rents. They burned houses, murdered landlords, and rallied behind Parnell.

Parnell, born of an American mother, raised a Protestant, and educated at Cambridge, brought together the Home Rule League, founded in 1870, and the more active Irish Land League, formed in 1879. He was a commanding leader, totally dedicated to winning home rule for the Irish. The sustained agitation he led destroyed Gladstone's policy of pacification, and Gladstone yielded to those who wished to imprison him. But imprisoning Parnell solved nothing. Gladstone released him and then made a bargain called the Kilmainham "treaty." In it Gladstone agreed to an Arrears Bill by which 100,000 Irish tenants would be freed from debt; Parnell for his part agreed to work for peace. Things looked hopeful. Then in May 1882, Irish extremists murdered the new Chief

Secretary for Ireland, Lord Frederick Cavendish, and his undersecretary while they walked in Phoenix Park, Dublin. The murder discredited the Irish nationalists and the use of violent tactics. In the next three years Parnell dropped obstructionism in Parliament, built up a strong Irish National League, and used his eighty-six votes to bargain with each party for concessions. In June 1885 he brought down Gladstone's government by allying with the Conservatives, but won little.

After the elections of 1885, he used the eighty-six Irish nationalist votes to defeat the Conservatives and bring back Gladstone. Gladstone proposed a Home Rule Bill in 1886 that would establish an Irish Parliament and an Irish executive in Dublin. The Irish Parliament and executive would control domestic matters but not defense, foreign policy, or customs and excise taxes. Gladstone, who for years had championed the independence of Italians and Poles and other oppressed peoples, decided (unhappily with little consultation with others), that the Irish deserved home rule. Increasingly remote from his colleagues and the public's belief in a British Ireland, Gladstone found that ninety-two Liberals, including the Radical Joseph Chamberlain, were irreconcilable, a position that led most of the ninety-two to become Liberal Unionists and eventually Conservatives. Gladstone split the Liberal party that he had done so much to weld together. In 1846 he had watched Sir Robert Peel split the Conservative party; now he did the same to the Liberals. The result was that the Conservative party ruled England for seventeen of the next twenty years.

Political parties are powerful, elusive, and unpredictable entities. The Conservative party, closely tied to the upper classes, revering established institutions, respecting authority, and cherishing the wisdom of the past, has enjoyed a continuity that runs from the younger Pitt to Margaret Thatcher. The Liberal party, born in the 1850s and rising to greatness under Gladstone, faded away before the power of the Labor party in the twentieth century. It built its greatness on two elements, a coalition of all classes and an ideology that stressed individualism, equality of opportunity, justice, and morality. These ideals appealed to a mobile, prosperous, and earnestly religious society, but they were not as solid and enduring a basis for a party as one whose strength lay in tradition, established institutions, deference, and the support of an aristocracy and plutocracy whose interests were bound up with the status quo. When the class consciousness of the workers grew strong and assertive, the Liberal coalition fell apart; and when Victorian individualism and the evangelical conscience declined before the forces of collectivism and secularism, liberalism decayed. But before that day came, liberalism was to flourish once more.

FURTHER READING

BEST, GEOFFREY. *Mid-Victorian Britain, 1851–1875.* London: Weidenfeld and Nicolson, 1971. A social history of England which deals with family, birth, marriage, death, kinship, households, and does so with colorful and pungent insights.

BLAKE, ROBERT. *Disraeli.* New York: St. Martin's Press, 1967. The best life of Disraeli, written by one sympathetic to that complex statesman yet sharply critical of his inconsistencies and defects.

CHAMBERS, J. D. *The Workshop of the World, 1820–1880.* Oxford: Oxford University Press, 1961. A master at clear exposition, Chambers brilliantly describes the British economy when its manufacturers, traders, and bankers enjoyed a near monopoly in the world.

CROUZET, FRANCOIS. *The Victorian Economy.* New York: Columbia University Press, 1982. A straightforward analysis of the Victorian economy done by a Frenchman who takes nothing for granted, defines all institutions, and admirably simplifies some complex developments.

HANHAM, HARRY. *Elections and Party Management: Politics in the Time of Disraeli and Gladstone.* London: Longmans, 1959. A remarkably detailed and shrewd discussion of late Victorian politics, one that goes into the constituencies, examines the candidates, the voters, the parties, and the organizations.

HOBSBAWM, E. J. *Industry and Empire.* London: Penguin Books, 1968. An economic interpretation of the herculean strength of Victorian capitalism and its harsh impact on the less favored.

MAGNUS, PHILIP. *Gladstone.* London: Murray, 1954. A sympathetic portrait of the great commoner that is sound and discerning about his religious earnestness, political charisma, vast industry, and psychological complexity.

SEAMAN, L. B. *Victorian England.* London: Methuen, 1973. A brilliant evocation of an age, written with elegance and understanding and in a lively prose, hence a most illuminating and delightful history of England under Queen Victoria.

SMITH, PAUL. *Disraelian Conservatism and Social Reform.* London: Routledge and Kegan Paul, 1967. A searching and critical study of social reform under Disraeli, refreshingly candid in admitting that Disraeli did not push reforms vigorously and that they did not do much for the poor.

SOUTHGATE, DOUGLAS. *The Most English Minister: The Policies and Politics of Lord Palmerston.* London: Macmillan, 1966. The best one-volume study of Palmerston, one that follows Sir Charles Webster on foreign policy but is perceptive and original on Palmerston, the Tory who became Whig and ended Liberal.

VINCENT, JOHN. *The Formation of the Liberal Party.* London: Constable, 1966. A brilliant analysis of liberalism and the Liberal party, shrewd and realistic and abounding in sharp observations that undermine older myths.

Victorianism

24

The English people in the nineteenth century not only achieved economic supremacy, world empire, and political democracy, but created that formidable outlook called Victorianism. It was an outlook quite as important to their lives as universal suffrage or the marvels of industry. It was complex—sometimes earnest, vigorous, sober, and elevated, at other times smug, complacent, indulgent, and vulgar; sometimes tolerant, individualistic, and honest, at other times dogmatic, conformist, and hypocritical. It could passionately pursue the heroic and the beautiful, or settle into materialism and philistinism. But though complex and many-sided, the outlook of educated Victorians contained a core of moral seriousness that distinguished them from their easygoing ancestors of the eighteenth century. No one could mistake William Gladstone for Sir Robert Walpole, nor Alfred Lord Tennyson for James Boswell.

The moral seriousness of the Victorians owed its greatest debt to that evangelical revival that created Methodism, revived Dissent, and inspired nearly a third of the Church of England. The Evangelical revival was not, however, the only tributary of Victorian earnestness: the Puseys and Newmans of the High Church, the Arnolds and Kingsleys of the Broad Church, and secularists like John Stuart Mill and George Eliot were no less moral. Moral seriousness in fact did not decline with the erosion of theology since many found in morality its substitute. That a self-reliant morality had brought them economic success also heightened their seriousness. The growth of Victorianism in fact owed much to the interplay of economic and intellectual developments. Millions had advanced themselves through industry, thrift, sobriety, honesty, and decency. Virtues that work become the firm axioms of a moral code. They found the same code in the Bible they read in Methodist chapels, Congregational services, and Anglican schools. No book could begin to rival the Bible in its influence on the outlook of the Victorians. In 1837, when Victoria became Queen, it was the bedrock on which ordinary people based their view of the world. It told them that Christ was divine, suffered death on the cross for our sins, and rose from the dead. It told them that God created the earth in six days, that humankind began with Adam and Eve, and that there was a heaven and a hell. In 1901 when Victoria died, the Bible had lost its infallibility and religion its certainty, undermined by Victorian rationalism and prosperity and weakened by urban pleasures and greater longevity. It was for many a painful loss. Although rationalism undermined religion in many ways, the public saw as the chief culprit or hero all-conquering science. The triumphs of science were astonishing. Its conquests form one of the most dramatic events of the Victorian Age, one of the chief forces defining Victorianism.

THE CONQUESTS OF SCIENCE

The greatest book of Victorian science was Charles Darwin's *On the Origin of Species*. It was published in 1859 and aroused fierce controversy. Scandalous and irreligious, cried the theologians, it denies the Book of Genesis. Brilliant and revolutionary, proclaimed the scientists, it explains the origins of the earth's many species. It did in fact do both. It did explain the evolution of species, but it did so in terms of millions of years, not six days, and in terms of scientific laws, not God's will. For a great many people the book came as a shock, since they believed that in the beginning God created the vast variety of plant and animal life that lay before them. They had been raised on the Book of Genesis and Milton's *Paradise Lost*. In Milton they had read

The earth obey'd and straight
op'ning her fertile womb, teem'd at birth
in numerous living creatures, perfect forms
Limbed and full grown

Charles Darwin told them that God did not create "numerous living creatures . . . limbed and full grown." Eons ago, said Darwin, such creatures did not exist. What did exist were simpler organisms from whom "limbed and full grown" creatures later, at different places and times, evolved. Some "limbed and full grown" species even became extinct. Darwin, the son of a physician, was educated at the public school of Shrewsbury, and at Edinburgh and Cambridge universities. He had little formal training in biology, but he did, at Cambridge, take walks with his tutor to examine the nearby flora and fauna. These increased his enthusiasm for collecting and examining the works of nature that led him in 1831 to join the *H. M. Beagle*, a naval ship commissioned to make a five-year survey of the coastline of South America. It was an enthusiasm that led him to examine fossils in Argentina and turtles in the Galapagos islands off Ecuador. A centuries-old fossil, the Megatherium, both differed from and resembled the existing armadillos just as the turtles of one island differed from and resembled those of the other islands. Species were not only multitudinous in variety but were related, and some, like the Megatherium had died out. Perhaps species were not so immutable! As Darwin collected more and more fossils, he wondered if they did not form a gigantic succession of types, one that ran back millions of years. As he collected related but different species, he also wondered if their similarities did not reflect common ancestors and their differences adaptations to different environments.

In 1836 Darwin arrived in England loaded with specimens. He married his cousin, a member of the wealthy Wedgwood family, and retired to a country home in Kent. There he raised children, collected specimens, published voluminous works on barnacles and coral reefs, talked with breeders of animals and plants, and suffered from Chaga's disease, an illness he contracted on the Pampas. He also examined the embryos of various mammals and found some interesting resemblances. The embryos of apes, for example, resembled those of humans far more than those of dogs. Did not these resemblances suggest a chain of evolution? Also what of those rudimentary but useless organs that persisted in many species, organs like the shriveled wings of certain beetles. Were they not once used at a different stage of evolution? Embryological resemblances and vestigial organs, when combined with the fossil remains of extinct species and the variations of related living species, provided evidence suggesting that species had evolved over time.

But why? What mechanism explained these profound changes? Darwin speculated that those best able to survive the struggle for scarce food and the battle against predators led to the evolution of new species, an idea that took deeper roots in 1838 when he read Thomas Malthus's *Essay on Population*, with its argument that because population grew more rapidly than food supply, there ensued a constant struggle to survive. Darwin had long known that plants and animals of an area maintain a stable population even though they reproduce in excess of its food supply. Obviously some survived and some died. Darwin was also aware that no two offspring were ever exactly alike, that each had its own individual variation. Could it not be that variations determined who survived? Mammals, for example, with long necks could eat the leaves of tall trees. They could survive droughts, and so they, and not those with short necks, would have offspring. These offspring would have long necks and some, by the chance of mutation, necks a bit longer again and would survive in another drought. Ultimately the giraffe evolved. In a similar way gray rabbits that blended with the landscape and wolves fast afoot evolved because they could survive. The original occurrence of, for example, a longer neck or a grayer skin was a mere accident of inheritance, but the fact that they and their favored offspring survived and evolved into new species, that was determined by a universal law, the law of natural selection. Darwin had thus provided two theories, the theory of evolution, which stated that the astonishing plenitude and variety of life evolved slowly and at different times and places, and the theory of natural selection, which asserted that this evolution resulted from two factors, those chance varia-

Charles Darwin whose *Origin of Species* in 1859 shook the Victorians' picture of the world (Gernsheim Collection, The University of Texas at Austin, Humanities Research Center).

tions which defined inherited characteristics and the ability to survive by adapting well to a particular environment.

The first of these theories was not original. In 1789 Darwin's own grandfather, Erasmus, published *Botanic Garden*, a long poem celebrating evolution's varied creativity. From 1749 to 1822 French scientists—Buffon, Maupertuis, Lamarck—had expounded evolution in detail, and in 1844 a Scot, Robert Chambers, popularized evolutionary theory in a best seller, *Vestiges of Creation*, that caused a scandal. Geologists from James Hutton in 1785 to Charles Lyell in 1830 had shown that the earth's mountains and valleys, rivers and oceans, had resulted from slow, uniform evolutionary changes. Lyell also raised the key problems that puzzled Darwin, the problems of embryonic resemblances, the variation of related species, their different distribution and adaptation, and the existence of fossils of extinct species. Darwin read Lyell and Lamarck on the *Beagle*. When he examined fossils and turtles, he did so through mental lenses ground according to an evolutionary prescription.

The idea of evolution had, in fact, become commonplace. In history, philosophy, anthropology, archaeology, and the study of society, all was development, growth, progress. Had not humankind itself advanced by stages? The German philosopher Hegel viewed history as the evolution of the absolute spirit, and the German historian Herder viewed nations as biological species, and the results of unique organic developments. In England historians traced the evolution of institutions from Anglo-Saxon beginnings through medieval stages to their modern form. History gained a greater scope for evolution with the emergence of archaeology and anthropology. The archaeologist Henry Layard found from his excavations in the Near East that great civilizations could rise and fall. His *Nineveh*, published in 1848, sold 8,000 copies in the first year. Anthropologists wrote of the Old Stone Age, of the Bronze Age, and of humankind's long history. The discovery of the skull of the Neanderthal man in 1846 made it necessary to measure human history in hundreds of thousands of years. Modern society too advanced in stages. In France Auguste Comte said those stages were the religious, the metaphysical, and the positive; and in England Herbert Spencer, in his *Social Statics* of 1850, argued that society progressed according to evolutionary principles, one of which was the survival of the fittest. All these ideas appeared before Darwin's *Origin of Species*.

The climate of opinion in early Victorian England rested not only on new evolutionary assumptions but on old Newtonian ones. As sovereign as ever was the belief that universal laws lay behind all natural phenomena, that mechanical laws governed matter in motion throughout the universe, and that these laws could be measured empirically and stated mechanically. In 1808 Dalton, in 1839 Faraday, and in 1849 Joule astonished the learned world with such laws for gases, electricity, and heat. In 1843 John Stuart Mill, in his *Principles of Logic*, even asserted that universal laws of development could be found in history, thus fusing the nineteenth-century idea of evolution with the seventeenth-century idea of fixed, universal laws. Such a fusion lay behind Malthus's laws of population and helped define Darwin's frame of reference—and that of Alfred Wallace. In 1858 Wallace, a young naturalist, sent Darwin a paper in which he, independently of Darwin, outlined the theory of natural selection. Darwin gave him full credit for what was now a joint discovery. Wallace, like Darwin, lived in an intellectual world of evolutionary assumptions and Newtonian models. Like Darwin he grappled with the urgent problems posed by recent geological and biological discoveries. It was from these assumptions, from accumulated data, and from problems crying out for solution that Darwin's and Wallace's great discoveries came.

These discoveries presented a chilling view of creation. Even Darwin realized it: he told a friend that his first avowal that species were, after all, not immutable was like confessing to a murder. For that murder many theologians condemned him, and scientists denounced him. The astronomer John Herschel called natural selection "the law of higgeldy piggeldy"; the geologist Adam Sedgwick said parts of it were "utterly false"; and the anatomist Richard Owen declared it faulty in logic and inadequate in fact. There is today sufficient evidence to prove evolution and natural selection true, but there was not in 1859. Darwin's theory was a brilliant, educated guess, one that owed as much to his intuitions and to the climate of opinion as to the order inherent in the data he observed.

Darwin was also criticized for creating a mechanistic, materialistic, and meaningless world, a world partly the result of accident, partly the result of brutal determinism. But to a great extent such a world was the result of a phenomenon greater than Darwin—the triumph of Victorian science. Darwin was one among many great scientists. In physics James Joule, Lord Kelvin, and Clerk Maxwell made brilliant advances. Joule and Kelvin discovered the laws of the conservation of energy, including the gloomy second law of thermodynamics, which asserted that the ability of the world's energy to do work—heat a building or power an engine—declines steadily and inexorably. It was this law, not natural selection, that led the poet Alfred Lord Tennyson to become so pessimistic. But the physicists were impressive. Heat and energy could be treated mathematically, as could, because of the genius of Clerk Maxwell, electromagnetic induction. Maxwell explained the laws of energy in terms of a kinetic theory of matter—in terms of molecules and atoms—and he integrated heat, light waves, and electromagnetic force into a field theory of energy that replaced the old Newtonian emphasis

The Baptists' Metropolitan Tabernacle (*Aberdeen University*).

on mass. In discussing Faraday's experiments in electrolysis he even wrote of "molecules of electricity," molecules J. J. Thompson discovered in 1897 and called electrons. From Faraday and Joule to Clerk Maxwell and Thompson physicists quite equaled Darwin in discovering the laws of nature, laws many saw as no less mechanistic and materialistic.

Science made conquests on every front. Surgery became sophisticated and its findings helped psychologists to develop neuroanatomy, to study the functions of the brain, to locate the reflexes in the spinal cord. Anesthesiology developed. Doctors isolated the bacteria that caused disease and in some cases found cures. Medicine for the first time became scientific and effective. It was another triumph of science, as palpable and beneficial as the miraculous steam engines, machine tools, and advances in chemistry that lay behind England's remarkable industrial performance.

Scientific societies of every kind were formed. Amateurs swarmed over the countryside with butterfly nets and geological hammers. A literate public bought and read scores of scientific publications, recondite and popular. A rain of material goods flooded England, proving that people were the masters of nature, but it was accompanied by a stream of scientific fact that showed people were the slaves of nature's mechanical forces. Victorian science, like Janus, had two faces, and both were formidable. It was this conquering colossus that Victorian religion had to confront.

RELIGION AND DOUBT

When Queen Victoria died in 1901 the majority of her subjects were religious—many intensely so. During her long reign both the Church of England and the free churches greatly increased their membership. New sects were born or, like Mormonism, imported. Missionaries preached the Gospel throughout the world and in British slums. In 1844 some devout linen drapers began the Young Men's Christian Association, and in 1877 General William Booth founded the Salvation Army; today both are active throughout the world. The older churches grew in numbers. From 1861 to 1901, the Baptists tripled and the Congregationalists and Roman Catholics doubled their places of worship. One of these, the Baptist's Metropolitan Tabernacle could seat 6,000. Its great minister, the Reverend Charles Spurgeon preached, in his lifetime, to 10 million people and published sermons for 50 million to read. Sermons, in fact, vied with novels as the popular reading of the day. The great Methodist Hugh Price Hughes also won converts. His New Forward Movement of the 1890s had a phenomenal growth in London's West End. The Church of England held firm in its parishes and cathedrals, its schools and universities. Religious belief, though less literal-minded, was a fact of life for millions of late Victorians.

The majority of the working classes attended no church and had little faith, the result of poverty, ignorance, and neglect, not skeptical reason. Skeptical reason, of course, did make inroads into the educated classes. An expanding, all-encroaching rationalism had produced a self-conscious, earnest, aggressive agnosticism among a few of the educated. Far broader was a pervasive and expanding secularization of society, a secularization reflecting the growth of wealth, population, literacy, cities, longevity, pleasures, and, above all, knowledge of all kinds. It was a secularization that allowed a parallel advance of both religion and doubt, belief and unbelief. The conflicts that resulted and the battles that ensued created tensions and anxieties which many Victorians, however complacent about material success, could not avoid.

That an earnest Christian faith constitutes part of Victorianism is clear in the case of the growth of the Nonconformist conscience. During the nineteenth century the membership of the free churches more than doubled, rising from less than 1 million to more than 2 million. In 1800 their chapels were modest and few: in 1910 their sumptuous churches had seats for 8,788,285 worshippers, compared to the Church of England's 7,236,427. The Congregational and Baptist churches also became more unified, and the Methodists more democratic. For the Methodists, reform did not come easily. In 1849 the Reverend Jabez Bunting expelled three ministers as part of his despotic rule. A widespread revolt followed, one that lost the official Methodist Church 50,000 members, but that led to democratic reforms, a greater role for the laity and, in the next fifty years, 340,000 new members, the end of divisions, and a United Methodist Church of nearly 1 million.

The laity had long dominated the Congregational and Baptist churches. Disunity was their problem, one they solved through the creation of the Congregational Union and the Baptist Union, with their annual conferences, periodicals, and London offices. The establishment of the Free Church Council in 1892 also brought greater unity. Its president in 1897, Hugh Price Hughes, the gifted Methodist leader, said that its aim was to apply the law of Christ to every relation of human life. The free churches promoted what Hughes proudly called "the Nonconformist Conscience." It could be an awesome and puritanical force. It warred on all forms of sin and pursued all paths to virtue. It invaded homes, workshops, slums, suburbs, and politics. In the home it brought family prayer, Bible reading, Sundays devoted to piety, and the rule of a stern father. It won many workers to self-improvement and abstinence from alcohol. It provided the urban middle classes with a focus for their social and intellectual life. In an age without cinema or television, the chapel, its sermons, meetings, social gatherings, and charities, formed the center of the member's life. The Nonconformist conscience also inspired philanthropies. Among the most renowned of these were the many orphanages of the Methodist Dr. Barnardo, but there were many others. The free churches even established missions in the slums to reduce squalor and destitution. Hugh Price Hughes preached on "Christ the Social Reformer," while the Congregationalists shook the conscience of the nation in 1883 by publishing *The Bitter Outcry of Outcast London*.

The Nonconformist conscience was not shy about politics. It imposed its view of the law of Christ on town councils, formed peace societies, demanded that shops be closed on Sunday, called for fewer beer shops, and denounced corruption. The Nonconformist conscience ruled over Birmingham, Leeds, Leicester, Bradford, and many other towns. Nonconformists also sent MPs to Parliament and became the principal bulwark of the Liberal party. In 1890 they were powerful enough to destroy the career of Charles Stewart Parnell because he had committed adultery. As Lord Palmerston remarked, "In the long run English politics will follow the conscience of the Dissenters."

Lord Palmerston was only partly right. The Church of England remained a power. In 1870 and 1902 it defeated the Dissenters on the education question. The Education Acts of those two years preserved the Church of England's right to educate over half the pupils in elementary schools. For those parishioners long familiar with the Book of Common Prayer, Sunday matins and even-songs, and the celebration of village baptisms, marriages, and burials, the Church unobtrusively provided a moderate and satisfying faith. In its loud, very obtrusive quarrels, however, the Church may have helped to undermine that faith.

It was the quarrels that won the headlines. One of the most dramatic arose over gowns, candles, and incense. The ritualist controversy grew out of the tractarian movement's emphasis on the importance of sacraments. The tractarian movement began at Oxford, where John Henry Newman and others wrote tracts arguing that the Church of England was an apostolic and catholic church independent of state and Pope. Only its proper rituals could impart holiness to a sacrament involving the presence of Christ. The High Church clergy thus dressed in white surplices, made the communion table into an altar, decorated it with candles, and used incense and holy water in celebrating the eucharist. Romish! Popery! Idolatry! shouted the critics. In 1850 the shouts turned to riots. But even more damaging, these rituals drove many to leave the Church. Alarmed bishops ordered their end while a worried Parliament passed an act in 1874 declaring them illegal. Some High Churchmen defied the act and went to jail. That in turn made parishioners angry. Living in drab towns, they found in processions, rich vestments, altars, candles, and incense a beauty absent elsewhere in their lives. In more than one case they demanded the release of the jailed clergymen. Ritualism held its own as an important part of the Church of England.

There were also quarrels over doctrine in which the High Church again took the lead. In 1847 Henry Phillpotts, Bishop of Exeter, refused to allow an evangelical to hold a Church living because the clergyman did not recognize the full efficacy of baptism in regenerating souls. In the same year Phillpotts and a majority of the bishops opposed, though in vain, the appointment of a liberal Broad Churchman, Dr. Hampden, to the bishopric of Hereford. In 1851 the Bishop of London persuaded King's College to dismiss another Broad Churchman, Professor F. D. Maurice, for having doubts about eternal damnation. These quarrels increased the press's appetite for such scandals and did little in defense of religious faith. Some Anglican clergymen could be stupidly dogmatic:

in a Suffolk village one clergyman refused to bury a Dissenter's infant because it had not been baptized. The village was in an uproar, and the clergyman retreated behind a 9-foot wall he had built around his garden.

Although damaging quarrels hurt, the Church grew silently stronger. Absenteeism, pluralism, and gross inequalities of income were reduced. Parliament from 1828 to 1900 also gave the Dissenters greater equality. At midcentury they won the right to bury their own in the parish cemetery, attend Oxford and Cambridge, and be excused from Church rates. The Church ceased to appear oppressive. It also ceased to be the haven of the indolent younger sons of the aristocracy and gentry. The late Victorian clergy, from curate to bishop, became more professional. They were better trained in theology and more dedicated to parish work. Oxford and Cambridge no longer had a monopoly of their education; diocesan theological colleges now graduated conscientious priests.

The new breed of clergy also penetrated the urban wastelands to preach that moderate Christian socialism which Charles Kingsley and Frederick Maurice worked for in 1850. In 1877 Stuart Headlam established the Guild of St. Matthew and in 1884 Samuel Barnett founded Toynbee Hall, both in the slums of London's East End and both dedicated to the alleviation of poverty. In his periodical, *The Christian Reformer*, Headlam argued for a more just society, a plea taken up at a higher level in 1889 by the Christian Social Union, an Oxford-based body that included 1,436 clergymen. Its president was Brooke Westcott, Oxford's renowned theologian. Westcott had attended Trinity College, Cambridge, with Fenton Hort and Joseph Lightfoot, two theologians who, with Westcott, brought to the Church of England a learned and modern theology, one combining biblical scholarship with the social gospel. It was a social gospel not greatly different from that of the Methodist the Rev. Hugh Price Hughes and the Baptist the Rev. John Clifford, a gospel based more on the morality of the sermon on the mount than on the theology of St. Paul's epistles, a morality reflecting that secularization that even within the church could erode dogma.

All was also not well with the working class and their unbelief. It took two forms, the age-old ignorance and indifference of the working class and the new skepticism of the Victorian intelligentsia. The problem of a near-pagan working class was a persistent one. A great gulf divided that class from the Church of England. To the poor and weak, the Church represented the wealthy and powerful. The clergy became magistrates and poor law guardians and sent the erring and negligent to jails and workhouses. Many clergymen also seemed more assiduous in collecting pew rents, church rates, burial fees, and tithes than in ministering to the poor. And bishops of enormous wealth and aristocratic friends seemed always to oppose reform. It was still the Church of the wealthy and privileged. The elite of the Congregational and Baptist churches were also the wealthy and privileged, though in a society of a lesser order, that of the manufacturing towns. The theology of these Puritan churches was often too narrow, cold, and dogmatic for the workers. The simple, emotional appeal of the Methodists best met the religious needs of that class, but chiefly of those on the way up. Hugh Price Hughes's greatest successes came in London's West End, not the East End.

The second evangelical revival that occurred between 1850 and 1880 came in an era of prosperity. For many persons, religious belief was a reflection of prosperity. Membership in the Methodist Church fell during depressions and rose with prosperity. A religion that preached discipline, industry, and abstinence proved socially and psychologically functional. Its Puritan ethic led to better jobs for laborers and greater prosperity for businesses. For those who arrived in the middle class, it provided a formula for respectability. Their cleanliness and sobriety would distinguish them from the ill-kempt and drunken masses. Methodism became bourgeois. "It is the rarest thing," said the *Methodist Times* in 1892, "to find a genuine representative working man on any of the governing bodies of the Church." East End missions and sermons on Christ as a social reformer proved too little to bridge the gulf that divided the workers from the people of property in the free churches and those of privilege in the Church of England.

It is a fact that helps explain the success of William Booth's Salvation Army and the labor churches. Booth's army penetrated the slums, established outposts there, and won the desolate by offering not only edifying sermons but soup, beds, and colorful ceremonies where bands in uniforms played hymns with a music hall robustness. The labor churches gave the intelligent artisan socialist doctrines, ethical ideas, fellowship, and no theology. The Salvation Army, because of its soup and beds, has held its own. The labor churches proved ephemeral. The more secular-minded workers found fellowship in cycling and football clubs, pleasure in music halls and public houses, and socialism in the Labour party and trade unions. British socialism, though, had an ethical seriousness that owed much to the ideals of the free churches. The result was that British workers never developed the strong anticlericalism of the European working classes. But neither did most of them believe in the divinity of Christ or in heaven and hell.

Some of the upper classes also ceased to believe in the literal truth of the Christian story. By 1900 agnosticism threatened to become the new orthodoxy among the Victorian intelligentsia. It, along with a general indifference to religion in an age of prosperity, led to a decline in churchgoing among the middle and upper classes after 1886. Skepticism became pervasive. It reflected three powerful intellectual forces: the appeal to reason, the ethical imperatives of a serious Christianity, and the advance of knowledge on all fronts.

The first of these forces, the appeal to reason, was an old one. In the medieval era it informed the thought of William of Ockham. In the Renaissance it inspired Francis Bacon's dreams of the advance of learning through the empirical sciences. In the eighteenth century David Hume showed how the appeal to reason could lead to religious doubt. In the Middle Ages an immovable faith held reason tightly in check, while in the Renaissance the doctrine that faith and reason had separate spheres sheltered faith. But at the end of the eighteenth century Thomas Paine, Joseph Priestley, and Jeremy Bentham denied faith its sheltered sphere. That aggressive rationalism grew stronger in the nineteenth century. Philosophers became ever more critical. They questioned everything and bowed to no authority. John Stuart Mill wrote of the new disposition to demand the why of everything. In 1843 he published the *Principles of Logic*, an impressive demonstration that knowledge arises from careful observation and exact reasoning and not from divine revelation, historical or mystical. He also presented the argument of the French philosopher Auguste Comte that an age of science had replaced the ages of religion and of metaphysics. Others expounded the rationalism of the German idealists, Immanuel Kant and George Frederick Hegel, or reprinted the great works of the French Enlightenment. The river of rationalist thought had many tributaries.

Many religious persons could accept this appeal to reason by accepting Bacon's separation of faith and reason. There were, however, Christians whose earnest convictions led them to condemn such a separation as Latitudinarian gloss. They were often children of evangelicals, from whom they imbibed an earnest devotion to such ideals as justice and compassion, which they could not square with the old theology. Two young evangelicals who worried over that reconciliation in the 1840s were the novelist Mary Ann Evans, soon to be known as George Eliot, and James Anthony Froude, later the historian of Tudor England. Froude's doubts led in 1849 to the publication of *The Nemesis of Faith*, a book that shocked the faithful and was publicly burned at Oxford. What bothered Eliot and Froude and many others was the injustice of the atonement. Was it just that a blameless Jesus should suffer the pains of crucifixion? Was it just that deeply sinful humans, because of that sacrifice, should go to heaven? And how just is a God who sends the virtuous to hell because time, place, and accident kept them from conversion? Justification by faith fell far short of the compassionate morality taught in the Sermon on the Mount.

Historical research also threw doubts on Christianity. George Eliot met that fact in 1846 while translating David Frederick Strauss's *Life of Jesus*. Strauss applied the exacting standards of historical scholarship to the four gospels. He found their miracles unsupported by evidence, their account of Christ's life inconsistent, and their story of the resurrection a myth. The book caused a revolution in nineteenth-century religious thought, a revolution which widened in 1862 when the French novelist Ernest Renan published his popular *Life of Jesus*. Educated Victorians also read about primitive cultures and ancient civilizations, the newest discoveries of geology and biology, and scholarly studies of the religions of the world. This vast outpouring of knowledge, this expansion of historical time and geographical space, widened their mental horizons. Paleolithic ages and ancient societies dwarfed the events of Galilee. Probing reason, serious morality, and advancing knowledge raised doubts at every level about the literal truth of the Christian story.

In quite a few cases, these developments led to atheism or agnosticism.

For Darwin faith was lost privately and quietly; for others, like T. H. Huxley and Charles Bradlaugh, loudly and publicly. Huxley in fact coined the word "agnostic" to apply to those who claimed they did not know whether God did or did not exist. Charles Bradlaugh, founder of the National Secular Society of 1860, was less modest when he told the House of Commons that its oath was not binding on him because he was an athiest. A deeply religious and outraged Commons refused to admit him. An unseemly quarrel, it led Bradlaugh and fellow atheists to organize local societies where with religious intensity they denounced religion. Bradlaugh's societies soon declined, but not agnosticism. In the 1830s the twelve most promising undergraduates at Cambridge became priests in the Church of England; in the 1880s the twelve most promising became agnostics. The same change, though not so complete, occurred throughout the intellectual world.

But not all of the intelligentsia became agnostics. Many sought instead to replace their lost faith in the Resurrection by a broader, more philosophical faith, one based on morality or intuition or the course of history. The historian Thomas Carlyle, for example, found God in the course of world history. History and its heroes, men like Dante, Luther, and Cromwell, revealed the moral law of God, a law which punished the wicked and rewarded the virtuous. Faith consisted in saying an everlasting yes to the spiritual and moral laws that, behind the superficial and ephemeral world of the senses, controlled the destiny of peoples. In *Sartor Resartus*, in *The French Revolution*, and in *Heroes and Hero Worship*, all published between 1833 and 1841, he startled the Victorians with his erudition, his powerful style, and his repeated assertion that history, reason, nature, and the moral law all reveal an omnipresent God. His resounding affirmation of a divine and moral universe had a profound impact on the art critic John Ruskin, on the novelist Charles Kingsley, and on many others.

The liberal Christianity of Thomas Arnold likewise had a profound impact on hundreds of Rugby boys. Religious truth, he told them, does not lie in theology but "in a certain moral state. . . ." Arnold represented the Broad Church movement, one that sought to place Christianity on a rational and liberal basis. In 1860 seven Broad Churchmen at Oxford carried that task further by publishing *Essays and Reviews*. By giving the Christian story a symbolic and metaphorical interpretation, they reconciled Christianity with biblical criticism and the new geology. The orthodox condemned it as rank heresy, but it was an outlook that prevailed.

Carlyle's God in history and Thomas Arnold's ethical Christianity did not allay everyone's doubts. The young Alfred Tennyson in 1851 published *In Memoriam* and in 1867 Thomas Arnold's son Matthew published *Dover Beach*. Both poems reflect the search for religious meaning in a world of doubt. Tennyson wrote of "doubts and fears," the "Godless deep," and of voices that say "Believe no more." Arnold laments the ebbing away of "the sea of faith," and the onrush of "winds of doubt." But both affirm, as did George Eliot and J. S. Mill that there is a religious meaning to life. Tennyson and Arnold believed in transcendent powers beyond themselves; Eliot and Mill, in the ethics of Jesus as a religion of humanity.

The poet's intuition of transcendent powers, Carlyle's God in history, the liberal's belief that the ethics of Jesus is the essence of Christianity—these and their many variations created a religious modernism which, along with the continued vigor of traditional faiths, made the nineteenth century far more religious than the centuries which preceded or followed it. But it could not last. The modernist had, to be sure, reconciled science and reason with religion, but by abandoning a belief in the revelations central to Christianity. The traditionalists kept those revelations, but only by denying some of the most cogent arguments of science. And both modernists and traditionalists faced the growth of that prosperity, greater longevity, and exciting urban world of pleasure that distracted people from thinking of the next life. But that event belongs to the twentieth century. In the reign of Queen Victoria, religious belief in all its forms never declined so much that it ceased to be the most important force defining the morals and mores of her majesty's subjects.

MORALS AND MORES

A serious morality lay at the center of Victorianism. It defined both the character of countless individuals and the mores that ruled society. It produced an intense purposefulness that was far removed from the relaxed urbanity of the eighteenth century. Preached by ministers, extolled by fathers, taught by schoolmasters, proclaimed by judges, and praised by poets, this seriousness permeated all classes. It had its center in the middle classes and in evangelical religions, but it radiated upward to the aristocracy and downward to the working classes. It informed the outlook of all religious faiths and most of the philosophies, religious or agnostic.

It did not, of course, touch everyone. There were still peers devoted to pleasure, manufacturers who worshipped Mammon, laborers indifferent to moral principles, and beggars, pickpockets, and prostitutes, driven by poverty into the vast Victorian underworld. Victorian society was too complex and Queen Victoria's reign too long to have produced only one morality or one set of social mores. There were many moralities (and immoralities) and various rules and customs. Yet from about 1840 to 1880 certain ethical values and certain social ideals came together to form the strenuous moral code of the mid-Victorians.

That code had strong roots in the evangelical family, the reformed public schools, and a more serious Oxford and Cambridge. To many Victorians, the family was sacred. It was the first and most crucial school of character. With its prayers, Bible reading, and severe discipline, it formed a far more closely knit unit than the looser unregulated early eighteenth-century home. Its typical father insisted on a stern and pious puritanism, one that led some, like William

"Family Prayers," as painted by the novelist Samuel Butler (*The Library, St. John's College, Cambridge University*).

Wilberforce, to refuse to send their sons to public schools known more for bullying, fighting, flogging, and sexual looseness than for learning and religion, in both of which they were deficient. Great was the relief among serious fathers when Thomas Arnold at Rugby, C. J. Vaughan at Harrow, and Christopher Wordsworth at Winchester replaced, as best they could, the rote teaching of Greek and Latin, the riotous violence and bullying, the neglect of religion, and the corruptions of drink and sex with a broader more demanding curriculum, an improved discipline, daily chapel, strict morals, and an intense participation in soccer, cricket, rowing, boxing, and athletics. Long edifying sermons, the orations of Cicero, and the history of England's past joined with a hierarchical system in which older students commanded and bullied the younger to inculcate in all the pervasive and unquestioning conservatism of the privileged. These expensive Anglican boarding schools, and scores of imitators (a few nonconformist), thus became the training ground of the Establishment's future governing class, a class that the sons of merchants and manufacturers would join. By 1902 there were 64 such schools, schools dedicated to the formation of a manly, godly, Christian character.

These new ideas won great popularity in a novel by Thomas Hughes, one of Thomas Arnold's prize students, entitled *Tom Brown's School Days*. First pub-

At the great public schools the young of the wealthy learned Greek, Latin, and Victorian manliness (*Illustrated London News*).

lished in 1857 it became a classic rivaled only by Frederic Farrar's *Eric or Little by Little*. Farrar taught at Harrow. Both books celebrated a morality based on a Christian and patriotic manliness and a boyish, high-spirited, but pure, zest for life and success. In more mature form these ideals won out at Oxford and Cambridge, in simpler form at the grammar schools that sought to emulate the public schools in pursuit of godliness and good learning. In these various schools and universities, the upper and upper middle classes came together to form the governing class.

A morality not too dissimilar arose among the producing classes. It found expression among apprentices to newspaper editors, booksellers, and printers and found its centers in Sunday schools, mechanics' institutes, and improvement societies, centers where the more ambitious sons of the middle and artisan classes sought self-improvement. In the printing offices of Mr. Walker's *Preston Guardian*, for example, three young apprentices learned the skills, disciplines, and self-reliant morality that led them to become editors of the *Liverpool Mercury*, *Preston Pilot*, and *Leeds Mercury*. Edward Baines, editor of the *Leeds Mercury*, attended the local grammar school (the same school Wordsworth attended earlier), joined a reasoning society "to improve the mind," read Benjamin Franklin, and attended the Congregational Church. In Baines enlightened ideas combined with evangelical piety, just as they did with the Scottish publishers Robert and William Cham-

At new elementary schools young maidens learned to read, write, sew, and always act properly and morally (*Bettmann Archives/BBC Hulton*).

bers. The Chambers brothers, by dint of hard work and intelligence, rose from being apprentices to an Edinburgh bookseller to become publishers and editors of *Chambers Edinburgh Journal*, which was widely read throughout Britain. They filled it with editorials on "Self Helpfulness," "Right Conduct," "Savings Banks," and "Chastity."

In 1859 another self-made Scot, Samuel Smiles, celebrated the same virtues in *Self Help*, one of the age's most popular books. By 1900 it had sold a quarter of a million copies. By 1900 Smiles had also published *Character*, *Thrift*, *Duty* and a five-volume *Lives of the Engineers*. For Smiles the engineers were the heroes of Victorian England, the apotheosis of industry, intelligence, discipline, and work. Smiles, like Arnold, was a believer in self-control and discipline. Humans were not naturally good, but lazy and sensuous. The first step was to resist these proclivities. The second was to form habits of thrift, punctuality, industry, cleanliness, sobriety, modesty, and deference. These habits, once learned and made a matter of discipline, became as deeply rooted in the middle classes as Christian manliness did in the upper classes. Both were different but functional expressions of a Puritan morality.

The same morality permeated part of the working class, what the Victorians called the respectable part. Victorian morality could find a home in a weaver's cottage or a farmer's kitchen quite as well as in Arnold's Rugby or Walker's printing office. It was indeed in a weaver's cottage in Preston that young Joseph Livesley found that the declining trade of weaving meant poverty and hunger and that the only escape was through self-reliance, thrift, and canniness. His canniness was crucial. It led to small profits selling cheese, much frugality and saving, larger profits, and success, and not only as a cheese wholesaler but as editor of the *Moral Reformer*, a journal preaching total abstinence. By 1862 Livesley and many like him had created a million teetotalers.

The larger part of the Victorian working classes achieved a morality and respectability not unlike that which the middle classes preached at them, but for reasons usually very much their own. Their culture was also centered on the home and on a closely knit nuclear family in which the father, often with a strap, was an absolute sovereign, a family in which from eldest to youngest and from male to female hierarchy ruled. The home of course was small—if very poor confined to a one-room-up, one-room-down, rowhouse, if better off to a two-up and two-down rowhouse, in both houses all rooms small. For a family of six or seven (by 1900 five or six) the closeness of quarters demanded fixed rules of behavior—of order, sobriety, cleanliness, sharing, cooperation, respect—rules also needed because of the barely sufficient resources on which they lived. Some of the working class, the idle and drunken or the disadvantaged and neglected, fell below the great divide distinguishing the degraded from the respectable, but for the more than four in five who lived outside the slums and had jobs, the family and the neighborhood with its games and traditions molded a culture full of affection, caring, tolerance, and independence, one however in no way radical since all knew their proper sphere.

The strength and pervasiveness of Victorian morality arose from its usefulness. Economically, it brought success and social advance; intellectually, it buttressed religion and assuaged doubt; psychologically, it brought order, cleanliness, and chasteness to a world of drunkenness, dirt, and profligacy. In an economy of unprecedented growth Victorian virtues led to jobs and prosperity. Men of steady employment, said the journalist Henry Mayhew in 1849, were the "enlightened, provident, and sober." Most were married and their homes tidy. They belonged to trade societies that assisted the old and disabled. Many among them loved manly sports like cricket. Thomas Arnold never tired of teaching manliness. It would enable young men to succeed in a civil service about to reform itself, in the expanding professions, in the world of commerce, and in the Empire.

For England's million servants in 1851 (the second largest occupation after farm laborers) sobriety, industriousness, modesty, deference, and neatness were not merely attractive but absolutely necessary. For many of the servant girls from the countryside, moral training began with the strict regimen of the farmer's kitchen, a regimen as exacting as any public school, and ended under the sway of a mistress to whom Mrs. Beeton's *Book of Household Management* was the gospel. The gospel included sixty-four pages on the duties of servants.

The emphasis on self-control, discipline, prudence, and a chaste life also meant a psychologically more secure world. The unreformed public schools and the London slums were miserable places. The schools had brawls and riots, bullying and fagging, and sexual play; the slums had violence and drunkenness, dirt and crime, prostitution and incest. Moralities arise in part from psychological revulsion at the deficient mores of an earlier age. The "steady, sober chap" brought peace to the drunkard's child. At Buckingham Palace Queen Victoria found in her husband, the steady, sober Prince Albert, and in a life of respectability a happiness not present when, as a child, she suffered in the world of her wicked, adulterous uncles. The drunkard's child, the adulterer's niece, the public school boy revolted by bullying and homosexuality, and the lodger in the teetotaler's home all found happiness in an ordered, disciplined, and moral life. The twentieth century, which revolted against the extreme prudery and priggishness of the late Victorians, often forgets the moral squalor that led to an earnest and serious puritanism.

Victorian society benefited in many ways from its exacting morality. Not only did its gospel of work and achievement produce an economic cornucopia and a prodigious outpouring of learning, but its insistence on honesty brought high standards of rectitude to public life, its cultivation of the independent mind led to a sturdy individualism, and its call for higher ideals than self led to a philanthropy and statesmanship that helped millions. Even its harsh discipline and stern manliness produced a stoicism, self-control, and sense of duty that in workers and soldiers as well as in industrialists and proconsuls, strengthened Britain and its Empire. Neither was it all that grim and dour an outlook. There were countless families for whom a tidy hearth, a good library, arduous labor, genuine Christian affection, and a Sabbath of hymns and prayers brought a deep and joyful contentment.

But there was another side to the coin. Victorian morality could also hurt. It was often hard, insensitive, and too exacting, three traits that produced much pain. It was certainly hard on disobedient children and erring adults. This stern code was cruel when carried to extremes or when made part of institutional life. The grim workhouse was far too severe a punishment for being destitute. The treadwheel, solitary confinement, and reduced diets brought far more pain than reform in England's prisons. The flogging of juvenile delinquents did no better. Flogging was a favorite form of punishment. Magistrates ordered it for young poachers and military officers for the insubordinate. Parents birched rebellious children, as did schoolmasters—Eton's John Keate flogged ten boys a day. There was in the Victorians a streak of cruelty dramatic in the case of flogging and fifty-round, bare-knuckled prize fights, coldly quiet in the severe rules of the workhouse, the repressive codes of the family, and men's insensitivity toward women.

Victorian men considered women inferior and conditioned them to believe it. John Ruskin, the greatest art critic of the age, declared that men were doers, creators, discoverers; women were created for "sweet ordering, arrangement,"

With bare knuckles, one either hits the opponent's body and not his head or breaks one's hands—hence the astonishing feat of fifty-round fights (*Bettman Archives/BBC Hulton*).

and praise. Alfred Tennyson, the greatest poet of the age, depicted in his poem "Locksley Hall" a heroine praiseworthy because utterly obedient to a boorish husband. And William Gladstone, the great Prime Minister, opposed granting women the vote because it would damage their purity. Sara Ellis, in *Letters to the Mothers and Daughters of England*, advised them to "be content to be inferior to men" and to view good men as approaching "the nature and capacity of angels." Learned scientists told them feminine cells had a unique metabolism that made women passive; learned doctors told them that during menstruation they tended to be listless and cruel and that if they became doctors they would endanger their ability to have children.

At midcentury Victorian wives had also to suffer the tyranny of husbands. Until the Married Women's Property Acts of 1874 and 1882, whatever personal property a woman brought to a marriage and whatever she earned subsequently belonged absolutely to her husband. Absolute too was his custody over their children if a separation and his sway over his wife as to whether there should be a divorce—or whether she could even leave home.

An awakened feminist movement, inspired by J. S. Mill's *On the Subjection of Women* of 1869 and by such feminist periodicals as the *English Woman's Review* and led by the intrepid Josephine Butler and the irrepressible Emmeline Pankhurst, succeeded in giving women rights over their own property and reducing the husband's power over divorce and the custody of children. Other acts ended the husband's right to imprison or confine wives.

Acts that lessened legal tyranny did not, for upper-class women, lessen the tyranny of the empty life as a perfect lady. In a house full of nurses and domestics, a perfect lady was not to sully her crinoline in housekeeping or fray her delicate nerves with child raising. For many a job was also unthinkable, though not charitable work. In 1893 over half a million women did philanthropic work, work of all kinds, work in local coal, clothing, and blanket clubs; in the town medical dispensaries and hospitals; in church choirs, bazaars, and visiting societies; in great national causes of reform and world missionary organizations; or in the village caring for stray cats and dogs. Nor was philanthropy the only activity: some worked in the emerging political parties, others as local officials. Many, to be sure, endured long hours of empty leisure, but the number of claustrophobic housewives anonymously imprisoned in an impersonal suburb was the fate of women far more often after than before World War I.

In Victorian times the cruelest fate fell upon the spinster. Forty-two percent of women between the ages of 20 and 40 were spinsters. Those from the middle classes were called "redundant." They could, if lucky, be governesses. It was a genteel vocation, but also a lonely, ill-paid, and lowly one. If not a governess, one became part of a brother's household. In such a house they, like the wife, did not enjoy the conversation with men after a dinner party. After dessert the men withdrew and drank, sometimes until inebriated. Sexual pleasure was also not for genteel women; their doctors told them that proper women had no desire for it. The Victorians had primitive views of sex. Boys were told that nocturnal emission was a disease, that masturbation caused insanity and excessive intercourse debility. While the daughters were kept in innocence, the sons learned sex from servants, boarding school boys, and prostitutes.

Victorian morals were, in fact, far too demanding. The result was indifference in the lower classes and hypocrisy in the upper. Many Londoners did not practice Victorian morals. Henry Mayhew estimated that only one London worker in ten was of the superior sort. Many of the rest, such as ill-paid seamstresses and tailors, sought solace in drink and profligacy. And with them was the Victorian underworld, a vast army of scavengers, beggars, hawkers, cart-pushers, pickpockets, housebreakers, gamblers, swindlers, prostitutes, and pornographers. Every evening they emerged from the dismal tenements of the East End to do business in the bright, gaslit, sinful streets around Piccadilly Circus and Leicester Square.

Pickpockets and prostitutes were the most numerous, and both callings attracted the young. Small, delicate fingers allowed boys to divest the rich of watches, while the virginal lures of young girls won large fees from the lecherous. Charles Dickens's portrait of Fagin's gang of pickpockets in *Oliver Twist* was as true as Frank Harris's account in *My Secret Life* of girls becoming prostitutes in order to buy sausage rolls. In 1851 the police counted 8,000 prostitutes in London. It was the tip of an iceberg that Henry Mayhew estimated at 80,000. Although the majority of their clients came from the working classes, the upper classes formed a fair share of customers. Because society frowned on marriage without an adequate income, the average age of marriage for a man was 26. Before that age, many sought pleasure with the girls driven by poverty to prostitution.

Poverty drove many others to crime. While workhouse governors preached self-reliance and industry, experience taught that sweated labor and 5 shillings a week did not compare to stealing a watch worth £3. The ablest pickpockets became "swells" with their own gang, a villa, servants, and a wine cellar. If charming, they became swindlers; if bold, housebreakers; if violent, garroters, that is, muggers. These criminals mixed with the respectable at racetracks, dance halls, and supper places and with the less respectable at cockfights or rattings where bulldogs tore rats apart. Age and repeated prison terms reduced many to begging. The immense and varied underworld had its hierarchies and leaders and even ethic. It would be false to romanticize that code or the quality of the life, which could be insecure and wretched, but the underworld did have an earthy, frank openness that offered a striking contrast to the cant and hypocrisy of many among the respectable classes. There were also many from that class whose patronage fostered vice and whose sweated trades drove some of the poor to crime.

The middle and upper classes of Victorian England did not always measure up to the code they preached. Some violated it, others let it turn into rigid conventionalities. Clergymen who countenanced corrupt charities preached against venality, bankrupt businessmen lectured on thrift, men who visited brothels banished the word sex from their drawing rooms. Only a minority, admittedly, were so hypocritical. But a more extensive cant lay behind the puritanism and piety of those who so avidly pursued wealth and prestige in a society full of poverty and injustice. The worship of Mammon was the greatest passion. In 1874 Anthony Trollope made it the main theme of his searing exposure of materialistic England, *The Way We Live Now*. A second passion was social advancement, a passion Charles Dickens exposed in *Our Mutual Friend*, a story of the new rich, of the Veneerings, "bran-new people in bran-new houses in a bran-new quarter of London." The pursuit of respectability by these insecure classes spawned not a little bigotry, a bigotry that rejoiced when, in 1861, the courts sentenced Annie Besant and Charles Bradlaugh to prison for distributing books on birth control and in 1881 when a doctor lost his place on the register for selling the *Wifes Handbook* for 6 pence. This guarded sexual manual, admissible for the wealthy, was too dangerous for the poor. A double standard, class and sexual, vitiated Victorian society.

Yet Victorianism was many-sided. It had tough idealists, many of them in the feminist movement. Josephine Butler was one of the most audacious. She defended the rights of prostitutes who, by the Contagious Disease Acts of 1864–69, had to endure compulsory vaginal tests while the soldiers, often the source of the disease, went unexamined. Mrs. Butler and her allies forced Parliament to repeal the acts. Mrs. Annie Besant took one step more—a gigantic step—and demanded the spread of birth control. She too won out, though not without enduring persecution. By 1911 the upper- and middle-class families had only, on average, 2.8 children. Gone too were corsets and tight lacing. Women now had their own schools and journals and at Oxford and Cambridge their own colleges. Dressed in loose skirts or knickers they played tennis, rowed in boat races, competed in field hockey, and climbed mountains. Newly established teacher colleges produced women physical education instructors who brought gymnastics to the girls of the new secondary schools. Women also became lawyers, architects, accountants, and, for some 212 by 1901, doctors. It is one of the paradoxes of Victorian morality that it could lead both to male chauvinism and to a feminist movement, both to a calloused capitalism and to socialist ideas. It was often harsh, often generous, sometimes callous, sometimes noble, but never weak and insipid. It was a formidable force, one that influenced for good and for ill the Victorians' taste in art and literature.

TASTES AND MOODS

For many, "Victorianism" means a tasteless, philistine art—sentimental paintings, pretentious Gothic buildings, ornate furniture, ostentatious wallpaper, gauche *objets d'art*, and bric-a-brac run riot. The charge that the Victorians were philistines is an old one. Poet and critic Matthew Arnold in his *Culture and Anarchy* of 1869 labeled the middle class "philistine" and accused them of narrowness, materialism, and blindness to beauty.

Is the charge true? The answer is no if a love of beauty is measured by the energy and intensity with which it is pursued, but a qualified yes if it is measured in terms of esthetic quality. The energy and intensity with which they approached painting, for example, can be measured in pounds and shillings and in art periodicals and gallery crowds. The Victorians bought, viewed, read about, and argued over art as never before. At no previous time, nor since, did more painters make a better living. Art periodicals proliferated, private galleries multiplied. The aristocracy bought grand historical scenes, the gentry pictures of sporting life, and the wealthy bourgeoisie domestic paintings of moral uplift. The petty bourgeoisie settled for engravings, while the artisans saw the pictures of the day badly reproduced in such periodicals as the *Illustrated London News*. The better sort patronized galleries in great numbers, even though the cost was a shilling at new shows. They were so eager to see William Frith's newest paintings that guard rails were needed.

It was certainly not great art. In 1848, however, seven young painters,

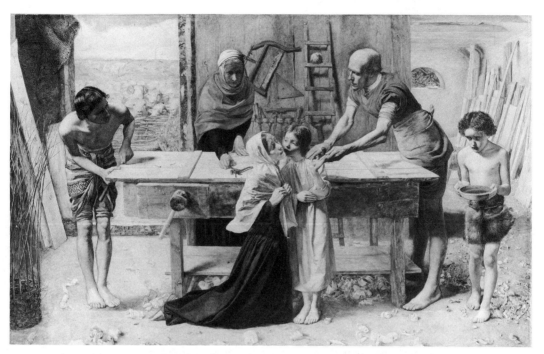

"Christ in His Father's Carpenter Shop" by John Everett Millais (*The Tate Gallery, London*).

who called themselves the Pre-Raphaelites, revolted against the dominance of the Royal Academy and the primacy of historical scenes and idealized landscapes. They painted earthier and simpler subjects, with a realistic attention to detail. Three of the Pre-Raphaelites were Dante Gabriel Rossetti, John Everett Millais, and William Holman Hunt. Their champion and the inspirer of many of their ideas was John Ruskin. The Pre-Raphaelites wished to return to the precise treatment of nature and the luminous spirituality of the Italian painters before Raphael. They painted every blade of grass, every hair on a maiden's head, with painstaking exactness. Since they did so on canvasses with a wet white base, this gave their work a bright luminosity. Millais's "Christ in His Father's Carpenter Shop," because it treated Christ as an ordinary person, brought outcries from the devout. Others found it refreshing and exciting. A great controversy followed, but no grand style in art, no creative revolution. The Pre-Raphaelites looked too much to the past to achieve that original and creative vision which gave birth to French impressionism. By 1854 the revolt was over and the movement dissipated. Rossetti retired to a bohemian life and to his dreamlike paintings and poetry, both of which have an exquisite and haunting beauty. Millais and Hunt went on to make fortunes. Both found their greatest popularity in narrative paintings.

Narrative painting had a long tradition in England. Hogarth had pioneered

"Derby Day" by William P. Frith (*The Tate Gallery, London*).

in it in the eighteenth century. In the Victorian age it never rose to high art, but it reflected the taste and mood of the middle classes. These paintings told stories that touched the heart, celebrated the goodness and plenitude of life, preached a respectable morality, and poured forth warm sentiments. No painter celebrated the plenitude of life better than William Frith and no picture did so more exuberantly than his "Derby Day." In it mingled all types from all classes: acrobats, beggars, gypsies, peers of the realm, farmhands, thieves, and multitudes of the middling sort. It is a festive crowd, gathered for the year's greatest race, a harmonious crowd, a crowd in no way threatening to established hierarchies, but a robust, competitive crowd, befitting a robust, competitive age. It reflects mid-Victorian prosperity in the same vital way that William Bell Scott's "Iron and Coal" reflect the power of industry and the morality of work.

Many narrative paintings preached a moral, but few did so as melodramatically as Holman Hunt's "The Awakened Conscience." In a cluttered parlor a woman sits on the lap of a man, a position Victorian husbands and wives rarely assumed and one that bespoke adultery. Suddenly the woman realizes the sinfulness of her affair. The presence of a cat playing with a bird provided an additional clue that the mischievous lover was playing with the woman's affection. Clues occurred frequently in narrative paintings. A black-rimmed letter meant news of a death and a racing form an addiction to gambling. These many clues symbolized powerful sentiments crucial to the drama of Victorian narrative painting and novels, sentiments whose excesses also reflect a pervasive sentimentality. Victorian painting was meant to adorn the parlors of the middle classes. Whether a narrative painting of domesticity or an engraving of Lord Leighton's grand historical scene, whether a shimmering topographical vista by David Roberts or the great Landseer's lovingly portrayed dogs, the Victorians wanted painting that was respectable, edifying, and comfortable.

The same Victorians wanted their buildings stately and impressive. Victorian architecture, of debatable greatness, was at least vast. It was vast in the numbers and kinds of buildings and in the wealth available for their construction. It was vast in the number of architects, mostly self-taught, willing to lend a hand. Vast, too, was the incredible profusion of styles—Georgian, Gothic, Classical, Renaissance, Egyptian, Moorish—and the new materials and techniques—iron, steel, plate glass, concrete, cantilevering, and prefabrication. And vast also was the outpouring of books, journals, opinions, and polemics, many vainly seeking to bring order to the anarchy of styles. But order, in the sense of unity of style, never came.

The reason the Victorians created no unified style was that the forces for fragmentation were too great. The Georgian style itself, so beautifully ordered and rational, could not survive the onset of Romanticism, the Industrial Revolution, and the advance of historical knowledge. Augustus Welby Pugin, a scholar of medieval times and a Romantic, favored Gothic as the grand style. Architects like Sir Gilbert Scott had a flair for gigantic Gothic structures like the St. Pancras Hotel, while George Street excelled in lovely Gothic churches. Gothic in these many forms made a significant impression on the English city, but faced with rival enthusiasms for classical, Renaissance, and baroque styles, there was no chance that it would become the dominant style.

But why a revival? Why not an indigenous style? Why not the functional style of Sir Joseph Paxton's Crystal Palace? To a great extent such a style did develop, but mostly where function was a paramount concern, for factories, railway stations, warehouses, docks, greenhouses. Many were handsome as well as useful. The Chatham naval dockyard, with its modern simplicity, and the huge iron and glass railway sheds at St. Pancras and Paddington still impress the tourist. To the Victorians these sheds, like the giant railway bridges and docks, partook of the sublime. The massive and the monumental, the ornate and the decorative, also impressed and led lordly aristocrats and captains of industry and the architects in their pay to turn from the neat and functional to the ornamental and grandiose. Whether classical or Gothic made no difference if it excited awe. If that awe could be evoked by combining styles, so much the better. The majestic Houses of Parliament combined Pugin's Gothic decoration with Sir Charles Barry's Renaissance plan.

The ornateness and stateliness of Victorian architecture, like its eclecticism and occasional vulgarity, reflected the tastes of successful, self-made men, poorly educated in the arts. England had no schools for architects as did France, and no strong monarch to plan a Paris or a Berlin. English architects expressed their pride in as impressive a manner as they could. The world's leading industrialists needed monumental factories, so in Leeds John Marshall, the wool baron, constructed his mill in the heavy Egyptian style. The town halls of these centers of cotton, wool, and iron must also inspire awe—thus the towering Gothic halls

"Iron and Coal" by William Bell Scott (*National Trust*).

in Manchester and Leeds and the opulent classical hall in Birmingham. For men who governed an empire there was a need for sumptuous clubs, so along Pall Mall arose the Reform Club and the Travellers' Club, palaces in the Italianate style. An empire that had bought the marbles of the Parthenon and was a center of learning needed an imposing museum, so in Bloomsbury rose the British Museum, in a monumental classical style. The pride of success even infected the Nonconformists. Having surpassed the Anglicans in attending members, they turned from modest, boxlike chapels to such monstrous churches as the Baptists' Metropolitan Tabernacle in a Gothic-Romanesque-Rococo style. These grandiose buildings, some successful, some not, represent a proud and wealthy age prone to overstatement and exaggeration.

It is the poets' function to see clearly, feel intensely, and express concretely the experiences and moods of their times. In the 1850s and 1860s Alfred Lord Tennyson and Matthew Arnold did so in a poetry that was both pessimistic and affirmative, a poetry in which doubt of God and anxiety about life alternated with strenuous moral truths and joy in nature's beauties. These qualities imparted a tension that many Victorians felt about the ambiguities of the new age of science and industry. Tennyson's *In Memoriam* plumbed deep into the realms

"The Awakened Conscience" by Holman Hunt (*The Tate Gallery, London*).

of grief and despair; Arnold's *Dover Beach* had a mellower sadness to it. A loss of faith in Christianity was crucial to both, though Tennyson rallied from unbelief to a faith in an "eternal process moving" toward "one far off Divine event," while Arnold consoled himself with the thought that the "Eternal not ourselves" would bring a better age. That a nontheistic religion could survive reason and science was also evident in the opulent verse of Robert Browning. A believer in Platonic ideas and Christian morals, he infused his poetry with positive values, but values found more in the past than in the present.

It was the present, with its flux of uncertainties, that disturbed Tennyson, Arnold, and many ordinary people. Factory towns devoured villages, railways disfigured landscapes, London became a monstrous megalopolis, and Parliament welcomed the strident voices of industry. The quarrels of High, Low, and Broad

Churchmen and the polemics of Dissent turned serene faiths into a tower of Babel, a tower soon to be undermined by biblical criticism and science. Prosperity there was, to be sure, but it produced misery for the poor and arrogance in the rich. Old certitudes and loyalties dissolved. "Truth," lamented Arnold, had become "Flexible, changeable, vague, multiform, and doubtful," while life has "really neither joy nor love nor light." The loss of old things held dear is hard to bear. The death of a youthful friend led Tennyson to compose passages of intense grief in *In Memoriam*. It became the great Victorian poem because it plumbed so deeply the anxieties of an age in which the old seemed doomed and the new fearful.

It was also an age of struggle. The poetry of the high Victorians was seldom a poetry of total despair—that was to come in the twentieth century. Grief and melancholy there was, but also struggle and moral conquest. *In Memoriam* is a struggle as well as a lament, and it ends with a promise that spiritual forces will overcome material ones. For the Victorians great forces were at work in the world. It was a competitive age in business, in the empire, in politics. It was an age filled with battles, intellectual and moral as well as military. On Matthew Arnold's "darkling plain" "armies clash by night," while Tennyson pictures nature as "red in tooth and claw." Yet Arnold is still hopeful that reason and learning will bring "sweetness and light," while Tennyson celebrates in *The Charge of the Light Brigade* the heroism of the British soldier, a heroism he also extols in every person's struggle for self-knowledge, self-conquest, and obedience to the moral order. Browning also celebrates the excitement of battle, the exhilaration of struggle and conquest. In his *Childe Roland*, he writes in tense and sinewy verse about "passions too fierce to be in fetters bound."

Tennyson and Browning tell entertaining stories of medieval romance and chivalry, just as Arnold does of the ancient Greeks. Victorian poetry not only expressed the anxieties of a new age and the moral struggle they bring, but also a delight in the rich and colorful world that travel, books, periodicals, and cheap prints had opened up for so many. Its poetry also brought a delight in the sheer beauty of verse, whether in Tennyson's ornate imagery and idyllic moods or in Browning's dramatic, tense, and spirited rhythm. The English esthetic sense, weak in the visual arts and even weaker in the creation of music, throve on the written word—hence its splendid poetry and hence its crowning achievement, the Victorian novel.

In the 1840s Charles Dickens wrote about one novel a year, a first printing (after running as a serial in a periodical) averaging 30,000 copies. Captain Marryat and Mrs. Charlotte Gore wrote two a year, and the most sensational sold more than 30,000 copies. The Victorians loved to read novels, especially gripping stories of romance and adventure. By 1858 periodicals that serialized them reached 3 million people. By the 1890s, at 4 shillings a copy, they were sold everywhere. A quarter of a million people also read copies that had been checked out of private circulating libraries, while the burgeoning public libraries loaned out more than 20 million copies a year.

The Victorians who read these novels were part of a prosperous, mobile world, people who worked at new jobs, lived in new towns, had new homes, rose in the social scale, gained better education, bought a flood of new goods, gained the vote, entered politics, and attended concerts, music halls, lectures, and sporting events. There was much that was strange, bewildering, and even frightening. For these people the Victorian novel did three things: it provided a map, a picture, a panorama of that society; by suggesting a meaning to modern life, it helped these mobile people find an identity; and finally it entertained them.

Its panorama of society was sweeping, crowded, varied, and truthful. It dealt with all classes and all places. A particular locality was crucial to many of them and accounts for much of their truthfulness. Gone were historical romances of a medieval past; now one read Anthony Trollope's *Barchester Towers* to discover the nuances of a cathedral town, Elizabeth Gaskell's *Mary Barton* to learn of factory life in Manchester, Charlotte Brontë's *Shirley* to savor life in a Yorkshire manufacturing town, or Dickens's *Dombey and Son* to experience the overwhelming size of commercial London. Many of these novelists also focused on the classes they knew best, those in the middle. But some transcended locality and class, particularly William Thackeray in *Vanity Fair*, and George Eliot.

In *Adam Bede*, Eliot studied a rural people, in *Daniel Deronda*, London's high society. It was, however, the new towns, with their squires, bankers, doctors, clergymen, artisans, and wives, all jostling together, as in *Middlemarch*, that brought out George Eliot's genius as a social cartographer. With the exactness of a scientist she delineated the town's social classes and with the controlled sympathy of a great artist she portrayed these individuals as they struggled to relate to the groupings and institutions of society. She sought to discover in her characters laws of the mind and in the conflict of classes the underlying laws of society. In *Mill on the Floss* she saw that the good society, the society of "claret and velvet carpets," of operas and "faery ballrooms," rests on a "national life condensed in unfragrant, deafening factories, cramping itself in mines, sweating at furnaces. . . ." The Victorian novelist did not flinch at criticizing the rich. Mr. Merdle in Dickens's *Little Dorrit* was "simply the greatest Forger and the greatest Thief that ever cheated the gallows." The wealthy in *Vanity Fair* were, in Thackeray's words, "greedy, pompous, mean, perfectly self-satisfied." Trollope's railway king Melmotte was a swindler and an impostor. But what really appalled Dickens, Thackeray, and Trollope were the people who fawned upon, bowed to, and praised the Merdles and Melmottes.

Although the novelists exposed the faults of the rich and the injustices of society, they preached no revolution. Gaskell in *Mary Barton* and Dickens in *Hard Times* were as vivid as George Eliot in depicting "unfragrant, deafening factories," but nowhere do they, or she, suggest a change in the capitalist system. They preached instead a change of heart, a greater benevolence, a warmer sentiment. Their readers and critics, like they themselves, were of the middle classes; even excessive exposure was to be avoided. Some critics found *Vanity*

Fair too relentless in its exposure of the follies and wickedness of high society. Others charged Dickens with bad taste in dealing at such length with the world of crime in *Oliver Twist*. Charlotte Brontë in *Jane Eyre* and Emily Brontë in *Wuthering Heights* also came perilously close to writing too frankly about sex, passion, and the tyranny of males. Novels should end happily. Particularly satisfying were marriages leading to blissful domesticity or a benevolent godfather rescuing an orphan. Victorians bathed such scenes in a sentimentality that provided a release from the tensions caused by a keen awareness of injustice and an inability to remove it.

The greater of the Victorian novelists also sought to find some meaning in this flux, to give to those caught in it some identity. This was particularly true of the women novelists. In the 1840s Elizabeth Gaskell, George Eliot, and the Brontë sisters—Charlotte, Anne, and Emily—emerged as major novelists. Many other women filled the ranks of minor novelists, and many of them, like the Brontës, Eliot, and Gaskell, sought to find a role for women in a world of scarce opportunities and hostile values. In Mrs. Gaskell's *Ruth* and in George Eliot's portrait of Dorothea in *Middlemarch*, that search is portrayed in a sympathetic but conventional vein—for Dorothea meaning comes in the moral resolve "to do some little good in Middlemarch." In Charlotte Brontë's *Jane Eyre* the intensity and passion are greater, yet morality and convention are not defied, seduction is resisted, and the story ends in marriage.

Men too lived in a bewildering world. No author described the mysterious, impersonal, and haunting forces that buffeted Londoners with greater genius than Dickens. His London is an illogical, crowded world of colliding people, most of them unable to relate to each other, many of them as helpless as young Oliver Twist, caught in a life of crime, or Paul Dombey "with an aching void in his heart, all outside so cold and bare and strange." In his later novels Dickens offered no clear meanings and no neat formulas for identity, but only a deeper, gloomier exploration of human nature in all its grotesqueness, cruelty, and nobility. In these later novels he depicted the world of London with an imaginative genius, a brilliance of style, a sense of the comic, and a range of sympathy that none could rival.

Although Dickens offered no clear solutions, he did entertain. So did all the great Victorian novelists. They were incomparable storytellers: witty, satirical, picturesque, suspenseful, romantic, exciting. Novels good and bad gave millions long hours of pleasure. What drama was to the Elizabethans and television is to us, the novel was to the Victorians. It had rivals, to be sure, in the music hall and traveling stage companies, and in the 1880s in the operettas of W. C. Gilbert and Arthur Sullivan. Victorians liked all diversions. But the novel held primacy of place. Written in the solitude of a study and read in a corner of a parlor or library, the novel allowed the individual to create his or her own imaginary world. It could be an escape or a search, but whichever it was, it was the activity of a single person. It thus reflected that sturdy self-reliance which, along with a seriousness about morality and an earnestness about life, formed the core of Victorianism.

FURTHER READING

ALTICK, RICHARD. *Victorian People and Ideas.* New York: W. W. Norton, 1973. A highly intelligent survey, ranging from an analysis of the class system to the ruling religious and political ideas of the age and including discussions of the press, books, and sex.

BRIGGS, ASA. *Victorian People.* Chicago: University of Chicago Press, 1955. Fascinating portraits of eight distinguished Victorians and two dramatic events that bring out both the variety of ideas, passions, and moralities of the Victorians and their common characteristics.

BURN, WILLIAM. *The Age of Equipoise.* New York: W. W. Norton, 1969. A penetrating study of the rural half of Victorian England, and of the professions, the rectory, the mansion and farm house, the courts, clubs, and public offices.

BURNETT, JOHN. *Useful Toil, Autobiographies of Working People from the 1820s to the 1920s.* London: Penguin Books, 1974. An unusual book, one that allows working people to express their hopes, worries, dreams, anxieties, and ambitions in their own blunt, plain, and pungent words.

GATHORNE-HARDY, JONATHAN. *The Old School Tie: The Phenomenon of the English Public School.* New York: Viking Press, 1977. The outlook of the Victorian governing class had its roots in those public schools that Gathorne-Hardy describes with a profound understanding of their importance and idiosyncracies.

HARRISON, JOHN. *The Early Victorians.* London: Weidenfeld and Nicolson, 1971. A comprehensive and revealing social history done with a special emphasis on the working classes and the conditions that they endured and overcame.

HOUGHTON, WALTER. *The Victorian Frame of Mind.* New Haven, Conn.: Yale University Press, 1957. A remarkable profile of the Victorian mind; classifies and analyzes its leading ideas and attitudes even when contradictory—as "the critical spirit" and the "will to believe."

IRVINE, WILLIAM. *Apes, Angels and Victorians.* New York: Meridian Books, 1959. A sprightly and bright discussion of the impact of Darwin on the Victorian scientific and religious establishments with special emphasis on the crusading work of T. H. Huxley.

THOMPSON, F. M. L. *The Rise of Respectable Society: A Social History of Victorian Britain.* Cambridge, Mass.: Harvard University Press 1988. A perceptive account of the rise of the working class to cleanliness, order, sobriety, improved standards of living, and respectability. A superb social history.

VICINUS, MARTHA, ed. *Suffer and Be Still: Women in the Victorian Age.* Bloomington: Indiana University Press, 1980. Thirteen authorities analyze with sympathy and insight the role of women in Victorian England, whether the neglected governess, abused prostitute, overworked shop girl, or bored wife.

YOUNG, G. M. *Portrait of An Age.* Oxford: Oxford University Press, 1977. A classic portrait, short but dense with brilliant perceptions and stimulating ideas, all focused on those characteristics that defined the eminent Victorian.

The British Empire

25

Britain had long been an Empire when Victoria became Queen in 1837. There was an Angevin Empire in the twelfth century, ruled over by Henry II and extending from Aquitaine to Ireland. His son Richard sought kingdoms in distant Palestine. Edward I conquered Wales, and Edward III and Henry V both won and lost great parts of France. The continental empire had no sooner ended with the loss of Calais in 1558 than Queen Elizabeth sent Sir Francis Drake to the Spanish Main, the Earl of Essex to Ireland, and Humphrey Gilbert to Newfoundland where, in 1583, he founded the first British colony in the new world. Newfoundland was the first of many colonies that by the end of the eighteenth century formed the basis of a colonial Empire that stretched from Calcutta to Toronto.

Two principal drives led to this Empire: the desire of traders to make profits and the desire of the British to emigrate. Emigration seemed a British habit, whether it was to create New Jerusalems in Massachusetts or build fortunes in the West Indies. Cromwell and Charles II also found colonies profitable. Inspired by mercantilist doctrines, they passed trade ordinances and navigation acts which reserved all colonial trade to British ships and which decreed that colonies must import all manufactures from Britain.

The American Revolution tore a large hole in this system. Economists like Adam Smith also attacked the mercantilist assumptions that lay behind the Empire. Monopolistic regulation, said Smith, hampered economic growth. Furthermore colonies were expensive and might rebel and be lost. Enthusiasm for Empire ebbed at the end of the eighteenth century, but the Empire itself, because of the war with France, led Britain to acquire Cape Colony in South Africa, Ceylon, Mauritius, and the Seychelles in the Indian Ocean, Tobago and St. Lucia, Mauritius and Trinidad in the Caribbean, Heligoland in the North Sea, and Malta and the Ionian Islands in the Mediterranean.

From the very beginning of the overseas Empire, the pursuit of power had been as significant a motive for conquest as trade and emigration. After the destruction of the French and Spanish fleets at Trafalgar, Britain had the high seas all to herself, a supremacy her iron and steam ships only strengthened. Britain had, of course, long enjoyed naval superiority, a fact which allowed imperial expansion. Captain Cook, an explorer, staked out claims in 1769 in New Zealand; the evangelicals, leaders of the campaign against the slave trade, established Sierra Leone in West Africa in 1787; a year later the government colonized Australia in order to rid itself of convicts; and in 1792, 1795, and 1799, Baptists, Congregationalists, and Anglicans formed missionary societies that sent to Africa and Asia the first of a stream of missionaries. The activities of these restless groups were yet another force behind expansion.

As the Empire grew, so did criticism of it. By 1850 a powerful manufacturing class and the adherents of the new political economy had repealed the tariffs on foreign grain and sugar and abolished the Navigation Acts; ideas of free trade had overthrown mercantilist doctrines. Middle-class radicals also denounced colonies as expensive and useless. Colonies, wrote Adam Smith, were a costly burden. Others condemned them as the cause of needless wars and bloodshed. William Gladstone shared many of these views, and even Disraeli had doubts. "These wretched colonies," he said in 1852, "are millstones around our necks."

Yet nothing slowed the acquisition of new territories. Free traders who were also imperialists urged the planned and systematic colonization of new Zealand and Australia, self-government and federation for Canada, utilitarian law codes for India, and an open-door policy in China, even if it required a war. Expansion reflected forces within the Empire itself far more powerful than intellectual doubts in London. These forces, in conjunction with Britain's naval power, industrial superiority, and worldwide entanglements, led to the imperceptible growth of the largest, wealthiest, and most populous Empire the world had ever seen, the basis of a veritable *pax Britannica*.

PAX BRITANNICA

The British Empire in 1900 included a quarter of the people of the world and nearly a quarter of its lands. Its variety was immense; its differences in topography, climate, flora and fauna, cultures and peoples staggering. Since 1880 it had made ninety-five additions. The Union Jack flew over the frozen tundra of Arctic lands, the jungles of Nigeria, the sunlit veldt of South Africa, and stormy mountain passes in the Himalayas. In New Zealand English-like landscape lay beneath Alpine peaks; in Ceylon's capital, Kandy, high in the mountains and alongside a lovely lake, were marble temples and bazaars crowded with exotic wares and people; and in the South Pacific lay 250 Fiji islands, the larger ones with mangrove forests, fertile sugar plantations, and volcanic mountains. Every possession was different in size; Australia was a continent and India a subcontinent; St. Helena, where Napoleon was held prisoner, was a mere dot in the South Atlantic. Islands and ports provided coaling stations. Whether it was Gibraltar and Malta in the Mediterranean, Bermuda and Halifax in the Atlantic, Singapore and Hong Kong in the Far East, or Aden in the Indian Ocean, steamships could fill their holds with coal and stock their shelves with ale, bacon, and marmalade. Although most colonies were a loss to Britain, some did produce great wealth. In the 1860s Australia's gold fields produced a third of the world's gold, and its sheep provided a sixth of Britain's raw wool. In 1900 one in three miners and quarrymen in the world mined and quarried in the British Empire. By 1913 nearly half of Britain's £3.9 billion overseas investment was in the Empire and 60 percent of her cotton cloth and 19 percent of her total exports went to India.

Diversity also marked the Empire's many cultures. The Aborigines of Australia and the Bushmen of South Africa had yet to move beyond a Paleolithic culture, while the Hindus of India and the Muslims of Egypt belong to civilizations renowned for their art, literature, philosophy, technology, and government. The diversity of the Empire's peoples was kaleidoscopic: thousands of languages and dialects were spoken and hundreds of religious sects and modes of worship prospered. The governments also varied; the British never chose to emulate

In the most resplendent of Oriental courts, the efficient British soon became the courts' imperial rulers (*Illustrated London News*).

the Romans by establishing a uniform law and government. They ruled through more than forty different governments, most of them some form of despotism. In the Malay states it was indirect, though there were British residents at the courts of the sultans; in India rule was both direct and indirect; in Africa trading companies often governed extensive areas. Behind all these governments stood the British army and directing them were governor generals, viceroys, captain generals, and in the field the ubiquitous district officers, young Oxford and Cambridge graduates whose scores on Colonial or Indian Office examinations entitled them to become minor proconsuls for one-fourth of the world's peoples. One half of Oxford's Balliol graduates found jobs in the Empire.

The British Empire was not a legal entity. In Egypt the fiction was carefully observed that Lord Cromer was only an advisor to the khedive, the country's formal ruler. Egyptian Muslim law ruled in the courts as did tribal law in Uganda and Chinese law in Hong Kong. Yet in all the courts of the Empire an aggrieved person could appeal ultimately to the Judicial Committee of the Privy Council, whose judges sat in London and who guaranteed not a uniform code of law, but fair enforcement of the various laws. It insisted on a just hearing and a due process of law. This committee, along with the Crown as an object of loyalty and the army as a power, gave some unity to the kingdoms, princedoms, protectorates, dominions, suzerainties, paramountcies, concessions, and spheres of influence that constituted the "formal" part of the British Empire.

There was also an informal empire. It took the form of an endless flow of goods, services, people, and ideas to the four corners of the earth. The goods ranged from cheap cottons and ironwares to railway lines and waterworks, and the services from banking and insurance to shipping and communications. Throughout the world there were agents of Lloyds of London to insure ships and of Barclay's Bank to grant loans.

British steamships, telegraphs, and submarine cables spanned the globe. In 1902 a cable from New Zealand to British Columbia completed the famed "All-Red route," a world-circling cable that passed only through British territory. Britain's economic imperialism could be both beneficial and harmful. In Argentina Britain built waterworks and railways and organized and ran its beef industry, yet cheap British textiles also ruined Argentina's small spinners, weavers, and traders. Argentina, like many other Latin American republics, became an economic dependent of Britain. The power of English finance, the skill of English engineers, and the cheapness of English manufactures made Britain powerful throughout the world. British capital had an astonishing influence on the world's economy, often so great that the line between formal and informal empire became blurred. Treaties of trade with Persia in 1836 and 1857 and Turkey in 1838 and 1861, for example, brought both countries under British political influence.

Equally astonishing was the export of ideas and people. Twenty million Britons emigrated from 1815 to 1914. They populated Canada, Australia, and New Zealand and helped to populate the United States, South Africa, and the

Without the ironclad steamboats, navy, and merchant marine, there would have been a smaller British Empire (*Illustrated London News*).

West Indies. Even small islands like the Falklands, Bermuda, or tiny Tristan da Cunha developed English settlements. Britons also went to India, Burma, Singapore, Malaya, and China in Asia; to Cairo, Teheran, and Baghdad in the Near East; to every capital in Latin America; and to all of Africa. There were even sizable groups in Florence, Rome, Nice, Paris, and other European cities. Wealthy British tourists went everywhere, demanding afternoon tea and displaying a smug superiority. They were generally hated. There was something galling in their achievements, their insularity, their patronizing air. They were the first to climb the Alps; they invented the new games—lawn tennis, soccer, rugby, squash—and won at them. They managed other people's travel. Thomas Cook & Sons built and ran the funicular railroad up Mt. Vesuvius. At any given moment British ships were carrying 200,000 passengers and as many merchant seamen. Half the merchant ships on the seas flew the Union Jack. Then there were the missionaries building churches, schools, and hospitals and everywhere preaching Christ's word. They were soon followed, in a more secular age, by British colleges teaching Western literature, history, philosophy, and science. Aloof and proud, the late Victorians abroad kept to their own compounds, and in summer to their own hill stations, with tennis courts, racetracks, and clubs.

In 1841 James Brooke, recently of the East India Company, journeyed to Sarawak in North Borneo. He was so charming, efficient, strong-willed, and eager to improve affairs that the bankrupt ruler of Sarawak abdicated in his favor. For forty-five years Brooke and his nephew ruled wisely as the white rajahs of Sarawak. Robert Hart went to China in 1854, stayed fifty-four years, and created and managed the Chinese maritime customs. Brooke and Hart were typical of legions of Britons whose restless energy carried them abroad and whose commanding will and sheer ability made them the rulers of men. Like the Castilians who poured forth from Spain in the sixteenth century to build its vast empire, these Britons formed a creative elite of unusual talent, boldness, courage, and ruthlessness.

THE SELF-GOVERNING DOMINIONS

Canada, Australia, and New Zealand are proud members of the British Commonwealth, that association of independent nations that have remained loyal to Elizabeth II. They remained loyal because the majority of them were British and self-governing. In 1837 they were not self-governing and possibly not loyal. In both Toronto and Montreal, small, all-powerful, Crown-appointed councils ruled in disregard of the wishes of elected assemblies. In lower Canada the elite of the councils were British and Protestant; the majority of the people, French and Catholic. So angered were the people at the oligarchy's irresponsibility and misgovernment that their elected assemblies refused to vote taxes, while the more violent rioted. There were also riots in upper Canada. Would Canada go the way of the United States? In London an alarmed Whig government sent the Earl of Durham to investigate and report.

The liberal Earl and his radical aides produced the famous Durham Report of 1839, the Magna Carta of colonial liberty. It recommended greater self-government, the union of upper and lower Canada, and an executive more responsible to the elected assembly. The Canadian Act of 1840 united the two provinces and created a two-house legislature, one elected and one appointed, but remained silent on whether the executive should be responsible to the elected house. Yet responsible government did evolve when the Whig colonial secretary, Earl Grey, and the governor general for Canada, Lord Elgin, appointed as ministers only those who had the confidence of the elected lower house. The same principle had come earlier to Nova Scotia, and as Canada moved toward federation it was adopted in other provinces. In 1867 the British Parliament passed the British North America Act, which united Ontario, Quebec, Nova Scotia, and New Brunswick into the Dominion of Canada. By 1876 the railway had crossed Canada, the prairie provinces and British Columbia had joined, and Canada had become the most powerful of the self-governing dominions.

Australia and New Zealand, like Canada, lie in a temperate zone, were sparsely settled and rich in land and resources. They thus attracted thousands of emigrants, emigrants who also demanded an independent and democratic government. The Australian Colonies Act of 1850 created elective assemblies in its six colonies, while the New Zealand Act of 1852 created a national bicameral legislature and, for its six provinces, unicameral legislatures. The executive was still answerable to the governor general sent from England, but not for long. As in Canada, the governor general, faced with truculent politicians and a resolute people, appointed as ministers those who had the confidence of a majority in the assemblies. Parliamentary government had become one of the most successful of British exports, but only to colonies whose peoples were mainly British.

In colonies as vast as Canada and Australia, this parliamentary government combined successfully with the federal system that had developed in the United States, one in which central and provincial governments shared power far more evenly than in Britain. Australia, roughly the size of the United States but far less fertile, achieved federal unity in 1901. In New Zealand, closer to England in size, federation gave way to a centralized unitary government in 1876 when the provincial governments lost most of their power. In both Australia and New Zealand, a democratic and egalitarian society flourished. In 1860 universal suffrage had come to Australia. In 1893 New Zealand became the first country in the empire to give the vote to women. Australia and New Zealand also led in developing a welfare state. Both established old age pensions, courts to arbitrate labor disputes, and heavy taxes on large landed estates. New Zealand went further: the government owned coal mines and railways, sold life insurance, managed land transfers, and regulated wages and hours.

Both Australians and New Zealanders had strong racial prejudices. They passed laws excluding Asians, seized lands from the Aborigines and Maoris, and destroyed their cultures. They acted as ruthlessly as the Canadians had toward the North American Indians. Had the natives been more numerous, self-government would have faced greater difficulties, as is evident in the tragic history of a fourth self-governing dominion, that of South Africa.

South Africa joined the Commonwealth in 1910 and withdrew in 1961. It is now an authoritarian and racist nation, isolated and friendless. The cause of this development lay in the fact that South African blacks were far more numerous and powerful than the Maoris, Aborigines, or Canadian Indians, but not sufficiently powerful or advanced in weaponry to defeat the white settlers. The most dominant of the white settlers were the Boers, a people of Dutch origins and Calvinist religion. They first came in the seventeenth century and were well entrenched in 1808, when Britain seized Cape Colony in order to protect the sea route to India. As the Boers and other white settlers increased in numbers and power, they grew restive at the lack of fertile land and angry at the British insistence that they quit treating blacks as virtual slaves. To escape these problems the Boers in 1835 began the Great Trek north. The result was the establishment of two independent republics, the Transvaal and the Orange Free State. To check the Boer republics the British created the colony of Natal to the east of them and on the west two trusteeships, Bechuanaland and diamond-rich Griqualand West. In 1877 Disraeli's government tried to annex the two Boer republics, a plan Gladstone denounced in the elections of 1880 but, once in office, carried out. He did so because of the pressure from humanitarians who knew that the Boers were cruel to blacks and wanted their power checked.

These annexations so angered the militarily powerful Boers that, in 1881, they destroyed an inadequate British force at Majuba Hill. In South Africa the British faced two dilemmas: Should they annex the Boer republics outright or recognize their sovereignty? Should they pursue trusteeship (direct rule from London) to protect blacks, or self-government, which would mean whites would use elected assemblies to oppress blacks? They vacillated disastrously on both questions. They recognized the Boer republics, but asserted a suzerainty over them that they could not enforce. They also chartered Cecil Rhodes's British South Africa Company and allowed it (and a host of adventurers scenting gold) to move into the land north of Transvaal. The shrewdest of these adventurers, Rhodes's agent, Dr. Jameson, won treaties from the King of the Matabele that paved the way to white subjugation of blacks. The British, having surrounded the Boer republics, asserted their "paramountcy" over all of South Africa; the Boers, growing wealthy from the world's richest gold fields, asserted their independence, including the right to deny white immigrants to their lands the vote. As these immigrants, called *uitlanders*, grew in numbers—some 44,000 in 1896—and in discontent, Rhodes, Jameson, and the Colonial Secretary, Joseph Chamberlain, worried over the Boer threat. In 1895, falsely believing the *uitlanders* would revolt, Rhodes and Chamberlain allowed Dr. Jameson and 500 men to invade the Transvaal. The Jameson raid was a fiasco. No one revolted, Jameson was captured, Rhodes fell into disgrace, and Chamberlain survived only by an adroit coverup. Boer not British paramountcy seemed the wave of the future.

To Alfred Milner, a brilliant graduate of Oxford who had been trained in Egypt under Lord Cromer, it seemed apparent that a Boer instead of a British paramountcy would cause reverberations that would weaken the British Empire. Chamberlain had appointed Milner High Commissioner to South Africa in 1897. In 1899 Milner demanded that the *uitlanders* be given the vote after five years' residence. The Boers offered seven years and had the Transvaal's legislature pass such a reform. Milner now demanded a high tribunal to clear up Britain's right to suzerainty. The Boers offered a compromise which Milner rejected. He then issued an ultimatum that the Transvaal must acknowledge British suzerainty and its right of intervention. The Boers refused, and the Boer War began in October 1899.

It lasted three years. The British needed 400,000 troops—including detachments from Canada, Australia, and New Zealand—to defeat 60,000 Boers. They also used concentration camps to subdue civilians. Some 117,000 were herded together in abominable conditions, from which 20,000 died. In 1910 the British, with the assent of the Boers, formed the Union of South Africa, the fourth unified, self-governing dominion. But except in the Cape, only whites could vote. Some 840,000 whites, nearly half Boers, ruled over 3.2 million blacks.

The Victorian imperialists never discovered a formula for developing non-white self-governing dominions. Their timid attempts in Jamaica, Trinidad, and other sugar islands came to naught. At midcentury, inspired by Lord Durham's report, they granted some self-government to the West Indies, but one based on a high property qualification. The result was rule by white oligarchies indifferent to the needs of the blacks. They also had no solution to the acute poverty that inefficient absentee landlords, cheap Brazilian and Cuban sugar, and the advent of free trade brought to the West Indies. The wealthiest parts of the eighteenth-century colonial system became the slums of the Victorian empire. In 1865 some Jamaican blacks rioted and killed eighteen whites. Governor Eyre put down the riot with savagery, executing nearly 600 blacks, burning a thousand of their homes, and flogging men and women alike. The rebellion led to the end of elected assemblies. Jamaica became a crown colony, administered as a trusteeship.

INDIA AND BEYOND

In 1784 Pitt's India Act established a government-appointed Board of Control in London and a Governor General in Calcutta to supervise the East India Company. In 1784, that company ruled over Bengal and factories at Madras and Bombay. The 1784 act condemned all conquests of territory. With the company's 2,000 servants confronting more than 100 million Indians and controlling less than one-thirtieth of India, it seemed unlikely that the company would create an empire. But conquest came, gradually and inexorably. Sometimes it was by treaties, sometimes by the subtle intrigues of resident advisors, and often by war. It took four wars to make Mysore in the far south a dependent state. Helping the company do so in the 1790s was Hyderabad, a princedom just to the north and as large as England and Scotland combined. In time the restless intrigues of Hyderabad forced the company to defeat that kingdom's forces and control its rulers. North of Hyderabad were the Maratha chiefs, a powerful group who, if united, could have thrown the British out of India, but whose factional wars so weakened these chiefs that the company assumed control in 1818. The same story repeated itself elsewhere.

By 1830, the East India Company ruled, directly or indirectly, all India except the northwest and Oudh, nestled against Nepal. By 1856 the company's armies had conquered Oudh and Sind, Punjab, and other states of the northwest. Their armies conquered lower Burma and attempted and failed to acquire Nepal and Afghanistan. It was an achievement at odds not only with the belief that conquest was repugnant, but with the rule of the company's first governor that it should seek profit only in quiet trade. In 1784 the company did not wish to found an empire. There was no pressure from Parliament or London businessmen. How and why, then, did the unintended happen?

The answer lies in British strength and Indian weakness, and in the forces this inequality released. At first the company wished only to profit from trade, but when confronted with corrupt governments, extravagant rulers, huge debts, and constant strife, brigandage, and war, it felt constrained to help restore order. Its agents became advisors, raised troops, loaned money, managed finances, collected taxes, made alliances, and took over bankrupt properties. Tax collecting, as Robert Clive and Warren Hastings had learned, was remarkably profitable, and they discovered this just at a time when the company's trade was less so. Once established in an area, the company became involved in other wars and reform of other states, thus widening contacts with a turbulent frontier of warring and corrupt rajahs and princes which, like a vacuum, pulled the company toward empire.

But not all was pull. As the East India Company grew more powerful, it developed its own not inconsiderable push. The push came not from London, but from British proconsuls in India. Having the best army in India, the generals could not resist using it. Neither could the subcontinent's ablest administrators forgo a display of talent at governing. From 1790 to 1860 a series of extraordinary governor generals journeyed to Calcutta: in 1798, the Duke of Wellington's older brother, the domineering Marquess of Wellesley; in 1828, the reforming Lord William Bentinck, zealous that "British greatness should be founded on Indian happiness"; in 1837, the aggressive would-be conqueror of Afghanistan, Lord Auckland; and in 1848, the restless, railway-building, imperious Lord Dalhousie. All were peers, all landowners, all held their right to rule others as God-given, and all won from London repeated complaints that they were driving the company along the path of empire.

In their employ were intrepid generals like Sir Charles Napier, conqueror of Sind. "We have no right," said the candid Napier, "to seize Sind, yet we shall do so and a very advantageous, useful, piece of rascality will it be." Napier's feats were astonishing. With twelve guns and 2,200 men, of which 500 were British, he defeated 22,000 Baluchis. In another battle his troops killed 5,000 and lost only 270. Superior weapons and training helped create British India. So did steamboats on the Ganges and Brahmaputra and, after 1870, 5,000 miles of railways, instruments never available to Hindu Emperors or Moslem Moguls and instruments that, when combined with the administrative skills and the adroit diplomacy of experienced imperialists, led to a unified India.

Once established, the rule of these proconsuls allowed other imperialistic forces to emerge—missionaries, investors, promoters of steamship lines and jute plantations, and the constant, swelling numbers of the British governing class in the Indian Civil Service. These forces, carefully guided by the Governor Generals, made the first half of the nineteenth century an age of reforms that accorded with Western values. *Suttee* and *thuggee*, for example, were abolished. *Suttee* was the Hindu practice of burning a widow on the funeral pyre of her deceased husband; *thuggee* was the belief that the plunder and murder of travelers was a religious rite. The British outlawed both, as they did infanticide and prohibition of remarriage for widows. The British also reformed the land laws, ending a maze of communal customs that defined village holdings and rent payments. In its place they created, in some areas, peasant proprietors, called *ryots*, and in others landed gentry, called *zamindars*, who leased land to tenants. Land was now private property, salable like its produce, in a market economy.

The British reformed India's criminal laws as well. In 1834 the government sent out the brilliant Thomas Babington Macaulay, historian and Whig politician, to bring order to India's tangled customs. He drew up a criminal code which reflected the best in English common law and the wisest of Bentham's admonitions for clarity, universality, and efficiency. Utilitarian, too, was Macaulay's famous Education Minute, with its recommendation that government-supported schools teach Western literature and science in English, instead of Oriental languages and literature. In a subcontinent of hundreds of languages, the choice of English was practical, but the Minute was nevertheless arrogantly insensitive to the achievements of Hindu and Muslim learning. Macaulay's reforms, like the land reforms, the coming of railways, telegraphs, and cotton factories, the work of missionaries, and the burgeoning of English newspapers and presses, meant that Britain was shaping India in a Western mold.

The changes finally caused a fearful explosion. In May 1857 the sepoys of the East India Company's Bengal Army mutinied. They had learned that the bullet cartridges, whose ends they had to bite off in order to load, were greased with the fat of cows or pigs. To eat beef is as much a sin for Hindus as eating pork is for Muslims. The grease was in fact from corn oil, though earlier it had been from cows. The rumor alone was sufficient, particularly since the sepoys' pay was in arrears and their English officers had grown arrogant and neglectful. The sepoys also had to fight beyond India, which lost some of them caste, and in disastrous Afghan campaigns. The Bengal sepoys were also Hindus who saw some of their most venerable customs threatened by reforming missionaries and bureaucrats. The Earl of Dalhousie's aggressive incorporation of Hindu states and his avid seizure of land by acts of resumption hurt many Hindu rulers and landowners. All these grievances led the sepoys to mutiny and civilians in Delhi and Oudh to support them.

The rebellion was quick and fierce. In May three regiments rebelled, murdered their officers, marched on Delhi, aroused its garrison, and slew every European they could find. At Cawnpore the sepoys promised 400 British civilians a safe exit and then massacred them. But the mutiny failed because the telegraph allowed commanders in other areas to disarm native troops and the railroads to rush in loyal reinforcements—superior technology again making imperialism possible. The repression that followed was full of atrocities that showed that the British too could throw off the mask of civilization. But the repression was brief. Lord Canning, the new governor general, insisted that only murderers proved at law should be punished.

The mutiny profoundly changed British India. Parliament finally abolished the East India Company, and Britain now ruled India through its viceroy and Indian Civil Service. The British army in India was increased, with a third of

A procession of elephants in honor of Lord Curzon's, Viceroy of India, state entry into Delhi (*The Mansell Collection*).

it and all officers to be white. The policy of ardent Westernization also yielded to a more detached and aloof paternal government. The mutiny had added an edge of hatred and fear to the attitude of the rulers and deepened the guilt that only a belief in the benevolence of paternalism could assuage. From 1857 to 1914 that paternalism was put to a test: Would it prove itself benevolent, efficient, and liberating or selfish, stultifying, and oppressive?

British historians tell a story of progress: of modern medicines and public health; of population more than doubling in the nineteenth century; of 40,000 miles of railway by 1914; of 30 million acres of land opened up by irrigation; of textile, jute, and steel mills; and of exports rising from £8 million in 1834 to £137 million in 1910. Their account also tells of intellectual and political improvement; of schools and colleges; a new intelligentsia, educated in science; elected councils where democracy was learned; civil liberties never before enjoyed; and above all a unified, ordered, and peaceful India.

Indian historians tell a story of poverty and oppression. They not only recall the naked plunder of the East India Company in the eighteenth century but consider the company itself a cause of the very chaos the British said required their intervention. That intervention, and the army and administration it brought, cost the Indians millions of pounds a year—in 1913 some £19.4 million. The intervention also destroyed the communal village and brought landlords, middlemen, tax collectors, heavy debts, and extortionate moneylenders, the total burden of which destroyed all incentives to improvement. The peasant was as poor in 1914 as in 1800. From 1877 to 1900 five famines carried off 15 million people. Britain's machine-produced goods wiped out the silks and cottons of India, heralded in the eighteenth century as the world's finest. India's incomparable metallurgists and shipbuilders bowed to the same force, and India's once-balanced economy became more one-sidedly agricultural.

Both British and Indian accounts have much truth in them. British rule was a mixed blessing. It did bring peace, it did create order and unity, and it did cause modernization. No irrigation works in history could rival British India's 40,000 miles of canals, which turned the once-arid Indus Basin into a fertile land. Yet modernization went only halfway. It built canals, but it did not effect a land reform that would provide incentives; it built jute plants, but it fell short of making India industrial. India in 1914 was still an impoverished country, with four-fifths of the people living off a stagnant agriculture. The poverty arose largely from a population explosion that was part of a larger worldwide increase—an increase not the result of British rule. Machine-made goods from the industrial countries of the world would have destroyed handicraft industries even if there had never been British rule. In a material sense, the British case for imperial rule was strong, as it was in terms of peace, good government, and a Western-educated intelligentsia.

Gains there were, but also British insensitivity to Hindu and Muslim traditions and their failure to allow India to grow toward self-government. At the beginning of the twentieth century Britain, instead of giving India an elected Parliament, gave it the Tory Lord Curzon, Viceroy from 1899 to 1905, and the embodiment of imperiousness. He ruled brilliantly, giving the peasants rural banks and canals and demanding administrative efficiency and better education. But he treated Indians as children and did little to further that token role in municipal government that the Liberals had introduced. Instead, full of paranoid fears of Russia, he ordered and completed the conquest of Tibet, of little economic value but satisfying to Curzon and his government's unquestioned faith in Britain's imperial destiny.

India lay at the center of the British consciousness of empire. It was a center of almost mystical attractiveness, as Disraeli realized when he created Victoria Empress of India. The possession of ancient, colorful exotic India was itself a reason for acquiring more lands. It was in fact a source of great wealth, and its self-supporting army was a formidable weapon for expansion. The conviction that every route to this priceless jewel in the British crown needed safeguarding led Britain into Egypt and East Africa, and into conflicts with Russia in the Mediterranean and the Boers in South Africa. The profits of Indian trade also led the British into Burma, Singapore, Malaysia, Borneo, Hong Kong, and parts of China.

The government in London had no plan to acquire these territories. Once again it was piecemeal, once again it arose from local situations, and once again each situation was different. Stamford Raffles in 1816 personally bought the island of Singapore. He realized its strategic importance to trade with China and Indonesia. The East India Company fined him and London condemned him, but he kept it. Burma came piecemeal by way of three wars in 1824,

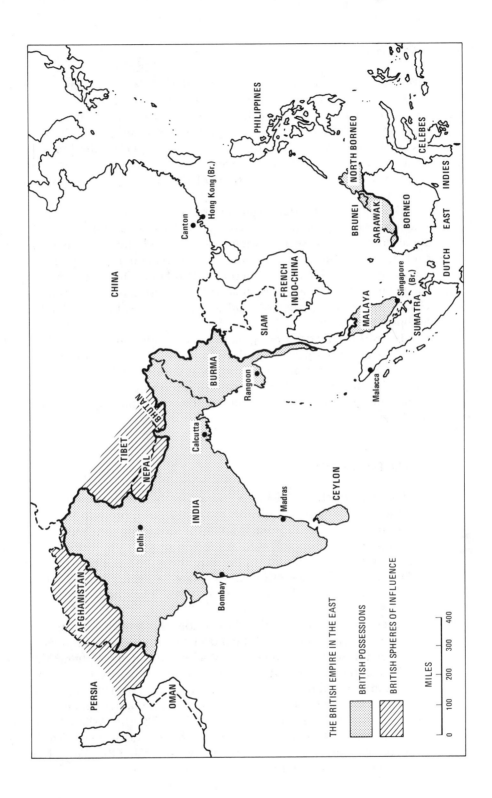

THE BRITISH EMPIRE IN THE EAST

BRITISH POSSESSIONS

BRITISH SPHERES OF INFLUENCE

MILES

0   100   200   300   400

CHINA

Hong Kong (Br.)

Canton

PHILIPPINES

NORTH BORNEO

BRUNEI

SARAWAK

BORNEO

CELEBES

EAST INDIES

FRENCH INDO-CHINA

SIAM

MALAYA

SUMATRA

DUTCH

Singapore (Br.)

BURMA

Rangoon

Malacca

TIBET

BHUTAN

NEPAL

Calcutta

INDIA

Madras

CEYLON

Delhi

Bombay

AFGHANISTAN

PERSIA

OMAN

1852, and 1855. Aggressive Burmese invaders of Bengal's Assam Province caused the first war; a King who abused Britons and an expansionist Governor General of India quick to exploit such behavior caused the second; and the vicious King Thebaw of Upper Burma the third by his intrigues with the French and his addiction to massacres. All three were won quickly, the first witnessing the earliest use in battle of those steamships that from the Yangtze to the Niger would win Britain an Empire. In 1874 the British began the slow infiltration of the Malay states.

By 1898 their resident agents were powerful enough to form a federation under a resident general and a civil service. In Malaya civil wars, piracy, disputed successions, Chinese secret societies, and valuable tin and rubber provided the pull; the push came from Singapore, from merchants, naval captains, and authoritarian Governor Generals trained to rule others. The larger the Empire grew, the greater the number of local situations offering a new class of proconsuls a chance to use a superb navy and a good army to bring order to the region and profits to traders.

In 1874 the British even took the Fiji Islands. They did so because internal disorders made it their moral duty to bring order, because they believed the islands to be of strategic value, and because of possible American and German encroachment. It was a familiar pattern, even to London's reluctance to annex them. The pattern was repeated in Egypt in 1882 and helped begin the scramble for Africa.

THE SCRAMBLE FOR AFRICA

In 1664 the British established a fort at Gambia on the west coast of Africa. It was trade that brought the British to Gambia, as it brought them to the rest of the world. It also led to the establishment of forts along the Gold Coast. Missionaries and philanthropists followed at the end of the eighteenth century, bent on converting the heathen and suppressing the slave trade that had originally led to the forts. In 1787 the evangelicals created at Sierra Leone, between Gambia and the Gold Coast, a home for freed slaves. They hoped to make it a model colony.

After the abolition of the slave trade, the British government found its costly forts useless and turned them over to a committee of merchants. In 1829 the merchants sent Captain George MacLean to supervise them. MacLean, with no official authority, proved a masterful arbitrator of disputes among the coastal tribes, and asserted over them an informal rule. This rule and continued trade led Britain to take back the forts to assert paramountcy, to ally with the Fante tribes against the Ashanti—only to see in 1873, the Ashanti rout the Fante and threaten the British forces. Britain's honor was in peril. To defend it the local commander, the Colonial Secretary, the War Office, the London press, and the public demanded the suppression of the Ashanti.

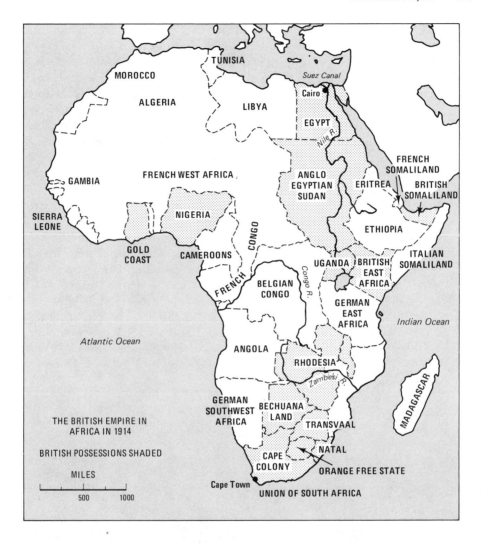

THE BRITISH EMPIRE IN
AFRICA IN 1914

BRITISH POSSESSIONS SHADED

MILES

500   1000

Farther along the coast was the delta of the Niger River, rich in palm oil, and also rich in malaria and strife. The year 1805 that saw the first European venture up the Niger also saw the death from disease of the entire expedition. But by the late nineteenth century, by trial and error, it was discovered that quinine taken daily would prevent, if not malaria itself, death from it. The British, with iron steamships soon dominated the Niger's trade, which earned £300,000 a year. That trade proved, as elsewhere, disruptive to existing tribal governments; warfare and strife increased. At the same time, the French were closing in. In London Parliament wanted no more expensive colonies. What should be done? George Goldie, entrepreneur and builder of a trade monopoly on the Niger, had a solution, an old eighteenth-century one: create a chartered company and let it profit and rule. In 1886 the British chartered the Royal Niger Company, which made Nigeria a part of the Empire.

Lord Salisbury, the prime minister who gave Goldie his charter, found trading companies useful in the scramble for Africa. He gave Cecil Rhodes a charter in 1889 to rule the lands of the Zambesi basin, lands David Livingstone, armed with his daily two grains of quinine, had explored between 1858 and 1864. Many missionaries had followed in Livingstone's wake. Salisbury, a genial, philosophical, and cynical aristocrat, cared little for missionaries and traders. He told them the government would not protect them if they plunged into dangerous lands. Yet Salisbury gave Rhodes a charter to advance north. He did so in order to assert British, and curtail Boer, paramountcy over South Africa. A second reason was to check Germany's intrusion into Africa.

Germany, united as an empire in 1871, and ruled by the Iron Chancellor, Otto von Bismarck, annexed German Southwest Africa in 1884. In the same year the Society for German Colonization sent Karl Peters into East Africa. The French and Portuguese were also expanding. Bismarck, who liked order, convened the Conference of Berlin in 1885 to define the rules of occupation, the main one being that a nation could claim no territory not occupied. The scramble that ensued quite astonished Salisbury. He told an audience that in 1880 "nobody thought about Africa," and in 1885 everyone was quarreling over it. Salisbury claimed he did not know why. His disclaimer was a bit disingenuous, since the British occupation of Egypt in 1882 had helped initiate that scramble.

Victorian view of Africans as primitive and inferior (*Illustrated London News*).

As usual Britain did not intend to occupy another territory; events compelled it, said the government. Had troops not been sent, Egypt would not pay her debts, anarchy would reign, the Suez canal would be endangered. Gladstone, in asking Parliament for £2.3 million to pay for the invasion, referred to Egypt's "anarchical condition," Britain's mission to spread the "blessings of civilized life," and the need to protect the canal. Parliament voted 275 to 19 for an expedition which, on August 16, 1882, defeated the Egyptian army of Colonel Arabi.

Egypt did have a large debt. Ismail, the Khedive of Egypt from 1863 to 1879, was extravagant. He commissioned Giuseppe Verdi's opera *Aida* for the opening of the canal, improved agriculture, poured gifts on corrupt officials, spent profusely on himself and his concubines, and ran up a debt whose interest payments took two-thirds of Egypt's revenue. A debt commission made up of Europeans took control of finances, and foreign advisors moved into key ministries. It did no good, for Ismail dismissed the foreigners and continued to spend wildly. The British and French forced him to abdicate in favor of his son Tewfik, who did no better. Conditions were ripe for Colonel Arabi to lead his fellow officers in a nationalist revolt that demanded government by Egyptians, not foreigners. The revolt did not cause anarchy, did not lead to talk of repudiating debts, and did not threaten the Suez Canal. To talk of occupying Egypt, wrote Disraeli in 1876, was "moonshine," a view Gladstone and the public shared. Yet Britain went in. The main reason given then and since was the need to defend the canal as a sea route to India.

British troops after defeating the Egyptian army in 1882 (*Radio Times, Hulton Picture Library*).

PUNCH, OR THE LONDON CHARIVARI.—February 26, 1876.

THE LION'S SHARE.

" GARE À QUI LA TOUCHE ! "

Disraeli in 1875 buys the Suez—to the English, the key to India (*Punch*).

Disraeli in 1875 had bought Ismail's 44 percent of the Suez Canal shares. Britain had long considered its influence in Constantinople and the vigor of the Ottoman Empire the principal bulwark against Russian threats to the route to India. As the Ottoman Empire tottered and British influence weakened, Egypt itself became more valuable to the defense of the canal. Gladstone's conversion came, said his foreign secretary, "when he admitted for the first time that we were bound to protect the Suez Canal."

Strategic worries, like fears of anarchy, are matters of subjective perception as well as objective reality, perceptions that reflect one's conditioning. Gladstone was a Christian who considered Muslims backward, a landowner who shared Coleridge's philosophy of paternalism, and a Briton who had been High Commissioner of the Ionian islands. He was also Prime Minister of a Cabinet whose Whigs thought in terms of spheres of influence, of a Liberal party split over Ireland, of a country whose pride in Empire ran deep, of a foreign office whose man-on-the-spot exaggerated Egypt's anarchy, and of an army and navy easily superior to Arabi's forces. Given these conditions, and given the sincerely held illusion that the occupation would only last a year or two, the paradox of a reluctant Britain occupying Egypt is understandable.

Imperial expansion tends to be self-generating—there is always the magnetic attraction of neighboring territories. In Egypt it was the Sudan. A large part of Ismail's extravagance arose from efforts to annex the Sudan. An uprising of a Muslim Messiah, the Mahdi, and his followers in the Sudan threatened the British in Khartoum. General "Chinese" Gordon was sent to rescue them in February of 1884. He dallied, was surrounded, and in January 1885, massacred. The massacre came two days before the arrival of a relieving force delayed because of confusion on the part of Gladstone, Lord Cromer, and its commander, Garnet Wolseley. Gladstone told Lord Cromer to settle the finances of Egypt and leave. Cromer stayed to rule over the khedive and Egypt for twenty-four years and to give Egypt, as Curzon had India, a paternal rule that improved life but in no way prepared its people for self-government.

Gladstone's government fell in 1886, and Lord Salisbury took over. Until then the Conservatives had been no more expansionist than the Liberals. In Parliament Salisbury had spoken disdainfully of lakes in Africa whose names he forgot and which were perhaps only swamps, yet he painted more bright red on the map of Africa than any other Prime Minister. Under his ministries of 1886–92 and 1894–1902, the Sudan, Kenya, Uganda, Nyasaland, Northeast Rhodesia, and Nigeria became British.

The British Empire was created, as many have said, in a fit of absence of mind. Salisbury no more than Gladstone or Disraeli, desired a larger empire, but neither he nor his predecessors could resist the demands for military assistance of those on the frontier, traders like Goldie, missionaries like Livingstone, generals like Wolseley, and governors like Rhodes. Neither would nationalism at home or a balance of power diplomacy tolerate other countries acquiring territories that could be British. Thus when Germany's Karl Peters moved into what is today Tanzania, when the Portuguese pressed up the Zambesi, and when the French moved on Nigeria, Salisbury checked each move. He directed Britain's consul in Mozambique to make treaties in Nyasaland and Northeast Rhodesia; he gave William McKinnon, the steamship magnate of the Indian Ocean, a charter for a British East African Company and urged him to move into Kenya and Uganda; and he granted Goldie a charter for Nigeria.

The main challenge came from Germany in East Africa. Salisbury met it by offering Germany Heligoland in the North Sea in exchange for Kenya, Uganda, and a protectorate over the Sultan of Zanzibar, an offer Germany accepted.

France was less amenable to deals. In 1897 Captain Marchand left the

The Gatling gun, an early form of the machine gun, was as powerful an instrument of imperialism as the ironclad steamboat (*Illustrated London News*).

Congo for the upper Nile. After an eighteen-month advance through jungle and desert, he, 7 Frenchmen, and 120 Senegalese raised the French flag at Fashoda. Two months later, on September 19, Lord Kitchener and an entire army met Captain Marchand and the 7 Frenchmen and made it clear that the Sudan and upper Nile belonged to Britain. Kitchener's main enemy had never been the French but an army of 50,000 Dervishers, Dervishers who in 1885 had massacred General Gordon's army. Gordon's men did not have, and Kitchener's did, the Maxim, a breech-loading and repeating rifle. The result, reported the young Winston Churchill, of a five-hour battle was "a hell of whistling metal" and 11,000 Dervishers "in tangled heaps." British and Egyptian losses were 80. The breech-loading and repeating rifle is second only to quinine as an explanation of why Europe, after centuries of contact, could partition Africa in but 16 years.

British territory ran from Cairo to Uganda and Nyasaland to the Cape, with large possessions on both east and west coasts. Salisbury said he acquired these territories for strategic reasons: Uganda and Sudan controlled the headwaters of the Nile, vital to Egypt's agriculture, while Rhodesia and Nyasaland checked the Boers, whose expansion would threaten British control of South Africa, which, like Egypt, was strategic to the route to India. Considerations of strategy had led British soldiers to the empty, barren, rocky, outpost of Fashoda, thousands of miles from London, Bombay, and Cairo.

The Nile River and its source had long had a magical hold on the British mind, almost as magical as the words "route to India." To defend that route and river, Gladstone seized Egypt and Salisbury the Sudan, areas of no great economic value, either as markets or fields for investment. In 1892 McKinnon's company spent £80,000 and earned £35,000. Most African colonies proved an economic loss to their proud occupiers; a colony's strategic value thus remained the only rational reason for acquiring it. It was the reason the philosophical Salisbury gave. But Salisbury's perceptions were, no less than Gladstone's, conditioned by his situation. He lived in a Britain of unparalleled industrial, technological, and imperial triumphs and in a Europe fraught with industrial competition, arms races, diplomatic rivalries, and a bombastic nationalism that gloried in Empire. These and other events came together in the Britain of the 1880s and after to produce an intense and passionate imperialism.

IMPERIALISM AND EMPIRE

In 1883 Sir John Seeley, professor of history at Cambridge, published *The Expansion of England* and awoke countless Britons to their imperial greatness. Other writers also opened floodgates of imperialist sentiment. In 1885 the idea that the dominions should form a closer union inspired the establishment of the Imperial Federation League; in 1883 W. T. Stead became editor of the *Pall Mall Gazette* and in 1888 W. E. Hanley founded the *National Observer*, both journals championing the cause of Empire, a cause that in 1899 won a much larger audience among the half-million readers of the *Daily Mail*, the first of the cheap, sensationalist dailies. Neomercantilist ideas of a grand imperial trade area led in 1891 to the United Empire Trade League, followed in 1903 by Joseph Chamberlain's campaign for imperial tariffs. In 1887 the government and zealous friends of Empire organized the first Colonial Conference, and in 1890 and 1891 G. A. Henty published *Bombardment of Alexandria* and *The Dash for Khartoum*, two of some thirty popular tales for boys. In 1900 Karl Pearson, foremost of Social Darwinists, lectured the British on the struggle for existence as a mechanism of progress, and in 1899 the poet Rudyard Kipling urged the reader to

Take up the White Man's Burden
Send forth the best ye breed
Go bind your son to exile
To serve your captives need.

Enthusiasm for imperialism was irrepressible. "They are tumbling over each other, Liberals and Conservatives," said Cecil Rhodes in 1899, "to show which side are the greatest and most enthusiastic Imperialists."

In 1897 the whole Empire celebrated Queen Victoria's Diamond Jubilee. Troops from every corner of the empire, some 50,000 splendidly attired, marched down the Strand and Fleet Street to St. Paul's. The Queen sent telegrams of gratitude to celebrations throughout the Empire. The people of London cheered. The masses cared deeply about the Empire. During the Boer War they agonized over the fate of the British troops besieged for six months in Mafeking. When news arrived from South Africa in July 1900 that the British had relieved Mafeking, Londoners poured into the streets for an orgy of drunken and riotous celebration. As the century ended, nationalism reached fever pitch in Britain as it did in France and Germany, and its favorite mode of expression was imperialism. It touched all classes, every religious faith, all political parties. Radicals like Charles Dilke proclaimed its virtues in a book entitled *Greater Britain*; the Liberal prime minister, Lord Rosebery, bowed to no one in its defense; scarcely a Tory doubted its rightfulness; and the Fabian Socialist and playwright, G. B. Shaw, announced that "a Fabian is necessarily an Imperialist in theory."

Three powerful developments explain this fervid imperialism: intellectual and social trends in England, economic and diplomatic rivalries abroad, and the overwhelming fact of empire. The intellectual and social trends were many and complex, ranging from learned Social Darwinist works like Benjamin Kidd's *The Control of the Tropics* to Kipling's poems and the jingoist songs of the music halls. There was, of course, the persistent call by Christian evangelicals to go forth and convert heathen. Persistent, too, since the eighteenth century, were humanitarians anxious to end slavery or protect the aborigines. Much newer was that pseudoscience, Social Darwinism, which proclaimed the supremacy of the Anglo-Saxon race. The new science of anthropology also claimed that whites were superior to the colored races. By 1900 this belief permeated imperial thought. Urbanization, increasing wealth, and popular education had meanwhile produced rootless, lonely, and often bored city dwellers, avid readers of newspapers, biographies, and novels, of Kitchener's triumphs, Livingstone's heroism, Kipling's tales of India, and the incredible wealth of Cecil Rhodes. The incomes of most city dwellers were no greater because of the Empire, but their fantasy life was richer and their pride in being British immeasurably greater.

The rise of Germany as an economic, military, and imperial power, the restless, defiant probings of a chauvinistic France, and the threats to the Near East of the Russian colossus created among the British and their leaders a deep anxiety, one that made more strident their imperialist boastings and strivings. German ships took German goods everywhere. Leading English economists and businessmen formed Imperial Federation Leagues demanding imperial tariffs. For statesmen like Salisbury, a deft player of the diplomatic game, the rise of Germany, Bismarck's formidable alliances, and the intrusion of Germany and France into Africa posed a serious threat to the balance of power. The nationalism of the populace, the economic fears of businessmen, and the diplomacy of statesmen all led to an anxiety and defensiveness that could best be assuaged by a stronger affirmation of the need of a great British Empire.

The existence of an Empire on which the sun never set also caused the British to become devoted imperialists. For more than a century the fact of Empire had insinuated itself into their lives, defining the very image they had of themselves as superior people. Millions had emigrated, populating the dominions, ruling India, trading in China, preaching in Africa, making fortunes in Latin America. Visits and letters home and the return of imperial servants gave succeeding generations a personal and intimate picture of the wealth, excitement, and color of Empire, pictures enhanced by a stream of novels and journals telling of Britain's achievements. For more than a century, trade and investment had brought wealth. Tours abroad on British steamers, with stops at British hotels in Cairo, Aden, and Bombay, made vivid the fact of Empire, especially for those of the governing class who found pride and incomes in military and administrative service abroad. It was a cumulative process, a multiplying experience.

The fact of Empire helps explain the wave of imperialism far more than the wave of imperialism helps explain the fact of Empire. The building of the Empire began in 1583 in Newfoundland and, except for the Boer War and the League of Nations Mandates in 1919, ended in 1898 at Fashoda. Nine-tenths of the Empire was acquired before imperialism became a popular passion. The piecing together of the British Empire was steady and gradual, like the growth of a coral reef. The main cause of that steady accretion of territory was British power, military and economic. From 1740 to 1815 ruinous wars weakened the continental powers, leaving the British navy supreme and trade free to establish posts throughout the world. The Industrial Revolution converted that naval and commercial supremacy into a near monopoly.

During the first century of this unrivaled power it was trade that gave the greatest push to Empire; it took the British to Lagos, Rangoon, and Mandalay and up the Niger, Ganges, and Yangtze (Changjiang) rivers. There were of course other propelling agents: pilgrims, explorers, missionaries, adventurers, foes of slavery, the land-hungry in the thousands, convicts against their will, fleeing embezzlers, and naval and army officers in search of fame. Yet it was still profit that supplied the pervasive drive: the mere mention of gold in Australia sped thousands on their way, the slimmest chance of a clothing contract in Bolivia brought a Manchester agent, and talk of profitable coffee plantations in Ceylon brought investments from London. So great were the investments and trade that the economist John Hobson argued in his *Imperialism, A Study* of 1902 that capitalism was the main force behind imperialism. Capitalism had created a wealthy and powerful elite of investors, traders, and manufacturers anxious to make profits. Capitalism had also, by its unequal distribution of wealth, given so little purchasing power to the workers that they could not buy all the goods produced. This underconsumption forced the elite to search for markets abroad and so to persuade their government to acquire territories abroad as markets for goods, places for investment, and sources of raw materials. Hobson's arguments impressed Lenin, who in 1916 carried them further in his *Imperialism: The Highest Stage of Capitalism.*

Because traders were initially so crucial and because many did profit from Empire, Hobson's book has remained a persuasive interpretation of imperialism. But when each accretion to the Empire is examined closely, the London banker or Manchester cotton agent either vanishes or appears small. Looming much larger is the man on the spot confronted with a turbulent local situation. No one in London directed Stamford Raffles to buy Singapore, James Brooke to become Rajah of Sarawak, or India's Governor Generals to acquire hundreds of princedoms. Neither did London businessmen cause governors in Singapore to persuade a reluctant Colonial Office to move into Malaya. No London investors forced the Colonial Office to allow General Wolseley to wage war on the Ashanti or to agree to the annexation of the Fiji Islands; in both cases, local wars and chaos led local administrators to urge the Colonial Office to act. Economic gain sent thousands of Britons to Canada, Australia, New Zealand, and South Africa, but not at the behest of bankers and captains of industry; nor did bankers and captains of industry persuade Gladstone to take Egypt or Milner to precipitate the Boer War.

Traders were not unimportant, but they were often, as in Malaya and Burma, local traders whose security and honor, like the security and honor of missionaries and settlers and district officers, demanded protection. Such protection meant more troops and perhaps British advisors for neighboring chiefs, rajahs, or sultans. Britain in the nineteenth century became entangled in hundreds of local situations, each potentially troublesome. The governors and commissioners in these areas were often military men trained in imperial rule who believed in white supremacy and were thousands of miles from London. Before the telegraph and the Suez Canal, it took months to send a message from India or South Africa to London and months for the return, and if the Colonial or India Office dallied, a year could go by. The steady growth of Empire in fact owed much to decisions necessarily made by the man on the spot.

But though much of the drive for Empire arose from local situations, London still remained in control. The Prime Minister and Cabinet still had to assent before a Burma or Bechuanaland could be annexed. Although the new colonies proved very disappointing as markets for investment or exports, some capitalists did prosper, and many more had large hard-to-quench expectations of great profits, expectations that, in the depressed 1880s and with German and American goods everywhere, became urgent ones. Although Rhodes exaggerated in claiming that if no markets existed abroad there would be civil war at home, it did reflect a pervasive belief that more Empire was good for economic ills. And equally pervasive was the belief that more Empire was strategically necessary.

Assertions of strategy often covered up a more profound paternalism. The governing classes had an Olympian conviction in Britain's mission to govern inferiors. It was a conviction with many roots. One of the sturdiest was overwhelming military and industrial power. Another was the achievement of ruling an Empire well and the habits of authority it engendered. Frederick Lugard, the founder of Uganda and architect of Nigeria, was born and raised in India, as was Kipling, the imperial poet. General Roberts, conqueror of the Boers, first spent some forty years in India; the two governors at Singapore who insisted on British control of Malaya had learned warfare and administration in Africa and India. Milner, High Commissioner on the Cape and more than any person the author of the Boer War, served under Lord Cromer in Egypt. The Empire begat its own imperialists. But the roots of paternalism also run back to a landed aristocracy that for centuries had ruled over English farmers and Irish peasants, an aristocracy which learned in public schools and universities that it was their duty to govern others. Gladstone was reluctant to take Egypt, Lord Carnarvon hesitated about Malaya, and Salisbury scoffed at Africa. But when local officials implored them to intervene in order to end anarchy and bring order, they relented. Britain must, said Gladstone of Egypt, bring "the blessings of civilized life."

Nationalism as well as paternalism played a role. It was not an intense force until the end of the century, but it was always latent. Public opinion seldom pressed the government to intervene or send troops, but once an area was occupied or troops engaged in battle, Britain's honor was involved. There was also, in patricians and masses, a strong racism. "The Africans," wrote General Wolseley from the Gold Coast, "are like monkeys, they are a good-for-nothing race." In 1849 Thomas Carlyle pronounced Europeans wiser than Africans and said inferior races must obey the superior. It was an idea that by 1900 most English men and women held, one that fit the paternalism of the governing classes and the jingoism of the lower classes. The Empire had created a nation of imperialists.

FURTHER READING

The Cambridge History of the British Empire, Vols. 1–8. Cambridge: Cambridge University Press. The second edition 1963 has made many corrections and valuable additions to this majestic and patriotic survey of the creation of the world's largest empire.

CURTIN, PHILIP. *The Image of Africa: British Ideas and Action, 1780–1850.* Madison: University of Wisconsin Press, 1964. A probing examination of the least agreeable side of British imperialism, its pervasively racist and arrogantly paternalist view of the blacks in Africa.

FIELDHOUSE, D. D. *Economics and Empire: 1830–1914.* London: Weidenfeld and Nicolson, 1973. A balanced and finely tuned analysis of those political, intellectual, social, personal, and economic forces that led to imperialism, one dubious of the role of investment but not of trade.

HEADRICK, DANIEL R. *The Tools of Empire*. Oxford: Oxford University Press, 1981. A concise but most illuminating study of how technological advances furthered nineteenth-century imperialism.

HOBSON, JOHN. *Imperialism: A Study*. Ann Arbor: University of Michigan Press, 1968. The first definitive statement that a fully developed capitalism's needs for markets, raw materials, and areas of investment led to imperialism.

KNAPLUND, PAUL. *The British Empire, 1815–1939*. New York: Harper and Brothers, 1941. A comprehensive and sound textbook on the rise of the British Empire that emphasizes the vast variety of races, cultures, nations, and geographies that evolved into the variegated British Empire.

McINTYRE, W. DAVID. *Colonies into Commonwealth*. London: Brandford Press, 1966. The clearest account of the formation of the British Empire, its evolution into a Commonwealth, and its decline; good on recent research and different interpretations.

MORRIS JAMES. *Pax Brittanica: The Climax of Empire*. London: Faber, 1968. Not a narrative but a survey of the British Empire at its height around 1900, a vivid survey full of color, excitement, and brilliant insights.

NAIDES, MARK. *The Second British Empire, 1783–1965: A Short History*. Mass.: Addison-Wesley, 1970. An impressionistic interpretation of British imperialism, providing an outline of crucial facts and an analysis of the relation of the British to the indigenous people and institutions.

ROBINSON, RONALD, and JOHN GALLAGHER. *Africa and the Victorians*. London: St. Martin's Press, 1961. A powerful, scholarly, but overstated argument that the principal motive leading Britain to dominate Africa was strategic concern, especially over the route to India.

WIENER, JOEL, ed. *Great Britain: Foreign Policy and the Span of Empire, 1689–1971*, Vol. 3. New York: Chelsea House, 1974. A collection of important documents on the Empire from 1852 to 1913, including reports of select committees and royal commissions, treaties, dispatches and propaganda, and speeches for and against.

An age of crisis: 1873–1914

26

From 1847 to 1873 sustained economic growth assured most English people of the soundness of capitalism, the merits of parliamentary government, the importance of the Empire, and the wisdom of Victorian morality. It was a solid, secure, confident age. It had, to be sure, crises and anxieties, but crises could be settled and anxieties repressed. After 1873, economic and political events began to undermine the Victorian belief that all was well. The year 1873 saw a sharper than normal fall in prices, and declining interest rates and profits. By 1896 commodity prices were a third less than in 1873, though the fall was sporadic. The year 1879 saw the invasion of cheap grains and the plummeting of rents. The years 1884–89 brought an average unemployment rate for skilled workers of 7 percent—and it was much higher for the unskilled.

Prosperity and growth continued, but at a slower rate and with ups and downs. Some "downs" were so severe they led to doubts about the soundness of capitalism. Boom and bust created an atmosphere of crisis that spread to society and politics. Workers became belligerent. They established unions, struck for higher wages, organized socialist and labor parties. Businessmen organized and sought to break unions. Women, refused the vote, became violent; the Irish, refused home rule, grew bellicose. There was also a crisis of conscience as increasing prosperity made wretched housing, poverty, the suffering of the aged and ill, and the cruelties of unemployment seem indefensible. A secure age that trusted in prosperity, *laissez-faire*, and self-help became a nervous age of crises. Of these many crises, one of the most disturbing was the state of the British economy. Though still a colossus, it was beginning to flag in its race with America and Germany.

A FLAGGING COLOSSUS

British capitalism from 1873 to 1914 was a formidable force in the world economy and, despite rumors to the contrary, a growing one. But some of its arteries were hardening, allowing youthful America and Germany to challenge its ascendancy. Since bad news, not good, makes headlines, journalists and historians have underestimated the strength of Britain's economy from 1873 to 1914. An able reporter would have insisted that his editor consider four items about the economy's strength: its continued growth, its active role in the second Industrial Revolution, its leadership in world trade and finance, and the rising standard of life of the people.

Britain's economic growth was slow, averaging about 2.2 percent per person a year from 1870 to 1914. Yet it was growth. Between 1870 and 1914 the annual production of cotton and iron, those great staples on which the industrial economy rested, nearly doubled, that of wool and coal more than doubled, and shipbuilding increased two and a half times. From 1871 to 1911 output per textile worker increased 35 percent, and the cost of steel, £40 in 1860, was only £4 in 1895. England, in 1911, supplied 59 percent of the world's cotton manufactures, exported more cars than it imported, and produced steel as efficiently as in the United States. In 1871 the national product was worth £782 million; in 1901, at constant prices, it was worth £1.9 billion. Much of that increase came in the service trades, especially with the growth of the more efficient and accessible department and chain stores. Much of it also came from abroad, with huge dividends on investments for the rich, and for the masses, cheap food.

At the heart of the second Industrial Revolution were two new forms of power, electricity and the internal combustion engine, but there also appeared a host of new products, the result of advances in chemistry, precision machinery, mechanization, and the assembly line. Britain made significant contributions in chemistry—soaps, paints, fertilizers, and explosives sold widely—and in precision machinery. Its real genius lay with metals and machines, and after 1870 Britain continued to create harder and better steel from which, with improved lathes, milling, and grinding machines, it produced not only industrial machines of all sorts, but also sewing machines, clocks, and (in 1913 alone) 150,000 bicycles.

Britain's £4 billion in overseas investment nearly equaled the £5.5 billion Germany, America, the Netherlands, and Belgium together had invested abroad. British ships dominated the sea lanes, its banks served the world, the pound was as solid as gold, and the Empire afforded a vast market for goods. And although Britain exported only £635 million in goods, as compared to the £769 million worth imported, it still enjoyed a favorable balance of trade of £239 million because of £367 million in invisible earnings. Most of these came from shipping, but much also from interest in overseas investment and from large profits as the world's supreme bankers, brokers, insurers, and trusted guardian of that gold-based pound that underlay the world's finance.

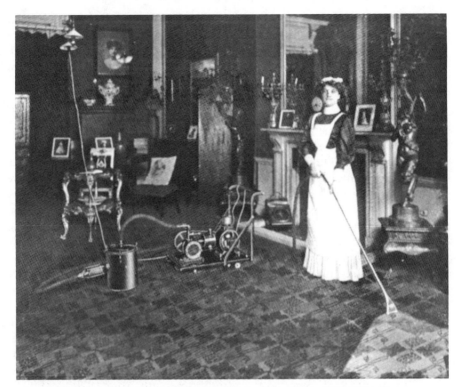

The wonders of electricity give birth to the vacuum cleaner (*The British Vacuum Cleaner Company Ltd*).

In 1870 the average yearly income (at 1913 prices) was £26.8, in 1910 it was £48.2. For most citizens of Britain, the most important economic event between 1870 and 1900 was the fall in the price of food and manufactures. The price of wheat was halved, meat and dairy prices fell by 10 percent, and shops were crowded with inexpensive ready-to-wear clothing, machine-made shoes, glass and pottery, and hardwares. One could also buy at reasonable prices watches, bicycles, cameras, sewing machines, and, at higher prices, gramophones, automobiles, electric vacuum cleaners, and washing machines. The standard of living in 1914 was nearly twice as high as it was in 1870.

Yet all was not well. There were disquieting symptoms, a slower growth rate, a hesitancy to adopt technologies, recessions, and gross inequalities of incomes.

"Slower growth" is a relative concept, relative not only to America's and Germany's more rapid growth but to Britain's growth earlier in the nineteenth century. From 1819 to 1853, Britain increased its gross national product 3.5 percent each year; from 1870 to 1913, by only 2.2 percent. From 1870 to 1913 annual industrial growth was 2.1 percent, while America's was 4.9 percent. Britain produced a third of the world's steel in 1880 and only a seventh in 1902. That seventh, however, consisted of 5 million tons, whereas the earlier third amounted to only 1 million. Britain enjoyed 41 percent of world trade in 1870 and only 30 percent in 1914, but since world trade was worth £5, not £4, billion, the absolute amount of British trade abroad slipped but little. Although the giant was still growing, it now faced faster-growing economies that were quicker to adopt the new technologies.

Britain's hesitancy to adopt new technologies was disturbing. Its scientists, Faraday and Clerk Maxwell in electricity, W. H. Perkin in dyes, and Bessemer and Gilchrest-Thomas in steel, led Europe in inventions and discoveries; yet it was Germany and the United States who led in their industrial development. Critics of Britain's late Victorian economy accuse her of sticking with less efficient spindles in spinning, the open hearth in steel, and the Le Banc method for producing soda, while Germany employed more efficient furnaces, ring spindles, and the Solway process. Given the hard wrought iron and superior thread produced by the open hearth and mule spindle, there were good reasons to continue their use, but in no way was Le Blanc the equal to the Solway method nor was there any reason to avoid the use of standardized parts and the assembly line in automaking.

The economy's severe fluctuations, its booms and slumps, was a third disturbing sign. British capitalism had a manic-depressive quality to it, now buoyant and spirited, now depressed and gloomy. In 1882, 1889, and 1899 only 2 percent of trade union workers were unemployed; in 1879, 1886, and 1910 it was around 10 percent. Real wages rose around 35 percent from 1870 to 1900, then fell 8 percent from 1900 to 1914. These fluctuations were unsettling. Parliament and the press called the earlier period of rising real wages and economic growth but falling prices and profits the "Great Depression," while they called the later period of rising prices and profits but falling real wages and declining growth a period of prosperity. These descriptions reflect the inequitable distribution of wealth and power that characterized late Victorian and Edwardian capitalism.

When Edward VII became King in 1901, economic inequality was, as it had always been, enormous. Nearly one-third of the national income went to but 3 percent of income earners, another third to another 9 percent, and just over a third to the 88 percent at the bottom. These inequalities along with the 8 percent fall in real wages after 1900, seemed to confirm Karl Marx's prediction that the rich would grow richer and the poor poorer, and that capitalism would produce fierce class conflicts. That the poor would grow poorer proved false in the long run; the fall in real wages was temporary. Not so temporary was the British loss of industrial leadership and the relative slowness in adopting technological changes.

In any analysis of why the rate of British economic growth slowed, two facts must be made clear: first, Britain could not have preserved its near monopoly of manufacturing forever, and, second, Britain was not responsible for the world-wide depression in prices between 1873 and 1896. In 1870 Britain controlled

Huge steamships like the S.S. *Titanic* lead Britain to become number one on the sea lanes and in world trade and empire (*Radio Times, Hulton Picture Library*).

75 percent of the world's production of cotton, iron rails, galvanized iron, tin plate, locomotives, ships, and coal, a position the healthiest economy could not sustain once other countries industrialized. Neither could a healthy economy have prevented the so-called Great Depression. The prosperity of the 1850s and 1860s owed much to the heavy investment in steel mills, railways, shipyards, docks, and warehouses, investments which resulted from inventions in the manufacture of steel. The building of these mills, railways, shipyards, docks, and warehouses meant the hiring of many workers. Their incomes in turn drove up prices, especially since these capital improvements temporarily did nothing to produce a flood of consumer goods. After 1873 capital expansion in these industries abated, workers were laid off, and incomes declined. Meanwhile mills, shipyards, ships, docks, and railways all over the world began to disgorge an unprecedented quantity of cheaper goods onto the market. Furthermore, no great discoveries of gold were made until 1898 in Alaska. As a result, the supply of money based on gold contracted and with less money chasing goods, prices fell and with them, profits. Investors grew cautious; plant, dock, and railway expansion slowed down; unemployment rose. But then around 1890 innovations in chemicals and electricity and the internal combustion engine led to heavy investment in new industries. After 1900 gold supplies also increased, and there was a housing boom. A new cycle of growth came, though far more for America and Germany than Britain. In Britain, from 1870 to 1913, productivity per worker increased a slim 0.6 percent a year. In Germany it increased a healthy 2.6 percent a year, an alarming difference and the key to the fact that Germany's gross national product increased 4.1 percent a year, compared to Britain's annual increase of 2.2 percent.

Many facts about the British economy help explain its failure to equal Germany's and America's rate of growth. As the pioneer in industry, Britain built the first spinning mills using the "mule" and the first steel mills using the Bessemer open hearth. These profitable mills were connected to other steps in cotton spinning and steel making and were accordingly located near large railway terminals, warehouses, and coalyards. To build a new mill meant moving away from these advantages. Although these mills could not compete in efficiency with those using the improved Gilchrest-Thomas process and ring spindles, they could make a profit, a profit that discouraged innovation and diversification.

The rational response would have been to build new plants and produce a greater variety of goods, acts too bold for conservative late Victorians who preferred sending their steels and cottons that could not compete in Europe to the Empire and Asia. Britain also sent capital overseas—in 1913 half of all her savings. By 1914 her overseas capital was worth as much as her industrial and commercial capital, land excluded, at home.

The financial houses of London had long looked to overseas investments. Overall investments declined after 1900, as the rich spent more and saved less. German banks and industry cooperated more closely and planned their investments in such areas as steel, chemicals, and electricity more intelligently; they

The most resplendent, exciting, and revolutionary product of the second Industrial Revolution was the automobile (*The Science Museum, Kensington*).

even poured money, as the British did not, into scientific research. Their efforts proved effective, since a few great firms, united into cartels, dominated each industry. In Britain the family firm prevailed, a very efficient unit for early Victorian textile mills but not for automobiles. It took the Wolseley firm 4,000 men a year to make 3,000 cars, a fact which explains why, in 1913, America produced 462,000 cars and Britain only 13,000.

Historians differ on how flagging was the British colossus. Many are critical, pointing to the persistence of the small family firm, the neglect of the assembly line and standardized parts, the inertia of old plants and old ways, the complacency of owners less businesslike than their grandfathers, and the failure to educate engineers and businessmen. Britain's universities graduated less than 200 engineers a year, Germany's over 3,000. Other historians present a different story. They deny that, despite fewer engineers, English industry was in anyway hurt by a lack of scientific skills. They also doubt that talent for business declines with generations, that family firms are necessarily inefficient, and that old staple industries—cotton, coal, steel, and ships—either decayed or prevented the emergence of new products. In 1914 cotton was a booming industry; productivity in coal was superior to all European countries and equal to Germany's; the price and quality of the Morris auto equaled Ford's Model-T, and car ownership proportionately was as high as in America; England's rayon industry was superior to Germany's and her shipyards produced half the world's tonnage. Moreover, England remained the financial and business center of the world, her national income at an all-time high. It was not, however, equally shared, and hence many were impoverished.

THE IMPOVERISHED

In 1889, Charles Booth, a businessman turned amateur sociologist, said that 30 percent of Londoners lived below the poverty line. His estimate was not hearsay, since he and his helpers had visited thousands of homes. Investigating the poor was an old art; in 1797 Sir Frederick Eden published *The State of the Poor* and in 1851 Henry Mayhew brought out *London Labour and the London Poor*. Both works described a society much poorer than that which confronted Booth. The average income in the 1890s was double what it was in the 1850s. Yet since poverty is relative to one's expectations and to one's neighbor's wealth, there were in Britain in 1889 many poor people. There was also a fervor greater than usual to investigate them. A Congregationalist, the Reverend Andrew Mearns, published *The Bitter Cry of Outcast London* in 1883, and the founder of the Salvation Army, William Booth, published *In Darkest England, The Way Out*. Both displayed an intimate knowledge of the wretched life of London's poor and both, unlike many early Victorians, believed that society, as well as the individual, was responsible for poverty. The problem was not so much the improvident and lazy pauper but a crowded, cruel London that produced the

A London slum in 1889 (*Radio Times, Hulton Picture Library*).

improvident and lazy. With expanding wealth poverty ceased to seem inevitable, but rather something that could be reduced. Certainly something should be done about London's slums, some of which were more miserable in the 1890s than they had been in the 1850s.

Three thousand Londoners, said Charles Booth, live in rooms with eight or more persons, while a half million live in rooms with three or more. These slums "reek of malaria," said William Booth, and of a "foul and fetid breath that is poisonous." The walls and ceilings were black with filth. Broken windows stuffed with rags kept out not only the wind but fresh air and light. Sometimes an old broken chair, a rough table, and a bed of rags and straw might be found, sometimes a couple of boxes and a plank held up by bricks, and sometimes no furniture at all. Coal was costly, rooms often cold, and cooking infrequent, hence the swarms of costermongers on the streets peddling hot food. Water was obtained either at filthy cisterns from courtyard pipes that were turned on twice a week for twenty minutes. Dismal as these were, their rents rose as wider streets, railways, docks, warehouses, offices, and shops destroyed already scarce worker's tenements: by 1900 rents took from one-fourth to one-half of the earnings of nearly one-half of London's working class. It left little for other necessities. A person unable to pay the rent fell into a semisavage world of the "submerged tenth," Booth's world of "occasional labourers, loafers, and semi-criminals," many of whom spent the nights huddled together on the Thames embankment or under railway bridges. They preferred this to a night on the planks of the Poor Law Union's Casual Wards, a night followed by labor at stone-breaking.

Charles Booth placed all those who had to struggle to gain the bare necessities of life below the poverty line. In London they included the average-size family who lived on 20 shillings a week or less, who spent some 14 shillings for food, 3 or 4 shillings for rent, and the rest for clothing, lighting, fuel, and (to escape

Some of the waifs and strays of London (*Barnardo Publications*).

Some unemployed in 1911 (*The Mansell Collection*).

the utter grimness of it all) drink and gambling. For many it left nothing for a half-penny newspaper, an ale at the pub, a tram ticket, or a penny for their children. The pretty clothing and amenities of all kinds that brightened the lives of the other 70 percent lay far beyond their incomes but not their gaze as they looked about them. The diet of the poorest was monotonous and depressing. Seebohm Rowntree, a chocolate manufacturer who investigated the poor of York, found their food "totally inadequate . . . a dreary succession of bread, dripping and tea; bread and butter and tea; bacon, bread and coffee, with only a little meat and none of the extras." The clothing, he said, was just as inadequate. He found that 28 percent of the people of York lived in poverty, a figure close to Booth's 30 percent of Londoners.

The greatest reason for this poverty was low pay. Miserable wages, said Rowntree, accounts for 52 percent of primary poverty. The worst pay and the worst poverty came in the sweated industry and the casual labor of the East End of London. Parliament in 1888 called industries "sweated" if they paid inadequate wages and worked employees long hours in unsanitary conditions. In small tailor, millinery, and fur shops, floors strewn with dirty materials and the air dusty, close, and fetid, men, women, and children worked 12-hour days for wages running from 5 to 15 shillings. In match, rope, cap, and box factories girls worked for 7 to 10 shillings. Some worked at home or in backyard shacks, sewing shirts, pounding nails, and making chains, again at 7 or 10 shillings. Better wages were made in cutting files, enameling wares, and packing powder, but these were the dangerous trades. The dust from the files and the lead used in enameling damaged the workers' health. The powder packers, their bodies greased and wrapped in newspapers, their heads swathed in wool, and their eyes protected by goggles, still suffered burns in the chlorine-heated chambers. A surplus of laborers, especially in London and especially among young women, was the main reason for these low wages.

Casual unemployment was a second reason that 40 percent of the working class fell into poverty. Dockers got good wages, but only when they worked. To get that work they had, said one of them, "to struggle like wild beasts." Most failed to get enough work to make 21 shillings. At the very bottom was the submerged tenth—some 3 million unemployed and unemployable, the casuals, vagrants, loafers, criminals, and lunatics. The working class was not homogeneous; the bottom tenth knew nothing of the life of the 15 percent who constituted the labor aristocracy, nor did the casual and sweated workers know the life of the steady workers in a unionized industry. Yet all feared old age and illness. Two-thirds of all workers would be paupers at some time in their lives. The aged and ill could look only to niggardly poor law guardians and charities for help, and both proved inadequate. The ill were numerous and the healthy few, since the slums produced disease, stunted growth, rotten teeth, fever, listlessness, and rickets. The height of boys at public schools was 5 inches greater than the height of boys the same age in the slums. In the Boer War, 60 percent of the recruits from the slums were rejected as unfit. In the slums of Glasgow, almost every child had rickets.

The poverty the lower third suffered in the 1890s and 1900s was not new: what was new was its extensiveness in massive slums and its grim contrast to the prosperity of everyone else. These two facts were fundamental to the new awareness of poverty that emerged in late Victorian England. The monstrous slums had a traumatic effect on the more sensitive and conscientious. Given a doubling of the national income in forty-four years, such misery seemed shameful. Heightening this shame were two other factors, the greater concern of modern Christians and ethical rationalists about social distress and the marked failure of old solutions. Charles Booth was a Unitarian, Rowntree a Quaker, William Booth a Methodist, and Canon Barnet, founder of Toynbee Hall in the East End, an Anglican. All saw Christianity more in social and moral terms than theological. In part they had to meet the competition of such rationalists and socialists as H. M. Hyndman, Beatrice Webb, and Annie Besant. It was Hyndman's claim that 20 percent lived in poverty which led Booth to make his inquiry; it was Beatrice Webb, the Fabian Socialist, who helped Booth carry it out. The secularist Annie Besant organized the match girls in a struggle to improve conditions. The match girls provided a vivid example of inequality and exploitation: they were paid 4 shillings a week, while the owners earned dividends ranging from 23 to 38 percent. Rationalists like Annie Besant acted with a moral fervor that posed a challenge to liberal Christians who had already begun to buttress their faith by portraying Christ as a moral and social reformer. Both rationalist and Christians found that the sheer massiveness of poverty and the variety of its causes made a mockery of the old Victorian view that such misery arose from personal failings. Many became convinced that stern poor laws and voluntary philanthropy were woefully inadequate. They also faced the fact that workers, who now had the vote, were forming trade unions and Socialist parties.

THE EMERGENCE OF LABOR

In 1844 some 600,000 workers belonged to trade unions, 30 years later over 4 million. This increase was a development as decisive in defining modern Britain as the growth of democracy, and one just as liberating for the working classes. But many in the governing class thought it the road to ruin; for them it was the greatest crisis in an age of crisis. In 1871 and 1875, it is true, Liberal and Conservative governments had passed laws protecting union funds and the right to picket, but the protected unions were the "new model" unions. These unions of skilled carpenters, engineers, and printers avoided strikes, established insurance schemes, and kept full treasuries. They were respectable and deferential. Much more alarming were the general unions of the unskilled—of dockers, miners, railway men, gas workers, and farm laborers. By 1874 the infant TUC could boast of 1.2 million members. But by 1884 it could speak of only half that amount, for employers used the depression of the early 1880s to destroy or weaken it.

But as the economy turned up, there were more strikes and more union activity. It started in 1888 with a successful strike by the grossly underpaid match girls. In 1889 London's gas workers struck, formed a union, and won the 8-hour day, a victory also won by provincial gas workers. The London dockers struck. "We are," said the prime minister, Lord Salisbury, "in a state of bloodless civil war." The dockers' strike was much tougher than that of the gas workers, since the employers were determined to destroy the union. A gift of £30,000 from Australian workers, public opinion made sympathetic by recent revelations of social distress, and the intervention of Cardinal Manning and the Lord Mayor of London helped the workers win 6 pence, rather than 4 pence, an hour and recognition as a union. Dockers in other ports also won recognition, as did many miners. Most of these dockers, miners, gas workers, and match girls were not skilled. The unions they formed had low dues, welcomed the unskilled, and promised aggressive strikes for higher wages rather than insurance schemes for old age. These general unions formed a "new unionism," one that competed at trade union congresses with the once "new model" unions that had now become the "old" unions.

From 1892 to 1910 new unionism suffered bitter defeats. Employers declared war on it. They strengthened their already powerful employers federations, established the National Free Labourers Association to provide strike breakers, denounced in pamphlets the insidious trade unions, forced workers to sign "yellow dog" contracts never to join a union, won the press and judges to their cause, and at the first sign of a strike, locked out employees. By such means they routed both miners and engineers in 1897. More threatening were three decisions by the courts between 1893 and 1901 that declared picketing and boycotts illegal and held unions liable for any damages suffered in a strike. The last of these decisions found a Welsh railway union to be liable for £23,000 worth of damages caused by its strike against the Taff Vale Railway Company. If this decision became law, future strikes would bankrupt the unions. Since the judges were almost all Conservatives, it spurred the unions to support Liberal or Labour MPs in the election of 1906.

The election produced twenty-nine Labour MPs and a landslide victory for the Liberals. A Liberal government then passed the Trades Dispute Act, which legalized picketing and declared that union funds were not liable to suits. Legally secure, the unions now fought to protect their workers from a decline in real wages. From 1909 to 1913 the cost of living rose 9 percent. Since wages rose more slowly, the workers' standard of living deteriorated. They therefore struck and joined unions as never before. From 1910 to 1914, membership in the TUC rose by 67 percent.

During those same years, some union leaders grew impatient with the Conservative and Liberal parties. In 1893 some 120 delegates, most but not all trade unionists, gathered at Bradford, a mill town in Yorkshire. The promoter of the meeting was Keir Hardie, illegitimate son of a servant girl, an errand boy at 8, and soon thereafter a trapper in a coal mine. He learned to read and write at night school and, appalled by conditions in the mines, organized the Scottish Miners Union. In 1892 he became the first independent laborer to win a seat in the House of Commons. His entry caused a great stir. Defying the customary top hat and formal suit, he arrived in yellow tweed trousers, serge jacket, and tweed cap. Keir Hardie was convinced a labor party could succeed. One delegate who was not was George Bernard Shaw, music critic, Fabian Socialist, and future playwright. Shaw said such a party would only be "another SDF." By 1893 the SDF, or Social Democratic Federation, had spent fourteen years vainly attempting to convert the British to Marxist socialism. Its founder was Henry Hyndman, educated at Eton and Cambridge, and author of *England for All*, which was taken from Marx. In top hat and frock coat, Hyndman expounded Marx on street corners. Among the SDF were England's more impatient socialists, Tom Mann and Ben Tillet, leaders of the dockers' strike, John Burns and H. H. Champion, heroes in 1887 of the Trafalgar Square protest against unemployment, and William Morris, author of utopian socialist schemes and famous as an artist, designer, and poet.

Far different from the SDF was the Fabian Society. In 1883 it began a long career of advocating a democratic, gradualist, peaceful, and pragmatic socialism. Among its members were some of London's ablest intellectuals, Sydney and Beatrice Webb, pioneers in social investigation, Graham Wallas, historian and political philosopher, and Hubert Bland, a learned and urbane journalist. For more than a decade the talented socialists of London had responded to the bleak years of the 1880s by urging that the means of production should be publicly owned and that the nation's riches should be employed to help all. But little had been done. Where such talents had failed, how could Hardie, a self-educated miner, succeed? Yet Hardie and the Independent Labour party, the ILP, did succeed. Shaw, despite his doubts, stayed and helped draw up both a socialist platform—a very practical one—and a title that Keir Hardie insisted should not include the word "socialist." Keir Hardie and the ILP succeeded because they accomplished three difficult tasks: they won over the trade unions, brought together most of the quarreling socialists, and won the votes of the workers.

Keir Hardie and most of the 120 delegates were from the industrial north, the home of factory people, unions, and Nonconformity. Their ideas were not socialistic, as Hardie realized. Many were Conservative; many more were Gladstonian Liberals. Some laborers represented the Liberal party in Parliament and were known as Lib-Labs. From 1895 to 1898 the TUC defeated Hardie's annual motion that the unions give financial support to Independent Labour candidates. In 1899 that motion finally won, and it won because the TUC had had enough of the Tories. Tory employers had used black legs (scabs) and lockouts to destroy unions, Tory courts declared picketing and boycotts illegal, and Tory governments did little to help the poor. The Liberals, too, did little for labor. Out of office in 1891, they promised extensive reform; in office in 1893 and 1894, they did nothing. Furthermore, Liberal caucuses in northern constituencies, even where the overwhelming majority were workers, chose businessmen and professional men, not union officials or workers, as candidates for Parliament. That these business and professional men persisted in their devotion to *laissez-faire* and their hostility to collectivism only increased the union leaders' awareness that they needed an independent labor party.

Hardie's victory in 1899 meant that union money would finance independent labor candidates. It thus led to a renewed interest in reconciling the divided socialists. In 1900 the socialist scene was diverse and chaotic. In London, the SDF and the Fabians were still strong; meanwhile, the new Socialist League doggedly pursued anarchist ideas. In the north there were Robert Blatchford and his newspaper the *Clarion*, John Trevor and the labor churches, and labor institutes. Blatchford's *Merry England*, with its picture of socialism as fellowship, his lively and popular *Clarion*, and his cycle clubs won more people to socialism than did the turgid Marxism of the Social Democratic Federation or the prodigious researches of the Fabians. Just as diverse as these organizations were the ideas that inspired them. For them, the writings of John Ruskin and William Morris on the ugliness and selfishness of capitalism were crucial. For others, it was Henry George's *Progress and Poverty*, with its attack on idle landlords and rents. Many read Marx.

For yet others, it was a personal conviction that capitalism was unjust, that the poor deserved help, and that the working class had a right to a fair share of the wealth it produced. These convictions had roots in the Nonconformist religions, particularly Methodism. The meeting at which the Labour Representation Committee (LRC) was formed in 1900 was held in Memorial Hall, London, a temple of Nonconformity. At that meeting the delegates decided that the executive committee of the LRC should consist of twelve members from the ILP, two from the SDF, one from the Fabians, and seven from the trade unions, a ratio that roughly reflected their respective contributions to the founding of the committee.

In 1900 the LRC, weak and fragile, faced the task which has so often destroyed third parties, the winning of votes. Although the LRC, after 1906 called the Labour party, never won as many votes or elections as did the Liberals—in 1910 only 40 MPs to the Liberal's 273—it did put down deeper roots into the clubs, friendly societies, and trade unions of a growing working-class culture. The momentum was shifting to Labour, especially since the Liberals had difficulty firmly supporting an eight-hour day or a trade union's right to strike, difficulties that in 1908 led the Miners Federation, long a bastion of Liberalism, to go Labour.

The Liberals were also both slow and ineffective in meeting the problems of unemployment and poverty, problems that Lord Salisbury and the Conservatives had the first chance to resolve.

SEVENTEEN YEARS OF CONSERVATIVE RULE

From 1572 to 1611, William Cecil and his son Robert managed England's government under Queen Elizabeth and King James I. For his services, Robert became the Earl of Salisbury and gained the wealth to expand Hatfield House, his magnificent country home. From 1885 to 1906 except for three years of Liberal government, Robert Cecil, third Marquis of Salisbury, and his nephew, Arthur Balfour, managed England's government under the sovereign sway of the people. At Hatfield House Robert Cecil met with his advisors not to devise measures to please the Queen, but to prepare plans for winning the votes of the workers who gained the franchise in 1867 and 1884. The aloof, detached Lord Salisbury led the Conservatives in five elections, won three handily in 1886, 1895, and 1900, lost one clearly in 1885, and in 1892 gained more than the Liberals but not the Liberals plus the Irish. In England itself the Conservatives won five elections in a row. Democracy brought neither socialism nor radical Liberalism; it brought Conservative government led by aristocrats whose forefathers had served the Tudors and Stuarts.

Any explanation of this paradox must start with the fact that British democracy was still limited. Only those who owned a house or rented lodgings at more than £10 a year could vote. They also must have resided in the constituency for one year. Only three out of five adult males met these requirements. Furthermore some men, usually rich, could vote twice or more—once as a householder, once as an owner of a business premise, and perhaps a third time as a university graduate. Many of the rich living in suburbs enjoyed this plural voting. Many of them were also frightened by Gladstone's radical talk of leading the "masses against the classes" and of his insistence that Ireland be given home rule. The shrewd Lord Randolph Churchill, observing the disenchantment of the middle classes with Gladstone, urged Conservatives to organize "villa Toryism." They did and from 1885 on most of the middle class of England's affluent and expanding suburbs voted Conservative.

The disunity of the Liberals, which encouraged this trend, offers a second reason for seventeen years of Conservative rule. Gladstone's Home Rule Bill of 1886 not only split his party, forcing ninety-two Liberal MPs to leave and become Liberal Unionists, but alienated millions of voters who viewed the Irish as lazy drunkards and the loss of Ireland as the beginning of the loss of the Empire. Most Englishmen agreed with Lord Salisbury that the Irish were no more capable of self-government than the Hottentots. In 1899 the Boer War, fought on behalf of the Empire, deepened the split in the Liberal party between the supporters of that war, led by Lord Rosebery, and the critics led by Henry Campbell-Bannerman. Salisbury, architect of a large empire in Africa and a constant foe of Irish home rule, used the glitter and patriotism of Empire to attract thousands to the Conservative fold. This appeal to pride in Empire constitutes a third reason for the Conservatives' ascendancy.

A fourth reason was a paternal and aristocratic image that appealed to the deferential of all classes. Deference, of course, was strongest in rural areas, where the agricultural workers tended to support the squire's candidate. The 1884 Reform Act which gave the rural householder the vote and the 1885 Redistribution Act which gave rural England more MPs greatly increased the voting power of those deeply deferential to property. But even in urban England, in London and Lancashire, where Nonconformity was weak and the immigrant Irish numerous and disliked, English workers voted Conservative. They liked the Conservatives for their imperialism, their support of the drink trade, their opposition to home rule, and their rhetoric, which was freer of *laissez-faire* doctrines. For many workers, the aristocracy were their natural rulers, their governors or "guvs." They looked to them for good government, both at home and in the Empire.

From 1886 to 1892 and from 1895 to 1906 Lord Salisbury and his nephew Arthur Balfour gave them such a government. Salisbury was a wealthy, skeptical, and blunt-spoken aristocrat whose shrewdness and pessimism made him doubt the possibility of progress, the desirability of democracy, or the efficacy of bold reforms. Balfour, more polished and urbane, but equally aloof, skeptical, and pragmatic, was chief secretary of Ireland under Salisbury. Under orders to provide a rule that "does not flinch and does not vary," Balfour pursued a policy of coercion and conciliation. By tough enforcement of the Crimes Act of 1887, he hoped to put down violence, and by aiding peasants to purchase land, by building railways, and by establishing boards to promote industry, to "kill home rule with kindness." Both worked, temporarily.

Enforcement of the Crimes Act decreased violence, while a generous Land Act, which gave tenants a 12 percent down payment and a low-interest loan, created a small proprietor class that became the economic backbone of the new Ireland. The Conservatives brought twenty years of good government to Ireland. The fall of Parnell also brought peace. The revelations of his adultery with Mrs. Kitty O'Shea led Ireland's Nationalist party to disown him. The Nationalist party itself was also tired and spent. The agitations, expectations, and failures of the Parnell years led the pendulum to swing from violence to quiescence, allowing coercion and conciliation to work. But the deep passions of Irish nationalism did not expire. After 1900 they were displayed at Dublin's Abbey Theatre in the plays of William Butler Yeats, Lady Gregory, and George Moore and in the Gaelic League's effort to revive the Gaelic language. An unflinching and unvarying firmness from London could never end the Irish resolve to rule themselves. Salisbury and Balfour had provided good government, made significant reforms, created a prosperous peasantry, but in the long run these policies only strengthened Irish nationalism.

Salisbury's government also brought many reforms to England. They made for a more efficient government, but left the deeper social problems unsolved. His most revolutionary reform was the Local Government Act of 1888. Before 1888 the power to govern the countryside lay with 27,000 independent local authorities, the most powerful of which was the magistracy, an appointive, not an elective, body. The Reform Act of 1884 provided that rural householders could elect MPs. If they could elect MPs, why could they not elect local officials? Pressure for a democratic local government mounted and led Salisbury's government to create sixty county councils and sixty-two boroughs which acted as county councils. These elected councils took over most of the powers once dispersed among 27,000 local authorities.

The government made still other reforms. In a complex industrial society, with pressure groups and a bureaucracy, every year brought more acts of Parliament. Under Salisbury Parliament passed acts amending and consolidating earlier acts on factories, mines, tithes, health, housing, safety in industry, fraudulent shops, cruelty to children, and allotments of land to workers. All these acts were progressive, but they were mere scratches on the surface of the problems of poverty, distress, and exploitation. In 1895 Salisbury said no question was more important than the social condition of England. He was particularly anxious to build new houses, but his act promoting them led to only 18,000 new units by 1910. Salisbury, like most Conservatives, had great faith in the virtue of self-help, the sanctity of property, and the rights of local government. He also had a great fear of a powerful central government and of heavy taxes. He even opposed compulsory education as an intrusion on the liberty of the family, though in 1891 his government passed an act making all education free. He

The bulwark of the Conservative party was the prosperous governing classes, here enjoying themselves at the Henley Regatta (*The Mansell Collection*).

cynically told his friends that if the Conservatives did not do it, the Liberals would. Salisbury frankly admitted he usually acted only when forced to do so. He was a traditionalist who valued old ways, old institutions, and vested interests. His social policy, admits his biographer, was feeble.

His nephew Balfour was both bolder and more imaginative, passing the revolutionary Education Act of 1902, which established a public system of secondary schools, and the Workmen's Compensation Act of 1903, which made employers liable for injuries to workers on the job. The Education Act was passed because the law courts in 1901 ruled that local school boards could not use money raised from the rates for secondary schools. Secondary education in England was woefully inadequate. School boards and other authorities had tried to meet the need from local rates, but the court decision now made that impossible. Balfour secured the passage of the Education Act which abolished all school boards, placed all elementary and secondary schools (Anglican, Catholic, and board) under the education committees of the county councils, and supported all by local taxes. The Nonconformists raised a howl. Eighty of them refused to pay a tax that supported Anglican and Catholic as well as board schools and were imprisoned. It is unjust, they protested, to tax them for the propagation of a false religion. The Act left the Nonconformists so angry that they bent every effort to defeat the Conservatives at the polls. Their efforts were one of the reasons the Liberals defeated the Conservatives in 1906.

Another reason was trade union anger at Balfour for his failure to press Parliament to correct by legislation the Taff Vale decisions that made picketing illegal and unions liable for damages. Balfour was also unmoved by the social question, which he turned over to Joseph Chamberlain, the sole Liberal Unionist in his cabinet. Chamberlain, as the Radical mayor of Birmingham and the progressive minister of Gladstone's government, had long spoken out for social reform. In 1892 he had urged state-financed old age pensions. Balfour asked him in 1902 to deal with the problem of accidents in industry. Chamberlain's answer was the Workmen's Compensation Bill, which required that employers pay injured workers half their weekly wage when injured. It seemed for a moment that Chamberlain would channel his vast energies and great intelligence into forming a viable social philosophy for the Conservatives. But as colonial secretary he chose rather to pour his energies into the cause of Empire. The result was that the money and effort that ought to have gone to the aged and the ill went into the Boer War. To further imperial unity, to find a source of revenue, and to protect British industry, Chamberlain, in May 1903, proposed that the Empire become a free trade area, one with tariffs directed only against those outside the Empire. It was a radical proposal that would overthrow the policy of free trade which, from the days of Cobden and Bright, had helped bring England unprecedented growth. The slowing down of that growth, the competition offered by German and American goods, a desire for imperial unity, and the intellectual criticisms of *laissez-faire* economics all led Chamberlain and others to demand a 2 shilling tariff on corn, a 5 percent tariff on meat and dairy produce (except bacon), and a 10 percent tariff on manufactures.

Balfour said that although he would support retaliatory tariffs aimed at countries which imposed heavy duties on British goods, he would not accept general tariffs on countries outside the Empire. But a tariff on such countries was necessary if an imperial free trade area was to be attractive to colonies like Canada. In fact, even that idea was not very attractive to Canada, to Australia, or to New Zealand. Chamberlain's plan won little colonial support. Its main appeal was to manufacturers who wanted a 10 percent tariff on foreign goods and to ardent imperialists, two groups active in Conservative constituencies. Chamberlain, who resigned in 1903, and his allies won most of these constituencies. In the House of Commons Balfour adroitly balanced his views halfway between free trade and protection. He was utterly opposed to the 2 shillings on corn and the 5 percent on meat and dairy products as politically disastrous in an industrial country that imported nearly half its food. Tariff reform was unpopular with the public, and that issue more than the Education Act explains why the Liberals won their great victory in 1906. The 1906 election ended seventeen years of good, efficient government and some valuable reforms, but years in which great inequalities of income, the poverty of the lower third, the suffering of the aged, jobless, and ill, and squalid housing remained essentially untouched. It was now the Liberals' turn to grapple with these problems.

THE LIBERALS' CHANCE

The Liberal party in January 1906 won the greatest electoral victory ever recorded in Britain. It won 401 seats to the Unionists' 157, Labours' 29, and the Irish Nationalists' 83. Since Labour and the Irish Nationalists were friends of the Liberals, the defeat was devastating to the Unionists, as the Conservative party was then called because of its devotion to the union with Ireland. The 157 Unionists even fell short of the nearly 200 Nonconformists who now sat in Commons. Everywhere aroused Nonconformists had fought the Conservatives. They were angry at an Education Act that used public funds to support Anglican and Roman Catholic schools; they and others also opposed laws that favored public houses and the trade in drink. Though the school and drink issue hurt the Conservatives, it was the issue of tariff reform that did the most damage. The belief that a prosperous people, enjoying the import of cheap food and raw materials, experiencing a buoyant export of manufactures, and profiting from the vast earnings of international trade and finance, would want to erect tariffs restricting those imports and exports was absurd. The cry "free trade endangered" was just what was needed to unite the Liberals. Its appeal even led Winston Churchill to abandon the Conservatives for the Liberals.

The Conservatives had also done little about the 12 million citizens judged underfed, badly housed, and impoverished. That Tory judges, Tory press lords, and Tory employers showed hostility toward trade unions did not help the Conservative party. More workers voted Liberal or Labour than ever before. Never before, in fact, had the electorate divided more sharply on class lines. The Liberals, admittedly, did not win all the workers' votes—but Labour victories were made possible by an electoral pact between the Liberals and Labour which allowed Labour candidates to run alone against the Conservatives in thirty-five constituencies. Most workingmen still voted Liberal: twenty-three of them even became Liberal or Lib-Lab MPs. Many of the middle class also voted Liberal. The Liberal triumph was indeed an astonishing and puzzling victory, since this party was, after 1915, never to rule England again.

The Liberal party of 1906 was as heterogeneous and motley as the ideas it represented. Its 401 MPs included peers, squires, manufacturers, barristers, shopkeepers, miners, and trade unionists. Anglicans, Nonconformists, Catholics, Jews, and free thinkers were active in its ranks, as were temperance reformers and land tax zealots, staunch imperialists and staunch anti-imperialists, worldly London Fabians and Welsh Methodists. They represented both the old and the new liberalism, with most of them favoring the old. The old liberalism espoused liberty and equality at home and peace and national self-determination abroad, with liberty meaning civil and religious rights, a laissez-faire economy, low taxes, and democracy. Equality meant equality of opportunity, not incomes, equality before the law, not common ownership. Above all there should be no special privileges for any particular class, church, university, or school system. Their ardor for peace and national independence had, under Gladstone's influence, led them to support Irish home rule—though not every Liberal was enthusiastic about it. Neither did all Liberals agree that liberty meant an unqualified *laissez-faire* economy: a concern for social equality led many to espouse a "new" liberalism, one in which the state would promote a fairer distribution of economic and social rewards by promoting jobs, health care, housing, old age pensions, and minimum wages. From 1906 to 1908 it was the job of Henry Campbell-Bannerman to lead this diverse and motley group, a job that from 1908 to 1915 fell to Herbert Asquith.

Before 1906 Asquith had been a Liberal imperialist and Campbell-Bannerman a Little Englander, but in 1906 Campbell-Bannerman wisely made Asquith the Chancellor of the Exchequer. He also put two other Liberal imperialists, Sir Edward Grey and Lord Haldane, at the Foreign Office and the War Office. Unity now prevailed. Campbell-Bannerman was a shrewd Scottish businessman, a poor speaker, not particularly progressive, and no crusader for social reform. Yet he was liked by all, led a talented Cabinet with firmness, and gained a remarkable ascendancy over the House of Commons. He had the canniness and generosity to give the Boers of Transvaal their independence and the trade unions at home their own bill exempting them from strike damages in lawsuits. Asquith was colder and more formidable. A masterful debater and parliamentarian, his arguments always went to the heart of the matter. By patient and judicious compromises and by a quiet and smooth perseverance, he piloted many a controversial bill through Parliament and weathered many crises. Born in Yorkshire into a Nonconformist family in the woolen business, he rose through Oxford, success as a barrister, and marriage into the fashionable society of the wealthy. Bridge games, dinners, automobiles and yachts were his delight. He, too, was no crusader for social reform—though no enemy either. He earned the nickname "wait and see" by following that maxim; he acted in the spirit of Campbell-Bannerman's words, "we will toddle along until it is settled." Both men guided rather than pushed the emergence of a "new" liberalism.

It was Campbell-Bannerman's duty to see that the grievances objected to by the old Liberals were settled first. He did so by proposing five bills dealing with education, trade unions, drink, plural voting, and land. The Education Bill of 1906 made all schools receiving local rates state schools and required them to give only nondenominational religious instruction. The only exceptions would be schools—largely Roman Catholic—in towns of over 5,000 population in which four-fifths of the students were of a single faith. The four-fifths clause was a political concession to Irish Catholics whose votes the Liberals needed. The Trades Dispute Bill of 1906 exempted all unions, as friendly societies had long been exempted, from any liability in the courts for civil suits. Strikes would no longer mean bankruptcy. The bill also legalized picketing.

The Plural Voting Bill of 1906 prohibited owners of many properties from voting more than twice. Some half million, in fact, voted more than twice, while 4 million adult males could not vote at all. The Scottish Land Bill of 1907 would have protected tenants from unjust evictions and the Licensing Bill of 1908 would have reduced the number of public houses. Either by damaging amendments or by rejection, the House of Lords wrecked all of them except the Trades Dispute Bill. The workers' vote was far too important for a weakened Conservative party to continue its hostility to unions. The Reform Acts of 1867 and 1884 had established a new era in politics, one based on three not a half million voters, and most of them workers. Far less numerous than the workers were temperance reformers, old Liberals obsessed with land reform, and Nonconformists angry at the Education Act of 1902—and so the Lords gave short shrift to their bills.

The Lords was not entirely negative. In 1908 it passed Winston Churchill's Wages Board Bill, Unemployment Workman's Bill, and Labour Exchange Bill. Churchill was the new president of the Board of Trade, placed there by Asquith, who in April had replaced the dying Campbell-Bannerman. Churchill's first bill created boards made up of an equal number of employers and employees which could set minimum wages for tailors, seamstresses, lacemakers, chainmakers, and makers of paper boxes—some half a million workers in the sweated industries. His second bill required local authorities to form distress committees to employ the jobless. Little came of this measure, but much good was done by Churchill's third bill, which established some 180 labor exchanges that greatly facilitated the problem of unemployed workers finding jobs. The enthusiastic, restless, brilliant Churchill, son of a lord, nephew of a duke, and at 33 famous as an author, journalist, adventurer, and politician, considered these measures as part of that "big slice of Bismarckianism" which industrial Britain sorely needed and part also of what Churchill himself first dubbed the "new" liberalism.

Although Asquith was cooler to Bismarckianism than Churchill, he was sensitive to social distress and realistic about the workers' vote. His greatest contribution to the "new" liberalism was the Old Age Pension Bill, which he introduced in 1908 in his usual low-key and pragmatic manner. The bill's payments were modest. It gave 5 shillings a week to single persons over 70 if their income from other sources was less than 10 shillings. Married couples received only 7 shillings 6 pence. But the principle was revolutionary. The state had ended all distinctions between the deserving and undeserving poor, had abandoned workhouse tests, and now promised every poor person over 70 a pension.

To pay for these pensions, to support Churchill's labor exchanges and wage boards, and to build battleships to meet the threat of Germany, Lloyd George at the Exchequer had to find new sources of taxation. He found them in the incomes of the wealthy, particularly those whose wealth consisted of land. His "people's budget" proposed an inheritance tax that ranged from 1 to 15 percent on fortunes over £100, a graduated income tax varying from 4 to 20 percent on incomes over £500 (with child support for families with incomes below £500) and, most alarming of all, three taxes on land, a 20 percent tax on any increase in the value of land (to be imposed when it was sold), a 10 percent tax on the increased value of leased land, and a yearly tax on the value of underdeveloped land, including the value of the minerals beneath its soil.

The "people's budget" announced a revolutionary principle, the calculated and self-conscious use of the power of the government to tax and to spend to promote a fairer distribution of the national income. The rich would be taxed in order to help the poor. Lloyd George also, after a visit to Germany, had become an advocate of Bismarckianism. He was the son of a farmer (who died when he was a year old) and the nephew of a shoemaker who raised him in the Baptist faith and in the Liberal politics of the Welsh village, villages in which the Anglican squire, parson, and schoolmaster represented a dominant and oppressive establishment. But despite his humble birth, this self-made attorney was as confident and ebullient, as brilliant and audacious, as Churchill. Indeed, according to Churchill, Lloyd George's magnetism, charm, and persuasiveness made him the unrivaled master of getting things done.

One thing he "got done" was the National Insurance Act of 1911. It paid those, both men and women, who became unemployed 7 shillings a week. To men who fell ill it paid 10 shillings a week for thirteen weeks, and 5 shillings a week thereafter; to women who fell ill it paid only 7 shillings 6 pence. The scheme applied to only 2.25 million workers, each of whom paid into it 4 pennies a week. Employers contributed another 3 pennies and the state 2. It was administered by friendly societies, insurance companies, and trade unions under state supervision. Lloyd George gave these vested interests and the doctors key roles in order to buy off their opposition.

The National Insurance Act was the capstone to a welfare state that the Liberals began building with free school meals for children in 1906, medical inspection of children in 1907, and old age pensions in 1908. The new welfare state also included eight-hour days and fixed wages for miners and Churchill's labor exchanges and wage boards. Although it lessened the distress for some of the aged, ill, unemployed, overworked, and jobless, it did so by partially taxing the pay of a working class whose share of the national income in 1910 was 11 percent less than in 1890, and a working class that faced rising prices, periodic unemployment, and hostile, strike-breaking, less paternalist employers. The Liberals began the construction of a welfare state in part as a response both to the threat of the Labour party and to the proddings of the bureaucracy. It was a Labour MP who pushed the School Meals Act and a bureaucrat who smuggled into a larger bill the medical inspection of children. Three successive Labour party victories in by-elections also warned the Liberals that they must, as Churchill said to Asquith, fight socialism with social reform.

The Conservatives did not oppose most of these measures. No great initiators of social reform, the party of Disraeli was not composed of heartless opponents of measures to help the poor. But there was one thing they could not abide:

taxes on land and great wealth. They therefore vetoed the people's budget in November 1909, thereby plunging England into a constitutional crisis unequaled since 1832.

It had been more than two centuries since the Lords had rejected a money bill. By 1909, such a veto was considered unconstitutional. That the Lords also vetoed bills on education, land, plural voting, and drink only made the veto of the budget more intolerable. The Liberals in the Commons at once passed a resolution condemning the Lords' rejection as unconstitutional. Asquith dissolved Parliament, thus taking the issue to the public. In the January 1910 general election, the electorate gave an ambiguous answer. They elected 275 Liberals and 273 Conservatives. The victory of 82 Irish and 40 Labour MPs along with the 275 Liberals was fatal for the Lords since neither of these three parties would tolerate 653 peers, mostly Tory, governing Britain's destiny. In April 1910 the Commons passed a Parliamentary Bill denying the Lords the right to veto money bills and limiting the veto of ordinary bills to two years. If the Commons passed a bill in three successive sessions, it became law. In May the Lords rejected the Parliamentary Bill, as they had, in May 1831, rejected the Reform Bill. The stubborn Lords were unwilling to give up their power to reject bills.

The only way to effect change was for the King to threaten to create new peers. This move was delayed by Edward VII's death on May 6. The new King, George V, was reluctant to create peers. To make the people's will clear and decisive, another election was held in December 1910. This time the electorate returned 272 Liberal, 272 Conservative, 42 Labour, and 84 Irish MPs. The Irish held the balance and would support the Parliamentary Bill only if Asquith promised a Home Rule Bill, which he did. Attempts to settle the issue by conferences between Conservative and Liberal leaders failed. Asquith finally told Balfour that George V had agreed to create new peers—some 500. It was now up to the Lords. Party passion became intense in the hot summer of 1911. The drama now centered on the Lords, who divided into "hedgers" (willing to yield) and "ditchers" (willing to fight to the last ditch). As in 1832 the fact that a last ditch stand would not only not defeat the bill but would also cheapen the peerage by bringing in hundreds of new ones, persuaded the Lords to pass the Parliamentary Act of 1911.

The Liberals from 1906 to 1911 had made Britain a more democratic state, and a state more concerned than ever with the welfare of its citizens. From 1912 to 1914 it accomplished little, for its time and energy became enveloped in three major crises that arose out of profound unrest among women, workers, and Tories.

WOMEN, WORKERS, AND TORIES

At four in the afternoon on March 1, 1912, groups of respectably attired women with muffs moved into Haymarket, the Strand, Regent Street, and Bond Street, the principal thoroughfares of London. Suddenly there came the sound of breaking glass, as the women took hammers from their muffs and smashed shop windows on these elegant streets, causing nearly £4 million of damage. The police arrested 124 of these militant suffragettes. They were members of the Women's Social and Political Union, an organization established in 1903 by the Pankhursts, Emmeline, the mother, and Christabel and Sylvia, her daughters. Aiding them were loyal lieutenants: factory operatives like Annie Kennie, prosperous wives like Mrs. Pethwick-Lawrence, and Oxford graduates like Emily Wilding Davison. In 1914 these women were still angry. The Liberal government had repeatedly refused to sponsor a bill giving votes to women. It also refused to give a private member's bill for women's votes enough time in the Commons to gain passage. The indignant suffragettes had, by 1914, burned down 107 buildings, including the Oxford boat club, slashed paintings in art galleries, assaulted Mr. Asquith, chained themselves to the rails of Buckingham Palace, stuffed burning rags into mail boxes, and used acid to burn onto golf greens the words "VOTES FOR WOMEN." Mrs. Pankhurst believed that breaking windows was "the most valuable argument in modern politics." Emily Davison believed that the sacrifice of her life would be even more persuasive. On June 4, 1913, at the Derby, she threw herself under the hooves of the King's horse and died.

Mrs. Pethwick-Lawrence speaks at a rally for votes for women at Trafalgar Square (*Radio Times, Hulton Picture Library*).

The women finally won the vote in 1918. They owed their victory in part to their active role in the war effort, but they owed it in larger measure to their sustained clamor, which led Asquith in July 1914 to promise a delegation led by Sylvia Pankhurst that Parliament would grant them the vote. The Pankhursts and the militant suffragettes of the WPSU were not the only women who agitated for the vote. By 1914 53,000 women joined 480 branches of the National Union of Women's Suffrage Societies, an organization that believed that peaceful agitation made a stronger argument than did broken windows. These constitutional "suffragists" accused the window-smashing "suffragettes" of creating a backlash. How else, they asked, can one explain the fact that a bill granting votes to women that passed the second reading in the Commons by 167 in 1911 lost by 14 votes in 1912. The violent suffragettes retorted that neither bill meant a thing since Asquith was resolved to allow no third reading. From 1867 on, the issue had been raised and discussed but nothing was done. The shattered window at least created a sense that something must be done.

The suffragette violence created both a strong impetus for and a strong backlash against votes for women. On the whole it hastened the grant of the vote, for although fires and picture slashing angered many persons, without violence Parliament might have delayed and delayed. The effects of violence, however, cannot be calculated in precise columns, nor could those who used it turn it on and off like a water tap. The broken windows and the marches and rallies were not merely political arguments; they were also symbols of the emancipation of women and a release from long-smothered indignation at being the pristine Victorian wife, the bird in the genteel cage, the tightly corseted matron in the cluttered drawing room. The suffragette movement was a rebellion against such slavery, and it led Christabel Pankhurst to write of "the exaltations, the rapture of battle." Violence can be a form of self-expression and emancipation, of the assertion of new identity and a new sense of power. This was true from 1910 to 1914 not only for women, but for workers.

In the summer and fall of 1910 a wave of strikes spread over England. Workers in mines, shipyards, docks, railways, and mills walked off their jobs. The miners of South Wales stayed out until August 1911, when starvation drove them back in defeat. In 1911 the seamen and firemen of Southampton and Hull, the dockers of London, and the women confectionary workers of Bermondsey all struck, as did, once again, the railway workers. All the strikes of 1911 meant the loss of 10 million working days, an alarming figure, but less so than the 40 million lost in 1912 when dockers, railway workers, miners, and many others again struck. For the miners, the happy result was that Parliament established boards which set the minimum wages at 5 shillings for men and 2 shillings for boys. Trade union membership increased as rapidly as strikes. In 1910 there were 2.5 million members, in 1913, 4 million, an expansion that resulted from the organization of the unskilled into general unions. Of these, 1.3 million belonged to the Miners Federation, the National Railway Union, and the Transport and General Workers, the big three who in 1914 formed a Triple Alliance

A meeting of the gas workers, one of the new industrial unions (*Illustrated London News*).

and who boasted that they could paralyze the country through a general strike. In 1912 there had been some 850 strikes; by July 1914 there had been nearly 940. The anger of workers threatened to wreck Liberal England.

The main cause of this anger was a fall in real wages, a fall that resulted from a refusal to raise wages in a period of rising prices. From 1909 to 1913 prices rose 9 percent, a rate clearly in excess of the rise in wages. A worker in 1913 could buy less food, clothing, and fuel than in 1909. Since the 1909 wage bought only the barest necessaries, a drop brought suffering and anger. Many of these strikes were about wages: the miners wanting a guaranteed 5 shillings a day and the dockers an 8-penny hourly rate. The dockers also fought, as did the railway men, for union recognition and collective bargaining.

There were other causes behind the unrest. Syndicalist doctrines, for example, influenced London and Liverpool dockers, South Wales miners, and Dublin transport workers. Tom Mann led the Liverpool strike in 1911 and Ben Tillet commanded London dockers in 1911 and 1912, and these two heroes of the 1889 dock strike forged in 1910 the potent Transport and General Workers Union. Both were syndicalists, as were A. J. Cook and Jim Larkin, leaders, respectively, of the South Wales miners and the Dublin transport workers. Syndicalism, a doctrine developed by the French philosopher Georges Sorel, urged workers to paralyze the economy by general strikes and to seize the factories, shops, banks, and land. The next step would be the abolition of the state and the creation of a society based on democratically elected workers' associations, which would own the means of production. It was an attractive dream, one even taught at Manchester Central Labour College. But its call for violence, general strikes, and common ownership of property frightened the governing class and not a few workers.

Syndicalism meant much less to the ordinary worker than such day-to-day experiences as the constant fall in real wages, the continuance of long hours, the refusal to bargain collectively, and the crass display of wealth by the new plutocracy. When anger at these daily annoyances combined with impatience of the Labour party, the workers turned to direct action. The Liberals' insurance scheme took 4 pennies a week from them and (like the old age pension) added nothing immediately to falling real wages. Like the women of Britain, the workers were also gaining power, self-consciousness, organization, and expectations—developing, in short, an identity, pride, and confidence in themselves. The workers, like the women, burned down and otherwise destroyed not a little property. Liberal ministers, despite their belief in *laissez-faire*, were forced to take an active role as mediators. None was more successful than Lloyd George. By persuasion, cajolery, and appeals to patriotism, he settled the miners and railway strikes and in doing so increased the role of government and the tendencies toward collectivism. But not far enough to give workers a fair share of the expanding wealth of Edwardian capitalism. Given their greater education, better organization, higher hopes, and deeper frustrations, it is not surprising that the workers occasionally rebelled. What is astonishing is that the frock-coated, top-hatted wealthy Tories also rebelled.

The Tories rebelled over Ireland. They had long disliked, and still disliked, all talk of abandoning this ancient jewel of the imperial crown. Particularly galling was the prospect of losing Ulster, with its 886,000 Protestants. These vehement Protestants constituted one of the three elements that made Ireland one of the most complicated problems in all Europe. The other two were the 3.7 million Irish Catholics (690,000 of whom lived in Ulster) who wanted home rule, and the English people, who for centuries had ruled and exploited the Irish. In April 1912, when Asquith proposed a Home Rule Bill for Ireland, the Irish Catholics and the English were inching toward a moderate solution. The bill gave Ireland (including Ulster) its own Parliament and executive, which would deal with almost all domestic matters. Foreign affairs, defense, and some economic and police matters would belong to the Parliament in London, to which Ireland would send forty-five MPs. It was a moderate but substantial devolution of power to Dublin, not particularly displeasing to an English public bored with Irish conflicts. The eighty-two Irish nationalist MPs, sixteen of whom came from Ulster, favored the bill, though seventeen other MPs from Ulster opposed it. Asquith, in fulfillment of his promise to the Irish MPs, had introduced the Home Rule Bill in January 1911. In 1912 and 1913 the Commons passed and the Lords rejected it. In 1914 the Lords' veto would not hold, as the bill would have passed in three successive sessions. This fact, known in 1912, persuaded the Conservative leaders to counsel rebellion.

Rebellion is a strong word, inappropriate for the party of law and order. Yet Bonar Law, who replaced Balfour in 1908 as the Conservative leader, declared, in July 1912, "I can imagine no length of resistance to which Ulster can go in which I should not be prepared to support them." That Bonar Law was the son of Ulster-Scots Presbyterians, born in Canada, educated in Scotland, and a tough Glasgow businessman explains both his strong attachment to the Empire and his willingness to tell Sir Edward Carson, leader of the Ulster Forces in Parliament, that the Conservative party would support his every step, constitutional or unconstitutional. Carson was a somber, ruthless, and brilliant politician, single-minded in his hatred of home rule. To kill home rule he was prepared to lead the Ulster volunteers to battle against the constitutional authority of his majesty's government. And to give effect to that resolution, he had both the financial backing of the Conservative party and the use of a private army of 100,000 in Ulster.

The growth of the Ulster volunteers engendered the growth of the Irish volunteers. By 1914 the Irish volunteers numbered over 100,000, and they too had arms. Civil war seemed imminent unless Asquith and the army intervened decisively and firmly. They did not. In March 1914, sixty of the eighty-two cavalry officers in the British army stationed at Curragh, outside Dublin, resigned rather than commit themselves to fighting against the Ulster rebels. It was a mutiny, but it brought no censure from their superiors, since they, including the head of the War Office and the Commander-in-Chief, had given them permission to resign. The Curragh mutiny enjoyed official blessing. Asquith dismissed the War Secretary and Commander-in-Chief (but no one else), and even though he took over the War Office himself, he pursued, from March to July, his usual "wait-and-see" policy. He attended conferences, procrastinated, and began to hedge on including Ulster in a united Ireland. He told Bonar Law and Carson that six out of the nine counties of Ulster could remain separate from Dublin for six years, after which the public, through a general election, could decide their fate. Bonar Law and Carson refused even that concession and prepared for civil war. Only the outbreak of World War I ended the threat.

Whether Asquith's patience and delay could have undermined the determination of Carson and Bonar Law or whether civil war would have broken out in Ireland is difficult to say. After World War I, with the Liberal party divided and the Tories powerful, six of Ulster's counties gained a separate status. Ulster's 886,000 Protestants were delighted, but not the 690,000 Catholics, who made up majorities in seven of the nine counties. For four decades the Catholics suffered civil disabilities, inferior jobs, and the rule of the Protestants; then in the 1960s they rebelled and continue to struggle today against the Ulster Protestants. Had Asquith been decisive and had the Tories not used Ulster to fight home rule, the problem might have received the same solution in Irish history that the South received in American history. The British Tories prevented such a solution. They did so not merely from a dedication to Ulster Presbyterians, but from a propensity to violence, one akin to that exhibited by the suffragettes

Sir Edward Carson in the center with the young F. E. Smith on his left attend a rally in Ulster against Home Rule (*Radio Times, Hulton Picture Library*).

and syndicalists. This propensity of all three groups—so at variance with liberalism—ceased in August 1914 when Britain became engulfed in World War I, a far more traumatic and destructive theater of violence.

FURTHER READING

DANGERFIELD, GEORGE. *The Damnable Question: A Study of Anglo-Irish Relations.* Boston: Little, Brown, 1976. A story of inevitable conflict, sympathetic to the Irish, critical of Britain, and perceptive and poignant on the deeper forces and tragic consequences.

FULFORD, ROGER. *Votes for Women: The Story of a Struggle.* London: Faber, 1957. A full and fair account of British women's battle for the vote, without sensationalism or condescension, but judicious and sympathetic.

GILBERT, BENTLEY. *The Evolution of National Insurance in Great Britain: The Origin of the Welfare State.* London: Michael Joseph, 1944. A probing analysis of the welfare legislation which the Liberals passed from

1906 to 1911 and of the forces behind them.

GRIGG, JOHN. *Lloyd George: The People's Campaign, 1902–1911.* Berkeley: University of California Press, 1978. The dramatic story of the radical Lloyd George at his most idealistic, free of charges of duplicity, the crusader for equality and compassion for the poor.

HUNT, E. H. *British Labour History, 1815–1914.* London: Weidenfeld and Nicolson, 1981. The story of ordinary workers and the growth of those trade unions that were so crucial for them, but which were so neglected by historians.

LEVINE, A. L. *Industrial Retardation in Britain, 1880–1914.* London: Weidenfeld and Nicolson, 1981. A careful assessment of the degree of economic retardation before 1914, one that was no absolute decline but a slower advance than those of America and Germany.

O'FARRELL, PATRICK. *Ireland's English Question.* New York: Shocken Books, 1971. A shrewd, clear analysis of the rise of Irish nationalism and the achievement of independence—all from the Irish point of view.

PELLING, HENRY. *The Origin of the Labour Party: 1880–1900.* London: Macmillan, 1954. A study of the intellectual, economic, social, and political forces that led to the birth of the Labour party, one that also asks why such a party won out in Britain but not America.

PIKE, E. ROYSTON. *Busy Times: Human Documents in the Age of the Forsythes.* New York: Praeger, 1970. Documents revealing the life of all classes, with budgets for families receiving 30 shillings a week and £10,000 a year and vivid depictions of sweated labor.

READ, DONALD. *England, 1868–1914.* London: Longmans, 1979. The most recent, liveliest, survey of the period, sound on political developments and full and illuminating on social history.

THOMPSON, PAUL. *The Edwardians: The Remaking of British Society.* Bloomington: Indiana University Press, 1975. An unusual survey based on interviews with survivors, concrete and vivid, dealing with drink, religion, crime, leisure, politics, class, education, and social mobility—and the lack of.

Britain and World War I

27

Three quarters of a million British soldiers died in World War I. Nearly 2 million more were wounded, hundreds of thousands hopelessly maimed and disfigured. Many suffered war's newest curse, shell shock, and spent years in mental hospitals. Shock of all kinds lodged itself in the memories of front line soldiers, the shock of the most horrible of wars, of muddy trenches, murderous shell fire, the constant fear of death, the tediousness of endless watches, the stupidity of blundering attacks, and the overwhelming sense of the war's futility.

The home front also experienced shock. German zeppelins and airplanes killed 1,413, wounded more, and destroyed buildings. German submarines sank British ships so rapidly that they threatened to shut off Britain's food and raw materials. Rationing and conscription and a war socialism were adopted. Total war had engulfed the British for the first time.

Total war and the unparalleled horrors at the front also sent shock waves through the most deeply rooted of British beliefs and institutions. Progress no longer seemed inevitable. Human nature was not, after all, rational and good, but, as the Viennese psychoanalyst Sigmund Freud had written, irrational and neurotic. The religion of the Prince of Peace became a mockery as German ecclesiastics blessed the war. Civilization and decency seemed cast aside, while morality became the handmaid of propagandists. All was changing. Women were no longer housewives but ran lathes at munition factories, won the vote, and smoked cigarettes. Workers formed stronger unions and demanded a greater share of income. New ideas and new groups acted as a dissolvent in these four years of bewildering events. No other four years of British history can compare with these, either in terms of sheer suffering and tragedy or of the shattering impact on the nation's beliefs. It was the most traumatic event the British had ever experienced. It closed the door on the secure nineteenth century and opened the way to the uncertainties of the twentieth. Its very importance prompts the question of why Britain became involved in such a holocaust.

WHY ENGLAND WENT TO WAR

It was Sir Edward Grey's unhappy duty, on July 24, 1914, to tell the Cabinet that Austria had delivered an ultimatum to Serbia. It was, to Grey, "the most formidable document ever addressed by one state to another that was independent." As tragic as it was that Slav nationalists had assassinated Austria's Crown Prince, Archduke Ferdinand, and his wife, at Sarajevo on June 28, no connection at all had been established between the nationalists and the Serbian government. Austria had slight justification for the ultimatum, one that Russia, deeply committed to the defense of Serbia, could not accept. Grey's prediction of war stunned the Cabinet. Serbia was so remote, so unimportant. And why support Russia, long England's rival in Persia, Afghanistan, and the Far East?

Why, indeed, get involved in Europe's endless quarrels at all? Many who sat in the Cabinet and many more in the Liberal party represented that isolationist sentiment that Canning had employed so spiritedly in the 1820s and that later inspired millions of Victorians to denounce European entanglements. The same isolationist tradition defined much of British foreign policy after the Crimean debacle. With its navy ruling the seas, its goods flooding the world, its Empire expanding everywhere, and Europe divided, Britain needed no alliances.

By 1904 that situation had changed. A rival tradition, that of using alliances to create a correct balance of power, reasserted itself; the spirit of Elizabeth and William III and of the armies of Marlborough and Wellington had not died out. The Boer War had revealed both England's military weakness and its isolation. Germany's growing power, its insistence on building a navy to rival Britain's, its rejection of British efforts to negotiate an overall understanding, and its clumsy attempts to bully France all forced Britain in 1904 to come to an "understanding" with France over the many colonial disputes that had divided them. In 1907 Britain came to a similar "understanding" with Russia, resolving their rivalries in Persia, Afghanistan, and the Far East. Neither was a formal alliance. The only alliance made was in 1902 with Japan. After 1906, however, the "understanding" with France was strengthened by military arrangements in which the French navy was to patrol the Mediterranean, the British navy was to guard the English Channel and the French coasts, and far more loosely promised, the British Expeditionary Force was to support the left flank of the French army. It was an informal commitment kept secret from the Cabinet until 1911, but a commitment that carried a moral obligation to defend France.

These understandings with France and Russia, along with France's and Russia's defensive alliance of 1902, formed the basis of the Triple Entente. Opposing it was the Triple Alliance of Germany, Austria, and Italy. Since Italy was a reluctant and unreliable ally, it was the two German states of central Europe against Russia, France, and Britain. In a sense Germany and Austria were encircled, but it was an encirclement caused by their own actions. Germany's seizure of Alsace-Lorraine in 1870 made France forever hostile, while Austria's annexation of Bosnia and Herzegovina in 1908 inflamed Serbia and humiliated Russia, the protector of the slavs in the Balkans. Germany completed its encirclement by its Moroccan adventures and naval building.

The encirclement had in fact no great influence on the mind of the Kaiser and his ministers. That they had little fear of encirclement is evident in their aggressive support of a bellicose Austria. The Kaiser and his Prime Minister, Bethman-Hollweg, not only gave Austria a blank check to do whatever she wished but urged her to settle the Serbian affair quickly. They did this even though their ambassador in London had told them of Grey's prediction that if Germany did attack France England would find it difficult not to support France.

Grey was a wise but not a forceful diplomat. He was no Palmerston. Palmerston would early on have told Germany to tell Austria to back off or it would be war. But even that might not have worked so disdainful were the Kaiser and his officials of the tiny British Expeditionary Force. Grey preferred conferences to ultimatums, a preference all the stronger after 1913 when he helped settle the Balkan war crisis by presiding over a conference of ambassadors in London. His main effort to prevent war was thus to urge Britain, Germany, France, and Italy to mediate the issues in dispute. It was not an effective move. The use of conferences and the idea of a Concert of Europe had long been in decline, receding before the emerging modern state, bristling with armies, navies, tariffs, alliances, and colonies. Both Germany and Austria rejected the idea. A fatal and rapid plunge toward war seemed inevitable. Austria, having received a blank check from Germany, was resolved to eliminate Serbia. Russia, knowing France would support it, was resolved to defend Serbia. What could Sir Edward Grey do? Some critics, like the *Manchester Guardian*, urged a declaration of neutrality; others, like Sir Eyre Crowe of the Foreign Office, urged a declaration of support for France and Russia so firm that it would deter Germany from war.

Grey chose neither. He was not a great foreign secretary but an honest, reticent, punctilious English gentleman, a graduate of Winchester and Oxford, a passionate lover of fishing. At the Foreign Office he exhibited a judicious understanding of European affairs, a firm control of his staff, and a suppleness and tact in diplomacy, but he had no boldness, no imagination, no ability to command men and events. He pursued a cautious, moderate policy, one that not only fitted his temperament, but also reflected the deep split in the Cabinet, in the Liberal party, and in public opinion. Those for intervening on behalf of France were few, those for defending Russia fewer. On August 2, the Cabinet was 12 to 6 against the war. Had Grey announced British military support for France Asquith's government would have fallen, or at least Grey thought so. The entire labor movement, half the Liberal party, and a large part of the public opposed British military support of France and Russia. Rallies in Trafalgar

Square demanded neutrality, as did all but one of the Liberal newspapers. At Cambridge eighty dons joined the newly formed Neutrality League.

On August 1, 95 percent of the English, said Lloyd George, were against hostilities; on August 4, he added, 99 percent were for it. The Commons on that fateful day voted to declare war on Germany. Only two in the cabinet resigned. What had happened? Why the somersault in opinion? The German invasion of Belgium, a state whose neutrality Britain had held to be inviolable, caused the shift. Nations often enter war for moral as well as calculating motives, particularly when an injustice as cruel and blatant as the German sweep through Belgium occurs. That sweep also forced the British to look to England's security and the balance of power. A defeated France and a German-occupied Lowlands posed an awesome threat. The thought of a German Middle Europe was as alarming to the English as the presence in the Lowlands of Philip II, Louis XIV, or Napoleon. It is a cardinal rule of British foreign policy that no one power should dominate Europe. On July 26, when Grey told the cabinet of the Austrian ultimatum, few saw such a threat as imminent. One week later, after mobilizations and declarations of war of unprecedented rapidity, a shocked public began to realize that England could not afford to allow France to fall. On August 3 England declared war and the crowds cheered, just as they had in Vienna, Berlin, Moscow, and Paris.

The principal cause of World War I was the rise of a powerful, wealthy, militaristic, and nationalistic Germany whose enormous power led its autocratic emperor, dominant military, and chauvinistic statesmen to support the attempt of another autocracy, Austria, to solve the inner contradictions of a polyglot empire filled with nationalistic movements. On a later occasion Russia might have been as aggressive, but in 1914 it mobilized only to defend Serbia's independence. Germany, which had urged Austria to discipline Serbia, refused to attend a conference to settle the matter, precipitously declared war on France and Russia, and attacked Belgium. Britain had little choice but to go to war or to allow Germany to dominate Europe.

A CONFUSION OF STRATEGIES: 1914–1915

To the keen eye of Germany's General Schlieffen, who died in 1906, the flat, open farmlands of Belgium and northern France formed the easiest entry to France. In a two-front war the conquest of France had to be swift, so that troops could be released to take on Russia. To invade through the forests, forts, and hills west of Alsace-Lorraine would be difficult. The small left flank of the German army in that region was thus to move forward slowly, doing little more than acting as a hinge from which the huge right flank could rotate like a giant swinging door, a door that would open to Belgium and northern and western Europe. These forces would then encircle Paris. From August 6 to 17, 11,000 trains carried over 3 million Germans across the Rhine. One month later, on September 9, these 3 million, who constituted the finest military machine ever built, ground to a halt at the Marne River just north and east of Paris. Two months later, having retreated from 5 to 50 miles along a front that ran from Switzerland to the North Sea, they and the Allies dug in. They were not to move more than 10 miles either way until March 1918. Germany had not won the quick victory that would have changed the course of European history.

Why had Schlieffen's plan failed? German critics blame General Moltke for his confused and weak generalship. French historians praise General Joffre's and the French army's intransigence in retreat and General Gallieni and his hastily formed army that was driven to the front in Parisian taxis. Others argue that more troops on the right flank, as Schlieffen urged, would only have overburdened transportation and already clogged supply lines. Also of help, however minor, was the British Expeditionary Force. The BEF, numbering some 100,000, arrived by August 20, met the Germans in battle at Mons on August 23, and checked this formidable force for some days. But for British resistance, said the German commander, General Kluck, I would have taken Paris. The BEF, after Mons, retreated south to play a confused but important role on the Marne. After that battle it slowly moved north to man a 100-mile sector running from the North Sea to the river Oise. From October 23 to November 11, at the Belgian town of Ypres, later to be the scene of great and costly battles, the BEF fought desperately and successfully to keep the Germans from sweeping west and seizing the Channel ports. The BEF lost 50,000 men, but stopped the Germans.

In early 1915 Sir John French, Commander-in-Chief of the British army in France, and Lord Kitchener, Secretary of State for War, persuaded the war council that first priority should be to help throw Germany out of France and Belgium. Joffre, commander of the French forces, had convinced General French, who convinced Kitchener, that it could be done. Three major offenses on the German trenches followed. The first onslaught came from March 10 to 13 at Neuve Chapelle on the southern end of the British sector, the second at Ypres from April 24 to May 31, and the third at Aubers Ridge near Neuve Chapelle on May 9. All failed. Nevertheless, on September 15, at Loos, the British tried and failed again, an attempt that cost over 60,000 casualties, roughly the same as had fallen at Ypres. The losses were great, the lessons many, but not learned. Heavy artillery did not destroy fortifications, preliminary barrages only led to stouter defenses, attack on narrow sectors only increased enemy concentration, and dogged persistence after initial rebuffs only wasted life. Even if there was a breakthrough, it only created an exposed salient as that at Ypres which was exposed to German fire. After Aubers Ridge, Kitchener, who earlier had confessed to Sir Edward Grey, "I don't know what is to be done," concluded that "the lines cannot be forced." Yet in September he agreed to the attack at Loos "even though by so doing we suffer heavy losses." The murderous machine gun had given defense an overwhelming advantage, an advantage also made

The trench, for four years the home of young men caught in a grim, muddy, hopeless stalemate (*Imperial War Museum*).

insuperable by concrete fortifications, barbed wire, breech-loading, rifled-steeled artillery, and screeching, terrifying high-explosive shells.

Aware that the Western Front was impenetrable, many looked for a way around it, for some back door. Winston Churchill was one of the first to find one—the Dardanelles, those narrow straits leading from the Mediterranean to Constantinople. Capture those straits and Constantinople, and Turkey, which had entered the war on the side of Germany, would surrender: munitions and supplies would flow freely to Russia and the Eastern Front. The capture of Constantinople would also buoy up Greece and Bulgaria, relieve Serbia, encourage Balkan nations to join the Allies, and lead to the fall of Austria. "If the straits are breached," said the German chief of staff, "the war would be lost."

Some historians have pronounced this a vast exaggeration, arguing that the Allies had little to send Russia, that Russian problems were far too great for increased supplies to solve, and that the Balkan mountains are not avenues for invasion. In any case the straits were not breached. Gallipoli, that long, slender peninsula which guarded the Dardanelles, was never conquered. Every attempt came too late and by forces that were too small. On at least three occasions in 1915 Gallipoli could have been taken. On March 19 a second naval attack would have routed the few Turks, who were running out of ammunition and mines. The attack was called off because the admiral was frightened by the sinking of three old ships. From May 6 to 8 the better employment of British forces would have defeated the Turks. The unimaginative commander simply sent the men marching into the fire of unlocated machine guns. And finally, on August 6 and 7, after a surprise landing far up the peninsula, the Turks could have been encircled but for the dallying and confusion of a 61-year-old general who had never been in battle before. By January 8, 1916, the British had evacuated the peninsula. The casualties came to 250,000.

Although the delays at Gallipoli were costly, the most fatal came from London, where the war council first followed French's and Kitchener's recommendations to concentrate on the Western Front. Then, as cries for reinforcements came from Gallipoli and the Western Front proved impenetrable, it sent more troops out under inept generals. There was no clear strategy, no clear priorities, no firm leadership, no command of events. The Admiral of the Fleet, Lord Fisher, would not send steel-armored landing craft to Gallipoli because he wanted them for landings in the Baltic that existed largely in his fantasies. Haig thought of landings in Holland. Lloyd George pushed for the French scheme of a landing in Salonika in northern Greece, a landing that did occur and was for three years a useless drain on resources. Useless also were the many divisions who lost and won battles from 1914 to 1918 in Mesopotamia, Palestine, and Syria.

The year 1915 was most disheartening. True, Italy had entered the war on the side of the Allies and the British ruled the seas, but otherwise all went wrong—in France, in Gallipoli, in Mesopotamia, and at home, where zeppelins bombed London. England was plagued by a serious munitions shortage, a confusion of strategies, an indecisive prime minister, statesmen cowed by the military, a military ignorant of the new warfare, a public enjoying business as usual, labor unions jealous of old rights, war profiteers piling up wealth, a decline in volunteers, and dismay at the most futile of wars. It was increasingly clear that victory would never come until the problems of the home front were first solved.

THE HOME FRONT

On May 14, 1915, Lord Northcliffe's *Times* and *Daily Mail* denounced the Asquith government for the serious shortage of shells that had forced a premature end to the attack at Neuve Chapelle. On the same day, Lord Fisher resigned as admiral rather than send ships to a Gallipoli campaign desperately in need of reinforcements. The two events awoke the British from the business as usual attitude that prevailed for more than a year after the outbreak of war. Parliament demanded a stronger government based on all parties. Asquith then formed a

A U-boat firing on a merchant ship (*Radio Times, Hulton Picture Library*).

coalition government of twelve Liberals, eight Conservatives, one Labourite, and Lord Kitchener. Asquith also later made Lloyd George head of a new ministry of munitions. It would be Lloyd George's job to end the shortages that so hampered the armed forces.

Shortages of all sorts formed the central problem on the home front. There were shortages of explosives, machine guns, and artillery, and shortages of tents, sandbags, blankets, boots, uniforms, and steel helmets. There were also shortages of raw materials to make these necessities, materials such as iron ore, chemicals, wool, leather, jute, and sugar. The thousands who died created a shortage of soldiers and the thousands who volunteered to replace them created a shortage of labor. Ships too were in short supply as German submarines, in the first six months of 1917, sank 600,000 tons a month, far more than could be replaced. These losses also meant fewer imports, which caused shortages of raw materials and food. From the very beginning there was a housing shortage, a shortage no public housing program could relieve, since there was also a shortage of taxable revenues in a war that, by July 1915, cost £3 million a day. During the war national expenditure increased sixfold, converting a £650 million debt into a £7.4 billion debt and raising the income tax to 6 shillings on the pound and

Some of the nearly million women who produced the instruments of victory (*Radio Times, Hulton Picture Library*).

taxes on luxuries to 33 percent. There was also a dire shortage of imagination, energy, understanding, and resolution among the generals and statesmen.

The War Office, to be sure, imposed in early August a ban on exports of chemicals needed to produce explosives and requisitioned all existing supplies, but it did little else with any vigor. Under the self-satisfied Secretary for War, Lord Kitchener, it moved slowly. Its officials seriously underestimated the needs of an army that had grown ten times larger. Lord Kitchener's indiscriminate recruiting also made the shortage of labor in war industries more severe; by June 1915, one-fifth of the urgently needed munitions workers had joined an army that an undermanned industry could not fully equip. The army's demands for industrial goods outran supply on every item. Kitchener's War Office was also parsimonious and unimaginative. It turned down the Stokes light mortar—one of the most effective of the new weapons—and it ordered only two machine guns per brigade, though in 1909 the British army schools had recommended six per brigade. Kitchener discouraged the development of the tank, which he called "a pretty mechanical toy."

Herbert Asquith directed the home front from August 1914 to January 1916, and Lloyd George from that date until the war's end. Asquith, a first-rate peacetime prime minister, was a second-rate war leader, while Lloyd George, superb as a war leader, was later a disappointment in peacetime. Asquith, though agreeing with the new liberals that government could mitigate poverty, was at heart a believer in the two pillars of Victorian orthodoxy, voluntarism in social matters and *laissez-faire* in economics. He and Kitchner thus agreed the government should rely on patriotic Englishmen volunteering instead of conscription, and that industry should be left alone. But dire events, the shortage of shells, ships, food, uniforms, boots, and skilled labor, forced Asquith to take the first, tentative steps toward a managed war economy. In May 1915, for example, he created a Ministry of Munitions, made a bargain with the trade unions, and decided to purchase sugar in bulk and to control credit. But this use of government was slow, piecemeal, and ad hoc, responses guided by no plan or strategy. The bargain with the unions, for example, did end some restrictive practices, did bring in women to skilled jobs, and did bring promises of no strikes, promises given in exchange for government promises that it would limit profits and give workers a say in management. But the promises were voluntary and didn't hold. Prices and profits rose and rose far faster than wages, leading to many strikes. By war's end 2.5 million workdays had been lost. The *Manchester Guardian* in December 1916 exploded: "Nothing is foreseen, every decision is post-poned. The war is not really directed—it directs itself."

The most active and interventionist minister in Asquith's government was Lloyd George at the Ministry of Munitions. He established numerous government munitions factories, bought raw materials in bulk, fixed prices, negotiated wages, and doubled and redoubled production. It not only impressed many MPs but press lords like Lord Northcliffe and Sir Max Aitken (later Lord Beaverbrook). These two men joined with discontented Liberals and restive Conservatives to bring down the Asquith coalition.

On December 1, Lloyd George demanded that the management of the war be given to a council of three, with himself as chairman and without Asquith, though he would remain Prime Minister. Asquith at first agreed. But the *Times's* demand on December 4 that he be denied responsibility for the war so injured his pride that he insisted on retaining "effective control," a demand that led the Conservative ministers to resign and the government to fall. George V invited Bonar Law to form a government but he refused because the Tories were a minority party. Bonar Law strongly recommended Lloyd George, who became Prime Minister. Lloyd George constructed a coalition government by winning over Tories and Labourites. He immediately galvanized the war effort. He had the electric energy of the elder Pitt and the uninhibited audacity of Winston Churchill, the two other great war ministers of modern Britain. He established four new ministries for shipping, labor, food, and national service; created an efficient war cabinet of five ministers; established an air board and through it a Royal Air Force independent of army and navy; brought to government the ablest captains of industry; and pushed through Parliament statute upon statute giving the government greater powers. Asquith's war socialism was pallid compared to that of Lloyd George; not since Cromwell had a British leader enjoyed such powers. By the war's end Parliament and the government had created 10 new ministries and 160 new boards and commissions.

Lloyd George tried his best not to use those powers. He preferred conciliation to coercion, cooperation to conflict. No theories of collectivism inspired him; he was instead a supremely gifted problem solver. To get striking miners back to work in 1917, he raised their wages somewhat and nationalized the mines—largely on paper. To get shipbuilders to expand rapidly, he blended cost-plus contracts with patriotic appeals and made Glasgow's ablest shipbuilder Minister of Shipping. He let food retailers run his rationing of food and landowners the local agricultural committees. Results were what he wanted. In 1917 shipyards added over a million tons of shipping to the merchant marine, while farmers plowed an extra million acres. Greatly increased airplane production gave Britain an air force superior in quality and quantity to that of Germany. RAF planes now flew 140 miles an hour! The widespread use of allotments—quarter-acre plots—produced 800,000 tons of extra food. Churchill, at munitions, produced hundreds of improved tanks, a weapon he had pioneered in 1914 at the Admiralty and that in 1918 would finally penetrate the German lines.

These remarkable results of necessity put a strain on the economy. They led to both inflation and to "dilution," that is, the use of unskilled workers, particularly women, at machines previously reserved for trained workers. In the autumn of 1917 inflation and dilution, combined with long hours, poor housing, disasters on the Western Front, and some early Russian revolutionary events, led to strikes and discontent. Lloyd George responded by holding down prices, subsidizing wheat and potatoes, rationing scarce foods, giving bonuses to workers, and limiting excess profits. The result was that for the first time wages led prices, real incomes increased, and workers were no longer bearing, through inflation, the chief burden of the costly war.

Lloyd George also helped win the battle of shortages by helping to win that battle of the seas. The British had cleared the German navy from the high seas by December 7, 1914, when, off the Falkland Islands, they sank all but one of Count von Spee's squadron of cruisers. On May 30 and 31, 1916, when the British fleet met the German fleet in the North Sea off Jutland, Britain preserved its control, but at a cost. The British lost 14 ships and some 6,000 men, the Germans 11 ships and 2,500 men. The Germans not only suffered fewer losses but they escaped a trap that might have destroyed them. For them it was a tactical success. The British fleet, under the cautious Admiral Jellicoe, missed a great opportunity, on the evening of May 30, to destroy the German fleet. By morning it had scurried back to port, never again to sail out. The British still dominated the North Sea. The British blockade of Germany continued. Jutland forced Germany to turn once more to submarine warfare as a means of starving Britain out of the war. From February 1917 onward that warfare was unrestricted. German U-boats sank all ships trading with Britain and France and all Allied ships in the Mediterranean, North Sea, and Atlantic.

Losses rose to 600,000 tons a month in April, a month in which only two U-boats were destroyed. Britain had food for only six more weeks. The Admiralty could no more solve this problem than the War Office could end the deadlock in the trenches, even though in the convoy the Admiralty had an answer as promising as the tank would prove against the trenches.

Commander Henderson had used armed trawlers to convoy coal barges across the Channel for some time and had lost only 9 of 4,000 ships. The Admiralty still pronounced ocean convoys utterly impossible. Lloyd George, an unconventional Prime Minister, interrogated the Admiralty's junior officers and discovered convoys did work. He then ordered the Admiralty to use them, which they did with astonishing success. In September 1917 shipping losses had fallen to 200,000 tons and German submarine losses had risen to an unprecedented 10, figures depressing to the Germans since, though submarines could be replaced easily, crews could not, nor could the morale of existing crews be maintained. Britain once again won the battle of the seas.

To win that battle Lloyd George had asserted his ascendancy over the Admiralty. It was an ascendancy he could never gain over the army. He had the greatest doubts as to the wisdom of battering away at Germany's impregnable Western Front, but as Minister to a King who admired General Haig, Commander-in-Chief in France, and as a colleague of Tories who admired Haig, he felt inhibited. He was not as confident of his skill as a strategist as were the elder Pitt or Winston Churchill, nor did he enjoy their dominance over the generals. The result was that the military alone was responsible for the many tragedies and the final victories on the Western Front.

THE WESTERN FRONT: 1916–1918

The names Somme and Passchendaele have etched themselves into British memories as symbols of horror and futility. The Somme, a quiet-flowing river 75 miles north of Paris, and Passchendaele, a peaceful village in Belgium, were the bloody scenes of great summer offenses that were to blast a hole through the German lines, open the way for the cavalry, and end the war. Neither offensive came even close to doing so. The battles of the Somme—for there were many, not one—began on July 1, 1916, a bright summer day, and sputtered out fruitlessly four months later in the cold and rains of November. The struggle for Passchendaele was part of the larger Third Battle of Ypres which began on July 31, 1917, and dragged on for three months in the mud-sodden plains of Flanders. The battle of the Somme repeated the errors of the campaigns of 1915; Passchendaele repeated the blunders of the Somme. The Somme cost some 420,000 British casualties, 60,000 of them on the first day; the Third Battle of Ypres caused 340,000 casualties, 31,000 on the first day. The Somme advanced the lines only 2 to 3 miles, much of it in more exposed positions; at

The barbed wire could be exceedingly dense, and so murderous to advancing troops (*Radio Times, Hulton Picture Library*).

Ypres the Allies advanced 4.5 miles and finally occupied the village of Passchendaele, by then a sea of mud.

In these two campaigns, and others of a lesser scale, the British High Command repeatedly pursued unsuccessful tactics: week-long bombardments that only warned the enemy of attack; a mistaken optimism that artillery fire could silence the enemy's artillery and machine guns; and, those guns not silenced, ordering long lines of infantry, all with 66-pound packs, to go over the top in daylight and walking slowly. But the artillery had not knocked out an enemy which for two years had built deeper and stouter trenches and sturdier pill boxes for machine guns. As the British went over the top, the German machine-gunners rose from their sunken forts. Their withering fire felled the advancing waves like sharp scythes mowing grass. The British made no sudden assaults with special squads, mounted no night attacks, poked for no weak spots. There were only massive attacks, incredible courage, over a churned-up terrain of shellholes and wire that no British general had ever examined. It was the tactics of the eighteenth century ineptly applied to mechanized warfare of the twentieth century. On some occasions the sheer mass made a breakthrough, but nothing came of it, for there were no reserves ready to exploit the advantage.

Why did the British High Command persist in these costly errors? Why the repeated blunders? Any answer must begin with the deep conservatism and traditionalism that most armies, and particularly the British, engender. The generals were trained in a different warfare and their mentalities were stolid and fixed. Kitchener and French were in their sixties, Robertson and Haig in their mid-fifties. Kitchener, imperial overlord of millions in India and

Egypt, conqueror of the Sudan, author of the scorched earth policy in South Africa, and universally venerated in England, was an aloof, unpleasant, autocrat whose stubborness only the humorless, violent-tempered General French could equal. Both being jealous and egotistical, neither could abide the other. The self-willed French, ignorant and untrained in staff work, was sometimes so indecisive, sometimes so reckless, that he had to be replaced by Haig, another cavalryman steeped in conservatism. But conservatism was not the only drawback; they also faced baffling and insuperable problems. After Gallipoli few believed there were any back doors. The only place to defeat the Germans was at the Western Front, where they were massively arrayed and dug in. Yet how could Britain defeat them without sacrificing thousands of men? Some said the tank. The tank, dismissed by Kitchener, viewed with prejudice by Haig, called a "desperate innovation" by the chief of the Imperial General Staff, was first pushed by Churchill at the Admiralty and in 1915 by Colonel Swinton and the War Committee of the Cabinet.

On September 15, 1916, Haig used tanks prematurely and badly on the Somme. He dispersed them among the infantry battalions instead of, as Swinton urged, concentrating them in large numbers. In November 1917, at Cambrai, they were still not used as Swinton urged, yet 381 of them advanced 4 miles, breaking into open country. But they came to a stop, many broken down, others knocked out by enemy artillery, and the rest unsupported by needed reserves and support troops. Slow, armed only with a machine gun, and not heavily armored, they were largely designed to cross trenches and muddy shellholes, crash through barbed wire, and silence machine guns. Thin in armor and prone to breakdowns they could help the infantry break through but could not take on the artillery. No magic key to the Western Front and no substitute for infantry, they still proved useful in the key battles of October 1918 in breaking through the German lines. But they should have been used far earlier, in far larger numbers, and with heavier arms and armor.

The personality of General Haig also helps explain the blunders of the Somme and Passchendaele. His confidence in himself was complete. He was, like Cromwell, convinced that God directed him. Lord Haldane, when Secretary for War in 1914, called Haig the best military mind of the century. Others called him bull-headed and self-righteous. A master of timetables and logistics, he could be ignorant of tactics and terrain. He seldom surveyed the battlefield closely. He was doggedly courageous, like the troops he ordered into slaughter. From 1915 on, two beliefs possessed Haig, the war could only be won on the Western front and by attrition. By 1917 his hope of a breakthrough followed by a cavalry charge had yielded to the conviction that, just as the remorseless action of a grindstone wears tough metal thin enough to break, so remorseless allied attacks would wear German toughness to the breaking point. Part of the explanation of the horror and futility of the Somme and Passchendaele was the subservience of Asquith and Lloyd George to the stern Kitchener and the unconquerable Haig.

In 1918 the Allies won the war in part by attrition, horrible as it was. British doggedness did wear down the Germans, though not without nearly losing the war. Freed in November 1917 from the Eastern Front by the Russian Revolution, the Germans had their last chance to win in the west before the Americans arrived. Ludendorff, in February 1918, had 200,000 more fighting troops than the Allies. In the north, by the adroit use of railways, Ludendorff threw 62 divisions against 26 British divisions and 2,508 heavy guns against 976. He drove at the juncture of British and French forces and broke through. Once again German troops reached the Marne, and once again they were stopped. Haig ordered his troops to defend all positions to the last man. The American troops at the Argonne Forest, more tanks, and British perseverance around Amiens turned the tide. On August 8 Ludendorff told the Kaiser that the war was lost, and by November 11 the armistice was signed.

The Allies' great superiority in men and materials, even though badly deployed at first, had worn down the morale and resources of the Germans. There was no decisive battle; attrition won the war. At first it was the French who, with enormous sacrifices, blunted and held off the Germans; then, after 1916, it was the unflinching and often poorly directed attacks of the civilians of Britain, who though hastily trained still constituted an army so indefatigably stoical that it kept the Germans off balance and drained away their strength. In March and April they stemmed the German offensive at Arras and Amiens, as four years earlier they had at Ypres. Then, for a few glorious months. Haig came into his own as a tactician who could deploy troops and tanks with skill and imagination.

The tank, for Lord Kitchener, a "pretty mechanical toy"; for Haig by 1918, a great help in defeating the Germans (*Imperial War Museum*).

The extraordinary courage of the half-trained soldiers was matched by their endurance of trench life. It was muddy, wet, cold, and smelly; full of lice, rats, and the stench of dead horses and soldiers. In two and a half miles of trenches at Passchendaele, wrote Captain Wilfred Owen, "there was not one inch of dry ground—and a mean depth of two feet." Owen was the best of an extraordinary group of war poets. Into his dugout, which had one to two feet of water and four feet of air, twenty-five tightly packed men spent fifty hours during a deafening bombardment. Outside "the sentries . . . were blown to nothing" and all was mud, "an Octopus of sucking clay, 3, 4, 5 feet deep." Later he writes, "For 12 days I did not wash my face, nor take off my boots, nor sleep a deep sleep," and then, after an attack, he writes of "the ground all crawling and worming with wounded bodies." Four days before the armistice, a German bullet killed Wilfred Owen.

When there was no battle, the trenches were all monotony and drudgery, with a tedious diet of canned corn beef and canned stew and the tedium of waiting and waiting. By 1917 the constant tedium of sentry duty and the futility of attack encouraged the belief that the war would never end. Another war

The airplane, like the tank, had its first trial by battle in World War I (*Imperial War Museum*).

Behind the lines, mud, desolation, and duck boards; further to the front, just mud and desolation (*Imperial War Museum*).

poet, Captain Edmund Blunden, spoke of "the prevailing sense of the endlessness of the war." He also spoke of 1916 as a year of "deepening despair and horror," a year in which "madness seemed to rule the hour." The trenches were dreadfully confining. They cut one off, said Blunden, "from the common sights and scenes of life." It allowed, he added, "two views of the universe: the glue like formless mortifying wilderness of the crater zone above, and below, fusty, clay smeared, candlelit wooden galleries, where the dead lay decomposing." The trenches were also noisy and dangerous. Wilfred Owen writes of "the shrill, demented choirs of wailing shells," while another war poet, Siegfried Sassoon, likened the barrage before the Somme to a tornado, through whose "sustained uproar" one could hear the "tap and rattle of the machine gun." That night "the fear of death and the horror of mutilation took hold of my heart." It did the same to another captain, who wrote: "I could see no valid reason I should escape mutilation or death. All reasonable odds seemed to be against it."

Despite the stupidity of futile and murderous attacks and the mud, cold, stench, noise, and tedium—conditions that led the French to mutiny—the British soldiers slogged on, showing a phlegmatic indifference to misery and death that few professional armies have ever exhibited. The reasons for this stoicism are elusive. The rigid class system of British society and the deference long inculcated into the lower orders, which prevailed even at the front, certainly played a role. So did British patriotism, which could be not only insufferably

Death was the great reality of World War I (*Imperial War Museum*).

smug and irresponsibly jingoist, but also proudly defiant and brave. Britain's deep Puritan tradition, its underlying sense of predestination and calling, its proud disregard of pleasure, its masochism even, its sense, as in Bunyan's *Pilgrim's Progress*, of the valley of death and the coming Armageddon, all led men to follow Haig as they once followed Cromwell or, at the Crimea, the foolish Earl of Cardigan. And finally, so horrible were the trenches that the death wish, deep in all, found an expression, a relief in going over the top. All these motives and more are needed to explain the phenomenal bravery of the British in this the most vivid and long-lasting holocaust ever to engulf a British army.

THE COUPON ELECTION
AND THE PEACE OF VERSAILLES

A frenzy of church bells, horn-honking, toy trumpets, tea-tray banging, whistle-blowing, singing, and shouting followed the announcement of the armistice on November 11. People poured into the streets, jammed taxis, overflowed buses, crowded pubs, kissed, hugged, waved flags, drank, and for three days exulted in their victory over the Germans. At the front the soldiers were more subdued: sheer relief that the horror had ended was quite enough. Lloyd George, always a shrewd politician, decided to exploit the people's exultation and their admiration for "the man who won the war" by holding an election in December. The Parliament had run for eight years, three years beyond its legal term.

Lloyd George also made the fateful decision to run as the head of a coalition instead of attempting to reunite the Liberal party. There were reasons why he did not wish to go with the Liberals, one of them being Asquith's entrenched position and another the Maurice debates of January 1918. Major-General Maurice, director of military operations, charged in the *Times* that Lloyd George had lied to the Commons when he said that the British had more troops in France in January 1918 than in January 1917. Herbert Asquith unwisely moved for an investigation of these charges. It was in reality, though he denied it, a vote of censure against Lloyd George. Although it met defeat, 293 to 108, it further split the fragmented Liberals. Lloyd George increased that division by agreeing to run as the head of a coalition. One became a coalition candidate for a constituency by receiving a letter of endorsement signed by Lloyd George and Bonar Law. Asquith called the letter a "coupon," hence the "coupon election." Coupons were sent to 159 Liberals and 364 Conservatives, leaving 229 Liberals without Lloyd George's backing. When Lloyd George became Prime Minister in 1916, the Liberal and Conservative MPs were roughly equal. For Lloyd George to head a coalition that included 386 Conservatives (some Conservatives won without the coupon) and only 136 Liberals could not but damage the Liberal party. The electors returned only 26 Asquith Liberals, a humiliating figure for a party that won 401 seats in 1906. With 364 Tories dominating the coalition, it was impossible for Lloyd George not to become a prisoner of the Conservatives and impossible too for the 26 Asquithian Liberals not to fail in preventing Labour from becoming the leading opposition party.

The election was fateful in a second way. Held when hatred of Germany was fierce, it led Lloyd George and his coalition to promise a harsh peace. Germany must pay the whole cost of the war, demanded Lloyd George. "We will squeeze Germany till the pips squeak," shouted Eric Geddes, president of the Board of Trade. "Well I am for hanging the Kaiser," said G. N. Barnes, a Labour member of the government. The result of this anti-German hysteria was that Lloyd George went to Paris committed to a more severe peace than he privately wanted. The coupon election also returned 225 new faces, faces the Tory leader Stanley Baldwin described as part of those "hard faced men who looked as if they had done well out of the war." In April 1919 many of them were among the 200 who sent a telegram to Lloyd George complaining he was too soft on Germany.

Lloyd George was not too soft on Germany. He had, though, become its moderate defender against France's Clemenceau and Clemenceau's desire for a severe, Draconian peace. Woodrow Wilson was often Lloyd George's ally in checking Clemenceau, though at other times Lloyd George and Wilson were unalterably opposed. These three great leaders dominated the Paris Peace Conference that met from January to June in 1918. The 77-year-old Clemenceau was shrewd, cunning, stubborn, and patriotic, a cynic about men, a realist about power, and a skeptic about utopias. He could never forget that in his lifetime Germany twice invaded France. He wanted two things above all: firm guarantees against German aggression and heavy reparations for the havoc wrought on France. Wilson was profoundly different from Clemenceau. An idealist rather than a cynic, he was not skeptical of building a new and better world order. The two things he sought were a League of Nations and a peace based on the self-determination of peoples. To gain these and other points, the idealist Wilson could also be, in Lloyd George's words, "the implacable, unscrupulous partisan."

Lloyd George was quite different from both Wilson and Clemenceau: neither as cynical or revengeful as Clemenceau (except in his election speeches), nor as visionary and trusting as Wilson. Lloyd George's quick, sharp, pragmatic mind made him the most perspicacious of the three, but his position was weakened by a reputation for trickery and by the fact that Britain was no longer the world's greatest industrial and naval power. The two things Lloyd George wanted most were a disarmed but intact and contented Germany and a stable Europe. The Big Four at Versailles and their many experts failed to achieve these two aims. They failed both because of the extraordinary complexities of war-torn Europe and the extraordinarily strong passions of revenge and fear.

The main result of their labors, the Treaty of Versailles with Germany, has not had a good press. That a second world war followed twenty years later seems to prove it a failure. But though it had faults, it also had merits.

The treaty can be analyzed in three parts: the territorial settlement, the arrangements for security, and the problem of reparations.

Its territorial settlements in Europe were not unwise. The problem of redrawing the boundaries of Europe after the defeat of the German and Austrian empires was baffling. Powerful nationalities had emerged, among them the Poles, the Czechs, and the Slovaks. They demanded statehood, even though German minorities lived in their midst. France, Denmark, and Belgium also had territories they wished to regain. Denmark annexed Northern Schleswig and Belgium took tiny Eupen and Malmedy. Poland received a corridor to the sea in which many Germans lived. The peacemakers deemed this departure from self-determination necessary to strengthen Poland's economy. Lloyd George warned that a Polish corridor to the free city of Danzig (one with 2 million Germans) "must . . . lead sooner or later to a new war." Although Lloyd George's warning was not heeded, he did, on behalf of Germany, prevent Poland from gaining Upper Silesia and France from taking the Saar by persuading Wilson and Clemenceau that plebiscites should decide the future of these areas. In 1921 Upper Silesia and in 1935 the Saar voted to unite with Germany. The territorial arrangements in Europe, given its ethnic complexities, were not particularly unjust to Germany.

Less just was the seizure of Germany's colonies. In an age of colonialism and at a time when no other power gave up any overseas possessions, it seemed

EUROPE AFTER WORLD WAR I

GERMAN LOSSES SHADED

MILES

0   100   200   300   400

FINLAND

NORWAY

SWEDEN

ESTONIA

LATVIA

North Sea

DENMARK

POLISH CORRIDOR

LITHUANIA

SCHLESWIG

DANZIG

EAST PRUSSIA

SOVIET UNION

Danzig

GREAT BRITAIN

Berlin

POSEN

Warsaw

NETHERLANDS

GERMANY

POLAND

Brussels

EUPEN, MALMEDY

UPPER SILESIA

BELGIUM

LUXEMBOURG

Prague

Paris

CZECHOSLOVAKIA

ALSACE-LORRAINE

Vienna

Budapest

FRANCE

SWITZERLAND

AUSTRIA

HUNGARY

RUMANIA

Bucharest

Belgrade

YUGOSLAVIA

BULGARIA

ITALY

ALBANIA

GREECE

Mediterranean

Sea

particularly unjust. Lloyd George bowed to Australian and South African pressure when he allowed them to take New Guinea and South-West Africa. He also bowed to his own imperialists, who insisted that German colonies had provided bases for German naval raiders and should not be returned. All of Germany's colonies became, formally, mandates to be administered under the supervision of the League of Nations. In reality these mandates became colonies of Australia, South Africa, and Britain. Ex-Turkish territories also became mandates, France picking up Syria and Britain Iraq and Palestine. The latter were used to fulfill the promise Lord Balfour made to the Jews in his declaration of 1917, namely, that they should have a homeland.

The security arrangements, while not particularly unjust, were to prove inadequate before a resurgent Nazi Germany. Clemenceau wanted Germany's west boundary to be at the Rhine, with the Rhine's west bank an independent state and with France in control of the key bridges. Wilson and Lloyd George said no. It would, said Lloyd George, create a resentful Germany bent on revenge. Clemenceau had to settle for a fifteen-year Allied occupation of the Rhineland, a German army of only 100,000, a Germany without submarines and air force, and a treaty of mutual security in which Britain and the United States promised to come to France's defense if attacked.

There would also be the League of Nations. Clemenceau wanted the league to have its own army and the Allies to dominate the league. Wilson and Lloyd George again said no. They wanted a league whose action against aggressors was defined in Clause 16, which called on league members to sever all relations—economic, diplomatic, cultural, and personal—with any nation the league Assembly declared an aggressor. Such a league, said Clemenceau, would offer no security. Lloyd George liked the league's idealism, which was espoused by a surprising number of British statesmen and intellectuals. But for security Lloyd George looked, as Castlereagh and Canning had, to a proper balance of power in Europe. With Russia weak and Communist and viewed as a pariah, with the Austrian Empire broken up, and with the German population nearly double France's, such a balance was hard to construct. The treaty's security arrangements were not adequate to contain for long a Germany humiliated by defeat, resentful over its stolen colonies, and angry at being made the only one to disarm. It was a resentment and anger that reached the boiling point over reparations and the war guilt clause.

So great was the damage done to France by the war that some reparations were just. John Maynard Keynes, a severe critic of the final settlement, thought that a definite sum of $10 billion would have been fair. Although the treaty set no fixed sum, the reparations commission in 1921 decided Germany should pay $33 billion. Germany might in fact have paid that figure—it spent much more rearming in the 1930s—but it would have been at a huge physical sacrifice and an even greater psychological one. The problem of how to pay such a vast sum was also insurmountable, since Britain and France, increasingly protectionist, hardly wanted German goods pouring into their countries and ruining home industries. The reparations clause was one of the worst parts of a treaty that, as a whole, had fallen between two stools: it was too severe on reparations, colonies, and the claim that Germany and Austria alone were guilty of causing the war; it was too generous, or weak, in its security arrangements.

THE IRISH WAR OF INDEPENDENCE: 1916–1921

For Dubliners walking by, it was an astonishing sight. There in front of the Post Office was an unknown man proclaiming an independent Irish Republic— which few wanted—while inside gunmen cleared the building. Some jeered, some were derisory, most were simply stunned. The rebels on that Easter Monday in 1916 had seized eleven other buildings, and, unhappily, shot some Dubliners, one a boy of 12. It took the British artillery and troops five days to oust the rebels. Much of inner Dublin lay in ruins, 134 British soldiers and 285 Irish were dead, and many more Irish wounded. When the rebels surrendered, Dubliners booed them, while the press called their venture a foolish, futile, cruel, and mad act. One year later, with the new green, white, and orange flag at

A street barricade in Dublin during the Easter Rebellion of 1916 (*Radio Times, Hulton Picture Library*).

half mast at the Post Office, Dubliners lifted their hats in honor to the rebels. Six years later Ireland was independent, the rebels heroes, and their act celebrated by William Butler Yeats, Ireland's greatest poet, as a "terrible beauty." Yeats also sang the praise of Padrick Pearse, the unknown man who proclaimed the republic, and James Connolly, commander of those who cleared out the Post Office. The explanation of this reversal of opinion lies in the confrontation of a powerful but latent Irish nationalism with an arrogant and insensitive British imperialism.

Hopes for home rule had run high from 1912 to 1914. Conservative and Liberal legislation had given much land to the peasantry. Local government had fallen into Irish hands. The war brought high agricultural prices and prosperity. There seemed no reason for rebellion. But in reality hopes of home rule had worn thin: Sir Edward Carson, the Ulster volunteers, and the Tory party had vetoed it and would continue vetoing it. Ardent Irish nationalists who realized this fact thus drilled with the Irish Volunteers and joined the political party called Sinn Fein, which means "ourselves alone." The most resolute of them— the Pearses and Connollys—also joined the Irish Republican Brotherhood or IRB, a secret society which by 1917 had considerable control of the Volunteers. To these men the Home Rule Bill was a paltry bit of domestic government; it did not even apply to all Ireland, and fell far short of independence. They wanted Ireland, all Ireland, a free republic. So too in their deeper feelings, though inhibited by a sense of propriety and a fear of extremism, did most of the Irish. It was the brilliance of Pearse and Connolly to guess that a foolish, visionary, and sacrificial act would release the volcanic emotion of Irish nationalism.

Both expected failure and death, and both sought through sacrifice and martyrdom to arouse the Irish from their fears and apathy. The gentle Pearse, poet, schoolteacher, Catholic, lover of all things Gaelic, compared his sacrifice to Christ's death on the cross; while the belligerent Connolly, labor organizer, socialist, and journalist, wrote that "without the shedding of Blood there is no redemption." The theme of redemption and the absence of socialist dogmas allowed the Catholic hierarchy and its worshippers to see these men as heroically devoted to Ireland. The suddenness with which they emerged and the suddenness of their execution precluded those divisive, dogmatic quarrels that weaken so many revolutionary movements. Militarily the rebellion was foolish, futile, and bungled; theatrically it was brilliant and moving, a tragic act of singular dramatic power. It released the nationalist feeling that forms one of the most powerful forces in modern history. At his execution, one rebel said proudly: "Ireland has shown she is a nation."

The British response to the rebellion not only made the rebels heroes, but drove the ordinary Irishman into the Sinn Fein party. The British quickly executed fifteen rebels, most of them guilty of conspiracy, but some of them innocent. Another martyr, Sir Roger Casement, was hung in London for conspiring with the Germans to aid the rebellion. The trial afforded this brilliant and courageous

Irishman an opportunity to plead eloquently for Irish freedom. Asquith turned to Lloyd George, and he called a conference of all parties to settle the question. At that conference Lloyd George secretly promised Sir Edward Carson, in writing, that Ulster would be permanently separate, while orally promising John Redmond, head of the Nationalist party, that separation would be only temporary. Lloyd George also refused to give Ireland immediate home rule. The refusal wrecked John Redmond's Nationalist party, long-time champion of the parliamentary method of gaining Irish freedom. In Ireland the Sinn Fein party grew more popular.

A foolish act of Parliament for the conscription of Irishmen for the war passed in April 1918. It led many young men to join the Volunteers and the Sinn Fein. The arrest in May 1918 of the leaders of the Sinn Fein opened up that party to extremists. The arrests were made in order to stop a German conspiracy that existed largely in the mind of the Viceroy, Sir John French. Having blundered in Flanders, French was sent by Lloyd George to blunder in Ireland. His repressive measures, along with previous errors, made heroes of the rebels and caused the Sinn Fein to win seventy-three seats in the general election of December 1918. The Sinn Fein MPs, having won every seat outside Ulster except those from protestant Trinity College, refused to go to Westminster and met instead in Dublin as the Dail Eireann. They declared themselves to be the republic Pearse had proclaimed in 1916. It marked the beginning of the Irish War of Independence.

The Dail Eireann proceeded to form a provisional government. It appointed Eamon de Valera, a commander in the Easter Rebellion, president, placed Arthur Griffith in charge of home affairs, and Michael Collins of finance. Collins was also director of the volunteers, which now became the Irish Republican Army. In control of money and armies, Collins was the real leader of the government. De Valera, after being sprung by the IRA from a British prison, went to America and raised $5 million. Griffith, founder of Sinn Fein, was the front man, always urging peaceful means and winning adherents. Collins saw that peaceful means would not suffice. The provisional government needed power, particularly police and judicial power, and that power was in the hands of the British. In 1919 the provisional government succeeded in taking into its hands both police and judicial power. The Sinn Fein party set up courts and appointed police. The British-controlled Royal Irish Constabulary and court system were both bypassed. That shift was, as Griffith wished, largely peaceful. Much of it, as de Valera had recommended, was based on the refusal of loyal Irishmen to have anything to do with the RIC or magistracy. This ostracism led many Irishmen to resign, thus weakening these institutions. But boycott and ostracism were not, as Collins knew, sufficient. From the beginning he used violence against the RIC and the detectives of the central G division.

Local members of the IRA went further, as at Soloheadbog in January of 1920. Dan Breen began his career of ambushing, raids, and escapes by helping seize a cartload of explosives. The IRA did use violence, but under Collins with restraint and selectivity. In 1919 only eighteen men of the RIC and G division were killed. Daring raids for arms, boycotts, and intimidation were also used in the struggle for the right of self-government, but with a minimum loss of life.

Lloyd George's government, finding Sinn Fein gains as the actual governors of Ireland intolerable, reinforced the depleted RIC with the Black and Tans and Auxis, and increased to 50,000 the troops in Ireland. The Black and Tans, named for their uniforms, were part of the RIC. Most of them were unemployed British ex-soldiers whose years in the trenches had eroded all sense of decency and released voracious appetites for violence. The 1,500 Auxis were auxiliaries of the RIC, and also ex-soldiers. They moved through the countryside in bands of 100 in search of the IRA. Between the IRA and the Black and Tans and Auxis, a savage war ensued. The IRA, formally numbering 15,000, had around 3,000 active at any given time. They had the advantage of a fixed target, the 15,000 RIC and 1,500 Auxis, and their convoys, munitions, barracks, weapons, and lives. The RIC and Auxis confronted only civilians in blackened faces and no uniforms. The IRA ambushed police cars, raided and burned barracks, kidnapped police and army officers, seized arms, interrupted communications, and murdered key detectives. They were violent, but for the most part in a disciplined way. The Black and Tans and Auxis were not only a rougher, wilder lot, but knew their enemy only as the Irish; they thus used reprisals, burnings, and indiscriminate shootings. They burned down the center of Cork, raided homes, stripped and flogged the innocent to find the guilty, disobeyed laws they swore to enforce, and became brigands.

The Black and Tans were, in part, an offspring of the Home Secretary, Winston Churchill. They would, said Churchill on October 16, 1920, "break this murder gang [the IRA] . . . utterly and absolutely." Lloyd George echoed these sentiments when he said, on November 9: "We have the murderers by the throats." But it was only an illusion. Michael Collins's spies gave him information on the British detectives of the G division. On November 21 his men shot twelve of them in their Dublin hotels. The detectives, however loyal from the British point of view, were enemies of Irish freedom. That afternoon the Black and Tan shot twelve civilians at a football game, none known to be enemies of the British. The Bloody Sunday of November 21, the burning of Cork, the Auxis brigandage, and other atrocities drove the Irish to unite against the British. Devout Catholics, whose bishops denounced violence, allied with the IRA, as religion and nationalism, the two most powerful forces in Ireland, united.

From the Easter uprising onward the British acted from an arrogant, imperialistic blindness, writing a scenario that would repeat itself in places as diverse as Algeria, Cyprus, Ghana, and Vietnam, a scenario in which a minority of passionate nationalists provoked their imperial rulers into measures so repressive that they caused the people to resist with increasing violence. Though in July 1921 the IRA were, physically, nearly beaten, the British government had lost the psychological and moral struggle: the Irish nation not only hated British rule but in England the press, the churches, and the Liberal and Labour parties denounced British barbarities. The Tory-dominated coalition thus had to agree to a truce with men they had denounced as murderers and to a peace giving Ireland independence, under a dominion status, though without the six Ulster counties.

Lloyd George, whose stubbornness had prolonged the Irish war, negotiated the peace with skill, though also with duplicity. He won Collins and Griffith over by promising them a boundary commission that would take Catholic Fermanagh and Tyrone from Ulster, leaving the remaining four counties so economically weak that they would have to join Ireland. The boundary commission proved as illusory as Lloyd George's earlier promises that partition would be only temporary; the six counties of Ulster remain separate today.

Lloyd George persuaded the Irish to accept dominion status, to take an oath to the British Commonwealth of King George V, and to allow Britain certain reserved powers. De Valera and the fiery republicans opposed these concessions and declared a civil war. It lasted a year and ended with the defeat of de Valera's republicans. Ireland remained a dominion until 1937, when it became a republic with de Valera as president. For the British, however, 1922 was the crucial year, the year that ended six centuries of British rule in Dublin. The British could now turn to myriad domestic problems that plagued England between the wars.

FURTHER READING

FUSSEL, PAUL. *The Great War and Modern Memory.* New York: Oxford University Press, 1975. A moving description of the mud and horrors of trench warfare that makes excellent use of poets, memoirists, and other literary figures.

GUINN, PAUL. *Britain Strategy and Politics, 1914–1918.* Oxford: Oxford University Press, 1965. An examination of the interaction between war strategies and domestic policy that shows how strategy reflects many aspects of national life.

LIDDEL HART, HENRY BASIL. *A History of the First World War.* London: Cassel, 1970. The best one-volume history of World War I in terms of strategy and tactics, one with a wise understanding of what could and could not be done to end the tragic stalemate.

MACDONALD, LYN. *They Call It Passchendaele.* London: Michael Joseph, 1978. A vivid description of the muddiest and costliest campaign of the war as told from more than 600 eyewitness accounts.

MARWICK, ARTHUR. *The Deluge: British Society and the First World War.* Boston: Little, Brown, 1965. The story of how "business as usual" yielded to a total war effort including socialism, women in workshops, conscription, and a revolution in manners and morals.

O'BROIN, LEON. *Dublin Castle and the 1916 Uprising.* London: Sidgwick and Jackson, 1966. A day-by-day narrative of the Easter Monday uprising, of its nationalist aspirations and dogged courage, a poignant picture of defeat and a bitter criticism of the British.

SASSOON, SIEGFRIED. *Memoirs of an Infantry Officer.* London: Faber and Faber, 1930. The memoirs of a poet whose writings plumb the depths of this grim and awful war with sensitivity and compassion.

STEINER, ZARA S. *Britain and the Origins of the First World War.* New York: St. Martin's Press, 1977. The most intensive and recent study of the origins of the war in terms of Britain's role; emphasizes the role of public opinion.

TAYLOR, A. J. P. *English History, 1914–1945.* Oxford: Clarendon Press, 1965. The most brilliant, witty, and opinionated of the Oxford series on English history—sharp, imaginative, and occasionally perverse, but useful and a delight to read.

WOODWARD, SIR LLEWELLYN. *Great Britain and the War of 1914–1918.* London: Methuen, 1967. A detailed and broad survey of the war including not only the Western Front, but Gallipoli, Bagdad, Macedonia, the Battle of Jutland, and the submarine threat.

Britain
between the wars

28

Life in Britain in the 1920s and 1930s was varied and changeable. There was something for everyone in its kaleidoscopic patterns: drowsy vicarages and rose gardens for leftover Victorians; nightclubs and the Charleston for the moderns; destitution, unhappily, for the jobless; riches, happily, for land promoters; tumultuous strikes for shop stewards; deferential waiters for rich diners; and politics of every variety—Tory, Liberal, Labour, Communist, Fascist, and Vegetarian. The tempo of life was often hectic and the tone strident, as insecurity and class hatreds mingled with brashness and cupidity. The 1920s were haunted by nightmares of the last war; the 1930s were haunted by fears of the next. But even more profound than these fears and nightmares in defining the reigning mood of the interwar years was the erratic behavior of the British economy.

THE ECONOMY

From 1918 to 1939 booms, slumps, strikes, recoveries, crashes, depressions, and revivals followed one another with a suddenness and unpredictability that puzzled the economist and frustrated the statesman. No single phrase can describe its ebb and flow, its eddies and currents, unless it is the phrase "age of unevenness." It was uneven in the ups and downs of the business cycle; it was uneven in its geographical variations. The years 1919–20, 1924–29, 1934–37, and 1939 witnessed growth; 1920–24, 1930–34, and 1937–38 saw slumps, crises, and depression. Expanding industries graced the south and Midlands of England, while declining industries plagued Scotland, Wales, and the north. Uneven, too, was the impact of events on classes: unemployment in 1931 was 30.4 percent among unskilled workers and 7 percent among white-collar workers; 10 percent of income earners took 42 percent of the national income, while millions lived on a dole that paid a family of five a miserable 29 shillings 3 pence a week. The unevenness allowed socialists to pronounce that capitalism had died and capitalists to praise free enterprise for bringing Britain a quick recovery. In the deserted shipyards, desolate coal mines, half-time cotton mills, and rusting iron works of the north capitalism decayed; in the Midlands' auto factories and in the chemical and electrical firms around London it was its Promethean self.

The uneven economic events of the interwar years began with an exhilarating postwar boom. In 1919 people spent their wartime savings on goods that war had denied them. The buoyant market that resulted spurred business to expand. The workers hired, many of them demobilized soldiers with discharge pay, increased further the brisk demand for goods. In the euphoria of good times many capitalists invested unwisely, particularly those who invested in cotton, steel, shipping, and engineering, since their investment expanded a productive capacity already too large. Some of these new empires were amalgamations based on watered stocks. The boom raised prices 10 percent in one year. Because wages lagged behind prices, some 2,000 strikes, involving some 2.5 million workers, occurred in 1919 and 1920. Some workers won raises, others did not. At the end of 1919 real wages thus varied from 67 to 118 percent of the 1914 level—again unevenness.

The government heightened the boom both by spending money on housing, education, and national insurance programs and by legally going off the gold standard. Without government support the pound fell from $4.76 to $3.50 and the cheap money led to a brisk economy. To return to gold, the government would have had to contract the supply of pounds, which in turn would have lowered prices and checked prosperity. Yet to orthodox financiers, and almost all financiers were orthodox, deficit spending could not go on forever. In 1920 the government therefore cut spending drastically. World markets also suddenly collapsed, and confidence evaporated. By 1922 prices had fallen 20 percent from the high level of 1919. Unemployment rose to 18 percent. England had entered a slump.

That slump owed much to the damaging impact of World War I, a war that destroyed a third of Britain's shipping tonnage, denied her railways and manufactures the capital to prevent deterioration, and diverted resources to tanks and explosives instead of autos and electrical goods, the mass production of which America took an unsurpassable lead. Heavy war debts, the loss of 10 percent of overseas investment, and the loss of markets in South America and Asia also made America not Britain the center of world trade and finance.

Other reasons than the war also explain these grim figures: the efficient competition of other nations, high tariffs, and the decline in the purchasing power of agricultural and raw material producing countries—many in the Empire—that had long bought British goods. As world commodity prices fell, so did the power of these countries to buy British.

But the trouble ran even deeper than declining markets. Britain's great staple industries lost their gargantuan share of the world market. Some, as coal, lost their share from inefficiency; others, such as cotton and shipping, from the unavoidable expansion of world competition. In coal Britain failed to follow the German and Dutch in mechanizing and amalgamating their pits. From 1913 to 1936 while Dutch and German efficiency rose 112 and 81 percent, respectively, Britain's rose only 28 percent. Little wonder that by 1929 exports of coal had fallen 18 percent below the prewar level. Although cotton and shipping and steel were more efficient they too suffered loss of markets. It was inevitable that India and Japan would spin and weave their own and much of the world's cloth just as it was certain that Italy and Greece would produce ships and the United States and Germany tons and tons of steel. Hence, although British shipbuilders grew even more efficient, they still built in 1938 only half of the 1 million tons of ships that they had built in 1913. Also promoting the relative decline of Britain's old staple industries is the fact that not every firm made sufficient improvements: some cotton mills clung to the old "mules" rather than the efficient "ring" just as steel mills clung to the open hearth instead of the superior Gilchrist Thomas basic process.

The government did little to stop the decay of the old industries. In 1921 it hastily divested itself of its wartime control of the coal mines. Lloyd George bought the miners off with generous wage increases and the mine owners with subsidies. He was only buying time. It was also to buy time and avoid a strike that he created a royal commission to inquire into the mining industry. Sir John Sankey, a judge favorable to nationalization, presided over an evenly balanced group of mineowners, businessmen, union officials, and liberal economists. By one vote it recommended nationalization. Lloyd George rejected the recommendation and returned the mines to private ownership. From 1922 to 1924 the coal industry, aided by a subsidy and a strong European market, prospered. Then in 1925 disaster came, as Europe's own coal production rose and as the British government returned to the gold standard.

The return to gold meant that possessors of pound notes could now turn them in for gold. Furthermore, the government decided to adopt the prewar rate of $4.86 a pound, not the existing rate of $4.40 a pound. The appreciation of the value of pounds meant that it required more francs and marks to buy them and hence more francs and marks to purchase a ton of British coal. British coal thus became more expensive in France and Germany, and so less was bought. The mineowners responded by attempting to lower prices by cutting wages and increasing hours of work. The workers flatly refused. "Not a penny off the pay, not a minute on the day," was their leaders' repeated refrain.

Stanley Baldwin, who became Prime Minister for a second time in 1924 (the first time coming in 1923), also refused, in 1926, to extend the subsidy. The owners announced a wage cut, even though the miners' wages were already near the subsistence level. The plight of the miners moved other unions to come to their aid. Ever since the war, the unions felt a need for united action. Even practical union leaders talked of a class war. From 1910 to 1920 union membership rose from 2.5 to 8 million, but from 1920 to 1926 it fell to 5.5

million. Baldwin's statement that, for the good of England, all workers should take a wage cut hardly lessened their fears. Increasingly union leaders spoke of a sympathetic strike in favor of the miners. The Triple Alliance of the Railway, General Transport, and Miners' unions had long championed the idea. In 1925 the threat of a sympathetic strike forced Baldwin to extend the coal subsidies that had kept up wages. This triumph greatly encouraged the idea of a general strike. What better cause for its use than those miners whose real wages had steadily fallen since 1900? The resolve of the coal owners not only to lower wages but to increase the hours of work led to a crisis, which ultimately led to negotiations between the government and the leaders of the TUC. Stanley Baldwin, who had ended the coal subsidy and who took no action against the wage cuts, broke off negotiations on May 2, 1926.

The next day Britain experienced its first general strike. Printers, steelworkers, railway men, dockers, bus and truck drivers, and workers in chemicals, metals, electricity, and gas all left their jobs. Other unions followed, but by no means all. Union leaders wanted no disruption of society, no overturn of the constitution, no revolution. They only wished to help the miners. But a general strike proved about as effective as a sledgehammer would be for swatting a flea. Another reason the unions lost was that the government was as meticulous as the unions were lax in preparing for the confrontation. Under vigorous government supervision middle-class volunteers ran trucks and buses, distributed food, ran milk trains, and denounced the TUC as revolutionaries. There was some violence over scabs driving buses, but generally a holiday air prevailed, with police and strikers playing football together. On May 12 the TUC, persuaded by the government's promise that the Liberal's Sir Herbert Samuel would negotiate a fair settlement, surrendered. The miners continued the strike for another six painful, agonizing months. Then they capitulated. The miners had to return, at lower wages, for longer hours. Coal was the sickest of the staple industries, and the government gave it no relief.

Recovery, slow after 1924, picked up after 1927 and not just in the new industries such as autos, electricals, and chemicals, but in cotton, steel, and shipping. But the recovery was not sufficient to cure the ailing coal industry nor reduce unemployment below 10 percent. In 1930 the recovery ended. The trouble began on October 24, 1929, in the New York Stock Exchange, when investors, realizing that speculative buying had grossly inflated the value of stocks and bonds, suddenly sold 13 million shares. The bubble had burst. Business confidence plummeted, factories shut down, and unemployment soared. The American depression had worldwide repercussions. Prices fell everywhere. Countries producing foods and raw materials suffered the most and therefore purchased far fewer British manufactures. In Germany, which had borrowed heavily from Britain, banks failed, which in turn weakened confidence in British banks and the British pound. The Labour government, which in 1930 had liberalized unemployment benefits, found in 1931 that mounting unemployment had produced a large deficit in its budget. These developments made foreign holders of English pounds so nervous that they turned them in for gold. In July 1931, gold flowed out of English banks at the rate of £2.5 million a day. At that rate England would soon have to abandon the gold standard.

In August came the worst financial crisis in British history, one that caused the fall of the Labour government. A national government was quickly forced to defend the pound by making huge cuts in the budget, including cuts in the pay of sailors. Those cuts provoked the sailors at Invergordon, the majority of whom lived just above the poverty line, to mutiny and the mutiny, though quickly settled, led to even less confidence in the pound. On September 21, four weeks after the Labour leadership abandoned the Labour party rather than abandon gold, a national government did just that. It went off the gold standard and the pound ceased to be convertible. Its value sank to $3.80.

The financial crisis so undermined business confidence that investment fell and unemployment rose to nearly 3 million. The Great Depression engulfed Britain like a storm. In 1934, however, the British economy began to recover. Recovery was as unpredictable as the collapse; no one seemed in control. A government forced to defend the pound had devalued it. The learned Sydney Webb, colonial secretary in the Labour government, said pathetically, "no one told us we could do that." The economist John Maynard Keynes had in fact recommended devaluation and had argued that cheaper money would stimulate prosperity. But the flow of cheap money that continued after 1931 did not

An armored car, during the general strike, escorts some food wagons (*Radio Times, Hulton Picture Library*).

The assembly line comes to English automobile production (*Radio Times, Hulton Picture Library*).

come because of Keynes's advice, but largely because it offered a golden opportunity to refinance war debts. The government had been paying 5 percent to holders of government bonds. By lowering the bank rate to 3½ percent, the government was able to refinance its debt at great savings.

The availability of money at low interest encouraged investment in the production of automobiles, buses, radios, gramophones, rayons, cameras, films, airplanes, and all sorts of electrical, chemical, and aluminum products. New inventions and innovations brought prosperity to many. The miracle of the radio simply could not be ignored: in 1922 there were 36,000 sets; in 1929, 3 million. Radios needed repairs, so thousands set up repair shops. The radio, like the electric light, stove, refrigerator, and vacuum cleaner demanded electric power: 730,000 used it in 1920; 10 million in 1939. Industry, which found electric motors far more mobile and efficient than steam engines, also demanded electric power. The output of the electrical power industry grew 10 percent a year, as did the production of motor vehicles. In 1914 only a few in Britain had electricity in their homes and there were only 387,000 autos, buses, and trucks; in 1939 77 percent of the homes had electricity, and there were 3 million motor vehicles on the road. The production of these vehicles demanded quantities of steel, lumber, glass, paint, aluminum, brass, and copper, so plants sprang up to produce them.

Plants also multiplied for the production of artificial silks, whose output increased 15 percent a year. Britain soon produced 27 percent of the world's rayon. Dyestuffs increased at 5 percent a year. Most of the new industries were around London and in the Midlands since they could now use electrical not steam power and no longer needed to be close to the coal fields. The workers who poured into these areas needed houses, and since rents brought better returns than stocks and bonds, money flowed into housing: no industry experienced a greater boom in the 1930s, and with the aid of government subsidies it built 2.5 million private homes. The service trades—restaurants, hotels, dry cleaners—and entertainment were also prosperous. Far from having empty shipyards, as the north did, the south experienced an expansion so exuberant that despite the depression, the rate of industrial growth from 1924 to 1935 averaged 2.7 percent a year and per capita income rose 13.7 percent from 1929 to 1937, the greatest increase since the 1890s.

"Per capita" of course does not mean equal. In an age of unevenness, the 13.7 percent increase was not shared equally by all. The miners and cotton workers received far less of it than the airplane and auto workers or the new managers of those great cartels—like British Steel and Imperial Chemicals—that concentrated control of Britain's industrial capitalism into the hands of a few. Certainly it did not apply to the unemployed, who formed the leading social problem of a society still profoundly unequal.

UNEMPLOYMENT, POVERTY, AND INEQUALITY

In 1920, a year that began bright with hope and prosperity, a pall fell over Britain, one that lasted nineteen years, the pall of unemployment. By December 1920 1 million were jobless; six months later there were 2.5 million. Never during the 1920s did unemployment fall below 1 million. In 1933 it rose to just shy of 3 million, or one in four of insured workers. In 1939 it was still 1.6 million. It was a curse no government could lift. It was also a curse that touched more than the nearly 3 million who, in 1933, were officially jobless, since it also fell on their families—some 6 million more. Then there were the unofficially jobless—vagrants in the countryside, derelicts in London, beggars, touts, and con men; and the semi-jobless who clung painfully to respectability, thousands of door-to-door canvassers of newspaper subscriptions and whatever else they could sell.

The pall of unemployment also fell on whole towns. In Jarrow, a shipbuilding town on the river Tees, the income of shopkeepers shriveled as 68 percent of its workers became unemployed. Few, too, were the neighbors and relatives who did not help, and thereby suffer with, the unemployed. The very appearance of the town deteriorated. Jarrow became a desolate place, filled with empty shipyards, locked-up iron works, boarded shop windows, old row houses of crumbling brick and broken slate, and 73 percent of its workers jobless. On the street corners broken and idle, hopeless men loitered. Jarrow, a town of 35,000, was not the only industrial graveyard in the northeast. On the Tyne and Tees, the two main rivers in the northeast, most shipyards, iron and steel works, and coal mines lay idle, and 165,000 were without jobs. It was labeled a "distressed area," as were South Wales, West Cumberland, and industrial Scotland. At Rhondda, in South Wales, 100,000 out of 200,000 miners were without jobs; this 50 percent ratio also held true for Glasgow. Areas not labeled "distressed" also suffered: in Blackburn, a cotton town in Lancashire, 28 percent were unemployed, half of them for over five years.

In 1921 Parliament met the challenge of unemployment by greatly expanding the National Insurance Act. Almost all large-scale employers now had to

Jarrow unemployment march to London (*Keystone Press*).

contribute, along with their employees and the government, to an insurance fund from which an unemployed man would receive 15 shillings a week for himself, 7 shillings for his wife, and 1 shilling for each child. The payment would last 26 weeks. Long-term unemployment on a vast scale soon made a mockery of the 26-week clause and bankrupted the fund. The government then gave the unemployed "transitional payments." To get the transitional payment a person had to appear before a local Public Assistance Committee, or PAC, and answer questions about all income coming into the household. After 1928 those not on National Insurance also had to come to the PAC to get poor relief. For nineteen years these payments, and not public works, provided the unemployed relief. It was the age of the dole.

In 1931, because of the financial crisis, payments to the unemployed were cut 10 percent. The PAC now gave less to the unemployed and reduced even that sum if anyone in the family brought in extra income. The inquest into the family's income was called "the means test" and was bitterly resented. These inquisitions invaded privacy and disrupted families. Sons and daughters retreated to cheap rooms away from home and grandfathers and grandmothers to common lodging houses (or were driven to them) in order that their 20-shillings wage or 10-shilling pension did not diminish the desperately needed PAC payments.

The effect of massive unemployment on the life of millions was tragic. For most it brought material hardships—scanty diet, squalid quarters, threadbare clothing, much cold and damp. In Liverpool the unemployed head of a family of four confessed, "We go to bed early so as not to feel hungry." Too proud to leave their middle-class flat, this family existed on a diet of bread, margarine,

The unemployed queuing up before a Labour Exchange in 1925 (*Radio Times, Hulton Picture Library*).

potatoes, weak tea, and, on occasion, a hot dish. Others moved to smaller cellar rooms, rooms with little light and ventilation and only a table and a couple of broken chairs, since the best pieces had been sold or pawned. Thousands of unemployed families in Liverpool crowded into cellars long declared unfit for habitation, and hundreds of single men hired beds in the dormitories of common lodging houses, many of them turning to the streets for a bite of food. On payment day it might be that rare treat, fish and chips, or a sweet. "The pay day and the day after," said one of the unemployed, "is the only day you can relish; otherwise it is bread and butter." The wives who scrimped on their own diets in order to keep the working husband fed and the children healthy, grew emaciated, tired, and ill.

The material hardships of the unemployed were not as painful as the psychological. It was shameful to live on dole. For men proud of thirty years of hard, steady, honest labor, nothing was more humiliating than to be useless, to be idle. The unemployed were not shiftless. In the full employment days of World Wars I and II they broke production records. Work gave them pride and a sense of belonging, sometimes oddly expressed: "When you've a job," said one of them, "you feel you're doing your bit for the Empire." Work also prevented boredom. Without a job, time, with its long, vacant spaces, became as excruciating as the cold, and to escape both men crowded into public libraries, went to the

The slums of Nottingham (*University of Nottingham*).

cinema, slept through public lectures, went to settlement houses, joined unemployed clubs, talked interminably, and bet on the football pools, a foolish expenditure but their only way of escaping a sense of hopelessness.

Long periods of joblessness also bred apathy. After fruitless job searching acquiescence to the dole came easy. The low wages and harsh working conditions of many jobs furthered that apathy. Why work in mines where one in six each year was injured and most contracted diseases of the eyes and lungs? Why be a cotton weaver in an industry which in the 1930s demanded that one attend to six rather than the customary three looms? And why be either, when relief payments for a father with four children equaled the pay of a miner or a weaver?

The unemployed were not the only ones to suffer poverty. Sharing their trials were the poorly paid and the aged. The miner's 45 shillings a week and the cotton weaver's 48, though far below the wages of most workers, did guarantee a bare subsistence—that is, if a full week was worked throughout the year, an unlikely event from 1930 to 1938. Thousands of weavers, said the *Cotton Factory Times*, received only 15 or 25 shillings a week; two-fifths of the miners in a northern coal field, said a union official, take home only 30 shillings in cash. The agricultural worker, at 35 shillings a week, was almost as poor and he received that for a 48-hour week. Mining, agriculture, and textiles were the three leading employers in England and the wages they paid put most below the poverty line. Yet they were still better off than the aged poor, who received only 10 shillings a week per person. That pension was not meant, said the Tory Neville Chamberlain, to provide the aged with "complete independence," an assertion that Labour's Ramsay MacDonald echoed when he claimed that unemployment assistance was "never meant to be a living wage." The aged poor thus joined millions of unemployed, the part-time worker, and the underpaid to create a world where wretched housing, deficient diet, and poor health placed its citizens below the poverty line.

But poverty is a relative concept. The poor in the 1930s lived better than their Victorian counterparts, not to mention the Tudor vagrant or Norman serf. A 1934 survey revealed that the percentage of the population in poverty in the East End was one-third of the percentage that Charles Booth found in 1900. The lower classes ate more fish, consumed more potatoes, drank more tea, wore better clothing, and enjoyed better plumbing. But they were also aware that the affluent ate far better. The rich, and the not so rich, also had more comfortable houses. It was not the suburban villas and London flats alone that boasted electric stoves and lighting and the most modern toilets and baths, but the modest middle-class home and the new council houses inhabited by the steadily employed. Illustrated magazines and the cinema made the comforts of the affluent vivid. What a bitter experience for those in houses without indoor water supply, sinks, or wastepipes (the condition of one-fifth of Birmingham's houses) to see model homes with model bathrooms. One-third of Birmingham's houses did not even have a private toilet. The slums of Glasgow and Liverpool were worse, while in North Oxfordshire only six out of fourteen villages had piped water. While the rich enjoyed ample rooms, central heat, refrigerators, vacuum cleaners, and the smartest furniture, most of the poor crowded into small houses damp from leaky roofs and deteriorating plaster, infested with bed bugs, and heated only by a coal stove on which all cooking was done. In 1931, 35 percent of the British lived more than two to a room, and 15 percent more than three to a room. These conditions were not as extensive as in Victorian England and they grew less in the 1930s, yet they still formed a dismal contrast to the smart new houses of the middle and upper classes.

In the 1920s and 1930s social scientists sought to use statistics to measure poverty more objectively. Sir John Boyd Orr, a student of food and nutrition, found that the diet of the lowest 10 percent of income earners was deficient in every respect—in calories, proteins, minerals, and vitamins. He also found that a fourth of the nation's children fell into this bottom tenth. The diet of the next 20 percent was also inadequate. Their diet of bread and potatoes led to rickets, TB, anemia, stunted growth, and dental decay. Toothlessness became the stigma of the poor.

The English between the wars became a healthier people. The National Insurance scheme provided medical care to 19 million workers, the death rate fell, infectious diseases declined, the young grew taller, and medicine made astonishing progress. In 1931 life expectancy was 58.7 years, compared to 40 in 1870. But again the results were uneven. National Insurance covered only half the workers and never spouses or children. Those in distressed areas got TB twice as often as did those in the south, the death rate in Rhondda's mining towns was twice that of rural Cambridgeshire, and infant mortality in Jarrow was twice the national average. Only one-fourth of all births took place in hospitals; the rest occurred at home. Health and medical care, like housing and food, reflected the most basic fact about English society, its inequality.

That inequality, whose roots ran far back into the past, was based on an unequal distribution of wealth and a rigidly stratified educational system. In 1929, 2.5 percent of the people owned two-thirds of the nation's wealth and 1.5 percent received 23 percent of its income. The lower two-thirds—the wage earners—received one-third of the nation's income. But even among wage earners there was inequality: printers earned 75 shillings a week and agricultural workers only 35; a railway hand took home 68 shillings, a cotton weaver only 50; and in all trades men's wages were twice those of women's. There was, notwithstanding, a long-run trend toward equality, one that reflected the rise of trade unions, the beginning of a welfare state, and the full employment of World War I. Whereas in 1913 only 3 percent of the national income went to social services, in the 1920s social services counted for 10 percent. That 10 percent increased very little in the 1930s and did not reach all the poor equally. One-third of those in poverty actually received no social services.

The educational system furthered the gulf between the classes by providing three different sets of schools. The upper classes sent their offspring—some 6 percent of all children—to the very expensive so-called "public schools" such as Eton and Harrow; the middle classes, at costly fees, sent their children to grammar schools; while most of the working classes received, until age 13, a mediocre elementary education, though in the 1930s some authorities provided secondary education for those between 11 and 14. By law 25 percent of the places in grammar schools were to be free to scholars in elementary school who did well in the Free Place Examination, the remaining places in these semi-private schools costing parents a sum beyond the reach of most workers. Passing the Free Place Examination was difficult for children of the working classes, with the result that in London's seven poorest boroughs only 1.3 per 1,000 children won a scholarship to a grammar school. The remaining pupils stayed on in elementary schools until age 14 and were taught little. Meanwhile, at the grammar schools 14 percent of the nation's 11-year-olds, the children of the middle class, learned modern languages, mathematics, history, and science. Some 86 percent of them would go into the world of business and the lesser professions and would become accountants, solicitors, clerks, and civil servants. Only 14 percent would go to the universities.

The universities were largely the preserve of those whose friendships and upper-class consciousness were formed at the privileged public schools. They would go to Oxford and Cambridge, and then to Parliament, to the Inns of Court, to the higher civil service, to the officer corps of the army and navy, to the summit of the financial world, to the best clubs in London, and to the leadership of the Tory, Liberal, and Labour parties. These different educational channels molded three different worlds—that of the governing classes, that of business and professionals, and that of the wage earners. From these three worlds came the votes and the leadership on which the Liberal, Labour, and Tory parties depended. It was the shifting fortunes of the three parties that formed the fundamental problem of British politics, a problem that had to be resolved before a serious effort could be made to solve economic and social problems.

THE RISE OF LABOUR
AND THE DECLINE OF THE LIBERALS

In 1910, when the Liberal party's 275 MPs constituted the largest party in the Commons, Labour had only 40 MPs. In 1924, when Labour's 151 MPs made them the second largest party (to the Tory's 412), the Liberals had only 40. In fourteen years the Liberals had lost the leadership of the left and the Labour party, whose popular vote was now 5.5 million, had become the alternative to the Conservatives. In those same years a similar attempt by the American Socialist party to replace the Democrats had failed. On the Continent, socialist parties were either submerged by fascism, as in Germany, Italy, and Spain, or weak, as in France.

There are four important reasons for the success of the Labour party: its alliance with the Trade Union Congress, the Liberals' ambivalent ideology, World War I, and the quarrels of Herbert Asquith and Lloyd George. The first two reasons emerged before the war. Some historians believe they were so powerful that by 1914 the Liberals were doomed. Certainly the vote of the TUC in 1899 to support, financially and otherwise, the Labour Representation Committee posed an ominous threat to all Liberal candidates contesting working-class districts. In the world's most industrialized society, the decisions of its trade unions to go Labour made the growth of that party difficult to stop.

Many manual workers—three quarters of the population—also had doubts about a Liberal party deeply wedded to an individualistic morality and a *laissez-faire* economics. The Liberals, frightened by Labour victories in by-elections, moved toward collectivism from 1908 to 1911, with old age pensions, wage boards, labor exchanges, and national insurance. Then they did little more, leaving the party ambivalent about the role of the state in economic life. In 1918 that ambivalence was still unresolved.

World War I did the Liberal party no good. It not only brought a halt to the growth of the new more collectivist liberalism, but doubled trade union membership—the main base of the Labour party. The 1918 Act giving the vote to all men over 21 and all women over 30 also so decisively increased the working-class vote that it greatly strengthened the Labour party. World War I also shattered some of the pillars of Victorian liberalism. Victorian liberalism was based on a belief in individual liberty, free trade, world peace, democracy, morality, and progress, beliefs ill-suited to the regimentation, expediencies, deceits, and jingoism needed to win a war. The war, in revealing Asquith's mediocrity and Lloyd George's genius as a leader, hopelessly split the Liberals. The war also hastened the decline of religion, particularly that of the Nonconformists, one of the chief pillars of the Victorian Liberal party. In 1918 the party was in no position to withstand Asquith's touchy vanity and Lloyd George's rootless ambitions.

The vanity of Asquith, though the lesser of these two disruptive forces, could hurt. His demand for a select committee to inquire into Sir Frederick Maurice's charges that Lloyd George had lied about troops in France was foolish. A greater error, but understandable, was Asquith's failure to urge Lloyd George to lead the Liberal party to victory. Lloyd George, whose ambitions far exceeded his loyalty to the Liberals, never even inquired if this was possible. Instead, he asked the Tories to join him in an effort to continue the wartime coalition. With his power and fame at their zenith, he agreed to the coupon election. The result was a Parliament with only 28 independent Liberals, a group much smaller than the 63 Labour MPs who emerged as the leading critics of Lloyd George's capitulation to the 335 Conservative MPs. Lloyd George, in 1920, yielded to Tory demands for a cut of £100 million from the budget, cuts that drastically reduced the government's efforts in education and housing, and that also lessened unemployment payments and curtailed the work of labor exchanges. He even agreed to abolish the taxes on land begun in his people's budget of

1909 and to adopt protective tariffs. These actions, like his repression in Ireland, alienated millions of Liberals. In 1922 the Tories tired of Lloyd George. They became restive when he urged that armed forces be sent to help the Greeks fight the Turks over an area south of the Dardanelles. When Lloyd George than talked of another general election to continue the coalition, the Tories rebelled. At the Carlton Club on October 19 they deposed him. The Tory, Stanley Baldwin, soon to be Prime Minister, urged his deposition. He was, Baldwin admitted, a dynamic force, but such forces he added are terrible things. Had it not, he asked, "shattered the Liberal Party?"

Later in October, the new Prime Minister, Bonar Law, led the Tories to a great victory, with their 345 MPs far exceeding the Liberals' 116 and the 142 of the surprising second-place finishers, the Labour party. Bonar Law, ill with cancer, resigned in May 1923 in favor of Stanley Baldwin. Baldwin called an election, in which the Tories won 258 seats, Labour 191, and the Liberals 158. The formal reconciliation of Asquith and Lloyd George in 1922 convinced few people. Lloyd George had the ideas, charisma, and money (some of which he gained from the sale of honors), while Asquith had the party organization. Asquith himself admitted that people viewed Liberal unity as a farce. The Liberals were also still beset by ambivalence over *laissez-faire* and collectivist ideas. Furthermore, their base was weak, since workers increasingly turned to a party supported by the trade unions and property increasingly saw the Tories as the best defense against socialism. The Liberals by 1924 were no longer an effective alternative to the Tories. The principal party of the left was Labour, and in 1924 and 1929 its leader, Ramsay MacDonald, was Prime Minister.

The domestic achievements of the two Labour governments were unimpressive. The first accomplished little besides passing a good housing act and increasing grants for education and unemployment assistance. The Housing Act was the centerpiece. It authorized the treasury to give local councils £9 a year for forty years for each house it built. The council had to add its own subsidy of £4/10, had to meet standards of sanitation and size, and had to rent it at no more than 9 shillings a week. The act resulted in half a million low-rent houses. The second Labour government lasted longer, but accomplished equally little. It raised unemployment payments and made them easier to obtain, reduced the hours of coal miners, established agricultural marketing boards and coal committees to set quotas, and gave subsidies for slum clearance and public housing. But it did nothing to repeal the hated Trades Dispute Act or to reduce millions in unemployment and poverty. Ramsay MacDonald was far more anxious to show that Labour could govern respectably than to promote a socialism not a little at odds with his Victorian individualism.

The Labour government also failed to meet the financial crisis of 1931. It did not understand the new economics of John Maynard Keynes, whose advice it sought and received, but rejected. The Cabinet thus defended the gold standard by drastic cuts in spending. No one in the Cabinet, curiously, doubted that a balanced budget was needed; no Labour minister urged deficit spending or public works. All were Victorian about finances. What did split the Cabinet was a proposal to cut unemployment assistance by 10 percent. To make the poorest in the country a tenth poorer seemed morally unjustifiable. It also raised the wrath of the trade unions. The government split over this small but vivid issue and fell. Having done little to create a better world, the government failed to take the measure of the world depression.

The reasons for the meager accomplishment of the two Labour governments are many. One of the more obvious is that both were minority governments, dependent on the votes of Liberals. Their fall in 1924 was a result of the Liberals' censuring them for dropping a prosecution against a Communist editor. It was a petty issue, though it did touch on a second obstacle facing Labour, the country's hysteria about Bolshevism. The Tory press played on that fear by denouncing the Labour government for granting diplomatic recognition to Russia and for negotiating trade treaties with it. Four days before the October elections, the Tory press published the Zinoviev letter. Zinoviev was president of the Comintern and the letter, addressed to the British Communists, urged revolution. What impact this letter, probably a forgery, had on the election is hard to estimate, but it is certain that the press lords' exploitation of the red scare of 1924 did Labour no good.

Three other factors, all internal to the party, also inhibited it: its heterogeneity, its lack of a coherent outlook, and Ramsay MacDonald. The Labour party of the 1920s was a federation of various opinionated groups with no experience in government. They came in all sizes and shapes: dogmatic Socialists from the Independent Labour party; aged, narrow-minded trade union officials; Fabians, hoping to be social engineers; Christian pacifists; misty idealists; Cooperators; guild socialists; Prohibitionists; and intellectual Marxists.

The Labour party was, of course, socialist, but in a vague, amorphous way. It believed that social evils came from capitalism and would melt away with its abolition. It was a vision so exhilarating and distant that it led the leaders to skip over such hard questions as how to manage budgets, how to employ the unemployed, and how to revive ailing industries. For most Labourites, socialism was a moral vision more than an economic system, a moral vision that still possessed Victorian elements. Beatrice Webb still worried that indiscriminate relief would promote idleness; Philip Snowden, the flinty Chancellor of the Exchequer, disapproved of extravagant spending and large deficits, and MacDonald called "the State as Lady Bountiful" a Tory idea and the idea of reducing unemployment by government spending "humbug."

Ramsay MacDonald, the son of a farmhand, was born in Scotland in 1866. He was raised on Scottish individualism and Celtic romanticism. As a young man he went down to London, where he lived on oatmeal, tea, and the ideals of brotherhood. Tall and handsome, a superb organizer and an eloquent orator, he became secretary of the Labour Representation Committee in 1900 and an MP in 1906. His pacifism, which during the war lost him his seat in Parliament and won him much abuse, made him by 1922 a heroic figure and the chairman of the Labour party. Beneath his commanding presence lay a reserved, shy, and somewhat naive man, a man proud of his successes, eloquently idealistic, compassionate, pleased with the company of the wealthy and aristocratic, and, after the death of his wife in 1911, remote and aloof. He had little understanding of economics and no blueprint of a socialist society. Lenin called his ideas "the best example that could be given of that smooth, melodious, banal and Socialist-seeming phraseology under which British Labour concealed its bourgeois origin."

MacDonald's Victorian morality and Victorian economics led him to defend the capitalist views of Treasury officials and bankers, to oppose his own party, and to urge a reduction in assistance to the jobless. It was a tragic mistake that did the economy no good and the Labour party great harm. He then compounded his error by abandoning his party in order to become the prime minister of a Tory-dominated coalition, one that in the election of November 1931 swept away Labour MPs as decisively as Lloyd George's coalition had swept away Liberal MPs. But he also had successes. He was an able diplomat and a highly respected statesman who proved that the Labour party was safe, respectable, and fit to govern. In 1924 MacDonald presided over the London Conference that adopted the Dawes plan for reducing Germany's reparations payments and in 1930 he presided over another conference in London at which the British, the Americans, and the Japanese agreed on the relative tonnage for cruisers, destroyers, and submarines. MacDonald was a well-informed, skillful, and refreshingly open negotiator, and these qualities won him deserved acclaim. A critic of the general strike, he appeared a man of peace standing above the class war. A man of mixed qualities, he worked conscientiously to build a viable Labour party, only to undo much of that work by ineffective domestic programs and by the debacle of August 1931. That debacle brought the Tories to power.

THE ASCENDANT TORIES

The most important fact about British politics between the wars was the dominance of the Tories. For more than eighteen years they were the largest party in Parliament and for sixteen years enjoyed a majority of its seats. Their majority kept Lloyd George in office after 1918 and Ramsay MacDonald after 1931. Majorities supported Bonar Law in 1922, Stanley Baldwin in 1923, 1924–29, and 1935–37, and at the end of the 1930s, Neville Chamberlain.

The leading Tory between the wars was Stanley Baldwin. Not even in the Cabinet before September 1921, he became prime minister by May 1923. Good luck, astuteness, and an attractive personality help explain this rapid rise to power. The good luck came in 1922 when the ablest politicians in the Conservative party—Austen Chamberlain, Lord Balfour, Lord Curzon—refused, from loyalty to Lloyd George, to enter Bonar Law's government. Their refusal created a vacuum that allowed the newcomer, Baldwin, to become Chancellor of the Exchequer. Cancer then forced Bonar Law to resign, leaving Baldwin with only one competitor, Lord Curzon. It was King George V's task to choose between the proud, aristocratic, and brilliant Curzon, once Viceroy of India, or the modest, unassuming Baldwin, a Worcestershire iron manufacturer. George V chose Baldwin after Lord Balfour told him that not only was Curzon quarrelsome and haughty and Baldwin amiable and modest, but that Curzon did not, as did Baldwin, sit in the Commons, and thus could not lead the party in its daily battles to govern England.

Baldwin won the job and promptly committed a political blunder by holding an election on the issue of protection. He did so in part because he believed tariffs on foreign goods would reduce unemployment, an evil that worried him deeply. But his protectionist cry only united the Liberals, invigorated Labour, and aroused fears of costly food; the result was 87 percent fewer Tory seats and England's first Labour government. Ten months later, after the Labour government fell, Baldwin buried the issue of protection and campaigned on moderation and stability. In 1924 Baldwin promised to return to old ways, to reduced spending, to the gold standard, and to a *laissez-faire* economy. The result, however, was not stability. In 1926 came the general strike, which Baldwin did little to prevent. Yet so firm, calm, and conciliatory was he during those nine tense days that the public saw in him a tower of strength.

Toward Tory extremists in business, in the courts, and in Parliament, Baldwin was not a tower of strength. Over a thousand strikers went to prison for seditious speeches, many more were refused reemployment, and throughout England employers drove down wages and discouraged union membership. Parliament also passed the Trades Dispute Act of 1927, which outlawed sympathetic strikes and made it more difficult for unions to raise money for political activities. Baldwin even allowed the police to raid the Russian trade delegation and the Foreign Office to break diplomatic relations with Russia. These extreme measures were a reflection of Baldwin's weakness before powerful interests and the dominance of Tory attitudes.

Baldwin was also happier to drift with, rather than direct, events. From 1925 to 1929 he allowed the organization of the Conservative party to grow slack and left most social evils to fester. The one exception to the policy of drift was the work of Neville Chamberlain at the Ministry of Health. Once mayor of Birmingham, as was his father, he had the same intimate knowledge of local government and the same skill in legislation. He drew up, and Parliament passed, an act making old age pensions part of the national insurance program. Previous to this act, the treasury gave pensions only to the poor over 70, a kind of pauper relief. Old age pensions now became a benefit earned by weekly contributions, not a payment from the Treasury to all who were elderly and poor. The act also provided payments for widows, orphans, and dependent children. Though the act expanded the welfare state, it still left gaps—namely, the millions not enrolled in the national insurance program. But it pleased Chamberlain because it preserved the Victorian belief that by contributing to the fund, workers became independent.

In 1929 Chamberlain also drew up an act establishing public assistance committees in Britain's 140 county councils and giving them power to grant unemployment assistance and poor relief to the able-bodied. The act reduced significantly the power of the old poor law boards. The same act exempted agricultural property from local taxation and granted a partial exemption from such taxes to manufacturers. It also gave "block" grants to local government. Before 1929 the Treasury gave grants proportionate to the amount of local taxes, a policy favoring the richer areas where taxes were higher. Now the Treasury gave grants according to the needs and population.

Old age pensions, PACs, and block grants all meant a greater role for government, as did the establishment in 1926 of a Central Electricity Board and the British Broadcasting Corporation. Baldwin's government did not hesitate to call on the state to solve technical problems, to improve the efficiency of local government, or to apply palliatives to the worst abuses, but it did hesitate long and hard before using the state to attack the larger problems of unemployment, poverty, and inequality. In the face of these massive evils, the Tories stuck to a policy of *laissez-faire*, which helped cause their defeat in the general election of May 1929.

By October 1931 Baldwin was back in power, though in the discreet form of a supporter of Ramsay MacDonald's national government. The Tories had 11 places in the Cabinet to Labour's 4 and the Liberal's 4, and 473 sat in the Commons. It did not displease Baldwin that MacDonald was Prime Minister, since the two had much in common. Both sought to bring people together, to dampen extremism, and to unify the nation. At election time they competed for the votes of the center by promising to lead all classes. The speeches of both were moral and vague, Baldwin finding the solution to social distress in four monosyllabic, Anglo Saxon words, "faith, hope, love and work," and Mac-Donald promising "to make the land blossom like a rose and contain houses and firesides where there shall be happiness and contentment and glorious aspiration."

In 1935 ill health led MacDonald to resign in favor of Baldwin, who, since October 1931, had in fact been calling the tune. That tune had two major themes—protectionism and economy. In November 1931, Parliament passed an act giving the Board of Trade the power to impose temporary tariffs of 10 to 20 percent on any foreign goods flooding British markets. In February 1932, Parliament passed the Imports Duties Act, which placed a fixed duty of 10 percent on nearly all manufactured goods and gave the Treasury the power to raise some of them to 20 or 33 percent. Most foods and raw materials were free of import duties.

Protectionism lost the national government little in popularity. The same could not be said of its other economic measures. In its first budget, in October 1931, it proposed a 10 percent cut in the salaries of all civil servants and a 15 percent cut for teachers. The teachers rebelled, marched 10,000 strong through the streets of London, lobbied their MPs, and forced MacDonald and Baldwin to cut the teachers' salaries only 10 percent. Unemployment assistance was also reduced 10 percent, and the means test was employed to reduce the sums given out to some half-million persons. Stricter standards also deterred some quarter of a million from applying. Many Public Assistance Committees gave relief more generously than the law stipulated. To end such illegalities the government created the Unemployment Assistance Board whose large staff resolved to make all payments uniform and smaller. In striking contrast to this niggardliness was government generosity to farmers, manufacturers, and builders.

The government aided agriculture in three ways: first, by creating marketing boards to fix prices for milk, bacon, potatoes, and hops; second, by giving subsidies to producers of bacon, wheat, and sugar beets; and third, by imposing import quotas on eggs and poultry. In 1936 the government also created coal-selling committees and cotton spindle boards to set quotas for each colliery and mill, gave the steel industry a 50 percent tariff, and granted subsidies to shipbuilders and house builders. The Tories had proved themselves even more interventionist than Labour. They also departed from their campaign oratory by going off the gold standard and running up budget deficits. To refund the debt, Chamberlain reduced the Bank of England's rate on loans from 5 to 3½ percent, and to give subsidies to industry and agriculture, he ran a deficit, a deficit that grew larger when in 1934 he reduced the income tax. By 1937 most incomes over £500 paid no more in taxes than before the war—which was about 5½ percent. Those earning incomes around £100 fared worse: their rate was 11 percent. The rich and powerful carried considerable weight in Tory England.

The school children of Britain carried nowhere near such weight. The government, economy-minded as ever when it came to the poor, ordered that school lunches for the poor, granted by an act of 1921, should go only to those whom a doctor had certified to be suffering from malnutrition, a requirement that limited lunches to 4 percent of the children. One local medical officer called the order, "brutal, inhuman, and barbarous."

The economy after 1934 slowly revived. The low interest rates that resulted from both debt refinancing and a world depression encouraged investments, investments also encouraged by cheap imports of raw materials and foods. The high tariffs, cartel arrangements, and restrictive quotas of 1936 and 1937, all of which drove up the cost of living, neither stopped the decline of British exports nor prevented the slump of 1937–38. Only heavy spending for rearmament in 1939 brought a sustained revival.

In 1935 the suave and complacent Baldwin led the Tories to a great election victory. A fall in unemployment, a declining Liberal and discredited Labour party, Baldwin's enthusiasm for the League of Nations and peace, his consummate skill in the use of the government and Tory-dominated newsreels and radio, and promises of no great armaments, all these factors explain the Tory triumph.

It was also in 1935 that Parliament passed the Government of India Act. The act reflected the partnership of Baldwin and MacDonald at its best. It was Baldwin who sent a commission in 1927 to investigate the rising clamor for independence and the conflict between Muslims and Hindus, and it was Mac-Donald in 1929 who promised India dominion status as an "ultimate solution." MacDonald also presided over three roundtable conferences in London, the second of which brought Mahatma Gandhi to London to argue the cause of independence. Gandhi was head of the Indian Congress Party and leader of massive civil disobedience campaigns that were undermining British rule in India.

The conferences led to the Government of India Act, which called for the creation of a federal government and greater autonomy for each province. World War II came before the act could be carried out, and it had little effect other than to make independence all the more likely and to anger Winston Churchill. The issue of India made Churchill a rebel, critic, and backbencher (that is, one who, not holding any government office, sits on a back bench rather than the front or Treasury bench). Being a backbencher gave Churchill the opportunity to criticize Baldwin, which he did on the embarrassing case of the romance of the new King, Edward VIII, with the American divorcee, Wallis Simpson. George V, Edward's father, had set the same high standard for the British monarchy as had his grandmother Queen Victoria. His indefatigable laying of cornerstones, his assiduous attention to government, the homely wisdom and charm of his Christmas radio messages, and his tolerance and respectability revealed a simple, straightforward servant of the people. Not so dedicated and simple was his son, Edward. King by succession in 1936, he immediately planned to marry Wallis Simpson. The Anglican church said divorce was a sin and millions agreed. There were other reasons for disliking the marriage. Was not Wallis a commoner and an American? Baldwin, sensing the mood of the public, told Edward he could have Wallis or the crown, but not both. The romantic Edward chose Wallis and abdicated in favor of his brother, who became George VI. The marriage crisis had ended, and soon a more fearful international crisis would arise. But in the meantime people continued to enjoy that revived prosperity which, along with an unparalleled technological revolution, was transforming their lives.

PROGRESS AND DISILLUSIONMENT

Progress, material and cultural, was a fundamental fact of England between the wars, yet the mood of those years was disillusionment. Never had the English enjoyed such technological advances, never were they so free and emancipated, and never so overwhelmed with amusements. It was also a time of cultural creativity, of poems, novels, paintings, sculptures, dramas, symphonies, and ballets. Yet for all the progress, the novels spoke of alienation and the poetry of despair. It was a paradox that began before World War I, grew in strength between the wars, and still exists.

The progress in technology was the most revolutionary. Never before or since has technology made such profound changes in the daily life of a generation. The steam engine, though it gave the Victorians cheaper manufactures and trips on railways and steamships, did not enter into their daily lives—nor today do rockets and hydrogen bombs. What has entered daily lives are radios, televisions, motor cars, gramaphones, hair dryers, the cinema, frozen food, electric mixers—all features of English life by 1936. Television broadcasting began in London in 1936, only thirty-nine years after Marconi's radio, Daimler's first automobile, and the Lumiere brothers' first moving picture. The radio, auto, and cinema were all invented around 1895. After World War I, they suddenly flooded the Western world. So did a host of other inventions using the magic of electricity: light bulbs, stoves, heaters, telephones, flashlights; and from the electric motor, vacuum cleaners, fans, hair dryers, mixmasters, coffeegrinders, and refrigerators—which in turn meant frozen foods of all sorts and drinks with ice. The internal combustion engine was the electric motor's great rival, producing the automobile, bus, truck, airplane, tractor, bulldozer, road grader, and power mower. Chemistry too transformed the daily lives of people with plastics, cellophane, gasoline, cosmetics of all kinds, medicines, and improved rubber. Improved rubber in turn made possible smooth automobile and bicycle rides and condoms and diaphragms—the latter allowing birth control, small families, and promiscuity.

Hamstead Gardens, one of those suburbs in the green belt to which the wealthy with their automobiles fled (*Aerofilms*).

Prosperity and improved building techniques also created a housing boom, with the houses being more widely scattered because of the automobile. By 1939 3 million people owned homes and 2 million owned cars. They went largely to the richest third of the population, though the spillover in used cars and houses helped the middle third to move to older suburbs. The autos, buses, and trams created greater London, greater Birmingham, and greater Manchester, those huge conurbations crowded with suburbs. Highways spun out in all directions with a randomness that the rigid railway had happily been unable to achieve. Cinemas, factories, filling stations, stores of all kinds, and giant impersonal pubs sprang up, and on the branch roads, semi-detached villas. The less affluent lived in council houses, smaller still, yet also cluttered with the paraphernalia of the new life—radios, phonographs, electric fires, and cheap, grandiose furniture, almost all of it bought on the installment plan.

It was an age of material things, of objects that consoled bored and lonely housewives. The neighborliness, the belongingness, of a mining town, rural village, or industrial slum did not exist in the suburbs. There was no one pub, no one parish church or chapel, only auto rides to various pubs and cinemas or bus rides to Woolworth's or Marks and Spencer, chain stores that were the temples of the new materialism and whose items crammed the shopping bags of devoted worshippers. The shopping bags were also crammed with canned foods. Falling world prices meant cheaper and more food, though not better nutrition: consumption of ice cream and chocolates rose far more rapidly than did consumption of fresh vegetables and fruit. Although the English ate more, they drank less. The cinema, the pleasant home, and the radio kept men from the pubs and from drink, as did many other delights. As amusements few things

For the lucky among the less affluent, there were the council houses (*Radio Times, Hulton Picture Library*).

could compare to the cinema and radio. Nine out of ten homes had a radio, and each week some 40 percent of the English went to the movies, 25 percent of them twice. For a few pennies the unemployed found in the cinema warmth and distraction, the lonely wife a dream romance with Rudolph Valentino, the young boys adventures in the Wild West—and for all the troubled and harassed there were glamorous musicals, the antics of the Marx Brothers, and the poignant comedy of Charles Chaplin.

The government wanted the radio to be less escapist. It therefore appointed a Scottish Presbyterian, John, later Lord, Reith, to rule it with an iron hand. He allowed no broadcasts, besides the weather, on Sunday morning, and no news on any day until 6 P.M. He believed in giving the people what they ought to want. What they ought to want included lectures and sermons, Mozart operas and Shakespearean tragedies, and for relaxation dance music from the Savoy. All the announcers spoke a precise, upper-class, standard English. Austere, learned, Puritan, and stodgy, the BBC nevertheless set standards of taste, integrity, and excellence that, uncorrupted by advertising, led after World War II to the world's finest radio and TV.

In an age when people were determined to have fun, the amusements were endless. The educated still went to operas, concerts, ballets, plays, and the art galleries; the lovers of sport played tennis, golf, cricket, soccer, Rugby, or swam, hiked, and ran. Far more watched the best at tennis, golf, and football than ever before. The workers jammed football stadiums, flocked to greyhound racing, packed dance halls, enjoyed prize fights, and bet on everything. Wealthy youth threw bizarre parties, flocked to nightclubs, drank cocktails, danced the Charleston, and pursued fun so furiously that the head of the Lord's Day Observance Society said, "We have gone recreation mad."

That holidays were a most desirable form of recreation Parliament recognized in 1938 by passing the Holiday with Pay Act, an act that added 11 million to the 3 million enjoying that week of heaven. Not a few went to "Billy" Butlin holiday camps to swim, bask in the sun, dance, have romances, play games, and be entertained. Everything had to be fun, even reading. Newspapers were full of pictures, huge headlines, and simple, snappy stories of crime, gossip, scandals, sports, and features giving advice on gardening, love, and investment. They also contained crossword puzzles, recipes, and racy accounts of mountain climbers and air heroes whose stunts they financed. The novels of the period were no less exciting. Six pence bought stories of Tarzan, the villainous Fu Manchu, or the sheik of Araby. Lending libraries did a land-office business, especially in the detective novel, which became the rage of the 1930s. But nonfiction held its own as the English, possessing one of the worst public education systems in Europe, continued to be the best at self-education.

The 1920s also experienced a social freedom previously unknown, particularly for women. The war, prosperity, social mobility, and the city weakened old conventions; science, skepticism, modernism, and relativism undermined moral certainties. Few understood Freud, fewer Einstein, but the word got out:

The radio, today the poor cousin to television, was between the wars technology's revolutionary miracle (*Radio Times, Hulton Picture Library*).

space and time and morals were relative, and sex should not be repressed Newspapers now wrote freely about sex. The courageous Dr. Maria Stopes argued at a packed Queens Hall for birth control, and the Cambridge Political Union voted it wise and moral. The size of families grew smaller, as it had for some time, and some observers claimed that adultery was increasing. Family and school discipline also relaxed as psychologists condemned corporal punishment and progressive schools espoused a free and spontaneous education.

Women also gained more rights. The Matrimonial Act of 1922 allowed them to sue for divorce on the same grounds as men. During the 1920s women also could become barristers, sit on juries, join the higher civil service, and earn degrees at Oxford. Many became secretaries, typists, schoolteachers, factory workers, and some journalists, professors, executives, and doctors. They expressed their independence in a new style of dress, and cut their hair short.

For most of the 15 million now with paid holidays, it was not the costly Riviera but a holiday camp in Britain (*Radio Times, Hulton Picture Library*).

The style expressed movement, freedom, and independence, as did their way of life—cigarettes and cocktails in public, cheek to cheek dancing, and banter about sex. They read Virginia Woolf and applauded the acting of Edith Evans, women of fame who were part of the cultural scene.

The cultural scene was anything but in decline, and the same was true of the intellectual scene. In physics the advances were extraordinary. "We are living," said Lord Rutherford in 1923, "in the heroic age of physics." In 1923 Rutherford's colleagues at Cambridge proved him right by discovering the neutron, demonstrating the existence of the electron, and splitting the atom. Rutherford was the first to describe the structure of the atom, and his experimental work, along with Einstein's general and special theories of relativity, led to a revolution in physics equal to that which occurred in the age of Galileo and Newton. Advances in biology, chemistry, and biochemistry, while not as epoch-making, were impressive. And complex as these discoveries were, popular versions at the book stalls, in newspapers, and on the BBC told the educated more about the world than Newton or Galileo ever knew.

Historians, philosophers, and social scientists also added to the advance of knowledge. By rigorous attention to biographical and social detail, the historian

Sir Lewis Namier attempted to dissect the political life of England under George III as precisely as Rutherford had the atom. Many other historians followed in his steps or made other advances. No less rigorous were the investigations of the Viennese Ludwig Wittgenstein. Wittgenstein, who taught at Cambridge, published his revolutionary *Tractatus Logico-Philosophicus* in 1922. It was an attempt to build a strictly logical system of knowledge, one that eschewed metaphysics and intuition. It fitted with the empirical outlook of the British philosophers, of Bertrand Russell, G. E. Moore, and A. J. Ayer, and with their desire to sweep away the philosophical "rubbish" of the past and to subject everything to logical analysis. Sociologists, anthropologists, psychologists, and economists were no less bent on being thorough and analytical, and all expanded human knowledge, none more relevantly than, in 1936, John Maynard Keynes in his *General Theory of Employment, Interest, and Money*.

The progress of knowledge was abundant, rigorous, and exciting, and yet in its fragmentation, relativism, and multiplicity, disquieting. Physics revealed various truths: there were three different worlds—the old Newtonian one measured in feet and miles; the world of galaxies where time and space were relative to the position of the observer and measured in light years; and the world of the atom, infinitesimally small, full of megatons of energy, yet a world the exact measurement of which was so difficult that it led the physicist Heisenberg to speak of the principle of uncertainty. Psychologists also talked about different worlds: behaviorists about stimulus and response, the environment and condition-

"A Battery Shelled" by Wyndham Lewis in 1919 (*Imperial War Museum*).

ing; psychoanalysts about sexual and destructive instincts, the existence of which behaviorists denied. In 1930 Freud's *Civilization and Its Discontents* told the English once again that the repression of these instincts was the source of neuroses.

The arts were also characterized by variation, multiplicity, and uneven progress. The Royal Academy artists were moribund, while the students of the Slade Art School were alive with talent and ideas. Although Walter Sickert still painted lovely scenes in an impressionistic manner and Augustus John did powerful portraits, what really startled the art critics were the angular, geometric, metallic figures of novelist, critic, iconoclast, and painter Wyndham Lewis and Stanley Spencer's vivid and mystical paintings in which even dustmen and scorpions radiated beauty. Two sculptors, Henry Moore and Jacob Epstein, won applause for their innovative techniques. English taste in art lagged behind that on the Continent: the English now liked Cézanne but could not endure Picasso. They responded in a more sophisticated manner to music, attending concerts in great numbers and listening to the works of modern British composers like Vaughan Williams and Benjamin Britten.

They also read poems and novels that reflected the deeper moods of the

"Travoys arriving with wounded at a dressing station" by Stanley Spencer in 1919 (*Imperial War Museum*).

age. For many of the educated, that mood was one of disillusionment, and its most powerful expression came in 1923 with T. S. Eliot's *Waste Land*, a poem about a civilization that has become:

> A heap of broken images, where the sun beats
> And the dead trees give no water, the crickets no relief
> And the dry stone no sound of water.

It was a world of lonely, separated, soulless people, people whose religious faith had been shattered, people restlessly seeking but not finding. By 1925 they had become Eliot's "hollow men," men who, with "voices dry as grass," were lost in rats' alleys.

Others besides Eliot despaired of the state of civilization. The novelist D. H. Lawrence pronounced Christian and Liberal ideals dead, industrialism heartless, modern life unloving, sexual life repressed, and revolutions pointless. The very popular novels of Aldous Huxley satirized everything, including that hedonism with which cynical moderns consoled themselves in the wasteland. But not everyone despaired. No age is homogeneous; and most people never read anguished poets or bitter novelists. For the bright young people, life was as gay as Noel Coward's witty, clever, risqué comedies and as bittersweet as his songs; for the satisfied and wealthy—always more numerous than the despairing—there were the fascinating stories of Somerset Maugham and delightful tales of P. G. Wodehouse, and on the stage endless plays of no distinction and much fun. For the literati there were the daring innovations of James Joyce's *Ulysses* (1922) and Virginia Woolf's *Mrs. Dalloway* (1923), with their abandonment of rigid narrative, chronologies, and sentences, and their use of a large canvas filled with memories, dreams, streams of consciousness, shifting times, comic scenes, and poetic brilliance. These esoteric and private experiments, however, had no public theme, espoused no public cause, offered no hope of a less bleak world.

The young poets of the 1930s reacted to the bleakness of the 1920s by seeking some cause in which to believe. Faced with depression at home and fascism abroad and with a blundering Labour and a smug Tory party, they found that cause in radical politics. W. H. Auden, son of a doctor and a graduate of Oxford, was the best poet of the young radicals, but their ranks were rich in talent, including the poets Stephen Spender, C. Day Lewis, Louis MacNiece, and the novelist Christopher Isherwood. Middle-class, from the public schools and universities, and all friends, they became part of a world of proliferating literary reviews, experimental theater groups, radical journalism, public causes, manifestos, and marches—all on behalf of a vision of a brave new world, a world Auden wrote of, saying

> We shall build a tomorrow
> With new clean towns
> With no more sorrows.

In the 1930s there were fascists and pacifists, communists and Trotskyites, Christian Socialists and believers in social credit, nudists and vegetarians. Most joined left-wing causes. By 1938 the Left Book Club had 100,000 subscribers and over 1,000 discussion groups. After 1936 the greatest passion for these on the left was the fight of the Spanish Republicans against the fascist General Franco. Auden, Spender, and C. Day Lewis went to Spain, as did George Orwell. Auden, Spender, and Lewis went as communists; Orwell, a brilliant essayist with a passion for independence, fought with the anarchists. The Spanish experience, like that of being a communist, was disillusioning. For Orwell, Spain showed how ruthless communists could be, a fact he made clear in 1938 in *Homage to Catalonia*. Auden and Isherwood left Spain, and then Britain, for America, and quit the Communist party. Disillusionment persisted in the 1930s and grew acute over the government's policy of appeasement, a policy that belongs to the story of Britain and World War II.

FURTHER READING

ALDCROFT, DEREK. *The Inter-War Economy: Britain 1919–1939*. London: Batsford, 1970. An analysis which, never attempting to cover every area, focuses on key issues and developments, such as aggregate growth, fluctuations, government policy, and the crucial industries.

BLYTHE, ROLAND. *The Age of Illusion: England in the Twenties and Thirties*. Boston: Houghton Mifflin, 1964. A colorful, humorous, and perceptive portrait of two decades, finding its meaning in priggish Tory ministers and adulterous Anglican rectors, as well as in ordinary people.

FEILING, KEITH. *The Life of Neville Chamberlain*. Cambridge: Cambridge University Press, 1970. The standard life of the most important statesman of the interwar years, a sympathetic account that demands a critical reading.

GILBERT, MARTIN. *The Roots of Appeasement*. London: Weidenfeld and Nicolson, 1966. A wise interpretation of British appeasement because it is not viewed as mere cowardice or folly but as sometimes a viable policy—though not with Hitler.

GRAVES, ROBERT, AND ALAN HODGES. *The Long Weekend: A Social History of Great Britain, 1918–1939*. London: Faber and Faber, 1940. A kaleidoscopic picture ranging from nudism to socialism and card playing to detective novels; a picture that despite its great variety brings out common attitudes and themes.

MCELWEE, WILLIAM. *Britain's Locust Years, 1918–1940*. London: Faber and Faber, 1962. A critical review of two decades whose record McElwee judges not a proud one but still one that saw rapid changes, crises, and war without violence or loss of liberty.

MARQUAND, DAVID. *Ramsay MacDonald*. London: Jonathan Cape, 1977. A monumental portrait of a self-made Scotsman who rose from poverty to the highest office in the land, told with admiration for MacDonald but awareness of his defects.

MIDDLEMAS, KEITH, AND JOHN BARNES. *Baldwin: A Biography*. London: Weidenfeld and Nicolson, 1969. A definitive study of an enigmatic man who was Britain's commanding power for sixteen years, whose influence the two authors measure and explain with discrimination and sympathy.

MOWAT, CHARLES L. *Britain Between the Wars*. London: Methuen, 1955. A thorough and always sensible survey of the political, economic, social, and diplomatic events of these years, liberal if not a bit socialist in its point of view, but always fair.

RAYMOND, JOHN, ED.   *The Baldwin Age.* London: Eyre and Spottiswoode, 1960. Fourteen eminent writers explore the byways of Baldwin's age, whether mass entertainment and churches, or physics and the League of Nations.

STEVENSON, JOHN.   *The Slump: Society and Politics during the Depression.* London: Jonathan Cape, 1977. A discerning look at the paradox of the 1930s, of a society that produced a million cars while a million men were unemployed and both Labour and the Tories stumbled.

Britain and World War II

29

For Britain World War II lasted nearly six years, during one of which the British stood alone against Germany. It was a different war from World War I; 324,000 not 750,000 were killed, and of these 70,000 were civilians. It was also a sprawling, mobile war. Instead of trenches, mud, and stalemate there were naval battles in the Pacific, desert war in Africa, jungle fighting in Burma, submarine pursuit in the Atlantic, and the battle for the skies. Surprises came at every turn—the fall of France, the invasion of Russia, Japan's bombing of Pearl Harbor, the arrival of the United States, and the invasions of Italy and France. While not as horrible as the first war, it was far more taxing on the British people and destructive of their land and Empire.

THE COMING OF WAR

Few British men and women could forget the horror of World War I. It was engraved on their memories, informed some of their most powerful literary statements, and inspired the learned to search out the causes of war. It also led idealists to propose panaceas and politicians to promise the end of war. The search for the causes of war led to the system of alliances and the armament races that preceded World War I, part of the balance of power diplomacy that had always led to war. The conviction that modern war had become unendurable and that a new way must be found to settle international disputes was the most powerful legacy left by World War I.

A second legacy was a deep feeling of guilt about the Treaty of Versailles. It was not great in 1918, when hatred of Germany was intense, but it grew strong as hatred faded and as books told of the Allies' postwar blockade, the inequities of the treaty, and the role of all nations in causing the war.

A revulsion against war and guilt over Versailles were ill-suited to realistic grappling with the third and knottiest legacy left by World War I: the problem of Germany's dominance in Europe. Despite the loss of Alsace-Lorraine and some Polish territory, despite clauses against an air force and navy, and despite an army limited to 100,000, Germany was still potentially Europe's strongest power. In wealth, population, technology, and drive, it excelled all. Germany was still a giant and, because of defeat, an angry one. The German problem, the problem that led to World War I, still existed. With Russia looking inward, America isolationist, and France weakened by four years of carnage, it fell to Britain, head of the world's greatest empire, to lead in the rebuilding of Europe and the fashioning of a new diplomacy.

It is not easy to fashion a new diplomacy. In trying to do so Woodrow Wilson helped create the League of Nations, only to have the United States Senate spurn the idea. Yet the League built its marble palace at Lake Geneva and resolved to guarantee peace through collective security, which in the 1920s had become the great alternative to balance of power diplomacy. Article 10 of the League Covenant required all to aid any member that was attacked, and Article 15 called for the arbitration of all disputes. But neither was explicit about when and how this would be done. At Geneva Ramsay MacDonald urged the adoption of the Geneva Protocol, which required immediate arbitration of disputes and military aid by every member to any nation attacked. But the protocol died when MacDonald left office; Stanley Baldwin let the idea drop. He also dropped MacDonald's treaties with Russia, thus neither advancing the idea of collective security nor establishing a basis for a future alliance with which to contain Germany.

Indeed, Baldwin and his Foreign Secretary, Austen Chamberlain, even weakened the alliance with France by merging it with the Locarno Agreements of 1925, in which Germany, France, and Belgium promised to submit all disputes to arbitration. Britain and Italy also promised to join in the defense of any victim of aggression—a promise that was utterly redundant, for the same promises were contained in the League Covenant. Locarno brought Germany into the League and into the concert of Europe; it was admirable in its conciliatory aims, but it neither put teeth into collective security nor strengthened any alliance. Like the Kellogg-Briand Pact of 1928, in which fifteen nations, including Britain, renounced war, Locarno was not an alliance but only a series of vague promises that did little to strengthen the League.

In 1931 Japan's attack on Manchuria, a province of China, posed a serious challenge to the idea of collective security. It was repeated in 1935 when Italy invaded Abyssinia in Africa. The League did nothing but procrastinate about Japan, but then Japan was far away. Italy was much closer. Furthermore, Italy was vulnerable, since it had no oil and had to send supplies and troops through the Suez Canal. Had Britain wished to support the League, it could have closed the canal or denied Italy oil or both. Britain did neither, despite the fact that the Foreign Secretary, Sir Samuel Hoare, in September 1935 promised the

League Assembly that Britain would be steadfast in any "collective resistance to all acts of unprovoked aggression." Hoare reversed himself in December by joining France's Pierre Laval in a plan to lure Mussolini away from Hitler by giving him two-thirds of Abyssinia. News of this sellout, leaked to the press, shocked the public, who accused Hoare and Baldwin of betraying the very League they promised steadfast support. Hoare resigned in disgrace. Baldwin gave a rambling, inept, and vague apology that revealed his ignorance of foreign affairs.

Despite Hoare's resignation and Baldwin's apology, the government did not close the canal, did not embargo oil, and did not abandon an effort at a private deal. Mussolini arrogantly refused the deal and conquered all of Abyssinia. The failure to stop Mussolini was a fatal blow to the League's effort to use collective security to deter aggression. Never before and never since had that idea enjoyed a more favorable climate of opinion or a better chance to be put into practice. That it was not was due less to the League's failure than to the failure of Britain and France to support the League. An embargo on oil, a closed Suez, a defeated Mussolini, and an independent Abyssinia would have alarmed Hitler, who was watching these events closely. It would also have given the League a new buoyancy and confidence in its resolve to make collective security work.

Collective security can take many forms—economic sanctions, courts of arbitration, pooled armed forces, and solemn promises. Of its various forms, few were more popular than universal disarmament. The British Labour party and its leader, Ramsay MacDonald, made it the centerpiece of their diplomacy. In 1933 MacDonald, now prime minister in a national government, proposed a grand plan to the Disarmament Conference at Geneva. The plan ran into difficulties when Germany's demand for equality clashed with France's insistence that only a larger French army could guarantee its security. The French did contemplate some reduction, but only if there was an effective system of international inspection and supervision. The insistence on supervision led Germany to leave the conference. A week later Germany also left the League. It then rearmed, a fact Hitler boasted of in March 1935, when he announced military conscription and bragged about his air force, both proscribed by the Treaty of Versailles. The dream of universal disarmament was dead.

Collective security was collapsing. In 1933 Germany had scuttled disarmament, and in 1935 Britain had let down the League on the question of Abyssinia. In 1936, Germany's occupation of the Rhineland, in violation of Versailles and Locarno, undermined the idea of a peace based on treaties. The Germans could, of course, claim that the Versailles treaty was imposed on them. But Locarno was not. In signing it, the Germans freely and solemnly promised to keep their troops out of the Rhineland. Germany, by reoccupying it in 1936, and Britain and France, by doing nothing, made it clear that treaties and promises would provide neither the basis of a new diplomacy nor a secure peace.

By 1936, hopes of a new diplomacy, of open covenants openly arrived at, of reduced armaments, of mutual guarantees, of promises kept and treaties respected all melted away. Was it not time to return to the old diplomacy, to the balance of power, alliances, and rearmament? Winston Churchill reminded Parliament that Elizabeth I, William III, and William Pitt had formed such alliances. But the Prime Minister, Neville Chamberlain, pursued a different policy: appeasement. The course of the government, he told Parliament, was "the appeasement of the world."

In 1936 appeasement—the resolution of conflict by conciliation and concessions—was neither new nor a necessarily unwise policy: it could serve well in some situations. It was not an unwise policy when it inspired MacDonald to negotiate a reduction in reparation payments or when Chamberlain arranged Locarno. But it was inappropriate when Mussolini was in Abyssinia and Hitler in the Rhineland—though perhaps understandable, since these were the first aggressive moves by the two dictators, and since they caught Britain by surprise. By 1938 the situation was different: the untrustworthiness of Hitler and Mussolini had become undeniable and the threat of German power unmistakable. The Spanish Civil War, in a most brutal way, made both self-evident. Anthony Eden, resolved on neutrality, established a Non-Intervention Committee in London which Germany and Italy joined. When Germany then sent General Franco an air force and Italy some 100,000 soldiers and numerous tanks, Eden was silent. The British sent nothing. Britain not only kept its promise not to intervene, to the detriment of Spain's legitimate government, but sent no protests to Hitler or Mussolini for their wholesale violations. Most Tories both sympathized with Franco and feared the Communist's role in the Republican government, though it was a minor one.

The duplicity of Hitler and Mussolini did not faze Chamberlain; he still believed he could win them over by persuasion. His government denied the army an expeditionary force able to fight on the Continent by refusing it the needed tanks and motorized weapons. He had great faith in the air force— especially its bombers—and in 1937 urged it be strengthened, but not too much, as undue expenditures on arms would ruin the economy. Instead of arming Britain, he allowed Lord Halifax in November 1937 to visit Hitler. Halifax told Hitler Britain would agree to territorial alterations in relation to Austria, Czechoslovakia, and Poland—if done peacefully.

Hitler responded in March 1938 by invading Austria and annexing it to Germany. The Labour party called on Chamberlain to recognize the danger and to form an alliance with France and Russia. He refused, saying that alliances would "plunge us into war."

He also declared that Britain had no obligation to defend Czechoslovakia, an invitation to the Germans to move. Hitler did so by demanding settlement of the problem of Czechoslovakia's Sudetenland, where some 3 million German-speaking people lived. They had never been part of Germany and only a few had agitated for autonomy until Hitler's paid agents organized them. Their agitation subsided in August when the Czech leader Eduard Benes gave them a large degree of autonomy. Chamberlain believed, wrongly, that autonomy for the Sudetens would satisfy Hitler and that if he could talk to him personally all would be well. But on September 15, when he met Hitler at Berchtesgaden, he was confronted by the demand that the Sudetenland be annexed to Germany. He agreed, if it was done slowly and by a plebiscite. To cement this agreement, Chamberlain flew to Godesberg on September 22. Hitler now demanded more territory and all within six days.

Chamberlain returned a crushed man. His more spirited Cabinet and Parliament were ready to fight: gas masks were distributed and trenches dug. Yet the Prime Minister continued to seek appeasement. On September 28 he flew to Munich and conceded most of what Hitler had demanded. He also asked Hitler to sign a separate piece of paper bearing a promise to settle disputes peacefully. Upon landing in England he waved the paper and announced, "peace in our time." A public that remembered World War I cheered and rejoiced until, on March 15, 1939, Hitler seized all of Czechoslovakia.

The collapse of appeasement made two things imperative—rapid rearmament and alliances with other powers opposed to Hitler. Chamberlain did both,

A smiling Adolph Hitler beguiles a smiling Neville Chamberlain (*UPI*).

but the first slowly and at the prodding of Parliament and the second in a way that produced confusion and weakness. Parliament established a Ministry of Supply, adopted conscription, and voted money for an expeditionary force. France in the winter of 1939 was Britain's only ally. By spring there were four more: Poland, Romania, Greece, and Turkey. With little consultation—and impulsively—Chamberlain had promised that Britain would help defend all four if they were attacked. Britain in fact did not have the forces to defend even Poland, nor were any of these powers themselves strong. The only great power in the east was Russia.

During the Czech crisis, and later, the Russians asked for such an alliance. In April 1939 the Foreign Office finally began negotiations, but the talks went nowhere. Britain never pushed them vigorously. While the Russians urged dispatch and sent top-ranked officials to the negotiating table, the British sent nonentities and procrastinated. Chamberlain never really wanted a Russian alliance. He told Parliament in 1938 that he had "the most powerful distrust" of the Soviets. The depth of that distrust encouraged Stalin to sign a Nazi-Soviet nonaggression pact in August 1939. Germany could now safely attack Poland, and did so on September 1. Britain then declared war on Germany, and Poland fell. Britain and France now faced a powerful Germany, without Russia as an ally and without the support of Czechoslovakia and its thirty-six divisions.

Would it have been wiser for Britain and France to have fought Germany in 1938 with Czechoslovakia, Russia, Romania, and Poland rather than with Poland alone in 1939? Historians now and generals then differ on this question. British generals told Chamberlain that Britain and France could not prevent the fall of Czechoslovakia. At the same time, German generals told Hitler they could not take Czechoslovakia and defend Germany against the French. Historians critical of Munich compare Czechoslovakia's thirty-six and France's eighty divisions with Germany's twenty-one fully and fourteen half-formed divisions and note the potential value of Russia as an ally. Those favoring Munich not only emphasize Czechoslavakia's geographical vulnerability but point to the low morale of the French army, the nonexistence of an equipped British force, and a Russian army that, if it did join in, had been decimated by Stalin's purge of its officers. That Germany rearmed faster than Britain in the year after Munich does pose a problem for the defenders of Chamberlain.

Although the strategic balance sheet of 1938 is a matter of debate, the other policies of appeasement, a trust in dictators, a belief in the efficacy of concessions, a failure to arm, a distrust of alliances, are not. The adoption of these policies raises the deeper question of the sources of appeasement. The principal source was a deep revulsion against those alliances and arms races that many believed had led to the ghastly horrors of World War I, a pervasive revulsion, one not only held by Labour leftists and moral idealists, but by a Tory elite of peers of the realm, lords of the press, industrialists, City financiers, publishers, Oxford fellows, and Chamberlain's Cabinet. By September 1938 and the Munich crisis the public's fear of Germany and its indignation at Hitler's conquests had supplanted its revulsion of war quite sufficiently to support a war against Hitler. But Chamberlain's government said no!

Its official reason was that it was unprepared for war and that it needed a year to complete the radar system, build up the air force, and equip the army. That it had not done so, that it gambled on conciliating Hitler, was due, in large part, to a fear that rapid armaments would ruin the economy, one heavily burdened by the cost of social services and by a war debt eleven times greater in 1918 than in 1914, a debt that took 40 percent of the central government's expenditure. That high taxation would ruin a capitalist economy was the unquestioned assumption of the all-powerful Treasury, many businessmen, and the Cabinet. It restricted defense spending two years after Hitler came to power to but 15 percent of the budget. The lion's share of that 15 percent went to the navy and air force, a revival of the Tory's old "blue water" tradition of a quasi-isolationist Britain financing and supplying continental armies, a tradition that Chamberlain and others fused with the new belief that bombers would win and lose the next war. And in addition to economic retrenchment, quasi-isolationism, and faith in bombers was a fourth attitude, a hatred of communism which saw Hitler as the scourge of bolshevism. It was a hatred that in precluding an alliance with Russia made the war, when it broke out, a grim battle for survival.

THE BATTLE FOR SURVIVAL

On May 20, 1940, ten days after they began their invasion of France, the Germans reached the English Channel. By June 4 the British had evacuated 338,226 soldiers from the beaches of Dunkirk, leaving behind all their heavy equipment. France surrendered on June 22. By August, German U-boats had sunk 1 million tons of British shipping, and the German air force, the Luftwaffe, had begun the destruction of the planes and bases of the Royal Air Force. If successful, Hitler would win the air cover needed for Operation Sea Lion, the invasion of a defenseless Britain. Not since Napoleon formed his grand fleet in 1805 had England been so vulnerable.

This sudden peril was in some ways as unexpected as the phony war between September 1939 and April 1940. In 1939, many expected the dreadful conflagration promised by novelists, pacifists, scientists, militarists, and moviemakers. When war was declared the sirens did sound and people did scurry to bomb shelters carrying gas masks. A million and a half children and mothers were evacuated to the countryside, bomb shelters dug, hospital beds kept open, and a blackout decreed. But the heavens did not pour down destruction. Hitler did not even invade France, and the British public continued to support the complacent Chamberlain. To business as usual came war as usual. There were cautious increases in spending and taxes but little rationing or control of capital, no crash program to arm, a million still unemployed, and no women at the lathes. There was also no coalition government, no rallying of public opinion, no call to make sacrifices—only a belief that France would hold on, that "time was on our side," that the blockade would ruin Germany, and that the service chiefs would run the war handily. There were some energetic actions: airplanes were built in large numbers, Churchill was busy at the Admiralty, and an expeditionary force was sent to France (to serve under the incompetent General Gamelin).

Churchill, the only bold minister, was perhaps too bold toward Norway. In the northern part of Sweden were mines that sent iron to Germany, most of it through the Norwegian port of Narvik. To stop the flow, Churchill suggested sending troops through Narvik to help Finland resist the Russians (who had invaded that country in 1939), with some of the troops also seizing the mines. It was a foolish idea, snuffed out by Finland's surrender. Churchill then urged the mining of the Norwegian coast as a means of blocking the export of iron to Germany. This, and British preparation to move into Norway, led Hitler on April 9 to outwit the British navy and seize Norway. Churchill then persuaded the government to seize Narvik and other ports. The government agreed, the ships and troops went in, but because the RAF could offer no air cover, they

Confident, buoyant, courageous, and eloquent, Churchill made Britain's darkest hour its finest.

were soon thrown out. The fiasco brought down Chamberlain and brought in as Prime Minister the man most responsible for Narvik—Winston Churchill. Churchill was not at that time overly popular. Nevertheless Chamberlain, the King, and important MPs realized that the times required an energetic and determined leader, one whose confidence and eloquence could inspire the people to heroic efforts.

Churchill took office on May 10 and immediately formed a national government in which Labour and Liberal leaders played key roles. He created a small War Cabinet with himself as Minister of Defense. Trained at Sandhurst, an officer in India, a major on the Western Front, and twice First Lord of the Admiralty, Churchill made it clear, as Lloyd George could not, that he would run the war. It was a formidable task. On the day he took command, Germany's *blitzkrieg* tore France apart as lightning splits a tree.

The bold strategy and brilliant tactics of the Germans, joined to the incompetence of the French, led to catastrophe. The attack came where least expected, through the narrow roads of the Ardennes Forest, not on the open fields of Belgium and northern France. On the front as a whole, Allied troops and tanks outnumbered the Germans. But the few troops in the Ardennes were no match

The rapidly moving panzer corps sweep through France (*Imperial War Museum*).

for the swift tanks, trucks, motorcycles, and mobile guns that flowed in a long, endless line through the forests, crossed the Meuse on bridges captured by parachute troops, and then drove for the sea. It was a bold strategy, and its speed and surprise destroyed the morale of a slow-moving French army. The Germans could have wiped out the British except that Hitler ordered them to halt before Dunkirk. From May 27 to June 4 the British navy and some 870 ships—ferries, steamers, tugs, crabbers, yachts, lifeboats—evacuated 338,000 troops.

After Dunkirk Hitler decided that air dominance over the Channel would allow the Germans to drive the English fleet away and send across barges full of soldiers and tanks. Hitler ordered the Luftwaffe to destroy the RAF. The effort began on August 13 with a mammoth attack. The Luftwaffe had some 1,350 bombers and 929 fighters. Britain had 670 fighters, some 750 in reserve, and a monthly production of 470. What was in desperately short supply were pilots. The German aim was to destroy the RAF's airfields and fighters and those radar and telephone centers that formed its central nervous system. Radar, discovered in 1924, was not developed until 1936. Completed by a crash program in 1939, it gave the RAF a complete view, in all weather, of the skies over southeast England.

The air battle for England lasted a little over six weeks. By September 1, the Germans had destroyed 338 and damaged 104 fighters, while losing only 177 themselves, with 24 damaged. Bombs had also torn up airfields, smashed hangars, destroyed aircraft, and damaged six of seven sector stations so severely that the RAF's system of defense was about to collapse. Pilots were being lost at the rate of 10 percent a week. Not a few, having parachuted to safety in the morning, were back up in the evening. How long could they, their craft, and their fields take it?

The Germans also had to ask how long they could take it. Their bomber fleet took serious losses. Those lucky enough to return often carried wounded or dead crewmen. Morale plummeted. British planes never ceased to appear, even though intelligence reports pronounced most English airfields "permanently destroyed." These frustrations, and a British bombing of Berlin, led the Germans on September 7 to concentrate on London. Hundreds of tons of explosives fell on the East End. Goering, commander of the Luftwaffe, excitedly phoned his wife, "London is in flames!" On hearing the same news Keith Park, Air Vice Marshal of the RAF, said, "Thank God." He was thankful because the "methodical Germans had at last switched their attacks from my vital aero-dromes. . . ." The shift of targets diluted the German attack. But even without it they would have faced the improved tactics of the RAF. On September 7, after the Luftwaffe fleets had banked to return, the RAF's big wing dived down on them, broke their formation, and sent many crashing. The Luftwaffe that day lost 52 fighters, the British only 26. On September 27 it was 52 Germans down to 28 for the RAF. By September 30 the losses were worse. Hitler called off the invasion.

Marshall Goering, sixth from right, and his staff look at the white cliffs of Dover, 20 miles away, and plan the destruction of the Royal Air Force and Britain (*Franz E. Furst, Camera Press Ltd.*).

The British won the air war over England for many reasons: Goering's shift from airfields to cities, the improved tactics of the RAF, and a heroism that led Churchill to say, "Never in the field of human conflict have so many owed so much to so few." Yet those few also owed much to the many who backed them up: mechanics working around the clock, air observers in exposed positions, radar operators, and the thousands of aircraft workers who produced from April to September 1940, 650 more planes than expected.

From June 1940 to June 1941 Britain stood alone against Germany. Survival depended on imports brought in by the world's merchant marine. If we could sink, said Germany's Admiral Doenitz, 700,000 tons of that shipping a month, Britain would collapse. In September 1940 Hitler was in no position to sink 700,000 tons. He had poured Germany's resources into the Luftwaffe and tank corps, giving the navy a low priority. Still he had a fleet of surface vessels, small but new and efficient and with tougher armor and better engines. Before the invasion of Norway that fleet with the help of the Luftwaffe sank, each month, 100,000 tons of British shipping. But the British, with far more ships, proved more formidable. Germany lost in the Norway campaign half of her destroyers, three of her eight cruisers, and one of two pocket battleships. In May 1941 she also lost her most powerful battleship, the *Bismarck*. These losses drove Germany's surface ships from the Atlantic.

At that point Doenitz turned to the U-boats. Germany was now producing more than 200 a year. In 1942 these submarines, along with bombers taking off from France and Norway, sank more than 650,000 tons a month. In early

March 1943, 38 U-boats hit two huge convoys, sinking 141,000 tons and losing only one submarine. The Greenland Gap and Doenitz's "wolf packs" lay at the center of the problem, though inadequate air cover was a troublesome part of the picture. The Greenland Gap was a 300-mile-wide swath running down the mid-Atlantic, a gap Allied land bombers could not cover. German U-boats were thus free to surface, refuel, and move rapidly at night, faster even than the convoy's escorts. In mid-March German U-boats in the Greenland Gap and German long-range bombers on the Gibralter run threatened Britain's lifelines. Germany's long-range bombers had indeed become a greater menace than its U-boats and led the British to introduce the first escort carriers with catapult-launched fighters. These fighters, along with longer-distanced ones with improved radar and search lights, quickly took their deadly toll of Doenitz's U-boats. By June the U-boats had to call it quits. The number of Allied ships sunk in April fell to half those of March and in May fell still lower, while the loss of U-boats increased enormously. The British had found, and again just in time, the right technology, resources, and tactics.

The technology was once again radar, radar with a wavelength the Germans

From the Armada to World War II, the British navy has protected the island and its trade (*Imperial War Museum*).

Convoys and air cover thwart the U-boat attack on vital British supplies (*Imperial War Museum*).

could not pick up yet that allowed escorts and airplanes to locate the U-boats. The resources came from America in the form of long-range bombers and aircraft carriers that soon put an end to the Greenland Gap. With their bombs, improved depth charges, and new rockets, they made quick work of the U-boats. Better escorts, including 260 American destroyers, and better-trained naval and air personnel were also crucial, since it was the coordination of escorts and planes that destroyed the wolf packs. By May 1943 Germany had lost 30 percent of its U-boats, and in June Doenitz withdrew them. The battle for the seas had been long, bitter, and costly. By the war's end, the Axis powers had sunk 2,828 merchant ships, weighing 15 million tons, and 175 Allied warships—in both cases mostly British. The Allies in turn sank 789 U-boats, mostly German. Behind these statistics lay the vivid experiences of ordinary people, experiences that were frightening and heroic, ghastly and exhilarating. For the British soldier, the horrors of World War I were claustrophobic, intense, and prolonged—constant mud and endless, monotonous, hopeless days; for the British airman, seaman, and tank driver, the heroes of the Battle of Britain, the battle of the seas, and the struggle for the deserts, the horror was of an unexpected suddenness, of a torpedo slamming into an engine room, of screams, certain entrapment, and death; or in the Spitfire all exhilaration, clouds, sun, and beauty, until the fire of a Messerschmidt cannon hit the plane and sent it twisting downward.

Although different in so many ways from World War I, the second war did have, in the darkest hours of 1941, some similarities. One of them was the almost unanswerable question: How could Britain possibly defeat the Germans? A second was the belief that it might be done in the Mediterranean.

THE MEDITERRANEAN STRATEGY

From June 1940 to May 1945, Britain poured men and supplies into the Mediterranean theater of war. America did the same after November 1942. It was an effective strategy, argued Churchill and his generals, because it diverted German men and supplies from the Russian front, which opened up in June 1941. In the spring of 1944 and thereafter, it also drew German power away from the Western front. It was, said its critics, an ineffective strategy, one that by diverting vast resources to remote deserts, delayed by a year or two that invasion of France that alone would relieve Russia's blood-letting and bring victory. The debate on the wisdom of the Mediterranean strategy began in December 1941, when America and Britain established a Joint Chiefs of Staff Committee, and it has continued ever since.

The origin of the Mediterranean strategy was not, however, a matter of studied calculation. Pressing events and old commitments, not logistics, determined its adoption. In June 1940 Mussolini, finally convinced that Hitler would win, entered the war on Germany's side. He ordered his army in Libya to attack the British army in Egypt. The British instinctively defended Egypt, for Suez was the lifeline to the East, a route that also led to the oil fields of Persia. Battle then followed battle in a chain of events that brought the Allies into Morocco, Algeria, Tunisia, and Italy. British successes in Libya and German U-boat successes in the Atlantic (which ruined the idea of a second front in 1942) made a Moroccan and Algerian landing a good occasion for America to try out its new army. Defeats in Tunisia in the winter of 1942 and then success in early 1943 called forth more tanks and men, making it tempting to invade Sicily. The invasion of Sicily led to the invasion of Italy as the quickest way to divert German troops from the Russian and Western fronts.

Step 1 in the chain of events was the defeat of Italy's army in eastern Libya. Step 2 was the British decision in 1941 to help defend Greece and Crete. The triumph in Libya came as a surprise, since 50,000 British soldiers faced 500,000 Italians. A bold encircling movement led to the surrender of the Italian army. Control of North Africa was at hand. But instead of reinforcing the army in order to rid all Libya of Axis troops, Churchill and his generals ordered 56,000 men, 28,000 vehicles, and many aircraft to join other British forces in Greece and Crete in a forlorn effort to save those countries from German and Italian armies that had earlier invaded Albania, Yugoslavia, and Greece. Churchill, who liked to gamble, overextended himself once again, as he had at Narvik. Another Dunkirk ensued on May 2, 1941, as German tanks swept over Greece, but one in which 50,000 of 62,000 men were lost. German parachutists seized Crete and 18,000 more were lost. British and Greek forces outnumbered the

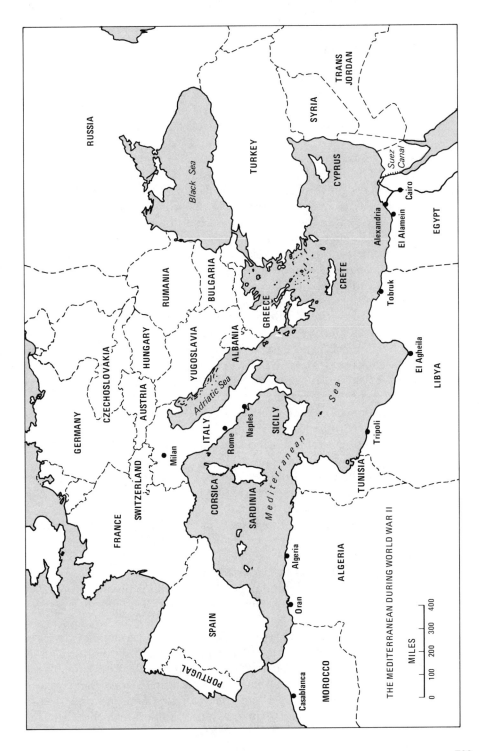

THE MEDITERRANEAN DURING WORLD WAR II

MILES

0   100   200   300   400

Germans in Greece and Crete, but they did not have air superiority. Neither had they learned how to check the swift thrusts of the German tanks, a failure that allowed General Rommel's two small-scale divisions, one light and one panzer, and some Italian forces, to inflict many defeats on Britain's North African army. With Rommel's appearance, the desert war began in earnest.

From El Agheila (some 450 miles east of Tripoli) it is about 700 miles of desert to El Alamein, 60 miles west of Alexandria. Halfway along the coast is Tobruk. On March 31, 1941, Rommel struck eastward from El Agheila; in April and May he drove the British beyond Tobruk, though leaving it in British hands. The British rebounded in June with Operation Battleaxe and blunted Rommel's advance. The war seesawed back and forth. In November, at Churchill's prodding, the British mounted the massive Operation Crusade. It resulted in enormous British losses and encouraged Rommel to dash for the Egyptian frontier. But Rommel outran his supplies and had to withdraw to positions near El Agheila held nine months earlier. Each side then replenished its armies with men and tanks and, on May 26, 1942, fought another great battle at Gazala, a line 100 miles west of Tobruk. The battle lasted until June 15. Although the British outnumbered the enemy's forces two-to-one in men and three-to-one in tanks, they still met defeat. Rommel, however, was also weakened: he had only 60 tanks. A conservative general would have consolidated his gains; Rommel did not. He plunged eastward, covering 300 miles in a week and capturing many tanks and guns. On June 20 a demoralized Tobruk fell, and by July Rommel was at El Alamein, 60 miles from Alexandria.

Rommel won because of his genius at swift movement and the shrewd combination of artillery and tanks at central points; the British generals lost because they dispersed their tanks among several divisions and then sent them a few at a time against entrenched positions. Until El Alamein the British were no match for the Desert Fox.

Then, however, Rommel met his match in General Montgomery and his superior numbers. Montgomery, who took over in August 1942, took a defensive position at El Alamein. Rommel, desperately low on supplies, had to attack. He did and met defeat. Montgomery's army of 230,000, with a six-to-one superiority in tanks, slowly, remorselessly and with little brilliance wore down Rommel's 80,000, only 27,000 of whom were Germans. A bold encircling move might have captured Rommel's army and ended the North African war, but audacity was Rommel's gift. Montgomery, the meticulous planner, took four months to drive Rommel to Tunisia, where, reinforced, Rommel took on the Americans and British.

While Montgomery was chasing Rommel, American and British troops landed in Morocco and Algeria, at Churchill's urging. Roosevelt agreed because he preferred some action in 1942 to none at all. The British generals urged landings in Tunisia as well, but the Americans vetoed them as too dangerous. The result was that Hitler had time to pour men and arms into Tunisia and Rommel had time to weld them together. Rommel's brilliance, American inexperi-

Vast, empty deserts provide a perfect stage for classical tank warfare (*Imperial War Museum*).

ence, and British slowness delayed the end of the North African campaign until May 12, 1943.

In a balance sheet on the Mediterranean strategy, Greece and Crete would be listed as grave errors. The desert war would be listed more ambiguously. It did save Egypt and the Suez, but it cost the Allies far more in men and arms than it did the Germans. Initially, the invasion of Morocco and Algeria meant an enormous expenditure of resources, but in the end Hitler, in a foolish attempt to save Tunisia, sent thousands to die and a quarter of a million to become prisoners—losses that no doubt pleased Stalin, who was angry over the delay of a second front in Europe. The *raison d'être* of the Mediterranean strategy was the draining off of Axis forces, and in this it succeeded. It was a success that led Churchill to persuade a more reluctant Roosevelt to invade Sicily, a decision that in turn meant the invasion of Italy.

If the invasion of Sicily had occurred a month earlier, victory would have been swift, allowing an earlier invasion of Italy, which if directed at Rome, would have brought its fall before the German army took over. But the overly cautious Montgomery delayed until he had assembled an assault force nearly as great than that which landed at Normandy—2,590 ships, 8 divisions, and 2 airborne brigades—a force he directed with such indifference to the coordination of air and naval forces and to American offers of help that the Germans, after taking a heavy toll of the British, escaped to Italy. The movement up the mountainous spine of the Italian peninsula went slowly. Amphibious landings at Salerno, south of Naples, and at Anzio, south of Rome, bogged down, as did the troops inching up the Apennines at Monte Cassino. The Germans held off the Allies in Italy from July 10, 1943, to May 2, 1945. In the spring of 1944 twice as many Allied as German troops were in Italy, a ratio roughly true for North Africa. The Mediterranean strategy drew Germans from the Russian and Western fronts, but it also drained off Allied troops and equipment—particularly landing craft badly needed for a second front in France.

WAR IN THE FAR-FLUNG EMPIRE

World War II was a more global war than its predecessor. Battles raged throughout the vast Eurasian continent, on the Atlantic and Pacific oceans, on their islands, and in Africa. The war thus involved the British Empire at every turn. When the British threw the Italians out of French and British Somaliland (which the Italians had invaded in 1940), and then Abyssinia and Italian Somaliland, their armies came from the Sudan and Kenya. The Sudanese army consisted of two Indian divisions and a Sudanese Defense Force; the Kenya army of 75,000 men, only 6,000 of whom were British. The Empire seemed to give the British an advantage.

But in December 1941, the Japanese undermined that assumption. On December 8 they invaded Malaya, on December 10 they sank the battleship *Prince of Wales* and battle cruiser *Respite* north of Singapore, on December 26 they took Hong Kong. The new year brought more bad news. On January 15 the Japanese invaded Burma, on February 5 they completed their sweep through Malaya (capturing 25,000 prisoners), and on February 15 they forced Britain to surrender Singapore, the strategic center of the Empire in Asia, and 85,000 troops. The principal reason for these disasters was the absence of an effective air force. It was Japanese aircraft, unhindered by British fighters, that won supremacy of the seas by sinking the *Prince of Wales* and *Respite*, just as it was Japanese air cover that allowed an outnumbered Japanese army to conquer Malaya.

British ineptness and smugness helped the enemy in Malaya and in Burma. Some British generals believed modern armies could not move rapidly through jungles; others, like General Wavell, supreme commander in the Far East, thought it would be a mistake to overrate the skill of the Japanese. The British dispersed troops throughout Malaya, leaving jungle routes on the east undermanned. Singapore was also poorly fortified, a mere half-garrisoned, halfway house, said the *Times*, yet no government, not even Churchill's, took action; nor did any government remedy the fact that its Burma army was ill-equipped, ill-trained in jungle warfare, and lacking in air cover. A smaller, more skilled, and better equipped Japanese army, one that enjoyed air cover, thus forced 60,000 British soldiers to retreat through a thousand miles of jungle leaving 3,500 casualties and encampments smelling of excrement and death—the work of malaria, dysentery, and the Japanese. Even the dauntless Churchill wished to write off Burma as lost, but not the Americans, who wanted to keep open the road to China and whose power and wealth enabled them to call the tune.

Thus in 1943 and 1944 the popular General "Bill" Slim rebuilt the army. To weaken the Japanese, he sent Brigadier Orde Wingate and his guerrilla forces, called the Chindits, deep behind enemy lines. Wingate, like Lawrence of Arabia, was a romantic figure, brilliant, imaginative, courageous, but unlike Lawrence, acerbic and arrogant. His Chindits performed heroic feats in the jungle but accomplished little of strategic value, although their raids did teach the British about the jungle. The Dieppe raid in France in 1942 was also a failure, yet it too taught the British lessons later used in the invasion of France. Many of the British military entered World War II, as their predecessors had World War I, stubbornly attached to outdated tactics and weaponry. But in both wars they finally did learn: the admirals that aircraft carriers were invaluable, the generals that a mobile, concentrated tank corps can sting, and the brigadiers that the jungle can be penetrated. That they did learn, though slowly, helps explain the old adage that the British lose all the battles but the last.

General Slim did win the last battle. He and his men learned about jungle warfare, the use of parachute troops, radio communications, camouflage, and air drops and air cover. In 1944 aircraft, mostly American, delivered Slim's army 94 percent of its supplies. The Americans wanted Slim to reopen the Burma road and upper Burma airfields so that supplies could reach a China which still held down the bulk of the Japanese army. The Chindit raids had another salutary effect. Because they originated in India, a Japanese army of 80,000 invaded, only to suffer, at Imphal, the worst defeat of its history. They lost 53,000 and had to retreat. Like the Germans in Egypt and Russia, they had overextended themselves. Germany and Japan won the first battles because they had long planned on war, had adopted advanced tactics and weapons, and had resolved to conquer. But because they unwisely took on nations larger, more wealthy, and more populated, they were doomed to lose the last.

FRANCE LIBERATED, GERMANY DEFEATED

The Alps and the mountains of the Balkans provided the Germans with a defensive barrier more formidable than the beaches of the Atlantic. To help Russia defeat Germany, Britain and America had to land somewhere along a 3,000-mile coastline that helped define the borders of Holland, Belgium, and France. In 1943, the Allies decided to make that landing on the northern shore of the French province of Normandy. The supreme commander was to be Eisenhower; Montgomery would lead the invading forces. The preparations were extensive and thorough. For four years the Germans had been fortifying the beaches of France. They had 60 divisions in France and the Lowlands, compared to the 37 Allied divisions available for invasion. Of the 37 divisions, only 8 could land the first day, and it would be seven weeks before they all arrived. It was a hazardous venture, yet it was done from strength.

The Allies, with 5,300 ships and 12,000 aircraft, dominated both sea and air. British intelligence deceived the enemy. In 1938 the British captured and reconstructed one of the machines on which the Germans enciphered key commands. Breaking the German code allowed the British to read the enemy's secret signals on critical occasions, to learn what the Germans feared would happen, and then to deceive them through the Double Cross System. The result was that almost all British operations came as a surprise. In 1943, for example, the British placed bogus documents on a dead body and had it washed ashore in Spain. The documents led the Germans to expect landings in Greece, not Sicily. Normandy also caught them off guard. Heavy bombing near Calais and false information to German agents led them to look for an invasion directly across the Channel. German air reconaissance also reported a massing of forces in Essex and Kent. What they saw were dummy landing craft, gliders, inflated rubber tanks, and recruits still to be fully trained. The fully trained troops and their equipment lay hidden in the New Forest in southern England.

The invasion was touch and go. Inaccurate parachute drops, rough seas, swamped tank carriers, congested beaches, lost tanks, and unexpected fortifications meant that on the first day a smaller beachhead was won than expected. Since Hitler, whose commands alone authorized troop movements, slept late and since on June 4 Rommel, thinking the seas too rough for a landing, was traveling, the nearby crack panzer divisions remained immobile. The Allies could thus enlarge the beachhead and anchor large floating harbors brought over from England. Through these harbors flowed masses of men, tanks, and guns for the six-week battle of Normandy. In that battle Montgomery's British troops on the eastern flank made a frontal attack on Caen and took on the best of the German tank corps, while the Americans on the west inched forward through heavily hedged and defended fields. On July 26 General Patton and the Americans broke through into Brittany, and on July 31 other American forces swept into a Loire Valley denuded of troops that Hitler had foolishly placed in beleaguered Caen. In mid-August Montgomery swept north; on August 26 Paris fell, followed quickly by Verdun, Brussels and Antwerp. The Germans now had their backs to their own frontier and faced an army with a twenty-to-one superiority in tanks and a twenty-five to one superiority in aircraft. "There were no German forces behind the Rhine," said the German Chief of Staff for the West, ". . . our front was wide open." Yet the war dragged on for eight more months.

This delay arose from Allied quarrels, a hesitant and compromising strategy, Hitler's suicidal stubbornness, and the courage of the German people. One of the quarrels was between Montgomery and Patton for supplies, another between Montgomery and Eisenhower over strategy. The supremely confident Montgomery was dogmatic and tactless in constantly demanding that all Allied forces be under one command and that some forty divisions concentrate on the northern avenue to Germany. Not gaining this goal, he then clamored for the lion's share of supplies for his British and Canadian forces. But his performance at Antwerp and at Arnheim in Holland only provided fuel for his critics. At Antwerp he neglected to seize key bridges, and at Arnheim, after an inaccurate drop of 10,000 parachute troops, his slowness in moving forward allowed the Germans to kill 1,130 and capture 6,450. The northern avenue was not an easy one.

But neither was Eisenhower's strategy of the broad front so easy. With Patton far to the south stalled before Metz and Montgomery in trouble in Holland, there was bound to be a weak link. On December 16 Hitler, who had furiously rebuilt his Western army, following precisely the *blitzkrieg* plan of 1940, broke through the forests of the Ardennes, gained 60 miles, routed the Americans, and then ran out of gasoline. By January the Germans were in full retreat, but for the Allies it was a costly setback. The Ardennes offensive had revealed the weakness of the broad-front strategy, just as Arnheim had revealed Montgomery's weakness as a tactician. The Allies, having no clear strategy, hesitated and compromised. Yet in the long history of alliances, one replete with mistakes and confusion, the story of the cooperation of the British and American forces in Europe will go down as a successful chapter. The hesitations and confusions were minor compared to the power and success of these vast armies. By May 2, the Allies and the Russians had defeated the Germans.

One reason why Hitler persisted so long was his wild hope that buzz bombs and rockets would win the war. A second reason was the failure of Allied bombing to ruin the morale of the Germans or seriously curtail German war production. Both sides shared the illusion that bombing would destroy morale and reduce war production, neither of which it did. The Germans fired their V-1s—a jet-propelled, pilotless plane—at London from June 1944 to March 1945. In September of 1944 came the V-2s, 50-foot-long rockets carrying a ton of explosive. The V-1 was noisy and terrified Londoners; the V-2 was noiseless because it traveled faster than sound. Both killed hundreds and made even more homeless, but neither blunted the British war effort. Neither did the Allies' saturation bombing destroy German war production or, as its supporters insisted, its war morale. The Allies' obliteration bombing of 1944 did not prevent Germany from doubling its aircraft production any more than it deterred one-fourth million in that year from joining the army. And although bombers did reduce German war production 9 percent, it took 25 percent of Britain's and 15 percent of America's war production to build these monstrous flying fortresses. The airplane as a tactical weapon, giving troops and ships cover, was invaluable, but as a bomber it brought mostly useless destruction. Had more tanks and landing craft and less bombers been built, the war would have ended sooner.

When it did finally end in May 1945, some of the greatest issues dividing the Allies were unresolved. There were two struggles for Europe: an avowed one against Germany and, toward the end, an unspoken one between the West and Russia. The peripatetic Churchill caused many conferences to be held during the war: with Roosevelt at Quebec, Washington, Cairo, and Casablanca; with Stalin at Moscow; and with Roosevelt and Stalin at Teheran and Yalta. For planning the war and preserving unity, these conferences were of great help, but they did little to solve the future of Europe. At Yalta in February 1945 the Big Three did decide to divide Germany into British, American, and Russian zones and agreed that both Poland's eastern and western boundaries should be moved some hundred miles westward. But it was the Russian army, not the

Yalta conference, which decided that Poland and the Balkans would fall under Russian sway. There was little America or Britain could do to stop it.

Roosevelt may have been unduly optimistic about Russian-American friendship and too naive about his amateurish and good-hearted diplomacy, but they made no more difference to the final outcome in Eastern Europe than did Churchill's sophisticated and persistent efforts to get the anti-Communist Polish government in London established in Warsaw. There was no sellout of Eastern Europe at Yalta, since the West had nothing to sell. Russia's national self-interest required friendly regimes in Poland and the Balkans. That these countries went Communist did not disturb the British people, for after five years of war they had far different concerns.

THE CITIZENS' WAR

Parliament in 1940 voted to have no general election until the end of the war. Each party also promised not to contest by-elections in constituencies held by the other. Party politics was banned for the war's duration; bipartisanship and unity were the new watchwords. Churchill led off by bringing Labour's top leaders into his government. Clement Attlee, Labour's quiet, unprepossessing leader became Deputy Prime Minister. Ernest Bevin, an earthy, blunt, self-educated leader of the Transport Union, became the czar on all matters concerning labor, which for him also meant all matters concerning economics. Herbert Morrison, son of a London policeman and long ruler of the London County Council, ran the Home Office, which provided the services needed to meet the strains of wartime and blitz. Sir Stafford Cripps, a brilliant, ascetic, highly independent leftist, became an extraordinarily efficient Minister of Aircraft and the leader of the House of Commons. Even Churchill was a nonpartisan figure. A Tory MP at 24, a Liberal minister at 33, a Tory Chancellor of the Exchequer at 50, and a backbench maverick at 60, he was in a sense above party, and to some an old Whig. Churchill's Cabinet, said Attlee, never divided on party lines.

During the Dunkirk crisis and the Battle of Britain he won over his detractors with his candor, eloquence, and resoluteness. He promised not "peace in our time" but "blood, toil, tears, and sweat" and spoke of the resolve that "We shall fight on the beaches, we shall fight in the landing grounds, we shall fight in the fields and in the streets, we shall fight in the hills, we shall never surrender. . . ." His eloquence and courage inspired a people tired of the prosaic and timid. During the dark hours of the blitz his stirring speeches gave an exhilarating sense of heroism to millions.

By 1942 that rhetoric had turned flat as the words Greece, Crete, Singapore, and Tobruk announced humiliating defeat upon humiliating defeat. Political criticism reasserted itself, though in a nonparty way. Criticism of poorly built tanks and scarce aircraft mixed with doubts about Churchill's reckless strategy.

Yet in June 1942 only 25 MPs voted for a motion of no confidence in Churchill and only 40 abstained. A healthy 476 supported him. Then, in November, came the victory at El Alamein, and the end of wartime criticism of Churchill. Throughout the war polls showed that 78 percent or more of the people approved of Churchill's leadership. Polls showed no such approval of the Conservative party. The ban on partisan politics did not extend to shifts in political opinion and hopes, and in the war years these opinions and hopes moved steadily leftward toward socialism. The movement received a large impetus from the communal experience of sharing the hardships and sacrifices of the bombing of Britain.

With the blitz, which began on September 7, 1940, came what the popular novelist and broadcaster, J. B. Priestley, called the citizens' war, one in which ordinary men and women become leaders and heroes. By February 1941 the government had given out 2.5 million Anderson shelters, tents of corrugated iron people buried in backyards and covered with earth. Each one held six persons. The government and the people also built public shelters for another 1.5 million. There were shelters in London for four out of five people. When the blitz began, many of the public shelters were without toilets and other needed services. The government was also unprepared at first to deal with those who crawled out of their Andersons to find their homes demolished. Where to go to eat? to sleep? to stay warm? By June 1941, the Luftwaffe had destroyed or damaged half a million houses in Britain, 60 percent of them in London, killed 43,000 civilians, and wounded thousands more. After one raid, 155,000 families were without gas, water, or electricity. To care for the homeless, to put out fires, and to warn of air raids, millions volunteered their unpaid services. They joined the Fire Guard, became air raid wardens, worked in community kitchens, ran rest centers, took hot tea, blankets, and solace to the bombed, worked in repair units—all without pay. It was voluntarism at its best, one with roots in the past yet able to work in harness with an expanded government.

Britons spent many nights during the blitz in all kinds of shelters—underground stations, the crypts of churches, hotel lobbies, caves, railway arches, and Turkish baths. Each shelter had a distinctive personality, but all had a neighborliness that came from a shared sacrifice. A similar equality was found in factories and fields, where citizens doubled their energies so that Britain could defy the Nazis. Chamberlain had dallied too long. In April 1940, a million were jobless and women were still in their kitchens. In late June, England had only 160 tanks. In August U-boats threatened the food supply and the Luftwaffe the cities. By September there was a shortage of Spitfires and convoy escorts. Aircraft and shipyard workers, farmers and merchant seamen, became as vital to the war as those in uniform. By and large they met the challenges of the war.

Food production soared as farmers plowed 18 million acres instead of the normal 12 million. They not only plowed up grassland long untouched, but golf courses, parks, the King's grounds at Windsor, and the downs of Sussex. Thousands of nonfarmers also cultivated 1.4 million acres of garden plots. Air-

Cleaning up the devastation of the blitz (*Radio Times, Hulton Picture Library*).

craft production multiplied, from 3,000 planes in 1938 to 26,000 in 1943. Tanks, artillery, explosives, trucks, shells, machine guns poured out of British workshops as the country devoted 55 percent of its national income and labor force to the war, the largest percentage of any ally, and far larger than America's 40 percent.

To muster such an effort, the government used a mixture of capitalism and socialism. The government's war powers exceeded those of World War I: it had complete control of raw materials and labor and enormous powers to determine wages and prices; it owned and ran 265 factories, its huge Royal Ordnance establishment at Chorley employing 35,000 in some 1,500 buildings. The government's greatest problem was a shortage of labor, solved by drafting all women 19 to 40. By war's end 6.75 million were in the services or at factories where ten-hour days and seven-day weeks had become the rule. To pay for this gigantic effort, the government taxed incomes at a standard rate of 50

Bomb shelter (*Radio Times, Hulton Picture Library*).

percent; imposed 100 percent purchase taxes on luxury goods; raised taxes on spirits, beer, and tobacco; and encouraged savings. The citizens responded by saving a fourth of their incomes after taxes. Despite full employment, higher wages, and government spending, prices rose only 50 percent during the war. But not everything went well with the wartime economy. Central planning was fitful, subcontracting excessive, the use of labor often inefficient, and absenteeism high. Powerful shop stewards, defying union leaders, led wildcat strikes. Coal production declined 15 percent; thousands of tanks had inadequate motors and guns, and 1,400 trucks had faulty pistons, a fault that hampered Montgomery's sweep to the Rhine.

British scientists played a crucial part in this citizens' war. It was not only a bombardier high up in the skies who released the bombs that sank the German battleships *Scharnhorst* and *Gneisenau* at Brest, but also a man in England sitting before a radar screen. Smaller radars worked from airplanes helped win the battle of the Atlantic. British scientists also led, before 1942, in the development of the atomic bomb, a bomb America completed because of its wealth and resources. British scientists were active in all fields, devising ways to escape damaged submarines, planning the precision bombing of French railways before D-Day, constructing nutritional diets for war workers, improving weapons, and saving lives by a medicine far in advance of that used in World War I. Penicillin, a British discovery, was the greatest saver of lives (and its greatest contribution to the twentieth century). The survival rate of the wounded was far higher than in any previous war, which for thousands was the most crucial fact about World War II. Social scientists also contributed to the war, running surveys of public opinion to determine what the public would endure in taxation and rationing—which they found was considerable—and studying the impact of the war on the citizens who fought it.

THE IMPACT OF WAR

World War II brought austerity to Britain, and its cold fingers touched every aspect of life. Almost everything was rationed except bread, tobacco, and beer—and the beer was diluted. Some foods were ample, usually the duller foods like milk, potatoes, and vegetables, whose consumption rose 30 to 40 percent. The consumption of the more desired foods—meat, fish, poultry, sugar—fell 20 to 30 percent and that of fruit 40 percent. There were no bananas and only thirty eggs per person per year. Rationing allowed a pound of meat a week, along with 4 oz. of butter, 8 oz. of sugar, 8 oz. of cheese, and 2 oz. of tea. The ration book for clothing had 48 coupons a year, with a lined wool overcoat taking 18 and a woolen dress 16. Utility clothes replaced the stylish, and wool socks or none at all took the place of silk or rayon stockings. A timber shortage limited furniture, and a metal shortage made men line up for razor blades.

Queues or lines became universal not only at grocers but at bus stops, railway stations, and fuel yards. The shortages that brought the most discomfort were in fuel, transport, and housing. Bombing made housing the cruelest of shortages, especially since Britain had three very cold winters and a shortage of coal. Wartime mobility also strained the railways and buses, which could not be replaced because tanks and planes had higher priority. Jammed railway corridors, long bus queues, and endless waiting became a part of life. And to all these were added darkness, as a complete blackout descended on England. Every window was covered, the edge of every door taped, and once brightly lit cities became as dark as tombs.

Although austerity touched almost everything, it did not drive the English to despair, or to jumping off bridges. The suicide rate actually dropped 25 percent and mental illness declined. The death rate, despite rationing and bombed houses and cold, fell, and the children of the poor ate better than ever. Infant mortality fell 10 percent. The young married more than ever, and the birth rate rose nearly 17 percent during the war. As a compensation for the physical shortages, there was a greater equality, neighborliness, freedom, and purpose.

Greater equality was inescapable. Bombs, ration books, and conscription are blind to class differences, and if wartime taxation was not, it was because the government's sights were fixed on the bank balances of the rich. Full employment also meant higher wages and so a fairer division of income. Before the war the top 1 percent of earners took 14 percent of the national income, while another 10 percent of earners took 38 percent. After the war, the top 1 percent took only 11 percent of the income, another 10 percent only 30 percent. These figures show a move to equality. They also show continuing inequality. The rich, titled, and well-educated did far better in the war. They still ate at fine restaurants, bought fine suits, sent their sons to Eton, had gin-and-orange at the club, collected rents, and bought and sold stocks. The shops in the West End had finer goods and more crowded shelves than those in the East End. Generous cost-plus contracts made some manufacturers rich. Skilled workers also did well. A skilled mechanic earned £7 a week, whereas the average male worker earned only £4; both figures, however, were higher than a woman's pay, even for the same work.

Yet none of these differentials overweighed the deeper feeling that all alike were fighting the Nazis. All classes met in the Home or Fire Guard where a workingman could command a banker. All but the very privileged also stood in queues, drank in pubs, waited for trains, went to the cinema, and spent nights in bomb shelters.

Austerity notwithstanding, World War II was not for the British a bleak and cheerless period. Cold rooms and dull diets there were, but also air warden jobs that gave the aimless a purpose in life and bomb shelters and communal kitchens for the lonely. After the blitz ended, some still spent nights in the bomb shelter. Pubs were friendlier, class divisions less sharp. With scarce goods and high wages, the British spent more on entertainment—on operas, concerts, stage plays, greyhound racing, soccer, cricket, and Rugby, and in night clubs and dance halls. They also went in droves to the cinema, where Hollywood reigned supreme. A whole generation was becoming Americanized. And the BBC was a godsend. It offered comedy to tired factory hands, hints on soil to farmers, Beethoven sonatas to music lovers, dramas to air wardens and fire watchers in their lonely stations, learned lectures for intellectuals, and after El Alamein, news of victory. Its most popular performer was Tommy Handley and his comedy show, with its zany parodies of pompous bureaucrats and stuffy colonels. The government also had Handley and other entertainers, such as the cellist Pablo Casals, go from factory to factory to entertain Britain's citizens at war. Never was entertainment so democratic and unifying.

The war was, for many, a liberating experience. That might appear paradoxical, since never before had there been so much compulsion and censorship. Churchill's government enjoyed powers beyond the dreams of absolute monarchs: it could order fashionable women into factories and young men into mines, and it closed down the Communists' *Daily Worker*. No news endangering security could be printed or broadcast, not even weather forecasts, since they would help enemy bombers. But despite conscription, censorship, and the ubiquitous economic directives, the war emancipated many, women in particular. As wage earners they gained the economic independence that comes from a purse full of pound notes. They also left home earlier. The divorce rate rose, as did the rate of illegitimate births. A Puritan sexual code long eroding eroded further. There was a greater tolerance for eccentricity and less hatred of the enemy. The government and the public treated conscientious objectors more humanely, and there was none of the hysterical hatred of the Huns that erupted in World War I. Geographic mobility also shook up the lives of many: in a country of 38 million there were 60 million changes of address. Religious dogma continued its long decline.

Churchgoing had dropped steadily since 1900. It was not high in 1939, but by 1945 it was lower. Faith in God, however, may not have declined; two-thirds of the men and three-fifths of the women polled in a London suburb confessed to a belief in God. Faiths of all sorts, whether Mormon, Jehovah's Witnesses, Hindu, Christian Science, or astrology prospered. What really suffered was the humanist faith in people and the socialist faith in an inexorable progress. The deepest mood of the war was a skeptical stoicism. "To fight without hope," writes the poet Herbert Read, "is to fight with grace." "To be sentimental or emotional now is dangerous," wrote another poet, Keith Douglas, ". . . to admit any hope for a better world is criminally foolish."

Not everyone shared his skepticism. A faith in collectivism replaced the skeptical stoicism of the early hours of the war as victory followed victory. One of its brighter embodiments was the famous Beveridge Report. Sir William Beveridge's report came out in December 1942, and soon 635,000 copies of it (or its abridgment) had been sold. It recommended a comprehensive scheme of social insurance, one based on a fixed weekly contribution, and a national health service for all. It also urged allowances for all children after the first, allowances to come not from contributions but from general taxation. It also urged that the government give direct assistance to those poor who were not helped by social insurance and that the government guarantee to every British man and woman a decent minimum income.

Despite its popular reception the report angered so many Tories that it was shelved. They preferred the more moderate collectivism of the Town and Country Planning Act and the Education Act, both passed in 1944. The first gave local authorities greater power to buy up private property and the second promised everyone a free secondary education until 15 years of age. But like Disraeli's paternalist measures, these collectivist acts were tentative and compromising. The Education Act preserved both the privileged position of Anglican and Catholic schools and the sharp distinction, made at age 11, between those who could go to academically strong, middle-class "grammar" schools and those who were consigned to overcrowded, working-class "modern" schools, a distinction that perpetuated class divisions. Gender divisions were also hard to end. Despite the fact that the war brought greater equality, class and sex differences were far too entrenched to be removed. While patriarchs at the Ministry of

Health refused to support day care centers, patriarchs in the industrial world kept 71 percent of female workers in unskilled jobs long classified as women's work. And though the war raised the workers' standard of living, it did not lead to any leveling up. Yet many wondered why, if government and people could pull together to defeat the Nazis, could they not work together to defeat poverty and inequality? The failure of the Tories to understand these sentiments helps to explain their defeat in the general election of 1945 and Britain's turn to socialism.

FURTHER READING

BARNETT, CORELLI. *The Desert Generals.* London: William Kimber, 1960. A drama of five British generals—O'Connor, Cunningham, Ritchie, Auchinlech, and Montgomery—and their defeats and victories in North Africa.

CALDER, ANGUS. *The People's War: Britain, 1939–1945.* New York: Pantheon Books, 1969. A close study of the effect of the war on civilian life and an examination of how events interacted, how book reading increased as theater declined, how women at work changed social mores.

CALVOCORESSI, PETER, AND GUY WINCH. *Total War: The Story of World War II.* New York: Random House, 1972. Battles and campaigns are described, but the main emphasis is on why they were fought, when and where, and what went on at home.

CHURCHILL, WINSTON. *Memoirs of the Second World War: An Abridgement of the Six Volumes.* Boston: Houghton Mifflin, 1959. Eloquently written by the leader of the alliance against Hitler, biased, but also unrivaled in knowing what went on and in portraying its drama.

DEIGHTON, LEN. *Fighter: The True Story of the Battle of Britain.* London: Jonathan Cape, 1977. A spirited and knowledgeable narrative of the most crucial battle of the war, one in which Germany by the narrowest margin failed to destroy Britain's air defenses.

LEE, J. M. *The Churchill Coalition, 1940–1945.* Hampden, Conn.: Anchor Books, 1980. A meticulous look at that coalition of Conservative, Liberal, and Labour MPs led by Churchill; an analysis of its economic policy, social reforms, strategies, and its successes and failures.

PAYNE, ROBERT. *A Portrait of Winston Churchill.* New York: Coward, McCann and Geoghegan, 1974. One of the best one-volume lives of Churchill, praising of the "man with the lion's roar, indomitable of spirit and defiant," but aware of his ambition, impetuosity, and errors of judgment.

SNYDER, LOUIS. *The War: A Concise History.* New York: Messner, 1960. The story of World War II told briefly and straightforwardly in terms of essential facts, crucial events, and clear interpretations.

WILMOT, CHESTER. *The Struggle for Europe.* London: Collins, 1952. A graphic account of how America and Britain were able to crush Germany after Normandy, and a brilliant analysis of why Russia came to dominate Eastern Europe.

WINTERBOTTOM, F. M. *The Ultra-Secret.* New York: Dell, 1974. A fascinating story, as exciting as any spy novel, of how the British obtained the Nazi's decoding machine, and code, and used it to help win the war.

Socialist Britain: 1945–1990

30

Few Parliaments in the 700 years of its existence have fundamentally changed the course of English history. The Reformation Parliament of 1534 did, and the Long Parliament of 1641. The first determined that Britain would be Protestant, the second that constitutionalism would prevail over absolutism. The Parliaments of 1832 and 1867 determined that Britain would be a democracy. The Parliament of 1945 belongs to these few, for, though socialist ideas and practices had roots in the past, not until the Labour government of Clement Attlee did England make a decisive commitment to its goals and principles.

THE COMMITMENT TO SOCIALISM: 1945–1951

Twelve million men and women, a great many of them young and voting for the first time, chose Labour in July 1945, 10 million chose the Conservatives, and 2.25 million the Liberals. Labour, which had never won over 39 percent of the votes, now won nearly 50 percent of them and did so by campaigning explicitly and avowedly for socialism.

It is doubtful if most of the 12 million knew what socialism meant. Many no doubt would nod affirmatively to the dictionary definition that socialism meant the public ownership of the means of production, a definition Clement Attlee, the leader of the Labour party, underscored by declaring that private property was capitalism's chief evil and public ownership its chief remedy. Yet most persons did not expect the nationalization of Britain's factories and workshops, nor did the Labour party's manifesto go much beyond calling for the public ownership of coal, railways, gas, and electricity—all of them already semipublic utilities. For many socialism also meant, however hazily, a larger welfare state and a more planned economy. High on Labour's agenda was a public health service and a comprehensive social security program. Labour also promised a planned economy that would prevent depressions, banish unemployment, and promote growth and further equality.

Public ownership, a welfare state, and a planned economy were the pillars of the new commonwealth, and all three reflected the deeper belief that government should guarantee social justice, equality, and security. The growth of a moral conviction that there should be greater social justice, more equality, and fairer shares, rather than any specific economic doctrine, explains why 12 million Britons voted against their victorious wartime leader and for socialism.

The reasons for the growth of these attitudes and for Labour's triumph over Churchill and the Tories are many. One of them was the memory of England between the wars—of poverty, unemployment, slums, ill health, distress, gross inequalities, and a Tory government that broke strikes, attacked unions, reduced the dole, imposed niggardly means tests, and neglected education. The Tories had also appeased Hitler. The Tories were the "guilty" men, the men most responsible for Britain's unpreparedness, diplomatic humiliation, and entrapment in war.

An even more important reason for Labour's victory was the experience of six years of war. Conscription, rationing, austerity, and injuries fell on all alike, giving each a sense of equal sacrifice. War also showed government intervention was not so harmful. Had it not helped defeat Hitler and brought greater justice at home? Wartime experience also gave the British a deeper sense of unity, of fellowship, of sharing. And finally the war's end led millions to hope for a new era, to expect a new dawn, a new Britain without bitter class war, a Britain moving toward social justice with the same vigor it had moved toward victory.

In July 1945, the Labour party, whose manifesto bristled with plans for a better world, seemed far abler to meet these new expectations than a Tory party whose leader said socialism would bring in a "Gestapo." Churchill, caught up in his love of rhetoric, had warned his radio audience that a Labour government would bring in a "Gestapo." But the British people knew that the diffident Attlee, the earthy Bevin, and the fair-minded Morrison had actually managed Britain's home affairs for four years, a fact which removed all fears that the socialists could not govern fairly and well. If anybody was to be feared, it was the impulsive Churchill of the interwar years, the man who sent troops against strikers in Tonypandy, Wales, who helped break the general strike, who sent the Black and Tan to Ireland, and who wanted to hold on to India.

The Labour party had 393 MPs in the House of Commons to the Conservatives' 213 and the Liberals' 12. With such a majority and with a five-year term, Labour had the power and time to carry out its vision of a new society. It did so with dispatch and boldness. The government nationalized 20 percent of British industry, built a comprehensive welfare state, and expanded economic planning.

The nationalized industries included coal, railways, electricity, gas, trucking, canals, docks, hospitals, the Bank of England, the air service, and iron and

Modest in appearance and manner, firm in command, steely in debate, Clement Attlee was Prime Minister from 1945 to 1951 (*National Portrait Gallery*).

steel. Already nationalized were telephone and telegraph, radio broadcasting, London's subways and buses, and the central grid for electrical power. Only the nationalization of gas and of iron and steel raised a controversy. Few contested taking over the Bank of England, since the government had long controlled it. Neither did many object to the government running the coal mines. Antiquated, inefficient, nearly bankrupt, yet vital to the whole economy, these mines required a capital, a direction, and an integrated and energetic management that only the government could supply. It also seemed natural that railways, canals, and electricity, all monopolies, should be nationalized—and they too needed modernization. In every case of nationalization, the government paid the owners a generous compensation. Many an owner of coal and the railway shares became wealthier by exchanging them for better paying government bonds. Independent public corporations, like the Coal Board and the Electricity Council, and not government departments, ran these enterprises, though the government did appoint them and could send them directives.

The various boards managed their industries with varying degrees of success. Coal did poorly at first. Full employment elsewhere attracted men away from

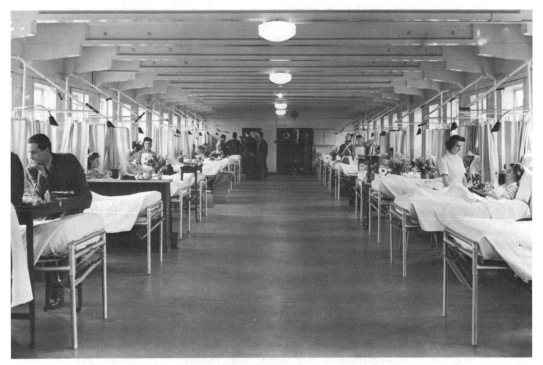

Because of war damage and austerity, the National Health Service's first hospitals were often prefabricated buildings—yet everyone was given good medical care without charge (*Radio Times, Hulton Picture Library*).

work in dangerous mines. Yet by 1967, when fully mechanized, production per man was twice what it was in 1946. With a healthy industry, such as British Airways, the nationalized companies could hold their own with private enterprise. Although nationalization produced no miracle of efficiency, neither did it prove a failure. Having met the needs of sick industries and natural monopolies, there was no further nationalization until the 1970s when near-bankrupt airplane-engine, ship, and auto firms needed government help.

The same cannot be said of the welfare state. It never ceased growing, a fact critics deplored, but a fact its supporters said reflected its popularity. The National Insurance Act of 1946 formed one of its bases. Following the principle of the 1911 National Insurance Act, employees, employers, and the state all contributed. The self-employed could also participate. The resulting National Insurance Fund provided old age pensions and weekly payments for those who were unemployed or ill. The fund also gave payments to widows and guardians of children, and grants to mothers when bearing children and to a family when burying its dead. Security was provided from cradle to grave, particularly since an Industrial Injuries Act gave ampler payments and coverage to those hurt on the job and because there was also a National Assistance Act, free legal aid, a National Health Service, subsidized housing, and expanded education. Monthly family allowances were paid for each child beyond the first, and that irrespective of the family's income. National Assistance went only to the very poor not covered or inadequately covered by National Insurance. Payments for legal aid were also given only to the poor.

At the apex of the welfare state was the National Health Service, which began operation in July 1948. After that month any person could go to a doctor or dentist of his or her choice and receive free treatment, including medicines, false teeth, and glasses. Hospital care was free, as was the most skilled surgery. It was not an insurance scheme; there were no contributions. The government paid the entire bill out of general taxation. The doctors received both a minimum salary and fees per patient call: the more popular doctors thus earned higher incomes. Regional boards appointed by the government owned and ran hospitals. Before the government took over, voluntary organizations and municipalities had run hospitals. Nationalization meant that the health service, like the coal boards, began the experiment in socialism severely handicapped by obsolete survivals of voluntarism and private enterprise. Difficult too was the fact that nine in ten doctors opposed the new service.

Subsidized housing and education rounded out the welfare state. Bombing had destroyed 208,000 houses, made 250,000 temporarily uninhabitable, and severely damaged another 250,000. The housing shortage was grim. To meet it, private builders, working under contract to local county councils and under the overall supervision of the Ministry of Health, built, from 1945 to 1951, 1 million new houses and repaired or temporarily constructed ½ million more. It could not quite compare to the 358,000 a year that private enterprise built (often with government subsidies) in 1934 and 1935, but those builders did not face the severe shortages of money, material, and labor of the late 1940s. Most of the new houses were council houses, that is, houses owned by local councils and rented at a loss, the loss being made up by central and local subsidies. It was a scheme generous to the working classes but not productive enough to meet Britain's pressing need.

The Labour party's education policy favored the working classes far less than did its policies in health and housing. This arose in part from a class-ridden and outdated education system and from the Education Act of 1944. In 1939 nearly half of all children were in all-age schools, schools which working-class children attended from 6 to 14. The children of the middle classes went on to grammar schools, as did the brighter working-class boys. The wealthy still sent their sons to such public schools as Eton and Harrow. The Education Act of 1944 sought to end the all-age working-class schools by creating secondary modern schools for those who, at age 11, had failed that examination that won the better prepared a place in a middle-class grammar school. Rich children, of course, went to costly boarding schools such as Eton or Harrow or St. Paul's School for girls. They were the favored students who, along with the brighter grammar school graduates, went on to university. The Labour party in six years

War damage to half a million homes also meant austerity in housing (*Radio Times, Hulton Picture Library*).

of office did little to change this rigid class system. Neither did they extend education in secondary modern schools beyond the age of 15. The socialism of the Attlee government was not all radical, but a mosaic of reform and conservatism. There was, for example, no significant redistribution of wealth: the top 10 percent still received nearly a third of the income.

But radical appeared the extent of economic planning, as much a part of socialism as nationalized industries and a welfare state. The Labour government showed no hesitation in using fiscal and monetary controls. It lowered and raised interest rates to encourage or discourage investment, and it ran deficits to increase purchasing power and prosperity. It also taxed luxuries to discourage consumption of valued exports and taxed the rich to equalize incomes. While import duties were raised to exclude goods costing dollars, credit for installment buying was tightened to deter consumption. It also relied on direct controls— buying meat in bulk from Argentina, subsidizing farmers, granting investment allowances to manufacturers, rationing goods, licensing plant expansion, and reserving 70 percent of nylons for export.

In the first two years the government also believed in directing the workers of the country. It wished, for example, to send workers to coal mines and farms, but the trade unions balked. Manufacturers also grew angry at Board of Trade's endless directives designating what goods they should produce. By 1948 it was clear that direct controls hindered more than helped economic growth. And despite these many controls there was still no overall planning, at least not until Sir Stafford Cripps took over the Treasury in 1948. The Labour government was learning in a painful way how to manage an economy, and one of the lessons was that fiscal and monetary controls worked better than direct ones. By 1951 business was largely free to respond to market forces, with the government's role being to see that the market was a healthy one.

From 1945 to 1949 direct controls had less to do with socialism than with the legacy of war, a war that not only demanded a multitude of boards and councils with vast powers but one that brought in its aftermath a series of grave crises. The first of these was Britain's financial condition in July 1945.

War damage at home cost Britain £3 billion and assets sold abroad another billion. War had also tripled the national debt. It was now £3.3 billion. To pay its way, Britain thus had to increase exports to 175 percent of 1938 and even farther above the exceedingly low levels in 1945. "The country is bankrupt," wrote Churchill privately, on leaving office. Rich America in August 1945 abruptly terminated all lend-lease supplies to Britain, that indispensable flow of goods that enabled Britain to win the war and to survive. With economic ruin a matter of months away, the government sent John Maynard Keynes to Washington. The result was disappointing. Washington would only grant a loan of $3.75 billion at 2 percent interest, payments to begin in 1950 and end in 2000. That Canada loaned another $1.2 billion was a help, and the loans did allow Britain to feed and clothe its people and to revive the export industries on which its well-being depended. The crisis prevented any sudden abandonment of that vast armory of controls that had been necessary for the winning of World War II. Also preventing the end of controls was the winter of 1947.

The winter of 1947 was the coldest and snowiest since 1880. Railway lines were buried, coal lay at the pit heads, and factories closed, closures that cost Britain £200 million in desperately needed exports. Dollars and gold flowed out of Britain, particularly in July, when the pound became fully convertible with the dollar. The government adopted convertibility only because the Americans had insisted on it as part of the loan. Within six weeks, the British abandoned it as bankers rushed to sell risky pounds for sound dollars. Labour's Chancellor of the Exchequer, Hugh Dalton, was also in part responsible for the weakness of the pound. His anxiety about unemployment (an anxiety widely held) led him to lower the interest rate on bank loans to 2 percent, which encouraged the banks to extend credit and so cause inflation. It was a good solution for a depressed economy with unemployment, but not for a full employment economy that would be weakened by inflation. Easy credit meant that ever more pounds chased Britain's scarce goods, leading to higher prices, fewer sales abroad, a trade deficit, and the depletion of Britain's gold and dollar reserves, without which the pound could not be kept at $4.03. Something had to be done.

Sir Stafford Cripps, Dalton's successor, had the answer: no increases in wages, no American cigarettes, no gas for pleasure driving, no trips abroad costing over £35, cuts in meat and cheese rations, tighter credit, and stricter controls on raw materials. An earlier crisis in world food in 1946 had added bread and potatoes to the many foods already rationed, and with a coal shortage

The queues of wartime continued after 1945, as Britain struggled to rebuild a bombed and war-impoverished economy (*Radio Times, Hulton Picture Library*).

and clothing earmarked for export, the British experienced a grim austerity. With the loan exhausted, dollars pouring out, the trade balance critically adverse, Cripps finally had to devalue the pound from $4.03 to $2.80. Devaluation lowered the price of British goods, which, along with Europe's economic recovery, led to brisk exports and a stronger pound. America's Marshall Plan aid also helped. America gave, not loaned, $4.9 billion to Europe, of which $1,263 million went to Britain. By 1950 Britain, with a 4 percent growth rate and most direct controls ended, had turned the corner to prosperity. The Labour government even squeezed through the general election of 1950 with a majority of eight over the Tories. Then came another crisis, the Korean conflict, and the Americans persuaded the Labour government to adopt a three-year rearmament program that cost £4.7 billion. America also drove up prices by stockpiling raw materials, and that, along with rearmament, led to inflation and another severe deficit in the balance of payments, one the Tories inherited when they won a majority of seats in the election of 1951.

YEARS OF AFFLUENCE AND TORY RULE: 1951–1964

By 1951 a chorus of critics had condemned nationalized industries as inefficient, the welfare state as costly, and economic planning as burdensome. To many of the 13.7 million who voted Conservative and returned 321 MPs, socialism meant crises and austerities, ration books and identity cards, and a drab, dispirit-ing life. But for the 13.9 million who voted Labour and who, because heavily concentrated in working-class districts, returned only 295 MPs, it meant jobs, security, health care, old age pensions, and in every way a better way of life. Churchill, who proclaimed "set the people free," denationalized iron and steel and trucking, ended rationing and food subsidies (though over a three-year period), and abolished countless regulations. But that was about all. The govern-ment did not dismantle the welfare state and made no move to return coal, railways, electricity, gas, and the airlines to private hands. Nor did it give up economic planning. Socialized medicine was left intact. The Conservatives, said one of their leading MPs, had accepted 1945 as they had 1832. Some even promised to outdo the socialists. Harold Macmillan, Minister of Health, promised to build 1,000 more houses a week than the socialists.

The thirteen years of Tory rule that followed made definite their commit-ment to a partly socialist society. By 1959, for example, the Tories were spending 16 percent of personal income on welfare, where Labour had spent only 14 percent in 1951. The Tories had expanded maternity benefits and child allow-ances, used progressive taxation to equalize incomes, built more than 300,000 houses a year, managed the economy with fiscal, monetary, and a few direct controls, guaranteed full employment, and fought the never-ending battle for a sound balance of payments. The growth of collectivism was not something one turned off like a faucet.

In the general elections of 1955 and 1959, 49 percent and 48 percent of the voters favored the Tories, as against 46.5 percent and 46 percent who voted Labour, and 4.5 percent and 5 percent who voted for lesser parties. In 1951 Labour had outvoted the Tories, but with Labour votes concentrated in dense working-class areas and wasted on lopsided victories, the Tories won a majority of 29 seats, a majority that became 67 in 1955 and 107 in 1959. In four successive elections the Tories had increased their share of the votes, a feat never before achieved. The Tories managed it because they maintained a large share of the manual workers' vote and because some 10 percent of the workers who had once voted Labour stayed home. The British electorate is basically divided on occupational and class lines: the white-collar workers and leisured rich vote Conservative and the blue-collar or manual workers, Labour. But there were variations to this rough-and-ready class division, since 33 percent of the manual workers voted Tory and 15 percent of white-collar voted Labour. Since manual workers made up 65 percent of all voters, their voting patterns were crucial— the 33 percent voting Tory made up half of that party's vote, with the 67 percent voting Labour making up 89 percent of that party's vote.

In 1955 and 1959 it was not the switch of manual workers from Labour to Tory that made the difference, but the failure of manual workers who had voted Labour to vote: in 1951, 13.9 million voted Labour; in 1959 it was only 12.2, with the Tory's 13.7 million remaining 13.7. The Tories thus enjoyed thirteen years of power.

Why did the Tories win a third of the votes of manual workers, and why did so many Labour voters abstain? The answer is that many workers had long voted Tory and did so from an historic deference, a deference strongest in small paternalistic firms and weakest in large factories where peer groups and trade union loyalties eclipsed paternal ones. The second reason why workers voted Tory is that the Tories supported the welfare state and economic planning for full employment. Under Winston Churchill, Prime Minister from 1951 to 1955, the Tories built more houses than had Labour. Churchill also granted generous wage increases and kept unemployment low. Eighty years old in his last year of office, this extraordinary man adjusted to the world of Keynesian economics and the welfare state. In 1955 Anthony Eden, Prime Minister on Churchill's retirement, continued the commitment to government action, as did his successor in 1957, Harold Macmillan—though both used a vigorous free enterprise rhetoric in their campaigns and both worked to promote a freer capitalism. While extolling *laissez-faire* and sound finance on the hustings, they cagily inflated the economy by tax cuts and government spending (in order to create full employment and prosperity) on the eve of the election. They did so even though it seriously weakened the pound.

While the grandly heroic Churchill, the austerely handsome Eden, and the raffishly elegant Macmillan appeared to many workers as their natural, paternal governors, the Labour party's leadership fell into disarray. Cripps and Bevin died, Attlee and Morrison had grown old, and Nye Bevan and Hugh Gaitskill, the young men of promise, quarreled bitterly. In the early 1950s the followers of the brilliant and eloquent Bevan urged more socialism and public ownership, less armaments, less dependence on America, no German rearmament, and friendlier relations with Russia. The followers of Gaitskill were for armaments, no more nationalization, a close alliance with America, German rearmament, and wariness toward Russia. In party conferences and at meetings of Labour MPs, in the press and pamphlets, the quarrel went on. In 1959 it suddenly ended as Bevan and Gaitskill had a rapprochement. But then the Committee on Nuclear Disarmament launched a crusade against building and deploying nuclear bombs. It demanded unilateral nuclear disarmament. In 1960, over Gaitskill's opposition, the committee won a majority vote in the annual Labour Conference. A year later Gaitskill and his followers reversed that decision, but the picture of a disunited, factious party, one flirting with pacifism, led some workers to vote Tory.

A third reason workers voted Tory or abstained was because many agreed with the boast attributed to Macmillan, "You never had it so good." Easily the most important fact about Britain in the 1950s was economic prosperity, in part a happy inheritance from Labour. From 1945 to 1951, despite fuel and food crises, Britain's economy grew 4 percent a year. A commitment to socialism had not hindered growth; neither had Tory welfare measures and planning. The real wages of the workers rose 50 percent during the Tory's thirteen-year rule, a salutary rise, though not as salutary as the 100 percent increase in the

In 1951, one hundred years after the Great Exhibition and six years of economic recovery, the British again celebrate the wonders of science (*Radio Times, Hulton Picture Library*).

capital of the wealthy. Farmers also prospered, agriculture production rising 160 percent from 1945 to 1957. In 1964 Britain also produced 1.9 million cars, five times the number made in 1938. In 1951, the British spent £90 million on cars; in 1964, £910 million. The age of consumption had arrived, of accelerating sales of TVs, radios, hi-fis, tape recorders, cameras, refrigerators, vacuum cleaners, smart suits, fashionable dresses. It was also an age of expanding production in which Britain held its own. In 1951–53, British products made up 22.2 percent of the world's exports of manufactures, only 0.2 percent less than in 1938. In the 1950s Britain's industrial output grew 40 percent, and from 1955 to 1960 output per person increased 12.5 percent. Overall, from 1948 to 1963 the increase in gross national product averaged 2.8 percent a year. In the early 1950s this growth occurred without undue inflation or unemployment. The weekly *Economist* pronounced it a miracle.

The principal cause of this prosperity was the rapid growth of the world economy. Advances in technology brought more efficient production and new and cheaper goods. In the outpouring of these goods, Britain played an important role. From huge modern oil refineries came fuel for autos, homes, and factories and raw materials for the new plastics and synthetics. Imperial Chemicals, Britain's largest cartel, turned the oil into lucite, polyvinyl, polyethylene, and teryline. Chemicals had created a new world of fibers. Electronics created a world of transistor radios, computers, tape decks, amplifiers, and color television. The optical industry, meanwhile, produced wonders in cameras, microscopes, and medical equipment.

British scientists, who won 35 Nobel prizes after 1945, did not take a back seat in this third industrial revolution. In aircraft Britain was first with the turboprop and the jet airplane, and led the world in the use of nuclear power. As a result there occurred a shift in what Britain exported: in 1937 the top four items were machinery other than electrical, cotton goods, coal, and iron and steel; in 1963 machinery other than electrical was still first, but the next three were vehicles and aircraft, chemicals, and electrical apparatus. The exports of these and other items rose 19 percent a year in the 1950s and helped produce a prosperity that made many manual workers think of themselves as middle class.

In a survey in 1961, 40 percent of workingmen called themselves middle class, and they voted Tory more often than those who called themselves working class. Had a planned capitalism, a welfare state, and class mobility made the workers prosperous and bourgeois, and so blunted Labour's call for a more socialist society? Many persons at the 1959 election said yes. Right-wing socialists like Gaitskill thus tried to purge clause 4, the clause calling for nationalization, from the Labour party's charter of 1918. It only further divided the party. It was also unnecessary since by 1963, as prosperity ebbed and financial crises intensified, Macmillan's reputation turned sour. Easier money and ampler wage rises led to inflation and higher prices for exports. Exports thus declined, the balance of payments turned negative, the pound weakened, and the Tory euphoria evaporated. Illness led Macmillan to retire, and in 1964 the voters turned out the Tories as a party of inflation, mismanagement, neglect, and elitism.

Exports had dropped because inflation drove their prices above those of their competitors. Since imports did not drop, the result was that dollars and gold flowed out faster than in. Britain's reserves of dollars and gold fell faster as speculators unloaded pounds for dollars. It was the perennial problem, a problem that has plagued Britain from 1945 until today.

There were two ways to solve it. One was to produce more and cheaper goods and services, the other was to reduce the money supply by less government spending and by tightening credit, measures that usually led to unemployment. Tory governments preferred the first, hoping that a buoyant capitalism would produce a flood of inexpensive exports and so reserves of dollars and gold. Tory paternalism could give people jobs, hospitals, schools, and pensions. But it did not work, because the flood of goods came from Germany, Italy, France, and Japan, not from Britain. Britain's 2.8 percent growth rate could not compare with West Germany's 7.6 percent, France's 4.6 percent, and Japan's 10 percent. While Volkswagens and Toyotas, Telefunkens and Sonys swept world markets, British cars and amplifiers sold poorly, as did British steel, ships, and (by the 1960s) its once-excellent aircraft. Although unions contributed to inefficiency by restrictive practices, strikes, and wage demands, so did management with its poor engineering, stodgy ways, and often hostile labor relations. Many of Britain's captains of industry had lost their touch.

Without the expected exuberant growth of exports, Macmillan in 1961 and 1962 had to tighten credit; increase taxes on beer, tobacco, spirits, candy, and ice cream; and call for a freeze on wages. The popularity of Macmillan, known in 1959 as MacWonder and Supermac, collapsed. Only Neville Chamberlain in 1940 had a lower rating at the polls. Part of that unpopularity also came from Tory neglect and elitism. Macmillan, member of Parliament in the 1930s for the distressed town of Stockton on the Tees, knew and cared about poverty. A disciple of both Keynesian economics and Disraelian paternalism, he had as Minister of Health pushed housing vigorously and as Chancellor of the Exchequer worked for full employment. But his paternalism had its limits and biases. Hospitals, prisons, reformatories, and schools were neglected, local government and law remained unreformed, a smaller percentage of the nation's income went to health service, unemployment rose, and old age benefits failed to keep up with rising prices. Despite a rising population, public housing fell below the much vaunted 300,000-a-year level, and homelessness increased. The number of hidden poor, those below the poverty line, grew quite as rapidly as did the rich. In 1961 the government reduced the tax on the rich and left capital gains untaxed; it nevertheless imposed a wage pause on all workers, including teachers and nurses, whose salary increases were long overdue. It was showing itself a class government, one that spent far less to expand comprehensive schools than the universities.

On education the government was also shortsighted about its economic advantages. Despite a baby boom, industry's demands for scientists and engineers, and the urgent pleas of two distinguished commissions, the government, in 13 years, left the secondary modern school leaving age at 15, increased the already small number going to university by a paltry 18 percent, and vetoed as many local schemes for comprehensive schools as possible. The comprehensive school in combining the local grammar and the local secondary modern school followed the model of the American public high school. Going comprehensive both improved the education of the majority and lessened class prejudices. But it was too egalitarian for Macmillan and a Tory party that were at heart elitist: three quarters of the Tory party came from public schools and ten of twelve in Macmillan's Cabinet came from Eton. Many members of the Cabinet were related to Macmillan or his wife, the daughter of the Duke of Devonshire. Macmillan loved to appear as a grouse-hunting squire and the habitué of the best London clubs. His selection as Prime Minister in 1957 came not from a party caucus but from the elite of the party guided by Lords Salisbury and Kilmuir, a mode used in 1963, with Macmillan as the guide and with Sir Alec Douglas-Home, a Scottish aristocrat, as his heir.

In both 1957 and 1963 the press expected the new Prime Minister to be R. A. Butler, one of the most liberal, most experienced, and ablest of Tories. Macmillan's tactful and shrewd leadership had edged the Conservatives further into the world of economic planning and social welfare, but by 1961 the intractable problem of a deficient balance of trade and a shaky pound came to the fore, revealing the limits of Tory paternalism. Then in 1963 the press claimed that the Minister of Defense, John Profumo, had had an affair with a call girl who also gave her favors to a Russian spy. Profumo denied it in the Commons, then confessed its truth. The scandal hurt an already weakened Tory government, one increasingly associated with a tired aristocracy and a high-living *nouveau riche*, an elite that did little about industrial efficiency or the improvement of hospitals and the very poor—or, more significantly, about workers' incomes. No longer convinced that they "never had it so good," the voters no longer deferred to their traditional governors or quietly abstained. The abstainers were now among the Conservatives and so the Labour party returned to power. It faced not just the perennial problem of balance of payments and the strength of the pound, but the fact that British power and Empire had collapsed.

THE COLLAPSE OF THE EMPIRE

Britain still ruled in 1947 nearly one quarter of the world's people. Twenty-one years later its Prime Minister, Harold Wilson, removed the last of its imperial forces from overseas. Aside from Hong Kong, Gibraltar, a few islands, and token forces, there was no British Empire. Britain was also, in 1968, surrounded by the vast armies, navies, and intercontinental missiles of America and Russia and could no longer count as a world power. Edward Gibbon's *Decline and Fall of the Roman Empire* covers more than a thousand years. To describe the decline and fall of the British Empire one need cover only the twenty-seven years that followed Japan's conquest of Malaya.

In 1945, few foresaw this sudden eclipse. Winston Churchill, speaking in 1948, said that Britain's unique position in the world rested on three roles: it was the head of the British Commonwealth, a chief power in Europe, and the special partner of America. On these three circles rested British power and policy. In 1948 Churchill's three-circle theory was a truthful one. In North Africa, Italy, and Normandy, British and American generals and statesmen had forged an intimate and special relationship, one that rested on a common language and culture and on mutual interests. The Empire and Commonwealth were also a reality, as were Britain's occupation of Germany, its role in liberating France, and four centuries of intervention to preserve Europe's balance of power. Yet in 1945 each of these three partial realities harbored dangerous illusions. Could a Britain with a damaged economy, bombed cities and factories, no atom bomb, huge debts, and but 47 million people be equal partners to an United States with the world's largest economy, an atom bomb, unrivaled resources, and 150 million people? And would a Commonwealth of newly independent countries jealous of sovereignty be as unified and enriching as the Empire or would a revived Europe look kindly to British leadership? From 1945 to 1968 the interplay of these realities and illusions defined Britain's foreign policy.

The de facto Anglo-American alliance was, after 1945, a crucial factor in the Cold War between Russia and the West. It was Churchill, not Roosevelt, who at Yalta viewed Communist Russia as a threat to Europe; it was Britain, not America, that mistakenly associated the Greek guerrillas too closely with communism and that believed Stalin had designs on Greece and Turkey. America shared Britain's misperceptions, which were understandable in view of Russia's conquest of ten Baltic and East European states. Russia's desire for such "friendly" states, though understandable in terms of her enormous losses from past Western invasions, nevertheless frightened British and American statesmen who watched Russia impose totalitarian regimes on East Europe, strip East Germany of machinery and food, and place armies on the Elbe.

These actions led to anxieties that multiplied in 1948 with the Communist *coup d'état* in Czechoslovakia and the blockade of Berlin. In 1949 Russia exploded the atom bomb and China fell to communism. In 1950 Communist North Korea invaded South Korea. These events deepened the West's fear of Russian aggression and exacerbated the Cold War. Britain's special relationship with America, its perception of the European balance of power, its democratic traditions, and its recent experience with the folly of appeasement led it to ally closely with America against the Russians. The Labour government's socialism was democratic, not Marxist, and its leaders had fought to keep communists out of the Labour party and the trade unions. No peculiarly socialist foreign policy thus emerged from 1945 and 1951, but one fashioned by the Cold War and the American alliance. The result was that Britain and America cooperated to set up an independent West Germany, to defeat the Berlin blockade by an airlift, and to establish NATO, the North Atlantic Treaty Organization, whose aim was to check Stalin's ambitions just as grand alliances had sought to check the ambitions of Louis XIV, Napoleon, and Kaiser Wilhelm. In 1951 the Labour government showed its pro-American Cold War resolve by tripling armaments and sending troops to Korea.

Neither Churchill, Eden, nor Macmillan departed from this special alliance in the 1950s. In 1952 Churchill announced that Britain, having exploded an atom bomb, was now a more powerful and so more independent ally. Churchill, master of phrases, spoke of ensuring peace by a "deterrence of terror." But Churchill was worried: not only because nuclear war would be suicidal for a crowded, small England, but because Eisenhower's Secretary of State, John Foster Dulles, spoke so belligerently of massive retaliation. To make peace through deterrence more likely, Eden and Macmillan, following Churchill, urged friendly approaches to Russia and the holding of summit meetings. Britain played a key role in arranging the Geneva summit meeting of 1955 and the Paris meeting of 1960, both of which were failures. One success, however, did come in 1963, the treaty ending the above-ground testing of nuclear bombs. Far weaker than America, Britain based its influence on the judiciousness of its advice. After the Suez Crisis of 1956, that advice was not worth a nickel.

The crisis began in 1955 when John Foster Dulles refused to help Egypt build the huge Aswan Dam it so desperately needed to improve its agriculture.

To get the money, General Nasser, the Egyptian head of state, nationalized the Suez Canal Company. Although the company's owners were compensated, it still aroused Anthony Eden's latent imperialism and his hypersensitivity about appeasing dictators. Eden, in collusion with Israel and France, ordered 100,000 troops to land in the canal zone. The spirit of Palmerston was reborn, but in the wrong century. America, not Britain, was number one. Dulles also disliked Eden and Eden, Dulles. America, not Nasser, forced the British to withdraw. In March 1957 the Chancellor of the Exchequer, Harold Macmillan, an enthusiast for invasion, suddenly declared for withdrawal. The United States' resolute opposition and a collapsing pound led him to be, in Harold Wilson's words, "First in and first out." The special partnership survived but much weakened, much tattered. Eisenhower met Macmillan at Bermuda and promised Britain the Skybolt missile. In return Britain gave America a Polaris submarine base. In 1962 America canceled the Skybolt as too costly and gave Britain Polaris missiles for British submarines. But since America controlled the fissionable materials of the warhead, Britain became a dependent, not an independent, nuclear power. With the pound weak and the need for American aid constant, a special partnership of equals became an illusion.

Also illusory was the belief that a collapsing Empire could become a viable Commonwealth. In 1945 few believed Britain could or ought to rule a quarter of the world's peoples. Even Churchill and the Tories voted for the act making India an independent republic within the Commonwealth. Churchill, of course, regretted the independence, but he was delighted that India had joined the Commonwealth. In 1948, Pakistan and Ceylon also joined the once all-white family of Canada, New Zealand, Australia, South Africa, and Britain. By 1966, South Africa had left the Commonwealth, and eighteen other colonies had joined it as independent nations.

The chief reason Britain gave these colonies independence was that otherwise they would have become ungovernable. The growth of the Indian Congress party, the ascendancy of the charismatic Mahatma Gandhi, the consummate political skill of Pandit Nehru, the determination of the Muslim League to create an independent Pakistan, and the determination of millions of Indians to oust the British all narrowed the choice to independence or ceaseless disorder. It was Indian and Muslim nationalism that formed the irrepressible force, a nationalism whose roots were British. Nehru attended Cambridge University, Gandhi read law in London, and for a century the language and literature of England formed the intellectual diet of India's governing class. They read Bentham and Mill, studied the French Revolution, and imbibed a passion for nationalism and liberty. It would have taken hundreds of thousands of troops to repress these forces.

But though independence was inevitable, its timing and mode were not. Britain might have persisted, as France did in Indochina. That Britain did not is due to the principles and prudence of the Labour government which, in 1946, announced firmly that India would be free in 1948. Although the handing over of power was done intelligently, there was bloodshed. Nearly a million persons lost their lives as Muslims fled to Pakistan and Hindus fled to India. Religious hatred ran deep—and this hatred, not British policy, led to the creation of two states.

Religious hatred and a blend of British principles and deception also led in 1938 to the partition and abandonment of Palestine. Ever since the Balfour Declaration in 1917, the British had tried, in the Mandate of Palestine, to combine two irreconcilable policies: promotion of a Jewish homeland and an independent Arab state. Ernest Bevin, by favoring the Arabs after 1945, aroused the enmity of powerful Jewish armed gangs determined on independence—a determination the United States supported. Britain, unable to reconcile the irreconcilables and to counter American power, bowed out and allowed the United Nations to partition Palestine between the Jews and Arabs.

The Labour government from 1948 to 1951 gave independence only to India and Palestine; no other colony received even a promise. The government even encouraged whites to settle in Kenya and southern Rhodesia. These settlers were to be part of a partnership in which the whites, possessing power, would tutor the blacks in self-government. This tutelary and paternalist principle, along with strategic concerns in the Near East and Asia, became the basis of the Tory defense of Empire from 1951 to 1959. It worked in the 1950s in Africa, where 60,000 whites in Kenya and 300,000 in southern Rhodesia, and colonial officials elsewhere, ruled as of old.

But it was clear that the proud, educated, and increasingly nationalistic Egyptians, whose formal independence of 1936 was blunted by the presence of the British army, would not accept British dominance. In 1952 revolutionary army officers overthrew Britain's friend, King Farouk, and set up a republic. In 1954 Britain yielded and took its 60,000 troops to Cyprus. But Greek Cypriots wanted union with Greece, not British rule, and to gain it they fought a guerrilla war with a heroism and terrorism that forced Britain to grant Cyprus independence in 1960. The British then moved their forces to Aden, at the bottom of the Arabian peninsula, until 1967, when Arab nationalists forced them to leave. They left, ending one of the grandest and most romantic principles of British foreign policy, that a presence in the Near East was needed to defend the route to India.

By 1967 the tutelary principle had also bowed to local forces in Africa south of the Sahara. The first breach came in 1957, when the Gold Coast became Ghana and a member of the Commonwealth. In 1960 Nigeria and Somali won independence, in 1961 Sierra Leone and Tanzania, in 1962 Uganda, and in 1963–64 Kenya, Zambia, Zanzibar, and Malawi. Britain's decision to grant independence was the product of enlightened self-interest more than the immediate pressure of arms and rebellion and nationalism. Britain could have, like Portugal, clung on for one or two more decades. It did not in large part because Macmillan had the foresight to see the pervasiveness and inevitability of what he had called in 1961 the "winds of change," winds that swept over Africa, winds that had their distant origins in English democratic and nationalist ideas.

The founding fathers of Tanzania, Malawi, Kenya, and Ghana, Julius Nyerere, Dr. Banda, Jomo Kenyatta, and Kami Nkruma, had studied or lived in Britain, while the father of Zambia, Kenneth Kaunda was the son of a Christian minister. Not only did missionaries educate Kaunda's father and Nyerere and Nkruma and thousands of others, but British schoolteachers, administrators, doctors, merchants, and editors taught Africans ideas of democracy, the rule of law, civil rights, and nationalism.

Throughout Africa these Western ideas mixed with older customs and values and transformed themselves in new forms, forms marked by tribal pride, one-party government, mixed socialist-capitalist economies, pan-African dreams, and an unquenchable desire to rule themselves. But these winds of change did not transform Africa without struggle. The British not only educated the founding fathers but, in order to hold back the winds of change, imprisioned them. Nyerere, Kenyatta, Nkruma, Banda, and Kaunda all spent time in British prisons. The British also created concentration camps, repressed freedom, broke promises, vacillated, and lied—particularly in Kenya, Nyasaland, and northern Rhodesia, where Britain persisted in the illusion of a tutelary partnership. That 60,000 whites could prevail over millions of blacks in Kenya was as vain a hope as that 300,000 whites could dominate the even more numerous blacks of the Federation of the Rhodesias and Nyasaland, particularly when most whites lived in southern Rhodesia. The British abandoned the attempt in 1964, but the white-dominated regime of southern Rhodesia declared itself independent, an act that led Britain and the United Nations to declare a boycott against it. By 1964 Britain had sided so strongly with the new African nations that South Africa left the Commonwealth. What was once a cozy family of white dominions was now a quarreling, polyglot club of Britain's former colonies. As the Commonwealth became more heterogeneous, British statesmen were drawn to closer links with Europe.

To be a leader in Europe was the second of Churchill's circles, and after 1945 a neglected one. Close cooperation there was in the Marshall Plan, in NATO, in the General Agreement on Tariffs and Trade, but these were Atlantic in scope. To the purely European schemes, such as the proposed European Defense Community of 1951 (which failed), the Coal and Iron Community of 1951, and the European Economic Community of 1957, Britain said no. Given no imminent threat, British diplomacy inclined to insularity: the spirit of Walpole and Canning was not absent in Bevin and Eden, the two foreign secretaries who, from 1945 to 1955, kept Britain out of Europe.

In the late 1950s and early 1960s three developments changed this insularity: a decline in the special relationship with America, the fading of the Commonwealth dream, and revived trade with a buoyant Europe. The trade statistics were telling. In 1950, 26 percent of British exports went to Western Europe and 46 percent to the Commonwealth; by 1968 it was 37 percent Europe and 28 percent Commonwealth. Britain's economic future lay across the Channel. De Gaulle and Adenauer also made it clear that power as well as wealth came

At first glance, another imperialist ceremony, but a closer look at the Ghana flag flying over Parliament House reveals the birth, in 1956, of the state of Ghana (*Associated Press, London*).

from European unity. Harold Macmillan and the Tories thus applied for membership in July 1961. The negotiations were protracted because of two problems, British trade with the Commonwealth and British agriculture. If entry into the Common Market meant tariffs against New Zealand dairy products and Canadian grain, and higher subsidies to European farmers, the cost of living would soar and Britain would sell less to the Commonwealth.

In January 1962, after many of these issues had been resolved, General de Gaulle, President of France, vetoed Britain's entry. Some pundits conjectured that the jealous de Gaulle resented Macmillan's special relationship with President Kennedy and was angered by Britain's special right to use American Polaris missiles. In effect de Gaulle told Britain to choose Europe or the special relationship with America. Other pundits believe that de Gaulle would always find a pretext to veto Britain since he feared that Britain would rival France as leader of Europe.

In 1967 Harold Wilson again asked to join the European community, and de Gaulle again vetoed British membership. In 1972, after de Gaulle had retired, the new Tory Prime Minister, Edward Heath, finally gained British admission. By that year the American partnership had suffered the strains of the Vietnam War and the Commonwealth had become a club so loose that two of its members, India and Pakistan, fought a major war against each other. The three equal circles had become one large circle, Europe, flanked by two smaller ones.

The Commonwealth, though psychologically a cushion for national pride and thus often only a matter of glowing rhetoric, was still not all illusion. A multitude of connections—cultural, political, economic, historical—tied Britain to its old colonies. In 1964 nearly 58 percent of British investment was in the Commonwealth. In 1966, 32 percent of British exports went to former colonies, and 32 percent of British imports came from them; and in 1966 more Britons worked in India than at the height of Empire. Thousands of future Commonwealth rulers went to British universities and schools. Commonwealth Prime Ministers still met to show that a heterogeneous club could contribute something to a more harmonious world. Britain and America also still had a special relationship of a kind, if only that American tourists, students, and entertainers flooded to the sole European country that spoke their language. Although the two decades after 1945 saw Britain lose the greatest Empire ever created and the decay of one of the most intimate of wartime alliances, the British did adjust to the new realities. Britain resumed its historic role as a European power.

THE WILSON ERA AND THE PROBLEM OF INFLATION

From 1951 to 1964 the Tories ruled in an age of affluence; from 1964 to 1979 (with a Tory interlude) Labour ruled in an age of inflation. The coincidence of affluence with Tory rule and inflation with Labour rule was accidental; deeper economic trends, like the changes of weather, are beyond the control of statesmen. This does not mean that statesmen are unimportant: it is good to put up storm windows in the winter and repair air conditioners in the summer.

In 1963 Harold Wilson, who had become leader of the Labour party, charged Sir Alec Douglas-Home, who had become Prime Minister, with allowing the economy to go unrepaired and exposed to stormy economic weather. With the five-year term of the 1959 Parliament expiring, Wilson set out to end Labour's string of defeats. In 1945 Labour campaigned on a socialist idealism that met the mood of a generation which remembered wartime sharing and a harsh prewar capitalism. In the affluent 1950s that idealism had little appeal to voters enjoying a rising standard of living. In 1964, the pragmatic Wilson sought to win their votes in a modern, scientific manner. He used polls to determine what the voters wanted and tailored Labour's campaign to them. He also promised "a white-hot technological revolution," full of computers, nuclear power, and electronics, and a government by planners and professionals not aristocrats

From 1966 to 1970 and 1974 to 1976,
Harold Wilson sought a socialist answer
to slow economic growth, adverse trade
balances, and inflation and had little
success (*Illustrated London News*).

and clubmen. Such efforts, managed according to sound socialist principles, would bring, in the next five years, a 25 percent growth in the economy. Sir Alec Douglas-Home's retort that Wilson was a "slick salesman of synthetic science" had some truth to it, but not enough to deter 44.8 percent from voting for Labour in September 1964. It was not an overwhelming vote, but it did exceed the 42.9 percent voting Tory. The 11.4 percent who voted Liberal proved crucial. They were middle-class voters, fearful of socialism but disenchanted with a Conservative party whose erratic economics, scandals, and inscrutable methods of choosing leaders suggested that Britain would not be modern and dynamic under Sir Alec Douglas-Home.

Labour's 44.8 percent won it an overall majority of four MPs, a majority that could not last long. The shrewd and agile Wilson thus spent his first year and a half as Prime Minister preparing for another election. In January 1966 he called for an election in March, which Labour won with 48.7 percent of the vote. The Tories received 41.4 percent, the Liberals 8.6 percent, and the lesser parties, 1.3 percent. Labour now had a majority of ninety-seven seats. Wilson's government had increased old age pensions, ended charges for prescriptions, passed a generous Housing Act, voted money for hospitals, and created a Department of Economic Affairs which drew up a national plan to modernize industry.

He also attacked the Tories for leaving an £800 million deficit in the balance of payments and an inefficient economy. The Tory party still lacked strong leadership since Edward Heath, though not an aristocrat, was no more dynamic than Douglas-Home, whom the Tories ousted in July 1965.

Heath and Wilson were both 49 years old in 1966. Although both were educated at Oxford, neither was upper class. Both labored long for their parties, outlasted more brilliant colleagues, and reached the top, only to depart, Heath at 58, thrown out by his party, Wilson at 60, resigning in frustration over a divided party. Heath was patient and industrious, not brilliant and inspiring. Although his colleagues admired his vision and purpose, some found him tetchy and abrupt of manner. A handsome bachelor and fine musician, his unpretentiousness was attractive, as was his clear exposition of Toryism on television. But he was no match for the nimble wit and corruscating polemics of Wilson. On television and on the hustings Wilson was persuasive, engaging, clever, and aglow with his vision of modern socialism. In the Commons he also bested the solemn Heath with wit and mockery. With a majority of ninety-seven, the formidable powers of a Prime Minister, a fervid faith in technology and planning, and the skill of a born debater, Wilson was the unrivaled leader who could guide Britain to the new socialist Eldorado.

But in 1966 Wilson faced a host of problems. The welfare state, though it alleviated much want, ill-health, distress, and ignorance, left much still unalleviated. It had also created problems by producing a costly, unwieldly, clumsy bureaucracy. Despite the Tories' good beginning in 1962, there was still a desperate shortage of hospitals. Poverty was again rediscovered, millions having either fallen outside the reaches of social insurance or seen their unemployment or old age benefits shrunk by inflation. One out of the three of the aged lived alone, most in poverty. For all the grand promises of public housing, many were homeless. Prisons were overcrowded and repressive and crime was rising steadily. Eleven-plus examinations still doomed many a bright working-class child to a drab secondary modern school with mediocre teachers. Very few of the children of the working classes received education beyond the age of 15.

The 1960s was also a decade of progressive ideas, of advancing liberalism, and so Harold Wilson faced demands for enlightened laws on divorce, abortion, homosexuality, drugs, paroles, and capital punishment. The Prime Minister's headaches were endless. They included traffic congestion, pollution, crime, prisons, juvenile gangs, university riots, immigrants, and those who disliked immigrants. The influx of immigrants led the Tories in 1962 to pass an act limiting Commonwealth immigration, previously unrestricted, to relatives of those already in Britain or to those with jobs. West Indian blacks, Pakistanis, and Indians, though less than 4 percent of the population, posed a problem in cities like London and Birmingham. Wretchedly housed, badly educated, denied jobs, discriminated against in pubs, some grew resentful and turned to riots, as in London's Nottingham Hill riot in 1958; others took drugs or committed crimes.

Harold Wilson faced no problem as intractable as Ulster where the three-

The increase of immigrants from the Commonwealth led the British to restrict immigration (*Radio Times, Hulton Picture Library*).

fifths who were Protestant not only excluded the two-fifth who were Catholic from the best jobs, schools, and housing but gerrymandered voting districts so as to deny them a fair share of office. One small group among the Catholics, the Irish Republican Army, used violence to end that dominance. Bombs and killings soon tore Ulster apart. Miserable as Wilson's Ulster and immigrant problems were, they were still small beer compared to the sluggish, creaky economy. Unemployment rose as growth slowed to 2.1 percent, a humiliating figure compared to Germany's and Japan's more than 5 percent.

It was the sluggish economy that underlay the greatest worry of all, inflation. In 1968 it accelerated to 5 percent, in 1969 to 8 percent. Distressing in any country, it was particularly so in Britain because it undermined the value of the pound. Inflation makes exports more expensive, which causes sales to drop. Since declining exports earn fewer dollars, marks, and francs, and since steady imports cost valuable dollars, marks, and francs, British banks found their reserves of foreign currencies falling as the volume of unwanted pounds rose and so became less valuable. As the pound dropped in value, rumors arose that it would be devalued. The rumors led international speculators in currency to sell pounds, thus making it difficult for the government to maintain the pound at $2.80. To keep the pound at $2.80, the government had the central banks buy up pounds with dollars borrowed from the International Monetary Fund.

There were other forces weakening the pound, especially the expense of capital investment abroad, aid and the loans to Commonwealth countries, and payments for armed forces and military bases abroad. The investments abroad were, of course, only a temporary loss if those investments became profitable and earned dollars or other needed currencies. The military bases, however, meant a constant drain and were a reason the Empire was so quickly liquidated. Harold Wilson, the Labour party, the Tories, the press, and most economists considered the defense of the pound at $2.80 the first priority. Since the international bankers holding pounds or able to give loans for its support had greater faith in its soundness when there was less government spending, tighter credit, higher taxes, and a balanced budget—the principal ways of checking inflation— enormous pressure fell on Wilson, as it had on Attlee, Eden, and Macmillan, to cut spending and tighten credit. This he did in 1965 and 1966.

When the balance of payments favored Britain and when international financiers trusted the pound, the government could expand credit, spending, and investment, and so promote full employment. When there was an adverse balance of trade and Britain's reserves of foreign currency fell, the government had to spend less and raise interest rates and taxes—that is, deflate the economy thus dampen growth and increase unemployment. It was a painful dilemma. One way out was to inflate the economy in the hope that renewed business activity would produce inexpensive, attractive, and salable exports which would earn the needed foreign currency and gold: it would be a gamble, a dash for economic growth by inflation.

At the center of Britain's economic problems was the fact that British products competed poorly with those of other nations. In 1953 British exports made up 20.9 percent of the world trade in manufactured goods, in 1964 only 13.7 percent. Harold Wilson's great hope was that technology and planning would help industry modernize, that government, unions, and management meeting together in councils could check rising wages and prices, produce efficiency, and win the dash for economic growth. In 1970 that hope was still unrealized, and inflation was brisker than ever. Yet all was not bleak. British did well in computers, aluminum, electronics, the entertainment and tourist industry, and such small industries as recycling paper and such gigantic efforts as North Sea oil. Production on a whole rose 14 percent from 1965 to 1970. From 1960 to 1970 productivity per capita rose 40 percent, compared to 30 percent in the 1950s. And after the pound was devalued in November 1967 British exports prospered, though only briefly.

Wilson's government also made significant social reforms. In 1959–60 the

Tory government spent £426 million on housing, £916 million on education, and £827 million on health. In 1969–70 the Labour government spent on housing, education, and health £1,089, £2,513, and £1,931 million, a quite astonishing increase, even if corrected for inflation, in expenditures for welfare. And yet many problems remained and much inequality persisted. Although comprehensive schools grew, educating 31 percent of students by 1970, and although the use of the eleven-plus examinations declined, slum schools and classes larger than thirty pupils persisted. Only 25 percent of the 16-year-olds went to school and only 15 percent of them received any form of higher education. Expenditures on education still favored those bright enough or rich enough to go to grammar schools and universities. Housing subsidies and tax allowances for mortgage payments also favored the better-off classes, while the very poor paid high rents to slum landlords for dismal flats and the homeless remained in dire straits. Social security was now more ample for those who earned more and so contributed more to the fund, but it still failed to cover the very poor. Five million fell below the government's poverty line.

Among the many reasons for these failures, the most important was inflation. By raising prices and hurting exports it furthered trade deficits, restrictive budgets, and unemployment. It was a specter that haunted Harold Wilson for six years, a specter economists and statesmen could not exorcise. They were in fact of an uncertain mind. Some said inflation reflected an increased supply of money and the answer was to reduce that supply, while others said it was due to the wage-cost push and the answer was to check the increase in wages. A third group pictured it as a spiral of prices and wages, both of which reflected people's rising expectations, and saw the answer in government price and wage boards. All three answers involved horrendous consequences: reducing the supply of money meant cuts in government spending, tighter credit, slower growth, unemployment, and a smaller welfare program; a check in wages would anger the trade unions, who were Labour's staunch supporters, and cause strikes; and the administrative regulation of prices and wages would distort the economy.

Yet inflation had to be checked. Wilson tried a bit of all three solutions. His budget of 1966 was full of higher taxes, higher interest rates, restrictions on installment buying, and checks on spending. He also pushed through a Price and Wages Act that called for a six-month wage and price freeze, the freeze to be followed by six months of restrained increases. The act also created a Prices and Incomes Board that could disallow increases. Since the board had no real power of enforcement, it delayed but did not stop inflation, nor did it and a deflationary budget defend the pound. The pound rested on too narrow a foundation to serve, as it long had, as a principal international currency. It should have been devalued in the mid-1960s and allowed to float. That it was not was due, in part, to Wilson's stubborn belief, one held by Winston Churchill in 1925 and Ramsay MacDonald in 1931, that there was something sacred about the pound. A devalued and floating pound, though it promoted rational budgets, would not entirely end inflation, which was a worldwide event. In 1969, with trade unions again demanding wage increases, Wilson once more tried to create a board with powers to regulate wages and prices. He also urged a bill giving the government the power to delay unofficial strikes and to poll union members on official ones. Both actions split the Labour party, a fact which did not help Wilson when in 1970 he held a general election, nor did an 8 percent inflation, or a series of stop-and-go budgets. He lost the election and handed these problems on to Edward Heath.

EDWARD HEATH AT THE HELM: 1970–1974

When Harold Wilson called for a general election in March 1970, the polls showed Labour 12 percent ahead of the Tories. During the election Heath seemed no match for the adroit Wilson. "Trust me," said Wilson, "I have piloted Britain through perilous waters." Heath replied with sober television speeches charging Labour with responsibility for the country's inflation, unemployment, and strikes. He promised instead better industrial relations, lower taxes, and reform of taxation and local government. He also promised to promote scientific management, to make the marketplace freer, and to make the economy take off. Buoyant exports would soon right the balance of payments deficit and check inflation. It was the old gamble—the dash for economic growth.

In its first two years the Heath government, enjoying a majority of thirty MPs, made massive tax cuts in the hope that by encouraging savings it would spur investments and by increasing purchasing power stimulate economic activity, reduce unemployment, and accelerate productivity. The government also cut its spending. It preferred, it said, the private to the public sector of the economy, and a society of self-reliant people. A means test restricted family allowances to the poor only. Many of them, from pride or ignorance, failed to apply, which meant great savings. Housing expenditures were reduced by urging local governments to raise the rents on council houses, cut subsidies, and offer council houses for sale to their tenants. Huge education cuts led to an end to free milk for those over 7, to fewer free meals, and to less effort to replace slum schools and limit class size to thirty. Margaret Thatcher, today's Prime Minister, became Minister of Education and did her best to protect grammar schools by stopping the growth of comprehensive schools. The Tories, like Labour, had a constituency that sent children to grammar schools, wished to own their own homes (and have tax writeoffs on the mortgage), and desired to pay lower taxes.

In both 1970 and 1971 with inflation reaching 21 percent and prices racing ahead of wages, it is little wonder that strikes reached a high not known since 1926. Edward Heath countered with the Industrial Relations Act of 1971. By making it illegal to compel a worker to join a union, it outlawed the closed shop so dear to all unions. It further angered them by requiring a sixty-day cooling-off period before they could strike and by making all union-management

From 1970 to 1974, Edward Heath sought
a capitalist answer to slow economic
growth, adverse trade balances, and
inflation and also had little success
(*Illustrated London News*).

agreements legally enforcible by a special Industrial Tribunal. That Tribunal
was also to define more strictly, and penalize by fines and imprisonment, unfair
labor practices. The act, though involving the state, would limit its role to that
of umpire. Industrial disputes would occur in a free market, with employers
occupying the front lines. Disputes did occur, more days being lost in 1972
from strikes than in any year since the 1920s.

Heath also wanted no government control of wages and prices; he abolished
Wilson's useful Prices and Incomes Board and Industrial Re-organization Corporation. Heath had no strategy to control inflation other than to gamble on an
expanding productivity, a happy event he expected to follow England's entry
into the European Common Market. In 1972 Heath, who had led the negotiation
team in 1962, finally won admission for Britain to that powerful club. It was
to mark Britain's entry into the modern age, one in which German, Italian,
and French goods would force British industry to become efficient. Heath, though
wedded to an economics of *laissez-faire*, was an administrator who believed in
scientific management. His Local Government Act reduced the number of local
authorities, especially borough councils, and created six large new metropolitan
councils. The government also created area boards to administer hospitals more
efficiently. Heath's mixing of *laissez-faire* policies and scientific management
seemed promising.

Then, suddenly, the roof fell in. The culprit again was inflation. Under Heath it rose to 10 percent and more a year. Although inflation was worldwide, it was worse in Britain, and partly because Heath's massive tax cuts increased personal incomes and his opposition to an incomes policy along with his assent to some generous wage increases did very little to stop inflation. In 1972 Heath, aware that he had not blunted inflation, made a U-turn, completely reversing his course. He called in the trade union leaders and mapped out three phases of a plan to check wages and prices: phase 1 called for a ninety-day freeze on wages, prices, rents and dividends (a freeze later extended sixty more days); phase 2 allowed a 1-pound-a-week plus 4 percent wage increase and price increases only if costs rose; and phase 3 authorized £2.25 a week or a 7 percent wage increase. Phases 1 and 2 worked, but phase 3 broke down. It could not withstand the accelerating prices caused by the Arab oil embargo which followed the Yom Kippur War of September 1973.

Neither could industry do without that oil. Its shortage not only forced Heath to declare a three-day week for industry but it made coal production even more urgent. But the miners were still recalcitrant and England's industry lay semiparalyzed. Heath dissolved Parliament in February and called for a general election on the issue of whether the trade unions or the people's elected representatives would govern Britain. He lost. He had not stopped inflation, had not reduced unemployment, had not tamed the unions, had not won the dash for growth, and had not returned Britain to a *laissez-faire* capitalism. The last goal was perhaps impossible. Heath, for example, had to nationalize most of the famous Rolls Royce Company, symbol of British majesty, because it was going bankrupt. He also had to use the National Enterprise Board, a Wilson creation, to give subsidies to, and increase government controls over, private business. Rhetoric had to bow to reality.

Having failed to check inflation and having lost two general elections in 1974, the Tory MPs replaced Heath with Margaret Thatcher. She promptly proclaimed in 1977 that Britain was ready to reject socialism and collectivism. But it was not her task, but Labour's, to grapple with an inflation now running at 12 percent.

WILSON AND CALLAGHAN: 1974–1979

In 1974 and 1975 Britain seemed to fall apart. Two elections in February and October revealed disillusionment with both major parties as millions voted for minor parties. In 1951 the Labour and Conservative parties won 97 percent of the votes, in 1974 only 75 percent. A disillusionment with the two old parties was beginning. Inflation raged unchecked. Trade unions were voracious for higher wages, business raised prices, real incomes fell, the balance of payments became negative, and the press wrote about the English disease, the suicide of a nation, and an ungovernable nation. In February voters returned 301 Labour

MPs, a majority of 5 over the 291 Tories, but a minority of 14 if the 14 Liberals, 7 Scottish Nationalists, 2 Welsh Plaid Cymru, and 11 Ulster Nationalists joined the Conservatives. But the Liberals and Scottish Nationalists supported Labour and Wilson became Prime Minister. Since this fragile alliance could not last, Wilson prepared for another election in October. It returned 315 Labour MPs, a majority of 39 over the Tories, and equal to the 315 non-Labour MPs, which included, besides the Tories, 13 Liberals, 13 Scottish Nationalists, 3 Plaid Cymru, and 10 Ulster Unionists. The strength of the Scottish Nationalist Party surprised many. Its success reflected England's long neglect of Scotland and the disillusionment of Scottish Labour voters with the Labour party. These voters, not liking Tories at all, went Nationalist just as middle-class voters, unwilling to vote Labour and disillusioned with Tories, voted Liberal. Although in 1974 some foresaw the political fragmentation of England, Wilson managed to persuade the Liberals and Nationalist parties to support Labour.

Wilson's own party was fragmented in October 1974. Wilson, who in 1967 supported entry into the Common Market, in 1972 opposed it. In 1974 many in the Labour party wanted him out. Wilson finessed the dilemma by calling for a referendum on the issue—the first ever held in Britain—and the electorate voted two-to-one to stay in, in part because Wilson had obtained a more advantageous arrangement for Commonwealth trade. But he still faced the problem of a brisk inflation and a sluggish economy. In the last half of 1975 prices rose 25 percent, in 1976 the standard of living fell 5 percent, and in the same year the car, steel, and shipbuilding industries did poorly; inefficient branches were kept alive because their demise would cause local unemployment. All looked gloomy and hopeless. American observers said that Britain would be the first to change from a developed to an underdeveloped country. Others argued that Britain was sick from excessive socialism.

Then, in 1976 and 1977, the economy turned around. In 1976, for the first time in three years, Britain became a net exporter. In 1977 British reserves of foreign exchange rose seven times. Inflation declined to 10 percent and promised to go lower. Trade unions, for the moment, no longer clamored for high raises. Productivity rose as exports of computers, electronics, machinery, clothes, and Scotch whiskey brought in foreign exchange as vigorously as did the tourist industry and the invisible earnings from chartering and insuring ships, which Britain did more of than all other countries combined. By 1978 British inflation was 8 percent, a rate close to the international average. Talk of the English disease and of the suicide of a nation died out. The Germans even inquired into Britain's successful incomes policy.

The answer to British success lay in three policies and a happy accident. The three policies were the government's social contract with the unions, its budget cuts, and government aid, in money and planning, to industry; the happy accident was the discovery of oil in the North Sea, oil that met two-fifths of Britain's needs in 1978 and that promised even greater yields.

The social contract consisted of agreements between the government and the unions in which the unions took a moderate wage increase and the government promised to keep inflation moderate, the workers' incomes steady, and social reform effective. The agreements were the result of hard bargaining at No. 10 Downing Street and the Treasury and some fierce battles at annual trade union conferences. Making the arrangement more palatable was the government's repeal of the hated Industrial Relations Act of 1971 and the passage of an act giving unions powers they had never before enjoyed. Wilson, who initiated these agreements, resigned as prime minister in July 1976 and the Labour MPs elected James Callaghan as his successor.

Callaghan, at 64, was a friendly, tough, and shrewd veteran from the conservative side of the party. He soon proved to be a more effective Prime Minister than Wilson. Quite as intelligent as Wilson, he showed himself sharper at analyzing economic dangers and more tactful and straightforward in dealing with the party. He could also cajole, entreat, bully, and charm the leaders of business and labor, leaders he invited to Chequers, the Prime Minister's country house in Buckinghamshire, in order to talk frankly of wages, prices, and trade deficits. He also won the Labour party over to cuts in government spending, thus attacking inflation at both ends by reducing the wage-cost push on prices and by reducing the supply of money and so the inordinate demand for goods. Through risking no dash for growth, Callaghan worked for greater productivity by aiding particular industries. Callaghan's government nationalized shipbuilding, the manufacture of aircraft, and Britain's major auto company, British Leylands. They did so not from a passion for nationalization but because the companies were near bankrupt.

Callaghan knew that from 1945 to 1979 capitalism had supplied the driving force in the British economy. He also knew that neither a welfare state, government planning, nor public ownership necessarily blunted that force. Statesmen of both parties had learned that judicious planning in an age of inflation was a necessity and that on occasion so was public ownership. The marriage of capitalism and socialism in the 1970s was far more a function of solving urgent problems than of the ideological stances of Tories and Labourites. The rhetoric of the Tory right and the Labour left tended to triumph when the parties were out of power; when in power, necessity forced their leaders to the center. Such was the remorseless pressure of late twentieth-century problems that it made Heath turn to nationalization and Callaghan to cuts in government spending.

There was thus, by 1979, among many in both parties a more realistic and sophisticated outlook about economic complexities and the need to subordinate doctrines to ad hoc solutions. But not all were so pragmatic. The left of the Labour party and the right of the Conservatives became more doctrinaire: the left, led by Tony Benn, won control of the Party Executive and, supported by unions angry that the social contract involved more sacrifice than gain, denounced Callaghan; the Tory right, having ditched Ted Heath, were galvanized by Margaret Thatcher's stirring promises that less government and a freer capitalism would solve both inflation and recession.

Britain in 1979 was more divided than ever, its left more bellicose and its right bolder. Class conflict persisted despite, at the center, a growing consensus. Britain had also had since 1963 nearly fourteen years of Labour government. Weariness with years of rising taxes and inflation, however much slowed down in 1978, also coincided with rising fuel prices from the OPEC oil cartel. It was all, despite Callaghan's achievements, too much. In the general election in May of 1979, 45 percent voted Conservative and only 38 percent Labour, with the Liberals garnering 14 percent and Nationalist parties the rest. The result was a Conservative majority of 43 MPs and from 1979 to 1983, four years of Margaret Thatcher's first government, followed by another victory at the polls and a second government.

MARGARET THATCHER'S ELEVEN-YEAR RULE

On May 15, 1990 Margaret Thatcher completed her eleventh year as Prime Minister. Only Robert Walpole's 20 years as chief minister (and the young Pitt's 18 and Liverpool's 15) exceeds her long and still uncompleted reign. It is a remarkable feat for a leader of a Conservative party that in the general elections of 1979, 1983, and 1987 never won more than 45 percent of the vote and a Conservative party that in its first three years saw unemployment triple, one-seventh of Britain's manufacturers close down, inflation reach 21 percent a year, and the party's ratings on the polls fall to 28 percent. But despite these difficulties the Conservatives, in the general election of 1983, won 43 percent of the votes, which gave them 397 MPs compared to Labour's 209 and the Alliances' 23. From 1984 to 1987 many observers felt that it was victory in the Falkland Island war that saved the day for Mrs. Thatcher's government. Nothing succeeds like success, especially if the success stirs the patriotism of a once great and proud country experiencing decline.

On April 20, 1982, 8,000 Argentine soldiers invaded the Falkland Islands some 400 miles off Argentina in the South Atlantic. Seventy-two days later 25,000 British soldiers and sailors and 100 ships threw them out. That Britain had occupied the islands since 1834 and that the 1,800 Falkland Islanders, largely of British extraction, wanted British rule to continue, gave Britain a clear legal and moral right to defend it.

But did that defense serve England's national self-interest? Some 1,000 Argentine and English lost their lives and 1,700 more were wounded. The war also cost Britain over £2.7 billion, or £1.5 million per islander, and all for islands nearly 8,000 miles away and of no strategic or economic value whatsoever, islands that the British diplomats in 1982 were actively negotiating away, a negotiation that even encouraged the invasion.

Legally the war was just, in terms of national self-interest, irrational, brilliant only in execution, and psychologically exhilarating. In pubs all over England the spirit of Agincourt and the Armada, of Trafalgar and D-Day were revived and with it the fortunes of Margaret Thatcher. The iron lady, as the Russians dubbed her, never flinched in defending the Falklands. Her resolution, her energy, her painstaking attention to detail, her eloquence, and her adamantine refusal to compromise had a Churchillian air. The Tory party immediately shot up 20 percent in the polls and provided historians a crucial explanation of their election victory in 1983.

It was an explanation that seemed less crucial after May 1987 when the Conservatives, with no Falkland war, still won 43 percent of the vote and a majority in the House of Commons. In constituency after constituency the Conservative's 43 percent—or thereabouts—returned MPs because the Alliances' 23 percent—or thereabouts—left Labour's 32 percent, seldom enough to return an MP. Not the Falkland Islands war but a deep split in the parties of the left allowed a Thatcher government resting on but 43 percent of the vote to rule on and on.

The deep split in the left, long a-brewing, erupted in the fateful years from 1979 to 1981. Radical left-wing activists of all kinds, ranging from idealistic peace workers to the ruthless Trotskyites of the Militant Tendency, won out in those local party constituencies where aging leaders no longer inspired loyalty. Militants also won out in some 20 trade unions, unions angry at the attempts of Wilson and Callaghan to discipline them and to hold down wages. These militants and constituency radicals arrived at party conferences in sufficient numbers to change the Labour party from a majority party of consensus to a minority party of radical causes. They took from the Labour Parliamentary party, always sensitive to the public that elected them, the power to choose the party's leader and gave it to an Electoral College, 40 percent of whom represented trade unions, 30 percent constituency parties, and 30 percent the one powerful Labour Parliamentary party. The trade unions, long the paymaster of the Labour party and enjoying huge block votes at its conferences, now had the leading role in selecting its leaders.

The conference then chose as leader of the Labour party the distinguished but ineffective, aging, and radical Michael Foot. They also called for unilateral nuclear disarmament, the abolition of private schools, the end of private health care, further nationalization, and the turning over of economic strategy to the trade unions.

It was too radical, too extreme, too removed from public opinion for four former Labour ministers, Roy Jenkins, Shirley Williams, David Owen, and William Rodgers. These four knew that while only 21 percent of the public opposed, a full 67 percent were for, a nuclear deterrent; nor did the public want the end of private schools and unions running the economy. They thus established a new party, the Social Democratic party. At first it won great support, especially when it allied with the Liberal party. In 1982 this Alliance won the approval of 50 percent of those polled. But soon weaknesses became apparent, most particularly since, as an alliance of two different parties, they had two leaders, David Owen from the Social Democrats and David Steel from the Liberals. David Owen was for and David Steel against a nuclear deterrent, just one of many differences that not only divided the two Davids but the rank and file. With no clear, fixed convictions and representing no clear social and economic interests, the Alliance was only strong enough to deny Labour victory at the polls.

In the general election of 1983 Labour won only 28 percent of the vote, a far cry from the 48 percent of 1966. It was the Labour party's lowest point. Michael Foot resigned. The Electoral College chose the young, attractive, Welshman Neil Kinnoch. Under Kinnoch's leadership from 1984 to 1987, the party expelled the militants, moderated its policies, sought to broaden its base, and, in the 1987 election, employed the best advertising agencies and movie directors to present a new, modern, bright image. But the party was still committed to abolishing nuclear arms, still dominated by trade unions, and its radicals still dominated town councils where they espoused such unpopular causes as homosexual rights and support of Nicaraguan communists.

There were also long-run causes for Labour's decline. Its electoral basis lay largely in an industrial North that was in decline. Also in decline was membership in trade unions—by 1986 25 percent less than 1980. Furthermore, the shift from large heavy to light technical industry and from manufacture to the service sector of the economy created a more independent-minded worker. In the marginal Midlands with its smaller firm industries, the skilled workers, not happy with radicalism and talk of disarmament and some resentful of blacks and Pakistanis seeking jobs and housing, voted increasingly Tory. They voted Tory particularly if they had taken advantage of Mrs. Thatcher's shrewd policy of selling council houses to its tenants. Of workers owning their homes, 31 percent voted Labour and 44 percent Tory.

Long-run economic and social trends also favored the Conservatives. The more affluent the British became, the more they voted Tory—or at least not Labour. The slow growth of the economy of the late 1970s led to heavier taxes and so to a tax revolt not unlike that which twice sent Ronald Reagan to the White House. People were tiring of socialism and its burdens, and even its crowded Health Service and deteriorating council housing.

To a split in the left, a radicalized Labour party, an Alliance lacking an electoral and ideological base, and long-run conservative trends, one can add a fifth factor in explanation of three successive electoral Tory victories, Margaret Thatcher. Born in 1925 in Grantham, Lincolnshire, to Alfred Roberts, owner of two grocery stores, she was educated at the local grammar school after which she took a degree in chemistry at Oxford University. She then married the wealthy paint manufacturer, Mr. Thatcher, earned a law degree, entered politics, won a seat in Parliament, became Minister of Education, overthrew Edward Heath, and became the first woman Prime Minister—all done in her inexorable, remorseless, ruthless manner. Her Methodist father had instilled into her the old fashion Victorian virtues of self-reliance, industry, frugality, ambition, forethought, and a rock-solid belief that in a world free of socialism these virtues would bring order, prosperity, and progress. To this rock-solid foundation she

later added a *laissez-faire* economics and a monetarist economics, one that believed
that inflation could be reduced by simply reducing the supply of money. And
thus armed in 1979 Mrs. Thatcher took on those three formidable challenges
posed by Britain's declining economy: inflation, slow growth, and socialism.

At first the curse of inflation seemed to doom Mrs. Thatcher's economic
policy: 10 percent a year when she took office, two years later it was 21.9 percent.
In fulfilling her election promises to raise wages in the public sector, she initiated
a general and substantial rise in wages, rises which were passed on in higher
prices. She also raised the value added tax (a hidden sales tax), adding 4 percent
to the cost of living. These inflationary pressures did not greatly worry Mrs.
Thatcher and her monetarist advisors because they insisted that wage and price
controls were unnecessary if one simply limited the supply of money. Since
bank credit even more than currency constitutes money, Geoffrey Howe, the
Chancellor of the Exchequer, raised the interest rates on bank credit to 17
percent, a figure that would discourage expansion of that form of money. But
a healthy return of 17 percent on loans to the British Treasury led the world
bankers to buy up pounds, thus driving up its value, a value already rising as
North Sea oil made Britain the world's fifth largest oil producer and its currency
desirable. By 1982 the pound, once worth $1.60 was worth $2.30. This expensive
pound, by making all British exports far more expensive than their competitors,
dealt a devastating blow to industry, a blow industry could not meet if borrowing
cost 17 percent. For many, the result was catastrophic. From 1979 to 1982
one in seven in manufacturing lost their jobs and manufacturing production
fell 17.3 percent. Unemployment tripled. By 1982 it was 3 million.

The 3 million jobless, barely existing on minimal benefits, along with many
other underemployed, had little to spend on goods. Prices thus rose more slowly,
a fact also reflective of a worldwide recession and a world oil glut. By March
1983 inflation was only 4.6 percent.

Mrs. Thatcher, with the help of unemployment and a world recession,
had solved the first of the three formidable problems, inflation, but at a huge
cost in terms of the second problem, Britain's slow rate of growth. Indeed, in
her first three years there was no growth but a 4.2 percent decline of the gross
national product. For the stern social Darwinist that Mrs. Thatcher is, such a
shakeout was needed so that the fittest could survive and could lay the basis
for efficiency. Nor would she allow trade unions to stand in the way. When
the radical Arthur Scargill called on his National Union of Miners to strike in
order to prevent the closure of inefficient mines, a year-long, violent strike
ensued, with Mrs. Thatcher and her special police defeating Scargill and his
10,000 flying pickets. Mrs. Thatcher's government also, in 1980 and 1982, passed
two Trade Union Acts that curtailed their powers. These acts, the coal strike,
and, above all, mass unemployment, so weakened the trade unions that Thatcher's
vision of a *laissez-faire* capitalism was a giant step nearer. And nearer too when
she abolished, as much as she could, the government's regulatory powers.

But by 1987 the economy was still plagued by slow growth since from

1979 on it averaged only 1.4 percent a year, far below the 3.1 percent of the socialist 1960s and a rate surprisingly low given the vast wealth flowing from North Sea oil. Much of the slow growth was inherent in British culture. Germans built Ford Escorts in half the time it took British workers because British workers arrived late, left early, took long meal breaks, and moved slowly. The managerial style was equally leisurely. British workers were also less educated. At age 16, 82 percent of British children, but only 10 percent of German, had left school; and of German school leavers, 50 percent became apprentices compared to Britain's 14 percent.

Germany and France also had clear-cut industrial policies, policies developed when government, banking, and industrial planners met and directed investment to their optimum use in a market-based capitalism. Mrs. Thatcher would have no such industrial policy just as in educational matters she wished no expansion. Indeed she even reduced university budgets 10 percent and phased out science colleges in the North. Her breaking of the overweening power of trade unions and her insistence that only efficient firms survive had salutary results, and much of the English economy is healthier today than in 1979 because of it, but she has left untouched those deep lying cultural weaknesses that make slow growth, the second of the three formidable problems, a problem still as formidable as ever.

Socialism was for Mrs. Thatcher, and increasingly for the 43 percent who voted for her, part of Britain's economic problem. In the 1950s Churchill, Eden, Macmillan—even the young Ted Heath—had accepted socialism, especially if dressed in the apparel of Tory paternalism. The Thatcher revolution was to reject that acceptance and to denounce socialism itself. Nationalization of the means of production was its worst evil. Economic planning was almost as bad. Even the welfare state was harmful as debilitating of moral fiber.

By the late 1980s Mrs. Thatcher had developed a passion for "privatization"—that is, for the conversion of publicly into privately owned industries. British Gas, British Aerospace, British Telecom (telephone and telegraph), and many other state enterprises were sold to private investors. By 1990 20 not 7 percent of the English owned stock, and £20 billion worth of public assets had become private. The windfall profits from these sales also greatly pleased those anxious to lower taxes. But the government's basic reason for privatization was the belief that free enterprise was more efficient than public, a conclusion that many studies supported. Even German and Swedish socialists had given up on nationalization. But European socialists do not have that disdain for economic planning that marks Mrs. Thatcher's *laissez-faire* economics. Neither are they as critical of that welfare state which Mrs. Thatcher and her advisors feel is so harmful to economic growth. Many in France and Germany—and not just socialists—are aware that although in the mid-1970s France and Germany spent 21 percent of their gross national product on education, health, and welfare compared to Britain's 17 percent, their economic growth rates were twice those of the British.

Margaret Thatcher never dared a frontal attack on the welfare state. She was not blind to the fact that surveys revealed that only 6 percent preferred tax cuts to a cut in the services of the welfare state. "The Health Service," she said, "is safe with us." But if no frontal attack there was much whittling away and foot dragging. Public housing was cut 50 percent, university budgets were so reduced that 30,000 qualified applicants were refused, teachers' salaries were kept low, student housing payments were dropped, some schools closed, and the Health Service deteriorated as more and more were encouraged to use private doctors. Overall expenditure did not, despite government promises of reduction, fall. Advances in medical technology made the Health Service more expensive; unemployment demanded millions in relief; riots in 1981 in the inner cities and a general increase in crime demanded expanded police, courts, prisons, and social agencies. Eleven years after Mrs. Thatcher took office the government, its expenditures, and the welfare state were all larger.

Not so intact were those local authorities where socialists held power. If Mrs. Thatcher could not overthrow socialism, at least she could overthrow some socialists. One of them was the flamboyant Ken Livingston, leader of the Greater London Council. Mrs. Thatcher's government abolished that council. It also abolished six other metropolitan authorities and reduced the power of all local governments to tax and spend. That centralization which the Victorian Tories had denounced Thatcherite Tories carried to new heights.

Thatcherite Tories also stopped the long-run trend toward equality. The income of the top 10 percent increased more than six times faster than that of the bottom tenth. The taxes on the rich were lowered more than for any other group. After 1989 they did not even have to pay a local property tax, such local taxes having been converted into a poll tax paid by all. In 1989 there were 33 percent more at or below the poverty line than in 1979. Even if the two English nations that Disraeli discovered, the rich and the poor, had never really ceased to exist, at least the gulf between them had lessened. Under Mrs. Thatcher it widened and took on geographical as well as social demarcations. The industrial North was declining and poorer, and voted Labour; the South was progressing and richer, and voted Tory; the inner cities were deteriorating and rioting; the suburbs proliferating in affluence. One nation owned their homes, had green lawns, lived in secure and racially free neighborhoods, worked for private enterprise, and sent their children to the best schools; the other nation rented aging council houses surrounded by littered concrete courtyards; lived in crime-ridden and racially divided neighborhoods; received unemployment, child, or old age benefits; and saw their children drop out of school. Mrs. Thatcher, perhaps the ablest, certainly the most resolute, Prime Minister of the postwar era, has a deep empathy with the nation of the rich, of the active, enterprising, ambitious, and in her eleven years she has shown great shrewdness and talent in furthering that world, but it is a shrewdness and talent not in empathy with the nation of the poor, of the disadvantaged, colored, ill-educated. The result is an England more deeply divided than at anytime since the 1930s.

Mrs. Thatcher faced other problems besides inflation, slow growth, and socialism. Northern Ireland, race, inner-city riots would no more go away than problems of Europe, defense, and foreign affairs. In confronting these problems Mrs. Thatcher's policy has largely been to contain the problem more than to solve it. In Northern Ireland containment, not solution, is almost inevitable since the passion of the Irish Republican Army and their friends in Eire and America for a united Ireland is as violent and unconquerable as is the passion of the Ulster Protestants never to be part of a united Ireland. Mrs. Thatcher's one imaginative move, taken with Eire's Prime Minister, Dr. Garret Fitzgerald, in 1981, for the creation of an Anglo Irish Council was so summarily and entirely rejected by the Protestants that containment of an irreconcilable struggle remains the only alternative.

Not so hopeless of solution was the problem of race and the inner cities, yet here Mrs. Thatcher again merely contained the forces. By the late 1990s Asians and blacks, who now account for 4.4 percent of the population, will account for 6.5 percent. Despite laws and commissions against it, racial discrimination is pervasive and deep-seated. One example of it is the dearth of blacks on inner-city police forces and the presence on those forces of whites prejudiced against blacks, and prejudiced too against the alienated, deprived, and angry, who, when provoked by police brutality, riot. Although it is an exceedingly complex problem calling for complex solutions, Mrs. Thatcher has done little more than reinforce police containment, an action that, along with no real action to lessen discrimination, constitutes a political containment of the Tory right wing.

That right wing is also delighted that Mrs. Thatcher is containing, as best she can, the European Community's encroachments on English sovereignty. Mrs. Thatcher has long been active in the European Community, active, that is, at opposing its progress until it reforms its overly liberal subsidies to agriculture and its excessive demands for English contributions. By her firmness, indeed by her truculence, she has redressed legitimate English grievances. But now, as the European Community plans a common budget and a common currency Mrs. Thatcher is vigorous in the containment of English sovereignty. The only strict monetarist in Europe she does not want nonmonetarists defining Britain's budget.

The same proud nationalism defines her defense and foreign policy—a policy of containment exactly in the sense George Kennan used that word in 1948 when he urged that the West contain Soviet aggression. Mrs. Thatcher is a cold warrior, but, says Gorbachev, after exchanging visits, a charming cold warrior. Although the Warsaw Pact is collapsing and Russia's economy and unity threatened, Mrs. Thatcher still tells Mr. Bush: Keep armed! Keep NATO armed! And resolved she is that Britain keep her Trident missiles and nuclear bombs. But why? Why, when Russia has already removed all intermediate-range missiles from Europe and when Hungary, Poland, Czechoslovakia and East Germany are all moving toward neutrality, should Britain possess such expensive toys? Are they not, like the Falkland Islands, mere symbols of former greatness, symbols furthering no national self-interest? So thinks Neil Kinnoch and the Labour party and so thinks Paddy Ashdown, head of the "Democratic" party, the offspring of the merged Alliance. So perhaps might some of the 67 percent who in grimmer times wanted a nuclear deterrent. At least if the nuclear deterrent no longer divides the left the left might unite, if not as one party, at least in an electoral compact to divide up constituencies. It would be a unity that might defeat a Conservative party that has not won over 45 percent of the vote in two decades. Mrs. Thatcher's eleven years' rule has defined the Britain of the 1980s. It is not so certain that she will define the 1990s.

FURTHER READING

BUTLER, DAVID, and DONALD STOKES. *Political Change in Britain.* London: Macmillan, 1974. A survey of politics in postwar Britain based on hundreds of interviews and statistics from elections; both show the continuity of parties and explain their changing fortunes.

CALVOCORESSI, PETER. *The British Experience, 1945–1975.* London: Pantheon Books, 1978. "A tale of hopes defeated by failures," says Calvocoressi, yet the author remains optimistic and liberal about socialist England.

CROSS, COLIN. *The Fall of the British Empire.* London: Hodder and Stoughton, 1968. Two themes define this story: how the Empire actually functioned at its height, and how and why it collapsed so suddenly.

GREGG, PAULINE. *The Welfare State: An Economic and Social History of Great Britain from 1945 to the Present Day.* London: George G. Harrap and Co., 1967. A favorable account of socialism and "the glory" of "the five shining years [after 1945] which saw idle wheels set busy . . ." but regretful that after 1950 it lost its impetus.

HARRIS, KENNETH. *Attlee.* London: Weidenfeld and Nicolson, 1982. A thorough and definitive biography that emphasizes Attlee's sense of duty, Christian fellowship, admiration for John Ruskin and William Morris, and toughness as prime minister.

HAVIGHURST, ALFRED F. *Britain in Transition: The Twentieth Century.* Chicago: Chicago University Press, 1979. A comprehensive and detailed history of twentieth-century Britain that is particularly useful because it brings the story down to 1979.

JENKINS, PETER. *Mrs. Thatcher's Revolution: The Ending of the Socialist Era.* Cambridge, Mass.: Harvard University Press, 1988. A shrewd, searching examination of Mrs. Thatcher's attack on socialism, an examination as willing to praise her vigorous and needed reforms of restrictive and stultifying institutions as to condemn those harsh measures that have polarized England.

NORTHREDGE, F. S. *British Foreign Policy: The Process of Readjustment.* New York: Praeger, 1962. An acute analysis of the decline of Britain from a world- to a second-rate power, concentrating on the crises that revealed her weaknesses.

SAMPSON, ANTHONY. *Macmillan: A Study in Ambiguity.* London: Penguin Press, 1967. A bright, shrewd journalistic biography of a prime minister who played an important role from 1937 to 1957 and a dominant role from 1957 to 1963.

SKED, ALAN, AND CHRIS COOK, *Post-War Britain.* London: Penguin Books, 1984. The best survey of the political events from 1945 to 1983, a fair and balanced account, one firmly rooted in a clear analysis of economic and social developments.

WILSON, HAROLD. *A Personal Record: The Labour Government, 1964–1970.* London: Weidenfeld and Nicolson, 1979. A memoir that reveals again the great defect in a prime minister's account of his own record—that he is biased—and the great virtue—that he knows so much.

WRIGHT, J. E. *Britain in an Age of Economic Management: An Economic History since 1939.* Oxford: Oxford University Press, 1979.

A broad but concise survey of nearly forty years of economic change, emphasizing those deeper trends in trade, finance, manufacturing, and technology beyond the control of government.

Life in Socialist Britain

31

"BALANCE OF PAYMENTS CRISIS" and "POUND IN PERIL" were the headlines greeting the British in 1947. The same headlines also greeted them in 1957, 1967, and 1976 and in many other years, though most readers skipped by them. Having heard the cry of wolf but never seen him, they left this headache to economists and statesmen and turned to the home department, to the fashion page, or to the car ads and read of a reality that in thirty years had transformed his or her life, a reality of increasing wealth, advancing technology, and "the good life." He or she also read newspaper reviews of plays filled with sex, of movies packed with violence, of revolutionary art shows, and of the newest books. Editorials told the reader of comprehensive schools, the Open University, and divorce and abortion reforms, issues that revealed a freer, more mobile, more open, and tenser world. It was these social developments, not debates on the pound, that defined the daily life of the English. Of these developments, easily the most profound was the simple fact that every year except 1976 and 1977 saw the British wealthier than the year before, a result of remarkable advances in technology.

TECHNOLOGY AND WEALTH

In 1977, the twenty-fifth year of the reign of Elizabeth II, her subjects were far wealthier than they had been at her accession. The economy in 1977 produced 70 percent more goods and services for each person than in 1952, a larger share of which went to male manual workers whose real wages had risen 89 percent—and that for a 44-hour, not a 47.7-hour, week. These added pounds meant that the now more-average-than-ever Englishman ate 24 percent more meat, 92 percent more cheese, 46 percent less potatoes, more frozen foods,

French cheeses, and exotics like artichokes and aubergines. The average Englishman also lived in a more comfortable house or flat. In 1952, 30 percent of
householders owned their homes; in 1977, 53 percent; and in 1977, of all households 91 percent had baths, 99 percent flush toilets, 92 percent TVs, over 75
percent refrigerators and washing machines, and over 50 percent telephones—
and outside the door, 74 percent had a car. They were particularly valued on
the three-and-a-half-week holidays that twenty-five years of advancing wealth
had brought to manual workers. The automobile also whisked newly affluent
children to their retired parents, an increasing class, since life expectancy had
grown from 71.2 years for women and 66.2 for men in 1952 to 75.5 and 69.3
in 1977.

Science and technology, along with hard, efficient labor, lay behind this
growth in wealth and the good life. The role of science in medicine never
ceased to astonish. Inconveniences the British did suffer, in queues at clinics
and in waiting time for hospitals, but they spent only 5.2 percent of their gross
national product on health, compared to America's 8 percent, and had a far
lower rate of child mortality—in 1977 half that of 1952. Technology also did
wonders for the economy. Computers and lasers were only the latest in a continuing process of automation and cost-cutting that began with the assembly line
and electric eyes of the 1920s. Britain in 1978 had the most advanced computer
industry in Europe and led in the development of robots as she still did with
jet engines and scanners for diagnosing illnesses. Mammoth projects were not
beyond its engineers.

The great Victorian engineers would have stood in awe at the "big hole"
at Loch Kishorn, near Inverness, where in 1976 some 850 men built a 170-
foot-high oil drilling rig, soon to be floated out to the North Sea to become
one of forty rigs on which engineers, roustabouts, and roughnecks drilled 11,000
feet down in search of oil. The work was dangerous and demanding, since
every 30 feet of drill penetration required the men to put in another length of
steel, a task demanding split-second timing and sure-footedness. Winds and
seas of gale force swept across these platforms. Fatalities on the rigs were ten
times those suffered by miners and fifty times those of the average industrial
worker. But these rigs promised Britain large supplies of oil in an era of energy
crises, the fields around the Shetland Islands equaled those of oil-rich Kuwait.

The workers on the oil rig were more efficient producers of wealth than
any of their predecessors, a statement also true of seamen and dockers, workers
in electronics and frozen foods, and airline clerks and farmers. In 1972 some
55,000 seamen manned ships carrying more goods to and from Britain than
the 120,000 of 1947. The reason was larger ships run by smaller crews. Many
of these goods came off the ships in containers designed to fit trucks and railway
cars, making many dockers redundant but the remaining few very efficient.
Efficient also were workers in electronics: in 1956 there were three times as
many of them as in 1939, but they produced ten times as much, which meant
cheaper radios and televisions. Efficiently produced frozen foods also added to

Giant floating oil rigs, some 170 feet high, gave to Britain gallons and gallons of North Sea oil.

the nation's wealth; frozen foods in 1972 cost only 9 percent more than in 1962, even though all other food prices had risen 30 percent.

Machines in every line of work enhanced efficiency—computers checked airline reservations and bank balances in seconds. Microcomputers also gave British autos better mileage and cut their pollution, just as they helped run the big air buses that took Britons on charter flights to the Spanish Riviera. Mechanization and chemistry, twin offspring of the all-conquering technology, even reached farms. Larger tractors plowed the fields, fertilizers and pesticides nourished growth and killed weeds, and vast battery hen and pig-fattening factories produced eggs and bacon in a massive, cheaper, more specialized, and, for the animals, more frightful manner. "There is no profit," said a factory farmer, "in eggs and hens unless one has 5,000 birds and works seven days a week."

In 1945 these eggs ended up in myriad small shops; in 1978 most went to supermarkets. Mass distribution and mass consumption went hand in hand. Marks and Spencer became the J. C. Penney of England, selling clothing of quality and style at low prices. Hand tailors lost out to men's stores with ready-made suits and polyester shirts. The more affluent substituted pressed gabardine trousers for the baggier woolens. There were also chain stores for electrical goods, stores gleaming with transistor radios, stereos, televisions, elegant lamps, radio-clocks, pocket calculators, and vacuum cleaners.

The production of such products was not the problem: the problem was to encourage their purchase, a job done with relish by mass advertisers and generous terms for installment buying. In 1954 commercial television arrived. Advertisers flocked to it with such zeal that one owner of a TV station called it a license to print money. The press, read far more widely than in any other country, grew fat on ads. In the 1960s the *Sunday Times*, *Observer*, and *Sunday Telegraph* began their colored magazine sections, three-fourths being bright, clever ads on how to lead the good life in the era of comfort.

To lead that life one needed a house. A smart flat with Swedish furniture might do until the children came along, or a working-class row house until promotion, and if no promotion still a chance, greatly increased by Mrs. Thatcher, to purchase one's rented council house. But the real ideal was a detached villa on a leafy road—or at least a semi-detached villa on a leafy road, and if not that, a modern row house at a new housing estate. And so the great trek went on to the suburbs. Some found beauty in mock-Tudor houses with half-timbered facades, others in neo-Victorian houses with oriel windows and gabled roofs. Builders in the 1950s built them as they had in the 1930s; only a few who made the great trek to the suburbs wanted contemporary houses of spare lines and much glass. But within these traditional houses, technology and the contemporary look made deep inroads. The television replaced the fireplace as the focus of the parlor, while in the kitchen refrigerators, washer-driers, electric stoves, garbage disposals, and frozen food lockers proclaimed the emancipation of the housewife. Stuffed sofas, bloated armchairs, and massive sideboards yielded to contemporary couches and chairs of metal, canvas, foam rubber, and fiberglass, all set around a glass coffee table.

To pay for this good life the wife had to work. Whereas in 1900 only one in ten did, by 1980 it was one in two. The new suburbanites also worked hard on their homes, with power saws and power drills humming and paint rollers making dull walls bright. But did this not, questioned the critics, destroy neighborliness, destroy the close intimacy of East End street life and the robust friendliness of the West End pub? Two sociologists, Peter Willmott and Michael Young, found that they did. Contact with parents and neighbors did continue in the new suburbs, though in different ways and less intensely: in the older neighborhood of Bethnal Green, 43 percent of couples saw one of their mothers

A British invention, the hovercraft has proven to be a great success for rapid crossings of the English Channel (*British Rail*).

daily; in the suburb of Woodford, 30 percent; while 31 percent in Bethnal Green and 30 percent in Woodford had weekly contacts. The Woodford couples were also friendly, but at clubs on weekends, not every day on the streets. The good life meant club life, whether tennis, church, political, flower arranging, or working men's. The clubs, along with television, the garden, and house improvement, left little time for the conviviality of pub or street life.

Suburban life was less lonely and fragmented than life in council housing, particularly in the new high-rises where the resident of flat 1005 cared nothing for the resident of flat 1006. For the people of Moss Side, in Manchester, the demolition of their Victorian row houses and streets and resettlement in huge, lifeless blocks of flats was devastating. Gone was the old corner shop, replaced in the plans for the new Alexandra Park with 1,408 dwellings and four shops. For the teenagers of Alexandra Park the good life meant immersion in the new world of consumption and pop culture, of record and clothing stores, of coffee bars and jazz cellars. Each year in the 1960s there were 5 million more teenagers. Most left school at 15 for good jobs. Since many lived at home, their pocketbooks bulged. In 1957 they spent £830 million on clothes, records,

Proliferating high-rises with scores of impersonal and anonymous flats (*Illustrated London News*).

musical instruments, and transistors. In the 1960s they spent far more as the gigantic world of commerce and advertising plied them with the endless products of the age's new demiurge, technology—small Italian motorscooters, large British motorcycles, smart shoes, flowered shirts, Edwardian frock coats, miniskirts, Italian blouses, beads, endless nylon tights, and endless recordings. From the technology of chemistry, if machines and electronics and textiles did not bring happiness, came amphetamines and LSD. For both teenagers and adults, the new technology ushered in an age of heightened hedonism. It was also to be an age of greater freedom though paradoxically also of authority.

FREEDOM AND AUTHORITY

In 1949 George Orwell envisioned in his novel *1984* a society in which a totalitarian state became everyone's watchful, spying Big Brother. When that ominous year arrived, it found the English little spied on and enjoying more freedom than ever. The state had, to be sure, grown larger, and its boards and police occasionally acted as Big Brother, but a Big Brother whose courts protected free speech and a free press and whose police guaranteed even the racist National Front the right of assembly. Big Brother also took part in a social, intellectual, and sexual revolution of astonishing and liberating proportions.

For many the sexual revolution meant a decay in moral standards that would bring a remorseless increase in extramarital sex and homosexuality. Moralists pointed to the rise of illegitimate births: in 1955 they amounted to only 4.7 percent of all births, in 1970 to 8.4 percent. Then there were stories of all-night teenage sex parties. Many of these stories were exaggerated; a study of women entering Durham University in 1970 showed 93 percent to be virgins. A later and broader study claimed that only 17 percent of 19-year-olds were virgins. Premarital sex was the rule, with marriage often following, a rule reflected in the fact that 60 percent of firstborns were conceived out of wedlock. Talk about sex, however, was much greater—a bold, unashamed, and free talk—in the press, in novels, at the theater, in films, at sex shops. The freedom to discuss sex openly, to view nakedness on the stage and in films, to feel unashamed about an illegitimate child, and to admit being homosexual lay at the heart of the sexual revolution and led to reforming laws. In 1959 Parliament allowed prostitutes, if they did not solicit on the streets, to ply their trade. Gamblers could also for the first time legally ply their trades, whether it was being a bookie or running a roulette wheel, and the government even joined in with state lotteries. Parliament in 1967 declared homosexual relations between consenting adults legal. In the 1960s the government ceased censoring the theatre and soon there were naked men and women on the stage, though very seldom. Pornography left the dingy, secretive back rooms of Soho for the carpeted front rooms of smart West End shops, shops full of everything a sex aficionado could desire. There were also unisex clothing shops, shops for homosexuals, and in 1977 three transvestite productions playing to full houses. London, but not the provinces, had become a free city, a city in which one could buy and wear anything one wished, since there was also a clothes revolution in the 1960s, what with miniskirts for women and colorful shirts for men. Long hair, enormous moustaches, and bushy beards were also popular.

Educators also were exuberant about freedom. The prewar days of chanted multiplication tables, rote learning, dictatorial teachers, and the birch were gone; in their place came open curriculums, free discovery, experimental methods, spontaneity, permissiveness, and finger-painting. The critics said the new progressives neglected reading and writing for finger-painting, though the Plowden

Committee in 1967 found that 11-year-olds in 1964 read as well as 12½-year-olds had in 1948.

Women, too, wanted freedom. In 1947 only 1 percent of women had higher education and 18 percent jobs, abortions were illegal and divorces rare as the only reason for them was proven adultery, and wages and salaries were well below those of men for the same job.

By 1978 much had changed. More than half of women 20 to 45 had jobs, most were educated beyond 15 years of age, and abortion was legal. The Divorce Act of 1969 made a marriage's breakdown grounds for divorce: by the 1980s one in three marriages ended in divorce. The Equal Pay Act of 1970 finally

Free, equal, and anything but deferential are these Teddy boys, the product of the affluent fifties (*Radio Times*).

Greater equality came through comprehensive schools where the working and middle class children received education suitable to their talents (*Aerofilms*).

stated that women should have equal pay with men for the same job, although more often than not the law was not enforced and the pay was not equal. Women debated in the Oxford Union, became jockeys, made up 73 percent of radiologists, and substantial percentages of other professions. Yet they still constituted only a fraction of the lawyers, doctors, executives, and MPs. Women had only dented a centuries-old masculine world, but many of them believed time was on their side.

Freedom came in all the interstices of society and arose for many reasons, one of the main being a markedly more humane view of criminals, the insane, drug addicts, and the down and out. In 1969 Parliament ended capital punishment, and in 1967 the home secretary ordered no more birching in industrial schools and reformatories. In 1970 the home office used paroles, probation, and sentences of supervision to give England's criminals the shortest prison sentences among industrial societies. The experiment worked: only 8 percent of those on parole committed crimes. Government commissioners also saw that one out of five mental patients were released each year, while government clinics gave heroin addicts free shots and psychiatric care. Views on mental illness and crime also became more flexible. The Scottish psychiatrist R. D. Laing argued that many of the causes of mental illness lay with the patient's environment—with other people—and not the failure of his reason, while criminologists increasingly described criminals as socially deviant, not wicked.

Technology, wealth, state benefits to poor families, urban anonymity, demanding shop stewards, persistent women, sit-ins, all played a liberating role by increasing mobility, offering alternative securities, and insisting loudly and defiantly on individual rights. "The days of deference have disappeared," said a leading businessman, "no manager in his senses tries to run a company by dictate from above."

Although freedom advanced in many of the interstices of society, it did not do so in government. Government under Mrs. Thatcher grew more arbitrary and secret, far more so than with the Presidency of the United States, a Presidency decisively checked by Congress and the Supreme Court. In England ministers, departments, and administrative tribunals were relatively free of law courts since their judges were Thatcher appointees and their power of review limited. The government was also relatively free of the House of Commons since not only was its majority Tory and loyal, but one-sixth of its MPs held well-paying offices given them by the Prime Minister. There was not much the government could not do. It could, for example, forbid the BBC television from showing interviews of members of the Irish Republican Army, could jail foreign office clerks for leaks about missiles, and could grant its intelligence service total secrecy. Serious scholars even claimed that England no longer enjoyed a government under law.

EQUALITY AND INEQUALITY

Serious sociologists also claimed that England still fell far short of its egalitarian ideals, that it was in fact still deeply unequal and class ridden. From 1381 when John Ball asked, "When Adam delved and Eve did span, who was then the gentleman" to the promises of the Attlee and Wilson Labour governments the ideal of equality has possessed millions of the English. But quite as deeply rooted in a hierarchical, property owning society was the reality of inequality—and between that ideal and that reality there has been an unending struggle.

In that struggle equality has advanced, though slowly and incompletely. It has done so in three ways in the twentieth century: first the labor shortages of two world wars brought to wage earners a larger slice of the cake; second, from 1900 to 1980 the cake grew three times larger, bringing more out of poverty and into a modest competence; and third, the welfare state in taxing the rich and helping the needy has redistributed some of the wealth. Of the three ways, the two wars proved the most decisive. The cake has, to be sure, grown larger, but larger too were the slices to the rich. Indeed since the 1950s the slices of the rich were proportionally larger than the increased slices to the working classes. The welfare state's redistribution of wealth was also not huge: in the 1980s before taxes, the top fifth received 47 percent, after taxes 39.4 percent of the market income, while before welfare payments the bottom fifth received but .4 percent of market income, and after payments only 6.9 percent. Much of the welfare state was not designed to promote equality. Its large educational grants, especially to universities, favor the rich, and many of its old age, sickness, and jobless payments are greater to those better paid employees who put more into these social insurance schemes.

The educational system in particular perpetuated inequality. Before World War II society spent seven times more on the education of the sons of the professional and managerial class than on the sons of agricultural laborers; after World War II it still favored the professionals by six times. Manual workers constitute half of the population, and yet only 5 percent of their children go to university and a full 40 percent leave school with no qualifications whatever, not even in car repair or plumbing. Fifty-four percent of those going to university came from a professional and managerial class that constitutes only 18 percent of the population while 64 percent of those going to Oxford and Cambridge hail from private schools that only the rich could afford. Even the fact that 70 percent of secondary schools are comprehensive has not promoted much equality since the richer suburbs have far better schools than the poorer. The tax and salary structure under Mrs. Thatcher has also increased inequality: from 1977 to 1984 the real income of the white-collar class rose 16 percent and the real income of the unskilled fell 9.9 percent.

But not all is inequality. Society's grand hotel is larger and mobility on its elevators brisker. The Edwardian hotel had elegant penthouses for its aristocrats and plutocrats—some 3 or 4 percent of its population—comfortable rooms for the next third, and barely adequate to inadequate cellars for the varied poor; Thatcher's hotel abounds in balcony suites for the top fifth which own and receive around 40 percent of the wealth, comfortable rooms for the next two-fifths, and dismal cellars for the inner city's small but underemployed and unprivileged underclass. Growing affluence and technology has opened up a larger world of affluent professional, managerial, technical, and administrative careers: a world of pilots, programmers, broadcasters, radiologists, TV producers, sales managers, engineers, draftsmen, and plant foremen, few of whom had attended Oxford and Cambridge, yet many of whom felt equal to such graduates since they too could live on leafy roads, drive Jaguars, join tennis clubs, and shop at smart boutiques. To the extent that the Thatcher hotel was open to merit and talent, England became a more open and mobile society; but to the extent that the merit and talent arose from unequal class and educational backgrounds, it was a closed society.

In fact it fell somewhere between. Fifty-five percent remained in the class into which they were born, while 45 percent left their class of origins, a few to fall into a lower class, most to go upward since the cake had tripled in size. The mobility was greatest from the lower middle class to the upper middle, the least from the less well-educated working class. Greatly helping the bright and energetic were 42 universities, the new polytechnics with a curriculum of university quality, and upgraded colleges that grew out of technical schools, schools of art and teacher training colleges. There was also the Open University whose 50,000 students viewed lectures on TV, received readings and lessons by mail, and attended class discussions run by local part time tutors. But with all this effort Britain still offered higher education to only 20 percent of its 18-year-olds compared to 75 percent in the United States. And even when the working- and lower-middle-class youth won scholarships to polytechnics and universities, it only resulted in their leaving their own class and assuming the life-style of their superiors, much as the sons of coarse Tudor yeomen rose to become polished Stuart gentry. Individuals were mobile, but class inequalities remained; the elevators went up and down, but the balcony suites were still far more posh than the cellars.

Some of the most luxurious suites were also open to the least aristocratic. High incomes knew no class barriers. George Best, the soccer star, and the Beatles, earned far more than did earls and dukes. Equality and mobility did not bring, as its critics feared, democratic blight, phillistinism, mediocrity, and the end of class: in a 1972 survey 69.8 percent said they were working class and of those 93 percent said a class system did exist. It was, however, a different class system from the old, a system where workers too pursued the true and the beautiful.

TRUTH AND BEAUTY

Just as the British of 1978 were wealthier, freer, and more mobile than ever before, so they were more active than ever in searching for truth and creating and enjoying beauty. That they had discovered the essence of truth and the essence of beauty they would deny. Yet if pressed they might admit that the educated Briton knew many more truths about the world—multifarious and fragmented though they were—than did their ancestors. Knowledge of all sorts was as abundant as nylons and transistors. Though it poured forth from the new media, from television, radio, films, records, its main form still remained the printed word. The British, more than any other people, love to read. In the 1950s they read more newspapers per person than the citizens of any other country. They also devoured books. One of every two was a book reader, and he or she averaged twenty books a year, placing Britain first among the six leading democracies. To help assuage this appetite, the government in 1974 spent £12.2 million on libraries and local authorities even more. But far more exciting than larger libraries was the arrival of the paperback in the 1950s. There was scarcely a subject in the world not covered by them. Nonfiction sold as briskly as fiction; accounts of the creation of the universe vied with accounts of the evolution of life.

For those too lazy to read about evolution, there was television. In January 1976 the BBC told of the discovery of "mitochondria," an internal organelle found in every living cell, though not in the cell's nucleus, where the DNA molecule was. Only a few years earlier TV had reported the discovery of DNA, the molecule that controls the reproduction of all cells and by its code determines all inherited characteristics. Scientists now found DNA had lost its monopoly as the sole determinant of inheritance. Since mitochondria can also be influenced by its environment, there suddenly appeared a loophole for the reemergence of Lamarckian ideas. A TV critic called the program "far and away the most exciting thing of the week . . . a soaring, mind-wrenching, speculation." Millions had learned a truth unknown to Darwin.

For those who wished to do more than look and listen, there were adult education classes in biology, sociology, history, and many other subjects, classes attended by one in seven of those between 30 and 40. The government in offering these classes made some amends for the sad deficiencies of English higher education. England, of course, had had such deficiencies for two centuries and yet had also produced one of the most literate of peoples. That the two characteristics coexisted is a paradox explicable only by the fact of self-education. In the 1970s, though only a few went to the university, all could buy paperbacks, attend adult education classes, and visit libraries, which they did in greater numbers than in any other country.

The result of this education and self-education was an unprecedented knowledge of one's own society, of one's past, and of the physical world. The English had numerous journalists, pollsters, sociologists, and statisticians to thank for the fact that they knew so much. A Victorian millhand knew little about what farmhands and bankers thought and did, of the problems facing Britain, or of the probable outcome of a coming election. The Victorian banker also knew little about the millhand or farmhand or of coming elections. By the 1950s, this had changed. The millhand could now know about both the coming elections and the views of bankers by reading the endless polls evening newspapers ran. The banker could also read the many reports drawn up by the 315 statisticians at the Government Statistical Office (140 more than in 1966) and the proliferating studies of sociologists.

They also knew far more about their past. The most historical-minded of peoples, the English in 1980 knew more of their origins than ever, and were more active than ever in increasing it. Sir John Neale's *Elizabeth and Her Parliaments* and G. R. Elton's *The Tudor Revolution in Government* gave their readers a close, detailed, accurate view of the inner politics of that glorious century. Sir Lewis Namier and his co-workers at the government-sponsored History of Parliament Project were writing detailed biographies of every person who ever sat in Parliament—an astonishing project, but only a small part of an avalanche of history books, both scholarly and popular, piling up in libraries and studies.

The British also wrote copiously about how to think clearly, an art that had become the central concern of British philosophy. Ludwig Wittgenstein, an Austrian-born Cambridge University don, had died in 1951, but his works still reigned supreme, only with a difference: whereas in the 1920s he argued that rigorous logic would produce propositions that corresponded to the structure of the external world, he now saw propositions as related to one another in groups or systems, each group having its own rules or grammar. The move was to a more subjective view of the world. The function of the philosopher was to make clear distinctions about the language and grammar of philosophical discourse, distinctions John Austin and Gilbert Ryle at Oxford and John Wisdom at Cambridge drew with a brilliance and imagination that made the school of linguistic analysis the dominant school in Britain and America.

The British also excelled in astronomy and physics, fields in which their discoveries were as "mind-wrenching" as those made by the British biologist Francis Crick and the American J. D. Watson when, working together at Cambridge University, they described the DNA molecule. Physicists continued their examination of the atom. To the long-known electron, proton, and neutron, they added pions, kaons, lambdas, sigmas, omegas, and other particles—a bewildering world whose infinite forces would supply the world's energy or blow it up. Astronomers described the earth's galaxy as spiral in form and rotating, a galaxy in which the sun was 27,000 light years from the center. It took the sun 270 years to make one full revolution of its galaxy. Some British astronomers argued that since this and other galaxies sped apart in the ever-expanding universe, there occurred a constant creation of matter, of new galaxies, to fill the void. Instead of a single creation, there is a constant trickle of creation. Other astronomers disagreed, arguing that the universe is not steadily creating itself, but was created by a great explosion which is now dissipating. They suggest that those strong distant radio sources called quasars, whose energy is of unprecedented magnitude, came from a far distant past. As fascinating as quasars were the universe's black holes whose extremely dense matter and powerful gravity prevented even light from escaping. At its very edge, its horizon, particles are created out of empty space and are emitted as radiation into the universe. Cambridge's brilliant physicist Stephen Hawkins, by a mathematical analysis of how these subatomic particles—the stuff of quantum mechanics—relate to black holes and the universe—the stuff of relativity—seeks that "Grand Unification" of relativity and quantum mechanics that Einstein sought but failed to discover. From DNA and kaons to quasars and black holes, the discoveries of science revealed a majestic, mysterious, awesome, and puzzling world, but an extraordinarily complex and varying one. As truths multiplied, the essence of truth grew elusive, a fate even more true of beauty.

Beauty is a dangerously subjective word, yet one whose widespread use attests to its reality. It would be hazardous to judge British buildings, furniture, interiors, cars, clothing, posters, shop windows—the environment of urban life—as more beautiful in 1980 than 1954, yet it would also be hazardous to deny the fact that never have so many Britons in so many ways sought to make their environment and culture more beautiful. Parliament in 1974 voted £50 million in grants to art galleries, opera houses, theaters, ballet companies, and painters and sculptors, four times more than in 1964. Local authorities also spent heavily on the arts, giving £12 million to museums and much more to architects who were to design public buildings.

In the 1950s avant garde architects like Peter and Allison Smithson and James Stirling judged most buildings, including the sleek Festival Hall of 1951 and the prettified public housings at Roehampton, as mediocre. They were mediocre because they compromised the bold, clean lines of modern architecture by adding the fussy decorative lines of the English picturesque. By the 1960s much of the picturesque had been abandoned, but only for the routine glass, boxlike high-rises of the international style, slabs that were dull compared with the Smithson's school at Hunstanton, Norfolk, or Stirling's Ham Common housing estate. The horizontal and vertical lines of Hunstanton integrate a basic symmetry with a geometric variety that is as pleasing as an eighteenth-century Palladian house It was also attractive in the frankness with which it left uncovered its steel frame and concrete, its pipes and rafters. For this frankness, critics called it part of the "new brutalism," a term also applied to Stirling because he left his concrete and interior brick uncovered. The exquisite harmonies of his windows and his imaginative use of materials won him international acclaim, as did his Sheffield Engineering building, with its geodesic-like skylights and cantilevered concrete buttresses. The row of skylights seemed like waves moving back and forth. Stirling and the Smithsons and others have proved that British architects could, like Christopher Wren, design works of great force and beauty.

English painting, in the decade after the war, maintained both its own traditions—as in the war and nature paintings of Graham Sutherland—and adapted to the latest styles from New York and Paris—surrealism, futurism, abstract expressionism. For some irreverent young painters like Richard Hamilton, Peter Blake, and Peter Philips, works in these borrowed styles seemed pompous, dry, academic, irrelevant. They wanted something lively, bright, earthy, and relevant, and so they (along with their peers in New York) created pop art. Hamilton in his ironical, playful "Hommage à Chrysler Corp.," found beauty in a car's front end, full of bulbous, breastlike forms and, said one critic, "Voluptua's lips." The pop artist loved the everyday world of technology, commerce, advertising, films, and sex—hence the miscellany of images, the pinups, postcards, cartoon heroes, film stars, machines, stockings, flags, and decals, images rendered graphic and blatant by bright, assertive colors and hard lines and made amusing and fun by parody and mimicry.

Pop artists were the masters of the collage, of finding beauty in a grab bag of objects. Peter Blake uses photographs of Elvis Presley in his bright and happy "Got a Girl," while Peter Philips in "Custom Painting No. 2" combines bumpers, pistons, pinup girls, and chemical works into a snapshot of the age of technology. Pop art was for the people; it could be reproduced, photographed,

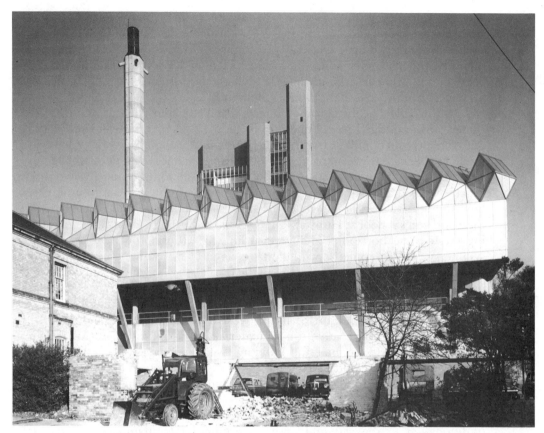

The engineering building at Leicester University, designed by James Stirling (*Archi-techts Journal*).

and even put on film, as it was in "Pop Goes the Easel," which delighted TV audiences in 1962. Its sprightly images also appeared on posters, advertisements, record covers, and book jackets. Only a few rich bought Joshua Reynolds's portraits in the eighteenth century and only a few hundred bourgeois Victorians bought engravings, but in 1960s millions bought pop art on record covers and saw it on subway posters.

Clothing too responded to a new zest for bright, beautiful things. In 1956 Mary Quant, from a Welsh working-class family, opened her Bazaar, a store full of low-priced, stylish, colorful, original clothes of her design. Other smart boutiques followed, and men's shops as well. Suddenly women appeared in miniskirts a full five inches above the knee and men in thigh-hugging, tapering trousers, and both with flowered shirts and beads. Then the pursuit of beauty through pop art dissipated, as its playful creators expected. Pop art was, said Richard Hamilton, "popular, transient, expendable low cost, mass-produced, young, witty, sexy, gimmicky, glamourous, and Big Business."

"Got a Girl" by Peter Blake (*The Whitworth Art Gallery, Manchester University*).

As ephemeral as pop art was op art, even the op art of its supreme practitioner, Bridget Riley. Riley, like other op artists sought geometric beauty. She used many parallel lines to produce secondary patterns that, though made solely of straight lines, appear to form curves which pulsate, forming waves that appear and disappear and appear. Her labyrinthine patterns sometimes give a sense of continuous movement, sometimes a sense of solidity, and sometimes the visual sense of heat, but always a pleasing formal grandeur, though one tinged with an uncomfortable vertigo. Op art has also become less fashionable. Bridget Riley's geometric patterns and James Stirling's geodesic forms have not captured the quintessence of beauty, no more than eighteenth-century Palladian architecture and Reynold's natural laws. Riley and Stirling and the twentieth century never expected they would. Yet if the essence of beauty escaped the pop artists, there was in its endless forms and experiments all kinds of beauty.

The architects, to be sure, could not end urban blight and there were many undistinguished buildings and much strip development, yet Britain was a brighter and more varied place in which to live. Beauty in all the arts was alive. Thousands attended Britain's twenty-six provincial repertory theaters, all founded since 1962. London's theater, the best in the world, prospered. Covent Garden, home of the opera and ballet, played to 96 percent capacity, and there was more opera and ballet elsewhere. In 1974 the new Hayward Gallery on the South Bank, massive and handsome, displayed to packed crowds the works of 122 contemporary British painters. In 1975 a book on British composers of music discussed the works of 100 British composers born since 1900. Both groups were but the tip of the iceberg of painters and musicians. There were some giants among them—in music, Benjamin Britten and Vaughan Williams; in sculpture, Henry Moore and Barbara Hepworth. The British love music, whether in their superb choral societies, distinguished civic symphonies, skilled jazz groups, or world famous pop groups. No one any longer pretended to know what beauty was, but the word was on more British lips than ever before, as they pursued it in all its fragmented and endlessly varying forms. For many it was also an escape from poverty.

THE POOR WILL ALWAYS BE WITH US

The agricultural and industrial revolutions offered humankind the opportunity of defying the biblical injunction that the poor will always be with us. The Victorians by moral reform, the twentieth century by socialism, and both by exploiting technology sought to banish poverty, but as of 1990 the poor were still in the land. Despite huge gains in productivity, neglect, the unequal distribution of wealth, and a more exacting standard of poverty meant that there were in Britain between 1 and 2 million poor. The government, having defined officially a level of poverty, found that in 1978 10 percent fell below it. By the mid-1980s that percentage rose as unemployment rose to 13 percent.

Unemployment, unofficially far greater, was the blight of the 1980s. The government, to be sure, paid the rents and rates of the unemployed and £21 a week for single men and £30 for couples if on supplementary benefits and more if on unemployment insurance benefits. For half of school leavers it was unemployment, supplementary benefits, and a corroding hopelessness, and hopelessness too for older men laid off from decaying industries. Another source of poverty were the three quarters of a million one-parent families with dependent children. Easier divorces, increasing illegitimacy, and more abandoned families all meant that thousands of children had only one parent at home and that usually a mother unable to hold a job because of the children. The result was the fact that a third of all the poor were children. The government's supplementary family income mitigated, but did not remove, this poverty, just as its pensions mitigated, but did not end, the wretchedness of the old. Old age was still, as it had always been, the main source of poverty. Fifteen percent of the people were over 65 and 36 percent of them lived alone, many in penury. Food and clothing they had, though some at the barest, but not most amenities. Dire poverty had receded: a 1968 survey showed the real income of the poor was 60 percent higher than in 1948.

But life was still dismal, a fact that largely arose from dismal housing. From Disraeli to Callaghan, governments had promised better housing—but, when built, it went largely to the affluent workers, leaving the poor in privately owned houses like those of Sunderland, where in the 1960s nine in ten had no indoor toilet, three in four no bath, and one in two not even cold water. A 1968 survey listed 1.8 million houses in England as uninhabitable and 4.5 million as lacking in amenities or in need of repairs—a staggering 40 percent of all houses. For thirty years the government spent millions to subsidize the mortgages of the salaried middle classes and the council rents of the well-paid wage earner (both heavy voters at elections) while neglecting the slums where the bottom two million lived in overcrowded, dilapidated tenements. In 1970 some 28,000 were not even lucky enough to have slum dwellings and had to tell local authorities they were homeless, a 15 percent increase over the previous year. Despite legal obligations to find them a home, authorities found houses for only 5,630. Many of the rest, out of desperation, became squatters. Any building emptied in preparation for demolition was open game for the homeless. In the London borough of Lambeth, 60 percent of the squatters were families with children. When evicted, as they were, they were again homeless.

There were also Britain's 50,000 gypsies and 42,000 prisoners. The gypsies, intensely familial, lacked sites for their caravans; the prisoners, anchored to a site, knew no family life. A local authority's usual response was to move the gypsies on and make no sites available. The government's response to prisoners was also harsh. It allowed a prisoner only one half-hour visit a month and one letter out a week. The overcrowding was also intense, the worst occurring if one were judged criminally insane, which meant assignment to the 110-year-old Broadmoor Hospital, where 691 prisoners were crowded into wards built for 500. The result was corridors filled with beds and day rooms with patients. The prisoners were a despised and forgotten minority. But far more ominous was British hatred for a larger minority, most of whom were poor: the new immigrants from the West Indies, Pakistan, India, and Bangladesh.

Blacks and Asians made up 4.4 percent of the population. They lived in miserable tenements, had the worst jobs, sent their children to the poorest schools, and suffered from racial prejudice. The chances of a black or Asian living in a house judged uninhabitable was twice that of whites. For the West Indians, who made up almost all the blacks in Britain, conditions were the worst. Two-thirds of them suffered from bad housing or unemployment or both. Many lived in conditions reminiscent of Victorian slums, with a husband, wife, and four children living in one room. One in five households had an unemployed male, most of them teenagers who had dropped out of school at 13 or 14 woefully uneducated. Drifting about London or Liverpool, 40 percent of them unemployed, some of these young blacks turned to pilfering and drugs, and most to loitering and disturbance. The police, feeling harassed, harassed them in turn. Tensions rose and in April 1981, in Brixton in South London, they rioted and looted and burned. It was not a race riot; nor were other riots that swept over several English towns in July 1981, except that in Southall which was led by white racist skinheads. The others were an explosion of white and black youth, youth without jobs, jealous of the extravagant wealth others enjoyed, and angry at neglect, a neglect vividly reflected in the crumbling houses and streets of their decaying inner cities—and no doubt, as Tory critics said, a crumbling of morality and discipline.

The Asians had closer-knit families and were more insistent that their children do well in school. While blacks ran London's transport and hospitals, the Asians worked in Lancashire textile mills and Midland iron works—as well as in hospitals and transport. Employers, allied with skilled white workers, denied the Asians skilled and supervising jobs, put them on night shifts, and dismissed them first in recessions. Asians also faced housing discrimination; some 21,000 Pakistanis had to live in the slums of Bradford. It was one of the most isolated immigrant communities in Britain, one where old customs persevered, including keeping wives indoors at all times, so that for them life in socialist Britain was the four walls of a slum house. That primitive custom was not the fault of the British—their fault was an equally primitive racial prejudice, one that led to signs on homes for sale saying TO BE SOLD ONLY TO WHITES, and to the emergence of the National Front.

It is unlikely that the National Front will ever become a national party that could threaten the Tories or Labour party—it averages only 4.6 percent at the polls. It is also likely that the Front will not fade away, not as long as the growing numbers of Asians and blacks strike fear in the parochial and narrow-minded British. Where there are many Asians and blacks, there is racial prejudice. Signs on flats read "No Pakis." In the East End 300 "Benghis" who were denied flats became squatters simply to get out of the rain and cold. Leather-jacketed youths on motor bikes boasted of "Paki bashing." One Asian woman in the East End recorded 100 instances where attacks by whites sent Asians to hospitals. She called pleas for help from white neighbors or town councilors vain and foolish, as vain and foolish as expecting police brutality to end. The government in 1977 created a Race Relations Board, but under Mrs. Thatcher it has been quiescent before the stubborn racial prejudice of the British.

The social composition of socialist Britain varied greatly. There was not only the gap between the banker with a country home and £30,000 a year and the jobless Pakistani squatter, but the gap between most wage earners and the black, jobless youth or an old-age pensioner. The dominant reality for the great majority was increasing wealth, freedom, equality, and cultural opportunities. Since the majority were doing well, they tended to forget the poor, a tendency the government did not oppose since the poor had few votes. No review of the buoyant progress most Britons enjoyed should obscure the fact that the poor were still in the land. But neither should a look at the poor distort the awareness that life grew better for the majority. For most Britons it was not poverty but prosperity that they would have to endure. It was a prosperity that, along with advanced technology, expanded education, and the new freedoms, collided with old orthodoxies and elites and defined the moods and ideas of postwar Britain.

THE CONTENTED AND ANGRY 1950s, THE SWINGING 1960s

In 1956 John Osborne, in his play *Look Back in Anger*, told the story of Jimmy Porter, a university dropout from the working class who found upward mobility into a society of middle-class respectability and into an age without noble causes bitterly frustrating. The play delighted affluent audiences. In 1956 the architects the Smithsons and the pop artist Richard Hamilton helped mount an exposition called "This Is Tomorrow," an iconoclastic blow at reigning architectural styles and one of the first pop art shows in the world. In 1960 came the first issue of the radical *New Left Review*. The historian E. P. Thompson, the literary critic Raymond Williams, and the novelist Doris Lessing brought to its editorial board great distinction and not a little anger at society's injustices. In 1961 John Lennon, Paul McCartney, George Harrison, and Peter Best, all from Liverpool's working classes, brought their heavy rock beat to Liverpool's Cavern under the name of the Beatles. In the same year Alan Bennet, Peter Cook, Dudley Moore, and Jonathan Miller, all from Oxford or Cambridge, presented at Edinburgh the funniest satire on British life since the war. And in 1962 Mick Jagger, Brian Jones, and Keith Richards started the Rolling Stones, a group that gave powerful expression to the frustrations felt by the Jimmy Porters of the world. From 1956 to 1962, from Oxford common rooms to Liverpool jazz cellars, from college dons to art school dropouts, an extraordinarily restive, rebellious, and creative mood swept England, a mood critics also discerned in the novels written by John Wain, Alan Sillitoe, and John Braine, the first of the angry young men.

To these young writers and artists the ideas, art forms, and attitudes that dominated the decade after 1945 were sterile, facile, and cloying, a charge that would have astonished the middle classes in the late 1940s, who regarded Graham Sutherland in painting, Henry Moore in sculpture, and Vaughan Williams in music as creative artists of the first order. In the late 1940s British drama also seemed of the first order. The verse plays of T. S. Eliot and Christopher Fry promised a renaissance of poetic drama. Fry's *The Lady's Not for Burning* in 1948 and his *Venus Observed* in 1950 were packed with dazzling verse, deliciously witty phrases, spirited comedy, and a pleasant melancholy. T. S. Eliot's *Cocktail Party* in 1949 offered a more subdued verse, but with Eliot's usual crispness, incisiveness, and angularity.

Fry's and Eliot's messages did not disturb their high-brow audience, no more than Henry Moore's lyrical forms or Vaughan Williams's pastoral harmonies. Fry told his audiences of Romans, Jutes, and medieval Englishmen, and of the passing of a noble and leisured world, offering as solace for that loss religion, resignation, and bright verse. Eliot also invoked religion and tradition, only more somberly. He argued in the *Cocktail Party* that people must look to the support of society and religion to hold their lives together in a world where democracy, skepticism, and hedonism threaten both old verities and the elites who guarded these verities. Equally delightful to the upper class was Evelyn Waugh's *Brideshead Revisited*, a novel written in 1945 that defended Toryism and Catholicism against socialism and skepticism. The late 1940s saw the last efflorescence of a traditional culture—nostalgic, secure, and conservative, one that could hardly accept the futuristic and technological promises which found expression in the Festival of Britain of 1951. The Labour government was determined that Britain should celebrate the one-hundredth birthday of the Great Exhibition and show the world it was still inventive and strong.

The Festival of Britain was held on the south bank of the Thames. Its Dome of Discovery was crammed with radar, jet engines, and ancient steam engines, all monuments to an undiminished technological genius. Its other buildings were filled with British products, mostly done in a contemporary style, light, airy, suave, and clever. These designs, and the designs of the buildings, delighted the 8.5 million who attended. "The people," said the *Times*, "are in a joyous mood." Up the Thames, at the Battersea Pleasure Gardens, there was also joy as 8 million visitors ate candy floss and rode a whimsically designed tiny railway. The festival was, observed one Englishman, "a rainbow—a brilliant sign riding the tail of the storm and promising fairer weather. It marked the ending of the hungry forties and the beginning of an altogether easier decade."

The sun had broken through the clouds of austerity and announced the new Elizabethan era. In 1953 the British celebrated another glorious festival, the coronation of Queen Elizabeth II. The death of George VI in 1952 marked the end of an Edwardian ethos that, battered and ridiculed, had proved durable, surviving one general strike, one depression, two wars and, almost, socialism. The future was with the affluent, multiplying, various middle classes and the 1950s was to be their decade, not one of creative art but of a rising gross national product.

Those most ancient of documents on the holding of a coronation say that it should be in the sight of all. Never were these instructions more fully carried out than in May 1953 when, on television, half the people of Britain watched earls in ermine and the Queen in diamonds march into Westminster Abbey. It was a coronation that promised another Elizabethan Age. The spirit of Drake and Raleigh still lived. The press that morning had announced that the British had made the first ascent of Mount Everest.

The people, with their new council houses, rising incomes, suburbias, Morrises, and Austins, enjoyed the new Elizabethan Age. They believed those who said they had never had it so good. Even the poets and novelists did not disturb the age's contentment with affluence and festivals. The poetry of F. W. Bateson, John Holloway, and Kingsley Amis avoided romantic anxieties and the obscurities of experimental forms, offering instead lucid verse in the rational eighteenth-century manner. "See, Pope, 'tis science holds the Muses hand/As laughing Ceres re-assumes the land." So wrote Bateson, with Kingsley Amis following in praise of an anti-romantic, anti-modern, anti-bohemian esthetic. In his very popular novels, particularly in *Lucky Jim* (1954), Amis uses the traditional modes of moral comedy and social realism to warn against intellectual pretensions and to celebrate the simple pleasures of life. Novels, he told the contented 1950s, were to be enjoyed, an argument the public accepted by making Nevil Shute Britain's best-selling novelist. Shute wrote exciting tales of airlines in Persia and forest fires in Australia, all replete with the newest technology.

The mood of the affluent 1950s was scientific, not romantic, pragmatic, not idealistic, just as it was complacent, hedonistic, bourgeois, and conservative. It was the decade of the ambitious, rising, conforming organization man, the suburban nine-to-fiver who sought contentment in musicals, a Shute novel, television, and the new Italian bistro. It was a pervasive, powerful mood and added a rocklike strata to British life. It was a mood that was anathema to Jimmy Porter, the *New Left Review*, and the Stones, and amusing and pompous to the Beatles, pop artists, and the four satirists of *Beyond the Fringe*. To the young in the late 1950s it seemed sterile, smug, irrelevant, trivial, and smothering; it drove them to want noise, excitement, activity, and daring.

The swinging 1960s began as an angry, generational revolt against the staid 1950s, a revolt that announced itself noisily in Osborne's very angry Jimmy Porter. Jimmy Porter went to a provincial university, married into the upper middle class, demonstrated his brilliance, and had great promise, yet he quit university, settled in dingy quarters, ran a candy shop, and declared verbal war on the very class that could have given him success. But the success called for servitude and fell short of that assured those from Oxford and Cambridge. John Braine's *Room at the Top* in 1957 expressed the same embittered class feeling of those who moved up into a tenaciously hierarchical society, a society that was also crass, competitive, ruthless, hypocritical, and cynical. Braine's hero uses those qualities to get to the top; the uncompromising Jimmy Porter rejects them with scathing vehemence. Alan Sillitoe's *Loneliness of the Long Distance Runner* and John Wain's *Hurry on Down* (1953) also express the frustration that working- and lower-middle-class youths met in trying to find a place in a new, rapidly changing, semi-mobile, moneyed, hierarchical society without certain standards and values. The loss of belief is particularly galling to Jimmy Porter. He laments both the loss of Victorian ideals—"Reason and Progress, the old firm is selling out"—and the political causes of the 1930s: "People of our generation aren't able to die for good causes any longer, we had that done for us in the thirties and forties."

Arnold Wesker dramatized this frustration in *The Kitchen*, a play about enslavement in a large restaurant and the exploitations of mass culture. Wesker saw in education and socialism a way out, and to hasten such opened an experimental theater for the working class. It was a flop. The workers wanted no socialist theater; they wanted flashy clothes, motorcycles, and Elvis Presley records. The young were in revolt against their parents and against stifling secondary modern schools. They wanted to plunge into a world made bright by electronics and plastics and the new rhythms of rock and roll. Working-class youth cared nothing for Osborne or Wesker, everything about the beat from America that the Rolling Stones fused so brilliantly with music hall sounds and with words and sounds of anger, vehemence, aggressiveness, and dark menace. In "Street Fighting Man," Jagger cries out, "My name is disturbance, I'll shout and scream, I'll kill the king." Jimmy Porter could hardly flay the square world more mercilessly than the Stones, and the mods and rockers, those teenage working-class Cockneys who emerged in the 1960s and exulted in it. The mods were passionate about elegant, rather feminine clothes, wore long hair, and took drugs; the leather-jacketed rockers were more manly, more heterosexual, more violent. Reinforced later by long-haired hippies from the middle class, they all formed an avid audience for the Stones, the Beatles, and the commercialism that always lay behind the swinging 1960s.

Mick Jagger, Brian Jones, and Keith Richards, the core of the Stones, were all middle-class, all university or college dropouts, all children of prosperity. They did not, like Wesker and the socialists of the 1930s, offer a magnanimous lament for the losers, but exploded with the angry cries of the half-successful and the frustrated among the successful, a cry that led 100,000 of them, most of them with full wallets and a good or fair education, to Hyde Park in 1968 to shout in sympathy as Mick Jagger sang his "Sympathy with the Devil."

Far more than anger lay behind the swinging 1960s. Indeed the Beatles, along with rock musicians, pop artists, poets, and the young of all sorts in flowered shirts and long hair, celebrated life far more joyously than did the angry young men of the 1950s. Riding the crest of three giant waves—economic affluence, social freedom, and a baby boom come of age—they found life worth singing and dancing about. Even their affluent parents joined in that exuberant consumerism and hedonism that underlay much of that swinging London that blossomed around boutiques, smart men's shops, coffee houses, jazz clubs, record shops and art galleries.

But it was the young who were the most joyously carried away by present delights and rising expectations. The great puritan "No!" was melting away and, where heard, was outvoted by a youth far more numerous than any equivalent older age group. Prohibitions were out, permissiveness in: pleasure extolled, freedom exalted, and love everywhere affirmed. The Beatles above all celebrated, almost as a ritual, the adolescents' new way of life, the free, loving happiness of togetherness, their early song "She Loves You" ending with the affirmative "Yeah, Yeah, Yeah!" Swinging London was a happy, liberated, world, one the Rolling Stones also celebrated, and one that gave the swinging 1960s a zest, an exuberance, a whimsy, a humor, and later a melancholy that blossomed in 1967 in the Beatles' record, *Sergeant Pepper's Lonely Hearts Club Band*. "It's wonderful to be here," they sang, "You're such a lovely audience. We'd like to take you home with us." The last thought had long sent thousands of girls into a

The miniskirt, like pop music, expressed a swinging, sexually freer age (*UP*).

frenzy of screaming, into Beatlemania. Not all was sexual with the Beatles, as it was not all anger with the Stones, for in both complexity and quality, the music and lyrics grew stronger and deeper.

The Beatles' *Penny Lane* of 1966, a teasing, whimsical satire of a suburban shopping center, was far superior to the earlier heavy rock recordings, as was *Sergeant Pepper*, which one critic said proved "conclusively that pop can be both art and pop, immediate and timeless." The same critic called the Stones' music as seminal as the Beatles'. Much in the 1960s was indeed seminal. In music, painting, clothing, writing, and life-styles, thousands created new forms. For decades middle-class liberals and socialists sought to spread culture—mostly at the level of Shakespeare and Mozart—to the people; now, unexpectedly, the people created their own culture—bright, cheerful, liberated, creative, yet also angry, ephemeral, and fragmented. There were many creators and creations but none established a great or lasting style. The swinging 1960s, born in anger, unhappily ended with anger, the angry violence of the rockers attacking the mods at seaside resorts, of students rioting at universities, of hooliganism at football games. As the 1970s began, people were reminded that from 1945 onward, the discontents of society had grown deeper.

THE WINTER OF OUR DISCONTENT

The great paradox of twentieth-century Britain was and is that, though a large majority had never been so wealthy, free, and equal, had never enjoyed more technological wonders, had never lived longer and in such good health, had never before known so much about the world, and had never pursued and enjoyed beauty of more kinds, they were discontented. Novelists, poets, play-wrights, and painters so testify, as do social statistics.

The novelists presented a grim picture from the first. In 1947 Malcolm Lowry's *Under the Volcano* told of the agonies of an alcoholic in a disintegrating world. Thirty years later, Muriel Spark in *The Take Over* told of crooked lawyers, thieving art historians, and dishonest servants and of fraud, pettiness, violence, and deception. Human nature seems not to have improved. The novels of Angus Wilson and Iris Murdoch, two of the age's most celebrated writers, were about the grotesque. For Wilson, the age's grotesqueries also reflected the dissolution of fixed manners and morals and the release of the darker forces of deception, disorder, and hate. In Iris Murdoch, all standards of truth, value, meaning, along with reality itself, dissolve away, leaving a welter of subjectivity and lost identities. A sense of meaninglessness reached its apex in Samuel Beckett's *How It Is*, his sixth work, eagerly read by the English. It tells the story of a naked being crawling through the mud and passing by old sacks, rusty cans, and debris. It ends in mere gabble, a sign of life's utter absurdity.

The poets were also gloomy. Two of the most read in the 1970s were Ted Hughes and Philip Larkin. In a poem about ghost crabs invading the land every night and withdrawing to the sea in the morning, Hughes writes of "our nothingness," of "brains jamming blind," of "the turmoil of history," and of monster ghost crabs tearing all apart. Philip Larkin has a brighter moment when he writes of a "sparkling armada of promises," but the armada disappears and all that is left are "wretched stalks of disappointment," "a huge and birdless silence," and a "black-sailed" ship which "In her wake no waters breed or break."

Intellectual uncertainty plagued the poets, forcing one of the best, Thom Gunn, to lament, "I, born to fog, to waste, walk through hypothesis."

Most Britons preferred to attend the theater rather than read poems, and the musicals still cheered them up, though the serious plays did not. John Mortimer's *Heaven and Hell* powerfully portrayed how emotional failure leads to a need for religion yet does so in an age disbelieving in God. David Storey's *Home* pictures that revered institution as an asylum of madness. Harold Pinter's *Room* was as claustrophobic and his hero also goes mad. It is a play of alienation, lost identity, decompositions, and, above all, absurdity. Pinter's many plays belong, as do Samuel Beckett's, to what became popular as the theater of the absurd.

Beckett in 1976 was still its high priest and the Royal Court, twenty-one years after Beckett's epochal *Waiting for Godot*, its shrine. *Waiting for Godot* was a play about two tramps who wait in vain for a mysterious Godot, or omnipotence, or God. It is full of a jaunty, stoical, human resilience. *That Time*, in 1976, by showing only his face with the voices of his past coming from offstage, portrayed a tramp whose life has disintegrated. *Footfall*, on the same bill, pictured a wretched hag walking to and fro, to and fro, puzzling over problems with no solutions. Beckett stripped away human disguises in the same stark manner as Francis Bacon, one of Britain's leading painters in this season of discontent. Bacon's people, half-animal and half-human, are invariably trapped in close, oddly proportioned, low-ceilinged rooms and often accompanied by slabs of raw meat, not unlike the torn flesh of the trapped, as if humankind belonged to a slaughterhouse. The faces are full of a mindless hate and greed, reminding viewers that Auschwitz and Hiroshima did happen.

In 1962 Britons thronged to the Tate Gallery to see these paintings. They also went to Beckett's plays. Were these searing, savage views of life simply the private agonies of a few or did they reflect far wider discontents? Certain social facts suggest the latter. Throughout the country discontent multiplied. Harried businessmen took to drink, cornered housewives to amphetamines, and the young to drugs of all kinds. The press reported drug waves and mounting alcoholism. More people than ever attempted suicide. Violence also increased: In 1974 the police arrested 100 students of the University of Essex after they had destroyed £32,000 worth of property. In 1970, at Derby, hooligans sent twelve football spectators to the hospital, which was mild compared to race riots and the sport of "bashing a Paki." Crime rose steadily from 1953 to 1978. After more than a century of unparalleled rectitude, corruption came to government. The divorce rate rose and the birth rate fell. Couples now averaged only 2.2 children.

There was a deeper sense of rootlessness in the new towns, in the high rises, even in ancient villages. "The biggest change in Akenfield," said its blacksmith, "is the growth of discontent." Akenfield was the pseudonym Ronald Blythe chose for his study of a Suffolk village that also showed a nearly empty parish church, a pub with declining customers and no more songs, and no end of

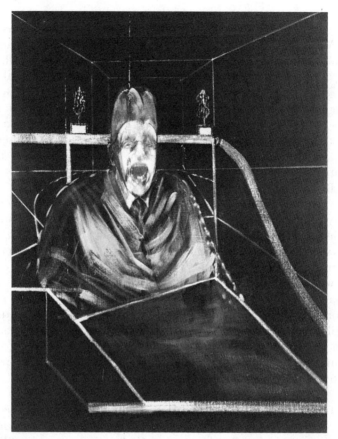

"Number VII from Eight Studies for a Portrait," by Francis Bacon, in 1953 (*Collection, The Museum of Modern Art, New York, Gift of Mr. and Mrs. William A. M. Burden*).

marriages breaking up. A once-poor but contented village had become one whose inhabitants talked of the "rat race," of "greed," of "people who no longer want to get together," and of those who are "locked in their houses with the TV." And Akenfield was a prosperous village that had finally thrown off feudal deferences.

Why should a prosperous Britain produce discontent? Conservatives pointed to permissive education and upbringing, the religious to declining faith, philosophers to the breakup of a liberal faith in reason, and moralists to materialism. Church membership and attendance was still declining. Only one in ten went regularly; such attenders constituting 1.2 million of the 6.7 million members of the Church of England and 1.3 million of the 3.5 million Roman Catholics. A staggering 70 percent of the 2 million Moslems seldom missed their services. The only Christian churches increasing in size were the Pentecostal and West

Indian ones, but they made up only 8 percent of the religious. It was a skeptical, confused, believing age, with beliefs ranging from yoga to Zen. Truth, even for the scientists, the high priests of the age, was fragmented, relative, and uncertain. The TV, popular press, radio, and paperbacks presented an abundance of facts and opinions, so copious on flying saucers and new atomic particles, so full of expanding galaxies and lost cultures, that it verged on chaos. Gone were the fixed articles of a thirteenth-century age of faith, of the natural laws of the Enlightenment, and the moral certitudes of the Victorian. In their place were materialism, envy, and growing expectations.

"The value system of most people," said the sociologist Mark Abrams in 1976, "is solidly grounded in materialism." It also, he added, is egalitarian and "tinged by envy." When people were asked whether they preferred a wage rise of £5 a week for themselves while others received a £6 rise or a flat £4 rise for all, 85 percent chose the flat £4 rise. Envy on an international scale was also present. Britain in 1978 was wealthier than ever, yet it had since 1945 fallen from third to eighth as an industrial power and its growth rate lagged far behind France's and Germany's. Articles appeared on the suicide of the nation as the English indulged in a favorite pastime, hypochondria. Much of that hypochondria was rooted in the frustrations of rising expectations, both the material ones of the affluent 1950s and the ideal ones of the swinging 1960s. The "sparkling armada of promises" had for many become "wretched stalks of disappointment."

Yet discontent in the Britain of the 1970s constituted but one of society's many moods and outlooks. Like geological strata, they were complex and varied. Discontent even overlapped and interwove with the more massive stratum of contentment. Tudor villas in suburbia and washer-driers and rising incomes have brought happiness to millions. The stratum of contentment even overlapped and interwove with Victorian morality and Edwardian elegance. On top of those was the stratum of the 1960s, of spontaneity, mobility, liberation, the beat of rock—and anger, drugs, and the delusions of flower power and beautiful people. Permeating all was a British wit, as old as Chaucer and Shakespeare, Dickens and W. C. Gilbert. It was a wit and humor that kept Beckett's tramps from despair, that added comedy and relief to the melancholia of *Sergeant Pepper*, and a freshness to the Rolling Stones' harder rhythms, a wit and humor that led three different critics to single out the music hall as a formative influence on Beckett, the Beatles, and the Stones.

It was that earthy humor and parodying mimicry that allowed many to endure nineteenth-century factory life; along with Cockney wryness and stoical understatement, it dissolved away many of the discontents of the 1970s, just as it had mitigated the tragic realities of trench warfare. That wit found brilliant expression in the plays of Tom Stoppard. It was a wit that admitted the world was absurd, truth fragmented, beauty relative, illusions many, but did so with dazzling inventiveness, elegant sophistication, and a flair for comedy that made the audiences forget inflation and slow rates of growth. In Stoppard's *Jumpers* gymnasts, philosophers, and detectives talk with dazzling wit about life's kaleidoscopic meanings while in *Travesties* Lenin, Joyce, and a Dadaist artist argue about painting, politics, and life. All is done spiritedly, is full of spoofs of moral seriousness and political causes, and contrasts the solidity of art with the relativity of history and the insubstantialities of life. As witty and brilliant as George Bernard Shaw, Stoppard's plays defy easy talk of cultural decline.

It also testifies to a wit and resilience centuries old. Much that has been related in this history of England has proved ephemeral. The institution of feudalism that brought order to England, the Elizabethan world picture that arranged all into exquisite and proper hierarchies, the British Empire itself, the world's greatest, and Britain's primacy in industry—all were gone. Yet some things remained the same. British history through all its twistings and turnings did produce a national character. In 1978 that character still had its flaws: it was as muddling and arrogant in its quarrels at British Leyland as it was in waging war in the Crimea. It was as smug and brutal in its treatment of Pakis and Benghis as it had been toward eighteenth-century poachers. It was as insensitive to the poor as it had always been.

But there were happier strains. British character and institutions have produced one of the world's most remarkable cultures. Courageous, dogged, phlegmatic, and stoical, the British foot soldier, despite his officers, won in the Crimea, overcame the Germans on the Western Front, and helped win an empire. Practical, inventive, empirical, and tenacious, the British plowed and enclosed their fields of heavy clay, discovered the steam engine, perfected the art of self-government and made it democratic. Inquiring, curious, and imaginative, they produced Newton, Darwin, Faraday, and Rutherford, and though inferior to Germany in music and France in painting, their love for and genius with words led to an unsurpassed literature, a literature of deep tragedy and noble eloquence, but also of parody, satire, and broad comedy—in short, of wit of all kinds, a wit that like a gold thread in an embroidery runs through all British history. That wit, joined to inventiveness, pragmatism, doggedness, and stoicism, will, barring an atomic war, assure Britain of a long history. "Wretched stalks of disappointment" mean less if one can joke about them.

FURTHER READING

BLYTHE, RONALD. *Akenfield.* London: Penguin Press, 1969. A brilliant portrait of a small Suffolk village and its inhabitants in the twentieth century; based on many interviews and told with the skill of a novelist.

COLVILLE, JOHN. *The New Elizabethans, 1952–1977.* London: Collins, 1977. A survey of Britain's politics, government, economy, men of business, and place in the world followed by a close look at its religion, morality, education, arts, and manners.

COX, C. B., and A. E. DYSON. *The Twentieth Century Mind: History, Ideas, and Literature in Britain.* Vol. 3, *1945–65.* Oxford: Oxford University Press, 1969. The best intellectual history of twentieth-century England, written by experts in each field willing to tackle the most difficult developments.

DAVIES, HUNTER. *The Beatles.* New York: McGraw-Hill, 1983. A lively, candid, perceptive, and thorough study of the Beatles by a person who traveled with them for sixteen months and interviewed nearly all who knew them.

HALSEY, A. H. *Change in British Society.* Oxford: Oxford University Press, 1978. An excellent sociological study of both continuity and change in today's Britain, one that emphasizes the persistence of class, racial prejudice, an uneven distribution of wealth and educational inequality but also sees considerable social mobility.

MARWICK, ARTHUR. *British Society Since 1945.* London: Allen Lane, 1982. A highly informed and imaginative analysis of forty years of social developments, one that emphasizes the loss of great hopes, the release from old restraints, and the persistence of tolerance.

MELLY, GEORGE. *Revolt Into Style.* London: Allen Lane, 1970. The most perceptive and sympathetic of interpretations of the pop music, literature, and art of the swinging 1960s and of that decade's films, TV, theater, and fashion.

SAMPSON, ANTHONY. *The Changing Anatomy of England.* London: Hodder and Stoughton, 1981. The most recent of his three *Anatomies of England*, chock full of information on every aspect of England—economic, political, social, ecclesiastical, and monarchical.

SISSON, MICHAEL, and PHILIP FRENCH, EDS. *Age of Austerity.* London: Hodder and Stoughton, 1963. The celebration of the fifteen years preceding the swinging 1960s by eleven intellectuals, and the story of how a great social experiment filled all with idealism and a feeling of involvement.

SHRAPNEL, NORMAN. *The Seventies: Britain's Inward March.* London: Constable, 1980. An indictment of the decade-long hangover that followed the swinging 1960s, a hangover marked by unemployment, class and racial friction, crises, violence, and deteriorating language.

YOUNG, MICHAEL, AND PETER WILLMOTT. *The Symmetrical Family: A Study of Work and Leisure in the London Region.* London: Routledge and Kegan Paul, 1973. Based on interviews and surveys, these two sociologists describe the changes in family structure as contraception, prosperity, and medicine brought fewer children, more jobs, and longevity.

Appendix

KINGS AND QUEENS, 1715–1990

George I, 1714–1727   (The monarchs of Britain from George I through Victoria were from the House of Brunswick, sometimes called the House of Hanover.)

George II, 1727–1760
George III, 1760–1820
George IV, 1820–1830
William IV, 1830–1837
Queen Victoria, 1837–1901
Edward VII, 1901–1910   (As the son of Victoria's Prince Consort, Albert of the House of Saxe-Coburg-Gotha, Edward VII was of that House; but the Germanic sound of Saxe-Coburg-Gotha led George V, during the anti-German hysteria of World War I, to change the name to House of Windsor.)

George V, 1910–1936
Edward VIII, 1936–1937
George VI, 1937–1953
Elizabeth II, 1953–

PRIME MINISTERS

Sir Robert Walpole, April 1721–   (The tenure of all the following Prime Ministers lasts until the date of their successor's appointment.)

Henry Pelham, February 1742
Duke of Newcastle, May 1754
William Pitt, the Elder, December 1756
Duke of Newcastle, October 1761
Earl of Bute, May 1762
George Grenville, April 1763
Marquis of Rockingham, July 1765
Duke of Grafton, August 1766
Lord North, February 1770
Marquis of Rockingham, March 1782
Earl of Shelburne, July 1782
Duke of Portland, April 1783
William Pitt, December 1783
Henry Addington, February 1801
William Pitt, May 1804
Lord Grenville, January 1806
Duke of Portland, March 1807
Spencer Perceval, September 1809
Earl of Liverpool, June 1812
George Canning, April 1827
Viscount Goderich, September 1827
Duke of Wellington, January 1828
Earl Grey, November 1830
Viscount Melbourne, July 1834
Sir Robert Peel, December 1834
Lord John Russell, July 1846
Earl of Derby, February 1852
Earl of Aberdeen, December 1852
Viscount Palmerston, February 1855
Earl of Derby, February 1858
Viscount Palmerston, June 1859
Lord John Russell, October 1865
Earl of Derby, June 1866
Benjamin Disraeli, February 1868
William Gladstone, December, 1868
Benjamin Disraeli, February 1874
William Gladstone, April 1880
Lord Salisbury, June 1885
William Gladstone, February 1886
Lord Salsibury, August 1886
William Gladstone, August 1892
Lord Roseberry, March 1894
Lord Salisbury, June 1895
Arthur Balfour, July 1902
Sir Henry Campbell Bannerman, December 1905

Herbert Asquith, April 1908
David Lloyd George, December 1916
Andrew Bonar Law, October 1922
Stanley Baldwin, May 1923
Ramsay Macdonald, January 1924
Stanley Baldwin, November 1924
Ramsay Macdonald, June 1929
Stanley Baldwin, June 1935
Neville Chamberlain, May 1937
Winston Churchill, May 1940
Clement Attlee, July 1945
Winston Churchill, October 1951
Anthony Eden, April 1955
Harold Macmillan, January 1957
Sir Alec Douglas-Home, October 1963
Sir Harold Wilson, October 1964
Edward Heath, May 1970
Sir Harold Wilson, October 1974
James Callaghan, April 1976
Margaret Thatcher, May 1979–

Index ————————————————————————————